Mobile and Ubiquitous Commerce:
Advanced E-Business Methods

Milena Head
McMaster University, Canada

Eldon Y. Li
National Chengchi University, Taiwan

T0321736

INFORMATION SCIENCE REFERENCE

Hershey · New York

Director of Editorial Content:	Kristin Klinger
Senior Managing Editor:	Jamie Snavely
Managing Editor:	Jeff Ash
Assistant Managing Editor:	Carole Coulson
Typesetter:	Michael Brehm
Cover Design:	Lisa Tosheff
Printed at:	Yurchak Printing Inc.

Published in the United States of America by
Information Science Reference (an imprint of IGI Global)
701 E. Chocolate Avenue
Hershey PA 17033
Tel: 717-533-8845
Fax: 717-533-8661
E-mail: cust@igi-global.com
Web site: http://www.igi-global.com/reference

and in the United Kingdom by
Information Science Reference (an imprint of IGI Global)
3 Henrietta Street
Covent Garden
London WC2E 8LU
Tel: 44 20 7240 0856
Fax: 44 20 7379 0609
Web site: http://www.eurospanbookstore.com

Library of Congress Cataloging-in-Publication Data

Mobile and ubiquitous commerce : advanced e-business methods / Milena Head and Eldon Y. Li, editor.
    p. cm. -- (Advances in electronic business series ; v. 4)

Includes bibliographical references and index.
Summary: "This book advances the understanding of management methods, information technology, and their joint application in business processes"--Provided by publisher.

ISBN 978-1-60566-366-1 (hardcover) -- ISBN 978-1-60566-367-8 (ebook) 1. Mobile commerce. 2. Electronic commerce. 3. Ubiquitous computing. I. Head, Milena, 1969- II. Li, Eldon Yu-zen, 1952-

  HF5548.34.M625 2009
  658.8'72--dc22
                        2008050169

British Cataloguing in Publication Data
A Cataloguing in Publication record for this book is available from the British Library.

All work contributed to this book is new, previously-unpublished material. The views expressed in this book are those of the authors, but not necessarily of the publisher.

Advances in Electronic Business (AEBUS) Series

Editor-in-Chief: Eldon Li, The Chinese University of Hong Kong, Hong Kong

ISBN: 1935-2905

Mobile and Ubiquitous Commerce: Advanced E-Business Methods

Edited By: Milena M. Head, McMaster University, Canada; Eldon Y. Li, National Chengchi University, Taiwan

Information Science Reference ~ 2009 Copyright ~ Pages: 347 ~ H/C (ISBN: 978-1-60566-366-1)
Our Price: $195.00

Mobile and Ubiquitous Commerce: Advanced E-Business Methods advances the understanding of management methods, information technology, and their joint application in business processes. This Premier Reference Source covers theories and practices of business technologies, enterprise management, Internet marketing, public policies, transportation and logistics, privacy and law, business ethics, and information technologies related to electronic business.

Agent Systems in Electronic Business

Edited By: Eldon Y. Li, National Chengchi University, Taiwan; Soe-Tsyr Yuan, National Chengchi University, Taiwan

Information Science Reference ~ 2008 Copyright ~ Pages: 408 ~ H/C (ISBN: 978-1-59904-588-7)
Our Price: $180.00

Agent Systems in Electronic Business delivers definitive research to academics and practitioners in the field of business automation on the use of agent technologies to advance the practice of electronic business in today's organizations, targeting the needs of enterprises in open and dynamic business opportunities to incorporate skilled use of multiple independent information systems. This comprehensive resource clearly articulates the stages (electronic commerce transactions, business processes and e-business infrastructure) involved in developing agent-based e-business systems.

Other Books in the Series:

Advances in Electronic Business, Volume 2

Eldon Y. Li, National Chengchi University, Taiwan & California Polytechnic State University, USA
CyberTech Publishing ~ 2007 Copyright ~ Pages: 332 ~ H/C (ISBN: 1-59140-678-1) ~ Our Price: $94.95

Advances in Electronic Business, Volume 1

Eldon Y. Li , Timon C. Du; uan Ze University, Taiwan; The Chinese University of Hong Kong, Hong Kong
IGI Publishing ~ 2005 Copyright ~ Pages: 356 ~ H/C (ISBN: 1-59140-381-2) ~ Our Price: $84.95

The *Advances in Electronic Business (AEBUS) Book Series* advances the understanding of management methods, information technology, and their joint application in business processes. The applications of electronic commerce draw great attention of the practitioners in applying digital technologies to the buy-and-sell activities. This book series addresses the importance of management and technology issues in electronic business, including collaborative design, collaborative engineering, collaborative decision making, electronic collaboration, communication and cooperation, workflow collaboration, knowledge networking, collaborative e-learning, costs and benefits analysis of collaboration, collaborative transportation and ethics.

Order Online at ww.igi-global.com or call 717-533-8845 x100 – Mon-Fri 8:30 AM - 5:00 PM (EST) or
Fax 24 Hours a Day 717-533-8661

Table of Contents

Section I
Overview

Chapter I
Jan H. Kietzmann, Simon Fraser University, Canada

Chapter II
Adrian Lawrence, Baker & McKenzie, Australia
Jane Williams, Baker & McKenzie, Australia

Section II
Mobile Business Models and Applications

Chapter III
Dietmar G. Wiedemann, University of Augsburg, Germany
Wolfgang Palka, University of Augsburg, Germany
Key Pousttchi, University of Augsburg, Germany

Chapter IV
Mikko Pynnönen, Lappeenranta University of Technology, Finland
Jukka Hallikas, Lappeenranta University of Technology, Finland
Petri Savolainen, Lappeenranta University of Technology, Finland
Karri Mikkonen, TeliaSonera, Sweden

Section III
Technical Considerations for Mobile and Ubiquitous Commerce

Detailed Table of Contents

Section I
Overview

Chapter I
    Jan H. Kietzmann, Simon Fraser University, Canada

The recent evolution of mobile auto-identification technologies invites firms to connect to mobile work in altogether new ways. By strategically embedding "smart" devices, organizations involve individual subjects and real objects in their corporate information flows, and execute more and more business processes through such technologies as mobile Radio-Frequency Identification (RFID). The imminent path from mobility to pervasiveness focuses entirely on improving organizational performance measures and metrics of success. Work itself, and the dramatic changes these technologies introduce to the organization and to the role of the mobile worker are by and large ignored. The aim of this chapter is to unveil the key changes and challenges that emerge when mobile landscapes are "tagged", and when mobile workers and mobile auto-identification technologies work side-by-side. The motivation for this chapter is to encourage thoughts that appreciate auto-identification technologies and their socio-technical impact on specific mobile work practices and on the nature of mobile work in general.

Chapter II
    Adrian Lawrence, Baker & McKenzie, Australia
    Jane Williams, Baker & McKenzie, Australia

As commercial interest in LBS increases, legal and regulatory bodies are becoming increasingly interested in the extent to which use of LBS may affect individuals' privacy. This chapter discusses the nature of the privacy-related issues arising from the use of commercial LBS and gives examples of approaches that might be taken to best address these issues from the perspective of users of LBS and commercial providers of LBS. It identifies and analyses some of the key privacy issues that arise from use of LBS and the ways in which these types of issues are being regulated in some jurisdictions. It also suggests some best-practice guidelines for how these issues might be best dealt with in order to ensure that individuals' privacy is protected. Given the increasing importance of privacy issues to consumers and their likely reluctance to use commercial LBS if significant privacy concerns are not addressed, this chapter concludes that both consumers and commercial LBS providers will benefit from privacy concerns being addressed appropriately. This chapter identifies and analyzes these issues on a theoretical level so that the issues and approaches suggested may be useful to both privacy advocates and regulators and providers of LBS, and will remain relevant as LBS become more sophisticated.

Section II
Mobile Business Models and Applications

Chapter III
    Dietmar G. Wiedemann, University of Augsburg, Germany
    Wolfgang Palka, University of Augsburg, Germany
    Key Pousttchi, University of Augsburg, Germany

A sizeable body of research on mobile payment evolved in recent years. Researchers analyzed success factors and acceptance criteria as well as strengths and weaknesses of different mobile payment service providers. This chapter explores business models for mobile payment service provision and mobile payment service enabling. While a mobile payment service provider offers a mobile payment procedure to end-users and merchants, a mobile payment service enabler targets on enabling other companies to offer mobile payment services. Our primary contribution is to demonstrate the applicability of a general mobile payment business model framework, which was proposed in prior research. In doing so, we analyze, as an example, the case of SEMOPS as a typical mobile service enabler. Representing any m-payment business model, the resulting framework enables researchers and practitioners for comprehensive analysis of existing and future models and provides a helpful tool for m-payment business model engineering.

Chapter IV
    Mikko Pynnönen, Lappeenranta University of Technology, Finland
    Jukka Hallikas, Lappeenranta University of Technology, Finland
    Petri Savolainen, Lappeenranta University of Technology, Finland
    Karri Mikkonen, TeliaSonera, Sweden

In a digital home a so-called multi-play system integrates networked entertainment and communications systems. Using a mobile phone, all those services can be controlled and used ubiquitously – from everywhere, at any time. Not much research has been conducted in the field of integrated communication offers. The novelty of this study is in that it addresses the ubiquitous communication system, called the multi-play service, from the perspectives of both the customer preference and operator strategy and transforms this into valuation of resources and capabilities. This chapter provides a framework to connect the customer value preferences to firm resources. The aim of the framework is to connect customer and resource-based strategies together. As a result of the analysis the authors reveal the most important resources in contrast to the customer value preferences.

Mobile government transforms many of the traditional governance practices. The citizens' adoption of M-Government services (e.g. voting, tax services, health services, etc.), however, is determined by a series of factors (e.g. ease of use, image, compatibility, etc.). This chapter investigates the predicting power of these factors towards contributing to theory building and providing direct implications that are useful for the diffusion and adoption of mobile government services in Greece. The study reviews the available literature on adoption and diffusion of innovation as well as the available relevant research insights on the mobile commerce landscape. Then, the study empirically tests the predicting power of a series of critical variables that are theoretically related to the Greek citizens' intention to adopt mobile government services. The findings imply that compatibility and ease of use have significant predicting power on citizens' intention to adopt M-Government services. Direct implications and further research directions are provided at the end.

Section III
Technical Considerations for Mobile and Ubiquitous Commerce

Mobile service providers (MoSPs) emerge, driven by the ubiquitous availability of mobile devices and wireless communication infrastructures. MoSPs' customers satisfaction and consequently their revenues, largely depend on the quality of service (QoS) provided by wireless network providers (WNPs) available at a particular location-time to support a mobile service delivery. This chapter presents a novel method for the MoSP's QoS-assurance business process. The method incorporates a location- and time-based QoS-predictions' service, facilitating the WNP's selection. The authors explore different business cases for the service deployment. Particularly, they introduce and analyze business viability of QoSIS.net, an enterprise that can provide the QoS-predictions service to MoSPs, Mobile Network Operators (as MoSPs), or directly to their customers (i.e. in B2B/B2C settings). QoSIS.net provides its service based on collaborative-sharing of QoS-information by its users. The authors argue that this service can improve the MoSP's QoS-assurance process and consequently may increase its revenues, while creating revenues for QoSIS.net.

Currently the most popular attacks to the E-Banking Web applications target the authentication systems relying on the single-side client authentication, showing their definitively ineffectiveness for financial services. Furthermore, most of the Web authentication systems have been developed on the classic username/password mechanism or One time Password systems using a single channel, either mobile or Web, generating an authentication system at inadequate level, enforcing a false perception of security, as phishing shows. The two factors authentication is not the panacea, but mitigates many threats, especially when combined with a Personal Trusted Device, as the popular smartphones represent. As a rule of thumb, the adoption of authentication systems to provide services B2C is driven by its ease-to-use more than the robustness of the adopted security system. For this reason, the proposed solution represents a system which tries to preserve the usability and to strengthen the authentication, with a combined Web/mobile authentication system.

Non-repudiation is an important issue in mobile business and mobile commerce in order to provide the necessary evidences to prove whether some party participated in a transaction. The basis to support non-repudiation is the electronic signature. In Europe, directive 1999/93/EC of the European Parliament and the Council establishes the conditions that should be fulfilled in order to provide an electronic signature legally equivalent to the handwritten signature. This chapter presents and analyses the different solutions that have appeared over the years to provide mobile signatures. This analysis will help to determine which mobile signatures solutions can be considered legally equivalent to the handwritten signature. Thus, this chapter allows people to get to know the different solutions that are available to build mobile commerce and mobile business applications that require the use of the non-repudiation service, and hence electronic signature in mobile devices.

Chapter IX

Soe-Tsyr Yuan, National Chengchi University, Taiwan
Fang-Yu Chen, AsusTeK Computer Inc., Taiwan

Peer-to-Peer applications harness sharing between free resources (storage, contents, services, human presence, etc.). Most existing wireless P2P applications concern merely the sharing of a variety of contents. For magnifying the sharing extent for wireless service provision in the vicinity (i.e., the wireless P2P environments), this chapter presents a novel approach (briefly named UbiSrvInt) that is an attempt to enable a pure P2P solution that is context aware and fault tolerant for ad-hoc wireless service provision. This approach empowers an autonomous peer to propel distributed problem solving (e.g., in the travel domain) through service sharing and execution in an intelligent P2P way. This approach of ad-hoc wireless service provision is not only highly robust to failure (based on a specific clustering analysis of failure correlation among peers) but also capable of inferring a user's service needs (through a BDI reasoning mechanism utilizing the surrounding context) in ad-hoc wireless environments. The authors have implemented UbiSrvInt into a system platform with P-JXTA that shows good performance results on fault tolerance and context awareness.

Section IV
Interacting with Mobile Devices

Chapter X

Dianne Cyr, Simon Fraser University, Canada
Milena Head, McMaster University, Canada
Alex Ivanov, Simon Fraser University, Canada

Anytime anywhere services offered through mobile commerce hold great potential to serve customers in wireless environments. However, there is limited understanding of how mobile Web site design is perceived by diverse users. This chapter explores how users who differ by culture, age, and gender perceive the design of a mobile device and their subsequent level of satisfaction with the device. Sixty subjects were tested in a controlled laboratory experiment on an Internet enabled phone. The results of a quantitative analysis were statistically inconclusive in terms of cultural and gender differences, but significant differences were found between older and younger users. However, an in-depth qualitative analysis of interview transcripts revealed some interesting differences among cultural, gender and age groups. Consistent with findings in the stationary Internet domain, design elements were found to impact satisfaction with mobile services.

Chapter XI

Douglass J. Scott, Waseda University, Japan
Constantinos K. Coursaris, Michigan State University, USA
Yuuki Kato, Tokyo University of Social Welfare, Japan
Shogo Kato, Waseda University, Japan

This study compared the exchange of emotional content in PC and mobile e-mail in business-related discussions. Forty American business people were divided into two groups (PC and mobile e-mail users) and were then assigned to anonymous discussion pairs who exchanged a total of six messages on a predetermined topic. When a message was sent, the writers completed two questionnaires related to 12 target emotions: One questionnaire assessed the emotions they experienced and another estimated their partner's emotional reaction. E-mail readers filled out similar questionnaires. Statistical analysis showed that when emotional exchange was successful, mobile e-mail users more accurately predicted positive emotions than did PC e-mail users. Conversely, when emotional exchange was unsuccessful, mobile e-mail users failed to accurately exchange negative emotions far more than their PC using counterparts. These findings indicate that the communication medium used may influence the exchange of emotional content in text-based communications.

Section V
International Perspectives for Mobile and Ubiquitous Commerce

The chapter aims to present an in-depth study of the factors influencing Mobile Internet adoption. The authors analyse the influence of Internet use experience, compatibility, perceived financial risk, credibility and attitude towards Mobile Internet in the M-Internet adoption decision. After identifying the key drivers of M-Internet adoption, the second part of the chapter presents an empirical study of the Spanish market. Results based on a sample of 213 Internet users show that Internet use experience, M-Internet compatibility, credibility and attitude are positive key drivers of M-Internet adoption. Perceived financial risk influences negatively on M-Internet usage intention. This chapter will give managers and students insight into the M-Internet industry and the different factors that influence M-Internet adoption. In addition, these factors can be applied to the specific context of the Spanish market.

This chapter introduces concepts, frameworks and possible models for introducing mobile payments in India. The introductory section defines mobile payments, outlines its characteristics and identifies the stakeholders. Ideally, mobile payments have to be simple and usable, universal, interoperable, secure, private, affordable and be available within the country wide as well as globally. There are various stakeholders in this context: the customer, the merchant, banks, mobile network operators, software and technology service providers, mobile device manufacturers, and the government. The technology considerations are addressed in a technological landscape with a wide variety of possibilities for implementing mobile payments. Implementations can be based on different access channels to the mobile device such as SMS, USSD or WAP/GPRS. The relative advantages and disadvantages each of these channels for mobile payments are discussed. Generic architectures that employ these technologies are modeled. The mobile phone carrying debit or card information (Track 2) within the device can act as a payment instrument. It can be used to extend the present day card based payment systems. This requires an independent entity called as a Trusted Service Manager (TSM) who provides the necessary hardware and software for handling transactions. The TSM is an intermediary between the financial institutions (banks) and the mobile network operators (telecommunications industry). Essentially the TSM accepts the information from the customer owning a mobile and it routes the financial transaction to the bank or an inter-bank clearing and settlement system (using an electronic interface – a financial switch) or to a payment systems operator (in the case that the customer is using a credit card). Possible models for one TSM in the country or having several independent TSMs are outlined. The TSMs may communicate with the financial system using the ISO 8583 messaging standards. Finally, technical standards and security issues are addressed. A symmetric encryption scheme (based on Triple DES or AES) can offer confidentiality of mobile payment transactions. However, for assuring integrity, authentication and non-repudiation a PKI scheme is required. Cost wise a PKI enabled scheme would be more than twice as costly as a symmetric scheme due to overheads in digital certificate transmission. Low value transactions may use the symmetric encryption standards whereas high value transactions can be done using asymmetric encryption standards.

Section VI
Additional Selected Readings

Chapter XIV

Over the years, computer systems have evolved from centralized monolithic computing devices supporting static applications, into client-server environments that allow complex forms of distributed computing. Throughout this evolution, limited forms of code mobility have existed. The explosion in the use of the World Wide Web, coupled with the rapid evolution of the platform-independent programming languages, has promoted the use of mobile code and, at the same time, raised some important security issues. This chapter introduces mobile code technology and discusses the related security issues. The first part of the chapter deals with the need for mobile codes and the various methods of categorising them. One method of categorising the mobile code is based on code mobility. Different forms of code mobility, like code on demand, remote evaluation, and mobile agents, are explained in detail. The other method is based on the type of code distributed. Various types of codes, like source code, intermediate code, platform dependent binary code, and just-in-time compilation, are explained. Mobile agents, as autonomously migrating software entities, present great challenges to the design and implementation of security mechanisms. The second part of this chapter deals with the security issues. These issues are broadly divided into code-related issues and host-related issues. Techniques, like sandboxing, code signing, and proof-carrying code, are widely applied to protect the hosts. Execution tracing, mobile cryptography, obfuscated code, and cooperating agents are used to protect the code from harmful agents. The security mechanisms, like language support for safety, OS level security, and safety policies, are discussed in the last section. In order to make the mobile code approach practical, it is essential to understand mobile code technology. Advanced and innovative solutions are to be developed to restrict the operations that mobile code can perform, but without unduly restricting its functionality. It is also necessary to develop formal, extremely easy-to-use safety measures.

Chapter XV

This chapter describes Finnish mobile telecommunications industry trends and prospects. In addition, it presents two theoretical frameworks based on the Finnish companies' experiences in the turbulent M-Commerce markets. First, the internationalization framework is targeted to facilitate C-Commerce actors to position themselves in the global telecom business. Second, the mobile media framework is targeted to facilitate analyses related to the emerging mobile media markets. Furthermore, the chapter presents five mini-cases of Finnish M-Commerce companies and concludes with theoretical and managerial implications to M-Commerce actors.

Chapter XVI

In a service-oriented enterprise, the professional workforce such as salespersons and support staff tends to be mobile with the recent advances in mobile technologies. There are increasing demands for the support of mobile workforce management (MWM) across multiple platforms in order to integrate the disparate business functions of the mobile professional workforce and management with a unified infrastructure, together with the provision of personalized assistance and automation. Typically, MWM involves tight collaboration, negotiation, and sophisticated business-domain knowledge, and thus can be facilitated with the use of intelligent software agents. As mobile devices become more powerful, intelligent software agents can now be deployed on these devices and hence are also subject to mobility. Therefore, a multiagent information-system (MAIS) infrastructure provides a suitable paradigm to capture the concepts and requirements of an MWM as well as a phased development and deployment. In this chapter, the authors illustrate their approach with a case study at a large telecommunication enterprise. They show how to formulate a scalable, flexible, and intelligent MAIS with agent clusters. Each agent cluster comprises several types of agents to achieve the goal of each phase of the workforce-management process, namely, task formulation, matchmaking, brokering, commuting, and service.

Chapter XVII

Bringing Secure Wireless Technology to the Bedside: A Case Study
of Two Canadian Healthcare Organizations 303

Dawn-Marie Turner, DM Turner Informatics Consulting Inc., Canada
Sunil Hazari, University of West Georgia, USA

Wireless technology has broad implications for the healthcare environment. Despite its promise, this new technology has raised questions about security and privacy of sensitive data that is prevalent in healthcare organizations. All healthcare organizations are governed by legislation and regulations, and the implementation of enterprise applications using new technology is comparatively more difficult than in other industries. Using a configuration-idiographic case-study approach, this study investigated challenges faced by two Canadian healthcare organizations. In addition to interviews with management and staff of the organizations, a walk-through was also conducted to observe and collect first-hand data of the implementation of wireless technology in the clinical environment. In the organizations under examination, it was found that wireless technology is being implemented gradually to augment the wired network. Problems associated with implementing wireless technology in these Canadian organizations are also discussed. Because of different standards in this technology, the two organizations are following different upgrade paths. Based on the data collected, best practices for secure wireless access in these organizations are proposed.

Preface

INTRODUCTION

Mobility and ubiquity are among the most important technological and market trends of the 21st Century. The wide deployment of wireless data communication networks and the explosive growth of mobile users have created incredible demand for mobile and ubiquitous commerce applications. For users, these applications can provide unprecedented flexibility and convenience in their professional and personal lives. Mobile devices allow users to work, communicate and transact anywhere/anytime. Ubiquity in mobile services implies that users need not even provide explicit input to communicate their current needs and context.

For companies, mobile and ubiquitous applications provide new opportunities to execute business transactions, interact with trading partners, improve customer service levels, extend brand presence, and enhance collaboration between an increasingly mobile workforce. While existing business models must be re-examined to enable these opportunities, companies also need to understand how to best cope with the burden of being "always on".

This volume of *Advances in Electronic Business* intends to stimulate discussion and understanding by presenting theoretical and empirical research on mobile and ubiquitous commerce. Research results and future perspectives are presented for the development and sustainable deployment of anywhere/anytime applications and services. This book is organized into five sections: the first provides an overview of mobility and pervasiveness as well as an emerging key issue of privacy; the second section examines various mobile business models and their applications in private and public sectors; the third section centers on technical considerations for various service models and security/authentication concerns; the fourth section explores individual differences and emotive aspects of interacting with mobile devices; finally, the fifth section provides an international perspective by highlighting mobile issues in Spain and India. Overall, this book helps to provide a roadmap for future scholarship and business success in this critical domain.

BOOK ORGANIZATION

Section I: Overview

Chapter I, *For Those About to Tag*, provides an overview of Radio-Frequency Identification (RFID) and its impact on creating a pervasive work landscape. Key changes and issues are presented and the author challenges the reader to consider the socio-technical impact of RFID tagging on work practices and the on the nature of mobile work in general.

Chapter II, *Privacy and Location-Based Mobile Services: Finding a Balance*, addresses a central concern with location-based mobile services: privacy. The authors identify and analyze the key privacy issues and present best practices for how to help mitigate some of these growing concerns.

Section II: Mobile Business Models and Applications

Chapter III, *Business Models for Mobile Payment Service Provision and Enabling*, explores business models for mobile payment service provision and mobile payment service enabling. The authors introduce a new mobile payment business model framework, which provides researchers and practitioners an analysis tool for existing and future models.

Chapter IV, *Ubiquitous Communication: Where is the Value Created in the Multi-Play Value Network*, addresses the ubiquitous communication system from both the customer preference and operator strategy perspectives. A framework is outlined that connects customer value preferences to firm resources.

Chapter V, *Predicting the Adoption of Mobile Government Services*, examines mobile government and its potential to transform many traditional governance practices. The authors present and empirically validate the key predictors of mobile government service adoption.

Section III: Technical Considerations for Mobile and Ubiquitous Commerce

Chapter VI, *Towards Mobile Web 2.0-Based Business Methods: Collaborative QoS-Information Sharing for Mobile Service Users*, presents a novel method for a mobile service provider's quality of service assurance process. The authors explore various business cases, focusing on QoSIS.net, which provides its service based on collaborative-sharing of quality of service information by its users.

Chapter VII, *Strong Authentication for Financial Services: PTDs as a Compromise Between Security and Usability*, outlines the flaws of current authentication systems in the banking sector that tend to rely on single-side client authentication. To address these flaws, the authors propose a system that combines and strengthens web and mobile authentication while preserving usability for the end user.

Chapter VIII, *Mobile Signature Solutions for Guaranteeing Non-Repudiation in Mobile Business and Mobile Commerce*, examines various mobile signature solutions, outlining their security and legal implications. Readers are provided with an understanding of how current and emerging mobile commerce applications can incorporate the use of e-signatures in their processes.

Chapter IX, *UbiSrvInt: A Context-Aware Fault-Tolerant Approach for WP2P Service Provision*, outlines the various potential advantages and challenges of wireless peer-to-peer applications. The authors present a novel UbiSrvInt approach that is highly robust to failure and capable of inferring a user's service needs in ad-hoc wireless environments.

Section IV: Interacting with Mobile Devices

Chapter X, *Perceptions of Mobile Device Website Design: Culture, Gender and Age Comparisons*, explores how users who differ by gender, age and culture perceive the design of a mobile device and their subsequent level of satisfaction with the device. Quantitative and qualitative analysis of a controlled laboratory study revealed some interesting differences among cultural, gender and age groups relevant for mobile interface designers.

Chapter XI, *The Exchange of Emotional Content in Business Communications: A Comparison of PC and Mobile E-Mail Users*, outlines an empirical study that compared the exchange of emotional content in personal computers and mobile e-mail in business-related discussions. The authors found that the communication medium influences the exchange of emotional content in text-based communications.

Section V: International Perspective for Mobile and Ubiquitous Commerce

Chapter XII, *Mobile Internet Adoption by Spanish Consumers*, examines the key drivers of mobile Internet adoption by Spanish consumers. Through an empirical study, the authors find that Internet use experience, mobile Internet compatibility, credibility and attitude are positive drivers of mobile Internet adoption in Spain.

Chapter XIII, *Framework for Mobile Payment Systems in India*, introduces concepts, frameworks and potential models for introducing mobile payments in India. The author outlines the needs/concerns of various stakeholders and presents a technological landscape of possibilities for implementing mobile payments.

Section VI: Additional Selected Readings

Four chapters have been carefully selected from recent publications to complement and provide additional support to the original 13 chapters presented in this book. They provide further background on mobile security issues (**Chapter XIV**, *Mobile Code and Security Issues*); international considerations (**Chapter XV**, *Finland: Internationalization as the Key to Growth and M-Commerce Success*); mobile workforce management (**Chapter XVI**, *Mobile Workforce Management in a Service-Oriented Enterprise: Capturing Concepts and Requirements in a Multi-Agent Infrastructure*); and wireless opportunities in healthcare (**Chapter XVII**, *Bringing Secure Wireless Technology to the Bedside: A Case Study of Two Canadian Healthcare Organizations*).

Milena Head
McMaster University, Canada

Eldon Y. Li
National Chengchi University, Taiwan

Acknowledgment

This book has been prepared in close cooperation with academicians and practitioners who are experts in the area of mobile and ubiquitous commerce from 15 universities and 4 companies spanning 14 counties. The editors would like to thanks all the chapter authors, including Jan Kietzmann, Dietmar G Wiedemann, Wolfgang Palka, Key Pousttchi, Adrian Lawrence, Jane Williams, Mikko Pynnönen, Jukka Hallikas, Petri Savolainen, Karri Mikkonen, Adam Vrechopoulos, Michail Batikas, Katarzyna Wac, Richard Bults, Bert-Jan can Beijnum, Hong Chen, Dimitri Konstantas, Gianluigi Me, Daniele Pirro, Roberto Sarrecchia, Antonio Ruiz-Martínez, Daniel Sánchez-Martínez, María Martínez-Montesinos, Antonio F. Gómez-Skarmeta, Soe-Tsyr Yuan, Fang-Yu Chen, Dianne Cyr, Alex Ivanov, Douglass J. Scott, Constantinos K. Coursaris, Yuuki Kato, Shogo Kato, Adrian Broz-Lofiego, Daniel Marchuet, Carla Ruiz-Mafé, Silvia Sanz-Blas and Mahil Carr for their tireless effort in preparing the manuscripts.

We would like to express our gratitude to the many reviewers for their assistance in reviewing the chapters to assure the quality of this book. Special thanks to IGI Global who published the book for its clear guidelines, help and support throughout the process. In particular, we would like to thank Rebecca Beistline for her professional assistance and encouragement.

Finally to all readers around the world, we thank you for using this book and hope you find it informative and valuable.

Milena Head
McMaster University, Canada

Eldon Y. Li
National Chengchi University, Taiwan

Section I
Overview

Chapter I
For Those About to Tag

Jan H. Kietzmann
Simon Fraser University, Canada

ABSTRACT

The recent evolution of mobile auto-identification technologies invites firms to connect to mobile work in altogether new ways. By strategically embedding "smart" devices, organizations involve individual subjects and real objects in their corporate information flows, and execute more and more business processes through such technologies as mobile Radio-Frequency Identification (RFID). The imminent path from mobility to pervasiveness focuses entirely on improving organizational performance measures and metrics of success. Work itself, and the dramatic changes these technologies introduce to the organization and to the role of the mobile worker are by and large ignored. The aim of this chapter is to unveil the key changes and challenges that emerge when mobile landscapes are "tagged", and when mobile workers and mobile auto-identification technologies work side-by-side. The motivation for this chapter is to encourage thoughts that appreciate auto-identification technologies and their socio-technical impact on specific mobile work practices and on the nature of mobile work in general.

INTRODUCTION

Mobile work is everywhere; and despite claims by vendors and organizational consultants mobility is neither new nor particularly novel. On the contrary, many traditional occupations have always been highly mobile, including the work of taxi-drivers, policemen, traveling merchants, entertainers and trades people, to name a few. Their degree of mobility may differ, but what mobile workers have in common is a fluid arrangement of workspaces, times and contexts. Despite a long tradition of mobile work arrangements, for example Hackney carriage drivers started in London, UK in 1622, the phenomenon of mobility has not received much attention by organizational scholars over time.

The advancement of modern mobile technologies from the heavy, transmission-weak and battery-hungry, expensive mobile phones of the 1980s to the omnipresent devices of today have raised mobility to the fore of both industry and academia. Interaction among mobile workers, but also with location-dependent colleagues, superiors and clients is carried out via technologies that allow subject-object-subject communication, with the device as a tool that facilitates the exchange of voice, video or data.

Surprisingly, until recently, the success of the mobile phone has not brought many radical innovations forward. Improvements of mobile technologies are seen primarily as incremental, with no new breakthroughs or killer-applications in sight. However, emerging mobile auto-identification technologies invite firms to connect in various ways to their mobile landscape. By strategically embedding technologies with a very small footprint, events involving individual subjects and real objects can be included within organizational information flows. Mobile radio-frequency identification (mobile RFID), for instance, allows firms to place transponders (i.e. tags) and transceivers (i.e. readers) throughout the terrain they cover to initiate object-to-object communication and drive mobile business processes.

In light of these developments, industry and academia have predominantly examined the increasing embeddedness of such context-aware technologies in terms of their impact on the information content of work. The imperceptible object-object interaction enabled by auto-identification technologies is hailed as a dramatic improvement for logistics and supply-chain management. However, along this path from mobility to pervasiveness, work itself, and the dramatic changes these technologies introduce to the organization and to the role of the mobile worker have so far been neglected. The introduction of mobile RFID is discussed here as an example of many auto-identification technologies that mark the move from a mobile landscape, in which mobile workers communicate at will with others as they navigate their terrain, to a pervasive ecosystems that exists as an interactive system between its living, human participants, the objects that shape their work and the environment in which they exist.

The motivation of this chapter is to discuss the fundamental difference of mobility and pervasiveness, with a focus on the user-technology relationship which, in today's attempts to optimize organizational effectiveness and efficiency through embedded technologies, has been entirely overlooked.

The aim of this chapter is to unveil the key changes and challenges that emerge when mobile landscapes are "tagged", and to prepare the reader for the impact that tagging technologies can have on mobile work environments. This chapter should be useful for developers of mobile technology, but also for application developers. Most importantly, this chapter is aimed at "those about to tag" – at practitioners who contemplate the adoption of auto-identification technologies to improve their organizational information flows.

MOBILE LANDSCAPES

The term and concept of mobility is difficult to delineate; and in many ways are any attempts to define mobility too restrictive or not focused enough to be meaningful in any way (Kristoffersen & Ljungberg, 2000). However, a discussion of changing mobile environments requires the delimitation of mobility and location. In this light, common approaches conceptualize mobility and mobile technologies as the opposite of the fixed-location devices.

In its early days, mobility indicated that a particular application could be carried out at different but specific geographical localities, whether within urban spaces or at remote sites. This notion of connectivity at different locales was of enormous significance when devices were first networked in a wireless fashion, and mobility referred more closely to the concept of portability of devices. Remember working on laptop computers and having to find a wired access point (in an Internet Café, possibly) to send your emails? How about the early adopters of mobile telephony, who were plagued by poor signal reception and widespread dead spots? Those were the days of portable technology, when the worker used to travel to the data. Under mobility today, at least in urban environments with the adequate infrastructure, users are less concerned with where they are. With GSM, 3G, GPRS etc., data travels to the mobile worker, and as conquering a larger terrain becomes less of a novelty, mobile connectedness across space, time and contexts becomes more of a necessity to the contemporary worker.

Space

The essence of *spatial mobility* lies in its independence from the concept of location, at least with respect to connectivity and data transfer. Viewed more conceptually, true mobility refers to nomadic arrangements that assume a convergence of systems and a compatibility of services across devices and operating systems independent of location. Kleinrock, the much acclaimed originator of the expression refers to this nomadicity as the arrival of the cliché of *Anytime, Anywhere* computing (1996), a concept approached with increasing capabilities of technology and infrastructure. Recent studies discuss the notion of hypermobility, signifying the "dynamic transformation in location, operation, and interaction in the workplace" (Kakihara, 2003, p. 238) facilitated through mobile technology.

In pursuits of higher degrees of spatial mobility, many seemingly new devices are introduced to the market, promising to bring altogether new technologies to the user. In many ways are such items not entirely new inventions, but rather products that incorporate numerous existing technologies in one device. For example, computing and telephony devices are becoming more indistinguishable as one is adopting features usually associated with the other. Traditionally distinctly different technologies are blending into hypermedia (Kallinikos, 2001(a)). Ljungberg and Sørensen (2000) describe such convergence as a combination of communication via wire, broadcast through the air and data transmission made possible through computers. The results are products such as mobile phones or satellite networks that make use of a host of these technologies. In addition to an increased depth through the convergence of technological features within devices, artifacts will assume new roles to facilitate amplified networking capabilities. Each new generation of mobile communication technology (e.g., infrastructure and mobile phones) allows for higher rates of connectedness and increased throughput for a range of devices that span spatial boundaries.

For practitioners, this often means that their workers are equipped with mobile technology, and that work that had to be pre-planned before could now be arranged more dynamically and on the fly. For many, the mobile phone is seen as a silver-bullet that enables mobile workers "to exchange and retrieve information they need quickly, efficiently and effortlessly, regardless of their physical location" (Hansmann, Merck, Nicklous, & Stober, 2003, p. 13). However, despite all of the new networking and communication choices, the concept of mobility does not suggest the "death of distance" (Cairncross, 1997), or more importantly that location may become inconsequential. Much of the work carried out by mobile workers is in fact location-dependent; it is in many ways about being at being somewhere, at sometime (Cousins & Robey, 2005), at a particular place, at a particular time (Wiberg & Ljungberg, 2000).

Accordingly, more and more people and devices are on the move, requiring more and more information to cross spatial boundaries. Nonetheless, mobility has not solved all of the problems. Many mobile activities are emergent, any upcoming tasks in the field might not even be known by mobile workers themselves, let alone their remote colleagues (Kakihara & Sørensen, 2001). Managing schedules, for example, has become much more difficult for on-site movers who move about at a specific work site, yo-yos who occasionally work away from a fixed location, pendulums who work at two different sites, nomads who work from many sites and carriers who work on the move (Lilischkis, 2003). While their work can be managed more flexibly, this flexibility requires increased communication between mobile workers and their peers. As a result, mobile work is most important for purposes of data exchange and communication but is still seen as practically exercised in many cases at particular times and places. In other words, while location does not matter from the perspective of connectivity, signal reception and the ability to use a mobile device, it not only plays an important role in the examination of where and how mobile work is carried out, but also in the mobile management of time.

Time

In addition to bridging spatial boundaries, mobile information and communication technologies allow people to communicate across temporal constraints. Particularly synchronous technologies have of course shaped interaction with workers in the field, and the mobile phone continues to be the communication medium of choice in most instances. Asynchronous technologies such as mobile email are also important, especially for those who work from areas that do not provide sufficient signal strength for mobile telephony or instant messaging. Either communication option allows mobile workers to plan their tasks with less of a focus on time, as site visits etc. can be rearranged flexibly with supervisors, colleagues or clients. Similarly, mobile workers can now use their time away from their real work to be productive. Mobile technologies are heralded as reviving dead time, time spent at airports, in traffic, or between meetings, thereby surpassing both the spatial and the temporal constraints of fixed-location technologies.

Context

Spatial and temporal dimensions of mobile communication are the more obvious improvements introduced through modern technology. Both are based on the objective affordances (Gibson, 1977) of the devices, infrastructures and supporting technologies. A more subjective affordance (Dourish, 2001) refers to how people and mobile technologies interact in different contexts (Perry, O'Hara, Sellen, Brown, & Harper, 2001). A call in the middle of a meeting, for instance, requires the businesswoman to shift from her work context to the context of being a mother, a text message during a security guard's site visit interrupts his work and requires him to shift contexts and pay attention to his mobile phone. With features such as call waiting, incoming calls even interrupt ongoing calls, requiring mobile workers to juggle two calls, and contexts, at a time, perhaps even while driving or carrying out some other mobile work tasks.

Most communication devices function in a binary fashion; based on signal reception they either render their users are generally available or not accessible to everyone. For the practitioner, this means that mobile workers need to be more flexible, and manage potential interruptions and the danger of communication overload through screening incoming phone-calls and selecting whom to answer or to ignore, prioritizing among different contexts. Nonetheless, even this process requires a shift in context for the user, a cognitive move away from his previous activity and towards the mobile device. These interaction modalities range from unobtrusive to obtrusive and from ephemeral to persistent (Ljungberg & Sørensen, 2000). As a result, individuals' work schedules, their tasks' start and completion times are harder to predict (Perry, O'Hara, Sellen, Brown, & Harper, 2001).

Today, context shifts and interruptions with email and particularly with mobile telephony raise expectations of responsiveness, and mobile workers spend a great portion of their days replying to a text message by sending another message, responding to an email with another email and so on. Repetitive non-responses on a mobile telephone cause unease, even suspicion, on behalf of the caller (Plant, 2001), whereas the same scenario on a landline would not nearly have the same effect. These examples clearly highlight how mobile information and communication technologies (ICTs) change the contexts in which people communicate and interact on a personal and professional level.

The following scenario is a common account of mobile work today, and the reader likely recognizes how mobile technology is deployed to span spatial, temporal and contextual constraints. It shows how the use of mobile ICTs is dramatically shaped by the situation in which this communication occurs, but also shows how mobile interaction shapes the mobile work activity itself.

VIGNETTE A: MOBILE WORK AT MORRISON SECURITY PATROLLING

Simon, a security guard for Morrison Patrolling starts his shift at 6pm, five evenings per week. He arrives at the main office, where he collects a worksheet that contains the various stops for his shift, a vehicle and a mobile phone. Throughout his twelve-hour shift, Simon does not return to the office. He patrols the assigned premises and ensures they are secure. In the event that they are not, he calls his superior to inform him that he will be late for his remaining stops. In the event of an emergency at a different site, a dispatcher calls Simon on his mobile phone to direct him away from his scheduled visits and towards the more urgent matter. For all activities, Simon keeps a paper-based log with the pertinent details. Of course, as security guards spend their days away, it is very difficult for the superior or dispatcher to know where Simon and his colleagues are throughout their shifts. As a result, guards, super-

visors spend an enormous amount of time on the phone, inquiring and reporting on mobile workers' progress, location or upcoming stops. Moreover, Morrison's customers, who never know if their sites have been checked and if they are secure, continuously call Morrison's managers, who then need to call the mobile security guards before they call their customer back with the respective information.

Communication involving mobile workers like Simon, in most cases, suggests that the communication is not carried out face to face, but via a mediating tool, a mobile communication device. This requires that any information from the field needs to be needs to be sourced, worded and communicated by the respective mobile workers in the field. Not only does this suggest that this information is highly subjective, but also that the mobile worker has a high degree of discretion with which he can shape the information passed on to others. In one instance, a mobile security guard could mistakenly report that a site was secure, when in fact it had been compromised. In the scenario above, the mobile worker could knowingly pretend to be at a different location to circumvent being sent to an emergency by the traffic dispatcher. As a result, the mobile worker is at the heart of mobile communication, in charge of mobile interaction even to the point where he could simply ignore an incoming call. In the mobile landscape, the mobile worker is in charge, not only of his work activities but also of communication with others (see also Kalakota & Robinson, 2002). The objects that shape the mobile landscape, including the tools the mobile workers uses and the sites he visits are marginalized, and details of mobile work are only communicated through subjective representations, via the phone or through documents, composed by the mobile worker (Kietzmann, 2008a).

THE MOBILITY OF THINGS

Mobility mostly refers to the extension of people's geographical reach, spanning both time and context. The mobile landscape is the result of communication carried out between different subjects, with the help of mobile phones, for instance, that enables and mediate the subject-object-subject interaction from a distance. Accordingly, mobility mostly refers to people who navigate the mobile landscape. But what happens when objects start to talk to each other? How does this influence mobile communication?

The movement of objects has traditionally referred to shipping and transporting goods from one location to another, to importing and exporting of merchandise and to carrying personal belongings to new locations while traveling (Kakihara, 2003). In discussions of mobile interaction, objects often refer to activity-supporting objects, including paper and pen, but also technological artifacts such as mobile phones, PDAs and BlackBerry terminals. Traditional mobility assumes that objects are inanimate goods, unable of initiating and maintaining any type of communication, and that human involvement is responsible for their movement and participation in any activity. As such, the involvement of objects in mobility discussions is of limited interest; *things* are seen as only supporting human activities on-demand. However, novel developments especially through mobile RFID and Near-Field Communication are giving life to objects.

Mobile Radio Frequency Identification

Traditional, non-mobile Radio Frequency Identification (RFID) is an auto-identification technology that has been available for several decades, perhaps with the first remarkable use in WWII, when the Royal Air Force employed RFID to differentiate between friendly and enemy aircraft. The planes of the Allied Forces were equipped with bulky RFID active transponders (tags) that

received power on board. On the ground RFID transceivers (readers) sent out signals that would communicate with these tags. When a plane was approaching, and a communication between these components could be established, it was assumed that it was a friendly plane. If however, the signal sent out by the reader did not trigger a response from the tag, the assumption was that it was an enemy aircraft that should be attacked.

Applications today still rely on similar communication between RFID tag and reader; although now the tags are miniscule microchips attached to an antenna, and are generally passive. This means, the tags do not have a constant power-source, but are powered by an electromagnetic field emitted by the reader. In most cases, radio signals inform nearby readers of a serial number stored on the tag, which uniquely identifies any item that bears it. So-called Smart Tags are used to track or trace objects everywhere. Think of the readers at the exit of a retail store that sound an alarm when an unpaid item is taken out of the store. Especially high value items, but also those that are popular store-loot are tagged, and the tag needs to be disabled at the register before they can be taken out of the store. Similarly, worldwide, such tags already help keep track of more than 100 million pets and 20 million livestock (Booth-Thomas, 2003).

The Auto-ID Center, initially established as an academic research project headquartered at the Massachusetts Institute of Technology, developed the architecture for creating a seamless global network of all physical objects (Auto-ID Labs 2005). The technology has since been transferred to EPCGlobal, which now oversees the development of standards for Electronic Product Codes (EPC). Such EPC tags attached to every imaginable item, and even people, are revolutionizing logistics, supply chain and inventory management around the world, based on three main advantages of RFID over current alternatives (e.g., barcode). First, RFID can identify items from a distance, without line of sight requirements. This means no more optical scanners at supermarket checkouts, for instance. Second, RFID can read multiple items at once. A truck can drive through the gates of a warehouse, and the inventory of the warehouse is automatically updated with all the items arriving at or leaving the premises. Third, RFID is unique. Barcode describes batches of items, for instance soda-cans from the same flat carry the same information. With RFID, each can can be uniquely identified and traced. Together, these three properties lead to a dramatic shift of interaction with and between objects. Especially when readers and tags communicate from a distance they transform subject-object-subject communication to object-object interaction.

But all of the readers mentioned above are stationary, attached to a store or a warehouse, and the tags are mobile. What would happen if the readers were mobile, too?

Mobile RFID was introduced only a few years ago, and surprisingly has so far stayed under the radar of industry and academia. Unlike other mobile technology developments, mobile RFID introduces entirely new affordances and interaction possibilities to mobile work. Mobile RFID utilizes the combination of a mobile phone, equipped with an RFID reader, a local interaction server and a large number of passive tags that work over a short distance (<3 centimeters). Passive tags, for instance, are able to initiate communication once they are in the proximity of a reader, and vice versa. Imagine the following:

VIGNETTE B: WORK WITH MOBILE RFID TECHNOLOGY

For Morrison Patrolling, tagging the mobile landscape and supplying the mobile security guards with mobile RFID readers promised to overcome many of the mobility-related difficulties. Simon and his mobile colleagues were trained to use the mobile reader, tags were positioned throughout their work environment, and Simon's office-bound co-workers were shown how to use the data coming from the mobile RFID driven system. Mobile guards then read tags attached to many objects within their mobile landscape (e.g., at gates, doors and windows) and selected status responses from the menu on their mobile phone. For instance, when a property was secured and checked, a security guard placed the reader close to the tag on a door and selected "all ok" from the phone's menu. This information was synchronously sent to the back-office. In other events, temperature sensors were attached to tags, and once a security guard with his reader was nearby, the tags queried him to conduct certain safety checks. In even more complex setups, a connected sensor measured the temperature in a room, and once it exceeded its allowable limit, it sent a text message to the mobile worker or even left a voice message, asking him to come to the room's rescue immediately. The auto-identification properties and the mobility and synchronicity of the RFID system virtually eliminated manual logs and work-sheets and drastically reduced the time guards had to spend on the phone to report on their whereabouts. Managers, too, had to spend much less time manually locating and coordinating the security guards, reports could be drawn up within minutes and Morison's customers could access RFID-events via extranet sites.

These advantages are compelling, and "those about to tag" have been convinced that auto-identification will solve their current mobility-related information flow problems. However, introducing mobile RFID, for example, is not just about adding a more advanced technology – it is a big organizational intervention. It is often unclear that everyday objects, as a result, become more active participants in mobile communication; they adopt an increasingly important role in our discussions of mobility.

While some might argue that this interaction is simply machine-to-machine interaction, mobile RFID still involves human participation. However, the important change is that in many cases it is the human involvement that is on-demand, requested by objects in motion, not the other way around. Mobile objects increasingly assume a heightened level of agency in mobile interactions that increasingly rely on mobile data, or information. In addition to, or perhaps as a result of more people and more devices on the move, the amount and depth of personal, public and organizational data transmitted is immense. In addition to wired artifacts (e.g., landlines, desktop computers), or fixed-location wireless devices (e.g., satellites), mobile devices supply an ever-growing share of data transmissions. Thanks to mobile phones, BlackBerry terminals, pagers and even short-range Bluetooth enabled devices, the need to be at specific locations to transmit, broadcast and receive data is at a decline. Moreover, wireless local-area networks, often open to the public or inviting customers at a minimal charge, and wireless broadband connections (e.g. WiFi cities) are increasingly popular, adding to the mobility of data and objects and bringing us ever closer to a truly pervasive ecosystem.

TOWARDS PERVASIVE ECOSYSTEMS

In order for auto-identification technologies to become useful for mobile work, they need to "know" more about the mobile context they are supporting. Basic mobile technologies are off-the-shelve devices that support workers across all possible activities, regardless of the context of their mobile landscape. A mobile phone knows nothing about its environment, and does not respond to unique changes other than signal reception. In a pervasive ecosystem; however, different technologies (e.g., embedded tags, sensors, webcams) must to varying degrees "understand" which environmental and use characteristics to reveal (e.g., the temperature of a room, users' facial expressions) (Höök, Benyon, & Monroe, 2003) and when to involve the human participant.

For the practitioner, this raises many new challenges. IT directors, systems designers, who previously often worked on technology outside of its future application, now increasingly focus on embedding technologies within their specific use context (McCullough, 2004). By building technology around everyday life their values shift from "objects to experiences, from performance to appropriateness, from procedure to situation, and from behavior to intent" (McCullough, 2004, p. 50). Thus argued, industry need to move from linear to more complex and interactive ways of viewing both technology and its future use. For pervasive environments, professionals have to learn how to capture, codify and represent mobile work contexts most appropriately, to "disregard irrelevant details while isolating and emphasizing those properties of artifacts and situations that are most significant" (Brooks, 1991, p. 53). Developing and implementing context-aware mobile auto-identification systems is tremendously difficult, and many developers of mobile information systems might find that they are not well suited for the challenge. In a different paper, the author of this chapter outlines an innovative approach to understanding mobile work and an interactive way to developing mobile information systems accordingly (Kietzmann, 2008a). In this discussion of tagged environments, the focus is more on the impact the technology will have on its users and their communication practices.

A Mobile World

In a mobile landscape, the interaction depends on the mobile worker's discretion and willingness to conduct mobile work accurately and disclose the requested information (e.g., location, time and the status of the object or activity). Details of mobile work are communicated directly through a mobile phone and through field notes, asynchronous logs and progress reports. In Simon's case, his patrolling logs were composed in his own language, according to his frames of reference. The resulting reports formed the most important representations of his mobile work, the only common objects shared by mobile workers, mobile colleagues and their remote supervisors. The worker's discretion and the accuracy of his representations of otherwise purely cognitive accounts of their work determine the overall reliability and validity of the interaction and its context. However, such subjective, imprecise evidence of details of mobile work requires extensive synchronization with other logs and legacy systems to replicate the chain of events of mobile actions and operations.

Who does not remember the countless calls that were necessary between manager and mobile worker to understand what had happened in the field? How about those necessary to understand the reports written by mobile workers? Some are illegible because they have been written in a moving vehicle; others are unclear because they refer to specific objects that are well known to the mobile worker, but not his manager. Due to this inherent ambiguity of details of mobile activities, the drawback of asynchronous representations and the challenge of interpreting others' externalizations, participants increasingly need to rely on synchronous verbal confirmations via the mobile phone for the coordination and control of mobile work activities. However, just as much as the asynchronous representations of mobile work, the mediating tool (e.g., a mobile phone) guarantees no meaningful, objective account of fieldwork for this subject-object-subject interaction; it is merely a conduit that enables the interaction.

In any event, the mobile worker maintains control over the technology and autonomy over the content of the interaction, his cooperation and participation in such communication (e.g., in some cases, disclosed information about location may be deliberately incorrect, in others the phone could consciously not be answered). Tools are neither cohesively embedded within the mobile work environment nor directly coupled to work activities. Attempts to exchange parameters of mobile work most definitely depend on the subject's willingness

to share details of their mobile work; the human remains at the core of the mobile activity.

A Tagged World

While such an understanding holds true for the majority of mobile activities today, the development of mobile RFID is an indicator of a changing level of coupling and embeddedness of computational devices for mobile work. Good practice of systems development is to focus on a high level of intra-activity cohesion and a low level of inter-activity dependencies, facilitating resilient relationships with minimal assumptions between interacting activity systems. As computers disappear and blend into the natural human environment (Weiser, 1991), they promise to become less distinguishable from human affairs and to support their practices. Mobile technology lacks this embeddedness; it is developed and diffused as a blank slate technology, one which has no built-in knowledge base or knowledge capability of its environment beyond the planning reasoning of its designers.

Pervasive computing, on the other hand, negates this concept and spirit of tabula rasa (McCullough, 2004) and relies on inscriptions into the social and physical environment (ibid.). For this, "no revolution in artificial intelligence is needed – just the proper embedding of computers into the everyday world" (Weiser, 1991, p. 3). As technology is becoming increasingly embedded and context aware, for instance through RFID or sensor technology, mobile and stationary people and objects can interact, collect and receive data from a distance. The embeddedness of pervasive technology meets current demands for an increased time and data-sensitive understanding of the contexts of mobile work, as employers of mobile workers and their customers insist on improving their insight into mobile work practices. By developing an infrastructure of embedded, physically nearly undetectable and location-independent tags and mobile RFID readers with inscribed rules, the resulting pervasive ecosystem provides cohesive, context-specific information directly to the tag-reading device. Given this increasing participation of information and communication devices, interaction becomes much less focused on the mobile worker and places greater emphasis on the tools at the core of work activities.

In these more advanced, pervasive activities, it is not only the mediated subject-object-subject interaction that is improved through this increased embeddedness and availability for participants to interact (e.g., through consciously writing to tags and sending messages that are associated with tag-events). Contradictory to mobile landscapes, in pervasive ecosystems, objects not only convey information and mediate the interaction between subjects, but rather adopt an active stance and add value through event-specific information, at times without the explicit permission or knowledge of the mobile worker. Through embedding pervasive devices among subjects (e.g., ID cards), tools (e.g., mobile phones) and objects (e.g., gates and doors) much more sophisticated and cohesive information systems emerge, in which subjects, tools and objects are beginning to talk to one another and, by extension, know about each another. It is this pervasive ecosystem, this interaction and embeddedness, that determines mobile behavior at work, rather than the free navigation of geographical spaces. A mobile worker no longer travels through his work world without traceable interaction (Sørensen, Fagrell, & Ljungstrand, 2000), but through a pervasive ecosystem (see Figure 2) in which "mobility becomes less of a description of an autonomous user freely moving in the world and more of a contingent subject-position made possible by object-object communication" (Elichirigoity, 2004, p. 10).

FOR THOSE ABOUT TO TAG

In pervasive ecosystems, all participants, human or not, are directly coupled and their activities are highly cohesive. In other words, mobile work practices are no longer communicated selectively and by the choice of the individual, but by object-object interaction. This, of course, has a tremendous impact on the mobile worker, her mobile and stationary colleagues, and their long-established communication protocols. Pervasive ecosystems query a number of details with each tag-reader interaction in the field, and synchronously communicate the results via an interaction server to the back-office. While this interrogation sounds highly complex, it is actually quite simple.

Once a system learns about four dimension of a mobile activity, it can provide a highly contextual picture of mobile work. Location, identity, status and time form the basis for this "individual pervasiveness" (Kietzmann, 2008b). For our security guard, this means that each time he approaches a gate, for instance, and tag and reader connect, information is sent to the back-office that contains the identity of the object (and hence its location), the identity of the worker, the status of the object ("all ok"), and the time of the event. Similarly, superiors or even objects can reverse this information flow and impose a "pervasive order" (ibid.) onto mobile work (e.g., a machine can call the worker, or traffic managers can liaise a message through a tag to the worker). This object-driven information flow changes mobile work, particularly as it relates to elements of transparency, control and discretion.

For those about to tag, this raises the following questions.

First, is the mobile landscape one that can be understood at all? Can the complexity of what mobile workers accomplish every day actually be captured and translated meaningfully into a context-aware auto-identification system?

Second, who owns the information that needs to be captured so that it can be codified? To a large extent, this will likely be the mobile workers, as they usually are the only individuals who know the mobile landscape in detail.

Third, why would these mobile workers support the new system? Why not? These are questions of control and discretion. If the mobile work environment was heavily regulated before, the new order that the pervasive system will introduce might not pose a great threat to mobile workers (e.g., heavily controlled occupations like bus drivers). If the mobile workers were left to their own judgment before, like taxi drivers, they might refuse to use the system outright. This relates to the second question. If the mobile workers are the only individuals who understand the context of their work, and if they resist the notion of working in a more closely controlled environment, where will the necessary context-information come from? Will it be reliable?

Fourth, how is agency affected by the tagged environment? In a mobile landscape, as outlined above, communication rests with the mobile worker and the phone and other interaction tools are simple conduits. In a pervasive ecosystem, the communication is driven increasingly by these tools, and the person becomes the conduit. If mobile workers like this new arrangement, the tagged environment has a much higher chance of success. Under pervasiveness, the mobile worker has much less control over the type of information revealed, and over the content that becomes visible to others. A previously sovereign mobile worker all of a sudden becomes dependent on the information system, and the discretion with which he carries out his work is now not up to the judgment of the worker but to the embedded knowledge and pre-programmed logic of the context-aware system. A security guard who previously used his expert-knowledge to navigate through traffic and might have changed the sequence of the stops along his route now is required to follow the sequence ordered by the mobile RFID system.

Fifth, who else is affected? Will everyone support the new system? Tagged environments not only change mobile workers' job description, but also affect everyone who works with data from the field. In the Morrison Patrolling case,

superiors and traffic managers who were able to schedule their mobile workers and trusted that they completed their work independently now had transparent data that they could not ignore. Some RFID driven events even demanded that superiors form decisions, which were previously left up to the mobile worker. This requires a system-wide look at users, not just a look at the mobile workers. If good data comes from the field, but those in the back office have no reason to use it, the auto-identification system will fail to live up to its promise.

Lastly, the perception of auto-identification technologies requires some attention. On the technology front, many seemingly futuristic developments are possible, if not already underway. Imagine introducing a GPS sensor to the security guard's mobile RFID tool, or add a techograph to the equation. The iPhone has already shown what is possible. How about connecting all of the mobile RFID events to each other to populate an "internet of things" that adds transparency and extensive data-mining capabilities to all mobile events? While these questions are of a much bigger Orwellian nature, they might be on the minds of the mobile users who are critical to the development and adoption of a tagging technology. Especially users who are technology savvy might envision how the following emerging trends might be adopted next, and how, as a result, their role might continue to change if they support the adoption of auto-identification technologies today.

Emerging Technologies

Mobile RFID is only the beginning of many context-aware technologies. And, in their current form, pervasive ecosystems are not yet entirely location independent since their read-range is still quite limited. However, the pervasive ecosystem marked by mobile RFID technology already points at what will be presented by the inevitable improvement of technology. Reading ranges are already projected to approach 20 meters for more stationary readers (Garfinkel & Rosenberg, 2006), on the mobile front this will only be a question of power management on the device. As more and more objects and tools of mobile work become embedded with tags and improved readers, we will witness a continuously increasing mobility with pervasive devices, ultimately approaching ubiquitous computing environments (Lyytinen & Yoo, 2002). Visions of the future home and retail organizations (Albrecht & MacIntyre, 2005), the next generation of cash (Angell & Kietzmann, 2006), interactive fashion and wearable computing (Mann & Niedzviecki, 2002) etc. contribute to the notion of a pervasive ecosystem.

Of course, improved devices alone will not change pervasiveness. Improved infrastructure and middleware technologies, including smart antennas, mesh networks and ad-hoc computing will elevate current networking technology towards pervasive data-throughputs, especially once agreed-upon standards are in place. Derived from nanotechnology's concept of swarm computing, amorphous technologies require that collective networks can be built on individual devices' capacities to transmit signals without intercepting them. This ad-hoc technology allows each client (e.g., mobile phone) to function as a server and signals to hop from device to device. This increasingly location independence of computing occurrences will render a fixed-location infrastructure of senders and repeaters unnecessary, giving way to a truly pervasive and ubiquitous world.

CONCLUSION

Many developments are at the horizon, and some, including mobile RFID are already commercially available. Of course, only the positive impact of auto-identification technologies is advertised to organizations. And indeed, the synchronous object-object information from the field enables altogether new forms of managing mobile work. Rightfully so, practitioners might be convinced that these advantages will improve their organizational metrics and success measures. Particularly once mobile RFID becomes more standardized, the advantages of auto-identification technologies might suggest an even stronger positive impact of tagging the mobile landscape.

This chapter outlines some of these positive affordances of auto-identification, but also aims to raise a word of caution. Tagging is a very complex and complicated process, which requires that a number of critical questions are asked and answered. In many cases, these are not of a technical nature, but relate to the social and socio-political environment that is to be tagged.

Certainly, mobility and pervasiveness are not the same. Each has its unique advantages and drawbacks. As this chapter outlined, the arguments that once led organizations to adopt mobile technology must be different from those that drive tagging decisions today. It was the ambition of this chapter to illustrate how a tiny technology, such as a mobile RFID tag, can change mobile work practices and the nature of mobile work entirely. Hopefully, this chapter has provided "those about to tag" with a number of interesting questions to ponder, and has informed their decision in favor or against mobile auto-identification technologies. It was not the motivation of this chapter to suggest that mobile RFID etc. are bad choices, but to endorse critical thoughts among "those about to tag" that will help determine if, and how, auto-identification choices will transform their mobile landscapes into pervasive ecosystems.

REFERENCES

Albrecht, K., & MacIntyre, L. (2005). *Spychips: How Major Corporations and Government Plan to Track Your Every Move with RFID*. Nelson Current.

Angell, I., & Kietzmann, J. (2006). RFID and the End of Cash? *Communications of the ACM, 49*(12), 90-96.

Booth-Thomas, C. (2003). The See-It-All-Chip, *Time Online Edition*.

Brooks, R. (1991). Comparative Task Analysis: An Alternative Direction for Human-Computer Interaction Science. In J. Carroll (Ed.), *Designing Interaction: Psychology at the Human Computer Interface* (pp. 50-59). Cambridge: Cambridge University Press.

Cairncross, F. (1997). *The Death of Distance*. Boston, Mass: Harvard Business School Press.

Cousins, K. C., & Robey, D. (2005). Human Agency in a Wireless World: Patterns of Technology Use in Nomadic Computing Environments. *Information and Organization, 15*(2), 151-180.

Dourish, P. (2001). *Where the action is: The foundations of embodied interaction*: MIT Press.

Elichirigoity, F. (2004). *Embedded Mobilities*. Paper presented at the The Life of Mobile Data: Technology, Mobility and Data Subjectivity, University of Surrey, UK.

Garfinkel, S., & Rosenberg, B. (2006). *RFID: Applications, Security, and Privacy*: Addison-Wesley Professional.

Gibson, J. J. (1977). The Theory of Affordances. In R. Shaw & J. Bransford (Eds.), *Perceiving, Acting, and Knowing,* .

Hansmann, U., Merck, L., Nicklous, M. S., & Stober, T. (2003). *Pervasive Computing: The Mobile World*. Heidelberg: Springer Verlag.

Höök, K., Benyon, D., & Monroe, A. J. (Eds.). (2003). *Designing Information Spaces: The Social Navigation Approach*. London: Springer-Verlag.

Kakihara, M. (2003). *Hypermobility: Emerging Work Practices of ICT-Enabled Professionals*. London School of Economics and Political Science, London.

Kakihara, M., & Sørensen, C. (2001). Expanding the 'Mobility' Concept. *Siggroup Bulletin, 22*(3), 33-37.

Kalakota, R., & Robinson, M. (2002). *M Business: The Race to Mobility*: McGraw-Hill.

Kallinikos, J. (2001(a)). *The Age of Flexibility*. Lund: Academia Adacta AB.

Kietzmann, J. (2008a). Interactive Innovation of Technology for Mobile Work. *European Journal of Information Systems, 17*(3), 305-320.

Kietzmann, J. (2008b). *The Dark Side of Mobile RFID and the Disappearing Computer*. Paper presented at the European Group for Organizational Studies, Amsterdam.

Kleinrock, L. (1996). Nomadicity: Anytime, Anywhere in a Disconnected World. *Mobile Networks and Applications, 1*, 351-357.

Kristoffersen, S., & Ljungberg, F. (2000). Mobility: From Stationary to Mobile Work. In *Planet Internet* (pp. 137-156). Lund: Studentlitteratur.

Lilischkis, S. (2003). *More Yo-yos, Pendulums and Nomads: Trends of Mobile and Multi-Location Work in the Information Society*: STAR.

Ljungberg, F., & Sørensen, C. (2000). Overload: From Transaction to Interaction. In K. Braa, C. Sørensen & B. Dahlbom (Eds.), *Planet Internet* (pp. 113-136). Lund: Studentlitteratur.

Lyytinen, K., & Yoo, Y. (2002). Issues and Challenges in Ubiquitous Computing. *Communications of the ACM, 45*(12), 6-65.

Mann, S., & Niedzviecki, H. (2002). *Cyborg: Digital Destiny and Human Possibility in the Age of the Wearable Computer*: Doubleday Canada.

McCullough, M. (2004). *Digital Ground: Architecture, Pervasive Computing, and Environmental Knowing* (Vol. The MIT Press). Cambridge, Massachusetts.

Perry, M., O'Hara, K., Sellen, A., Brown, B., & Harper, R. (2001). Dealing with Mobility: Understanding access anytime, anywhere. *ACM Transactions on computer human interaction (TOCHI), 8*(4), 323-347.

Plant, S. (2001). *On the Mobile.* from http://www.motorola.com/mot/doc/0/234_MotDoc.pdf.

Sørensen, C., Fagrell, H., & Ljungstrand, P. (2000). Traces: From Order to Chaos. In K. Braa, C.

Sørensen & B. Dahlbom (Eds.), *Planet Internet.* Lund, Sweden: Studentlitteratur.

Weiser, M. (1991). The Computer for the 21st Century. *Scientific American.*

Wiberg, M., & Ljungberg, F. (2000). Exploring the vision of anytime, anywhere in the context of mobile work. In *Knowledge management and Virtual organizations: Theories, Practices, Technologies and Methods*: Brint Press.

Chapter II
Privacy and Location–Based Mobile Services:
Finding a Balance

Adrian Lawrence
Baker & McKenzie, Australia

Jane Williams
Baker & McKenzie, Australia

ABSTRACT

As commercial interest in LBS increases, legal and regulatory bodies are becoming increasingly interested in the extent to which use of LBS may affect individuals' privacy. This chapter discusses the nature of the privacy-related issues arising from the use of commercial LBS and gives examples of approaches that might be taken to best address these issues from the perspective of users of LBS and commercial providers of LBS. It identifies and analyses some of the key privacy issues that arise from use of LBS and the ways in which these types of issues are being regulated in some jurisdictions. It also suggests some best-practice guidelines for how these issues might be best dealt with in order to ensure that individuals' privacy is protected. Given the increasing importance of privacy issues to consumers and their likely reluctance to use commercial LBS if significant privacy concerns are not addressed, this chapter concludes that both consumers and commercial LBS providers will benefit from privacy concerns being addressed appropriately. This chapter identifies and analyzes these issues on a theoretical level so that the issues and approaches suggested may be useful to both privacy advocates and regulators and to providers of LBS, and will remain relevant as LBS become more sophisticated.

INTRODUCTION

While the processing of location information in mobile communication networks is not a new phenomenon, increasing interest in use of location technologies for security and emergency purposes, as well as the numerous possible commercial uses of this information, has driven the development of higher-accuracy location techniques. As a result, there is now a broad and rapidly expanding range of commercial location-based mobile services (**LBS**) available to consumers. It is likely that the types of LBS available to consumers will become increasingly sophisticated.

A key concern arising from the use of LBS is whether use of individuals' location information for the purpose of providing LBS interferes with their privacy. A common theme that arises from research and discussions relating to privacy and LBS is that individuals want a level of control over the collection and use of their location information for commercial purposes.

Some jurisdictions have already implemented laws and regulations specifically aimed at protecting individuals' privacy in the context of LBS, while others have general privacy laws that protect location information to some extent. Some jurisdictions are yet to implement any laws that protect location information.

As the use of LBS becomes more widespread, it will be important that laws and regulations applicable to use of LBS continue to provide adequate protection for individuals' privacy and that such laws and regulations can adapt to new uses of LBS in the future. Further, as discussed below, given individuals' increasing concern with their privacy when using LBS and their reluctance to use services that do not ensure that their privacy will be protected, it is also in the interest of commercial providers of LBS to adequately address these privacy concerns in their development and provision of LBS.

A purpose of this chapter is to identify some of the key privacy issues that arise in the context of

LBS and analyze the ways in which these issues might best be addressed in order to ensure that individuals' privacy is protected. This analysis may be useful both to privacy advocates and regulators to assist them to identify what are the key privacy issues in the context of LBS, and to providers of LBS to assist them to understand the way that existing or proposed privacy laws may affect their practices and to develop privacy policies and practices that may assist them to comply with laws or otherwise gain consumer confidence.

As LBS are likely to become increasing sophisticated, and as privacy laws vary greatly among jurisdictions and are rapidly changing, this chapter aims to identify and analyze issues on a theoretical level so that the issues raised and suggested approaches are useful both now and as the issues develop.

BACKGROUND

Location information is information about the specific location of a mobile device at a particular time or over a period of time, such as a GPS-enabled navigation device, mobile phone, personal computer or personal digital assistant. Location information is obtained by telecommunications carriers through the integration of computing and wireless communications technologies and is obtained when individuals use such mobile devices or often simply when the device is switched on.

Some of the common non-commercial uses of LBS relate to emergency services, such as the E-911 feature in the United States and roadside assistance services, and law enforcement, such as investigation surveillance of people suspected of criminal activities and investigating the location of missing persons (Lockwood, 2004; Michael, Perusco & Michael, 2006).

Some of the common commercial uses of LBS involve individuals being sent information or advertising messages to their mobile devices, relating to things such as the location and availability of products and services in their local area, such as restaurants, cinemas and other businesses, maps of local areas and travel directions, local weather and traffic conditions, and travel-related services, such as the location of local hotels or hire-car businesses (Younes-Fellous, 2007; Stein, Hawking & Sharma, 2005).

Other commercial uses of LBS involve tracking services, which enable individuals to track their pets, children, aged people or friends. There are also tracking services that enable employers to track their employees and enable businesses to track the movement of their goods in transit (Hong, Boriello, Landy, McDonald, Schilit & Tygar, 2003; Kuchinskas, 2007; Bennet & Crow, 2005).

Online content providers can also use location information to identify the location of website users so the content provider can limit access to, or vary, content of the website in particular locations (Svantesson, 2005).

While there are many different types of LBS, they are often broadly categorized as either 'active' or 'pull' services or 'passive' or 'push' services. 'Active' or 'pull' services are those which are initiated by a specific request, such as a request by an individual who has entered a particular geographical area and wants to find a particular type of business or service in that location. 'Passive' or 'push' services are those which are not specifically requested by the individual at a particular point in time, such as services that send advertising messages to an individual when they enter a particular geographical area (which might be sent to an individual who has subscribed to receive such messages from time to time), or services that track an individual at the request of another individual (which involves the collection and use of location information from an individual who has not provided their consent to have this information collected and used for this purpose) (Australian Law Reform Commission, 2007, paras 63.91-63.94; Spiekermann, 2004). Some LBS, such

as friend-finder services, may be a combination of push and pull services.

The different commercial and non-commercial uses and different types of LBS are relevant when considering the privacy issues that arise from use of LBS because these different uses and types of LBS tend to raise different privacy issues.

NATURE OF LOCATION INFORMATION

Personal Information

Location information enables the location of individuals at a particular point in time, or over a particular period of time, to be ascertained and monitored. For the purpose of LBS, location information is usually collected by the telecommunications carrier and disclosed to a third party who provides LBS. The provider of the LBS may also disclose this information to other entities who provide services to the provider of the LBS. In these circumstances, an individual's location information may be collected, stored, used and disclosed by a number of different entities.

While location information in itself may not enable the identity of the individual to be ascertained, where that individual's identity can be ascertained either directly or indirectly from location information, that information will also be characterized as personal information about that individual.

To the extent that location information is personal information, it will be subject to data privacy regimes in many jurisdictions. Generally speaking, these regimes require organizations who collect personal information about individuals to handle this information in a way that ensures that individuals retain control over the information and protects the information from misuse. As discussed below, most jurisdictions do not have specific laws and regulations that relate to location information.

Sensitivity of Location Information

It is generally accepted that many individuals consider information about their location to be sensitive in some circumstances, either because they consider the fact of their specific location or movements private in themselves, or they are concerned about the extent to which their location at a particular time or over a period of time may reveal other personal information about them (Australian Law Reform Commission, 2007, para 63.86).

Early uses of location information were largely non-commercial, such as for security or law enforcement purposes. An example is the E-911 feature in wireless devices in the United States, which enables telecommunications carriers to locate emergency calls within a short distance of the origination of the call. Many individuals were not overly concerned about the privacy implications of these uses of location information, often on the basis that the benefit of the service outweighed any realistic privacy concerns (Ackerman, Kempf & Miki, 2003; Long, 2007; Dao, Rizos & Wang, 2002).

However, with the increasing advances in the accuracy of location information, and the numerous commercial LBS being offered and developed, individuals are becoming more concerned about the privacy of their location information.

Although in recent times there has been significant attention paid to individuals' attitudes to privacy and their use of the internet (for example, relating to what type of information search engines collect about individuals who visit particular websites and how long they keep this type of information), there are few studies examining the underlying need for individuals' privacy and the importance of privacy to individuals in the context of LBS (Wallis Consulting Group, 2007).

In their article entitled *Location-Based Services for Mobile Telephony: a Study of Users' Privacy Concerns*, Barkuus and Dey (2003) reported on a study in which they found that people were generally positive about LBS as long as they perceived such services to be useful. In relation to privacy issues, while they were in general not overly concerned about their privacy when using such services, they demonstrated greater concern for location-tracking services, which they considered to be more intrusive than simpler position-aware services.

It is likely that certain types of LBS, by their nature, will cause individuals to be more concerned about their privacy than others. There are a number of ways that use of location information may interfere with individuals' privacy or otherwise be detrimental to individuals.

One example of this is where individuals receive unwanted messages, such as advertising messages, on their mobile phones from businesses to which those individuals have not provided their personal information or otherwise given their consent to receive messages from. Spiekermann (2004) observes that it is feared that a spamming problem, similar to the problem that exists on the internet, may emerge in the mobile world and that such messages may be perceived by individuals as even more intrusive than email spamming (p. 16).

Another example is where location information is used to harass an individual. Tracking services, which enable the particular location of an individual to be tracked at a point in time or over a period of time by another individual without that first individual's consent, may be intrusive and may affect individuals' safety. (Minch, 2007, p. 2)

Use of individuals' location information at a particular point in time or over a period of time can also cause individuals to suffer embarrassment or discrimination. For example, use of this information might enable an inference to be drawn about individuals' health, relationships, or other personal aspects of their lives, which are intrusive or embarrassing. It might also have the effect that an individual seeking to use a service, such as to make an insurance claim from an insurance company, may be denied the service on the basis that the service provider is aware of particular information about that individual, such as that they recently visited a high-risk location (Mahmoud, 2004).

KEY PRIVACY ISSUES

The types of questions that are commonly asked when considering what type of privacy issues arise from use of any new technology include: whose information will be collected, what kind of information will be collected, who will the information be shared with and for what purpose, how will the information be stored, and what control will individuals have over the collection and use of their information.

As Minch (2004) observes in his article entitled *Privacy Issues in Location-Aware Mobile Devices*, LBS raise a myriad of privacy issues due to the capacity of these services to collect, store, use and disclose location information relating to users (pp. 2-6).

In this section, we identify some of the key issues arising from collection, storage, use and disclosure of location information. While the answers to the questions referred to above will be different depending upon the use and type of the specific LBS, there are some key privacy issues that are likely to arise in respect to most types of LBS. It is likely that, even as the sophistication of LBS increases, these issues will remain the key privacy issues arising from the use of LBS.

Further below we suggest some of the ways that these issues might best be addressed to ensure that individuals' privacy is protected.

A. Collection

The first key privacy issue is collection of information. Location information may be collected internally and independently by the mobile device (such as by a GPS-enabled device) or externally by other devices that the mobile device communicates with (such as telecommunications carriers' facilities).

Some factors that may influence the extent to which collection of location information affects individuals' privacy are whether they consent to their location information being collected or are aware that it is being collected, the collection is automatic and continual or only upon request and occasional, and whether individuals can control whether the information is collected and have the ability to opt-out of their location information being collected.

These issues are more likely to affect individuals' privacy in respect to collection of location information for the purposes of commercial LBS rather than collection for purposes such as emergency services or law enforcement where individuals are much less likely to object to the collection of the information or may not legally have an option regarding whether or not it is collected.

B. Storage

The second key issue is storage of information. Location information may be stored only on the individual's mobile device or also at other external facilities, such as on the telecommunications carrier's facilities. Even where the information is initially stored on the mobile device, it may be transmitted later to other facilities.

There are a number of factors that influence the extent to which storage of location information affects individuals' privacy. What type of information is stored and what level of detail this information contains will affect how the information can be used. Where the information is stored and at how many locations it is stored will affect what control the individual has over the information and how it might be used or disclosed. How long the information is stored for will affect whether the information can be used for long-term tracking or profiling purposes. Finally, how securely the information is stored will affect the likelihood of the information being lost or misused.

C. Use

The third key issue is use of information. As discussed above, there are many different uses of location information, ranging from use for emergency services and law enforcement purposes to the many different types of commercial services now available.

There are a number of factors that may influence the extent to which use of location information affects an individual's privacy. One factor is whether the individual consented to the specific use, or at least consented to receive the relevant service (for example, whether the individual specifically requested the service, such as a navigation assistance service, or whether the individual's movements are being tracked by another individual). Whether the individual directly benefits from the service (for example, whether the use is to assist the individual in the case of an emergency or, at the other extreme, whether the use is to advertise the services of a business to the individual) is also relevant. Another relevant factor is how intrusive the service is (for example, a service that creates a consumer profile based on purchasing behaviour is likely to be considered more intrusive than a service that sends a one-off message).

D. Disclosure

The fourth key issue is disclosure of information. Many LBS rely on the exchange of location information between the entity which collects the information, such as the telecommunications carrier, and third parties who provide LBS.

There are a number of factors that may influence the extent to which disclosure of location information affects an individual's privacy. One factor is whether the disclosure is made to assist third parties, such as for the purpose of an emergency, or is required by law or whether it is to benefit a third party service provider. Whether the individual consented to the specific disclosure or at least to receive the service that required the disclosure (for example, where the service involves the individual receiving marketing offers from a third party, the individual is likely to be aware that the relevant third party service provider will receive that individual's location information) is also relevant. Another factor is whether disclosure of information is made automatically and on an ongoing basis (for example, where the user has subscribed to receive a traffic-alert service), or only intermittently (for example, where a marketing business wants to advertise to consumers who are in a particular geographical location).

There are also security-related issues relating to disclosure of location information arising from the transmission of this information over wireless networks, both because of the additional disclosure of information and because of the increased potential that information will be intercepted by unauthorized parties.

A common theme among each these issues is what level of control users of the LBS have of the collection, storage, use and disclosure of their location information. This theme is discussed further below.

EXAMPLES OF CURRENT PRIVACY LAWS AND REGULATIONS

Although privacy issues arising specifically from use of LBS are being addressed by legal and regulatory bodies in some jurisdictions, there is little consistency among the approaches being taken. In some jurisdictions, there is as yet little or no legal or regulatory protection. As the use of LBS increases, there is increasing interest among non-governmental organizations and industry bodies in the way in which location information is regulated.

Below is a brief discussion of some examples of the way that some jurisdictions, namely the European Union, Australia and the United States, are handling regulation of location information. These jurisdictions have been selected as examples of jurisdictions that have varying levels of regulation of privacy both at a general level and more specifically in relation to protection of location information. The purpose of discussing the laws in these jurisdictions is simply to provide examples of some different approaches being taken to regulation of location information.

The European Union Directive on privacy and electronic commerce (Directive 2002/58/EC) contains provisions specifically dealing with location information, which it defines as "any data processed in an electronic communications network, indicating the geographic position of the terminal equipment of a user of a publicly available electronic communications service".

The provisions of this Directive relate to confidentiality, security and privacy issues that arise from the processing of location information. Some of its key features in respect to location information are (Spiekermann, 2004, pp. 17-18):

- Location information which has not been made anonymous must not be processed without the user's consent;
- Prior to giving their consent, users must be informed of the type of location information that will be processed, the purpose and duration of the processing, and whether the data will be transferred to a third party;
- Users must have the option at any time of withdrawing their consent regarding use of their location information;
- Only the entity who has entered into a contract with the user can use that person's personal information for marketing purposes and the user has the opportunity to object to such use;
- Electronic messages must not conceal the identity of the sender and must contain a valid reply address; and

- Automated calling is only allowed where a subscriber has given prior consent.

In Australia, there is telecommunications legislation that provides that use or disclosure of information relating to the location of a mobile telephone handset or other mobile communications device is permitted where the individual has consented to the disclosure or use. There are also privacy laws and regulations that relate generally to the collection, use and disclosure of personal information (*Telecommunications Act 1997* (Cth), s. 291; *Privacy Act* 1988 (Cth), Schedule 3). However, there are no specific laws that relate to handling of location information that apply specifically in the context of commercial LBS.

In the United States, there are several laws regulating location information to some extent, but no laws or regulations that apply specifically to information in the way that the European Directive discussed above does. The *Communications Act* of 1934 (as amended by the *Telecommunications Act* 1996, s. 122) requires carriers to only use proprietary network information for provisioning services requested by customers.

Under the *Wireless Communications and Public Safety Act* of 1999, the Federal Communications Commission (**FCC**) was authorized to deploy the E-911 feature in wireless devices mentioned above, but this legislation only authorizes the provision of "call location information concerning the user of a commercial mobile phone service" for the purpose of responding to an emergency situation.

In August 2002, the FCC rejected a proposal for specific location information privacy rules from the wireless industry association (**CTIA**) on the basis that it considered that existing privacy laws and regulations were sufficient (Smith, 2005). The rules proposed by the CTIA included a requirement that providers of LBS inform individuals about their information collection and use practices before they disclose such information and give individuals the option to choose whether or not to allow their location information to be used.

WAYS TO ADDRESS PRIVACY ISSUES

Approach to Privacy Reform

Generally speaking, the adequacy of existing laws and regulations relating to location information, and the need for new laws and regulations, should be assessed in light of the relevant jurisdiction's existing laws and regulations relating to privacy and related areas, such as telecommunications, surveillance and national security. It may also be appropriate to consider how such laws should apply to particular classes of individuals, such as children.

In jurisdictions which already have a relatively robust privacy regime, these laws and regulations may only need to be adapted to ensure they apply adequately to location information and to possible future uses of location information arising from development of LBS. In other regimes, where the current regime is less robust, a more comprehensive approach may be necessary.

A starting point, regardless of the level of complexity of the existing regime, is to consider how each of the key privacy issues that arise from use of LBS might best be addressed to ensure that individuals' privacy is protected.

The analysis in this section is based on current uses of LBS. However, as the level of sophistication of LBS increases, it may be necessary to reconsider how these key privacy issues are affected by new ways in which location information is collected and used.

Addressing Privacy Issues

This section considers how the key privacy issues arising from use of LBS discussed above, arising from collection, storage, use and disclosure of location information, might be addressed to ensure that individuals' privacy is protected. These suggestions draw on general privacy principles and the ways that privacy issues are handled in similar contexts, such as in an online context, and are suggested as "best practice" approaches to privacy protection. Many of these suggestions for how these issues should be addressed are similar to the principles adopted in the European Union Directive discussed above.

A. Anonymity

From a practical perspective, some commentators have suggested methods of collecting and using location information that would minimize the potential for privacy issues to arise from the use of such information. In particular, these methods rely on principles of anonymity and pseudonymity.

The reason that these methods may minimize the potential for privacy issues to arise from the use of location information is that, if such information cannot be traced directly or indirectly to a specific individual, use of this information will not interfere with an individual's privacy. This is the case both from a practical perspective and because, if this information is not characterized as personal information for the purpose of data privacy laws and regulations, any laws and regulations that govern how a provider of LBS must collect, store, use and disclose personal information will not apply to this information (Jorns, Quirchmayr & Jung, 2007, p. 2).

In an article published in 2007, Jorns, Quirchmayr and Jung suggest some of the specific approaches that could be taken to reduce the privacy issues arising from use of LBS. The first approach, which involves use of a random pseudonym, is to assign a randomly-generated pseudonym to each individual user of the LBS. The provider of the LBS would then associate any location information about that individual with the pseudonym, rather than the individual's real name or other identity details. This means that the individual can continue to use the service using that particular pseudonym and can have the benefit of maintaining that identity for a period of time (so that it could, for example, personalize a particular service or establish a reputation using that service), but would have the option at any time to simply cease using that pseudonym and commence using a different pseudonym that is not linked to location information that was linked to the first pseudonym (Langheinrich, s. 4.3).

The second approach, which involves the use of de-identified location information, is that providers of LBS could collect and use only de-identified location information (that is, information from which the individual's identity cannot be ascertained). This would mean that location information relating to a particular individual would be indistinguishable from information of other individuals within a particular group who are receiving the same services, such as in a particular geographical area. Although this would mean that particular location information could be linked to a limited set of individuals (for example, individuals in a particular geographical area), the particular identity of any one of those individuals would not be ascertainable from that information.

The third approach, which involves use of an intermediary organization, suggests that such an organization could be used to collect individuals' location information from a number of sources, such as different telecommunications carriers, and act as an information broker for providers of LBS. The carriers would attach a particular pseudonym to each piece of location information provided to the intermediary, and then the intermediary would assign a different pseudonym to that information when it provides the information to the provider of the LBS. The effect of this is that the provider of the LBS would only receive an individual's location information and pseudonym and would not have any way of linking that information or pseudonym to the individual's actual name or other personal information in order to ascertain the identity of that individual.

One way in which this third option may be less preferable than the first two is that the use of an intermediary organization, which involves an additional disclosure of information to an additional entity, increases the risk of misuse or disclosure of the information.

As mentioned above, the benefit of using these methods of anonymity is that, if an individual's location information cannot be directly or indirectly traced to that individual, use of this information will not interfere with that individual's privacy. However, in order for this benefit to be achieved, it is important that the anonymized location information cannot be reconciled with the relevant individuals' personal information. From a practical perspective, this may often be difficult for telecommunications carriers and providers of LBS to achieve.

B. Collection

One of the fundamental principles of data privacy regimes is openness (Langheinrich, s. 4.2). In particular, individuals should be informed about how their personal information is collected, used and disclosed. This principle is commonly satisfied in data privacy regimes by requiring that individuals are informed of specific information at the time that their personal information is collected.

In order to address the types of issues discussed above relating to collecting of location information in the context of LBS, telecommunications carriers and providers of LBS should be required to provide individuals with specific information either before or at the time that they collect location information, such as the purpose for which the information is being collected, how the information will be used, whether it will be disclosed to a third party for the purpose of providing the LBS, and how long the information will be retained.

If individuals are given notice of this type of information, they will be in a better position to control the collection of their personal information.

C. Storage

We identified above some of the factors that influence the extent to which storage of location information affects an individual's privacy. To best address these issues, providers of LBS should be only entitled to use and store location information to the extent necessary, to keep location information for as long as necessary to provide the particular service, and to implement appropriate security measures to ensure that the confidentiality and integrity of the information is protected.

Further, in order to ensure that individuals retain control over their location information, individuals should have access to personal information that is held about them and should be able to request that any incorrect information be corrected.

D. Use and Disclosure

We identified above the types of factors that influence how use and disclosure of individuals' location information may affect individuals' privacy. An issue that is fundamental to this is consent.

In order for individuals to maintain control over the use and disclosure of their location information, telecommunications carriers and providers of LBS should be required to obtain individuals' informed and freely given consent to any proposed use or disclosure of their location information.

A particular issue that arises in relation to consent is whether telecommunications carriers and providers of LBS should be required to obtain an "opt in" consent, which requires that individuals expressly indicate their consent, or whether it is sufficient to obtain an "opt out" consent, which requires only that individuals are notified that their information will be used for a particular purpose and are given the option to "opt out". "Opt in" consent is usually favored by privacy advocates, such as the Privacy Rights Clearing

House, because it is perceived to give individuals a greater level of control over the use of their location information (Wireless Communications: Voice and Data Privacy).

Whether "opt in" or "opt out" consent is appropriate is likely to depend on the type of LBS being provided. As discussed above, individuals are likely to be more concerned about some services than others. For example, individuals are likely to find services which rely on their location or purchasing habits being tracked over a period of time more intrusive than those that only depend upon occasional real-time location tracking or which depend upon a specific request from the individual.

Further, as Barkuus and Dey found in their 2003 study discussed above, the extent to which individuals are concerned about their privacy when using LBS may depend upon how useful they consider the service to be. On this basis, it may be appropriate that "opt in" consent is required for certain types of services but not for others.

Another issue relevant to consent is how easily individuals are able to withdraw their consent. Individuals will have most control over use of their location information if they have the option to withdraw their consent to a particular use of their location information at any time, and are able to do this easily, quickly and without any additional fee (Younes-Fellous, 2007).

Finally, in order for the option to consent to have the effect of enabling individuals to have a real choice about whether or not their location information is used for a specific purpose, the circumstances in which an individual is given an option to give (or withdraw) consent should be fair. For example, if a service will only be provided on the condition that the individual gives consent to a broad range of uses and disclosures of their location information that goes beyond an extent reasonably necessary for that individual to receive the service, this "choice" whether or not to consent will not amount to a real choice for that individual.

BENEFITS FOR LBS PROVIDERS

There are many obvious benefits for individuals of laws and regulations that adequately protect their location information. However, as discussed below, there are also likely to be benefits for providers of LBS if they have in place appropriate policies and procedures to protect individuals' location information.

In their 2007 article, Jorns, Quirchmayr and Jung argue that users' acceptance of LBS has been much lower than expected in some areas and that one reason for this is individuals' concerns regarding the privacy of their location information. Spiekermann (2004) argues that unproven economics and privacy concerns are the main reasons why "push services", where a user receives information without actively requesting it, have not come to flourish (p. 14).

Further, in their article entitled *Wireless Location Privacy Law and Policy*, Ackerman, Kempf & Miki (2003) observed that Japan has been the most successful jurisdiction at developing its LBS market and that one reason for this may be that it has, since 1998, had clear guidelines in place relating to the consent required to use location information.

It follows from these observations that it is likely that individuals who understand and are comfortable with how their location information will be used by providers of LBS will be more inclined to use the services.

This means that providers of LBS who can demonstrate that they are complying with laws and regulations relating to individuals' privacy and have in place policies relating to the way that individuals' location information is handled which are transparent and give users control over how their information is used will be able to market their services more successfully. To gain this benefit, providers of LBS may decide to implement "best practice" privacy policies and practices that are not currently required by applicable laws and regulations.

Given the increasing importance of privacy issues to consumers, having in place good privacy practices may enable providers of LBS to distinguish their services from those of other providers who cannot offer the same level of privacy protection. Gaining and maintaining individuals' trust is likely to be an important asset when offering increasingly sophisticated services to increasingly privacy-conscious individuals (Jorns, Quichmayr & Jung, 2007).

FUTURE TRENDS

Given the increasing commercial uses of LBS and the increasing awareness of the privacy issues among privacy advocates and consumers arising from use of LBS, it is likely that legal and regulatory bodies will continue to seek to introduce new laws and regulations to protect individuals' location information.

In addition to ensuring that individuals' privacy is protected, it is important that any new laws and regulations aimed at protecting location information are clear and consistent so that providers of LBS can easily understand and comply with them. Further, as the flow of data between different jurisdictions becomes more common, the laws and regulations in different jurisdictions would ideally be as consistent as possible.

Given the rapid pace at which new LBS are being developed, to the extent that it is possible, it is also important that any new laws and regulations are drafted in a way that enables them to be applied to new LBS developed in the future and new uses of LBS technology (Ackerman, Kempf & Miki, 2003).

In order to ensure that any new laws and regulations are practical and sustainable, legal and regulatory authorities would benefit from there being more research and discussion relating to the specific privacy issues that arise from use of LBS and the ways that these issues are being addressed in various privacy regimes. In order to ensure that these laws and regulations are effective, it will be important that the perspectives both of users and providers of LBS are considered.

CONCLUSION

The analysis in this chapter focuses on identifying some of the key privacy issues that arise in the context of LBS and analyzing, at a theoretical level, the ways in which these issues might best be addressed in order to ensure that individuals' privacy is protected. As those individuals who are comfortable that their privacy will be protected when they use LBS are the ones more likely to use LBS, it is in both individuals' and LBS providers' interests for privacy issues to be adequately addressed in the provision of LBS.

As a starting point for addressing privacy issues that arise in the context of LBS, the key privacy issues that arise from use of LBS in each jurisdiction must be identified and the ways in which these issues should be addressed to ensure that individuals' privacy is protected must be identified. The laws and regulations in jurisdictions which have already taken steps to address these privacy issues, such as the European Union, provide useful guidance on how these key privacy issues can be addressed from a legal and regulatory perspective.

In addition to changes to laws and regulations, there is also considerable scope for market-based regulation of these issues, such as by telecommunications carriers and providers of LBS adopting appropriate policies and procedures with respect to their handling of location information.

As there is more research and discussion relating to the specific privacy concerns individuals have about use of their location information and how these issues affect providers of LBS, legal and regulatory authorities will be in a better position to develop effective and sustainable laws and regulations.

REFERENCES

Ackerman, L., Kempf, J., & Miki, T. (2003). Wireless Location Privacy Law and Policy. *Internet Society.* Retrieved February 6, 2008, from http://www.isoc.org/briefings/015/index.shtml.

Australian Law Reform Commission. (2007). *Discussion Paper 72: Review of Australian Privacy Law (DP72).*

Barkuus, A., & Dey, A. (2003, July). Location-Based Services for Mobile Telephony: a Study of Users' Privacy Concerns. *Proceedings of the INTERACT 2003, 9th IFIP TC13 International Conference on Human-Computer Interaction.*

Bennett, C. J., & Crow, L. (2005, June). Location-Based Services and the Surveillance of Mobility: An Analysis of Privacy Risks in Canada. *A Report to the Office of the Privacy Commissioner, under the 2004-5 Contributions Program.*

Dao, D., Rizos, C., & Wang, J. (2002). Location-Based Services: Technical and Business Issues. *School of Surveying and Spatial Information Systems.* The University of New South Wales, Sydney.

Directive 2002/58/EC of the European Parliament and of the Council concerning the processing of personal data and the protection of privacy in the electronic communications sector (Directive on privacy and electronic communications).

Hong, J. I., Boriello, G., Landy, J. A., McDonald, D. W., Schilit, B. N., & Tygar, J. D. (2003). Privacy and Security in the Location-enhanced World Wide Web. *In the Proceedings of the Workshop on Privacy at Ubicomp 2003.*

Jorns, O., Quirchmayr, G., & Jung, O. (2007). A Privacy Enhancing Mechanism based on Pseudonyms for Identity Protection in Location-Based Services. *Australasian Information Security Workshop: Privacy Enhancing Systems (AISW).* Ballarat, Australia.

Kuchinskas, S. (2007). Is Privacy Where It's At. *Internet News*. Retrieved January 30, 2008, from http://www.internetnews.com/wireless/article.php/3718706.

Langheinrich, M. (2001). *Privacy by Design – Principles of Privacy-Aware Ubiquitous Systems*. Institute of Information systems, IFW, Zurich, Switzerland.

Lockwood, S. E. (2004). Who Knows Where You've Been? Privacy Concerns Regarding the Use of Cellular Phones as Personal Locators. *Harvard Journal of Law & Technology, 18*(1), 307-317.

Long, M. (2007, September). *Longitude and Latitude: location technologies and privacy concerns*. Paper presented at the 29th International Conference of Data Protection and Privacy Commissioners, Montreal.

Mahmoud, Q. H. (2004). *J2ME and Location-Based Services*. Retrieved June 21, 2008, from http://developers.sun.com/mobility/apis/articles/location/.

Michael, K., Perusco, L., & Michael, M. G. (2006, October). *Location-Based Services and the Privacy-Security Dichotomy*. Paper presented at Proceedings of the 3rd International Conference on Mobile Computing and Ubiquitous Networking, London.

Minch, R. P. (2004). Privacy Issues in Location-Aware Mobile Devices. *Proceedings of the 37th Hawaii International Conference on System Sciences*.

Spiekermann, S. (2004). General Aspects of Location-Based Service. In J. Schiller & A. Voisard (Eds.), *Location-Based Services* (pp. 9-25). Morgan Kaufman.

Stein, A., Hawking, P., & Sharma, P. (2005). A Classification of U-Commerce Location Based Tourism Applications. *Centre for Hospitality and Tourism Research*. Victoria University, Australia.

Svantesson, D. (2005). Geo-identification – Now They Know Where You Live. *Privacy Law and Policy Reporter*.

Wallis Consulting Group Pty Ltd. (2007). *Consumer Attitudes to Privacy 2007, prepared for the Office of the Privacy Commissioner, Australia*. Retrieved on April, 21 2008, from http://www.privacy.gov.au/publications/rcommunity07.pdf .

Wireless Communications: Voice and Data Privacy. *Privacy Rights Clearinghouse*. Retrieved April, 11 2008, from http://www.privacyrights.org/fs/fs2-wire.htm.

Younes-Fellous, V. (2007). Privacy and data protection in Europe (art. 29 Working Party representative). *Commission nationale de l'informatique et des libertés*. Retrieved on April, 21 2008, from ec.europa.eu/information_society/activities/esafety/doc/esafety_2007/data_privacy_ws_13feb/younnes_ppt.pdf.

Section II
Mobile Business Models and Applications

Chapter III
Business Models for Mobile Payment Service Provision and Enabling

Dietmar G. Wiedemann
University of Augsburg, Germany

Wolfgang Palka
University of Augsburg, Germany

Key Pousttchi
University of Augsburg, Germany

ABSTRACT

A sizeable body of research on mobile payment evolved in recent years. Researchers analyzed success factors and acceptance criteria as well as strengths and weaknesses of different mobile payment service providers. This chapter explores business models for mobile payment service provision and mobile payment service enabling. While a mobile payment service provider offers a mobile payment procedure to end-users and merchants, a mobile payment service enabler targets on enabling other companies to offer mobile payment services. The authors primary contribution is to demonstrate the applicability of a general mobile payment business model framework, which was proposed in prior research. In doing so, they analyze, as an example, the case of SEMOPS as a typical mobile service enabler. Representing any m-payment business model, the resulting framework enables researchers and practitioners for comprehensive analysis of existing and future models and provides a helpful tool for M-Payment business model engineering.

INTRODUCTION

Business models for mobile services that are based on direct transaction-dependent revenues need an adequate charging form between service providers and users (Pousttchi & Wiedemann, 2007). Moreover, the appearance of mobile services and mobile commerce with 2.5G networks by the end of the 1990s made it essential to develop an appropriate form of settlement that possesses the same properties, especially ubiquity, as the mobile offers for which billing occurs (Pousttchi, 2008).

For the purposes of this chapter, mobile payment is defined as a type of payment transaction processing in the course of which—within an electronic procedure—the payer uses mobile communication techniques (at least) in conjunction with mobile devices for initiation, authorization, or completion of payment (Pousttchi, 2008). We refer to the term payment systems whenever we discuss a general payment method such as cash, card payment or mobile payment. We refer to the term payment procedures whenever we talk about concrete solutions such as Paypal or Paybox (Pousttchi, 2003).

A sizeable body of research on mobile payment evolved in recent years (Dahlberg et al., 2008). This research mostly covers success factors (e.g., Zmijewska & Lawrence, 2005) and acceptance analysis (e.g., Khodawandi et al., 2003) as well as strengths and weaknesses of mobile payment service providers like banks, MNO or specialized intermediaries (Zmijewska & Lawrence, 2006). However, possible business models are neglected by most researchers.

For the purposes of this chapter, a business model is understood as a conceptual tool containing a set of objects, concepts and their relationships with the objective to express the business logic of a specific firm (Osterwalder et al., 2005). Moreover, research explicitly focusing on mobile payment service enabling has received less attention. While a mobile payment service provider offers a mobile payment procedure to end-users and merchants, a mobile payment service enabler targets on enabling other companies to offer mobile payment services. Thus, an enabler is typically in no direct relationship with end-users or merchants (Pousttchi et al., 2008).

However, a stringent and rigorous analysis of the business model of mobile payment service enablers is still lacking. Furthermore, the evolution in practice shows that mobile payment service enabling produces more and more interest. For instance, the German section of Paybox Solutions completely realigned their business model from a mobile payment service provider to a mobile payment service enabler. This opportunity also exists for other mobile payment service providers who have already launched a successful procedure in a particular market. They can act as a mobile payment service enabler and sell their solutions in other markets for other potential mobile payment service providers. Thus, a business model is required that both deals with the complexity and particular characteristics of mobile payments and related business issues for mobile payment enablers and effects as much rigor as possible to the analysis.

This chapter aims to show the applicability of the mobile payment business model proposed by Pousttchi et al. (2007) in view of mobile payment service enablers. In doing so, we elaborate a business model of the mobile payment service enabler SEMOPS (Secure Mobile Payment Service) which is a real candidate for being a European payment standard. The outcome of the chapter is a grounded understanding of the business model of a mobile payment service enabler.

The rest of the chapter is organized as follows. Section 2 describes the state of the art on the mobile payment service enabling market including SEMOPS. Afterwards, we review general literature of general business models and in the area of mobile payments. In Section 3, we present the mobile payment business model proposed by Pousttchi et al. (2007). Based on these results we develop the business model of the mobile payment service enabler SEMOPS in Section 4. Finally, we conclude, present limitations, and offer suggestions for future research.

BACKGROUND

State of the Art of the Mobile Payment Service Enabling Market

In this section, we present examples from the international mobile payment service enabling market to provide a better understanding of the niche of mobile payment service enabling. In doing so, we show three cases: Paybox Solutions, Mobipay, and finally, SEMOPS.

After restructuring the Paybox Group in January 2003, the German section of Paybox (renamed Paybox Solutions) offered mobile payment technology to banks and MNO as their core business. This case shows that a company completely realigned its business model from a mobile payment service provider to a mobile payment service enabler. Paybox Solutions was a specialized intermediary and became a mobile payment service enabler. The procedure is used for instance by Paybox Austria and enables among others money transfers between individuals. Further, users can make payments in online shops, train stations, taxis and other stores. Only a mobile phone, a checking account with a direct debit authorization and an online registration are required (Paybox.net, 2003; Paybox.net, 2007).

Mobipay is a Spanish mobile payment service provider and represents a Spanish alliance of all major banks and all MNO. This case shows that a company can do both, i.e., act as a mobile payment service provider and as a mobile payment service enabler. Like Paybox Austria the company offers a procedure that activates existing payment systems, normally a virtual credit, a debit or pre-paid card. The service principally allows executing all payment use cases transforming the mobile phone

into day-to-day payment means (Mobipay.com, 2007). The strategy of Mobipay International (as mobile payment service enabler) is to provide the Mobipay technology in other countries, especially in South America.

SEMOPS is a project funded by the Commission of the European Union (EU) to address as mobile payment service enabler banks and MNO. This case shows that a company can start as a mobile payment service enabler. Moreover, it shows that also government has an interest in this area of mobile commerce (Au & Kauffman, 2008). The project's idea is to transfer the thoughts of the Single European Payment Area (SEPA) to new channels. The consortium was supported by the EU IST program till 2005. Since the beginning of 2007 key consortium members of the original SEMOPS consortium, with the involvement of new partners, are committed to the commercialization of the SEMOPS service in a market validation program (eTen 029376 - "SEMOPS II."). In Hungary, Greece, and Italy the SEMOPS consortium provides its mobile payment technology to banks. In future also MNO will be addressed. The procedure is suitable for any mobile payment use case and enables also cross-border payments. The service concept is built on the credit push concept. Customers receive a kind of electronic invoice from the merchant, which they individually approve, (sign with a PIN) and forward to their selected mobile payment service provider to initiate the payment. For that, required funds have to be available, the amounts have to be reserved and the customer's mobile payment service provider has to advise merchant's mobile payment service provider. The latter provides a payment guarantee to its merchant partner. The whole authorization process is real time, while the actual settlement is performed using the usual interbank batch settlement functions. For more information please look at the project's website (http://www.semops.com) or the description provided by Karnouskos et al. (2003).

Literature Review

In this section, we present the state of the art in business model research, particularly in the IS domain. Afterwards, we review literature in the area of mobile payment business models.

The term business model is perhaps the most discussed and least understood term in electronic commerce (Timmers, 1998)—and thus in mobile commerce as well. The literature provides three different approaches in coping with this complex phenomenon.

The first approach reviews single business model classes, e.g., the auction business model; for an extensive literature review, see (Alt & Zimmermann, 2001).

The second approach deals with business model taxonomies. In the context of electronic commerce, Timmers (1998) developed taxonomy of nine business models along two dimensions— degree of innovation and functional integration. In the context of mobile commerce, Varshney and Vetter (2002) identified seven mobile commerce business model types.

The third approach considers generic business model frameworks including different partial models. Alt and Zimmerman (2001) introduced a framework including the mission, structure, process, revenues, legal issues, and technology of a business model. Buchholz and Bach (2001) differed in the same way between processes, transactions, participants, and revenues. Staehler (2001) proposed a framework including the value proposition, architecture of value creation, and revenues. The most promising way seems to be the business model framework of Wirtz (2001) who developed six essential partial models including the market, procurement, service compiling, offering, distribution, and capital model.

While the first and second approach refer to the way a company does business, the third stream of research emphasizes the model aspect and develops the proposition of business model meta-models in form of frameworks. However, all proposed frameworks and models are developed for electronic commerce and do not address the peculiarities of mobile commerce, especially mobile payments. For example, the proposed frameworks do not consider the partnering between the key players which is seen as critical success factor in mobile payment (e.g., Zmijewska & Lawrence, 2006).

Taga and Karlsson (2004) identified five mobile payment business models depending on which key player in the value chain has driven the market success. Pousttchi (2005) introduced a mobile payment reference model that provides tools for analyzing business models, roles of the market participants, and their interrelation from a value-based perspective. A recent literature review of mobile payment research proposed a framework of four contingency and five competitive factors (Dahlberg et al., 2008). While this framework provides a big picture illustrating how the various perspectives fit together, it lacks detailed referrals to build a concrete mobile payment business model. Based on a literature review and multi-case study analysis Pousttchi et al. (2007) identified relevant characteristics of a mobile payment business model and classified these within morphological boxes. As a result, Pousttchi et al. (2007) developed six partial models which allow for categorization of any given mobile payment business model and, based on this, structured comparison of different business models. The set also supports mobile payment service providers in defining and evaluating business models. In this chapter, we use the six partial models to develop a business model of the mobile payment service enabler SEMOPS. The proposed partial models are described in the next section.

BUSINESS MODELS FOR MOBILE PAYMENT PROVISION

This section will focus on the description of the framework developed by Pousttchi et al. (2007), containing six partial models: the market model, value proposition model, implementation model, capital model, distribution and communication model, and threat model.

Market Model

The market model analyzes the demand and the competitive environment on the target market. An overview of the complete model is represented in Table 1; the nine characteristics and their instances will be closely explained in the following.

An m-payment procedure involves many different stakeholders (Au & Kauffman, 2008). However, in order to develop an m-payment business model it is essential to define the target customers for direct business connection which accept the value proposition. Customers fall in one of five categories. A reseller redistributes the procedure to other merchants that charge their products and services. Also mobile payment service providers who use the technology of a mobile payment service enabler fall in the reseller category. An administration's intention is to collect taxes and charge government services whereas users are distinguished between corporate clients and consumers. With few exceptions, e.g., in customer-to-customer (C2C) or reimbursement payments, the user and the payer are the same entity.

The information relationship between users is important as this may disclose requirements and pitfalls of the business model. The used abbreviations in Table 1—A, B, and C—represent administration, business, and customer.

To characterize the user market we differ between mass and niche markets. In mass market strategy (Kotler, 2003), a mobile payment service provider conducts the implementation, distribution, and communication of the payment procedure as mass product. Thus, a mobile payment service provider aims at covering as much of the mobile phone user market as possible. An example is an MNO-independent mobile payment procedure which is offered to all mobile phone users in a country. In opposite, in niche market strategy (Kotler, 2003), a mobile payment service provider focuses on a small market and supplies a want of a special target group. An example is a mobile payment procedure that can be used only in a certain use case in a certain region.

The estimated number of transaction per payer has an effect, e.g., on users' decision to register for the procedure. Among others, the estimated number of transaction per payee has an effect, e.g., on the merchants' or administrations' decision to integrate the procedure in their existing infrastructure. The respective scales are provided by Pousttchi et al., 2007.

Table 1. Market model

Characteristic	Instances				
Customer	Reseller	Administration	Merchant	Corporate client	Consumer
Relationship between users	A2B	A2C	B2B	B2C	C2C
User market	Mass market			Niche market	
Number of transactions per payer	High			Low	
Number of transactions per payee	High		Middle	Low	
User's willingness to pay	High		Low	Nonexistent	
Competing payment procedures	Inside mobile payment market			Outside mobile payment market	
External effects from other markets	Yes			No	
Competitive strategy	Cost leadership		Differentiation	Segmentation	

In countries such as Germany user's willingness to pay is nonexistent (Pousttchi, 2003) because users were accustomed to a "for free mentality" through their Internet usage and may transfer this attitude to mobile commerce. In case of existing willingness to pay, we distinguish between high and low and fix the borderline at the average cost of credit card usage in the specific target market. Assessing the latter three characteristics, the mobile payment service provider can decide on which revenue types and sources are most suitable (see Table 5; Voelckner, 2006).

Considering the competitive environment on the target market, we have to take into account not only the competing payment procedures of other mobile payment service providers (see for examples Heinkele, 2003; Pousttchi, Wiedemann & Schaub, 2006), but also payment procedures outside the mobile payment market, e.g., cash, debit cards, credit cards, or electronic payment procedures (Kreyer et al., 2002).

An external effect from other markets occurs when a mobile procedure competes against procedures of other key players with high market power that result from their traditional business, e.g., against a monopolistic MNO who already exhibits a large customer base, or an existing vertical or horizontal alliance (Pousttchi, 2005). With regard to the relative positioning and strategies of competitors, we have to analyze a suitable competitive strategy (Porter, 1980).

Value Proposition Model

The value proposition model is used to represent the value of mobile payment procedure from the perspective of customers. An overview of the complete model is represented in Table 2; its five characteristics and their instances will be described in the following.

A basic set of seven exhaustive and disjoint use case types (Table 3) can be derived providing a reference point for any given mobile payment use case (Pousttchi, 2005; Pousttchi, 2008). The used abbreviations in Table 3—MC, EC, SMA, SMP, and C2C—represent Mobile Commerce, Electronic Commerce, Stationary Merchant Automat, Stationary Merchant Person, and Customer to Customer.

The applicability considers the geographic coverage of the mobile payment procedure. While regional transactions typically include payments for public transport or parking in a certain region, national transactions are common. However, some mobile payment procedures enable also international transactions.

An important strategic issue for mobile payment service providers is to choose the type of amount level they want to focus on. Micropayments refer to payments up to and including 10 Euros. Macropayments refer to payments above 10 Euros (Pousttchi, 2004).

Table 2. Value proposition model

Characteristic	Instances						
Use case type	A MC (premium rate)	B MC (fixed price)	C EC (digital)	D EC/MC (non-digital)	E SMA	F SMP	G C2C
Geographic applicability	International			National		Regional	
Amount level	Macropayments				Micropayments		
Payment guarantee	Yes				No		
Mobile marketing integration	Merchant	Major owner of a customer base	Mobile parking service provider	Public transport	Other	None	

Table 3. Use case types

Use case type	Description
A MC (premium rate)	Purchase or use of digital goods or services in mobile commerce with the use of premium fee charging
B MC (fixed price)	Purchase or use of digital goods or services in mobile commerce with the use of fixed price charging
C EC (digital)	Purchase or use of digital goods or services in electronic commerce
D EC/MC (non-digital)	Purchase of non-digital goods or services in electronic commerce or mobile commerce
E SMA	Purchase of goods or services at a physical point of sale—in the case that an automat acts as agent on the merchant side
F SMP	Purchase of goods or services at a physical point of sale—in the case that a person acts as agent on the merchant side
G C2C	Transfer of money between consumers

In view of merchants or administrations, providing a payment guarantee is also important, because it is in their interests to avoid sales shortfalls or charge-back cost.

The characteristic mobile marketing integration considers the possibility to couple mobile payment with mobile marketing (e.g., by the use of the confirmation for mobile coupons) and the company this kind of integration is offered.

Implementation Model

The implementation model describes the input factors needed to realize a mobile payment procedure. Table 4 displays an overview of the complete model with its seven characteristics and their instances. These will be closely explained in the following clause.

Traditionally, regulation of payment procedures, and thus also mobile payment, has been a part of banking regulation and/or monetary policy (Krueger, 2002). Thus, in case of charging products and services of third parties a banking license, at least a restricted banking license, is required.

In the EU the e-Money Directive (2000/46/EG) aims to establish a level playing field between issuers of electronic money (e-money).

In some cases, a registration of users is not required, e.g., when the mobile payment service provider possesses the relevant data or a prepaid procedure is offered. However, most procedures involve a registration before or at least after first usage—either registration on the cell phone, on the stationary Internet, or offline, in case, a pass port has to be posted or the registration requires the presence of the user (Zmijewska et al., 2004).

Several studies revealed that security is one success factor of mobile payment (e.g., Linck et al., 2006). For the purposes of this study, authentication considers the verification of the identity of the payer. Means of authentication can fall in three categories (Turowski & Pousttchi, 2004): (1) possession (e.g., of a subscriber identity module (SIM) card or credit card chip to carry out a mobile payment procedure with a dual-slot phone (Kreyer et al., 2002); (2) knowledge (e.g., about a personal identification number (PIN) or pass word); and (3) attribute (e.g., user's voice).

Table 4. Implementation model

Characteristic	Instances								
Requirement of a banking license	Full banking license		E-money license		No banking license needed				
Registration	Mobile registration	Internet registration	Offline registration		Pre-existing data		No registration		
Authentication	Possession		Knowledge		Attribute				
Realization technology	CLIP	IVR	SMS	USSD	WAP	PAN technologies	Java	Other	
Confirmation	SMS	System inherent display	Acoustic signal	E-mail		Sales slip	None		
Method of settlement	Mobile phone bill	Fixed line phone bill	Separate bill	Direct debiting		Credit card	Prepaid account/ card		
Partnering	Bank	Credit card company	MNO	Specialized intermediary	Internet service provider	Fixed network operator	Technology provider	Other	None

In general, the more means are incorporated the securer is the procedure.

Realization technologies for authorization, authentication, and payment confirmation mechanism have found broad discussion in mobile payment research (for an overview see Dahlberg et al. (2006)). The supplementary Global System for Mobile Communications (GSM) service Calling Line Identification Presentation (call capture, CLIP) is a convenient way for users to conduct mobile payments as authentication is done by a call in conjunction with the mobile telephone number (Mobile Subscriber Integrated Services Digital Network Number, MSISDN). The mobile payment procedure Paybox use Interactive Voice Response (IVR) and/or text messages (Short Message Services, SMS). IVR is a phone technology that allows a telephone caller to select options from a voice menu and interact with the phone system. The GSM service Unstructured Supplementary Service Data (USSD), used, e.g., by Mobipay, enables a session for mobile payment transactions and works with any GSM mobile phone since the coded commands are entered in the same way as an MSISDN (e.g., *105*1*4556#). Typically, Wireless Application Protocol (WAP) enables transactions in the use case types A, B, and D to pay services and products in mobile commerce, while Personal Area Network (PAN) technologies such as Bluetooth, infrared, and radio frequency identification (RFID) enable transactions in the use case types E, F, and G. Other procedures use Java applications that have to be downloaded on the mobile phone, but allow full application programming. However, the heterogeneity of devices is indeed a challenge.

After the payment authorization, a mobile payment procedure may not provide the user with any confirmation of the payment, e.g., when services or products are delivered immediately. In use case type F (and maybe in use case type E), traditional sales slips can be used as confirmation. An email is especially suitable for purchases on the Internet. An acoustic signal is conceivable, e.g., for IVR- or CLIP-based procedures as a sound and for Java- or NFC-based procedures as a beep. A system inherent display refers to visual confirmations that are displayed on the mobile phone screen and generated by USSD-, Java-, PAN-, or WAP-based procedures, but excludes SMS. All these considerations are important as a confirmation may increase the cost of operation—especially when using SMS.

In the background, the payments can be settled via various methods of settlements such as mobile or fixed line phone bills, separate bills (Khodawandi et al., 2003), direct debiting, credit cards or deduction from a prepaid m-payment account (Kreyer et al., 2002). Considering the implementation of a procedure there are various ways for partnering between the key players. For instance, cooperation between banks and MNO enables integrating existing infrastructures (Pousttchi, 2005). Henkel (2002) and Pousttchi (2004) stated that specialized intermediary start-ups have not enough strength to establish payment procedures on their own and maintain that such companies do require partnership.

Capital Model

The capital model analyses the sources and types of revenues, costs as well as the sources of financing. An overview of the complete model is represented in Table 5; the four characteristics and their instances will be closely explained in the following.

A major success factor for an m-payment system is to identify the right revenue model in order to convince both users and merchants to adopt the service. The revenue source and revenue type describe the incoming money streams from the value offered by the m-payment service provider. Revenue sources may be the user, the merchant, or a third party. The latter instance includes entities which are not involved in the payment process directly, e.g., resellers, mobile payment service providers, or administrations.

Moreover, we distinguish between transaction-dependent and transaction-independent revenue types (Turowski & Pousttchi, 2004). The former type includes revenues generated with each transaction, e.g., for the payment itself or the provision of transaction-based mobile marketing integration. The latter type includes customers' one-off cost plus period cost—independent from the volume of transactions. Examples are basic fees, royalties, proceeds of hardware sale, installation, integration, and support, as well as account-keeping and account set-up fees (Henkel, 2002; Salvi & Sahai, 2002).

Particularly, set-up costs (e.g., costs of foundation or royalties for the payment procedure) carry weight, when a banking license is needed. For instance, according to the e-Money Directive (2000/46/EG), a minimum capital of 1 million Euros is required to establish an e-money institute. Furthermore, we have to consider infrastructure setup cost or upgrade of their existing infrastructure; costs of operation include for instance salaries, servicing expenses, authentication fees, transport fees, and losses (e.g., bad debt and fraud losses); finally, promotion expenses accrue that can be reduced by the use of public relations or viral marketing.

Especially, for specialized intermediary start-ups assuring the financing of the enterprise with borrowed capital and/or equity capital is important.

Table 5. Capital model

Characteristic	Instances				
Revenue source	User		Merchant		Third party
Revenue type	Transaction-independent			Transaction-dependent	
Cost	Set-up	Infrastructure	Operation	Promotion	Other
Financing	Borrowed capital			Equity capital	

Table 6. Distribution and communication model

Characteristic	Instances					
Rollout	International		National		Regional	
Acquiring	Existing business connection		Explicit merchant acquisition		Acquiring service provider	
Issuing	MNO	Bank	Credit card company	Specialized intermediary	Merchant	Other
Market segmentation strategy	Concentrated		Differentiated		Undifferentiated	
Branding strategy	Own brand		Co-brand		White brand	No brand
Promotion	Print	Direct mail	POS	Radio	TV	Online marketing	Mobile marketing	Other
Partnering	Bank	Credit card company	Specialized intermediary	MNO	Merchant	Administration	Major owner of a customer base	Other	None

Distribution and Communication Model

The distribution and communication model denotes the two P′s of the marketing mix—place and promotion (McCarthy, 1996). Table 6 displays an overview of the complete model with its seven characteristics and their instances. These will be closely explained in the following clause.

It answers questions such as: How should the rollout of the procedure take place? Which strategies are mapped out for acquiring, issuing market segmentation, and branding? Which type of promotion (Kotler, 2003) should be used? Finally, which partnering strategy for distribution and communication purposes should be applied?

Acquiring refers to the acquisition of payees, normally merchants or administrations, whereas issuing refers the acquisition of payers, normally consumers or corporate clients (Pousttchi, Wiedemann & Schaub, 2006). With regard to acquiring, mobile payment service provider can offer the procedure to their existing customers, explicitly acquire new merchants or administrations, or mandate an acquiring service provider which also may be a payment service provider.

Issuing may conducted by the mobile payment service provider on its own or by a partner depending on the branding strategy.

The model provides three market segmentation strategies: (1) undifferentiated marketing in which the mobile payment service provider attempts to go after the whole market; (2) differentiated marketing in which the mobile payment service provider operates in several segments of the market with offerings and market strategies tailored to each segment; (3) concentrated marketing in which the business focuses on only one or a few segments with the intention of capturing a large share of these segments (e.g. Kotler, 2003).

Another important strategic issue is to choose the branding strategy. The instance no brand occurs, e.g., in system inherent payments of WAP services, when the mobile payment service provider or enabler brand is not disclosed. In the case of the procedure is issued by other partners under their own label, we define this branding strategy as white brand. Additionally, co-branding (in conjunction with partners) and establishing or extension of an own brand are possible (Zmijewska et al., 2004).

As in the implementation model (Table 4) partnering is important for acquiring, issuing, promotion and branding.

Threat Model

The threat model, as last model, describes potential and profound threats to the economic success

Table 7. Threat model

Characteristic	Instances					
Legal issues	Unsteady legislation		Regulation		Consumer protection	Other
Technology issues	Evolution of standard	Unreliable technology		Mobile device evolution	Scalability	Other
Objective security	Integrity	Authorization	Authentication	Confidentiality	Non-repudiation	Availability
Competitors' actions	By lawful means			By dubious means		

of an m-payment business model. Due to the peculiarities of m-commerce, the occurrence of unforeseen threats is much more likely. In contrast to fixed line Internet business it is typical here that stakeholders appear at different links in the value chain (Turowski & Pousttchi 2004), often acting with hidden agendas and using the market power they possess in or from other markets; their actions often compromise the success of other players. A further issue is regulation. While regulation in general shows already difficult and sometimes unpredictable effects, besides, m-payment is affected by two different regulatory environments, telecommunications and financial services. Finally, technology plays a particular role, characterized by the relatively low level of standardization in handsets, networks and software. Following experiences from practice, the explicit inclusion of a threat model aims at making these considerations an integral part of construction and assessment of m-payment business models, with special regard to the interrelations to other parts of the business model. An overview of the complete model is represented in Table 7; its four characteristics and their instances will be exactly expounded in the following clause.

The characteristic legal issues involves changes in legislation and regulation as well as consumer protection issues.

Also technology issues like the evolution of mobile payment standards are important. As the market for mobile payments still is in an experimental period, betting on an antiquated standard may be a severe competitive disadvantage. Moreover, the mobile payment procedure has to be tested against attacks on the payment infrastructure to detect unreliable technology issues. Also an assessment of the mobile device evolution is important. Varying implementations of standard environments and multiple proprietary environments on mobile devices has led to platform fragmentation—even the implementation of J2ME (Java 2 Micro Edition) is not consistent from device to device. Furthermore, care should be taken that the scalability (Bondi, 2000) of the procedure is given as far as the prospect exists that the transaction volume increases strongly in the future. Since financial services like payments can be subject to fraudulent activities, they require well-secured infrastructure.

Objective security (Linck et al., 2006) is a concrete technical characteristic, given, when a certain technological solution responds to all of five security objectives such as integrity, authorization, authentication, confidentiality, and non-repudiation. In recent years also the availability of a system is frequently called which provides functionality to ensure that the service is accessible and usable. Finally, we have to anticipate competitors' actions. On the one hand, these may conducted by lawful means, e.g., when a MNO refuses cooperation, and on the other hand, these may conducted by dubious means, e.g., a MNO delays the delivery of confirmation SMS.

APPLICATION OF THE BUSINESS MODEL FOR MOBILE PAYMENT ENABLING

In this section, we will use the six partial models described in Section 3 and originally developed to design a business model for a mobile payment service provider (Pousttchi et al., 2007). In particular, we will show their applicability for mobile payment service enablers and analyze, as an example, the case of SEMOPS as a typical mobile payment service enabler.

Market Model

As mentioned in Table 1, the market model analyzes the demand and the competitive environment on the target market. As SEMOPS exclusively concentrates on the mobile payment service enabling model, it does not intend to establish a direct relationship with end-users or merchants. Therefore, customers establishing a business connection with SEMOPS are resellers, i.e., mobile payment service providers. A mobile payment service provider falls in one of three categories. Either it is a MNO or it is a bank respectively financial service provider (FSP, especially credit card company) or it is a specialized intermediary (Pousttchi, 2004). From a business perspective SEMOPS is open; any of these may join to participate as mobile payment service provider. By adding one new mobile payment service provider to the SEMOPS network the number of possible transactions increases exponentially. This open structure allows fast penetration of SEMOPS. Principally, SEMOPS allows all kinds of relationship between users. Comparing the functional requirements of payment procedures for electronic government services (Pousttchi & Wiedemann, 2005) with the SEMOPS characteristics, e.g. payment guarantee, anonymity, and confidentiality, SEMOPS is also suitable for charging of electronic government services allowing A2B and A2C transactions as well. Thus, administrations subsidizing the mo-

bile payment procedure due to politico-economic motives may also be potential customers. The SEMOPS customers have complete freedom in defining their service structure. They may freely decide about important business issues like what use case type they offer, when and how they are timing the introduction of new transaction types, what fee structure they are using, when charging the users, what fee levels they are using, and how they are differentiating between the transaction types and users. Therefore, the description of the user market, number of transaction per payer, number of transaction per payee, user's willingness to pay, external effects from other markets and competitive strategy depends heavily on the mobile payment service providers' strategy and served market. However, with a direct transaction-based revenue model, SEMOPS is informed about the number of payment transactions by using special modules implemented in the mobile payment service providers' infrastructure.

The overall goal of the SEMOPS project is to become a trans-European payment network. In doing so, after the trial operations it will have to be introduced in new markets. However, these markets have to be carefully selected. Thus, competing payment procedures on future target market have to be considered and SEMOPS has to take into account not only existing mobile payment service providers, but also payment systems outside mobile payment market.

The classification of mobile payment markets in Figure 1 is based on the number, structure, progress, and diffusion of existing mobile payment procedures identified during a market research in 2007; the different categories should be interpreted not in absolute, but in relative terms, i.e., in comparison with the other EU Member States. Austria, Belgium, Spain, UK, and Estonia are considered to have the most advanced m-payment markets as in these markets mobile payment is dominated by co-operations between banks and/or MNO. For instance, in Spain Mobipay España exists which is a cooperation of about 80 per cent of Spanish

Figure 1. Development of the mobile payment market in the EU Member States

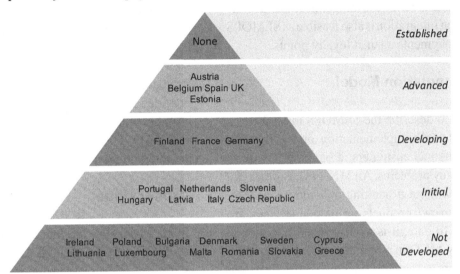

banks and all Spanish MNO. However, still many markets are in non-developed or initial stage and afford opportunities for new comers.

In most EU Member States, the most common instruments are payment cards and credit transfers (European Central Bank, 2006). Furthermore, some countries such as Austria, Germany, the Netherlands and Spain show a high number of direct debits per capita. Concerning the number of cheques per capita, a few EU Member States reach values higher than 25 transactions per capita. Taga and Karlsson (2004) suggest that a developed financial sector, especially a high usage of payment cards, is an important factor supporting the development of mobile payment. Summarizing the discussion above, the consortium's strategy should be to launch the procedure in countries with high usage of payment cards and low development of the mobile payment market. In countries with a high degree of mobile payment development a co-operation with these mobile payment providers would be preferable, especially, for cross-border transactions.

Value Proposition Model

As stated in Section 3, the value proposition model represents the value of the procedure from the perspective of customers which are—in case of SEMOPS—mobile payment service providers. With SEMOPS a mobile payment service provider is able to offer the procedure for each use case type (Table).

As SEMOPS aims at developing an international mobile payment system, it allows all types of geographic applicability: international, national, or regional. On the network level the different local operations are connected to each other through the local Data Centers.

The type of amount level is a strategic decision of the mobile payment service providers as SEMOPS enables micro as well as macro payments. According to the mobile payment reference model of Pousttchi (2005), generally, banks should conduct macropayments while MNO should conduct micropayments (especially in the use case types A and B).

With SEMOPS a mobile payment service provider is able to offer a payment guarantee, because, learning from earlier examples, SEMOPS established a real-time authentication. Mobile marketing integration is also feasible as SEMOPS enables payments against loyalty points.

Implementation Model

In order to describe the SEMOPS input factors, we focus on the implementation model (Table 4). With banks as customers, a banking license is without any problems. An MNO as customer can operate without a banking or e-money license, only when own products, i.e. mobile services, are offered. To date, it is unclear whether e-money issued by MNO in circumstances where prepaid consumers use some of their prepaid credit to buy services from third parties falls within the ambit of the e-Money Directive (Guidance note from the Commission Services, 2004).

The characteristics registration and authentication are important for the business connection between the mobile payment service provider and its customers. Typically, pre-existing data are available, while authentication is based on possession of the mobile device and (optionally) knowledge of a PIN.

SEMOPS is a very communication intensive service, but at the same time it has achieved great independence from any specific realization technology. The universal use and applicability of the service is achieved by a flexible technical design, where users and merchants can use any kind of mobile handsets or PC. To establish flexible and efficient communication, technologically a very versatile solution is realized. Around the core logic, which is the same in all different transaction types a modulated communication architecture has been developed. This allows the payment service to always use the most adequate method for communication, based on transaction channel and transaction type. In case of successful money transfer, the merchant's mobile payment service provider sends a notification to the merchant, and the customer's mobile payment service provider sends a notification to the customer. However, it depends on the use case which form of confirmation will be sent. For instance, in use case type C typically an email is used.

The various methods of settlements are a strategic decision of the mobile payment service provider. The basic principle of the SEMOPS business model is the partnering between banks and MNO. Thus, the benefits are among others the integration of existing infrastructures.

Capital Model

To get insights in the financial situation of SEMOPS, we take a look at the capital model (Table 5). In case of the relationship between SEMOPS and its customers the revenue source is a third party. Revenue types are mainly transaction-based. The present business model of the SEMOPS is like a cone structure, where each participant is directly and exclusively related to its own service partner and pays a transaction fee for the service received. The service is provided to customers and merchants by the mobile payment providers who decide its own fee structure. Not having so called interchange fees makes revenue calculation simple and completely predictable. Mobile payment service providers are paying for the service they receive from the Data Center. The Data Center is charging a transaction commission from the mobile payment service providers for each transaction it is processing. The transaction commission is transaction value related but it is only a fraction of the fees, the mobile payment service providers are collecting from their users. The Data Center is also performing other functions for the mobile payment service providers than just simple message routing. It is managing the daily reconciliation and closing process, it routes transaction lists between the mobile payment service providers, and also allows them data base update and synchronization. These are all services the mobile payment service providers need to pay for. Besides the key financial flows there are other players—also members of the consortium—and also services involved in the SEMOPS operation that need to be paid for, e.g., developers of the SEMOPS applications are entitled to a license fee for the use of the modules as well as the introduction, installation, integration, support, and maintenance of the modules, and in certain cases for the special tailoring to individual requirements. Additional, the mobile payment service provider must assure that all security solutions are in place and all security related rules and regulations are strictly followed. For this reason before launching a service in any country a security audit needs to take place and also before an individual mobile payment provider goes live an audit is performed. To ensure continuously high level security, the audit processes are repeated at predefined intervals. The cost of the mobile payment service provider audits is paid by the mobile payment service provider and the data center operators themselves. Last but not least the SEMOPS service needs external products and services to operate. These are consulting services that support the preparation and the operation of the service. Also hardware and software for running the various modules and infrastructure, telecommunication services, and other administration related products and services need to be acquired. The cost of all these products and services are paid by the actual users directly to the vendors.

Distribution and Communication Model

The distribution and communication model (Table 6) answers the question of the rollout of the procedure. With the e-Ten market validation project SEMOPS wants to establish itself, as the key candidate for being the trans-European payment network for mobile and internet transactions. Acquiring, issuing, and development of a market segmentation strategy and promotion depends heavily on the mobile payment service providers'

strategy and served market. Because of the direct, close relationship between the mobile payment service provider and its customer the service is branded by the mobile payment service providers under their own brand. As stated above, the basic principle of the mobile payment system SEMOPS is the partnering between banks and MNO. Regarding the distribution and communication model the benefits are for instance a combined customer base.

Threat Model

The threat model (Table 7) describes the potential and profound threats to the economic success of the business model. SEMOPS is one of the first payment services being secure and real-time. Thus, from the perspective of the characteristic legal issues, it fulfils consumer protection issues, and from the perspective of technology issues, it considers evolution of standard, a reliable technology, the mobile device evolution and scalability (Karnouskos et al., 2003). Regarding objective security the user and merchant are using the service provided by their own trusted partners and not by any third parties. The SEMOPS payment process enables integrity and confidentiality. Customers do not provide any sensitive information to merchants or to any other third parties except to their mobile payment service provider, while simultaneously merchants receive payment guarantee from their own mobile payment service provider which means that there is no possibility of identity theft, no fraudulent purchases, and no collection risk. The service relies on existing banking infrastructure including the legacy security systems and solutions. During the communication all sensitive information is end-to-end encrypted and the correspondence of the mobile payment service providers is digitally signed to ensure authenticity, and validity. SEMOPS provides a strong end-to-end encryption for the transferred data and allow the usage of various techniques for the authentication, defined by the mobile payment service providers, embedded into this encryption. On the merchant side the authorization is digitally signed by the mobile payment service provider ensuring authentication, non-repudiation, and validity of the message. Finally, SEMOPS has to anticipate competitors' actions.

LIMITATIONS AND FUTURE RESEARCH

We identify three major limitations to the mobile payment business model. The first limitation comes with the construction of a future mobile payment business model; the business model could limit practitioners' creativity. Although the business model is depicted as morphological boxes that are normally used as creativity technique, it allows only combining existing ideas. This issue in mind, practitioners should additionally include other creativity techniques such as brainstorming, synectics, or lateral thinking. As the second limitation, more work is necessary to test the artifact. During this research we demonstrated the soundness of the business model by using it in the case of SEMOPS. However, measures and evaluation metrics are crucial components of design-science research (Hevner et al. 2004). Therefore, to test the artifact within an appropriate context the next step in our research will be to develop such measures and evaluation metrics. Finally, the third limitation: the business model is not specified in a formal language.

Our future research will begin to tackle these challenges. We hope that these issues will also be given attention by other researchers in this area.

CONCLUSION

This research was motivated by the lack of an integrated view on mobile payment business models, especially for mobile payment service enablers. We aimed at reflecting the complexity of the m-payment task and the high interdependency of technical, human and market factors in order to serve researchers and practitioners alike. In response to these requirements we first presented the general mobile payment business model of Pousttchi et al. (2007) as a conceptual tool for comprehensive analysis and engineering of m-payment business models. Based on this prior theoretical work and multi case study analysis we have shown that this business model helps in defining business models of mobile payment service enablers. In doing so, we developed the business model of the mobile payment service enabler SEMOPS.

The SEMOPS service is built on cooperation. It was realized early on that a successful mobile payment service needs to assure the cooperation between banks and MNO. There were too many attempts on either side to capture the business alone without the participation of the other party, but they all failed. Also it was seen that within each sector wide collaboration is needed, one or a couple of active players cannot serve the market. If participation is limited to a couple of players then huge segments of the population will be left out, the service cannot reach its universal scope. The SEMOPS service aims to establish this wide cooperation along the lines of real financial benefits. It is obvious that the banking sector has different operating specifics from those ones the mobile communication sector operates. It is possible to elaborate a service structure, where these specifics are combined in a way that results in operating optimum, in terms of efficiency. In the SEMOPS service banks are processing typically macro payments, while MNO are processing micro transactions. This division of work results in substantial cost reduction, risk reduction, utilisation of a common back-end infrastructure and great market coverage. The involvement of a number of the banks and MNO further increases the market coverage by enabling transactions between any of their clients either on the customer or on the merchant side. Cooperation is not without consensus and some sacrifice. However it is important to see, that while earlier electronic and mobile payment solutions were trying to re-allocate the payment pie between established and new parties, the SEMOPS service, with the new transaction types, also increases the pie to such an extent that reallocation will probably not even be necessary, concentration can be devoted to new opportunities.

The SEMOPS consortium has finished an initial prototype of its service, and is working towards validating itself in real-life scenarios and testbeds in Hungary, Italy, and Greece with the aim to enhance, evolve and provide a commercial service in the near future.

ACKNOWLEDGMENT

This chapter describes work undertaken and in progress in context of SEMOPS II (Secure Mobile Payment Service, eTEN C029376) which is partially funded by the Commission of the European Union.

REFERENCES

Alt, R., & Zimmermann, H.-D. (2001). Introduction to special section-business models. *Electronic Markets,* 11(1).

Au, Y. A., & Kauffman, R. J. (2008). The economics of mobile payments: Understanding stakeholder issues for an emerging financial technology application. *Electronic Commerce Research and Applications, 7*(2), 141-164.

Bondi, A. B. (2000). Characteristics of scalability and their impact on performance. *Proceedings of the 2nd International Workshop on Software and Performance* (pp. 195-203). Ontario, Canada.

Buchholz, W., & Bach, N. (2001). *The Evolution of Netsourcing Business Models.* Giessen, Germany: University of Giessen, Chair of business administration II.

Dahlberg, T., Mallat, N., & Öörni, A. (2003). Consumer acceptance of mobile payment solutions—Ease of use, usefulness and trust. *Proceedings of the 2nd International Conference on Mobile Business* (pp. 211-218). Vienna, Austria.

Dahlberg, T., Mallat, N., Ondrus, J., & Zmijewska, A. (2008). Mobile payments: A review for past, present and future research. *Electronic Commerce Research and Applications, 7*(2), 165-181.

European Central Bank (2006). *Payment and securities settlement systems in the European Union and in the acceding countries.*

Guidance note from the Commission Services (2004). *Application of the e-money directive to mobile operators.*

Heinkele, C. (2003). *Überblick und Einordnung ausgewählter Mobile Payment-Verfahren.* Augsburg, Germany: University of Augsburg, Chair of Business Informatics and Systems Engineering.

Henkel, J. (2002). Mobile Payment. In G. Silberer, J. Wohlfahrt, & T. Wilhelm (Eds.), *Mobile commerce — Basics, business models and success factors* (pp. 327-351). Wiesbaden, Germany: Gabler.

Hevner, A. R., March S. T., Park J., & Ram S. (2004). Design science in information systems research. *MIS Quaterly, 28*(1), 75-100.

Karnouskos, S., Vilmos, A., Hoepner, P., Ramfos, A., & Venetakis, N. (2003). Secure Mobile Payment—Architecture and Business Model of SEMOPS. *Proceedings of the EURESCOM summit.* Heidelberg, Germany.

Khodawandi, D., Pousttchi, K., & Wiedemann, D. G. (2003). Akzeptanz mobiler Bezahlverfahren in Deutschland. *Proceedings of the 3rd Workshop on Mobile Commerce* (pp. 42-57). Augsburg, Germany.

Kotler, P. (2003). *Marketing Management*. Upper Saddle River, New York, USA: Pearson Education.

Kreyer, N., Pousttchi, K., & Turowski, K. (2002). Standardized Payment Procedures as Key Enabling Factor for Mobile Commerce. *Proceedings of the EC-Web, E-Commerce and Web Technologies* (pp. 400-409). Aix-en-Provence, France.

Krueger, M. (2002). Mobile Payments: A Challenge for Banks and Regulators. *IPTS Report, 63*, 5-11.

Krueger, M., Leibold, K., & Smasal, D. (2006). *Online Payment Methods from the Viewpoint of Customers—Results of the Study IZV8*. Karlsruhe, Germany: University of Karlsruhe.

Linck, K., Pousttchi, K., & Wiedemann, D. G. (2006). Security Issues in Mobile Payment from the Customer Viewpoint. *Proceedings of the 14th European Conference on Information Systems*. Gothenburg, Sweden.

McCarthy, E. J. (1996). *Basic Marketing: A Managerial Approach*. Irwin, Homewood, Illinois, USA.

Mobipay.com (2007). *How it works*. Retrieved May 11, 2007, from http://www.mobipay.com/en/home.htm

Mueller-Merbach, H. (1976). *The Use of Morphological Techniques for OR-Approaches to Problems. Operations Research '75* (pp. 127-139). Amsterdam, Holland: North-Holland Publishing Company.

Osterwalder, A., Pigneur, Y., & Tucci, C. L. (2005). Clarifying Business Models: Origins, Present, and Future of the Concept . *Communications of AIS, 15*, 751-755.

Paybox.net (2003). *The Paybox Group restructures*. Retrieved May 15, 2007, from http://www.paybox.net/327_378.htm

Paybox.net (2007). *Paybox Money Mobiliser*. Retrieved May 15, 2007, from http://www.paybox.net/download/paybox_fact_sheets/paybox_Money-Mobiliser.pdf

Porter, M. (1980). *Competitive Strategy: Techniques for Analyzing Industries and Competitors*. New York, USA: Free Press.

Pousttchi, K. (2003). Conditions for acceptance and usage of mobile Payment Procedures. *Proceedings of the 2nd International Conference on Mobile Business* (pp. 201-210). Vienna, Austria.

Pousttchi, K. (2004). An Analysis of the Mobile Payment Problem in Europe. *Proceedings of the Multikonferenz Wirtschaftsinformatik* (pp. 260-268). Essen, Germany.

Pousttchi, K. (2005). *Mobile Payment in Deutschland—Szenarienbasiertes Referenzmodell für mobile Bezahlvorgänge*. Wiesbaden, Germany: Deutscher Universitätsverlag.

Pousttchi, K. (2008). A modeling approach and reference models for the analysis of mobile payment use cases. *Electronic Commerce Research and Applications, 7*(2), 182-201.

Pousttchi, K., & Wiedemann, D. G. (2005). Payment Procedures for Electronic Government Services. *Proceedings of the 5th European Conference on e-Government (ECEG)*. Antwerp, Belgium, June 2005.

Pousttchi, K., & Wiedemann, D. G. (2007). Mobile Payment and the Charging of Mobile Services. In: Taniar, D. (Ed.): *Encyclopedia of Mobile Computing and Commerce*. Idea Group Inc., Clayton, Australia.

Pousttchi, K., Schießler, M., & Wiedemann, D. G. (2007). Analyzing the Elements of the Business Model for Mobile Payment Service Provision. *Proceedings of the 6th International Conference on Mobile Business* (pp. 201-210). Toronto, Ontario, Canada.

Pousttchi, K., Schießler, M., & Wiedemann, D. G. (2008). Proposing a comprehensive framework for analysis and engineering of mobile payment business models. *Information Systems and e-Business Management* (DOI 10.1007/s10257-008-0098-9) (in press).

Pousttchi, K., Wiedemann, D. G., & Schaub, J. (2006). Aktueller Vergleich mobiler Bezahlverfahren im deutschsprachigen Raum. *Studienpapiere der Arbeitsgruppe Mobile Commerce.* Bd. 1, Augsburg 2006, 50-96.

Salvi, A. B., & Sahai, S. (2002). Dial M for Money. *Proceedings of the 2nd ACM International Workshop on Mobile Commerce.* Atlanta, USA.

Schnell, R., Hill, P., & Esser, E. (1999). *Methoden der empirischen Sozialforschung.* Munich, Germany: Oldenbourg.

Staehler, P. (2001). *Geschäftsmodelle in der digitalen Ökonomie.* Lohmar, Cologne, Germany.

Taga, K., & Karlsson, K. (2004). *Arthur D. Little Global M-Payment Report.* Arthur. D. Little Austria GmbH, Vienna, Austria.

Timmers, P. (1998). Business models for Electronic Markets. *Electronic Markets, 8,* 1998, 3-8.

Turowski, K., & Pousttchi, K. (2004). *Mobile Commerce.* Heidelberg, Germany: Springer-Verlag.

Varshney, U., & Vetter, R. (2002). Mobile commerce: framework, applications and networking support. *Mobile Networks and Applications, 7*(3), 185-198.

Voelckner F (2006). An empirical comparison of methods for measuring consumers' willingness to pay. *Marketing Letter, 17*(2), 137-149.

Wirtz, B. W. (2000). *Electronic Business.* Wiesbaden, Germany: Gabler.

Zmijewska, A., & Lawrence, E. (2005). Reshaping the Framework for Analysing Success of Mobile Payment Solutions. *International Conference on E-Commerce*, Porto, Portugal

Zmijewska, A., & Lawrence, E. (2006). Implementation Models in Mobile Payments. *Proceedings of the IASTED International Conference Advances in Computer Science and Technology* (pp. 19–25). Puerto Vallarta, Mexico.

Zmijewska, A., Lawrence, E., & Steele, R. (2004). Classifying mpayments—a user-centric model. *Proceedings of the Third International Conference on Mobile Business.* New York, USA.

Chapter IV
Ubiquitous Communication:
Where is the Value Created in
the Multi-Play Value Network?

Mikko Pynnönen
Lappeenranta University of Technology, Finland

Jukka Hallikas
Lappeenranta University of Technology, Finland

Petri Savolainen
Lappeenranta University of Technology, Finland

Karri Mikkonen
TeliaSonera, Sweden

ABSTRACT

In a digital home a so-called multi-play system integrates networked entertainment and communications systems. Using a mobile phone, all those services can be controlled and used ubiquitously—from everywhere, at any time. Not much research has been conducted in the field of integrated communication offers. The novelty of this study is in that it addresses the ubiquitous communication system, called the multi-play service, from the perspectives of both the customer preference and operator strategy and transforms this into valuation of resources and capabilities. This chapter provides a framework to connect the customer value preferences to firm resources. The aim of the framework is to connect customer and resource-based strategies together. As a result of the analysis the authors reveal the most important resources in contrast to the customer value preferences.

INTRODUCTION

The connectedness with everything, everywhere, all the time is what surrounds us more and more in the modern information society. Synonymous to omnipresence, ubiquity is also provided by mobile phones that follow us nearly everywhere and all the time. In a digital home a so-called multi-play system integrates networked entertainment and communication systems, providing television, video on demand, music, telecommunications etc. Using a mobile phone, all those services can be controlled and used ubiquitously—from everywhere, at any time.

As the communication situation can take place in a stable or mobile location, and the need to enrich communication varies, the choice that the user makes between access types varies greatly. If ubiquity is added to an integrated offering, and the portable computer has the same dynamic and personal settings, it has all the potential to become a mobile communications center as well, especially for sessions demanding more rich media. When the user is physically moving, the usability and availability of a laptop computer decreases, and a mobile terminal becomes the choice. In the case of full integration, the user can still browse files from a PC with the mobile terminal. As those files are located in the network, they do not need to be sent through the radio network, which then also becomes an economic driver for ubiquity in the integrated model.

Not much research has been conducted in the field of integrated communication offers. Furthermore, there is not much literature or research available that profoundly considers the characteristics of a ubiquitous communication system. The novelty of this study is in that it addresses the ubiquitous communication system, called the multi-play service, from the perspectives of both the customer preference and operator strategy and transforms this into valuation of resources and capabilities (Srivastava et al., 2001). The multi-play offer is a new business concept consisting of an integrated set of features aiming to deliver greater systemic value to end customers (Gardner, 2001; Kothandaraman & Wilson, 2001).

The objective of this chapter is to provide a framework to connect the customer value preferences to firm resources. The practical suitability of the method is demonstrated with a relevant real-life business concept development case example of a Nordic operator (Mikkonen et al., 2008). The focus is in the resource analysis although the customer value and the business model analysis are also reviewed. This chapter and the method of a business model are based on several case studies on the subjects of the customer driven business model. The mapping framework connects different levels together in a system hierarchy. It consists of sequential steps from customer needs to the actor resources and capabilities in a value network. The aim of the framework is to connect customer and resource-based strategies together. As a result of the analysis we reveal the most important resources in contrast to the customer value preferences.

The chapter is structured so that first the backgrounds of the multi-play service and the integrated operator are discussed, second the research framework is introduced, third the customer value analysis and business model mapping are discussed, fourth the resource analysis is provided, and fifth the future trends concerning the multi-play and the method are discussed followed by the conclusion.

BACKGROUND

Multi-Play Service from Case Operator's Strategy Perspective

The business model of an integrated operator or a typical incumbent largely relies on available vendor technology and products enabled by highly standardized components. It can be broadly said that the ICT value network in the past consisted of operators who controlled the customer interface by selling end-user subscriptions to access networks, vendors who delivered network and customer equipment, and system integrators who co-developed services with vendors and operators, installed, operated and maintained the overall infrastructure, depending on the outsourcing structure of each geographic market (see e.g. Coursaris et al., 2008).

The operator typically gains its customers by offering value in forms of image, good network coverage and the degree of customer service and voice quality. The key activity that makes operators profitable is scaling up their subscription market share for different networks to drop the ratio of fixed costs and thereby increasing the return from network investments. A strong customer position is gained by developing long-term customer relationships and reacting to customers' problems. It is important to realize that the business model of an operator has long been an investment model, where operators invest in network equipment and manage end-customer subscriptions for the long term. Transaction costs increase when investments become more asset specific (Thompson & Yuanyou, 2004; Barney, 1999; Aubert et al., 2004). Good examples of this kind of investments in the ICT industry are the proprietary networks of operators (Li & Whalley, 2002). Vendors have to sell their equipment and software every year and, in the telecom industry, this power setting has driven the industry dynamics so that vendors actually have had a very significant role in developing new services for their customers' customers. This structure decreases the possibility for operators to differentiate themselves through products, as vendors want to sell their technology to all the competitors and, as everyone knows, equipment vendors have even standardized new services in collaboration to come to consumer markets. This situation is still an industry paradigm but it is gradually changing. New services, however, need different resources and capabilities.

Customer Oriented Business Model

According to Bowman & Ambrosini (2000), the power relations of the players in the network determine the capability of a firm to capture value. Power relations of firms, according to the resource-based view arguments, are related to the different resource profiles of the firms' business models. Because the firm often does not have direct access to all the resources it needs it has to cooperate and outsource (Barney, 1999). In value networks, even quite critical resources are often outsourced, and this gives a certain amount of negotiation power to the suppliers of particular resources. In other words, the aim of the strategy (and the business model) should be to create a relative monopoly situation (Cox, 1997) in terms of sustainable competitive advantage (Barney, 1991) for a firm in its market. However, the business model is not the same as strategy (Magretta, 2002; Mansfield & Fourie, 2004). Where business strategy defines the relationship between the firm and its environment, the business model is more an implementation tool for strategy (Mansfield & Fourie, 2004). This is why the business model implicitly reflects the firm strategy.

According to Margretta (2002), the business model is briefly a description of how the firm does business. This means that the business model is not the same as the firm; it is a more abstract concept. Business models have become common tools in describing the organization (governance structure) and its linkages to the value network. The business model concept based on Hamel (2000) describes the elements of a business model. These are customer interface, core strategy, strategic resources and value network (Hamel, 2000). Following this definition the business model actually describes the value network from the firm's perspective. The problem in many business model frameworks (Hamel, 2000; see e.g. Chesbrough, 2003) is that they are fairly static because of their descriptive nature. So far the frameworks have included a built-in assumption that change in some part of the system creates a completely new business model. To take change into account in the business model it has to be more than a descriptive framework. Timmers (2000) provides one such general definition: The business model is the architecture for a product, service and information streams. It also includes a description of the various business actors and their roles, of the potential benefits for the various business actors and of the sources of revenue. (Timmers, 2000)

Ineffectiveness is the motive for developing business models (Chung et al., 2004). Magretta (2002) argues that business models fail because they are based on wrong assumptions of customer behavior. The business model has to be aligned to meet the customer value preferences, and to be able to reconfigure the business model the firm has to have capabilities to innovate (Chung et al., 2004).

Customer preferences are an important element in the value network of actors, since the value is captured from customers (Bowman & Ambrosini, 2000). In consequence from the standpoint of value networks, customer requirements and preferences are essential in order to understand the changes in value network structures. Although it is important that customers are satisfied, it is the total value of the offering to customers that matters. As Gardner (2001) states, a perfectly satisfied customer can shift to the competing offering if it provides significantly greater value. Customer satisfaction does not create real (voluntary) customer lock-in (Hamel, 2000); it is the overall value of an offering that does (Gardner, 2001). The aim of the customer value analysis is to integrate the customer into the R&D process of the firm (Ulaga & Chacour, 2001). Although the idea was originally presented in a business-to-business environment, the basic idea can be transferred to the consumer markets as well (Thomke & von Hippel, 2002). One main view of the connection between the customer and the firm is the study of the customer need assessment (Kärkkäinen et al.,

2001; Kärkkäinen & Elfvengren, 2002; see e.g. Elfvengren et al., 2004). In this view the aim is mainly to recognize the unrecognized needs of customers. The customer need refers to what the customer ultimately wants. Customer value, on the other hand, refers to what the customer wants with certain limitations like money. Another approach for integrating the customer into the firm's processes is the customer value view (Thomke & von Hippel, 2002; Anderson & Narus, 1998; Flint et al., 1997; Flint & Woodruf, 1998; Ulaga & Chacour, 2001). This view is also linked to the value creation of firms (Wernerfelt, 1984; Bowman & Ambrosini, 2000; Clulow et al., 2007).

Integrating the customer into the R&D process certainly generates value to the customer, but to capture the value generated, firms have to reconfigure their business models accordingly (Thomke & von Hippel, 2002). Building a customer value model helps the firm to recognize the customer values and to modify the business model suitable for capturing them. The customer value model is a data-based representation of the worth (in monetary terms) of the product or service to the customer (Anderson & Narus, 1998). The customer value model can be opened and analyzed by defining the single attributes of value elements that can be technical, economic, service or social in nature (Anderson & Narus, 1998). Garvin (1987) has presented eight dimensions of product quality which are performance, features, reliability, conformance, durability, serviceability, aesthetics and perceived quality. A change in the customer-desired value is caused by trigger events (new opportunities, supplier problems etc.) that stimulate the customers to change their opinions (Flint et al., 1997). The value of some service to the customer is a subjective matter (Kortge & Onkonkwo, 1993), and it depends on the customer's user profile, namely, the way he or she likes to use the service, or is used to using it. In a group of people with similar user profiles, the value of the service is quite comparable.

DEVELOPING A CUSTOMER ORIENTED BUSINESS MODEL FOR MULTI-PLAY OFFERING

This chapter and the method of the business model are based on several case studies on the subjects of the customer driven business model (Pynnönen et al., 2008; Pynnönen et al., 2008; Pynnönen & Hallikas, 2008; Mikkonen et al., 2008). According to Voss et al. (2002) "case research is the method that uses case studies as its basis." Case studies are the preferred strategy when questions like *who*, *how* or *why* are being posed, when the investigator has little control over events and when the focus is on a contemporary phenomenon within some real-life context (Yin, 1994). The process has three phases and it is shown in Figure 1. The mapping framework connects different levels together in a system hierarchy. It consists of sequential steps from customer needs to actor resources and capabilities in a value network. The aim of the framework is to connect customer and resource-based strategies together. Customer needs are derived from the identifica-

tion and evaluation of the relative weight of the customer value attributes. This way it is possible to detect the features that the customer really values and select the customer segments that best fit with an offering. The resource-based strategy, on the other hand, determines the importance of resources and capabilities in a business model in order to maximize the supplier value. Each actor should develop itself, acquire or create partnerships with resources that are most critical in a business model.

The framework is based on the principles of Quality Function Deployment (QFD) which is used to connect the customer value preferences to the value streams of the business model and then to the resources in the network. The prioritization of the customer requirements is implemented with an Analytic Hierarchy Process (AHP) (Saaty, 1999).

QFD is an analytical tool that is designed to convert high level business objectives (what the business stakeholders want), into processes (how the business delivers those whats) (Clegg & Tan, 2007). QFD is also a method for converting cus-

Figure 1. The research framework

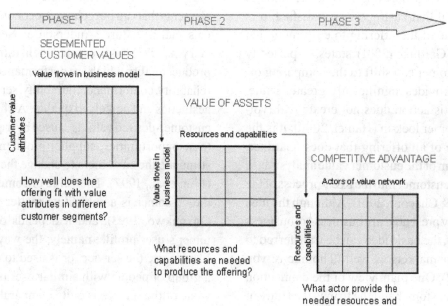

tomer demands into quality characteristics and for developing product design by systematically deploying the relationships of customer demands and product characteristics (Lee & Ko, 2000). The process is modified for assessing service qualities. The attributes of the service are the value streams from the main actor to the customer (e.g. TV, internet access, email).

The result of this analysis is the relative priorities for the customer value streams in the business model. These prioritized value streams are then connected to resources with a new QFD matrix. As a result of this transformation, the relative priorities of the resources of the business model can be evaluated.

Assessing the Customer Values

The first step in the research process is to assess customer value preferences with AHP method and to connect them to the business model of the firm. The second step is to connect the resources to the attributes of the offering of the business model. The third step is to relate the resource suppliers to the business model. The process has been tested in a real-life business concept development case of a multi-play offering for a Nordic operator (Mikkonen et al., 2008). These studies revealed that the framework is a powerful tool for analyzing customer value preferences and the results can also be linked to the business model of the firm.

The knowledge of customer value preferences is the key to creating a business model capable of producing voluntary customer lock-in. To gain this knowledge a firm has to create a customer value model of its offering(s). The customer value model can be opened and analyzed by defining the single attributes of value elements that can be technical, economic, service or social in nature (Anderson & Narus, 1998). Garvin (1987) has presented eight dimensions of product quality, which are performance, features, reliability, conformance,

durability, serviceability, aesthetics and perceived quality. These categories should be combined and modified to fit the assessed offering. In this example case the attributes are modified to fit the services of mobile communication systems. The example list of the modified value elements and their attributes is presented in Table 1.

For the assessment and prioritization of the customer value attributes the Analytic Hierarchy Process (AHP) (Saaty, 1999) decision model is used. The selection of the customer segment is the start point of building a customer value model (Anderson & Narus, 1998). We selected two of the most potential segments for adopting the multi-play offering to further analysis. The segments were based on the existing consumer market segmentation of TeliaSonera Finland (Mikkonen et al., 2008). When dealing with a consumer segment it is useful to form a customer panel of lead users and advanced users. According to von Hippel (1986), lead users are people who "face needs that will be general in a marketplace, but they face them months or years before the bulk of that marketplace encounters them, and ... are positioned to benefit significantly by obtaining a solution to those needs." Advanced users are users that are experts on the subject of mobile services through their personal interests or their work.

The data can be gathered by a web-based questionnaire where the attributes are placed as pairs so that every attribute is compared to another. The panelists are told to compare the relative importance of each attribute with respect to case mobile services. After the assessment, the AHP model is used to calculate the weighted preferences for each cluster of service attributes and the single items of the attributes. Finally the fit between the value attributes and the selected offerings are rated. The aim of this is to analyze what offering best realizes the desirable values. This part is also based on the AHP tool where a group of experts rates the attributes' realization in the case offerings. The assessment can be made, for example, on a scale from 1 to 9.

Table 1. Example of the customer value model for integrated communication systems

	Value attributes:	Description:
Service		
Performance	Bandwidth	Mbit/s
	Bandwidth effectiveness	Ability to throttle access bandwidth on-demand
	Software execution performance	Hardware & software layer optimization
	Response time	
		Network latency combined with response time of on-line services
	Customer service effectiveness	Minimum time to solution, with minimal customer effort
Features	Number of features	How many services are included in the bundle?
	Personalization of features	Ability to choose the services into the bundle & configure them
	Utilization of personal context	Use & management of location information, passwords
	Service provider neutrality	Customer can use other available (on-line) services
	Amount of available media content	TV, radio
	Potential new features	Possible new services in the bundle
	Tele-control of service	Ability to use services location-freely
Reliability	Customer care capacity	Can the firm handle the customer support?
	Access reliability	Can the device connect to the server without problems and fast enough?
		Are the services available if needed? Do they function as promised?
	Level of service error susceptibility	Firewalls, Spy-ware control, Virus scan
	Information security	Can the customer trust that the problems are fixed?
	Customer service reliability	Replacement and back-up systems
	Contingency policy	
Terminal device		
Usability	Low boot time	Device is usable quickly when started
	Ease of use	Remote control, connections
	User interface	Logical menus, controls and buttons
	Ease of install	"Plug and play" vs. program installation and configuration
	Installation and maintenance service	Availability if needed
Conform-ance fit	Compatibility	Compatibility with existing & potential complementary infrastructure
	Conformity to standards	Based on the commonly accepted standards
	Possibility of updating & customizing	Open or closed system? (hardware & software)
Appearance	Brand name	The brand of the device
	Terminal design	Fits with the other devices like DVD, size, weight, color
	Low noise level	Noise does not disturb the usage
Economic		
Costs	Low costs of initial setup	The costs of utilizing the offering
	Fixed fee	Monthly price including most services
	Fee per transaction	Most of the services are separately priced
	Bundled fee	The services and the terminal device in the same fee
	Low power consumption	No always-on, standby, effectiveness, hardware design
Socio-eco-nomic	Reduced complexity of billing	Saving time
	Reduced complexity of offering	Making purchasing easier
	Convenience	The influence on quality of life through easiness of the services
		Is the ownership of the offering socially desired?
	Status symbol aspect	No parasitic power consumption
	Energy effectiveness	

In our study of customer value preferences related to a multi-play offering the terminal device value element and the usability attribute were preferred. The value elements in the framework were pair-wise compared with the AHP to demonstrate the preference order in the selected segments of an integrated operator. The features of each segment profile were used in the analysis.

The general conclusion for the customer value preferences related to the multi-play offering is that attributes related to easiness of use and usability together hold a great deal of the value in the offering. This is a first signal of the possibility that specific values can be isolated, which in turn could lead to differentiated development between competing integrated offerings, related to the most important attributes. This differentiation is of a new kind, distinguishing easiness of use and usability created between different access types and services integrated together, not easiness and usability around one access type and its services.

Mapping the Business Model

Building a business model on customer needs is essential for the firm in order to recognize customer value and to create a suitable business model for capturing the value. The business mapping framework is based on a case study of ICT business models (Pynnönen et al., 2008). A value network of actors and value streams around an organization is thus constructed by identifying the consumed and produced value streams, precisely describing them, and associating them with required enabling resources. This can be thought of as a three-phase process consisting of

1. Offering investigation and decomposition
2. Value stream derivation and actor identification
3. Resource identification and association

Product and service offerings often initially seem equal to a single value stream that corresponds to the main deliverable of the offering. In reality, offerings are more complex product and service bundles or packages: they include various complementary elements associated with the main deliverable. Determining the structure of a complex offering may require domain-specific industry expertise. Value streams are discrete

product and service elements assigned to distinct categories and associated with the producing and consuming actor(s). This is an essential aspect of the framework. In this study, the value streams were categorized into the following categories:

- Goods (e.g. mobile phones)
- Free goods (e.g. web browser)
- Services (e.g. advertising space)
- Free services (e.g. e-mail)
- Information and knowledge (e.g. user information)

The case firm is of course always associated with a stream as either the producing or consuming actor. The other identified actors should be assigned a precise, domain-specific role, rather than just recognizing them as customers or suppliers. The actors and value streams can be conveniently presented using an illustration such as in Figure 2.

Figure 2 illustrates the business network formed around a multi-play service from an operator's perspective. The multi-play offering is illustrated with a bunch of value streams between the operator and consumer. The example is an early version of the business concept development work done in the case company. It reflects the possible future structure of the business network formed around the multi-play service.

The resources as enablers for the value streams were analyzed at this point. The traditional view is that capabilities enable the exploitation of resources. We have used an outcome driven view, where the producing of value streams is enabled by the resources which are categorized into software development capabilities, service capabilities, technological capabilities, information, ICT systems & technologies, immaterial assets, and contracts & partnerships categories. The aim of the resource analysis is to link the resources of the business model to the value streams. The resource analysis of the business models is based on the value stream analysis and it explains the configu-

Figure 2. Example of a multi-play operator's business model

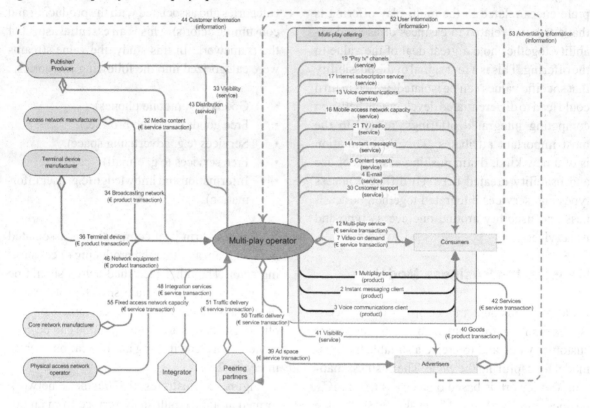

ration of the business concepts to the firm's business environment. The resources enable the value streams and they define the firm's possibilities to adopt new business concepts. The resources in our analysis are capabilities and assets for providing and consuming the value streams.

Connecting Customer Preferences to the Business Model

The prioritized customer value attributes from Table 1 are connected to the attributes of the offering (value streams from the operator to the customer) with the application of the QFD process. The importance weightings for the attributes are derived from the AHP analysis. The following Table 2 illustrates the QFD method applied here.

The result of this analysis is the relative priorities for the customer value streams in the business model. The results of this analysis are presented in Figure 3. The elements of offering are based on business model analysis in the case company. As stated earlier, the process reveals new value streams and therefore some new value streams. The new value streams identified in the process have been added to the analysis.

The user segments presented here as 'Hometown people' and 'Time balancers' are based on existing segmentation of the case company. The segments are family segments in which the biggest potential for these kind of offerings is estimated to be. The family in Hometown people segment lives in suburbs and has about two kids. The life of these families is quite stable and their average income is close to the average. The family in Time balancer segment is living in a city and

Table 2. QFD principle for connecting the prioritized customer values to the firm offering.

Value attributes	Weight	Firm offering				Sensitivity
		Value stream 1	Value stream 2	Value stream 3	Value stream 4	
		(Correlation: 0= No correlation, 1= Low, 3=Medium, 9=High)				
Attribute 1	0,50	1	0	9	3	6.5
Attribute 2	0,25	0	1	3	9	3,25
Attribute 3	0,25	9	3	1	1	3,5
Importance of offering elements		2,75	1	5.5	4	

Figure 3. Relative importance of value streams executing the customer values

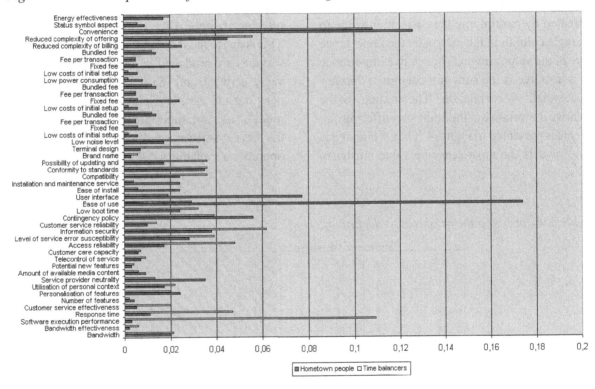

using public transport. Both parents are working. They have in average little fewer children than the other segment. The everyday life of the Time balancer family is busy. The different segments have different value preferences towards this kind of service because their life and communication needs are different.

Resources Needed to Deliver the Value for the Customer

To operate the business model the multi-play operator needs different resources and capabilities than traditional operators because of the emphatic role of the media and integration at the service layer. To access the resources that are critical we have applied a new QFD process (see Table 3). In this matrix we have connected the output value streams (elements of the offering) of the multi-play operator to the resources that are needed to produce those outputs. The resources in this analysis can be internal (company owned) or inputs from the value network (purchased resources) and they are identified in the business model analysis presented earlier. If a resource is needed in producing a value stream, it is marked with *1*.

The relative importance of a resource in producing the value streams (elements of the offering) and ultimately the customer value can be revealed by multiplying the correlation value in a single column in the matrix by the importance rate of the value stream. The relative importance of a resource is the sum of a column of "preference weighted" correlations. The summary of the relative importance of the multi-play offering elements is presented in Figure 4. The QFD analysis also reveals the most sensitive value attributes in contrast to the elements of the offerings. The sensitivity is calculated by multiplying the sum of a row with the importance rate of the value attribute. The most sensitive value attributes seem to be related to content services. This means that in this kind of an offering the greatest systemic value is locked in these value attributes.

The analysis shows that the most important resource of the multi-play operator is "integration services," which means that the devices and content must be integrated seamlessly together in order to produce the easiness and usability values to the customer. However, it seems that the most important resources in providing the multi-play offering are not in direct control of the operator. This is due to the fact that the devices and content services are produced by other members in the value network and the integration mostly happens outside the multi-play operator's business model. The most important internal resources are the "server software development" and "service operations capability." These capabilities are

Table 3. Connecting the resources to the firm offering

Columns C1–C13 fall under **Internal resources and capabilities**; columns C14–C20 fall under **Inputs**.

Outputs	Importance	Access network access	Broadcasting rights (IPR and Copyright)	Content ownership	Customer service capability	Infra provisioning capability (Includes billing)	Mobile access infra	Partnerships with content owners	Partnerships with publishers	Retail business	Scalability	Server software development	Service operations capability	User information	Integration services	Traffic delivery	Fixed access network capacity	Media content	Terminal device	Broadcasting network	Network equipment	Sensitivity
Multiplay box	3,12									1					1				1			9,35
Mobile device	2,59									1					1				1			7,78
Instant messaging client	0,29									1					1						1	0,86
Voice communications client	0,31									1					1						1	0,93
Multiplay-ready PC device	2,64									1					1				1			7,92
TV channels	2,22		1	1				1	1		1	1	1	1	1	1	1	1		1	1	31,11
Radio channels	2,14		1	1				1	1		1	1	1	1	1	1	1	1		1	1	29,97
Customer support	1,11				1										1							2,21
Installation and maintenance	0,90				1										1							1,80
E-mail	0,50											1	1	1	1	1	1					3,00
Content search	0,07											1	1	1	1	1	1					0,40
Voice communications	0,36											1	1	1	1	1	1					2,17
Program information	0,50		1											1	1	1	1				1	3,01
Instant messaging	0,29											1	1	1	1	1	1					1,73
Mobile network capacity	1,79	1				1	1								1	1	1	1			1	14,34
Fixed network capacity	1,79	1				1						1	1		1	1	1				1	14,30
Website space	0,73											1			1			1				2,19
Video rental service	1,94		1	1				1	1		1	1	1	1	1	1	1	1			1	25,25
Video on-demand service	1,94		1	1				1	1		1	1	1	1	1	1	1	1			1	25,25
Security service	1,43											1			1							2,87
Backup service	1,72							1	1			1		1	1	1	1					12,03
Telecontrol	0,60											1		1	1	1	1				1	3,62
Total		3,6	8,7	8,2	2,0	3,6	1,8	10,0	10,0	8,9	9,5	15,1	13,0	16,9	21,6	15,9	15,9	8,7	8,3	8,7	11,6	202,06
Relative Weight (Priority) %		1,8 %	4,3 %	4,1 %	1,0 %	1,8 %	0,9 %	4,9 %	4,9 %	4,4 %	4,7 %	7,5 %	6,5 %	8,3 %	10,7 %	7,9 %	7,9 %	4,3 %	4,1 %	4,3 %	5,7 %	

Figure 4. Relative importance of internal and external resources

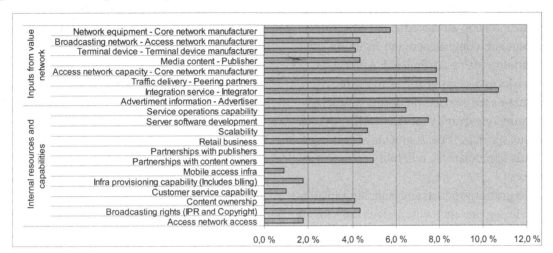

important because the customer preferred multi-play experience needs capabilities to operate the service seamlessly. The content services need servers that have to be reliable and to provide the services fast even though the number of simultaneous users increases.

When knowing the relative value of the inputs we can tell the importance order of the resource suppliers in the value network. In Figure 4 the inputs and the providers of them are connected so that the relative value of the input is also the relative value of the supplier of that particular resource. In our analysis, the relatively most important resource supplier is the Integrator. The Advertisers, Peering partners and Core network manufacturers are also quite important to the multi-play operator. These findings can be explained with the nature of the offering. The integration of services networks and devices is a difficult task and it requires the collaboration of different actors in the value network. The seamless operation of services regardless of the device requires much programming and standard development. This is usually time consuming and expensive.

FUTURE TRENDS

The future development of ubiquitous services is driven by the assumption that using a mobile phone, all ubiquitous services (TV, communication, music, video on demand) can be controlled and used ubiquitously. In other words, in our scenario the mobile device is an important and preferred device to access the Internet. Of course, there can be alternative service models, which use a different resource-base and value flow combination to provide an offering to the end-customers.

Several uncertain issues are related to the development of mobility driven ubiquitous services. Firstly, there is the question of whether the bandwidth of mobile networks becomes sufficient to provide all the demanded services effectively. Compared to fixed access networks, the speed of mobile networks will be sufficiently lower causing a conceivable difference to the customer perceived service quality. Another important issue is related to national regulation and whether regulators force the decoupling of mobile access and services. This would perhaps require new actors and capabilities for managing the service layer. Thirdly, devices and content must be integrated seamlessly together to fit the requirements of non-advanced users and segments that appreciate convenience and usability over other customer value attributes. Furthermore, if certain risks and security issues make the users of Internet-based service platforms suspicious, an emerging opportunity for the mobility driven ubiquitous services is the segments of end-users that highly appreciate the reliability and security of services.

As integrating products and launching an integrated offering presents some serious risks for an organization, constructing a systematic reasoning method for their configuration becomes necessary. Risks can be related to failures in customer satisfaction, economic investments in platforms and commercial launches, cannibalization costs and, very importantly, the brand of an operator. None of these single risks is affordable.

CONCLUSION

In this chapter we have addressed the business of an integrated operator by using the multi-play offering as a case example. The multi-play offering is a step towards ubiquitous communication systems. The difficulty in this kind of an offering to a traditional telecom operator is in the required, new kinds of capabilities and resources. We have provided an approach to recognize those resources and capabilities and to assess their relative importance in fulfilling the customer requirements. The main contribution of this chapter is the method and process to value the firm resources against the customer requirements.

The analysis revealed that the business model of a multi-play-operator does not include many resources that correlate with the device related value streams. This can be explained with the fact that the hardware included in the service is manufactured by a different firm and the operator bundles it with the services. The conclusion

is that one of the most valuable service elements for customers is provided with resources that are not controlled by the operator. Also, most of the service elements are produced with the resources of other players in the network. The multi-play operator has capabilities and resources that help its orchestration of the network and managing the bundle, like contracting capabilities. It also has resources that enable the delivery of the service to customers. The multi-play operator is, thus, dependent on the other players in the network.

The approach has some limitations. The assessment of the correlations between the customer value attributes and the value streams has to be validated. Moreover, it should be noticed that the selected case study business environment limits the generalizability of the results beyond the communication service business.

Despite the recognized advantages of the presented framework in the valuation of business concepts and resources through customer preferences, the valuation should also include the revenue model calculations to show the real business potential of a concept. This is a clear limitation of the presented framework, which is therefore best suited for the early concept development stages, where the initial concept value and potential is determined through perceived customer value.

REFERENCES

Anderson, J. C., & Narus, J. A. (1998). Business Marketing: Understand What Customers Value. *Harvard Business Review, 76,* 53-65.

Aubert, B. A., Rivard, S., & Patry, M. (2004). A transaction cost model of IT outsourcing. *Information & Management, 41,* 921-932.

Barney, J. (1991). Special Theory Forum the Resource-Based Model of the Firm: Origins, Implications, and Prospects. *Journal of Management, 17,* 99-120.

Barney, J. (1999). How a Firm's Capabilities Affect Boundary Decisions. *Sloan Management Review, 40,* 137-145.

Bowman, C., & Ambrosini, V. (2000). Value Creation Versus Value Capture: Towards a Coherent Definition of Value in Strategy. *British Journal of Management, 11,* 1-15.

Chesbrough, H. W. (2003). *Open Innovation.* Boston: Harvard Business School Press.

Chung, W. W. C., Yam, A. Y. K., & Chan, M. F. S. (2004). Networked enterprise: A new business model for global sourcing. *International Journal of Production Economics, 87,* 267-280.

Clegg, B. & Tan, B. (2007). Using QFD for e-business planning and analysis in a micro-sized enterprise. *International Journal of Quality &Reliability Management, 24,* 813-828.

Clulow, V., Barry, C., & Gerstman, J. (2007). The resource-based view and value: the customer-based view of the firm. *Journal of European Industrial Training, 31,* 19-35.

Coursaris, C., Hassanein, K., & Head, M. (2008). Mobile technology and the value chain: Participants, activities and value creation. *International Journal of Business Science and Applied Management, 3.*

Cox, A. (1997). *Business success: a way of thinking about strategy, critical supply chain assets and operational best practice.* Winteringham: Earlgate Press.

Elfvengren, K., Kärkkäinen, H., Torkkeli, M., & Tuominen, M. (2004). A GDSS based approach for the assessment of customer needs in industrial markets. *International Journal of Production Economics, 89,* 275-292.

Flint, D. J., & Woodruf, R. B. (1998). The Initiators of Changes in Customers' Desired Value. *Industrial Marketing Management, 30,* 321-337.

Flint, D. J., Woodruff, R. B., & Gardial, S. F. (1997). Customer Value Change in Industrial Marketing Relationships. *Industrial Marketing Management, 26,* 163-175.

Gardner, B. (2001). What Do Customers Value? *Quality Progress, 34,* 41-48.

Garvin, D. A. (1987). Competing on the eight dimensions of quality. *Harvard Business Review, 65,* 101-109.

Hamel, G. (2000). *Leading the revolution.* Boston: Harvard Business School Press.

Kärkkäinen, H., & Elfvengren, K. (2002). Role of careful customer need assessment in product innovation management - empirical analysis. *International Journal of Production Economics, 80,* 85-103.

Kärkkäinen, H., Piippo, P., Puumalainen, K., & Tuominen, M. (2001). Assessment of hidden and future customer needs in Finnish business-to-business companies. *R&D Management, 31,* 391-407.

Kortge, G. D., & Onkonkwo, P. A. (1993). Perceived Value Approach to Pricing. *Industrial Marketing Management, 22,* 133-140.

Kothandaraman, P., & Wilson, D. T. (2001). The Future of Competition - Value-Creating Networks. *Industrial Marketing Management, 30,* 379-389.

Lee, S. F., & Ko, A. S. O. (2000). Building balanced scorecard with SWOT analysis, and implementing ``Sun Tzu's The Art of Business Management Strategies'' on QFD methodology. *Managerial Auditing Journal, 15,* 68-76.

Li, F., & Whalley, J. (2002). Deconstruction of the telecommunication industry: from value chains to value networks. *Telecommunications Policy, 26,* 451-472.

Magretta, J. (2002). Why Business models Matter? *Harvard Business Review, 80,* 86-92.

Mansfield, G. M., & Fourie, L. C. H. (2004). Strategy and business models - strange bedfellows? A case for convergence and its evolution into strategic architecture. *South African Journal of Business Management, 35,* 35-44.

Mikkonen, K., Hallikas, J., & Pynnönen, M. (2008). Connecting customer requirements into the multi-play business model. *Journal of Telecommunications Management, 1,* 177-188.

Pynnönen, M., & Hallikas, J. (2008). Applying a Customer Value Model in Mobile Communication Business. *International Journal of Electronic Business, In Press.*

Pynnönen, M., Hallikas, J., & Savolainen, P. (2008). Mapping business: value stream based analysis of business models and resources in ICT service business. *International Journal of Business and Systems Research, 2,* 305-323.

Saaty, T. (1999). *Decision Making For Leaders: The Analytic Hierarchy Process for Decisions in a Complex World.* Pittsburgh: RWS Publications.

Srivastava, L., Fahey, L., & Christensen, H. K. (2001). The resource-based view and marketing: The role of market-based assets in gaining competitive advantage. *Journal of Management, 27,* 777-802.

Thomke, S., & von Hippel, E. (2002). Customers as Innovators: A New Way to Create Value. *Harvard Business Review, 80,* 74-81.

Thompson, S. H. T., & Yuanyou, Y. (2004). Online buying behavior: a transaction cost economics perspective. *The International Journal of Management Science, 33,* 451-465.

Timmers, P. (2000). *Electronic Commerce - Strategies and models for business-to-business trading.* London: John Wiley & Sons Ltd.

Ulaga, W., & Chacour, S. (2001). Measuring Customer-Perceived Value in Business Markets. *Industrial Marketing Management, 30,* 525-540.

von Hippel, E. (1986). Lead Users: A Source of Novel Product Concepts. *Management science, 32,* 791-805.

Voss, C., Tsikriktsis, N., & Frohlich, M. (2002). Case research in operations management. *International Journal of Operations & Production Management, 22,* 195-219.

Wernerfelt, B. (1984). A Resource-based View of the Firm. *Strategic Management Journal, 5,* 171-180.

Yin, R. K. (1994). *Case Study Research; Design and Methods.* (Second edition) (vol. 5) London and New Delhi: Sage Publications.

Chapter V
Predicting the Adoption of Mobile Government Services

Adam Vrechopoulos
Athens University of Economics & Business, Greece

Michail Batikas
Athens University of Economics & Business, Greece

ABSTRACT

Mobile government transform many of the traditional governance practices. The citizens' adoption of M-Government services (e.g. voting, tax services, health services, etc.), however, is determined by a series of factors (e.g. ease of use, image, compatibility, etc.). This chapter investigates the predicting power of these factors towards contributing to theory building and providing direct implications that are useful for the diffusion and adoption of mobile government services in Greece. The study reviews the available literature on adoption and diffusion of innovation as well as the available relevant research insights on the mobile commerce landscape. Then, the study empirically tests the predicting power of a series of critical variables that are theoretically related to the Greek citizens' intention to adopt mobile government services. The findings imply that compatibility and ease of use have significant predicting power on citizens' intention to adopt M-Government services. Direct implications and further research directions are provided at the end.

INTRODUCTION

The phenomenon of Electronic Government (e-government) attracts the attention of governments, worldwide. It is quite common for such evolutions to be linked to broader economic and social initiatives like the Information Society or the New or Knowledge Economy (Martin & Byrne 2003). Information Society programs in the e-government field are driven by technological, economic and social factors. However, improving the customer satisfaction with online government services is one of the leading factors driving e-government initiatives around the world.

Like e-commerce or e-business, e-government refers to the use of Information and Communications technologies (ICT) in the interaction process between the citizens and the government (voting, tax services, health services, etc.). These technologies could be the Internet, the Web, the mobile phone, the Interactive Digital TV, etc. Similarly, mobile government (M-Government) refers to the use of mobile devices (i.e. mobile phones, palmtops, PDAs) from citizens to interact with government. Therefore, among others, the major difference between e- and M-Government is the mobility that the latter offers to users (Turban et al. 2008).

Despite its infancy, M-Government is a growing and important set of complex strategies and tools that will completely change the roles and functioning of traditional governance. In advocating the existence and importance of M-Government, there are two basic facts to be considered:

• There are more people who have a mobile phone than there are people who have access to a desktop or portable computer and to Internet (Durlacher Research 2001), which will make government services available more to mobile subscribers than to PC users, even though M-Government is considered a subset of e-government. Especially in

Greece the above argument is quite applicable. Specifically, 24 per cent of the Greek population owns a desktop or a portable computer and also Greece has 3.8 million Internet users which corresponds to a 33.9 per cent penetration rate while the average Internet penetration rate in European Union member states is 48.1 per cent. On the other hand, Greece has 10.03 million mobile subscribers which corresponds to 92.8 per cent penetration rate.

• M-Government provides instant availability. Specifically, it helps people to access government services and useful information without the limitations of time and location.

Three interrelated evolutions accelerate the development of M-Government. These are: (1) advancements in mobile technology, (2) the wider acceptance of these technologies by the public, and (3) the development of government applications and services. Technological developments spawned by R&D initiatives in the private sector in concert with increasing consumer demand for improvements in e-government efforts are the foundation for M-Government (Kushchu & Boricki 2004). The above arguments emphasize the fact that mobile phones, and mobile messaging (mainly text messaging) in particular, can be one of the most appropriate mediums for the delivery of government services and public information. M-Government, especially in the case of Greece, can act as the introductory phase of e-government services, and help towards increasing the use of e-government services, with the optimum goal being the introduction and the wide use of ubiquitous e-government services.

Once citizens begin to use e-government services, they tend to continue using e-government (Council for Excellence in Government and Accenture 2003). However, in almost every E.U. member state more progress has been made during the last years concerning online services for businesses than concerning those for citizens (Cap

Gemini Ernst & Young, 2004). M-Government is a chance for each EU member state and specifically for Greece to accelerate e-government development. E-government is often now seen as a synonym, or a condition for good governance (Linz & Stepan 1996), which has been linked to the presence of democratic institutions and participation of their citizens (Lenk & Traumuller 2000).

Apparently, mobile government is a growing set of complex strategies and tools that will change the roles and functioning of traditional governance. Nevertheless, M-Government is considered as a subset of e-government that doesn't act as a replacement for e-government, but rather as a complement. However, it should be noted, that despite the obvious benefits of M-Government, the success and acceptance of such services rely upon citizens' willingness to adopt them.

The objective of this paper is to demonstrate and measure the factors that affect the adoption of potential M-Government services by Greek citizens under the Greek social, political, and legal context. To that end, the study employs the constructs reported in Tornatzky & Klein (1982) study as the most relevant to adoption research (i.e. relative advantage, compatibility, and complexity), as well as the image construct which is also noted as a considerable factor influencing adoption (Van Slyke et al. 2004). The paper then tests whether these factors have significant impact on M-Government adoption.

The interdisciplinary nature of the present study (i.e. Information Systems and Marketing) calls for the combined use of different theories and research perspectives. Specifically, the present study employs Rogers' (1995) diffusion of innovation (DOI) theory which incorporates a popular model used in Information System research to explain user adoption of new technologies. According to DOI, the rate of diffusion is affected by an innovation's: (a) relative advantage, (b) complexity, (c) compatibility, (d) trialability, (e) observability. Also, Moore & Benbasat (1991)

present image, result demonstrability, visibility, and voluntariness as additional factors that influence the acceptance and use of an innovation. The research objective of the present study is, therefore, to investigate which factor(s) significantly affect the intention to use M-Government services in the specific research context. This is accomplished through the employment of an empirical survey (quantitative study). The data collection instrument was a questionnaire. Specific research hypotheses were formulated, supported by corresponding references and tested through multiple linear regression analysis.

LITERATURE REVIEW

M-Government Dynamics

M-Government is basically a subset of e-government. The value of M-Government comes from the capabilities of applications supporting mobility of the citizens, businesses and internal operations of the governments (Kushchu & Kuscu 2003). M-Government can help make public information and government services available "anytime, anywhere" to citizens and officials, taking advantage of the characteristics of its medium, which is the mobile phone. We can define e-government as the use of information and communication technologies (ICTs) and in particular, the Internet, to deliver government information and services and to involve citizens in the democratic process and real-time government decision making in a much more convenient, customer-oriented (citizen-centric), cost-effective and potentially altogether different and better way (Carbo & Williams 2004). In the case of M-Government, those ICTs are limited to mobile phones and mobile messaging (Short Message Service and Multimedia Message Service). The synergy between e-government and M-Government may be of concern especially for those countries that are already gone ahead in making substantial investments in e-government implementations (e.g. EU countries). On the other hand, in developing countries M-Government applications may become a key method for reaching citizens and promoting exchange of communications especially when used in remote areas. The ultimate goal is the transformation of the government so as to be truly citizen-centric.

There can be three (3) levels of interaction between the administration and the citizen:

- **Push:** One way communication initiated from the administration
- **Pull:** Two way communication initiated from the citizen
- **Interactive dialogue:** Continuous two way communication initiated from any of the two parties of the communication channel (administration or citizen)

In reality, however, all three levels of interaction, still do not change the way the services are being designed and provided. But this is in fact only the very first step along the way ICTs coming to play a role in the modernization of the government's operations. We can label this first step "substitution", as traditional paper is being replaced an electronic interface. Beyond substitution, we can identify three additional steps in the way administration operations are going to be transformed by the ICTs. These are: (1) mirroring, (2) new digital products, and (3) total outsourcing of production (Finger & Pecoud 2003).

Based on various studies on M-Government applications (Yu & Kushchu 2004), and their use in practise (Cilingir & Kushchu 2004), a number of differentiating factors can be identified in terms of better precision and personalization in targeting users and in delivering content, more convenient accessibility and availability, and a larger and wider user base (Kushchu & Boricki 2004).

M-Government vs. E-Government

M-Government does not replace e-government, rather it complements it. While mobile phones are excellent access devices, are not suitable for the transmission of complex and voluminous information. Despite the emergence of more sophisticated handsets, mobile phones do not have the same amount of features and services as desktop or portable computers. For example, Short Message Service (SMS) has a limit of 160 characters, whereas e-mail allows a nearly infinite quantity of characters and multimedia content. Also, computers have wider screens with high resolution, compared to the small and low resolution screens that mobile phones have. Internet-connected computers are still the preferred device to take part in online political discussions, to search for detailed public sector information, and to transact most types of e-government service. No government can rely only on mobile technologies as a medium so as to offer value added governmental services to its citizens and businesses. Mobile applications also rely on good back-office infrastructure (e.g. ERP applications) and work processes: Government networks and databases, data quality procedures, transaction recording processes, etc.

M-Government does not mean only taking current e-government services and delivering them via mobiles, although, on the other hand, no one should understand M-Government as a ubiquitous solution to every need and want of public administration. Some aspects of governmental activities could only be solved by e-government, e.g., faster inter-departmental information flow. From a citizen perspective, M-Government stands for a new front-end access to public services that have been made available specifically for mobile devices or adapted from existing e-government applications.

Below are presented some key differences between M-Government and e-government in a more detailed way:

- More convenient accessibility and availability (power of pull):
  - M-Government enhances the adoption of online governmental services by citizens through the improved convenience it offers. Citizens can use the online governmental services not only "anytime" but also "anywhere".
  - Mobile phones are always on, and this is much different from personal computers. Usually these devices stay at an inactive state, but applications can "wake up" the device. In other words M-Government applications operate in a different way than e-government applications.
  - Mobile devices are designed to be carried around. As mobile devices are always carried around by the user, applications can be designed to provide instant information to the users. An example is to send out warnings during emergencies.
- Better precision and personalisation in targeting users and delivering content (power of push)
  - A personal computer can be shared among different users, but mobile phones are designed to be used by a single user. This means that personalized information can reach the same user at any time through that one specific device.
  - M-Government increases the acceptance, adoption and the usage of online governmental services by reaching the citizens through a more personal, familiar and user friendly way.
- Larger and wider user base (power of reach)
  - M-Government reaches a larger number of people through mobile terminals, which far exceeds the wired Internet user community. M-Government

reaches a variety of audiences, including people who have no training or experience with computers and the Internet, but are active users of mobile communication.

Current Practice

M-Government as a subset of e-government can be examined in terms of the interactions between sectors of government, business and citizens (Jaeger 2003). Government-to-Government (G2G) initiatives facilitate increased efficiency and communication between parts of a government. G2G initiatives can improve transaction speed and consistency, while reducing the time employees must spend on tasks. G2G interactions can also allow for much more proficient sharing of vital information between parts of the government. Government-to-Business (G2B) initiatives, involving the sale of government goods and the procurement of goods and services for the government, have benefits for both business and governments. For business G2B interactions can result in increased awareness of opportunities to work with the government and in cost savings and increased efficiency in performing transactions. For governments, G2B interactions offer benefits in reducing costs and increasing efficiency in procurement processes and provide new avenues for selling surplus items. E-government provides clear benefits for business and governments while at the same time citizens enjoy the widest array of benefits from e-government. Specifically, Government-to-Citizen (G2C) initiatives can facilitate involvement and interaction with the government, enhancing the "degree and quality of public participation in government". G2C interactions can allow citizens to be "more informed about government laws, regulations, policies, and services" (Muir & Oppenheim 2002). For the citizen, e-government can offer a huge range of information and services, including information for research, government forms and services, public policy information, employment and business opportunities, voting information, tax filling, license registration or renewal, payment of fines, and submission of comments to government officials. By giving geographically isolated citizens a greater chance to connect with the government and other citizens, e-government offers a new way to facilitate citizen participation in the political process.

Government-to-Citizen (G2C)

The Government–to–Citizen M-Government model provides direct benefits to the majority of the citizens and can be used as an introductory model of M-Government in countries where no e- or M-Government services exist. G2C model has 3 instances: (1) m-communication, (2) m-transactions, and (3) m-voting.

M-Communication

The most visible aspect of M-Government is the provision of information through mobile devices in two categories: (1) general information or alerts for citizens, business or government, and (2) important or legally binding communication and information provided by businesses or individuals to governments and vice versa (Zalesak 2003).

M-transactions

Mobile phones and text messaging not only provide a channel of communication between citizens and government; they also enable government-to-citizen transactions. While the use of m-payment in M-Government is still limited, it is expected that – as mobile payments systems evolve from simple payments for digital content and services to complex integrated handset, bank and operator payments – its use for transacting business with government will grow.

M-Voting (or M-Democracy)

M-voting and the use of text messaging and mobile devices for citizen input to political decision-making is an M-Government application with tremendous potential to enhance democratic participation. However, several concerns would have to be attended before voting over mobile phones. Specifically, questions of security and secrecy are top of the list. Another issue is to make the system as user-friendly as possible. Then, there is the problem of using a phone keypad to key in parties or candidate names. Finally, the voting procedure itself must allow voters at any stage to repeat the instructions and choices. In addition, the capacity of the system would need to be sufficient to deal with peak periods because congested telephone lines are as frustrating as long lines in the polling stations.

Along these lines, few people are willing to vote through their mobile phones. Specifically, the major concerns reported about m-voting are (Larsen & Rainie 2002):

- Lack of security
- Lack of knowledge about text messaging among older people
- Costs
- Psychological barriers

Research Objectives

While there seems to be substantial growth in the development of e-government initiatives it is not clear that citizens will embrace the use of such services. The success and acceptance of e-government initiatives are contingent upon citizens' willingness to adopt these services (Carter & Belanger 2004). Since M-Government is a subset of e-government the same argument can apply also for M-Government initiatives. Numerous studies have analyzed user adoption of electronic commerce (Vrechopoulos et al. 2001). Yet to date, few studies have explored the core factors that influence citizen adoption of e-government services and even fewer of M-Government services. Despite the global character of mobile technologies, a nation's and its citizens' needs and wants differ significantly, so governments should proactively consult with the public and take their opinions into account over implementation of M-Government strategies. So, the objective of this paper is to demonstrate and measure the factors that will affect the adoption of potential M-Government services offered by the Greek Government to Greek Citizens, under the Greek social, political, and legal context.

RESEARCH METHODOLOGY

Research Questions

Rogers' (1995) diffusion of innovation (DOI) theory is a popular model used in Information System (IS) research to explain user adoption of new technologies. According to DOI, the rate of diffusion is affected by an innovation's

- relative advantage,
- complexity,
- compatibility,
- trialability,
- and observability.

Also, Moore & Benbasat (1991) present image, result demonstrability, visibility, and voluntariness as additional factors that influence the acceptance and use of an innovation. The research objective of the present study is, therefore, to investigate which factor(s) significantly affect the intention to use M-Government services in the specific research context.

Research Hypotheses

Previous research has found that perceived characteristics of innovating (PCI) factors play a role in user acceptance of electronic commerce in the private sector (Gefen et al. 2003; Val Slyke et al. 2004). In the public sector, citizen adoption of e-government should be subject to similar factors (Warkentin 2002). Tornatzky and Klein (1982) conclude that relative advantage, compatibility, and complexity are the most relevant constructs to adoption research. Thus, these three factors are included in this study. Also previous research shows that image is also a considerable factor influencing adoption (Larsen & Rainie 2002) and, therefore, image is also included in the study. In sum, considering the similarities between electronic commerce, e-government, and M-Government these four factors (Compatibility, Image, Relative Advantage and Easy of Use) are used in this study to determine M-Government services adoption. In sum, it should be clarified that we decided to include in the research model these four factors (instead all the factors discussed in the previous section – some of them are common) since there is strong theoretical evidence that relates these specific factors to the "Intention to Use" M-Government services dependent variable of the model. In other words, the corresponding four (4) research hypotheses can be well supported by theory which is clear in the discussion below. For the remaining factors, their inclusion in the model and the formulation of corresponding research hypotheses would have as a major limitation the *novel character* of these hypotheses and, therefore, it was decided to not include them in the model. In other words, for the remaining factors there is not so strong theoretical evidence in the specific area of M-Government that relates then to behavioural intention.

Elaborating on the aforementioned theoretical insights, the following research hypotheses are formulated:

Hypothesis #1

As cited above and for the purpose of the present study *compatibility* is defined as the degree to which M-Government services are perceived as consistent with the Greek citizens' existing practices and habits. Specifically, if M-Government services will be designed and implemented in a way that it will not change Greek citizens' habits in terms of communication and transaction activities with the government, then Greek citizens are more likely to adopt M-Government services. Hence, it is hypothesized:

H1: *Higher levels of perceived compatibility with M-Government services will be positively related to higher levels of intention to use such services*

Hypothesis #2

For certain innovations, the social prestige that the innovation confers to its adopter may be the sole benefit that the adopter receives (Rogers 1995). In the context of M-Government services adoption by Greek citizens, those who have adopted the service may impress others that, for example, even though they are old in age, they are still able to learn and use new technologies, hence keeping up to date with changes in society. This may enhance their social status and also enable them to serve as role models for other senior citizens who have not adopted these M-Government services. Accordingly, senior citizens having a higher need for social recognition will perceive M-Government services to be beneficial to them. Hence, it is hypothesized that:

H2: *Higher levels of perceived image through the use of M-Government services will be positively related to higher levels of intention to use such services.*

Hypothesis #3

Previous innovation diffusion studies have identified the link between relative advantage (perceived usefulness in Technology Acceptance Model) and compatibility (Jaeger 2003). So, since it is expected that compatibility will have a positive effect on the adoption of M-Government services, it can derived that also relative advantage will have a positive effect on the adoption of M-Government services. Hence, it is hypothesized that:

H3: *Higher levels of perceived relative advantage through the use of M-Government services will be positively related to higher levels of intention to use such services.*

Hypothesis #4

Perceived ease of use is also hypothesized to directly influence the intention of using a technology. Although some studies (Szajna 1996) found that perceived ease of use has less significant effect on intention to use over a period of sustained usage, it has been decided to investigate this relationship in our study, since prior research found that perceived ease of use has a stronger effect on intention to use for individuals who are of older age (Morris & Venkatesh 2000). Hence, it is hypothesized that:

H4: *Higher levels of perceived ease of using M-Government services will be positively related to higher levels of intention to use such services.*

Research Model

The research model (Figure 1) derived through the aforementioned discussion serves as the theoretical framework for assessing the potential adoption and acceptance of M-Government services in Greece. In addition, it provides a useful tool to public sector managers and politicians needing to

Figure 1. The Research model

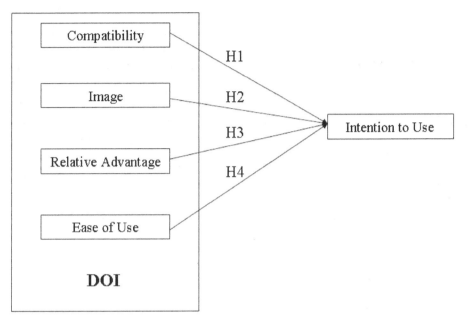

assess the likelihood of success for new technology introductions and helps them understand the drivers of acceptance, taking into consideration previous experience in e-government research.

Operationalization

An instrument anchored on a 7-Likert scale was constructed (i.e. 1 for Extremely Disagree, and 7 for Extremely Agree) based on the established measures of constructs. The items used in this survey were adapted from previous studies. Specifically, the measures of *compatibility, relative advantage*, and *image* were adapted from Van Slyke's et al. (2004) previous research while *ease of use* was measured using items adapted from Davis' (1989) TAM model. The items used to measure *use intentions* were adapted from Pavlou's (2003) and Gefen's et al. (2003) research. A list of the items is provided in the Appendix. Finally, all the items were translated in Greek so as only Greek citizens responded to this survey.

The next stage of the instrument development process was the creation of a pilot test of the overall

instrument. Specifically, questionnaires were distributed to a convenient sample of 15 postgraduate students from the Athens University of Economic and Business and the University of Crete. The aim of this test was to ensure that the mechanics of compiling the questionnaire had been adequate. This was accomplished by having respondents first complete the questionnaire, and then comment on its length, wording and instructions. The most considerable comments were accepted and incorporated in the final form of the questionnaire. Then, the questionnaire was published online and an invitation mail was sent to current and alumni students of the International M.B.A. program of Athens University of Economics and Business and current and alumni students of the Computer Science Department of the University of Crete. All recipients of the mail were asked to participate in the survey voluntarily and also to forward this invitation to any interested citizen they have thought of. A cover letter was included in the beginning of the survey explaining the purpose of the study along with a description about M-Government services, and seven simple usage scenarios of M-Government services. Finally, 121 citizens filled out the questionnaire.

ANALYSIS OF RESULTS AND DISCUSSION

Demographics

The survey gathered 121 responses. Most of the respondents was male (62.81 per cent) and had obtained one university degree at least (79.34 per cent). Respondents were almost equally divided into two age groups (18-25: 43.80 per cent, 26-35: 46.28 per cent) and likewise were divided into two major groups according to the respondents' job (Students: 40.50 per cent, Private Sector Employees: 38,02 per cent). Also, respondents have a fairly good level of experience with the government services (69,5 per cent of the respondents have enough or great experience interacting with the government), a fact that gives to this study a validity about its results. Finally, the vast major-

ity of the respondents (95.87 per cent) are mobile phone users.

It should be clarified that the sampling frames of this study (i.e. two universities) were selected having in mind that M-Government is an innovative service and therefore, according to the DOI theory the first group that will adopt such an innovation are the "innovators". This group usually is aware of technological evolutions and has high educational level. Therefore, the two sampling frames well served the purpose of the study, having also in mind that the Internet penetration rates in Greece is quite low compared to other European countries.

Validity

Factor analysis using Principle Components with Promax rotation was used to evaluate construct validity. As shown in Table 1, most items loaded properly on their expected factors. However, only two items from the Ease of Use construct either didn't get a high score in the factor analysis (above 0.70) or didn't load properly.

Table 1. Factor analysis

Item	Factor Loading				
	Compatibility	Image	RA	Use	Ease of Use
EOU1					,884
EOU3	,748				
EOU2					
USE2				,935	
IMAGE1		,829			
IMAGE5		,902			
RA3			,908		
EOU4					,830
RA1			,920		
IMAGE3		,879			
CT1	,839				
CT2	,793				
CT3	,799				
USE1				,831	

Table 2. Reliability analysis

Construct	Number of items	Reliability
Relative Advantage	2	,8582
Perceived Ease of Use	2 (4)*	,6769
Image	3	,8433
Compatibility	3	,7751
Behavioural Intention	2	,8264

* Two items were deleted because they didn't load properly

Reliability

The reliability of the constructs was evaluated using Cronbach's alpha variable. Table 2 presents the results of the reliability analysis, demonstrating acceptable reliabilities (above 0.70) for almost all constructs.

Hypothesis Testing

The data were analyzed using multiple linear regression analysis. Regression analysis was seen as the most appropriate analytical technique since the goal of this study is to determine the relationships between use intention (dependent variable) and Greek citizens' perceptions of M-Government services (independent variables). In other words, multiple regression analysis provides evidence about the predicting power of the independent variables on the dependent one. It is used when there is theoretical evidence that the independent variables are correlated with one another and with the dependent variable.

The model explains 30 percent of the variance in Greek citizens' adoption of M-Government services (adjusted R Square = .291, F=13.285, p<.0001). Two of the four adoption factors (Compatibility and Ease of Use) were found to be significant in predicting citizen intention to use M-Government services (Table 3).

Discussion

Compatibility

Higher levels of *perceived compatibility* are associated with *increased intentions* by the Greek citizens to adopt M-Government services. As shown in the first section of the manuscript most of the Greek citizens have embraced mobile phones and mobile services to their lives, so they are likely to adopt M-Government services as well. Citizens who have adopted mobile services can be expected to view M-Government services as compatible with their lifestyle. Mobile services adopters feel comfortable when searching for information, providing personal information and conducting transactions through mobile phones and mobile networks. These citizens will have higher intentions to adopt M-Government services than those who view these services as incompatible with their lifestyle.

Image

Higher levels of *perceived image* do not directly affect Greek citizens' *intentions to use* M-Govern-

Table 3. Hypotheses testing

Hypotheses	Variables	Coefficients	t	Sig.	Result
H1	Compatibility	,257	2,722	,007	Reject Ho
H2	Image	-,102	-1,291	,199	Cannot Reject Ho
H3	RA	,151	1,535	,128	Cannot Reject Ho
H4	Easy of Use	,291	3,207	,002	Reject Ho

ment services. Citizens do not view the use of e-government services as a status symbol. Previous work has also found image to be a less predictive indicator of use intentions when compared to the other DOI constructs (Larsen & Rainie 2002). Also the high penetration of mobile phones and mobile services cannot increase individuals' social statues or their social prestige.

Relative Advantage

Higher levels of *perceived relative advantage* are not significantly associated with the increase of citizens' *intentions to use* M-Government services. This unexpected outcome can be explained by the fact that M-Government have not yet been implemented by the Greek government so Greek citizens are not fully aware what M-Government can give them as a benefit in practice, in contrast with the traditional ways of interacting with the government (in-line, fax, landline telephone) which have been operated until now.

Ease of Use

Contrary to hypotheses 2 and 3, higher levels of *perceived ease of use* are significantly associated with increased *use intentions* of e-Government services. This predicted outcome is consistent with Morris and Venkantesh's (2000) previous research where it was found that perceived ease of use was more significant than relative advantage (perceived usefulness) in explaining use intention for older people in the workplace.

CONCLUSIONS AND IMPLICATIONS

This research is one of the initial studies that tried to focus on citizens in the context of M-Government's adoption services in Greece. The study shows that the Diffusion of Innovation theory is applicable in a new context (i.e., Greek citizens' adoption of M-Government services) Providing

clear evidence on the predicting power of these factors on the intention to use m-governemt services.

This study presents an introductory model that explains 30 percent of the variance in Greek citizens' adoption of M-Government services. However, since this percentage is relatively low the results should be interpreted with caution. Besides, the present study could be characterized as an exploratory one despite the fact that employs and tests research hypotheses (i.e. conclusive type of research designs do that). In other words, we tried to formulate and test some research hypotheses despite the fact that typically researchers approaching a new to the world phenomenon (i.e. M-Government) usually employ exploratory research designs avoiding, therefore, the formulation and testing of research hypotheses. In sum, employing a conclusive type of research for the present study, while it has major limitations, it enhances at the same time the value of the work reported in this chapter.

This model can serve as a starting point for other M-Government adoption research efforts, while encouraging further exploration and integration of additional adoption constructs, and using also other models like TAM and UTAUT. Also, Structural Equation Modelling (SEM) could be used in a survey with a greater number of respondents (>200) so as to predict more accurately the adoption factors of M-Government in Greece. Specifically, SEM could be used to investigate the *intention to use* as a dependent and independent variable simultaneously (for the latter case, the dependent could be the *actual usage* of the forthcoming M-Government services). Along these lines, further research should run as soon as M-Government services are offered to Greek citizens in order to investigate the *actual use* dimension (dependent variable) as well as evaluate the service-related variables (e.g. interface design, pricing and promotional policies, etc.).

The study reveals two significant indicators of citizens' intention to use M-Government services.

Therefore, state agencies should promote citizen acceptance and use of the future M-Government services by manipulating *perceived compatibility* and *perceived ease of use* in their communication strategies. Specifically, government agencies could increase citizens' perceptions of compatibility by noting the similarities between traditional government services and online government services and also by giving clear instructions about the use of M-Governments services. In addition, government agencies can promote the similarities between the mobiles services offered by mobile operators and third party providers, so as to depict the similarities between mobile services and M-Government services. Also, educational programs provided to adult Greek citizens about the use of M-Government could increase the adoption of such services.

In general, realizing the benefits of ICTs in the public sector requires organizations to understand its potential, overcome various problems and increase their efforts. The attempts by governments to improve and optimise their services are usually perceived positively by citizens. However, one of the central and frequently-voiced criticisms for governments is that they are slow, don't react to the demands of their citizens, and that they are generally bureaucratic and wasteful (Stahl 2005). Along these lines, IT initiatives in general, and e-government projects in particular, face multiple and complex challenges (Garson 2003). To that end, identifying and overcoming these challenges is not always easy. Technological complexity and incompatibility are, however, neither the only, nor the most difficult to overcome. Managerial, political, and legal factors have been also identified as important elements to take into consideration in the design and development of IT initiatives as well (Dawes & Pardo 2002). Furthermore, politics, privacy concerns, and other institutional arrangements can also affect the results of an IT project (Belamy 2000). Finally, whether e-government and subsequently M-Government in the future will be a method for including more citizens in

a government or excluding less technologically educated citizens remain a concern (Jaegar & Thomson 2003).

The study has some limitations. First, the relative small sample size may probably affect the statistical power of the findings. Second, future studies should target older citizens through other channels (e.g. street interviewing) since at the moment the majority of them do not use the Internet, and therefore they are excluded from the present study (i.e. from the online questionnaire). However, it should be clarified that M-Government services may not be the most effective G2C channel for older people in Greece (at least for the beginning of the 21st century!) mainly due to the serious difficulties they face towards using any of the ICT outcomes (e.g. Internet, 3G Mobile Services, etc). In other words, technology in general or M-Government services in particular seem to not have the chances to solve the problems of this group of citizens. For example, the majority of older people in Greece (i.e. +70) do not even use Banks' ATMs to get their pension because they: (a) do not know how to use them, (b) do not want to learn how to use them, (c) cannot find someone to learn them how to use them, (d) afraid to use them or (e) simply because they do not like to change their habits. Similarly, future research may investigate the factors influencing adoption among different age groups to see if there are differences in terms of the salient factors among them. This will help M-Government implementers to better design specifically-targeted services to citizens from different age groups. Besides, as it stands in B2C commerce, the multiple channel strategy (e.g. multichannel retailing) may be the most effective solution also in G2C.

REFERENCES

Belamy, C. (2000). The politics of public information systems. In G. Garson (Ed.), *Handbook of Public Information Systems*. New York: Marcel Dekker, Inc.

Cap Gemini Ernst & Young (2004). *Survey on Electronic Public Services in Europe.*

Council for Excellence in Government and Accenture (2003). *The new e-government equation: Ease, engagement, privacy and protection.*

Carbo, T., & Williams, J. (2004). Models and Metrics for Evaluating Local Electronic Government Systems and Services *Electronic Journal of e-Government, 2*(2), 95-104.

Carter, L., & Belanger, F. (2004). The influence of Perceived Characteristics of Innovating on e-Government Adoption *Electronic Journal of e-Government, 2*(1), 11-20.

Cilingir, D., & Kushchu, I. (2004). E-Government and M-Government: Concurrent Leaps by Turkey. *Proceedings of the 4ᵗʰ European Conference on E-Government,* (pp. 813-821).

Davis, F. (1989). Perceived Usefulness, Perceived Ease of Use and User Acceptance of Information Technology. *MIS Quarterly, 13*(3), 319-340.

Dawes, S., & Pardo, T. (2002). Building collaborative digital government systems. In W. Mciver & K. Elmagarmid (Eds.), *Advances in digital government. Technology human factors and policy.* Norwell, MA: Kluwer Academic Publishers.

Durlacher Research (2001). *UMTS Report, an Investment Perspective.* [Online] Available: http://www.durlacher.com [Accessed: 30 Jul 2002].

Finger, M., & Pecoud, G. (2003). From e-Government to e-Governance? Towards a model of e-Governance. *Electronic Journal of e-Government, 1*(1), 1-10.

Garson, G. (2003). *Toward an information technology research agenda for public administration.* In G. Garson (Ed.), *Public information technology: Policy and management issues.* Hershey, PA: Idea Group Publishing.

Gefen, D., Karahanna, E., & Straub, D. (2003). Trust and TAM in Online Shopping: An Integrated Model. *MIS Quarterly, 27*(1), 51-90.

Jaeger, P. (2003). The Endless wire: E-government as global phenomenon. *Government Information Quarterly, 20*(4), 323-331.

Jaegar, P., & Thomson, K. (2003). E-government around the world: Lessons, challenges, and future directions. *Government Information Quarterly, 20*(4), 389-394.

Kushchu, I., & Boricki, C. (2004). A Mobility Response Model for Government. *Mobile Government Lab.* Retrieved 9 March 2006 from http://www.mgovlab.org.

Kushchu, I., & Kuscu, H. (2003). From E-government to M-Government: Facing the Inevitable. *Proceedings of the 3rd European Conference on e-Government,* (pp. 253-260).

Larsen, E., & Rainie, L. (2002). *The rise of the e-citizen: How people use government agencies' Web sites.* Washington DC: Pew Internet & the American.

Lenk, K., & Traumuller, R. (2000). A framework for electronic government. *Proceedings of the 11th International Workshop on Database and Expert Systems Applications,* (p. 271). Baltimore, Maryland: ACM Publications

Linz, J., & Stepan, A. (1996). *Problems of democratic transition and consolidation: Southern Europe, South America, and post-communist Europe.* Baltimore: John Hopkins University Press.

Martin, B., & Byrne, J. (2003). Implementing e-Government: widening the lens. *Electronic Journal of e-Government, 1*(1), 11-22.

Moore, G., & Benbasati, I. (1991). Development of an instrument to measure the perceptions of adopting an information technology innovation. *Information Systems Research, 2*(3), 173-191.

Morris, M., & Venkatesh, V. (2000). Age Differences in Technology Adoption Decisions: Implications for a Changing Workforce. *Personnel Psychology, 53*(2), 375-403.

Muir, A., & Oppenheim, C. (2002). National information policy developments worldwide I: electronic government. *Journal of Information Science, 28*(3), 173-186.

Pavlou, P. (2003). Consumer Acceptance of Electronic Commerce: Integrating Trust and Risk with the Technology Acceptance Model. *International Journal of Electronic Commerce, 7*(3), 69-103.

Rogers, E. (1995). *Diffusion of Innovations*. New York: The Free Press.

Stahl, C. (2005). The Paradigm of E-Commerce in E-Government and E-Democracy. In W. Huang, K. Sisiiau, & K. Wei, (Eds.), *Electronic Government Strategies and Implementation,* (pp. 1-19). Hershey PA: Idea Group Publishing.

Szajna, B. (1996). Empirical Evaluation of the Revised Technology Acceptance Model. *Management Science, 42*(1), 85-92.

Tornatky, L., & Klein K. (1982). Innovation characteristics and innovation adoption-implementation: A meta-analysis of findings. *IEEE Transactions on Engineering Management, 29*(1), 28-45.

Turban, E., Lee, J. K., King, D., McKay, J., & Marshall, P. (2008). *Electronic Commerce 2008: A Managerial Perspective*. Fifth Edition, Pearson - Prentice Hall.

Van Slyke, C., Belanger, F., & Comunale, C. (2004). Factors Influencing the Adoption of Web-Based Shopping: The Impact of Trust. *ACM SIGMIS Database, 35*(2), 32-49.

Vrechopoulos, A., Siomkos, G., & Doukidis, G. (2001) Internet Shopping Adoption by Greek Consumers. *European Journal of Innovation Management, 4*(3), 142-152.

Warkentin, M., Gefen, D., Pavlou, P., & Rose, G. (2002) Encouraging Citizen Adoption of e-Government by Building Trust. *Electronic Markets, 12*(3), 157-162.

Yu, B., & Kushchu, I. (2004). The value of Mobility for e-government. *Proceedings of the 4th European Conference on E-Government*, (pp. 887-899).

Zalesak, M. (2003). Overview and opportunities of mobile government. *Mobile Government Lab*. Retrieved 9 March 2006 from http://www.mgovlab.org.

APPENDIX: QUESTIONNAIRE CONSTRUCTS AND ITEMS

Relative Advantage

| RA1 | Using M-Government services would enhance my effectiveness of my communication/transaction with the government. |
| RA3 | Using M-Government services would make it easier to complete my communication/transaction with the government. |

Ease of Use

EOU1	Learning to interact with the government via M-Government services would be easy for me.
EOU2	My interaction with M-Government services would be clear and understandable.
EOU3	I would find M-Government services to be flexible to interact with.
EOU4	It would be easy for me to become skilful at using M-Government services.

Image

Image3	People in my social environment who would use M-Government services would have more prestige than those who do not.
Image1	People in my social environment who would use M-Government services would have a high profile.
Image5	Using M-Government services could be a status symbol in my social environment.

Compatibility

CT1	Using M-Government services would be compatible with all aspects of my communication/transaction with the government.
CT2	I think that using M-Government services will fit well with the way I like to communicate/transact with the government.
CT3	Using M-Government services will fit into my style of communication/transaction with the government.

Intention to Use

| USE1 | Assuming I could use M-Government services, I predict I intend to use M-Government services the next 6 months |
| USE2 | Given the fact I could M-Government services, I predict I would use M-Government services the next 6 months |

Section III
Technical Considerations for Mobile and Ubiquitous Commerce

Chapter VI
Toward Mobile Web 2.0-Based Business Methods:
Collaborative QoS-Information Sharing for Mobile Service Users

Katarzyna Wac
University of Geneva, Switzerland, & University of Twente, The Netherlands

Richard Bults
University of Twente, The Netherlands & Mobihealth B.V., The Netherlands

Bert-Jan van Beijnum
University of Twente, The Netherlands

Hong Chen
Altran Netherlands B.V., The Netherlands

Dimitri Konstantas
University of Geneva, Switzerland

ABSTRACT

Mobile service providers (MoSPs) emerge, driven by the ubiquitous availability of mobile devices and wireless communication infrastructures. MoSPs' customers satisfaction and consequently their revenues, largely depend on the quality of service (QoS) provided by wireless network providers (WNPs) available at a particular location-time to support a mobile service delivery. This chapter presents a novel method for the MoSP's QoS-assurance business process. The method incorporates a location- and time-based QoS-predictions' service, facilitating the WNP's selection. The authors explore different business cases for the service deployment. Particularly, they introduce and analyze business viability of QoSIS.net, an enterprise that can provide the QoS-predictions service to MoSPs, Mobile Network Operators (as MoSPs), or directly to their customers (i.e. in B2B/B2C settings). QoSIS.net provides its service based on collaborative-sharing of QoS-information by its users. The authors argue that this service can improve the MoSP's QoS-assurance process and consequently may increase its revenues, while creating revenues for QoSIS.net.

INTRODUCTION

The last 15 years have been marked by the expansion, global adoption and seamless availability of the (fixed) Internet with a multitude of its ubiquitous services. In parallel, a new mobile era has undergone its preparation phase, driven by miniaturization and personalization of communication devices, as well as the rapid expansion and adoption of mobile voice and data services and heterogeneous communication infrastructures (Hansmann *et al.*, 2003).

In this era, ubiquitous Mobile Service Providers (*MoSPs)* bring to the market users' favorite Internet-services and start offering a wide range of new services. As a *mobile service* we define a data service that is delivered to (or from) a mobile device from (or to) the Internet. The service delivery is supported by the deployment of wireless communication infrastructures, enabling a user the Internet-connectivity while on the move. A MoSP is then an enterprise, which core business processes aim at providing mobile services to its customers (TMF, 2001).

The MoSPs are fully aware that to achieve their goals of gaining customer acceptance, secure their revenues and remain competitive, their services must provide users *Quality of Experience* (QoE) comparable to the QoE provided by the existing Internet-services (Afuah & Tucci, 2000). The QoE is "the overall acceptability of service, as perceived *subjectively* by the user" (ITU-T, 2007), and as a part of it, a MoSP must at least assure meeting user's *Quality of Service* (QoS) requirements, expressed quantitatively in terms of service speed, accuracy, dependability, security level and price related (performance) measures. The QoS is defined as "a collective effect of service performances which determine the (*objective*) degree of satisfaction of a user" (ITU-T, 1993). MoSPs unanimously indicate, that their *QoS-assurance process*, i.e., a business process related to service-management, and responsible for assurance that services provided to users are performing according to their QoS-requirement, is critical to their business viability (Andersson *et al.*, 2006; Nokia, 2004).

The challenge is that, the MoSPs' QoS-assurance process relies on the QoS provided by wireless communication infrastructures, supporting the mobile services delivery. Ideally, there would be infrastructures supporting anytime-anywhere services delivery to a user. However, in reality these infrastructures are beyond the control of MoSPs; they are owned and managed by enterprises called *Wireless Network Providers* (*WNPs*). A WNP core business processes aim at providing Internet-connectivity to its customers. A wireless communication infrastructure exhibits different QoS depending on the WNP it's owned by, a wireless technology used (e.g. WLAN/GPRS) as well as the mobile user's location-time.

Nowadays, in most countries, a number of WNPs coexist, operating different long-range wireless communication technologies. In particular, there exists at least one nationwide WNP called a *Mobile Network Operator (MNO)*. A MNO is an enterprise that, as a WNP, owns and manages its wireless network infrastructures. MNO's core business processes aim at providing voice services (primarily) and Internet-connectivity, using long-range wireless technologies (e.g. GSM/UMTS) (ITU, 2005) to its customers. A MNO can take a role of a MoSP, i.e., can also provide mobile services to its customers.

In parallel, WNPs like public-WLAN providers emerge rapidly, especially in big cities. Moreover, today's mobile devices embed multiple interfaces, thus supporting Internet-connectivity over various wireless technologies. Hence, the communications means tend to be ubiquitously available to mobile service users, and, at least in principle, these users must be able to choose a WNP (and a wireless technology) providing the QoS best meeting their QoS requirements thus facilitating meeting their expected-QoE. However, this assumption is far from the reality. The business strategy of existing WNPs, and particularly

MNOs, is based on a user 'lock-in', i.e., the user can access only wireless networks owned by 'his' WNP (Buschken, 2004). Moreover, the only disclosed information about the QoS provided by WNPs is based on the WNPs' marketing data about their network's theoretical performance—the real QoS (i.e. objectively measured) is unknown to the mobile users. Even mobile services provided by MNOs (taking a role of MoSPs), are based on estimations regarding their provided-QoS. A likely cause is the limited time/budget spent on service-user trials by MNOs (Tan, 2004). Moreover, it is widely accepted that performance tests conduced by WNPs, and particularly by MNOs, are coarse-grained 'drive-tests' over main streets in big cities and main highways (Gomez & Sanchez, 2005). These tests prove the availability of MNOs networks, i.e. their coverage at different locations; and the results are disclosed to a public as coverage maps. Current practices continue, despite the fact that the network's provided-QoS and user perceived-QoE are identified as one of the major factors for customers' loyalty, and moreover, a 'lock-in' practice is admitted to fail as a long-term strategy for customers' retention (Gerpott *et al.*, 2001; M.I.S Trend S.A., 2007; Nokia, 2004).

Effectively, WNPs networks provide 'best-effort' service quality-level to MoSPs. Additionally, MoSPs cannot select at a certain location-time a WNP, which provides a QoS that best meets their customer's required-QoS and their expected-QoE. MoSPs are constrained by the above situation and can only provide mobile services to their customers at a 'best-effort' QoS-level.

We envision that the above mobile user's restrictions on a WNP selection will be removed in the future. Already we see a role of *Mobile Virtual Network Operator (MVNO)* appearing on the market. A MVNO is a WNP (and particularly a MNO) providing voice services and Internet-connectivity over wireless network infrastructures owned/managed by multiple WNPs/MNOs (i.e. MVNO has business contracts with these WNPs/

MNOs to resell a use of their infrastructures). A MVNO's customer, i.e., a mobile user can therefore have an Internet-connectivity via set of network infrastructures. With larger number of WNPs/MNOs, with which a MVNO has a contract, a larger WNP/MNO choice becomes available to a mobile user at any location-time. However, this does not solve the problem of how the user will choose the most appropriate WNP/MNO, given his location-time, QoS-requirements and QoE-expectations.

As a solution, we firstly propose a novel *method* facilitating QoS-assurance business process of MoSPs. As a novel method we define a (business) method employed in an enterprise's business process(es), innovative in terms of technology and/or business contracts established between enterprises in a service-value chain (TMF, 2004).

Our method is technologically innovative because it incorporates fine-grained location-time-based predictions about the QoS-observed when given WNP is used, into the MoSP's QoS-assurance process. These predictions are denoted as *QoS-predictions*. They can be used to select a WNP (and a wireless technology) best meeting MoSP's user QoS-requirements. The goal of the proposed method is to facilitate MoSPs' to meet user's expected-QoE and thus increase own revenues. This follows the observation that a happy MoSP user is willing to continue using the service and paying for it (Andersson et al., 2006).

Our method is also innovative for a MoSP in terms of its business contracts. Namely we envision that there is a separate enterprise—a provider of the QoS-predictions (service), called *QoSIS.net*. QoSIS stands from *Quality-of-Service Information Service* embracing the QoS-predictions as part of its service. A MoSP has business relation with QoSIS.net in order to use the QoS-predictions.

Besides a novel method for a MoSP, we also propose a novel method for QoSIS.net. This method facilitates its core business process, i.e. a QoS-predictions service-fulfillment related process, embracing development and operation of the service, as requested by its customers (TMF, 2001).

The method proposed for QoIS.net is innovative technologically because it is based on user collaborative QoS-information sharing; QoS-information is acquired when mobile service users use different WNPs at different locations-times. The method's key feature is that QoSIS.net can provide accurate QoS-predictions only after having a large volume of historical QoS-information acquired from mobile users. Currently, we conduct the QoS-predictions feasibility assessment (including accuracy evaluation) in the mobile healthcare domain (Wac *et al.*, 2008).

To be more specific, QoSIS.net provides mobile service users (as a community) with QoS-predictions, as a value-added service. On behalf of these users, QoSIS.net exchanges between them the QoS-information about QoS observed when using different WNPs. This follows an idea behind all emerging *Web 2.0* services that gain an increasing users' acceptance in different domains (e.g. Facebook, Wikipedia) (Hoegg *et al.*, 2006; Martignoni & Stanoevska-Slabeva, 2007; Pascu *et al.*, 2005). Web 2.0 is a paradigm for "mutually maximizing collective knowledge and added-value for each *participant* (in a community) by formalized and dynamic sharing and creation of user-generated content" (O'Reilly, 2005). Its 'mobile' extension implies an implementation of Web 2.0 service as a mobile service. QoSIS.net, as a provider of QoS-predictions, based on QoS-information acquired from mobile users, adheres to a Mobile Web 2.0 paradigm. QoSIS.net customers are such 'participants' (also called 'prosumers' (Tapscott & Williams, 2006)) contributing to the community with their QoS-information.

In this chapter, the business viability of QoSIS. net is examined in detail, and it discusses possible technical solutions supporting QoS-predictions service fulfillment. We argue that the methods proposed for MoSPs and QoSIS.net have a strong potential to bring benefit to them in terms of revenue creation and customer satisfaction. Therefore, in the next sections we present current solutions for QoS-assurance process of MoSPs, then we present our approach for and the results of-QoSIS.net business viability study, after which we present our vision for MoSPs' QoS-assurance process.

CURRENT TRENDS

Internet was since its beginning, providing a 'best-effort' QoS-level. In the late 90's, first solutions for Internet-based SPs QoS-assurance business processes have been proposed, particularly for providers of real-time multimedia services (Shepherd *et al.*, 1996) (Hutchison *et al.*, 1997). From the technical perspective, these solutions were based on use of rigorous and complex QoS-management frameworks, including functions like QoS-negotiation and resource reservation (Andersen *et al.*, 2000; Xiao & Ni, 1999). Moreover, from the business perspective, these solutions required business contracts between SPs and Internet-providers (Afuah & Tucci, 2000). They contradicted with the 'open' nature of Internet-services, because they limited the SPs customer-base to that of the Internet-provider's base. In this situation, many SPs ignored the proposed solutions and learned to manage 'best-effort' QoS-level provided by Internet to assure meeting the QoS-requirements (and the expected-QoE) of their service users. The methods, employed in SP's QoS-assurance process, relied on estimations of QoS-provided by the Internet. This approach was feasible due to at least two factors: firstly, QoS-provided by Internet exhibits regularities and long-term estimations for e.g. months can be derived relatively accurately (claffy *et al.*, 1998). Secondly, if necessary, SPs could easily acquire information on provided-QoS via dedicated QoS-monitoring and all that without any degradation in the quality of their provided services (Michaut & Lepage, 2005).

With the dawn of the mobile era, history is repeating itself. The QoS-assurance process has been identified as critical to the business viability of MoSPs already in the late 90's (Chalmers & Sloman, 1999), when only basic voice and data services existed. The most critical factor in QoS-assurance is related to the user's mobility: a mobile user relies on the availability of different WNP/wireless technologies at different locations-times along his trajectory (Dekleva *et al.*, 2007). To deal with this, MoSPs are (again) advised to employ complex QoS-management frameworks in their QoS-assurance business processes. This solution (again) requires a close business relationship between MoSPs and WNPs, resulting in a WNP-centric business models. This solution is explored in research (Calvo *et al.*, 2004; Faber *et al.*, 2003; Robles *et al.*, 2002; Tan, 2004; Tsalgatidou & Pitoura, 2001).

From a technological perspective there are also other proposals. For example a proposal for MoSPs QoS-assurance process to employ predictions of user mobility path acquired from a WNP (Han & Venkatasubramanian, 2006; Soh & Kim, 2003), or to employ a QoS-broker for the reservation of WNP's network resources on behalf of MoSPs users (Nahrstedt *et al.*, 2001). Simultaneously, MNOs propose new concepts like Universal Mobile Access, Generic Access Network or IP-Multimedia-System (Cuevas *et al.*, 2006), aiming at a technical as well as a business solutions for MoSP's QoS-assurance process; aiming for MoSPs to have their core business processes tightly coupled with the business processes of MNOs. Such solutions contradict the 'mobile' nature of MoSPs' services, because business relations with MNOs limit MoSPs customer base and service-usage area to the MNOs customer-base and its coverage-area.

The MoSPs not following the WNP-centric business models emerge on a growing scale (Tan, 2004). Naming few, Skype is a VoIP provider (Osterwalder *et al.*, 2005), MobiHealth.com is a mobile healthcare SP (MobiHealth, 2007), while Digital Chocolate is a mobile gaming SP (Digital Chocolate, 2008). They all struggle to assure meeting their mobile users' QoS-requirements over unpredictable 'best-effort' QoS-provided by WNPs/wireless technologies (Bults *et al.*, 2005). Dedicated QoS-monitoring is not feasible due to the dynamic nature of QoS-provided by WNPs/wireless technologies (Dood, 2005) and the limited resources (e.g. battery) of mobile devices.

At the same time, new WNPs appear and new long-range wireless technologies (e.g. Ultra-Mobile-Wideband) are deployed by the existing WNPs. These are steps towards the vision of 4G, where wireless communication infrastructures are going to be plentifully available for mobile service users (De Vriendt *et al.*, 2002; Dekleva et al., 2007; Ortiz, 2007; Tachikawa, 2003). Yet, any new WNP or wireless technology when launched provides only a 'best-effort' QoS-level (Gomez & Sanchez, 2005) and uses the 'drive-tests' as performance tests.

A new trend of user-centric business models is arising in a mobile business research (Dekleva et al., 2007), aiming in the situation where a MoSP and its mobile service user can access any WNP anytime-anywhere. Towards this end, some technological solutions are proposed for signaling for inter-WNPs handover (Bless *et al.*, 2004; ITU-T, 2006) or for QoS-negotiations between a mobile device and a WNP (Manner *et al.*, 2001). From the business contractual perspective, an idea of 'ad-hoc' smart-business networks (van Heck & Vervest, 2007) between WNPs and MoSPs supporting delivery of service to a mobile user has been presented, while research in large EU projects focus on new methods for MNOs to support MoSPs, without locking-in the MoSPs' customers (Sanchez *et al.*, 2008). Still the question remains: how a MoSP chooses a WNP best matching his user's QoS-requirements and QoE-expectations at a given location-time. To the best of our knowledge, the kind of solution we propose has not yet been proposed in the literature.

RESEARCH GOALS AND APPROACH

The goal of this chapter is to analyze the business viability of the methods proposed for MoSPs and QoSIS.net. Our approach is as follows. The first step is the choice of the MCM-Business Model Framework of Hoegg et al. for analysis of QoSIS.net as an example of enterprise employing the Mobile Web 2.0 paradigm.

The MCM framework was initially based on a well-established definition of a *business model* being "1) an architecture for the products, services, information flows, including a description of various business actors and their roles, 2) a description of the potential benefits for the various business actors, and 3) a description of the sources of revenues" (Timmers, 1998). Furthermore, Hoegg et al. enhanced this definition to include a social environment component, and that based on examining the other existing frameworks being applied to the existing MoSPs (e.g. 'MediAlert' SP). Along this research they conducted surveys and interviews with mobile service users and domain experts. Finally, the framework presented by them in 2005 (Hoegg & Stanoevska-Slabeva, 2005), has been later-on successfully employed in analysis of existing businesses by other researchers, and in an analysis of (Mobile) Web 2.0 businesses conducted by the authors themselves (Hoegg et al., 2006; Martignoni & Stanoevska-Slabeva, 2007).

The second step of our approach is to apply this framework and conduct QoSIS.net business viability analysis. Particularly because the QoSIS.net is a non-existing enterprise, we conduct this analysis based on the intended QoS-predictions service usage scenarios. Therefore in the following paragraphs we provide the details of the framework, then the QoSIS.net usage scenario, and then its business viability analysis along the framework.

The MCM-Business Model Framework

The MCM-business model framework can be applied for a business viability of a MoSP, and particularly for an enterprise providing (Mobile) Web 2.0-services. The framework has the following components, that collectively expose enterprise's business model and factors influencing its design (Hoegg & Stanoevska-Slabeva, 2005), see also Figure 1:

- **Features of the service:** Design and operation of the service provided by an enterprise to its customers (i.e. the enterprise product)
- **Potential customers:** Aspects of target groups of customers (i.e. market segments) and expected service's value-added for them
- **Value chain:** Players involved in delivery of the provided service and their interrelations
- **Cost-revenue model:** Financial model explaining contribution of players in value chain
- **Features of the service medium:** Characteristics of means with which service is delivered and that may influence service interactions (e.g. service can be mobile)
- **Flow of supporting services:** Necessary for delivery of the service provided to customers
- **Social environment:** External influences—social, ethical aspects influencing the way the business is designed, implemented and operated.

QoSIS.net Viability Analysis

a. User Scenario

As every Saturday, Sophie, Maria and Eric meet in Westfield-London shopping center. Sophie is

Figure 1. MCM-business model framework

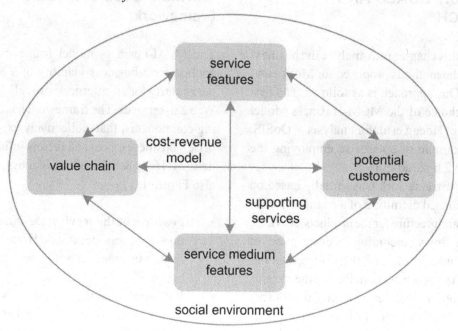

a young COPD (chronic obstructive pulmonary disease) patient and her health state is continuously monitored from the hospital with the MobiHealth's COPD Body-Area-Network (BAN) that she is wearing. She does not have to visit a care professional at the hospital frequently, she feels secure being remotely monitored. She is less restricted in her active life; she enjoys Saturday's habit of meeting her friends. In case of exacerbations, help from the hospital is dispatched to her, wherever she is. In the mall, her COPD BAN always uses the most suitable WNP/wireless technology as available there. The *"most suitable"* means sending her vital-signs data at the highest speed, i.e. with the lowest possible delay, to the hospital, and in a secure manner (i.e. not using unknown free WLANs). Netwrok usage price does not matter. The WNP/wireless technology selection process is transparent to her. In the mall her BAN uses most of the time the 3G-HSUPA network of Vodafone-UK, and when it is not available, e.g. inside the big shops, the BAN switches to 3G-UMTS network of T-Mobile. In such a way her

service-data is always sent at the highest possible speed to the hospital.

Maria and Eric are both typical technology nerds competing with each other. Maria has a newest mobile from 3UK with this fancy SeeMeTV application, which allows her to easily post short videos from her mobile on the SeeMeTV-web. She enjoys making jokes with Sophie and Eric, trying to get some catchy video that can bring her money if other SeeMeTV users watch it or even a prize of £1000 if they vote for it. To access the SeeMeTV-web her mobile always uses the most suitable wireless technology of 3UK, as available in this center. For her, the most suitable means that her videos appear online as quick as possible; price does not matter much to her; she can afford it. This time her mobile uses the 3G-UMTS network, because 3UK's GSM/GPRS network is, as always on Saturdays, saturated with voice/SMS traffic of users shopping in the same center.

Eric is a Facebook fan, and uses this social-networking community to stay in touch with his family and friends back home in Amsterdam.

He also enjoys making funny photos and movies along their day and posts them to his blog. He has just bought a fancy t-shirt for his brother, and he has posted a related movie and is now waiting for response—maybe it is not what his brother wanted? To access Facebook, his mobile always chooses the most suitable WNP/wireless technology available in the mall (in his case the cheapest but still as fast as possible!). Because he uses the latest phone with an integrated GPS, he was able to download an application from QoSIS.net website. This little application makes the WNP/ wireless technology choice on his behalf; he just needed to set his selection preferences. Since he installed it, he is very satisfied using his Facebook. com services which are provided to him without frustrating connection loses, as it was the case in the past. During this shopping-day, his mobile uses 2.5G-GPRS of O2 in the morning, and Orange-WLAN network in the afternoon, as they moved to the north part of this big center, where it has become available to him.

b. Features of the Service

The QoS-predictions service is a mobile service that provides MoSP and their users with fine-grained location-time-based QoS-predictions, about QoS-provided by different WNPs/wireless technologies at a given location-time. Each QoS-prediction is an estimation of QoS-provided by a WNP/wireless technology at a given location and time in the future, associated with its accuracy value.

The QoS-predictions service is a value-added service for MoSPs and their users. It is used by a MoSP in a WNP/wireless technology selection process; but it is transparent for a MoSP user like Sophie, Maria or Eric (the only effect a MoSP user may see is a changing WNP name on his/her device screen as an effect of a vertical handover of his mobile-device between different WNPs).

Although it was not shown in the QoSIS.net user scenario, the QoS-predictions service based

on the user's private mobility-map (stored on the user's mobile device) denoting nearby locations along with QoS-predictions for these locations in different times. The mobility-map is automatically updated, either at regular time-intervals or at the moment a new QoS-prediction is requested. The information in the map allows the mobile service user to get QoS-predictions even if the user is out of coverage of any WNP (although these QoS-predictions can be outdated depending when the map was last updated); in this situation a user can see where is the closest WNP available for him and what is its predicted QoS. If a service provided by a MoSP is critical, e.g. a MoSP is MobiHealth providing mobile healthcare service, the user can be warned explicitly via sound/vibration generated by the mobile device, when he a leaves the coverage area of any WNP.

The QoSIS.net operation is based on the QoS-information service; QoS-predictions service is part of it. The QoS-predictions service is based on users' collaborative QoS-information sharing, i.e. information is acquired from MoSPs users using different WNPs/wireless technologies at different locations-times. The collected QoS-information is used to derive QoS-predictions, used (back) by mobile users. The QoS-predictions are then validated along the new collected QoS-information; a feedback is implemented implicitly. Therefore, the QoS-information service contains of (Figure 2):

1. QoS-monitoring service
2. QoS-information processing service and
3. QoS-predictions engine (Pawar *et al.*, 2008; Wac, 2006).

Particularly, QoS-monitoring and QoS-prediction services are executed partially on a mobile device of the service user (see further paragraphs for details).

The *QoS-monitoring service* acquires QoS-information from mobile users (and actually from their devices) based on application-level measure-

Figure 2. QoSIS.net high-level system architecture

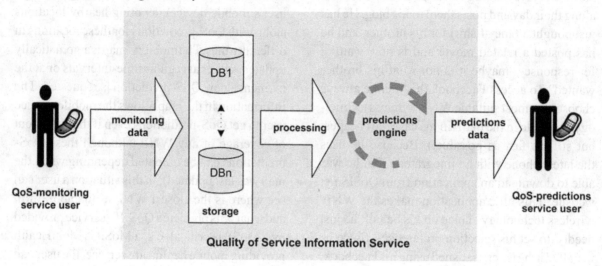

ments, i.e., measurements of the mobile service's observed QoS as well as users location-time and other parameters (see further details). Technically, QoS-monitoring service can be realized via passive QoS-measurements in MobiHealth or SeeMeTV service for users like Sophie and Maria, or via measurement-applications like AcbTaskMan (AcbTaskMan, 2007) or CoSphere (Peddemors, 2008) for Facebook users like Eric.

The QoS-monitoring service is transparent to the MoSP's users. The QoS-information is acquired to QoSIS.net, preferably via a lightweight protocol. The information is send with an hourly or daily frequency or even continuously (however that can be exhausting for mobile device resources). The information can be compressed (using lossless algorithms) before being send to the QoSIS.net, where is stored in databases (DBs).

The quality of the acquired QoS-information is critical to the accuracy of the QoS-predictions' service (and hence to QoSIS.net business viability). We argue, that the QoS-predictions' service cannot be more accurate than the historical QoS-information it is based upon. Particularly the location-time accuracy is critical; a user moving few meters away may observe a different QoS for a given WNP/wireless technology and hence

acquire different QoS-monitoring data (Dood, 2005).

The QoS-information acquired from MoSPs users includes:

1. the mobile user's location-time, mobility level (e.g. fixed location, walking, moving in a vehicle)
2. the WNP name and wireless technology used
3. the network usage price and security level
4. the mobile service's speed in terms of delay/throughput/loss (ITU-T, 1993, 2006; Seitz, 2003); detailed metrics depend upon the mobile service for which QoS-predictions are provided
5. the characteristics of the mobile device (CPU, memory, battery, network interfaces) and the location-determination system type/accuracy e.g. GPS system

The QoS-information does not have (nor needs) any notion of the mobile user's identity, all information acquired from mobile users is anonymous (but needs to be trustworthy).

The *QoS-processing service* (presented as an arrow in the figure) transforms the stored

QoS-information into a form suitable for a QoS-predictions' engine. The transformation may include annotation, rating, sub-sampling, discretization, obfuscation or any other method for information processing commonly used in data mining techniques (Mitchell, 1999).

The *QoS-prediction engine* continuously processes large quantities of collected historical QoS-information. The engine uses data mining techniques (e.g. Bayesian Networks or trees (Witten & Frank, 2005)) to discover QoS-information patterns. A QoS-prediction service request retrieves instantaneously the requested QoS-predictions for a given location-time. The result is returned to the QoSIS.net customer (i.e. a MoSP service user) in form of mobility-maps.

One of the mobile service users' characteristics, which we envision can facilitate QoS-predictions accuracy, is the fact that these users tend to have fixed mobility patterns, e.g. home, work, shopping-center at particular week-days on particular hours. Scientific research indicates that 45% of the people stay in a location area of a radius of ~10 km, while 73%—of radius of ~30 km and their mobility patterns can be learned for a history of 3 months (Gonzalez *et al.*, 2008). We anticipate that if the user's mobility pattern is highly predictable, a collection of large amount of QoS-information for WNPs/wireless technologies available to this a user along his movements, facilitates providing accurate QoS-predictions to this user.

Features of the Service vs. Mobile Web 2.0 Paradigm

The QoS-predictions' service is based on users-collaborative QoS-information creation and sharing. Hence, QoSIS.net can be seen as a specific example of *stand-alone Mobile Web 2.0 Service Provider* (Hoegg et al., 2006; O'Reilly, 2005). The content produced by MoSPs users is the QoS-information acquired by the QoS-monitoring service. This content is then processed in QoS-predictions engine and it is consumed by mobile

users via the QoS-predictions service. Mobile users are content 'prosumers' (Tapscott & Williams, 2006). We argue that while implementing the QoS-predictions service as Mobile Web 2.0, where users collaboratively collect QoS-information, QoSIS.net may benefit from the fact that MoSPs' users are very likely to be in a close location-time span, e.g. in one city, and therefore they collect overlapping QoS-information, which in turn increases the QoS-predictions service accuracy.

c. Potential Customers

The QoSIS.net market contains two types of customers:

1. customers in a Business-to-Business market segment, containing MoSPs and WNPs/MNOs/MVNOs acting as MoSPs and
2. customers in a Business-to-Customer market segment containing mobile service end-users (i.e. customers of MoSPs).

Recalling that in our scenario, Sophie is a MobiHealth.com customer and a user of its mobile health monitoring service. MobiHealth.com is an example MoSP (van Halteren *et al.*, 2004). Maria is a MNO-3UK customer and SeeMeTV mobile service user; her MNO acts as a MoSP (3UK, 2008). Sophie and Maria have role of QoSIS.net service users. Eric is a Facebook.com (MoSP (Facebook, 2007)) customer and user, and a customer and user of QoSIS.net.

Business-to-Business (B2B)
MoSPs like MobiHealth.com or MNOs like 3UK are potential business customers of QoSIS.net. They are particular mobile service providers in e.g. mobile information, healthcare or entertainment domains. Services provided by these types of MoSP require frequent exchange of service-data between (Internet-based) servers and mobile users and hence frequent use of WNPs. Mobile user's satisfaction depends on the QoS-provided

by the WNP used for service delivery. For MoSP, QoS-predictions can be used in a WNP/wireless technology selection process. For a MNO acting as a MoSP, QoS-predictions can be used in a selection process of a wireless technology (WLAN/GPRS/UMTS/HSxPA) at a given location-time for a mobile service user. The goal of MoSPs is to best meet users' QoS-requirements and facilitate meeting their expected-QoE. QoSIS.net can play an instrumental role in meeting this goal.

The QoSIS.net fulfills the MoSP's need of knowledge of QoS-provided by different WNPs/wireless technologies at mobile user location-time. For a MNO, it adds to its existing coarse-grained knowledge of its network; a MNO can analyze its provided-QoS to mobile service users at given locations-time and be willing to improve this QoS in order to stay competitive amongst the WNPs. The QoS-information can support the MNO's network planning, dimensioning and management, as well as better design of own mobile services provided to mobile users. Moreover, once encouraged, a WNP can even provide QoSIS.net with some additional information regarding its network configuration, which would facilitate more accurate QoS-predictions service. Without the existence of the QoSIS.net, MoSPs/MNOs try to assure QoS to its users by using coarse-level QoS-estimations (c.f. Current Trends). The advantage for QoSIS.net of entering in a business relation with a MoSP would be that they can be an equal copartner in designing the QoS-predictions and QoS-monitoring services (e.g. mobile device configuration), have integrated billing for both services, co-marketing and co-branding strategies, bringing even more customers to the MoSP.

When using QoS-predictions, a MoSP better manages user's resources involved in its services delivery e.g. lower service-data delays/improved throughput or optimizing user's device battery life. The biggest incentive for a MoSP to use QoSIS.net would be the fact that by using QoSIS.net, it can increase its customers' satisfaction and hence its revenues.

Although it sounds contradictory to what we have said earlier, we claim that MoSPs and particularly MNOs can use QoSIS.net services as a way to additionally 'lock-in' its mobile service users to their services/networks. It is because a customer satisfaction and QoE is a strong predictor of customer loyalty (Eshghi *et al.*, 2007), and QoSIS.net facilitates its improvement. Namely, if users are satisfied from the services provided to them, and they experience them at the expected-QoE level, they are more likely to use even more services from this MoSP. Additionally, the cost of switching to other MoSP for this user can be high: new MoSP may not use QoSIS.net, and even if they do, the user's historical QoS-information might not be portable to this new MoSP. In this situation a user need to accept that only after some service-launch-time (necessary for collecting of historical QoS-information), the service will be provided to him at the expected-QoE level, bringing him back satisfaction related to the service use.

Business-to-Customer (B2C)

Mobile service users like Eric are potential customers of QoSIS.net, but only if they have a mobile device with localization capabilities, e.g. an integrated GPS. Because their QoE while using their mobile services is related to the QoS-provided by the WNP/wireless technology used, they are interested in the use of QoSIS.net's value-added service in order to facilitate (proactive and automatic) choice of the WNP/wireless technology that fits best to their needs anytime-anywhere. The user grants responsibility to the QoSIS.net on how to use QoS-predictions, i.e., when to demand new QoS-predictions and when to choose another WNP/wireless technology.

QoSIS.net can equally target mobile users living a village or city suburbs with limited WNP/wireless technologies choice, as well as big number of users living in the city center with plentiful of available WNPs/wireless technologies.

A QoSIS.net user saves resources involved in e.g. Facebook.com services delivery e.g. money while choosing a WNP with cheaper tariffs, or mobile device's battery life. The incentive for a mobile user to use QoSIS.net is the improvement of his QoE when using his mobile services. Without the existence of QoSIS.net, Eric would be using an arbitrary WNP/wireless technology as available in his location-time, probably experiencing lower quality services and paying more than he expects.

QoSIS.net's Critical Success Factors

We identify that a critical success factor for the QoSIS.net service is to reach a critical mass of QoS-predictions service users. This is because QoSIS.net business thrives on large quantities of QoS-information for its QoS-predictions service. We envision that the primary market segment is B2B, and the secondary is the B2C. The B2B market entry strategy is to convince MoSPs and MNOs that QoSIS.net adds an accurate fine-grained location-time-based QoS-predictions service to their infrastructure that facilitates the improvement of QoE of their customers, hence increases their own revenues. This way the QoSIS.net user-base will be then equal to MoSPs/MNOs customer base. However, the initial hurdle of getting enough historical QoS-information for accurate QoS-predictions remains. QoSIS.net needs to agree with its customers on service-launch-time duration, after which it will provide QoS-predictions service with a given accuracy. We envision that the service-launch-time will be a function of mobility patterns of mobile service users (c.f. discussion on QoS-predictions engine) (Gonzalez et al., 2008). Once the QoSIS.net B2B market is substantial enough (i.e. sufficient QoS-information is available for QoS-predictions), the B2C market can be targeted.

d. Value-Chain

Value chain of QoSIS.net is different for B2B and B2C market segments and is presented in the following paragraphs.

B2B

In the value chain for business relation between QoSIS.net and a MoSP we distinguish QoSIS.net, MoSP like MobiHealth.com, and a MoSP user—Sophie (Figure 3a), who is also a QoSIS.net user. MobiHealth.com can have a business relation with one or more different WNPs/MNOs (via a MVNO). For a relation between QoSIS.net and a MNO acting as a MoSP, we distinguish: QoSIS.net, MNO like 3UK (three.co.uk) and its SeeMeTV service user—Maria (Figure 3b), who is also a QoSIS.net user. In both cases QoSIS.net is a 3rd Party SP, i.e., value-added SP for MobiHealth.com and three.co.uk (QoSIS.net customers). They provide QoSIS.net services to their customers as an integrated offer; these services are transparent for Sophie and Maria.

The *business relation* between QoSIS.net and MobiHealth.com/3UK is defined in a *contract* relationship. It is a negotiated and agreed between them formal document defining the terms and conditions for the delivery of the services (e.g. service availability of 99%), detailed services' usage specifications (e.g. user-pull or service-push) as well as the payment specifications (e.g. monthly, per-transaction post-paid) by MobiHealth.com and three.co.uk to QoSIS.net. this contract is also called a Service Level Agreement (SLA) (TMF, 2001).

Due to the nature of the service provided by QoSIS.net, a strong partnership trust (Ratnasingam & Phan, 2003) as well as technology trust (Ratnasingam et al., 2002) is required between MobiHealth.com, 3UK and QoSIS.net in order to assure the success of all businesses. Critical technological details of QoS-monitoring and QoS-predictions service delivery need to be included in SLA, maybe even in legal terms, e.g. which enterprise is responsible if QoS-predictions are not accurate enough and Sophie finds herself outside any WNP at the moment she requires urgent medical assistance?

Figure 3a. QoSIS.net as 3ʳᵈ party service provider for MobiHealth.com (a MoSP)

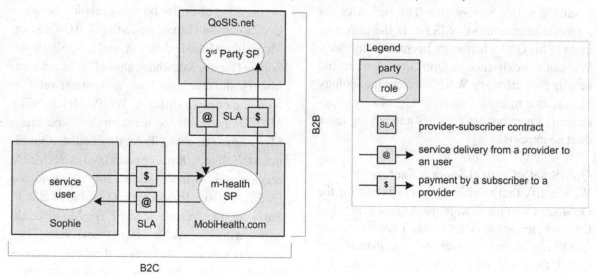

Figure 3b. QoSIS.net as 3ʳᵈ party service provider for 3UK (a MNO in a role of a MoSP)

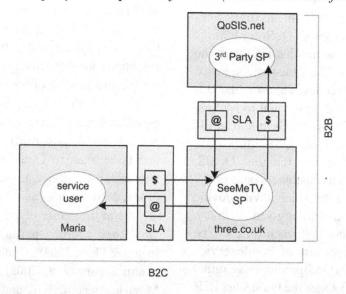

B2C

In the value chain for business relation between QoSIS.net and a MoSP user, we distinguish: QoSIS.net, Facebook.com and Facebook.com's user—Eric (Figure 4), who is also a QoSIS.net user. Eric can have a business relation with one or a more WNPs/MNOs (via a MVNO).

QoSIS.net is a value-added SP for Eric, and their business relation is defined by a SLA. The

payment relationship with Eric states that QoSIS. net services are free (as his Facebook.com services). It is important to notice that the terms and conditions specified in this SLA need to be agreed upon by Eric, before the QoSIS.net application can be used by him, i.e. installed on his mobile device. Moreover, Eric is responsible to make sure that by using QoSIS.net he does not violate an existing SLA between him and Facebook.com,

Figure 4. QoSIS.net as a service provider

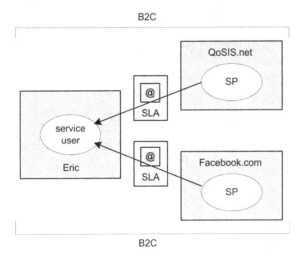

especially with regards to the (default) WNP use or use of any mobile device resources, for which these two SPs would now compete.

Facebook.com does not need to be in a business relationship with QoSIS.net, but it may benefit (in terms of revenues) from the services provided by it; satisfied Eric is more likely to use even more of Facebook.com services while on the move.

e. Cost-Revenue Model

In B2B settings, QoSIS.net has costs related to the setup and maintenance of its services, and to the marketing aiming to get new MoSPs/WNPs as customers. QoSIS.net's customers have costs related to QoS-predictions service usage (as agreed in SLA). We argue that any reasonable pricing model proposed by QoSIS.net can be beneficial for QoSIS.net's revenues, increasing also the MoSPs/WNPs revenues, depending nevertheless on the MoSP's application area and criticality on QoSIS. net service to the MoSP's core business.

QoSIS.net customers in B2C settings do not pay for a service usage. In these settings, the QoSIS.net marketing costs are small, as the major advertisement policy is a "word-of-mouth" going from one mobile service user to another (Tapscott & Williams, 2006). QoSIS.net can also launch an affiliation program, rewarding mobile users who helped to acquire a new QoSIS.net customer via their website.

Any QoSIS.net service user has costs:

1. Related to ownership of a mobile device with one or multiple network interfaces for wireless technologies like WLAN/ GPRS/UMTS/HSxPA to be used via different WNPs (or at least one WNP) and an integrated location-determination e.g. GPS module
2. Related to the mobile device's resources: computation, storage and communication capacity, as well as its battery used for the service delivery.

We would like to emphasize that particularly in Europe devices manufacturers are committed to increase the number of mobile devices with integrated location-determination technologies, like GSM-cell triangulation or GPS. Nokia committed itself that by 2012 50% of its phones will have GPS-integrated (Nokia, 2004). In the US having these technologies in a mobile-phone is mandated due to 911 number and the location-identification requirements, while in Asia it is widely accepted as a new fancy technology. Market analysts predict that overall, by 2011, 29.6% of all mobile phones will have GPS (comparing to only 11.1% for 2006) (ABI Research, 2007).

Once QoSIS.net has reached a critical mass of customers, it can reconsider its cost-revenue model. For example, possible revenue for QoSIS. net can be generated by selling its QoS-information acquired in B2C-settings to MoSPs (like Facebook.com) or MNOs, or any other interested enterprises. It can mean selling (anonymized) user profiles and information about used mobile services.

QoSIS.net can also differentiate its prices for B2B and for B2C (introducing 'premium' service). The transaction fee can depend on:

1. The number of WNPs/wireless technologies available to a mobile user at a given location-time (i.e. the price increases with the number of WNPs/wireless technologies, because the richer the choice, the higher probability that a MoSP can use WNP/wireless technology matching its user QoS-requirements, thus improving its user's-QoE),
2. The actual accuracy of the QoS-predictions, where this accuracy can be checked against the QoS-information acquired from user QoS-monitoring data
3. The accuracy of QoS-predictions, which would be (on purpose) lower for lower accuracy QoS-predictions, and higher for higher-accuracy QoS-predictions.

f. Service Medium

The QoSIS.net service is a mobile service—provided to its users from server on the Internet, accessible via a wireless medium. The features of this medium depend on WNPs/wireless technologies available at a particular location-time and used for QoS-predictions delivery. The QoSIS. net service may intentionally or accidentally be disabled/disturbed (Camponovo & Pigneur, 2003; Tsalgatidou & Pitoura, 2001), due to:

1. User communication-autonomy: (a) the user can deliberately configure his mobile device to use one particular WNP and wireless technology (b) user can be unreachable due to WNP lack-of-coverage or device's empty battery
2. Vulnerability of the user's mobile device (damage/loss) and its limited storage, processing, communication capabilities
3. WNP's wireless technology characteristics, e.g. asymmetrical throughput characteristics, variable delay characteristics and restrictions on volume of QoS-information exchange (hence lightweight protocols and

lossless compression of exchanged QoS-information can be required).

g. Supporting Services

From a business perspective, all QoSIS.net's services: QoS-monitoring, QoS-processing and QoS-predictions services are necessary to create a value to the QoSIS.net's service user. Supporting processes include processes for a WNP/wireless technology selection (i.e. handover to) and its enforcement. A technical realization of intra- and inter-WNP (i.e. vertical) handovers is an ongoing research issue (Chen & Shu, 2005; Dekleva et al., 2007; Pawar et al., 2008), outside of the scope of this chapter.

From the QoSIS.net perspective, its web-service provided to customers like Eric is a service supporting acquisition of new customers in the B2C settings. Moreover, due to the nature of services delivered by QoSIS.net, business-partnership management is one of the supporting services but still in the core activities of QoSIS. net, e.g. for generating service reports for its customers.

h. Social Environment

There are several influences of the QoSIS.net services provision rising from customer competition, legislation and social/ethical constraints. Firstly, competition amongst QoSIS.net customers (MoSPs/WNPs) requires QoSIS.net to be a trustworthy enterprise. It should apply strong security mechanisms to prevent competitive customer information being disclosed to others. Any information regarding MoSP service usage statistics or its customer's profiles should be protected. Similarly, WNPs' competitive market situation poses strong security requirements on the QoSIS. net information. Any information regarding QoS provided by a WNP should not be altered in favor of this WNP. Moreover, in order to secure QoSIS.

net revenues and its competitive advantage on the market, details of its QoS-information databases or QoS-predictions engine should not be disclosed to its customers.

An important social aspect of the provided service is related to the user-privacy consent. QoS-information acquired from QoSIS.net customers contains detailed location-time information of mobile service users. Therefore, it is required (at least in Europe) that a mobile service user is legally informed of the fact that this privacy sensitive information is acquired (Gorlach *et al.*, 2004), even if it is in anonymous form. In the B2B case, it is the responsibility of a MoSP as the QoSIS.net customer to provide user-privacy informed-consent and then to exchange all QoS-information respecting security, authentication/ authorization mechanisms. In the B2C case, all this is the responsibility of QoSIS.net.

QOSIS.NET-BASED METHOD'S FUTURE

There are many possible scenarios, in which Qo-SIS.net as a part of the proposed novel business method for a MoSP QoS-assurance can evolve. For example, regarding the cost-revenue model, QoSIS.net can provide QoS-monitoring and QoS-predictions services as separate services, and reward a user of QoS-monitoring service (i.e. producing QoS-information) while charging a user for using QoS-predictions service (i.e. consuming QoS-information). This however brings to QoSIS. net a risk of not having enough contributing users in B2C case; statistics for Web 2.0 indicate that at the launch of any service, only 1 % of users is willing to contribute and generate the content (Arthur, 2006).

The other possible future scenario in the B2C settings is related to the situation where a user would like to use QoSIS.net, however, he is not a frequent MoSP's service user (e.g. like Eric who is using his Facebook.com daily) and hence will not generate lots of 'real' mobile traffic. This kind of mobile user can be offered to use a QoSIS.net QoS-monitoring service as his mobile phone 'screen-saver'. Namely, when he would not use his mobile for a while, the QoS-monitoring service would take a role of an active mobile service user, using some WNP/wireless technology and imitating e.g. busty web-browsing, thus acquiring QoS-monitoring information at a given location-time. In such a way, QoSIS.net would acquire QoS-information enriching its databases and such a mobile user could be paid for information generation. However, the critical issue would be related to mobile device resources usage for this QoS-monitoring service (battery, capacity, storage etc.).

A scalable solution for QoSIS.net would be to limit its scope of operation to a particular city, region or country, limiting the scope of WNPs/ wireless technologies for which QoS-predictions can be provided. Scoping can be dictated by the need of limiting the QoS-information to be processed by the QoS-prediction engine, or the need for higher accuracy of QoS-predictions provided for a restricted location-area. Furthermore, QoSIS.net can be limited in terms of WNPs/ wireless technologies for which it acquires QoS-information. In the case of different QoSIS.net's location-based instances, they can form (short-term or a long-term) "smart-business-networks" for the purpose of delivering better services to their users roaming in locations areas belonging to different instances of QoSIS.net. All QoSIS.net instances collaborating in the business network could benefit from a larger QoS-information base for their QoS-predictions service.

Moreover, in order to enhance the QoS-information base and improve the QoS-predictions accuracy, we envision that QoSIS.net customers— MoSPs/WNPs whose users are likely to be in overlapping location-areas, can have a business relationship in which they agree to collaboratively share their QoS-information bases. All collaborating MoSPs could benefit from larger QoS-information base for QoS-predictions.

CONCLUSION

Mobile and ubiquitous service providers (MoSPs) emerge, struggling to provide to their users a QoE that is at least comparable to one the user is familiar with from the Internet. To bridge the gap regarding the lack of information about QoS-provided by different wireless network providers (WNPs) over diverse wireless technologies in a mobile users' location-time, in this chapter we have proposed methods enabling firstly a creation of an enterprise (QoSIS.net) providing such an information to MoSPs, and, secondly, usage of this information by an MoSP in its QoS-assurance business process. We emphasize that the aim of the proposed methods is to facilitate fulfillment of MoSP's user's QoS-requirements and his expected-QoE, hence securing the revenues of a MoSP, while creating revenues to QoSIS.net.

Future research opportunities within the domain of our topic relate to further advancements of the proposed methods for QoSIS. net and its customers, e.g. understanding the dependencies between the QoS-provided by a WNP/wireless technology and the MoSP user's QoS-requirements and his QoE-expectations, and this for MoSPs in different application domains. Related to this, a second research opportunity can focus on the efficient market entry approach for QoSIS.net as enterprise, such that it overcomes initial hurdle of attracting the required critical mass of users and start generating revenues. A third research opportunity lies in understanding the partnership-trust required in the QoSIS.net's value chain, as well as the challenges in QoSIS. net's customer management in the B2B and B2C market segments. Finally, we indicate a need for research on trust in technology. This research investigates dependability features of architec-

tural QoSIS-system design and technical details included in SLAs established between enterprises (QoSIS.net, WNPs/MNOs), e.g. security of QoS-information exchange between enterprises.

The future research opportunities relate particularly to research on new competitive methods that can be employed in existing management, operational (i.e. core) or supporting business processes of mobile and ubiquitous service providers as enterprises. These methods need necessarily aim in satisfying their customer, while increasing enterprise revenues. We propose these methods to be based on emerging trend of short- and long-terms business inter-dependencies (i.e. "smart-business-networks") between different enterprises, bringing into a value network different, but complementary expertise. This has a high risk of failure but also a huge potential to increase revenues of all of the involved enterprises and that by increasing a customer's QoE anywhere-anytime-anyhow.

Moreover we propose research on novel methods employing the user-collaborative information sharing paradigm, i.e. Mobile Web 2.0. The risk of these methods is mainly related to attracting a critical mass of contributing users. These methods would aim at creating new revenue streams from user-generated content-manipulation and enrichment. The enriched content could then be become a part of an enterprise service, consumed back by the users. The Mobile Web 2.0-based methods however require careful research upon the content type to be generated-consumed by the users. Therefore, answers for research questions like: what is the pre-existing offline information possessed by users, which, if available to be manipulated and shared online amongst them could empower them in some way?, Does this information violates in any way user's privacy?, And what is user's willingness to share this information online and with whom?, are critical.

We envision that in order to fulfill the dream of providing mobile services meeting users' QoE-expectations and generating revenues, MoSPs need to take a necessary risk and employ novel methods in their existing business processes.

REFERENCES

3UK. (2008). Retrieved Sep 05, 2008, from www.three.co.uk

ABI Research. (2007). *GPS-Enabled Mobile Devices—Key Drivers and Latest Trends Pushing GPS Penetration in CDMA, GSM and WCDMA Handsets* (White Paper).

AcbTaskMan. (2007). AcbTaskMan software. Retrieved Sep 05, 2008, from www.acbpocketsoft.com

Afuah, A., & Tucci, C. T. (2000). *Internet Business Models and Strategies: Text and Cases*. McGraw-Hill Higher Education.

Andersen, D., Bansal, D., Curtis, D., Seshan, S., & Balakrishnan, H. (2000). *System Support for Bandwidth Management and Content Adaptation in Internet Applications*. Paper presented at the 4th Symposium on Operating Systems Design and Implementation (OSDI), San Diego, CA, USA.

Andersson, C., Freeman, D., James, I., Johnston, A., & Ljung, S. (2006). *Mobile Media and Applications, From Concept to Cash: Successful Service Creation and Launch*. West Sussex, England: Wiley.

Arthur, C. (2006). What is the 1% rule? Retrieved Sep 05, 2008, from http://technology.guardian.co.uk/weekly/story/0,1823959,00.html

Bless, R., Hillebrand, J., Prehofer, C., & Zitterbart, M. (2004). Quality-of-Service Signaling for Next-Generation IP-Based Mobile Networks. *IEEE Communications Magazine, 42*(6), 72-79.

Bults, R., Wac, K., van Halteren, A., Konstantas, D., & Nicola, V. (2005). *Goodput Analysis of 3G wireless networks supporting m-health services*. Paper presented at the 8th International Conference on Telecommunications (ConTEL05), Zagreb, Croatia.

Buschken, J. (2004). *Higher Profits Through Customer Lock-In*: Thomson Texere.

Calvo, M., Rodríguez, C., & Dillinger, M. (2004). *Business models for reconfigurable communication systems*. Paper presented at the 13th IST Mobile & Wireless Communications Summit, Lyon, France.

Camponovo, G., & Pigneur, Y. (2003). *Business model analysis applied to mobile business*. Paper presented at the 5th Intl Conference on Enterprise Information Systems (ICEIS03), Angers, FR.

Chalmers, D., & Sloman, M. (1999). A survey of Quality of Service in mobile computing environments. *IEEE Communications Surveys and Tutorials, 2*(2).

Chen, W. T., & Shu, Y. Y. (2005). *Active application oriented vertical handoff in next-generation wireless networks*. Paper presented at the Wireless Communications and Networking Conference (WCNC05).

claffy, k., Miller, G., & Thompson, K. (1998). *The nature of the beast: recent traffic measurements from an Internet backbone*. Paper presented at the International Networking Conference (INET98), Geneva, Switzerland.

Cuevas, A., Moreno, J. I., Vidales, P., & Einsiedler, H. (2006). The IMS Platform: A Solution for Next Generation Network Operators to Be More Than Bit Pipes. *IEEE Commun. Mag., Advances in Service Platform Technologies, 44*(8), 75-81.

De Vriendt, J., Laine, P., Lerouge, C., & Xu, X. (2002). Mobile Network Evolution: A Revolution on the Move. *IEEE Commun. Mag., 40*(4), 104-111.

Dekleva, S., Shim, J. P., Varshney, U., & Knoerzer, G. (2007). Evolution and emerging issues in mobile wireless networks. *Commun. ACM, 50*(6), 38-43.

Digital Chocolate. (2008). Seize the Minute. Retrieved Sep 05, 2008, from www.digitalchocolate.com

Dood, A. (2005). *The Essential Guide to Telecommunications*. US: Prentice Hall PTR.

Eshghi, A., Haughton, D., & Topi, H. (2007). Determinants of customer loyalty in the wireless telecommunications industry. *Telecommunications Policy, 31*(2), 93.

Faber, E., Ballon, P., Bouwman, H., Haaker, T., Rietkerk, O., & Steen, M. (2003). *Designing business models for mobile ICT services*. Paper presented at the 16th BLED Electronic Commerce Conf.—eTransformations, Bled, Slovenia.

Facebook. (2007). A social utility that connects you with the people around you. Retrieved Sep 05, 2008, from www.facebook.com

Gerpott, T. J., Rams, W., & Schindler, A. (2001). Customer retention, loyalty, and satisfaction in the German mobile cellular telecommunications market. *Telecommunications Policy, 25*(4), 249.

Gomez, G., & Sanchez, R. (2005). *End-to-End Quality of Service over Cellular Networks: Data Services Performance Optimization in 2G/3G*: John Wiley & Sons, Ltd.

Gonzalez, M., Hidalgo, C. A., & Barabasi, A. (2008). Understanding individual human mobility patterns. *Nature, 453*(1), 779-782.

Gorlach, A., Heinemann, A., & Terpstra, W. (2004). *Survey on location privacy in pervasive computing*. Paper presented at the Workshop on Security and Privacy in Pervasive Computing (SPCC04) at PERVASIVE2004.

Han, Q., & Venkatasubramanian, N. (2006). Information Collection Services for QoS-aware Mobile Applications. *IEEE Transactions on Mobile Computing, 5*(5), 518-535.

Hansmann, U., Merk, L., Nicklous, M., & Stober, T. (2003). *Pervasive Computing: The Mobile World*: Springer.

Hoegg, R., Martignoni, R., Meckel, M., & Stanoevska-Slabeva, K. (2006). *Overview of business models for Web 2.0. communities*. Paper presented at the GeNeMe, Dresden, DE.

Hoegg, R., & Stanoevska-Slabeva, K. (2005). *Towards Guidelines for the Design of Mobile Services*. Paper presented at the 18th BLED Electronic Commerce Conf., Bled, Slovenia.

Hutchison, D., Mauthe, A., & Yeadon, N. (1997). Quality-of-service architecture: Monitoring and control of multimedia communications. *Electronics & Communication Engineering Journal, 9*(3), 100.

ITU-T. (1993). General aspects of Quality of Service and Network Performance in Digital Networks, including ISDNs (Vol. I.350): ITU.

ITU-T. (2006). Framework for achieving end-to-end IP performance objectives (Vol. Y.1542): ITU.

ITU-T. (2007). Vocabulary for performance and quality of service: Appendix I—Definition of Quality of Experience (QoE) (Vol. P.10/G.100): ITU-T.

ITU. (2005). *The Internet of Things (Statistical Annex)*.

M.I.S Trend S.A. (2007). *Study of use of mobile services in telecommunication (realized for Division of Telecommunication of the Federal Communication Office in Switzerland)*. Lausanne, CH: Institute for market and opinion surveys study.

Manner, J., Burness, L., Hepworth, E., Lopez, A., & Mitjana, E. (2001). *Provision of QoS in heterogeneous wireless IP access networks*. Paper presented at the Intl Symposium on Personal, Indoor and Mobile Radio Communications.

Martignoni, R., & Stanoevska-Slabeva, K. (2007). *Mobile Web 2.0*. Paper presented at the 20th BLED Electronic Commerce Conf.—eMergence, Bled, Slovenia.

Michaut, F., & Lepage, F. (2005). Application-oriented network metrology: Metrics and active measurement tools. *IEEE Communications Surveys & Tutorials, 7*(2), 2-24.

Mitchell, T. (1999). Machine Learning and Data Mining. *Communications of the ACM, 42*(11), 30-36.

MobiHealth. (2007). Putting care in motion. Retrieved Sep 05, 2008, from www.mobihealth.com

Nahrstedt, K., Xu, D., Wichadakul, D., & Li, B. (2001). QoS-aware middleware for ubiquitous and heterogeneous environments. *IEEE Communication Magazine, 39*(11), 140-148.

Nokia. (2004). *Quality of Experience (QoE) of mobile services: Can it be measured and improved?*

O'Reilly, T. (2005). What is Web 2.0? Retrieved Sep 05, 2008, from www.oreillynet.com/pub/a/oreilly/tim/news/2005/09/30/what-is-web-20.html

Ortiz, S. (2007). 4G Wireless Begins to Take Shape. *IEEE Computer, 40*(11), 18-21.

Osterwalder, A., Ondrus, J., & Pigneur, Y. (2005). *Skype's Disruptive Potential in the Telecom Market: A Systematic Comparison of Business Models*. Lausanne, CH: University of Lausanne.

Pascu, C., Osimo, D., Ulbrich, M., Turlea, G., & Burgelman, J. C. (2005). The potential disruptive impact of internet 2 based technologies. *First Monday—peer-reviewed Journal on the Internet*.

Pawar, P., Wac, K., van Beijnum, B. J., Maret, P., van Halteren, A., & Hermens, H. (2008). *Context-Aware Middleware Architecture for Vertical Handover Support to Multi-homed Nomadic Mobile Services*. Paper presented at the 23rd Annual ACM Symposium on Applied Computing (ACMSAC08), Ceará, Brazil.

Peddemors, A. (2008). CoSPhere NAL software. Retrieved Sep 05, 2008, from http://cosphere.telin.nl/nal

Ratnasingam, P., Pavlou, P., & Tan, Y. (2002). *The Importance of Technology Trust for B2B Electronic Commerce*. Paper presented at the 15th BLED Electronic Commerce Conf.—eReality: Constructing the eEconomy, Bled, Slovenia.

Ratnasingam, P., & Phan, D. (2003). Trading Partner Trust in B2B E-Commerce: A Case Study. *Information Systems Management, 20*(3), 39-50.

Robles, T., Mitjana, E., & Ruiz, P. (2002). *Usage scenarios and business opportunities for systems beyond 3G*. Paper presented at the IST Mobile and Wireless Telecommunications Summit 2002, Thessaloniki, GR.

Sanchez, A., Carro, B., & Wesner, S. (2008). Telco Services for End Customers: European Perspective. *IEEE Commun. Mag., 46*(2), 14-18.

Seitz, N. (2003). ITU-T QoS standards for IP-based networks. *IEEE Communications Magazine, 41*(6), 82-89.

Shepherd, D., Scott, A., & Rodden, T. (1996). Quality-of-Service Support for Multimedia Applications. *IEEE MultiMedia, 03*(3), 78-82.

Soh, W. S., & Kim, H. S. (2003). QoS Provisioning in Cellular Networks Based on Mobility Prediction Techniques. *IEEE Commun. Mag., 41*(1), 86-92.

Tachikawa, K. (2003). A Perspective on the Evolution of Mobile Communications. *IEEE Commun. Mag., 41*(10), 66-73.

Tan, S. (2004). *Evolution of mobile technology and business models (technical report)*: Center for Information and Communication Technologies, Lyngby, DK.

Tapscott, D., & Williams, A. D. (2006). *Wikinomics: How Mass Collaboration Changes Everything*. New York, USA: Portfolio.

Timmers, P. (1998). Business Models for Electronic Markets. *Journal on Electronic Markets, 8*(2), 3-8.

TMF. (2001). SLA Management Handbook (Vol. GB917-2001): TMF.

TMF. (2004). *Shared Information/Data (SID) Model; GB922 Addendum 0—SID Primer (ver.4.0)*. Morristown, New Jersey, US: TeleManagement Forum.

Tsalgatidou, A., & Pitoura, E. (2001). Business models and transactions in mobile electronic commerce: requirements and properties. *Computer Networks, 37*(2), 221-236.

van Halteren, A., Bults, R., Wac, K., Konstantas, D., Widya, I., Dokovsky, N., et al. (2004). Mobile Patient Monitoring: The MobiHealth System. *The Journal on Information Technology in Healthcare, 2*(5), 365-373.

van Heck, E., & Vervest, P. (2007). Smart business networks: how the network wins. *Commun. ACM, 50*(6), 28-37.

Wac, K. (2006). *QoS-predictions service: infrastructural support for proactive QoS- and context-aware mobile services*. Paper presented at the On the Move to Meaningful Internet Systems 2006: OTM Workshops, Intl Workshop on Context-Aware Mobile Systems (CAMS), Monpellier, France.

Wac, K., Hilario, M., Konstantas, D., & van Beijnum, B. J. (2008). Data Mining on Application-level QoS Traces: the MobiHealth System Case Study (forthcoming). *IEEE Trans. on Mobile Computing*.

Witten, I., & Frank, E. (2005). *Data Mining: Practical Machine Learning Tools and Techniques*: Morgan Kaufmann.

Xiao, X., & Ni, L. M. (1999). Internet QoS: a big picture. *IEEE Network, 13*(2), 8-18.

Chapter VII
Strong Authentication for Financial Services:
PTDs as a Compromise between Security and Usability

Gianluigi Me
University of Rome, Italy

Daniele Pirro
University of Rome, Italy

Roberto Sarrecchia
University of Rome, Italy

ABSTRACT

Currently the most popular attacks to the E-Banking Web applications target the authentication systems relying on the single-side client authentication, showing their definitively ineffectiveness for financial services. Furthermore, most of the Web authentication systems have been developed on the classic username/password mechanism or One time Password systems using a single channel, either mobile or Web, generating an authentication system at inadequate level, enforcing a false perception of security, as phishing shows. The two factors authentication is not the panacea, but mitigates many threats, especially when combined with a Personal Trusted Device, as the popular smartphones represent. As a rule of thumb, the adoption of authentication systems to provide services B2C is driven by its ease-to-use more than the robustness of the adopted security system. For this reason, the proposed solution represents a system which tries to preserve the usability and to strengthen the authentication, with a combined Web/mobile authentication system.

INTRODUCTION

A very crucial phase of a web transaction is represented by the user authentication. During this step many problems can occur and many attacks are possible, whose target is to access the restricted resources. In order to face this threat, current systems frequently adopt the HTTP basic authentication mechanism even if the applications are critical. Further authentication mechanisms, described in the following sections, have been proposed to improve web authentication security with regard to user friendliness, not yet representing a panacea, still being prone to different attacks. As Schneier (2005) suggests, two-factor authentication mitigates, but not definitively solves, this problem and no solution is foolproof.

According to the Gartner survey of 5,000 online adults in August 2006, an estimated 24.4 million Americans have clicked on a phishing e-mail in 2006, up from approximately 11.9 million in 2005, while 3.5 million have given sensitive information to the phishers, up from 1.9 million adults last year. Currently, the phishing effectiveness has not changed since august 2006, revealing, instead, a slight raising shape of the victims. For this reason, new forms of combined attacks appear, as for the man-in-the-browser attack, where trojan horses can modify the transactions on-the-fly. Furthermore, one of the most famous recent wiretapping scandal (Prevelakis & Spinellis, 2007), the greek cellphone caper, confirms that the definitive solution for financial services over external, untrusted networks is to embed security in the end-to-end partecipant terminals.

In this paper we firstly classify the e/m-banking threats, based on an attack tree model, then we introduce the state of the art of the e/m-banking authentication systems and, finally, we will present a new authentication system, based on a combined web/mobile procedure, taking into account security and usability as major requirements. The basic authentication mechanism is integrated with a challenge/response process and an One Time

Password (OTP). The challenge is issued from an authentication server and has to authenticate a mobile device, typically a cell phone with Java capabilities. This device can communicate with any other involved part through a fixed terminal, typically a personal computer, via a Bluetooth connection. The mobile device, once accepted, performs the authentication with the web site or application. This final step is accomplished using a temporary one-time password.

STATE OF THE ART

The Attack Tree for Bank Account Compromising

A threat model describes threats than can be realized by the exploitation of vulnerabilities, through attacks. The graphical description of the threat model is based on attack trees (Schneier, 1999), which provide a formal methodology to analyze the security of systems in a tree structure, with the goal as the root node and different attacks as leaf nodes. The Figure 1 presents the threat model, which studies attacks against e/m-banking applications through current and next generation terminals.

The root node represents the final target of the attacker, which is the compromise of the user's bank account: we characterize the attacks by four main targets, the User, the User Terminal, the communication link and the banking server. We will use the usual notation, per level: root node is level 0 (indicated as 0), the nodes at j-th level are numbered [0,..n] starting by the left side (e.g., the Web page obfuscation node will be indexed as 1.6.5.5).

Since many attacks are, unfortunately, well known, we define the most meaningful from an overall security perspective and new ones. (see Table 1)

1.1.2.1: *Hidden Code.* The use hidden code within a web-page that exploits a known vulner-

Figure 1. Attack tree for e-banking

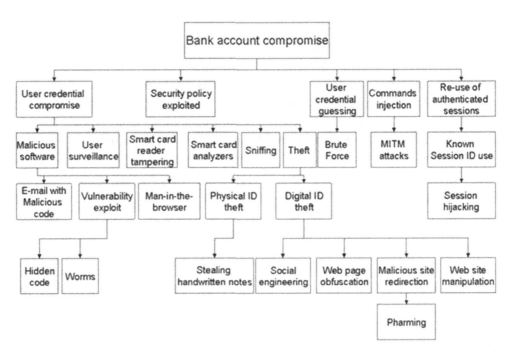

Table 1. Attack/resource matrix

Attack	Attack codes	User	User terminal	Link	Banking Server
E-mail with malicious code	1.1.1		×		
Hidden code	1.1.2.1		×		
Worms	1.1.2.2		×		
Man in the browser	1.1.3		×		
User surveillance	1.2	×			
Smart card reader tampering	1.3	×			
Smart card analyzers	1.4	×			
Sniffing	1.5			×	
Stealing handwritten notes	1.6.4.3	×			
Social engineering	1.6.5.4	×			
Web page obfuscation	1.6.5.5	×			
Pharming	1.6.5.6.1		×	×	
Web site manipulation	1.6.5.7				×
Security policy exploited	2				×
Brute force	3.7				×
MITM attacks	4.8			×	
Session hijacking	5.9.6			×	

ability of the customer's web browser and installs malicious software in the user terminal.

1.1.1: *Emails with malicious code.* Submission of e-mails or SMS, MMS for mobile devices, with malicious content, such as executable files, or HTML code with embedded applets.

1.3: *Smartcard analyzers.* Attacks against smartcards, such as the power consumption analysis or time analysis, may expose the security of the smartcard, by revealing cryptographic keys and passwords (Gandolfi, Mourtel, & Olivier, 2001). Such attacks are sophisticated and not easy to implement but very effective, especially in the case that the necessary countermeasures (noise generators, time-neutral code design) against these types of attacks are not implemented by the smart card manufacturer.

4.8: *Active man-in-the-middle attacks.* This type of attack regards a schema, where the attacker receives and forwards information between the user terminal and the e-banking server. The attacker sends malformed user packets or injects new traffic, such as transfer commands from an account to another. A new breed of this attack is provided by the man-in.the-browser attack, where trojan horses can modify the transactions on-the-fly, as they are formed in browsers, displaying the user's intended transaction to her (Gühring, 2006).

2: *Bank security policy violation.* Violating the bank's security policy, in combination with weak access control and logging mechanisms, a member of the personnel may cause an internal security incident and expose a customer's account.

1.6.5.7: *Website manipulation.* Exploiting the vulnerabilities of the Internet banking web server may permit the alteration of its contents, such as the links to the Internet banking login page. This may redirect the user to a fraudulent web site where his/her credentials may be captured.

Authentication Systems for Financial Services

The HTTP protocol provides two authentication methods: basic and digest, both unsecure (Franks, Hallam-Baker, Hostetler, Lawrence, Leach, Luotonen, & Stewart, 1999). For this reason many authentication techniques have been developed during last years, mostly employed on a secure channel, typically SSL/TLS:. The most diffused authentication mechanism for web authentication are:

- **Static password:** The most common authentication mechanism based on proof by knowledge. Password based mechanisms are widely utilized in e-banking applications. Static passwords however may be captured when attacking the secure channel establishment process (Hole, Moen, & Tjostheim, 2006), for example by deploying sniffing attacks as described below, where the SSL channel is split to one SSL channel between the user terminal and the attacker and another one between the attacker and e-banking server.
- **Soft-token certificate / SSL-TLS:** This mechanism conducts mutual authentication between the user terminal and e-banking server, based on certificates stored in the user's browser. The mechanism is prone to 1.1 attacks, which regard the compromise of the user terminal, where the user certificate is stored. The later may permit access to the user certificate by the attacker, causing identity theft.
- **Hard-token certificate / SSL–TLS:** This mechanism, based on the proof by possession principle, since the user possesses an object as a token towards authentication, is prone to a number of hardware (1.3,1.4) and software attacks, which target at analyzing the operation of the hard-token. Other attacks (1.1) exploit vulnerable interfaces of the hard-

token, which may permit unauthorized hard token commands, such as digital signing, leading to identity theft. Token stealing (1.2 and 1.6.4.3b) is also an issue but it has to be combined with the PIN compromise.

- **One-time password / time-based code generator:** One time passwords are generated by a pseudorandom calculator using a seed which is pre-shared between the user's device (protected by a PIN) and the e-banking server (or even by a counter where a new OTP is generated by pushing a button on the OTP dongle). In both cases OTPs, without a mutual authentication mechanism, such as challenge/response, don't provide anti-phishing security. These mechanisms are prone to a number of attacks, including the regular device stealing attacks (1.6.4.3), combined with user surveillance (1.2) or notes stealing for obtaining the PIN. This fact makes brute-force attacks possible (1.6.5.7,2,3.71), since the guessing possibilities are increased. Other attacks (1.1, 1.5, 1.6.5.6.1, 4.8, 5.9.6, 1.6.5.7, 1.2) are also possible since the codes are submitted through the browser but for a very limited time frame (as long as the code is active plus the time window). Hardware attacks (1.3,1.4), are also possible, by deploying the hardware analysis methods presented in the threat model.

- **HOTP:** A slightly different approach to OTPs comes from an HMAC-Based One-Time Password (HOTP) (Hoornaert, M'Raihi, Naccache & Ranen, 2005) algorithm applied on a mobile channel. This algorithm can be implemented by any hardware manufacturer or software developer to create interoperable authentication devices and software agents. The algorithm is event-based so that it can be embedded in high-volume devices such as Java smart cards, USB dongles, and GSM SIM cards. An in-depth security analysis (Hoornaert, M'Raihi, Naccache & Ranen,

2005) can demonstrates that the best possible attack against the HOTP is the brute force attack.

- **Challenge–response:** This mechanism is similar to the previous one, adding uniqueness to the each authentication process. The e-banking server generates a challenge, which is being processed by the client for producing a response. Challenge-response is prone to man-in-the-middle and session hijacking attacks (1.5, 1.6.5.6.1, 4.8, 5.9.6), since an entity may intercept the communication between the client (user equipment) and the e-banking server and capture and replay messages, or user the predefined session method described in the threat model.

- **Biometrics:** Biometrics provide strong authentication by adding the proof by property factor completing or substituting the existing proof by knowledge and proof by possession based mechanisms. Biometrics are prone to malicious code attacks (1.1), phishing attacks (1.6.5.4 and 1.6.5.5) and communication link (1.5, 1.6.5.6.1, 4.8, 5.9.6) that may expose the user's personal data and threaten the whole security chain, since biometric templates may be compromised and replayed.

- **Knowledge based:** Falling into behavioural authentication Although this mechanism is resistant to 1.2 and 1.6.4.3 attacks, it is prone to most of the remainder attack types, since malicious code may copy answers and create a knowledge database for the user (1.1). The user may also answer questions to an attacker, either tricked by phishing (1.6.5.4 and 1.6.5.5), man-in-the-middle attacks (generally 1.5, 1.6.5.6.1, 4.8, 5.9.6) or malformed e-banking server websites (1.6.5.7). Brute force attacks difficult to deploy due to the multitude of possible answers.

Another solution, presented in (Khu-smith & Mitchell, 2002), uses the authentication algorithm of the cards Subscriber Identity Module (SIM).

Figure 2. Architecture

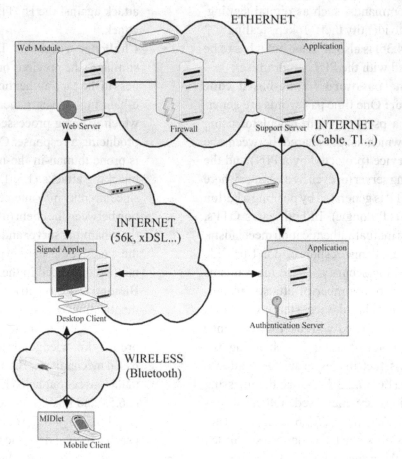

Every SIM contains a secret key, known only by the authentication center which has released the SIM. Without getting into details, one can meet security problems and various other issues related to the contractual agreements between telephone carriers and sellers.

In (Bellare, Al-Qayedi, Mabrouk & Zahro, 2004) the authors developed an architecture to resolve the weaknesses in the previous systems. The architecture is based on the basic authentication which is integrated with a challenge/response mechanism that functions on a mobile channel. A different approach has been presented in (Johnson & Moore), based on a further piece of hardware, an USB-attached device with a display, "the banking dongle" having an active role in the authentication protocol. Nevertheless, this kind of system represents a different approach to the problem, since our target is to enrich the user's smartphone with authentication/encryption software capabilities, as, e.g., has been shown in (Classens, Preneel & Vandewalle, 2001; Parno, Kuo & Perrig, 2006; Wu, Garfinkel & Miller), instead to deliver new hardware.

REQUIREMENTS AND ARCHITECTURE OVERVIEW

As we have seen, properly-managed multifactor authentication mitigates much of the risk associated with compromised passwords. OTPs can potentially be used anywhere passwords are used but we have to find a solution that makes all involved parts comfortable using OTPs. In order to provide a solution compliant with the our smart-phone-centric approach, the solution must:

- face the security presented threats;
- easy to deploy;
- as cheap as possible;
- easy to use, with respect to the definition in (Wu, Garfinkel & Miller),
- are reliably made aware of the security tasks they need to perform;
- are able to figure out how to successfully perform those tasks;
- don't make dangerous errors; and
- are sufficiently comfortable with the interface to continue using it.

Furthermore, we believe that using the same device to perform multiple tasks facilitates the deployment and familiarity with new applications/technologies even if the more complex the system is (e.g. lines of code) the more unsecure it is (e.g. bugs).

The architecture we propose (Figure 3) solves the problems previously underlined with a new approach to the combined web/mobile authentication based on the mechanism presented in (Bellare, Al-Qayedi, Mabrouk & Zahro, 2004).

The devices that compose the system are:

- *Desktop Client.* It allows mobile terminal to communicate with other entities.
- *Mobile Client.* Used for gaining access to the web site.
- *Authentication Server.* It carries out the main steps of the authentication procedure.

Figure 3. Extended authentication setup

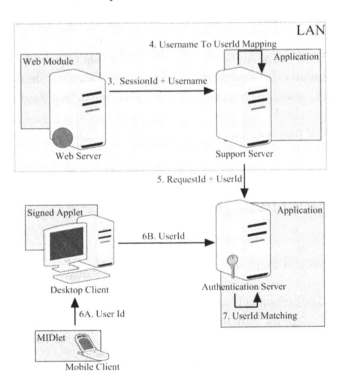

- *Web Server.* It supplies the web pages and manages the basic authentication.
- *Support Server.* It maps the username with the user identifier.

The first improvement we introduce with respect to the SMS-based system is the channel used to share the secret, a virtual private channel versus SMS/GPRS, with benefits regarding the costs cutting to zero. Another difference is that all the manual steps required are done before the extended authentication starts.

With this solution all the credentials are heavily distributed through many entities and none of them have access to all the required information.

The main steps involved are:

- *Web-Based Basic Authentication.* The user proves his identity through basic authentication.
- *Extended Authentication Setup.* The user inserts needed data, such as password and secret key.
- *Combined Web/Mobile Challenge/Response.* The Authentication Server issues a challenge to the mobile device.
- *Combined Web/Mobile OTP.* The Authentication Server generates an OTP sending it both to the mobile device and the Support Server. The latter then checks the correspondence between that password and the one forwarded to it by the Mobile Client.

AUTHENTICATION PROCEDURE IN DETAIL

The steps for a successful authentication are:

- *Username/Password.* The user submits username and password through the browser.
- *Username/Password Validation.* Submitted data is verified by the Web Server.

- *SessionId + Username.* The extended authentication setup (Figure 4) starts with the Web Server which sends a session identifier and the username to the Support Server.
- *Username to UserId Mapping.* The Support Server maps the received username to the Authentication Server's user identifier.
- *RequestId + UserId.* The Support Server generates a random identifier based on timestamp and sends it to the Authentication Server with the user identifier. This operation starts the extended authentication process.
- *UserId.* The user identifier goes from the mobile device to the Authentication Server.
- *UserId Matching.* The Authentication Server verifies that the two received user identifiers match.
- *Rand (Challenge).* The challenge/response mechanism (Figure 5) involves random data generated by the Authentication Server and sent to the mobile device.
- *Encrypted Shared Data.* The Mobile Client uses its secret key with the received random data to cipher the shared data with the Authentication Server, for example an image. AES algorithm is used.
- *Encrypted Shared Data.* The encrypted shared data is sent to the Authentication Server as a response to the challenge/request procedure.
- *Shared Data.* The Authentication Server uses the generated random data and the secret key to decrypt the received data.
- *Shared Data Matching.* Decrypted data is compared with the already owned shared data. Challenge/response procedure ends.
- *Encrypted TempPwd.* In the combined Web/Mobile OTP procedure (Figure 5), an OTP is generated and then encrypted with the random data and the secret key.
- *TempPwd.* The OTP is sent to the Support Server without being encrypted.

Figure 4. Combined Web/mobile challenge/response

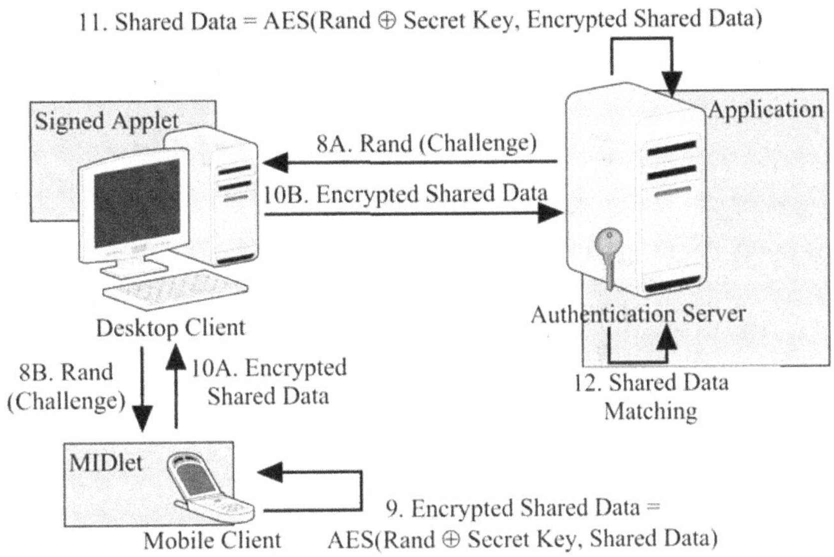

11. Shared Data = AES(Rand ⊕ Secret Key, Encrypted Shared Data)

- *Encrypted TempPwd.* The encrypted OTP is delivered to the mobile device.
- *TempPwd.* The Mobile Client, using the random data and its secret key, decrypts the received OTP.
- *TempPwd.* The decrypted password is sent to the Support Server through the Desktop Client and the Web Server. The Support Server, to recognize the request to handle, receives also the session identifier from the Web Server.
- *TempPwd Matching.* The Support Server verifies the correspondence between the two received OTP.
- *Authentication Success.* The extended authentication process ends successfully.
- *Page Redirect.* The Desktop Client receives from the Web Server the address of the 'welcome' and/or 'logged in' page.

If some errors, mistaken data or problems arise then appropriated warnings are exchanged between the involved entities. The user's devices communicate through a Bluetooth connection.

In order to avoid its security flaws, as shown in (Jakobsson & Wetzel, 2001; SANS Institute, 2001), an extra security layer has been added by encrypting the transmitted data with AES.

The Desktop Client communicates with the Web Server through HTTP or HTTPS protocol, depending on the security level which has to be reached.

SECURITY ANALYSIS

Since a comprehensive security analysis has been provided on authentication with Bluetooth in (Me, Strangio & Dellutri, 2005), a different perspective has been adopted in this work.

Even though not strictly necessary, a specific security mechanism has been implemented on the Bluetooth connection through the encryption of any exchanged data by AES algorithm.

AES is also used in the challenge/response procedure and in the dispatch of the OTP to the Mobile Device. As illustrated, AES is used with

Figure 5. Combined Web/mobile OTP

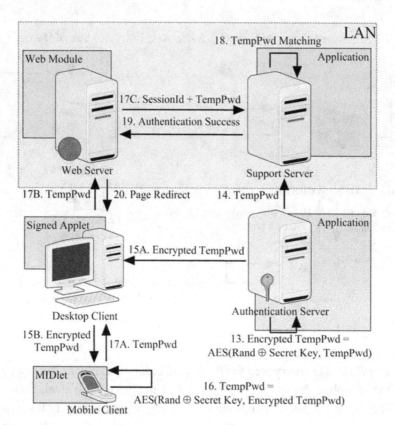

two elements: the secret key and the random data generated by the Authentication Server.

The usage of more communication channels, together with the concept of session, does not make the authentication, by intercepting and deciphering the data transmitted on a single channel, possible. For instance, to know the OTP exchanged between the Authentication Server and the Support Server is not enough to authenticate successfully.

In fact, the OTP is valid only if it is supplied within a certain time window through the active session of the web browser on a Desktop Client owned by the user.

Apart from the basic authentication, no data is submitted through the Desktop Client, avoiding keyboard sniffing.

Timestamps prevent replay attacks guarantying that no multiple authentication requests can occur.

In a real scenario, a phishing attack would fail because, even with the unauthorized usage of a user's basic authentication credentials, it would be impossible to complete all the steps involved due to the lack of the needed data, such as the secret key and user identifier that are stored in the Authentication Server, Support Server and Mobile Client. The system we presented could present some critical points related to the Support Server and Authentication Server security.

We assumed that the two servers are secured against attacks, since this argument does not involve the present paper.

Table 2. Security matrix

Auth. System	Attacks							
	Sniffing	User Surveillance	Malicious Software	ID Theft	Brute Force	Man-In-The-Middle	Phishing	Session Hijacking
HTTP Basic	×	×	×	×	×	×	×	×
HTTP Digest	√ Ciphered password	×	×	×	×	×	×	×
OTP based	√ OTP	√ OTP	√ OTP	√ OTP	√ OTP	√ OTP	×	×
HOTP based	√ OTP	√ OTP	√ OTP	√ OTP	√ OTP	√ OTP	×	×
Our solution	√ OTP	√ OTP	√ OTP	√ OTP	√ OTP	√ OTP	√ Mutual auth.	×

The Table 2 shows a "security matrix" that compares the solution we presented with the other ones previously discussed, specifying the countermeasures adopted to contrast the main types of attacks.

EXPERIMENTAL RESULTS

Our system has been fully implemented using Java technologies, including J2ME.

The functionalities integrated in the Web Server have been realized in a library called Web Module. It has been developed both in Java and Microsoft .NET for enhanced portability. For the same reason an applet has been chosen to run on the Desktop Client side. On the Mobile Client a Java MIDlet has been developed. Our solution has been tested using various scenarios. The Table 3 shows the results confirming that the system performs as expected. Scenario 1 is the only one in which the user is successfully authenticated supplying right credentials within the allocated time frame of N seconds. The scenarios between 2 and 7 show that at least one invalid information is found and, as a result, the authentication fails. In scenario 8 all supplied information is correct

Table 3. Security matrix

Sc	Un	P	Ui	Sk	Sd	Tp	T	AuR
1	✓	✓	✓	✓	✓	✓	< N	A
2	✗	✓	–	–	–	–	< N	R
3	✓	✗	–	–	–	–	< N	R
4	✓	✓	✗	✓	–	–	< N	R
5	✓	✓	✓	✗	–	–	< N	R
6	✓	✓	✓	✓	✗	–	< N	R
7	✓	✓	✓	✓	✓	✗	< N	R
8	✓	✓	✓	✓	✓	✓	> N	R

Sc: scenario   Un: username   P: password   Ui: user id
Sk: secret key   Sd: shared data   Tp: temporary password   T: timeout
N: chosen timeout   AuR: authentication result   A: accepted user   R: rejected user

but the process does not complete itself within the provided timeout and thus aborts.

CONCLUSION AND FUTURE WORKS

Our discussed combined Web/Mobile authentication system aims to improve the security of remote web access while maintaining a trade-off between system security and usability through the use of a standard mobile device and a tuneable timeout factor.

We introduced a solution that is also easy to integrate in new or existing web sites or applications. No variable costs are generated for its use because the inexpensive Bluetooth connection is used instead of GPRS, GSM or other costly methods (OTP keyfobs represent a cost for banks too).

From a managerial perspective there are some main advantages related to this new technology and the business potentially enabled:

- **Cross-selling opportunities:** The authentication service is deployed on the a user mobile device such as a cell phone, so it would be possible to implement cross-selling strategies to offer other value added mobile services (e.g. trading platform).
- **Brand awarness improvement:** It would be possible to embed one or more images on the application running at the Mobile Client side. That images could be arbitrarily customized by introducing a logo or other branded image.
- **No impact on existent privacy policy:** Both Authentication and Support servers don't access personal data.
- **Outsourcing:** Authentication Service is fully deployable as an outsourced service through a thirdy part Internet Service Provider.

- **Low impact on existent value chain:** The service can be deployed as optional and it requires only minor architectural changes as explained in the previous chapters. In addition, the eventual outsourcer should manage only cryptographic information without accessing to the enterprise database.

Currently, the only tangible drawback is represented by the digital divide, because not every Internet user (or bank customer) is supposed to own a Bluetooth enabled smartphone. However, this phenomenon is going to rapidly decrease, since smartphones are going to replace mobile phones in a very short time.

Finally, in particular for those company called "Multiunit Enterprise" (Garvin, Levesque,. 2008), as retail chains, banks, hotels etc, this could represent an effectiveness enhancement, due to the related capability to provide location-dependent authorized security (via mobile phone), namely secure access to the single unit services, where local services and local authentication systems are provided.

The system's security can be improved through some extensions such as the real-time capture of shared data from built in mobile cameras or microphones.

REFERENCES

Bellare, M., Al-Qayedi, A., Adi, W., Mabrouk, A., & Zahro A. (2004). Combined web/mobile authentication for Secure Web Access Control. *IEEE Wireless Communications and Networking Conference WCNC2004*. Atlanta.

Bellare, W., Hoornaert, F., M'Raihi, D., Naccache, D., & Ranen, O. (2005). *HOTP: An HMAC-Based One-Time Password Algorithm*. Network Working Group, Request for Comments: 4226.

Claessens, J., Preneel, B., & Vandewalle, J. (2001). Combining world wide web and wireless security. *Proceedings of IFIP I-NetSec.* Leuven (Belgium).

Franks, J., Hallam-Baker, P. M., Hostetler, J. L., Lawrence, S. D., Leach, P.J ., Luotonen, A., & Stewart, L. (1999), *HTTP Authentication: Basic and Digest Access Authentication.* Network Working Group, Request for Comments: 2617.

Gandolfi, K., Mourtel, C., & Olivier, F. (2001) Electromagnetic Analysis: Concrete Results. *Lecture Notes in Computer Science, 2162.* Springer-Verlag.

Garvin, G., & Levesque, C. (2008), The Multiunit Enterprise, *Harvard Business Review,* June 2008, (pp. 106-117).

Gühring, P. (2006). *Concepts against Man-in-the-Browser Attacks.* Retrieved April 01, 2008, from http://www.it-observer.com/pdf/dl/concepts_against_mitb_attacks.pdf

Hole, J. K., Moen, V., & Tjostheim, T. (n.d.). Case study: Online banking security. *IEEE Security and Privacy, 4*(2), 14-20.

Jakobsson, M., & Wetzel, S. (2001). *Security weakness in Bluetooh.* Murray Hill, USA.

Johnson, M., & Moore, S., (2007). *A New Approach to E-Banking.* Retrieved April 01, 2008, from http://mjj29.matthew.ath.cx/2007-Johnson-ebanking-full.pdf

Khu-smith, V., & Mitchell, C. J. (2002). *Enhancing ecommerce security using GSM authentication,* London, England.

Me, G., Strangio, M. A., & Dellutri, F. (2005). Local Authentication with Bluetooth enabled mobile devices. *Proceedings of IEEE International Conference on Autonomic and Autonomous Systems.*

Parno, B., Kuo, C., & Perrig, A. (2006). Phoolproof Phishing Prevention. In G. Di Crescenzo and A. Rubin (eds.), *Financial Cryptogra phy and Data Security,* vol. LNCS of 4107 (pp. 1–19). Springer-Verlag. Retrieved April 01, 2008, from http://sparrow.ece.cmu.edu/_adrian/projects/phishing.pdf

Prevelakis, V., & Spinellis, D. (2007). The Athens Affair. *IEEE Spectrum.* Retrieved April 01, 2008, from http://www.spectrum.ieee.org/jul07/5280

SANS Institute. (2001). *An overview of Bluetooth security.* Retrieved April 01, 2008, from http://whitepapers.techrepublic.com.com/whitepaper.aspx?docid=143972, 2001.

Schneier, B. (1999). Attack trees. *Dr. Dobb's J., 24*(12), 21-29.

Schneier, B. (2005). *Schneier on Security: The Failure of Two-Factor Authentication.* Retrieved April 01, 2008, from http://www.schneier.com/blog/archives/2005/03/the_failure_of.html

Wu, M., Garfinkel, S., & Miller, R. *Secure web authentication with mobile phones.* MIT Computer Science and Artificial Intelligence Lab.

KEY TERMS

Advanced Encryption Standard (AES): An algorithm for performing encryption and decryption adopted by the U.S. government and now used worldwide.

Applet: A program written in the Java programming language that can runs in the context of an HTML page.

Bluetooth: A short-range wireless protocol aimed at simplifying data transmission from fixed and/or mobile devices.

Ethernet: Ethernet is a family of computer networking technologies for Local Area Networks (see LAN).

Firewall: A device configured to permit, deny, encrypt, or proxy all data exchanges between different computers based upon a set of rules.

General Packet Radio Service (GPRS): A wireless data service used for services such as Wireless Application Protocol (WAP) access, Short Message Service (SMS), Multimedia Messaging Service (MMS), and for Internet communication services such as email and World Wide Web access.

Global System for Mobile Communications (GSM): An open, digital cellular technology used for transmitting mobile voice and data services.

HyperText Markup Language (HTML): The predominant markup language to build web pages.

Hypertext Transfer Protocol (HTTP): A communications protocol for retrieving interlinked text documents (hypertext) led to the establishment of the World Wide Web.

Hypertext Transfer Protocol over Secure Socket Layer (HTTPS): A protocol used to create a secure HTTP connection.

Java: A platform independent programming language originally developed by Sun Microsystems and released in 1995 as a core component of Sun Microsystems' Java platform.

Java Micro Edition (J2ME): A programming environment for applications running on mobile and other embedded devices such as mobile phones, personal digital assistants, TV set-top boxes, and printers.

Local Area Network (LAN): A computer network covering a small geographic area, like a home, office, or group of buildings.

Midlet: A J2ME program for special-purpose devices such as a cell phone.

Microsoft .NET: A software framework to develop applications for Microsoft Windows platforms.

Phishing: The fraudulent process of attempting to acquire sensitive information by masquerading as a trustworthy entity in an electronic communication.

Secure Sockets Layer (SSL): Predecessor of TLS (see TLS).

Transport Layer Security (TLS): A cryptographic protocol providing secure communications on the Internet for such things as web browsing, e-mail, instant messaging and other data transfers.

Universal Serial Bus (USB): A standard to interface devices to a host computer, specifically designed to allow usage flexibility and low-consumption without the need for an external power supply.

Web Server: A program that is responsible for accepting HTTP requests from web clients (usually browsers) and serving them HTTP responses (usually web pages).

Chapter VIII
Mobile Signature Solutions for Guaranteeing Non-Repudiation in Mobile Business and Mobile Commerce

Antonio Ruiz-Martínez
University of Murcia, Spain

Daniel Sánchez-Martínez
University of Murcia, Spain

María Martínez-Montesinos
University of Murcia, Spain

Antonio F. Gómez-Skarmeta
University of Murcia, Spain

ABSTRACT

Non-repudiation is an important issue in mobile business and mobile commerce in order to provide the necessary evidences to prove whether some party participated in a transaction. The basis to support non-repudiation is the electronic signature. In Europe, directive 1999/93/EC of the European Parliament and the Council establishes the conditions that should be fulfilled in order to provide an electronic signature legally equivalent to the handwritten signature. This chapter presents and analyses the different solutions that have appeared over the years to provide mobile signatures. This analysis will help us to determine which mobile signatures solutions can be considered legally equivalent to the handwritten signature. Thus, this chapter allows people to get to know the different solutions that are available to build mobile commerce and mobile business applications that require the use of the non-repudiation service, and hence electronic signature in mobile devices.

INTRODUCTION

Nowadays, mobile handsets (mobile phones, Personal Digital Assistants, etc) are an important element in our daily life. In fact, in developed countries almost everybody has a mobile handset and almost everybody has it on them every time. More and more these devices are reducing their size, and, even more importantly, they are incorporating new features of communication, entertainment and computation and storage capabilities. These improvements make possible the development, in different scenarios, of services that previously were not possible, such as in mobile commerce (m-commerce), mobile business (m-business) or multimedia. Among these services (Grillo *et al.*, 2008; Zmijewska & Lawrence, 2006; Dahlberg *et al.*, 2008) we can mention: m-payments, location-based services, banking transactions, contract signing, brokerage, mobile access to enterprise applications, e-health environments, and so on. These services, thanks to our mobile handsets, could be offered and used anywhere/anytime. Indeed, they could be used in pervasive environments in order to facilitate the daily life/work of the users.

Most of the m-commerce and m-business applications or services need to use some security services to guarantee the safety of the transactions that they perform. Of the different security services we can highlight non-repudiation because this service provides the necessary evidences to prove whether some party participated in a transaction. The basis to support this service of non-repudiation is the electronic signature since it allows the creation of evidences associated to a transaction and a user or entity (Zhou, 2001). Non-repudiation also needs other components or elements such as timestamping services, the participation of trusted third parties (TTPs), etc (for a deeper analysis see (Zhou, 2001)). However, as we have just mentioned, the basic element is the use of electronic signature. In this chapter we will focus on how to provide this service in mobile devices. From this basis we will be able to develop the rest of components or services needed and that are out of the scope of this chapter.

The goal of the electronic signature (e-signature) is to be equivalent to handwritten signatures, even in legal terms. In Europe, directive 1999/93/EC of the European Parliament and the Council (European Parliament, 2000) establishes the conditions that should be fulfilled in order to provide an e-signature legally equivalent to the handwritten signature. These conditions will be explained later in this chapter but we can release some details. Basically, it consists of generating the electronic signature by using a *Secure Signature Creation Device* (SSCD) with a qualified certificate. Previously, it was no possible to satisfy these conditions in mobile devices due to their limited cryptographic and computational capabilities. Today the situation is completely different and we are able to generate e-signatures based on asymmetric cryptography or even based on elliptic curve cryptography. Furthermore, there are now different technologies to provide e-signatures in mobile devices.

The aim of this chapter is to present the different solutions that have appeared over the years to provide mobile signatures (section 4). But before presenting these, we are going to describe the basic concepts related to mobile electronic signature (section 2) as well as the different technologies that we have available to build these mobile signatures (section 3). Furthermore, as well as reviewing the different solutions, we are going to analyze them from the security and legal point of view with the aim of determining whether the mobile signatures generated in these solutions can be considered legally equivalent to the handwritten signature (section 4). Therefore, this chapter will allow us to get to know the different solutions that we have available to build m-commerce and m-business applications that require the use of the non-repudiation service, and hence electronic signature in mobile devices. Thus, this chapter is useful to understand how current m-commerce and m-business applications as well as new ones that support new business models can incorporate the use of the e-signature in their processes. Finally, we have also decided to include an Appendix with a glossary of acronyms in order for the reader to find easily the meaning of each acronym used in this chapter.

(MOBILE) ELECTRONIC SIGNATURE: BASIC CONCEPTS AND BUSINESS APPLICATIONS

In this section we are going to introduce the basic concepts that will be used throughout this chapter: e-signature, secure signature creation devices, qualified certificates and mobile electronic signature. Then, we introduce some business cases where the use of the mobile electronic signature can be used.

An e-signature (European Committee for Standardization, 2004; Schneier, 1995) is a cryptographic operation based on asymmetric cryptography and hash functions that aims to provide the equivalent to the handwritten signature in the digital world. Thus, the e-signature guarantees three main security services: integrity, authentication and non-repudiation.

According to directive 1999/93/EC of the European Parliament and the Council (European Parliament, 2000), an e-signature is considered legally equivalent of the handwritten signature if the process to generate the e-signature is based on a Secure Signature Creation Device (SSCD) with a qualified certificate. A device is considered a SSCD (European Committee for Standardization, 2004; European Parliament, 2000) if it satisfies some requirements that are specified in the Evaluation Assurance Level (EAL) 4+ specification.

A certificate is considered qualified when it is issued by a (QCSP) (European Parliament, 2000). An entity is a QCSP if it copes with different security requirements that guarantee the security over the certificate life cycle. Furthermore, this device has to be liable for damage caused to any entity.

Finally, the European Telecommunications Standard Institute (ETSI) defines a mobile signature (ETSI, 2003b, pp. 12) as: "a universal method for using a mobile device to confirm the intention of a citizen to proceed with a transaction". Therefore, "this mobile signature is applicable to all kinds of applications and not just those which can be accessed through mobile devices" (ETSI, 2003b, pp. 13). Special scenarios of application of this mobile signature are mobile business and mobile commerce, because they need to guarantee the non repudiation of the transactions. Then, we introduce some case uses where the mobile signature would be needed.

The first two cases are related to e-health environment (more details of these cases can be found in (Grillo *et al.*, 2008)). In the first case, the mobile signature service can be used for a medical professional to send signed notifications to the user about the results for physical examinations. Thus, the user can be sure of the results come from the medical professional. In the second case, the user can use the mobile signature to confirm the request of services that the user has requested by phone, by e-mail, etc.

Other interesting use case is related to the use of mobile signature to top-up user's mobile with pre-paid account by debit card (more details in (ETSI, 2003b, pp. 18). In this user case, the client request to top up his/her mobile, after sending some information to carry out the transaction (his/her mobile number, the amount to top up and the payment information), the pre-paid system prepares a payment instruction request that the client has sign in order to confirm the transaction. Once the user has signed the payment instruction, the mobile phone is top up.

A very important use of mobile signature is to guarantee non-repudiation in mobile payments (see Hassinen *et al.*, 2006; Zmijewska & Lawrence, 2006; Dahlberg *et al.* 2008). In this scenario, first, a mobile user (acting as a customer) requests a service to a merchant. Then, the merchant provides the service options (short description of products and prices) and requests the user to create a payment order by signing his/her choice and his/her credit card information (the credit card information is ciphered in order the vendor can not obtain it). When the vendor receives the payment order, he forwards payment information to the bank and request the payment of the amount of the product chosen. Finally, if the bank confirms the payment, then, the vendor delivers the product.

In the academic world (University of Murcia and Telefónica, 2007; Sánchez-Martínez *et al.*, 2008), other useful scenario is the mobile signature of the official exam marks certificates. In this use case a lecturer is able to sign an electronic mark certificate related to each one of the subjects he teaches through a mobile device. Afterwards, the students receive a SMS notification instantly, so they can know these academic issues without any delay. Moreover, printable copies of these electronic documents are published on the official notice boards of the faculties in order to provide the students with the choice of the communication channel (physical or electronic).

In general, we could say that any business model that requires non-repudiation and that we want to translate to mobile environment would require the use of mobile signature. Other scenarios related to non-repudiation and electronic signature can be found in (Zhou, 2001), such as e-contract signing, certified e-mail, ticket purchase, etc.

(MOBILE) ELECTRONIC SIGNATURE: TECHNOLOGIES

In this section we are going to describe and analyse the main solutions that can be used to provide (mobile) electronic signature in mobile handheld. Generally speaking, the technologies can be classified into two main groups: technologies provided by the mobile network operator and

technologies provided by the mobile device. We describe into detail in the different technologies of each group next.

Technologies Provided by the Mobile Network Operator

As we have mentioned in the introduction, nowadays mobile network operators seek to offer advanced services to their clients. One of these services is the advanced electronic signature on documents and transactions. The mobile network operators must support different technological infrastructures in order to offer these e-signature processes. These infrastructures show some common specific characteristics. First, these network infrastructures are the property of an operator, which frequently charges an additional fee for the use of these services to the application providers or the final signer. In (Rossnagel and Royer, 2005) the benefits that can be reached from providing an e-signature service are analysed. Secondly, the application providers must usually reach commercial agreements with the operators in order to use these services. Thirdly, the e-signatures are conveyed over the Global System for Mobile communications (GSM)/General Packet Radio Service (GPRS) or Universal Mobile Telecommunications System (UMTS) layer according to the network capabilities. Finally, these electronic signatures can be performed through a Secure Signature Creation Device, which is commonly a Subscriber Identify Module (SIM) card.

Furthermore, these technologies are composed of some specific network elements. The first one is the SIM card inside the user's mobile device. This card is the core of the mobile communications and contains different applications, Application Programming Interfaces (APIs) and files, as we are going to see in the following section. Next we can consider a group of elements that are able to exchange messages between the network operator and the user's handheld. This communi-

Figure 1. Signature infrastructure provided by the mobile network operator

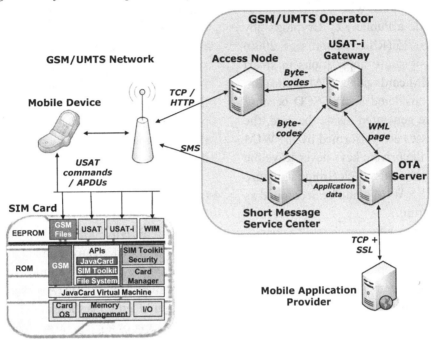

cation is normally provided by a Short Message Service (SMS) service centre for sending short messages, or by an access node for establishing Transmission Control Protocol (TCP)/Internet Protocol (IP) or HyperText Transfer Protocol (HTTP) connections, as we can see in Figure 1. In addition, there is another group of servers and gateways for different purposes according to the e-signature infrastructure. For example, in Figure 1, we can see a Universal SIM Application Toolkit – Interpreter (USAT-i) Gateway and an Over The Air (OTA) Server, which are commonly used by the application providers for sending e-signature requests to mobile devices. In the following sections we are going to introduce the SIM card and the most extended technologies that are able to perform digital signature processes through it. More details on the different technologies could be found in (Ruiz-Martínez *et al.*, 2007) as well as in the references included in each section associated to each solution.

SIM Card

A SIM card is a multi-application card, in which different applications can be integrated at the same time. In a SIM card we can usually distinguish between two different types of memory. The Read Only Memory (ROM) memory, as can be seen in Figure 1, has a physical layer with the SIM card operative system, the memory management and the input/output interfaces. In the figure, on top of this layer, there are several elements for managing the security and life cycle of each application (for example the JavaCard Virtual Machine) and the GSM application, which is burned in when the chip is manufactured. On top of the ROM memory, it is the Electrically Erasable Programmable Read-Only Memory (EEPROM) memory, which can be modified during the life cycle of the SIM card and which contains different applications (usually called JavaCard applets).

From a security point of view, the most important of these applications is the Wireless Identity

Module (WIM). This module is used to establish secure communications with applications as well as to provide a Public Key Cryptography Standard (PKCS)#15 (RSA Laboratories, 2000) interface for e-signature applications in smart cards. Thus, a SIM card with a WIM application inside can be considered as an SSCD because the key pairs are generated inside the card, the signature processes are performed by the WIM application and the private keys never leave the card. For all these reasons, an electronic signature obtained through a WIM could be accredited as a qualified signature.

Therefore, this technology should be considered as one of the base in the development of mobile electronic signature applications as regards the generation and management of keys. At present the manufacturers are including this application in SIM cards as a standard of e-signature. Although the WIM applet is defined as an independent smart card application, other mobile applications and technologies are able to use it in order to provide security processes with electronic signature. Some of these technologies are available in the SIM card (like proprietary USAT or USAT-i applets) or even in the mobile device (like Security and Trust Services API (SATSA) in J2ME Midlets). These technologies are described in more detail in the following sections.

SAT-USAT Application

SIM Application Toolkit (SAT) is a standard of the GSM system which enables the SIM to initiate actions which can be used for various value added services, for example electronic signature processes. SIM Application Toolkit consists of a set of commands programmed into the SIM card which define how the SIM should interact directly with the outside world and initiates commands independently of the handset and the network. This enables the SIM to build up an interactive exchange between a network application and the end user. The SIM also provides commands to the handset, such as display menu and asks for user input. SAT has been deployed by many mobile operators around the world for many applications, often where a menu-based approach is required, such as Mobile Banking and content browsing. At present, the SAT is broadly extended and it is the basis for implementing most added-value applications in mobile phones. Its equivalent in the third generation technology of mobile phones is the Universal SIM Application Toolkit (USAT).

A SIM Application Toolkit is a JavaCard applet (a small and secure Java program stored in the SIM card). These applets can be loaded on the card when the chip is manufactured (Rankl and Effing, 2004). After that, in any moment at the lifecycle of the card they can be dynamically downloaded and installed through an OTA server (see figure 1). This solution presents some drawbacks. First, the downloading of applets through an OTA server usually supposes the fragmentation of the applet into several linked short messages, which is a costly process, unless the operator uses a GPRS connection (Rankl and Effing, 2004). Second, the applet installation process involves security risks and performance problems. Third, the key generation and the signature process that a SIM Toolkit applet performs through the JavaCard API is between 10 and 20 times slow compared to executed it natively (Rankl and Effing, 2004). Last but not least, the asymmetric keys generated usually do not have a physically protected environment in which the secrecy of these credentials could be reasonably assured against attacks with high potential or against physical tampering (European Committee for Standardization, 2004). It is fundamental to make this aspect clear. Although the Java environment is executed inside the smart card, the protection of the contents of the applets is based on software executed on native operating system (Java Card environment), thus the keys are not protected with the same security mechanisms that offer the generation of the keys directly over the native operating system. Therefore, the signatures generated cannot be considered qualified signatures.

USAT-i Application

The Universal SIM Application Toolkit – Interpreter (USAT-i) is a SAT application for the 3G SIM cards. This application is a microbrowser that receives byte-codes enveloped by linked short messages, IP packets or HTTP messages in function of the transport layer. The USAT-i browser opens the envelopes, decodes, processes the byte-codes and finally deletes them. The decoded byte-codes are pages, similar to HyperText Markup Language (HTML) pages, written in a subset of Wireless Mark-up Language (WML). This small language provides application developers with particular tags to define a user interface or invoke to USAT commands. The network operator must deploy additional network infrastructure in order to support this technology. The most important element of this infrastructure is the USAT-i gateway, which is responsible for packing and codifying the application providers' WML pages into binary byte-codes. These byte-codes, optimized for small bandwidth, are sent to the mobile device through the transport layer which is usually the SMS, as we can see in figure 1.

Each manufacturer can extend the USAT-i browser of a SIM card through plug-ins. These plug-ins are different JavaCard applets installed on the SIM card during the manufacturer phase. The particular commands that implement these plug-ins can be invoked by the USAT-i browser. Furthermore, the manufacturers normally support a special kind of plug-ins, called (Public Key Infrastructure) PKI plug-ins, when the SIM card contains a WIM application. The PKI plug-ins are able to request security and cryptographic command from the WIM applet, for example the creation of an e-signature. As a result, we can state that the main advantage of USAT-i browser is that the installation of heavy applets "over the air" is not necessary. An additional advantage is the integration with the WIM application by means of the PKI plug-ins. Therefore, the private keys never leave the smart card and we can consider it a secure signature creation device. Thus, the electronic signatures could be considered qualified signatures. The main problem of this solution is that requires some investments by the mobile network operator so as to provide an additional network infrastructure to support this technology.

Technologies Provided by the Mobile Device

Mobile devices offer more and more powerful cryptographic functionalities. Windows Mobile Operating System (OS), Symbian OS and Java Mobile Edition (Java ME) constitute an example of technologies for handheld that make the use of cryptography in mobile environments possible. Next, we describe and analyse the basic characteristics of these technologies.

Symbian OS

Symbian OS is an operating system that was the result of the alliance of several cellular telephone companies, such as Nokia, Sony Ericsson, Samsung, Motorola and some more. The purpose was to create an OS for mobile devices that could compete with the Palm OS or the Windows Mobile of Microsoft. Symbian OS has been evolving until its latest version, Symbian OS v9.5.

As regards security in Symbian OS, we can emphasize that it is divided into two level components. The certificate management is in the base level. Thus, this level allows us to store and retrieve certificates, to assign a level of trust to a certificate based on the application, to perform certificate chain construction and validation, and finally, to perform a trust-based verification of a certificate. The other component is a cryptographic element, whose purpose is to provide secure mechanisms for data integrity and confidentiality, and authentication. Key generation and random number generation, hash functions, and standard cryptography algorithms, for example symmetric/asymmetric ciphers, are worth mentioning. Above this level there is a higher one composed of modules that use the cryptographic functionality offered by the low layer. This higher level includes secure communications (SSL/TLS, WTLS, IPSec, etc.), software installation (authentication/electronic signatures) and certificate Management user interface that provides certificate management.

There are difficulties with performing electronic signature in Symbian OS because the cryptographic functionality needed for the development of applications is provided only to Symbian OS partners and phone manufacturers. This restriction reduces the number of providers of applications that can make use of this solution to develop mobile application/service.

Windows Mobile OS

Windows Mobile OS is a compact operating system for handheld devices, with a basic applications suite based on Microsoft Win32 API. Pocket PC and Smartphone are the two main platforms based on it, although there is also another called Portable Media Center platform.

The architecture of security in Windows Mobile OS is based on Microsoft's security systems. Mainly it is made up of three layers; Cryptographic Service Provides (CSP), operating system and applications, as can see in the diagram bellow:

Figure 2 shows how the applications communicate with the operating system by means of Crypto API. This OS component is the cryptographic API that provides the functionality needed in secure environments. Some of these functions are the creation and verification of the electronic signature, data encryption and decryption, processing and management of certificates and finally, key generation and storage.

Next OS connects with elements called Cryptographic Service Providers (CSPs) through the Cryptographic Service Provider Interface (Crypto SPI). A CSP (Cryptographic Service Provider)

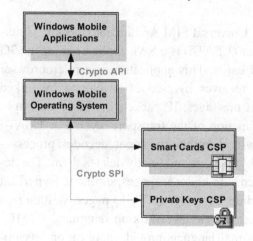

Figure 2. Windows mobile security schema

is an independent module that contains cryptographic implementations for a specific device of diverse algorithms and standards for authentication, encoding, encryption, key storage, and electronic signature. The job of a CSP is to facilitate the use of safe devices such as cryptographic smart cards or cryptographic USB tokens, to perform cryptographic operations based on such devices like creation of electronic signatures or the decryption of information based on a private key contained in these devices. Windows Mobile provides three preinstalled CSPs: RSA Base Provider, RSA Enhanced Provider, and DSS and Diffie-Hellman Cryptographic Provider. Thus, with a Smart Card CSP, another way of securing user credentials storage and compute electronic signatures is obtained, since these functions could be made directly by a cryptographic smart card. The generated signatures could be in standard formats such as PKCS#1 (RSA Laboratories, 2002) or CMS/PKCS#7 (Housley, 2004; RSA Laboratories, 1993). Thus, the use of the smart card for the safe storage of certificates and private keys and for performing the electronic signature is a secure option for mobile devices.

Once we have outlined the main characteristics concerning security in Windows Mobile, we can state that Windows Mobile OS offers mechanisms to support the lifecycle of the electronic signature.

Furthermore, since this solution can be based on the use of a cryptographic device such as a smart card, we can conclude that this solution can generate signatures legally equivalent to the handwritten signature. However, there are some elements that should be incorporated into this solution, as mentioned in (Barnés *et al.*, 2005). First, a certificate validation service that simplifies the building and the validation of a certificate chain up to a trusted certificate. This is required to simplify the components in the mobile device and therefore the capabilities required from this device. Second, the incorporation of functionality to support the PKCS#12 (RSA Laboratories, 1999) format. Thus, we can import keys and certificates from the Windows System.

Java ME

Java Mobile Edition Platform (Java ME. Formerly J2ME, Java 2 Micro Edition), is not an operating system itself. It is a collection of Java APIs for consumer-oriented products, such as Personal Digital Assistants (PDAs), cellular phones or home appliances. Within the Electronic Signature and Java ME environment, Security and Trust Services API (SATSA) is worth mentioning. SATSA is defined in Java Specification Request (JSR)-177 (Sun Java Specifications, 2007) and is made up of four optional packages. The main purpose of SATSA is to provide security and trust services for J2ME-based devices in particular processes where security is a required element, such as in authentication, payments scenarios and e-health (Grillo *et al.*, 2008). Security is obtained using, among other things, a Security Element. Smart cards are commonly used to implement it, since they are widely spread with mobile devices (SIM cards). Smart cards can provide the following characteristics: safe storage of confidential data, such as user's private keys, public key certificates and other personal information and they can perform cryptographic operations in secure processes in which non-repudiation, confidentiality and integ-

rity of information are required. The communication between Java ME applications (MIDlets) and a smart card uses SATSA-Application Protocol Data Unit (APDU) Optional Package, as can be seen in Figure 3.

As a special advantage of this technology, we can consider the use of smart cards in Java ME environment, which implements the WIM standard mentioned in a previous section of this chapter. Therefore, the e-signature generated using this technology could be considered legally equivalent to the handwritten signature.

In addition to SATSA, there are external Java libraries that stand out for performing cryptographic processes in Java ME devices, for example, Bouncy Castle, IAIK JCE Micro Edition (IAIK, 2008), Phaos Micro Foundation (Phaos Micro Foundation, 2008), and NTRU Neo for Java (NTRU, 2008). These libraries allow us to perform electronic signature, generate keys and manage certificates. More details on the features of the different libraries can be found in (Ruiz-Martínez *et al.*, 2007). However, it is important to point out that if the signature offered is only based on the use of these libraries in the MIDlet (without SATSA) and all the cryptographic material is not in the SIM card, then, the signatures created can not be considered legally equivalent to handwritten signature as in (Grillo *et al.*, 2008).

The only problem of this technology (Java ME with SATSA) is that, at the moment, there is no

Figure 3. SATSA scenario

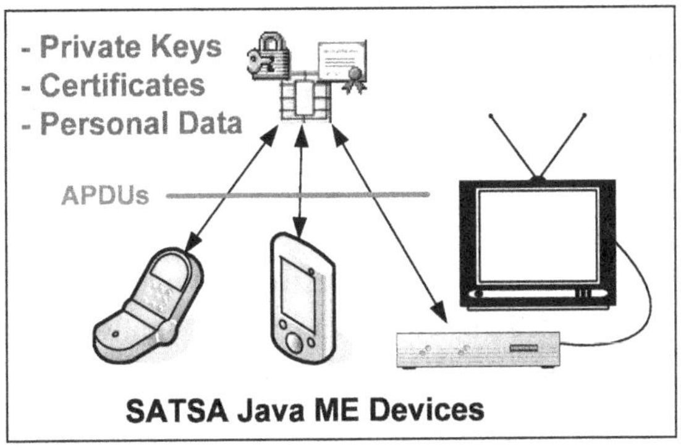

- Private Keys
- Certificates
- Personal Data

APDUs

SATSA Java ME Devices

broad range of mobile devices that incorporate it. However, we can observe a progressive incorporation of this technology in mobile devices which means that in the short term all mobile handheld will incorporate it.

TOWARDS A MOBILE SIGNATURE SOLUTION

Throughout the previous section we have reviewed different technologies that could be used to perform an electronic signature in a mobile device. These technologies are the base on which to build mobile signature solutions that require the use of electronic signature in mobile business or electronic commerce applications. However, there is an important problem for those wanting to develop that kind of solutions: there are a lot of different kind of mobile devices, each of them can support one or more of the already mentioned technologies to provide electronic signature. Therefore, mobile application/service providers would have to develop many different solutions. This supposes a lot of investment if we want to support a broad range of devices and scenarios. Some solutions have appeared aimed at facilitating the use of electronic signature in pervasive applications. As we will comment later, some of them could be based on the technologies previously mentioned. These solutions are: server-based signatures (Bicakci and Baykal, 2003; Bicakci and Baykal, 2004; Bicakci and Baykal, 2005), mobile signature service (ETSI, 2003a) and mobile signature application unit (Pisko, 2007). Then, we are going to describe each of them, taking into account that we want to satisfy the following requirements that we will use to compare them. These requirements are:

- We want to obtain electronic signatures that are legally equivalent to the handwritten signature. For this purpose, the electronic signature should be:

  - generated by a secure signature creation device (SSCD) that generates electronic signatures based on asymmetric or elliptic curves cryptography (that is, advanced signature).

  - based on the use of qualified certificates. On the other hand, for the complete verification of an electronic signature (including the certificate validation) it is not necessary that it is provided by a SSCD. This task could be left to a trusted third party and thus, we will simplify the features that we should require from a mobile device to perform electronic signature processes.

- In order to facilitate the exchange of signing information, the electronic signature should be generated and expressed according to a standard scheme and format such as PKCS#1 (RSA cryptography) (RSA Laboratories, 2002), X9.62 (Elliptic Curve Digital Signature Algorithm – ECDSA) (American National Standard Institute, 2005; Blake-Wilson *et al.*, 2005), PKCS#7/CMS (Cryptographic Message Syntax) (RSA Laboratories, 1993; Housley, 2004) or XML Signature (W3C, 2008). These standards are the basis for other standards that are used to store and validate the electronic signature over long periods of time such as (ETSI, 2006) and (ETSI, 2007).

- The independence of the mobile application/service provider should be facilitated regarding the technologies supported by the mobile device.

- In order to generate the electronic signatures in an efficient way, the solution proposed should not be based on a third party. The delegation on a third party of part of the signature process supposes the exchange of messages on the network with this party to generate the electronic signature. Therefore, the process is slower due to the communications costs.

- The solution should be independent of the mobile network operator and it should be possible for the mobile user and the mobile application/service provider to be different mobile network operators. Therefore, the solution should be independent of the mobile network operator used. Furthermore, it would be interesting to know if there are proposals that have implemented that solution (either research or industry).

Server-Based Signatures

The idea of a server-based signature is that, instead of performing the electronic signature in the mobile device, the signature is made in a server that can manage the private key and the certificate of the user. Therefore, the server has the responsibility of creating the electronic signature on behalf the end user. In this solution, the user's mobile device only participates in the signing process to approve the generation of the electronic signature in the server. In order to approve the transaction, a user's authentication based on either Personal Identifier Numbers (PIN) or One-Time Password (OTP) or Message Authentication Codes (MAC) with symmetric keys or One-Time Signatures (OTS) is requested. The whole process is shown in Figure 4. There are several solutions that are based on server-based signatures such as in (Bicakci and Baykal, 2003; Bicakci and Baykal, 2004; Bicakci and Baykal, 2005; Domingo-Ferrer, 2008).

This solution was initially proposed for mobile devices that had very limited capabilities (both cryptographic and related to network communication). Additionally, this solution can also be used to simplify the development of signature-based solutions for mobile/pervasive application providers in mobile business/commerce scenarios. As we can see in Figure 4, there are three main entities: mobile device, the signing server and the mobile application/service provider. Thus, the mobile provider will send the request to the server that will be in charge of requesting the confirmation

Figure 4. Server-based solutions steps

to the end-user. Therefore, as main advantage of this solution we can point out its simplicity. Another advantage of solutions based on PIN or OTP systems is that the users do not need any special device because the GSM phone that people already have it is enough.

On the other hand, its main drawback is that the electronic signatures generated by a server-based solution can not be considered legally equivalent to a handwritten signature because the electronic signature device is not under the sole control of the end user, it is under server control. Another drawback is that there is no standardised interface to access to this server-based server from a mobile/pervasive application provider. Furthermore, in OTP or OTS solutions, every time a signature is requested, it is required that the user enters a password or mnemonic that is used to generate a new OTP password or a new OTS signature that the user has to retype in order to send it to the server (Haller *et al.*, 1998).

Mobile Signature Service

The concept of Mobile Signature was considered very attractive by the European Commission because there is an important mass of mobile phone users that can take advantage of the use of electronic signature in their mobile phones. Therefore, they decided to allocate funds to ETSI (European Technical Standard Institute) in order to produce several specifications for a *Mobile Signature Service* (MSS). Hence, the main goal of this project was to try to standardize a mobile signature service that facilitates the development of applications, based on mobile signature, to the mobile application/service providers. Furthermore, they also wanted the definition of this service to be independent of the mobile device characteristics. Additionally, they took into account other aspects that were not previously considered, such as data formatting, roaming, etc. Thus, they proposed that the exchange of information between the Mobile Signature Service Provider (MSSP) and the mobile application/service provider was based on web services that are fully described in the ETSI specification (ETSI, 2003a). Furthermore, the mobile device should be provided with a smart card with crypto-processor, such as a SIM card. In fact, they propose that the electronic signature is calculated by using either SIM Application Toolkit (SATK) or WIM. Like this, the electronic signature generated would be legally equivalent to the handwritten signature.

Figure 5 depicts the different relationships that take place between the different roles that participate in the system. We can see the following roles: the user with a mobile device, the mobile application/service provider, the registration authority, the certification authority and the roaming mobile signature service.

In this specification, the user owns a mobile device (mobile phone, PDA, etc) that, in general, has a smart card, as mentioned previously. The smart card has a signing application that will be invoked by the Mobile Signature Service Provider (MSSP) in order to generate an electronic signature for the Mobile Service Provider.

The keys used to generate the electronic signatures are generated by the signing application. These keys will be certified by a Certification Authority (CA). The CA issues the certificates once the Registration Authority (RA) has validated the user's identity and the information that will appear in the certificate. The accesses to the keys of this application are protected by means of a PIN. This PIN will be requested before gen-

Figure 5. ETSI mobile signature service framework

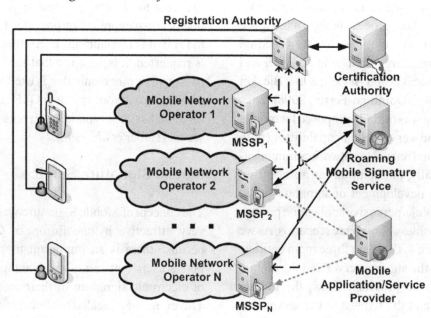

erating an electronic signature in this signing application. This smart card with this signing application is provided, in general, by the mobile operator although it could be provided by any smart card issuer.

Normally, in this solution, the Mobile Signature Service is provided by a Mobile Network Operator (MNO). However, it could be another entity that has a close relationship to the Mobile Network Operator. This entity is responsible for requesting an electronic signature from the mobile device. The way this request is sent to the mobile device depends on its capabilities and the smart card capabilities provided in the mobile device supplied by the MNO. In spite of this, the methods proposed are SATK or plug-ins based on WIM.

The MSSP, apart from requesting an electronic signature to the mobile device, is able to support other additional functions such as data hashing, data to be signed formatter, data to be signed verifier, etc (ETSI, 2003a). Thus, this entity encapsulates for the mobile application/service provider the complexity of the mobile devices and the different methods supported for generating an electronic signature, since the interface that the MSSP provides to the mobile application/service provider is based on web services.

Finally, the mobile application/service provider offers several pervasive solutions that as any moment could need to request the user's signature, e.g. in electronic payments, contract signing, etc. In this case, the mobile application/service provider requests a signature by using the web service provided by the MSSP. Once the MSSP obtains the signature from the mobile device, this is sent as a response to the invocation of the web service.

Until now we have considered that both mobile device and mobile application/service provider are in the network of the same mobile operator. However, in some cases, this is not the case. For these situations the mobile service signature has defined how to make roaming between different MSSP in order to be able to get the signature of a user in another network. Thus, the mobile application/service provider sends the request to its MSSP and this MSSP will send the request to the user's MSSP that will send the request of electronic signature to the mobile device. This task is carried out with the participation of the roaming mobile signature service that is responsible for sending the signature request from the MSSP of one mobile network operator to another MSSP of another different mobile network operator. When the electronic signature is performed, the user's MSSP sends to the (Mobile) Application/Service Provider (MASP)'s MSSP, which in turn, sends it to the MASP. Another way to tackle this problem is for the mobile application/service provider to be connected to different mobile network operators. Then, depending on the user's MNO, the request will be sent to the MSSP from that MNO.

Some of the ideas proposed in this solution have been implemented in the following projects: Mobile Signatures (MoSign) (Manhart, 2001) and Witness(European IST Project Wireless Trust mobile business, 2004). The MoSign project implements mobile signature for a mobile banking application that is based on SIM. The WiTness project provides a certification on demand infrastructure. This infrastructure allows different institutions to certify and enable mobile subscribers to use different services based on signature through the mobile terminal and the SIM. The scenario implemented is used to secure business information transmissions, especially within the corporate information system.

Finally, it is important to point out that a Finnish company named Valimo, Ltd, is offering a mobile signature service that allows the sending of signing requests to mobile phone subscribers by means of an MSS interface. This service is based on the proposal we have just explained in this section. The services provided by Valimo have been adopted by the leading mobile communications providers in both Spain and Turkey (Thomson Reuters, 2008).

The main advantage of this proposal is that the mobile application/service providers do not have to deal with different mobile devices that have different features. Therefore, they can develop signature-based solutions that are agnostic in terms of the mobile technology used in the end users' mobile devices. The MSSP is the entity responsible for coping with this problem. In this solution, the mobile application/service provider can also specify some advanced features in its signing request to the MSSP. These advanced aspects are: the signature format to be used, the data to be displayed to the end user, the format of the data to be signed, etc. Thus, the MSSP is facilitating the configuration of the different options to be used in the signing process to the mobile application/service provider.

On the other hand, this proposal has several drawbacks. First, the participation of a third party that manages the signing process is needed. This party is a Mobile Network Operator or an entity that is much closer to the MNO. Therefore, this limits the usability of the systems to reach agreements with the MNOs. Even more, in order to have a pervasive solution we will need every Mobile Network Operator to support it. They must provide the roaming between different MSSPs. Otherwise, this solution would be limited to users and mobile application/service providers from the same Mobile Network Operator or it would require the mobile application/service provider to work with several Mobile Network Mobile Operators.

Mobile Signature Application Unit

The previously commented solutions propose the generation of mobile signatures based on a third party. However, as mentioned in (Pisko, 2007), the development of mobile technology allows the definition of more efficient architectures of mobile services and applications. As a result of this development, the Mobile Signature Application Unit (MSAU) (Pisko, 2007) proposes an architecture for mobile devices in which the mobile signature service is fully integrated as an application unit in the mobile device. Hence, the MSSP has seen its work reduced to verifying the electronic signature and to providing the different components needed to build applications/services.

As we can see in Figure 6, the main components of this architecture are mobile device, mobile signature application, mobile signature application unit, communication interfaces and mobile service provider.

The mobile service provider exchanges information with the mobile service application that is installed in the mobile device. This exchange is made through a communication interface such as Bluetooth, NFC, 802.11, HTTP, etc. The mobile service application will make use of the MSAU in order to generate the electronic signature. The MSAU accesses to the WIM (see section 3.1.1) to generate this signature. This access is protected by means of a PIN.

Figure 6. Mobile service application architecture

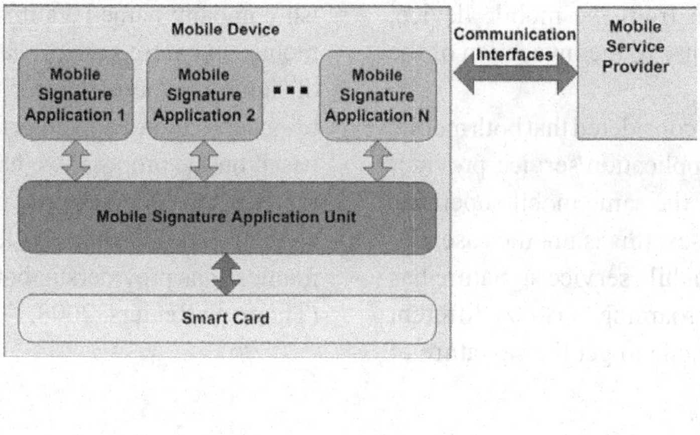

Several mobile service applications can exist at the same time in a device. For the mobile signature application unit to be used with several mobile signature applications, the standardisation of this module is proposed. The authors of MSAU mention that there are two possible ways to standardize this component. First, the standardisation of this module either in the mobile service providers or in a third party. Second, the provision of the mobile signature application unit as a part of the mobile operating system that will be used by the different mobile service applications.

This mobile signature application unit is based on Java Platform, Mobile Edition and SATSA. With SATSA the device is able to communicate with the smart card it has. These technologies (Java ME and SATSA) were already commented in section 3.2.3.

This proposal has two important advantages. First, the electronic signature is generated in a secure device (a WIM) that is under the sole control of the end user. Therefore, the electronic signatures generated with this architecture can be considered legally equivalent to the handwritten signature. Second, it eliminates the participation of a third party in the signature process. Thus, the process is faster because the number of messages and the amount of information to exchange is less.

As main disadvantage we can mention that, at present, there are not many devices that incorporate the use of Java ME with SATSA. Therefore, the number of users that can obtain benefit from this solution are very few. Another problem is related to the standardisation of the mobile signature application unit. At this moment, there is no standardized interface for the MSAU. Thus, the development of pervasive solutions is no easy and can not be extended between different mobile devices. As a result, this limits the development of mobile service applications that can be used in any device.

Comparison

In this section we compare the features of the three mobile signature solutions that we have presented in the previous sections. These features of each solution are summed up in a table (see Table 1), which allows us to compare them easily. The criteria used to compare them were commented at the beginning of this section.

From this table we can derive several conclusions. First, the server-based signatures can not be considered legally equivalent to the handwritten signature, unlike the mobile signature application unit (MSAU). As for Mobile Signature Service (MSS), we can say that it depends on the technology supported by the mobile device. If the solution was based on SATSA and WIM then, it could be considered legally equivalent to the handwritten

Table 1. Feature-based comparison table

Features / Solutions	Asymmetric Cryptography or ECC	Advanced Signature	SSCD	Qualified Signature	Standard Format	Signature based on a Third Party	Complete Verification based on a Third Party	OS-Independent device	MNO-oriented	Research	Industry
Server-based					x	x	x	x		x	
MSS	x	x	x_1	x_1	x_1	x_1	x	x	x	x	x
MSAU	x	x	x	x	x		x	x		x	

Notes: x_1 – It depends on the technology supported by the mobile device.

signature. Furthermore, in this case, the solution would be very similar to the MSAU. Second, in order to perform a complete verification of the signature and validate the certificate the use of a third party is required. Third, there is only one solution that is clearly linked to the mobile network operators, that is, the MSS.

Therefore, we can conclude that the most suitable solutions to build mobile commerce and mobile business services and applications based on mobile signature are MSS and MSAU. The choice between the two solutions will depend on the participation of a mobile network operator in the business model that we follow as well as the different communication technologies that are available in the user's mobile we are working with. Another aspect to take into account in this choice is the independence of the mobile application/ service provider the incorporation of the mobile signature in its applications and services. At this moment, in the MSS solution the interfaces to be used are standardised. However, in the MSAU there is no standardised interface as yet.

CONCLUSION

In mobile business and mobile commerce applications the use of mobile signature is essential to guarantee the non-repudiation of their transactions. Due to this importance, several technologies to provide electronic signature in mobile device have appeared. In this chapter we have reviewed them. As we have seen there are several possibilities that can be used in different ways and with different mobile devices. The fact that there are different solutions and different mobile devices with different features supposes an important problem for those mobile application/service providers that want to offer their services or applications based on mobile signature because they must support an important number of devices and technologies to be used in that solution. As a response to this problem, several mobile signature proposals have

appeared with the purpose of avoiding the mobile application/service provider's having to know the different interfaces and the different mobile devices. In this chapter we have described, analysed in detail and compared them in order to see which mobile signature solutions can provide electronic signatures legally equivalent to the handwritten signature as well as facilitating the development of application based on this technology to the mobile application/service providers. As a result, we can conclude that the mobile signature solutions that can be most suitable for mobile business and mobile commerce are the mobile signature service and the mobile signature application unit. In spite of this fact, there are two main issues open. First, the mobile signature application unit interface should be standardised in order to provide an interoperable solution. Second, the certification validation processes and their interfaces should be clearly defined in order to simplify this task in mobile devices.

REFERENCES

American National Standard Institute. (2005). *X9.62-2005, Public Key Cryptography for the Financial Services Industry, The Elliptic Curve Digital Signature Algorithm (ECDSA).*

Barnés, M. D., Gómez, D. S., Gómez-Skarmeta, A. F., Martínez, M., Ruiz, A., & Sánchez, D. (2005). *An Electronic Signature Infrastructure For Mobile Devices.* Securing Electronic Business Processes. Austria: Vieweg Verlag.

Bicakci, K., & Baykal, N. (2003b). *Design and Performance Evaluation of a Flexible and Efficient Server Assisted Signature Protocol. IEEE 8th Symposium on Computers and Communications.* Turkey: IEEE Press.

Bicakci, K., & Baykal, N. (2004). *SAOTS: A New Efficient Server Assisted Signature Scheme for Pervasive Computing.* 1st International Conference on Security in Pervasive Computing, LNCS No. 2802. Germany.

Bicakci, K., & Baykalb, N. (2005). Improved server assisted signatures. *Journal of Computer Networks, 47*(3), 351-366.

Blake-Wilson, S., Karlinger, G., Kobayashi, T., & Wang,Y. (2005). *Using the Elliptic Curve Signature Algorithm (ECDSA) for XML Digital Signatures.* RFC 4050. http://www.ietf.org/rfc/rfc4050.txt

Campbell, S. (2003). *Supporting Digital Signatures in Mobile Environments.* International Workshop on Enabling Technologies: Infrastructure for Collaborative Enterprises.

Chen, C., Chen, C., Liu, L., & Horng, G. (2007). A server-aided signature scheme for mobile commerce. *In Proceedings of the 2007 international conference on Wireless communications and mobile computing,* (pp. 565-570). Honolulu, Hawaii, USA: ACM.

Dahlberg, T., Mallat, N., Ondrus, J., & Zmijewska, A. (2008). Past, present and future of mobile payments research: A literature review. *Electronic Commerce Research and Applications, 7*(2), 165-181.

Dankers, J., Garefalakis, T., Schaffelhofer, R., & Wright, T. (2002). Public Key Infrastructure in mobile systems. *IEEE Electronics and Communications Engineering Journal, 14*(5), 191-204.

Ding, X., Mazzocchi, D., & Tsudik, G. (2002). *Experimenting with server-aided signatures.* Network and Distributed Systems Security Symposium.

Domingo-Ferrer, J., Posegga, J., Sebe, F., & Torra, V. (2007). Special Issue on Advances in Smart Cards. *Journal of Computer Networks, 51.*

ETSI (2003a). *Mobile Commerce (M-COMM); Mobile Signature Service; Security Framework. TR 102 206.* European Telecommunications Standards Institute (ETSI) Specifications.

ETSI (2003b). *Mobile Commerce (M-COMM); Mobile Signature Service; Business and Functional Requirements.* TR 102 203. European Telecommunications Standards Institute (ETSI) Specifications.

ETSI. (2006). *XML Advanced Electronic Signatures (XAdES).* TS 101 903 v1.3.2. European Telecommunications Standards Institute (ETSI) Specifications.

ETSI. (2007). *CMS Advanced Electronic Signatures (CAdES).* TS 101 733 v1.7.3. European Telecommunications Standards Institute (ETSI) Specifications.

European Committee for Standardization. (2004). *Secure signature-creation devices EAL 4+ in CEN Workshop Agreement (CWA) 14169.* European Committee for Standardization. http://www.cen.eu.

European IST Project Wireless Trust mobile business. (2004).http://www.wireless-trust.org.

European Parliament. (2000). *Directive 1999/93/EC of the European Parliament and the council of December 1999 on a Community framework for electronic signatures.* Official Journal of the European Communities. Belgium.

Fritsch, L., Ranke, J., & Rossnagel, H. (2003). Qualified Mobile Electronic Signatures: Possible, but worth a try? *Information Security Solutions Europe (ISSE) Conference.* Vienna, Austria: Vieweg Verlag.

Gao, J., & Küpper, A. (2006). Emerging Technologies for Mobile Commerce. *Journal of Theoretical and Applied Electronic Commerce Research, 1*(2).

Grillo, A., Lentini, A., Me, G., & Rulli, G. (2008). *Trusted SMS - A Novel Framework for Non-repudiable SMS-based Processes.* In L. Azevedo & A. R. Londral (Eds.), *HEALTHINF,* (1), 43-50. INSTICC - Institute for Systems and Technologies of Information, Control and Communication.

Gürgens, S., Rudolph, C., & Vogt, H. (2005). On the security of fair non-repudiation protocols. *International Journal of Information Security, 4*(4), 253-262.

Haller, N. et al. (1998). *The S/KEY One-Time Password System*. Request For Comments, 2289.

Hassinen, M., Hyppönen, K., & Haataja, K. (2006). An Open, PKI-Based Mobile Payment System. *In Emerging Trends in Information and Communication Security*, (pp. 86-100).

He, L., Zhang, N., He, L., & Rogers, I. (2007). Secure M-commerce Transactions: A Third Party Based Signature Protocol. *In Proceedings of the Third International Symposium on Information Assurance and Security*, (pp. 3-8). IEEE Computer Society.

Housley, R. (2004). *Cryptographic Message Syntax*. RFC 3852.

IAIK - Institute for Applied Information Processing and Communication (2008). *IAIK JCE Micro Edition cryptography library for the Java™ Mobile Edition platform*. http://jce.iaik. tugraz.at/sic/products/mobile_security/jce_me. Accessed on: 25th September 2008.

Malhotra, K., Gardner, S., & Mepham, W. (2008). A novel implementation of signature, encryption and authentication (SEA) protocol on mobile patient monitoring devices. *Technol. Health Care, 16*(4), 261-272.

Manhart, K. (2001). *Mobile digitale Signatur* (pp. 60-61). Germany: Funkschau.

NTRU (2008). *The NTRU Neo for Java*. http://www.ntru.com/products/index.htm. Accesed on: 25th September 2008.

Phaos Micro Foundation (2008). *Cryptographic library fro J2ME CLDC and CDC environments*. http://www.phaos.com/resources/datasheets/pmf_datasheet.pdf. Accessed on: 15th August 2008.

Pisko, E. (2007). Mobile Electronic Signatures: Progression from Mobile Services to Mobile Application Unit. *6th IEEE International Conference on the Management of Mobile Business*. Toronto, Canada: IEEE Computer Society Press.

Rankl, W., & Effing, W. (2004). *Smart Card Handbook* (3° ed., pp. 1120). Wiley.

Rossnagel H. (2004). *Mobile Qualified Electronic Signatures and Certification on Demand*. First European PKI Workshop: Research and Applications, EuroPKI. Samos Island, Greece.

Rossnagel, H., & Royer, D. (2005). *Making Money with Mobile Qualified Electronic Signatures*. *Trust, Privacy and Security in Digital Business*. Lecture Notes in Computer Science, vol. 3592.

RSA Laboratories. (2002). *PKCS #1 v2.1: RSA Cryptography Standard*. ftp://ftp.rsasecurity.com/pub/pkcs/pkcs-1/pkcs-1v2-1.doc.

RSA Laboratories. (1999). *PKCS #12 v1.0: Personal Information Exchange Syntax*. ftp://ftp.rsasecurity.com/pub/pkcs/pkcs-12/pkcs-12v1.doc.

RSA Laboratories. (2000). *PKCS #15 v1.1: Cryptographic Token Information Syntax Standard*. ftp://ftp.rsasecurity.com/pub/pkcs/pkcs-15/pkcs-15v1_1.doc.

RSA Laboratories. (1993). *PKCS #7: Cryptographic Message Syntax Standard*. ftp://ftp.rsasecurity.com/pub/pkcs/ascii/pkcs-7.asc.

Ruiz-Martínez, A., Sánchez-Martínez, D., Martínez-Montesinos, M., & Gómez-Skarmeta, A. F. (2007). A survey of electronic signature solutions in mobile devices. J. Theor. Appl. Electron. Commer. Res., 2(3), 94-109.

Sánchez-Martinez, D., Marín-López, I., & Jiménez-García, T. (2008). *Electronic Document Management in the University of Murcia*. 14th European University Information Systems Conference. EUNIS 2008.

Schneier, B. (1995). Applied cryptography (2nd ed.): protocols, algorithms, and source code in C (pág. 758). John Wiley & Sons, Inc.

Sun Java Specifications. (2007). *Security and Trust Services API for J2ME (SATSA); JSR 177.* http://jcp.org/aboutJava/communityprocess/mrel/jsr177/index.html

Thomson Reuters. (2008). *Turkcell's Award-Winning Mobile Signature Service: Success Powered by Valimo.* http://www.reuters.com/article/pressRelease/idUS125351+25-Jan-2008+PRN20080125. Accessed on: 10th September 2008.

University of Murcia & Telefónica. (2007). *Firma electrónica móvil de actas digitales en la Universidad de Murcia.* Sociedad de la Información, pp 48-49. http://www.socinfo.info/contenidos/pdf-40sep07/p30-50empresas.pdf.

Zhou, J. (2001). *Non-Repudiation in Electronic Commerce* (1º ed., pp. 234). Artech House Publishers.

Zmijewska, A., & Lawrence, E. (2006). *Implementation models in mobile payments.* In Proceedings of the 2nd IASTED international conference on Advances in computer science and technology (págs. 19-25). Puerto Vallarta, Mexico: ACTA Press.

W3C. (2008). *XML Signature Syntax and Processing (Second Edition).* W3C Recommendation. http://www.w3.org/TR/xmldsig-core/.

APPENDIX: GLOSSARY OF ACRONYMS

1999/93/EC	European Directive on Electronic Signature
3G	Third Generation of Mobile Phone Standards and Technology
APDU	Application Protocol Data Unit
API	Application Programming Interface
CA	Certification Authority
CMS	Cryptographic Message Syntax
Crypto SPI	Cryptographic Service Provider Interface
CSP	Cryptographic Service Provider
EAL 4+	Evaluation Assurance Level 4+
ECC	Elliptic Curve Cryptography
ECDSA	Elliptic Curve Digital Signature Algorithm
EEPROM	Electrically Erasable Programmable Read-Only Memory
ETSI	European Telecommunications Standards Institute
GPRS	General Packet Radio Service
GSM	Global System for Mobile communications
HTML	HyperText Markup Language
HTTP	HyperText Transfer Protocol
IPSec	Internet Protocol Security
J2ME	Java 2 Micro Edition
Java ME	Java Mobile Edition
JSR	Java Specification Requests
JSR-177	Security and Trust Services API for J2ME (SATSA)
MAC	Message Authentication Code
MNO	Mobile Network Operator
MoSign	Mobile Signature
MSAP	Mobile Application Service Provider
MSAU	Mobile Signature Application Unit
MSS	Mobile Signature Service
MASP	(Mobile) Application/Service Provider
MSSP	Mobile Signature Service Provider
NFC	Near Field Communication

OS	Operating System
OTA	Over The Air
OTP	One-Time Password
OTS	One-Time Signature
PDA	Personal Digital Assistant
PIN	Personal Identification Number
PKCS	Public-Key Cryptography Standards
PKCS#1	RSA Cryptography Standard
PKCS#7	Cryptographic Message Syntax Standard
PKCS#12	Personal Information Exchange Syntax Standard
PKCS#15	Cryptographic Token Information Syntax Standard
PKI	Public Key Infrastructure
QCSP	Qualified Certificate Service Provider
RA	Registration Authority
ROM	Read Only Memory
SAT	SIM Application Toolkit
SATSA	Security and Trust Services API
SE	Security Element
SIM	Subscriber Identify Module
SMS	Short Message Service
SSCD	Secure Signature Creation Device
SSL/TLS	Secure Sockets Layer / Transport Layer Security
TCP/IP	Transmission Control Protocol / Internet Protocol
TTP	Trusted Third Party
UMTS	Universal Mobile Telecommunications System
USAT	Universal SIM Application Toolkit
USAT-i	Universal SIM Application Toolkit - Interpreter
WIM	Wireless Identification Module
WML	Wireless Mark-up Language
WTLS	Wireless Transport Layer Security
W3C	World Wide Web Consortium

Chapter IX
UbiSrvInt:
A Context–Aware Fault–Tolerant Approach for WP2P Service Provision

Soe-Tsyr Yuan
National Chengchi University, Taiwan

Fang-Yu Chen
AsusTeK Computer Inc., Taiwan

ABSTRACT

Peer-to-Peer applications harness sharing between free resources (storage, contents, services, human presence, etc.). Most existing wireless P2P applications concern merely the sharing of a variety of contents. For magnifying the sharing extent for wireless service provision in the vicinity (i.e., the wireless P2P environments), this chapter presents a novel approach (briefly named UbiSrvInt) that is an attempt to enable a pure P2P solution that is context aware and fault tolerant for ad-hoc wireless service provision. This approach empowers an autonomous peer to propel distributed problem solving (e.g., in the travel domain) through service sharing and execution in an intelligent P2P way. This approach of ad-hoc wireless service provision is not only highly robust to failure (based on a specific clustering analysis of failure correlation among peers) but also capable of inferring a user's service needs (through a BDI reasoning mechanism utilizing the surrounding context) in ad-hoc wireless environments. The authors have implemented UbiSrvInt into a system platform with P-JXTA that shows good performance results on fault tolerance and context awareness.

INTRODUCTION

In recent years, new services have mushroomed all over the web world, and people can easily attain a great number of services from the Internet. A service usually performs in the role of computation facility or information provider. Popular examples include search services, agent services, entertainment services, transaction services, *etc*. Service composition then refers to the technique of creating complex services with the help of smaller, simpler and easily executable lightweight services or components (Chakraborty, 2001). That is, we can handily create novel, interesting and customized services by bundling existing services together to meet the demands of our customers.

On the other hand, mobile devices are in widespread use now, and myriad mobile ad hoc networking technologies (e.g., Bluetooth, IEEE 802.11) unfold dramatically. Clever design of mobile devices includes dramatically reduced size, enlarged storage, economic power consumption and accelerated CPU speed. This design not only improved the performance but also advanced the functionality of the mobile devices. The overwhelming majority of mobile devices launched recently are all capable of supporting wireless Internet access as one of their key features. The next era of network enables the integration of various heterogeneous networks and makes it possible for people to surf between them through different kinds of wireless device anytime, anywhere and anyway. People are striding forward to a completely new Wireless Age.

Accordingly, it can be envisioned that in the forthcoming future everyone (who is walking on the street, dining in the restaurant or working in the office) outfits with hand-held or wearable mobile devices as the standard equipments to access any nearby available network for wanted services. As you move around, a software agent residing in your wireless devices autonomously searches and collects information about what is available from your current location. You may carry with you some useful lightweight services downloaded from the Internet or any wayside provisioning server. You may provide services on hand for nearby people who need them and equally attain desired services from nearby people who possess them. You may, moreover, compose those available wireless services to form an aggregated service tailoring to your contextualized needs, exhibiting moment of values of the services. In other words, the demand to create novel functionalities out of composing wireless services in the vicinity is extremely indispensable.

The aforementioned envisions manifest the significance of the problem of wireless service provision that aims for providing contextualized customized services to meet the concrete needs or requirements of a given client who is equipped with wireless mobile devices by utilizing resources available in its vicinity.

Wireless service provision in the vicinity requires a certain service platform installed at the side of mobile devices. Most existing service platforms (Casati et. Al., 2002) (Mao et. al., 2001) (Mennie et. Al., 2000) (Schuster et. al., 2000) (Gribble et. al., 1999) have been designed on a wired environment that is of high stability and bandwidth, performing against the nature of ad hoc networks. Furthermore, their centralized approaches exerted for service provision have their innate drawback while transplanting them to the wireless environment. The drawback is three-fold:

- **Fault-tolerance:** In centralized architectures, if the server shuts down, everything else does as the server is the central point of failure.
- **Scalability:** The scalability is limited to the capacity of the central server. Should a large amount of requests be addressed to the server, the server easily becomes the bottleneck of traffic.

- **Extensibility:** Centralized architectures are also often hard to expand owing to the limited resources of the central server.

There have been a few published researches (Benatallah et. al., 2002) (Chakraborty et. al., 2002) (Sheng et. al., 2002) addressing the problem using decentralized P2P approach recently. However, when applied to wireless service provision they encountered certain problems mainly resting on the employment of the mediator (broker or coordinator) technique. This hybrid P2P architecture has drawbacks similar to centralized architectures. Exemplars of the hybrid P2P drawback primarily rest on existence of centralized nodes:

- **Quality of wireless connection:** This refers to the poor condition of the connection between mobile devices and the central node (e.g., intermittent disconnection and transmission latency). Information replied from a central node may take too long to reach the mobile device that originates the request. The client subsequently cannot attain the desired information in time, but be bothered by stale and useless information.
- **Real-time information:** Another question is about information updating. Information is unlikely to be always up-to-date on the central node in a dynamically changing environment, such as traffic information.
- **Infeasibility of mobile super peer:** Supposing a super peer in hybrid P2P architectures can be mobile, the aforementioned problem can be partially resolved. However, this leads to other problems. Qualified mobile devices (providing extraordinary computing power, storage capacity and sufficient bandwidth to take charge of a server's duty) are very uncommon in reality. Super-peers, if any, at proper place in proper time are not always reachable from all mobile devices.

Accordingly, (semi) centralized approaches cannot be served as a good solution to compose wireless services on the move. A better solution to wireless service provision is believed to have the duty segmented and delegated to peers (who are willing to and able to execute the proportioned duties, and bringing about the desired properties of salability and extensibility). That is, *a pure P2P solution could be further explored so as to unfold alternative forms of wireless service provision via* mobile ad hoc networking technologies (e.g., Bluetooth, IEEE 802.11).

Yet another inappropriateness of existing decentralized service provision architecture is that they did not take into account the issues of fault tolerance and context awareness. These two issues however are crucial especially dealing with mobile devices within wireless environments. The reasons are two folds: (1) Unreliability of between-peer wireless connection often results in unavailability of services. (2) Mobility of peers often engenders changes in user contexts and accordingly causes different needs. *This chapter aims to provide an approach for P2P mobile service provision, which is not only highly robust to failure but also keenly aware of the surrounding context in wireless environments.*

In this chapter, we present an approach named UbiSrvInt (abbreviation of Ubiquitous Services Integration) that is a pure P2P solution for wireless service provision that has the salient features of fault tolerance and context awareness (that are further described as follows):

- **Fault tolerance:** There are several solutions for handling system failures. The most common way is to re-execute it. It is indeed simple but very inefficient and not applicable in wireless mobile environments. The existing solutions (Chakraborty et. al, 2002) (Dialani et. al., 2002) to this problem for distributed service-based architecture are to employ checkpoints to guard against such faults. However, this method increases the traffic overhead of propagating checking message. It is too complex and only operable while using process-based service description. Such mechanisms adhered to service composition systems primarily rest on post-failure recovery. *In this chapter, a foresighted mechanism is exerted in the approach so as to improve the efficiency by delegating service execution to low-fault correlation peers.* Hence, it can reduce the percentage of failure taking place. Furthermore, the elimination of the central node can make the design of the system immune to single point of failure.

- **Context awareness:** Context awareness refers to the capability of adapting the involved decisions in accordance with the current user context and thus it is one of the most important preferred features from a mobile user's perspective (as mobile situations of the user change over time). In our approach, each peer acts as an autonomous entity whose behavior is governed and adapted by its beliefs, desires and intentions that are captured from user profiles and real-time contextual information in user's vicinity such as time, location, weather and so on. Thereby peers have the ability to reason and help users to get the right services in the right place at the right moment.

We have implemented *UbiSrvInt that is to be installed on each peer so as to realize pure P2P wireless service provision in certain application domains* (e.g., travel services, museum services, *etc.*). With UbiSrvInt functioning at each peer, the peer can avail itself of the available services of the peers in the vicinity, in a self-organized robust intelligent way. *UbiSrvInt is unique in its combined consideration of context awareness and fault tolerance for P2P-based customized service provision in unreliable mobile ad-hoc networks.*

The remainder of this chapter is organized as follows: Section 2 presents the contextualized fault-tolerant approach for P2P mobile service composition. A brief description of the implementation of UbiSrvInt is then provided in Section 3. Section 4 provides the performance evaluation of UbiSrvInt. Finally, Section 5 concludes this chapter with future fruitful research.

UBISRVINT

The UbiSrvInt approach serves as the foundation (equipped in each mobile device) upon which P2P mobile services are discovered, executed, and composed with a pure P2P interaction model. It is a general-purpose approach attempting to support a large cross-section of P2P mobile services. This section is unfolded with a description of the basic concepts (Section 2.1) followed by the detailed descriptions of the approach components (Section 2.2) (but with a strong emphasis on the component that is in charge of fault tolerance as addressed in Section 2.3).

Basic Concepts

The functionalities of the approach can roughly be structured into four layers shown in Figure 1 (a detailed structure of the approach will be shown in

Figure 1. Basic concepts of UbiSrvInt

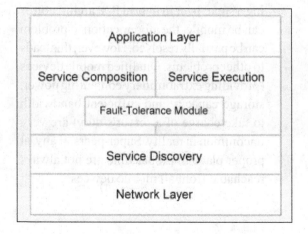

Figure 3). The network layer concerns controlling the routing of messages, masking the differences in characteristics of different transmission and sub-network technologies to provide wireless transparent transfer of data between peers. The service discovery layer is responsible for discovering the inferred services that are available nearby. With above discovered services as the inputs, the service composition layer carries out the integration of those services in a feasible order and ties in with the whole process of discovery. The service execution layer takes charge of the execution of assigned service components to yield services. The top of the approach is the application layer. It encapsulates different GUI facilities to serve as the means for the users to access different composite services.

One of the important characteristics of the approach is the use of a fault-tolerance module that provides capabilities for preventing failures in advance and recovering failures once any component fails. There are many useful ways to improve dependability, however, redundancy is the simplest technique typically employed in P2P systems. *Due to the time criticality feature of the P2P mobile services, physical redundancy is believed to be the most appropriate redundancy approach (as opposed to the time redundancy approach), replicating additional service components so as to assure the continued composite service in case the crash occurring to some of the service components.*

Furthermore, the probability of a wireless mobile peer failing while a transaction is in progress is dependent upon several factors such as network routings, access points, operating system types and releases, device brands, service types, and user behaviors. Therefore, all peers have their respective probability distributions of failures, which may be mutual correlated. *In UbiSrvInt fault tolerance is achieved through dispatching multiple replications of service components to different peers in the vicinity that fail independently.*

Figure 2. Triple component physical redundancy

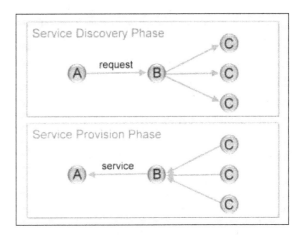

For instance, when peer A subscribes the service produced by peer B, a set of peers that fail with low correlation are delegated to produce the service required by peer A (as shown in Figure 2). In the example of Figure 2 this mechanism provides threefold active replications of the service component to prevent a single component failure. Peer A only interacts with peer B. Peer B handles peer A's request and sends back the service. Meanwhile, peer B replicates the component and dispatches them to peer set Cs. Each peer C executes the allotted component and returns the result of execution to peer B.

There are two possible worlds of exploiting this physical-redundancy concept: (1) The process of service provision may be interrupted because the provider crashes and consequently halts service or the provider omits to respond to incoming requests (as addressed in *fail-silent* (Powell et. al., 1988) or *fail-stop* (Schlichting et. al., 1983)). In this situation the faulty peer stops functioning and produces no ill output. For instance, peer A sends its request to peer B which handles the request and delegates peer set Cs to execute service. Peer B waits only for the first reply and returns it to peer A. (2) Unlike the first situation that assumes all peers are harmless and no incorrect response, the second situation allows the occurrence of the reality where peer sometimes continues to operate but produces wrong results to output (as addressed in *Byzantine faults* (Lamport et. al., 1982), which is obviously more troublesome to deal with). For instance, peer A sends its request to peer B which handles the request and delegates peer set Cs to execute the service. Peer B then acts as voter in this world, picks the majority winner of the three inputs obtained from peer set Cs, and returns the voting result to peer A.

The Architecture of UbiSrvInt

UbiSrvInt is composed of several components (as shown in Figure 3). As follows show what each component does and how the components interact with each other in the architecture: (1) Reasoning Agent collects context information of its surroundings from an external context handling system (e.g., provisioning server or context provider) and a user profile so as to reason rationally for furnishing the user with the tasks of adaptive service requests. (2) Sub-Tasking Agent is responsible for segmenting each task of service request into several subtasks. The sub-tasking information (i.e., the knowledge of the subtasks required to execute a particular task) is presumed to be attained from external systems (e.g., provisioning servers) or other peers. (3) Discovery Agent is in charge of discovering the services conforming to the functionality listed on the subtasks list of Sub-Tasking Agent. (4) Composition Agent receives services acquired by Discovery Agent and integrates them into a composite service in a proper order (based on certain task-related knowledge to perform service composition). (5) Execution Agent then works on service execution that would involve Fault-Tolerance Module (FTM). (6) FTM is the focus of our approach that provides capabilities for preventing failures in advance and recovering failures once any service component fails.

The underlying assumptions behind the approach are three folds: (1) Heterogeneous devices can effortlessly connect to each other through

Figure 3. The picturesque view of the UbiSrvInt infrastructure

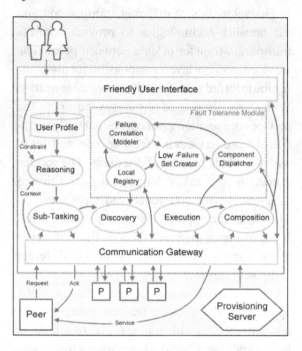

Figure 4. The BDI reasoning process

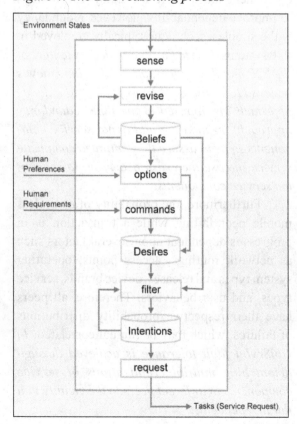

the component of Communication Gateway of the infrastructure. (2) Mobile services can be unfolded on the heterogeneous devices through transformation between different forms. The component descriptions of UbiSrvInt are then detailed in the following subsections.

Reasoning Agent

Reasoning is an implement to achieve the goal of taking possible courses of actions to provide adaptive services. The Reasoning Agent follows the belief-desire-intension (BDI) conception (Bratman et. al., 1988) and is responsible for receiving and interpreting service requests for its user, as shown in Figure 4.

The Reasoning Agent collects *contextual surrounding information* either from an external context handling system (e.g., provisioning server or context provider) or from a user profile in order to reason rationally. The types of context information can be identified into five categories: (1) Environmental contexts (date, time, location, nearby people, weather, light, humidity, altitude, velocity, etc.) (2) Informational contexts (news, traffic, transportation timetable, movie timetable, stock prices, sports scores, weather forecasts, etc.) (3) Personal contexts (sex, age, personality, health, mood, behaviors, schedule, activity, preference, economic status, etc.) (4) Social contexts (relationships, experiences, appointments, community activity, accessible personal contexts of people, etc.) (5) Resource contexts (network bandwidth, status of nearby printers, battery power, available services, etc.)

A variety of different context information can be gathered by external context handling systems (e.g., a sideway provisioning server available at a museum entrance) that often outfit sensors for collecting context information, such as environmental contexts, informational contexts and some resources contexts. As to personal contexts and social contexts, they are sensitive and therefore should be protected from strangers or unfamiliar

friends and thus retained in the user profiles at the side of mobile devices. Such kinds of information are only conveyed between peers according to the level of their relationships in order to keep the privacy of users. The P2P infrastructures enable the possibility of ubiquitous computing of all kinds of context information in contrast to a centralized approach, such as Client-Server infrastructures.

From the aspect of peers, the various context information is gained from outside except personal contexts, hence we generally called them *environment states* to distinguish from the contexts gained from inside. We assume that the state of a peer's environment can be characterized as a set of *environment states* $S = \{s_1, s_2, ...\}$. At any moment, the environment is in one of these states. The function *sense* represents the peer's ability to observe its environment and attain the environment information, outputting a percept. The perception of the peer is assumed to be represented by a non-empty set $P = \{p_1, p_2, ...\}$ of *percepts*. The *sense* function subsequently is formulated as follows:

sense: $S \rightarrow P$,

which maps environment states to percepts. The environment information is regarded as a true *belief* of the peer that will change over time. Let *Bel* be the set of all possible beliefs and the peer's belief revision function is a mapping that determines a new set of beliefs from the current percept and current beliefs:

revise: $\wp(Bel) \times P \rightarrow \wp(Bel)$

Note that the symbol $\wp$ denotes the powerset, the set of possible subsets, of any given set.

The user can directly invoke specific service requests with certain constraints or conditions. The requirements made by the user are defined as a set *Hr* of *human requirements*. Let *Des* be the set of all possible desires. The peer's *desire* can then be directly declared as shown in the *commands* function that receives the requirements from the user and then output the desires:

commands: $Hr \rightarrow \wp(Des)$.

Alternatively, the peer's desire can be indirectly derived from the user profile information. That is, Reasoning Agent can attain the information of the user's *preference* from the User Profile. The user's preference is defined as a set *Hp* of *human preferences*. Reasoning Agent subsequently can infer what the *options* available to the user are when there is no clear and definite instruction from outside. The option generation function, *options*, maps a set of human preferences and a set of beliefs to a set of desires:

options: $\wp(Bel) \times \wp(Hp) \rightarrow \wp(Des)$

The chosen options or commands become intentions, which then constitutes the formal service requests. Intentions are then fed back into the agent's future practical reasoning. Let *Int* be the set of all possible intentions. In order to make the final decision, the Reasoning Agent's deliberation process is represented in the *filter* function:

filter: $\wp(Bel) \times \wp(Des) \times \wp(Int) \rightarrow \wp(Int)$

which updates the agent's intentions on the basis of its previously-held intentions and current beliefs and desires. As the result of deliberating, it infers user's *intension* and outputs it as a formal service request for Sub-Tasking Agent. The service requests are regarded as *tasks*, which will be allocated afterward. The generated tasks are defined as a set of *tasks T*. The *request* function is assumed to simply return any executable intentions in a priority:

request: $\wp(Int) \rightarrow T$,

in which each intention is correspondent to a directly executable task. The state of Reasoning Agent at any given moment is, deservedly, a triple (B, D, I), where $B \subseteq Bel$, $D \subseteq Des$, and $I \subseteq Int$.

Sub-Tasking Agent

Sub-Tasking Agent receives the task information from Reasoning Agent and subsequently decides how to segment the task appropriately. That is, Sub-Tasking Agent is responsible for dividing a generic task into several subtasks.

Sub-Tasking Agent attains the sub-tasking information (i.e., the different subtasks required to execute a particular task) from an external system, such as Provisioning Server or other peers. We assume that the task-related knowledge can be characterized as a set *Kh* of all given *know-how* about sub-tasking a task. Subsequently, it generates a subtask list served as the input to Discovery Agent. Let *Ts* be the set of all possible subtasks, in which ts_i denotes *subtask* i of task *T*. The generated subtask list is represented as

$$T = [ts_1, ts_2, ts_3, ..., ts_N]$$

The service sub-tasking function, *decompose*, of the Sub-Tasking Agent is a function

decompose: $T \times \wp(Kh) \rightarrow \wp(Ts)$,

which maps the current task and corresponding know-how to determine a feasible set of subtasks.

There are two possibilities for the Sub-Tasking Agent to execute *decompose* function. The first situation is that Sub-Tasking Agent gets internal service request from Reasoning Agent. This kind of service requests will then be considered as initiating tasks. The other situation is that Sub-Tasking Agent works on task decomposition for external service request from other peers. In this situation it is Reasoning Agent that should decide whether the request can be handled or not. The factors that affect this decision are as follows: *user settings, remaining power, resource capabil-*

ity (e.g. computing capability, available storage, bandwidth, etc.), and number of tasks in hand. The capability of each peer can be represented as a capability vector *CV* of the form

$$\aleph \equiv CV(e_1, e_2, ..., e_M), e_i \in [0,1]$$

using the symbol $\aleph$, in which e_i denotes the standard normalized score of factor i. Let *J* be the set of two possible results of judgment, yes or no. Then the function *judge* is a mapping

$$judge: T \times \aleph \to J, J \in \{0,1\}$$

If the judgment result is positive, Sub-Tasking Agent will perform decomposition of the external service request to generate subtasks. Afterward, Composition Agent will execute the partial composition of those subtasks, which is introduced later.

Discovery Agent

In a WP2P environment mobile peers can share with each other nearby myriad types of resources (e.g., storage, cycles, contents, services and human presence). The locations of nearby peers are represented by a set of *peer locations* $L = \{l_1, l_2, ...\}$. Since peers can join and leave the environment at any time, the unpredictable movement makes resources discovering a challenge.

In this research services are the primary resource type concerned for the purpose of wireless service provision. A service is referred as the execution result of a service component of a peer. Let *Srv* be the set of all possible services. Discovery Agent is responsible for discovering the services conforming to the functionalities listed in a subtasks list $[ts_1, ts_2, ts_3, ..., ts_N]$. The service discovery function, *lookup*, of Discovery Agent is a mapping as follow:

$$lookup: Ts \to \wp(L),$$

in which Discovery Agent gets relevant peer location information from Local Register. The detail of Local Register will be described later. The service acquirement function, *acquire*, is a mapping as follows:

$$acquire: Ts \times L \to Srv,$$

which attains a service (i.e., just a look-up) via a remote call to an external nearby peer. The service will subsequently be delivered to Composition Agent immediately.

Composition Agent

Composition Agent is responsible for managing the order of integration of the discovered services. It receives services acquired by Discovery Agent and integrates them into a composite service in a proper order. Like Sub-Tasking Agent, Composition Agent requires task-related knowledge to perform service composition. The composite service is represented by a set named *CSrv* of *composite services*. The service composition function, *compose*, is now a function

$$compose: \wp(Srv) \to CSrv,$$

which produces an aggregate service from several pieces of input services.

Execution Agent

The Execution Agent as implied by its name is responsible for service execution. The process involves the FTM, which is the core of UbiSrvInt (and will be detailed in Section 3). If a peer plays the role of a service dispatcher as the peer B shown in Figure 2, it invokes Service Dispatcher to send a service component to peers (that fail independently) and waits for the result. On the other hand, if the peer plays the role of a service component receiver (as any peer in the peer set Cs shown in Figure 2), it executes the assigned component and returns its result to the dispatcher peer.

Peers that receive the same component executes works in parallel and return their results as soon as possible in order to save time. Because the receiver peers are failure independent to each other the dispatcher peer is supposed to get one result at least. The service provisioning function, *provision*, of the Execution Agent of receiver peers is a simple function

provision: $Ts \rightarrow Srv$,

which returns the execution result of a subtask as a service is sent to the one of dispatcher peers.

FAULT-TOLERANCE MODULE

The Fault-Tolerance Module (FTM) is the core mechanism of our approach. The main idea of the module is inspired by Introspective Failure Analysis (Weatherspoon et. al., 2002), which presumed that the probability of a component failing is independent of the duration of the coordination in progress, that all components have an identical probability of failure, and that components fail independently. However, their assumptions cannot faithfully reflect the reality (i.e., failures are often correlated) and will be relaxed in this paper.

FTM is composed of four parts (as shown in Figure 5): (1) Local Registry keeps monitoring nearby peers in order to collect such information as peer locations, user characters, device brands and types, operating system types and releases, access control settings, *etc*. (2) Failure Correlation Modeler draws upon peer user information of several failure dimensions to develop models that perform time-series prediction of the failure correlation among *peer types*. (A peer type is a tuple enumerating peer properties from three different dimensions including *human sources, software version*, and *hardware environment*. These dimensions directly affect the availability and reliability of a peer.) (3) Low-Failure Set

Figure 5. Fault-tolerance module (FTM) architecture

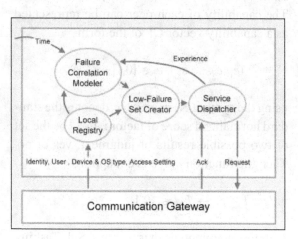

Creator receives as input the failure correlation model from Failure Correlation Modeler and produces the dispatch sets (of mutually highly failure-uncorrelated peers) using the most recent peer list recorded by Local Registry. (4) Service Dispatcher is responsible for delegating a service request to each peer listed in the dispatch set and waits for signed acknowledgement. Service Dispatcher records experience about the process of coordination and supply this information to Failure Correlation Modeler so as to refine the failure correlation model.

The main idea behind FTM is exerting physical redundancy for fault tolerance and fulfilled by a replication mechanism that mainly comprises two tasks: (1) the determination of a number of peer candidates for duplicating a service (enabled by the parts of Local Registry, Failure Correlation Modeler and Low-Failure Set Creator) (2) the execution of the replication process (enabled by the part of Service Dispatcher). The details of FTM's four main parts will then be detailed in Section 3.1-3.4.

Local Registry

Local Registry is responsible for monitoring peers in the vicinity. The information collected includes peer identity, user information, device brands and types, operating system types and releases, and access settings. We assume that the identities of nearby peers can be represented by a set *PI* of *peer identity* and the access settings of the peers can be represented by a set *PA* = {L, M, H}[1] of *peer access setting*. Through a user's access setting UbiSrvInt is able to know if a user is willingness level to host a specified function. Access settings are of three different levels: (1) low: willing to provide available services that it has on hand to the request peer automatically anytime; (2) medium: allowing only familiar or trusty peers to access the available services; (3) high: ignoring all requests the user has received and thus any forms of service provisioning are disabled.

Local Registry accordingly produces a list of nearby[2] peers, which is represented by a set *PL* of all possible peer entries. The monitor function is formulated as follows:

$$monitor - vicinity: \wp(PI) \times \wp(PT) \times \wp(PA) \to PL,$$

in which *PT* represents the peer type which is the combination of several peer attributes. The ideas of peer type will be introduced in the following sections.

Failure Correlation Modeler

Failure Correlation Modeler takes charge of building compact models in order to group highly correlated peers together. *Evolution* and *sharing* are the two distinctive properties:

- **Evolution:** It is imperative for failure correlation models to learn, adapt and grow toward maturity in a kind of continuous fashion rather than merely a one-shot experience. Fortunately, continued on-line data stream perfectly plays as the training examples to evolve the failure correlation models over time. What remains to require is an incre-

mental on-line learning algorithm that can process the on-line data so as to develop and then evolve the failure correlation models incrementally.

- **Sharing:** P2P communication enhances and glorifies the network effect through resources sharing. To make the best use of that, the models built by Failure Correlation Modeler is gifted with the feature of sharing. The models are constantly evolving and conveying themselves between peers to achieve the objective of Semi-Global so as to enable effective service provision. More details will be described afterward.

To cope with the required evolutionary property, the primary task of Failure Correlation Modeler is modeled as a time-series problem. The highly correlated peers exhibit similar temporal patterns scattering along various time frames. Hence similar series of input data that have a similar failure distribution will be clustered together. This time-series problem is then unfolded with the descriptions of its data sequence, pattern matching and clustering analysis as shown below.

Data Sequences

A task (service request) that has been assigned to a dispatched peer is called a *mission*. The charge of the dispatched peer is producing a service. Assuming that the outcome *o* of a mission is represented by 0 or 1 where 0 and 1 represent the outcomes of success and failure respectively:

$$o = \begin{cases} 0, success \\ 1, failure \end{cases}$$

A series of mission outcomes from a dispatched peer is regarded as an *experience*, which is the object of study addressing this problem. The time series data, *experience*, consist of a sequence of *N* observed pairs,

$$E_{peer} \equiv (o_i, t_i), i = 1, 2, ..., N$$

where o_i denotes the measured value of the *mission outcome* at *time* t_i and E denotes the set of experience.

A peer has several experiences corresponding to the number of the dispatched peers it has interacted. A peer classifies different experiences systematically according to different dispatched peers.

Sliding Windows

We divide the time period of the inputted time series data into fixed size units. In other words, a divided segment is an aggregate of successive time. Each segment could be visualized as a sliding window, whose size is twenty-four hours. We then subdivide the segment into smaller equal parts. Each divided equal part is called a *time slot* as shown in Figure 6.

For each time slot, we calculate *failure probability* in order to analyze failure correlation between different peers in different time periods. Supposed that the *number of experiences* (the number of outcomes) of each service request in a time slot is N_o, the failure probability of the time slot is then represented by P:

$$P_{peer} = f(t) = \frac{\sum_{i=1}^{N_o} O_i}{N_o},$$

where $\sum_{i=1}^{N_o} O_i$ denotes the total number of the failure occurrences in experiences of a specific dispatched peer in the time slot. Thus, a failure curve can be derived through counting failure probabilities of each time slot within a same sliding window. For different dispatched peers, the corresponding failure curves are preserved for further analysis.

In this research we use a time scale of *day* in our analysis to predict the failure correlation. The time series data segmented by the time scale of day is called *day-patterns*, which is represented by a set *DP* of all possible day-patterns. UbiSrvInt preserves a day-pattern for each peer. The newly attained experience will be used to refine the original day-pattern into a more updated day-pattern. The simplest way to get the new day-pattern is to average the data. The function of refinement day-pattern, *refine-day-pattern*, is formulated as follows:

$$refine - day - pattern\colon E \to DP$$

Enhanced Day-Pattern Matching

Data sequence matching finds those sequences that are similar to one other, which is useful for the analysis of failure correlation among peers. Accordingly, Fault-Correlation Modeler aims to locate peers that mutual correlated along the time axis. It is assumed that the fault-correlated peers have similar shapes of day-pattern in the space constructed by a vertical axle of failure

Figure 6. Sliding windows

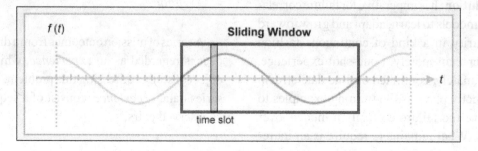

probability and a transverse axle of time. The similarity matching is then performed by computing the distance between sequences in the time domain.

Unlike common distance measures (e.g., Euclidian), a distance measure suitable for FTM has to be invariant of gaps, offsets and amplitudes. For instance, there are four day-patterns, A, B, C, and D shown in Figure 7. B and C as well as A and D exhibit the same tendency at the same time. Obviously, B has the higher failure correlation with C than that with A or D although B is of the closest distance to A (instead of C). Therefore, an *enhanced similarity* search method (Agrawal et. al., 1995) is necessary for matching pairs of subsequences *if they are of the same shape, but differ due to the presence of gaps (Figure 8(a)) within a sequence or differences in offsets (Figure 8(b)) or amplitudes (Figure 8(c)).*

Peer Types Grouping

Rather than analyzing failure correlations among peers in the real network environment, we profile *peer types* that enable the analysis of a more abstract level. This is more tractable because it greatly reduces the number of targets needed to be analyzed and clustered. We divide all peers into several groups according to their major properties. Three dimensions of properties for grouping peers are employed (and we believe these properties are staple sources of failure): (1) *User behavior*: Mobile devices are easily damaged from rough usage of users. On the other hand, human characteristics are believed to influence a user's behavior somehow. Therefore, it is possible that the characters of a user would correlate closely with the failure of her or his mobile device. Hence, we select *user characters* to be the first dimension of peer type, which includes constellation, blood type, age, sex and occupation, *etc. (2) Software*: Software is another factor causing failures. There are many kinds of software installed in a mobile device but the most likely reason for a system

Figure 7. Example of day-patterns

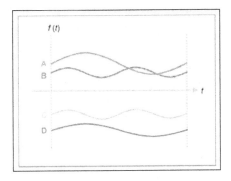

Figure 8. Enhanced similarity

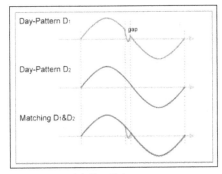

(a) Gap Existence

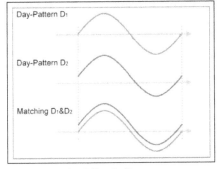

(b) Offset Difference

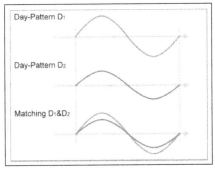

(c) Amplitude Difference

to fail is always because of its operating system (OS). Therefore, we select *OS names and versions* to be the second dimension of peer type. (3) *Hardware*: No doubt a breakdown of hardware will definitely cause failures and interrupt service provisioning immediately. Equipment failure is the most basic one of our concerns. Accordingly, we select *device brands and types* to be the final dimension of peer type.

The *peer type* can be represented as an attribute vector *PT* of the form as follows:

$$\Im \equiv PT(f_{user}, f_{os}, f_{device}),$$

where f_{user}, f_{os}, and f_{device} denotes the values of nominal variables, user characters, OS types and releases, and device brands and types.

Clustering Analysis

The objective is to merge similar day-patterns of peer types into clusters. Supposing *M* denotes the number of peer types. For each peer type, its day-pattern is being collected continuously. Accordingly, *M* sequences of day-patterns are summarized and each day-pattern P_j (*j=1,2...,M*) consists of a sequence of pairs shown below:

$$(p_{ij}, t_i), i = 1, 2, ..., N, j = 1, 2, ..., M,$$

where p_{ij} denotes the *failure probability* of peer type *j* at time t_i that has elapsed since midnight.

The clustering process starts with computing the mutual distances between all day-patterns, and ends with a pre-defined number of clusters formed. The two day-patterns which are most similar will be merged to a new day pattern. Such merging process is repeated until a pre-defined number of clusters are generated. The final day-patterns then become the clusters.

The distance measure employed should be invariant to offset and amplitude as addressed in Figure 8. Suppose that we have two day-patterns y_i and z_i, i = 1, ..., N. Combining the root-mean-square distance measure with *offset translation* and *amplitude scaling*, resulting in a distance normalization measure:

$$d_{nvm} = \frac{\sqrt{\sum \left(\frac{y_i - y_{min}}{y_{max} - y_{min}} - \frac{z_i - z_{min}}{z_{max} - z_{min}} \right)^2}}{N}$$

which can aid clustering patterns of similar shapes. The higher the value of the measure is, the higher failure correlation the two day-patterns have. The function of the complete distance normalization measure, *enhanced-distance-counting*, is then formulated as follows:

$$enhanced - distance - counting: DP_i \times DP_j \rightarrow D,$$

in which *D* denotes the distance between pair of day-patterns.

A number of methods can be used in clustering day-patterns, such as local k-means clustering, evolving clustering method (ECM) (Song et. al., 2001), evolving self organizing maps (ESOMs) (Deng et. al., 2000), or any other incremental distance-based clustering methods. The model produced by Failure Correlation Modeler is represented by a set *M* of all possible models. The *incremental-online-clustering* function is formulated as follows:

$$incremental - online - clustering: D \rightarrow M.$$

Semi-Global

When a new peer connects to the wireless service network (e.g. a new PDA user), it can rely on the experiences of other peers in the vicinity so as to promptly accommodate itself to the unfamiliar environment. Even though at the commencement of the whole service network where peers have only few experiences, peers can still gather these few experiences together to constitute a more reliable model and share.

Failure Correlation Modeler communicates with other ones so as to exchange models among peers. The collected models will be merged into a coherent model that will be then conveyed to other Failure Correlation Modelers. *The nearby peers can share the Semi-Global models in order to build a more precise Low-Failure set and prevent failure.*

Low-Failure Set Creator

Low-Failure Set Creator is responsible for creating dispatch sets grouping mutually highly failure uncorrelated peers together. The dispatch set is represented by a set *PS* of all possible peers. It uses the failure correlation models to choose several peer types that have the lowest probability of correlated failures. Subsequently, it attains a list of peers (registered in Local Registry) in which the most suitable peers for the chosen peer types can be selected. The *set-creating* function is formulated as follows:

$$set-creating: m \times PL \rightarrow PS.$$

Component Dispatcher

Component Dispatcher is in charge of delegating a specific service request to each peer listed in the dispatch set and waits for all acknowledgements from the service request receivers. If some of them are of no response, Component Dispatcher will send unacknowledged service request again to the other peers on the dispatch sets to ensure the dispatch is effective, realizing physical redundancy of fault tolerance.

Algorithm 2. Local registry

```
function LOCAL-REGISTRY (pt, pi, pa) returns a peer list
input:   pt, the peer type
         pi, identity of the peer
         pa, access setting of the peer
static:  pl, nearby peer list

pl ← MONITOR-VICINITY(pt, pi, pa)
return pl
```

Algorithm 3. Failure correlation modeler

```
function FAILURE-CORRELATION-MODELER(e, pt) returns a model
input:  pt, the peer type
        e, the experience
static: d, the distance between two day-patterns
        m, failure correlation model
        dp, day-pattern of any peer type

dp←REFINE-DAY-PATTERN(e)
for each peer type i do
        for each other peer type j do
                d←ENHANCED-DISTANCE-COUNTING(dp_i, dp_j)
        end
end
m←INCREMENTAL-ONLINE-CLUSTERING(d)
return m
function ENHANCED-DISTANCE-COUNTING (e_i, e_j) returns a distance
input: e_i, the experience of peer type i
       e_j, the experience of peer type j
static: d, the distance between two day-patterns

for   e_i and e_j do
      e←OFFSET-TRANSLATION(e)
      e←AMPLITUDE-SCALING(e)
end
d←DISTANCE-COUNTING(e_i, e_j)
return d
```

Algorithm 4. Low-failure set creator

```
function LOW-FAILURE-SET-CREATOR (m, pl) returns a dispatch set
input:  m, failure correlation model
        pl, nearby peer list
static: ps, a set of mutual highly uncorrelated peer

for each peer on the peer list do
        if the access control of the peer is low then
                ps←SET-CREATING(m, pl)
        end
return ps
```

Algorithm 5. Component dispatcher

```
function COMPONENT-DISPATCHER (ps) returns an experience
input:  ps, a set of mutual low failure correlated peer
static: e, the experience
        t, time
        o, mission outcomes

for each peer set do
        loop do
            WAKEUP-PEER()
            WAITING-ACK()
            if get ack before timeout then
                Dispatch-Component()
            if the dispatch number > the minimum limit then exit
        end
end
while not timeout do
        o ← GET-OUTCOME-REPORT()
        t ← GET-TIME()
loop
e ← REFINE-FAILURE-PROBABILITY(o, t)
return e
```

149

With the aforementioned descriptions of the FTM module, the overall processes of the module are then outlined by the following pseudo-codes (Algorithms 2-5).

IMPLEMENTATION

UbiSrvInt is implemented with the technology of JXTA (http://www.jxta.org) going with Personal Java that works for handheld devices such as iPAQ. JXTA is a modular platform that provides simple and essential building blocks for developing a wide range of distributed services and applications. Both centralized and de-centralized services can be developed on top of the JXTA platform. JXTA services can be implemented to interoperate with other services giving rise to new P2P applications. The overall operations of UbiSrvInt are to be depicted by a use case diagram and an activity diagram (represented in UML) as shown in the Appendix (Figure A1 & A2).

Ontologies are also extensively utilized in UbiSrvInt for capturing myriad types of resources and knowledge (context information, user and device profiles, composition knowledge and reasoning rules). Resource Description Framework (RDF) / Resource Description Framework Schema (RDFS) is employed to represent the ontologies in order to preserve the semantics of the above-mentioned resources. In our implementation Jena (http://www.hpl.hp.com/semweb/jena.htm), a full-featured Java API, is exerted to create and manipulate the RDF graphs required.

For a better understanding of the aforementioned resources and knowledge, as follows are the exemplar representations employed in the parts of Reasoning Agent, Sub-Tasking Agent and Fault-Tolerance Module.

Reasoning Agent

In order to provide users with personalized and contextualized service, a user intention reasoner is implemented conforming to the BDI conception. The knowledge involved in the BDI reasoning includes user profile, context information, and reasoning rules (that are subsequently represented with RDF graphs[3]).

The *resource*, user, is shown as an ellipse and is identified by a Uniform Resource Identifier (URI), in Figure 9 "http://....../user". Resources have several *properties* represented by arcs, labeled with the names of properties. There

Figure 9. User profile in a RDF graph

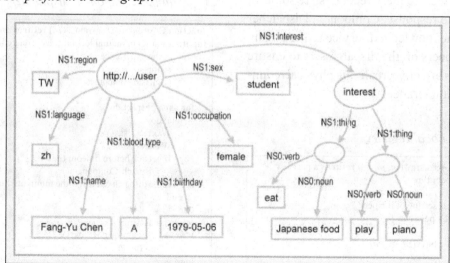

are eight properties in this case. The name of a property is also a URI, but as it is rather long and cumbersome, the following diagrams show it only in a brief form. A property is compound by two parts, a namespace prefix and a local name in the namespace. Every property has a value which is either a *literal* shown in each rectangle or a resource shown in each ellipse. RDF can take other resources as their value as the "interest" in this case for instance. Here we use a combination of two properties, NS0:verb and NS0:noun, to represent the structure of user's preferences, "interest".

Figure 10. Context information represented with a RDF graph

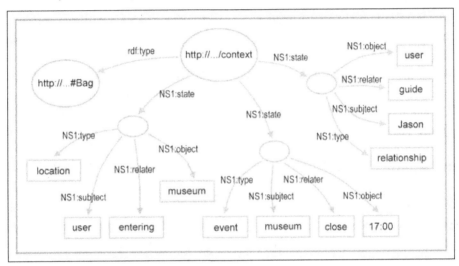

Figure 11. Reasoning rules in a RDF graph

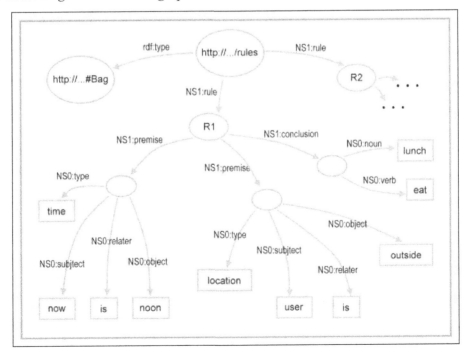

(<Verb> <Noun>)

Note that each property NS1:thing of resource "interest" is a *blank node* since it has no specific name.

Ranganathan's Context Model (Ranganathan et. al., 2003) is used to describe the context information captured from the surrounding of user. Each clausal model of context is presented in a tuple of the form: (*<ContextType> <Subject> <Relater> <Object>*) similar to English sentence. A simple exemplar is shown in Figure 10 in the format of RDF graph.

As to the BDI reasoning rules, the same expressions are used to represent the premises and conclusions of a single rule, which is exemplified as shown in Figure 11.

Sub-Tasking Agent

Subtask Agent decomposes a required service by user into several pieces of subtasks and then integrates the received pieces of services to fulfill

this service request. The service, i.e. task, decomposition knowledge used here is also described using RDF document.

RDF defines a special kind of resources for representing collections of things. These resources are called *containers*. In Figure 12, we use a specific kind of container, *BAG*, to represent an unordered collection of the decomposition knowledge. In this case, the resources is named "http://....../knowhow", having an rdf:type property whose value is rdf:Bag, "http://......#Bag". In this case, the two members of the bag are represented by the property NS0:task. The ordering of properties is not significant in a bag. Hence we could switch the values between two properties and the resulting graph would represent the same information.

Fault-Tolerance Module

Fault-Tolerance Module plays a critical role in service providing. It determines the dispatched peer lists by calculating the failure correlation

Figure 12. Decomposition knowledge in a RDF graph

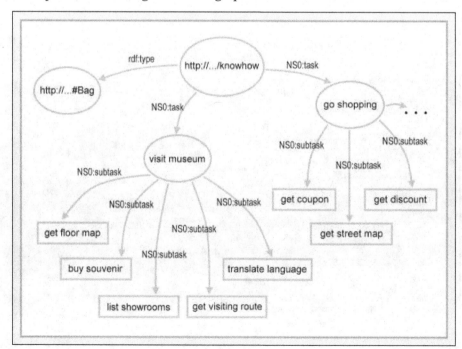

Figure 13. Handheld device profile in a RDF graph

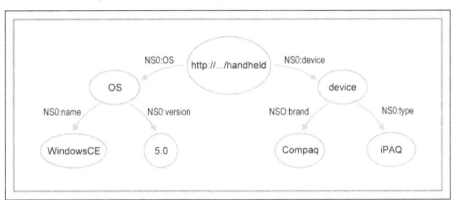

between different peer types, thus to create low failure correlation peer sets for service dispatching. Peers are grouped into different peer types regarding three dimensions: user characters, OS name and version, and device brand and type. Again, the knowledge of user profile and handheld device profile are described and stored in RDF forms as shown in Figure 9 and Figure 13.

On the other hand, in Fault-Tolerance Module we do not exert a sophisticated incremental clustering method since what we emphasis in the experiments is the fault-tolerance mechanism. A combination of the *k*-means clustering (Hartigan et. al., 1979) and a data compression technique (Chen et. al., 2004) is employed to effectuate the incremental clustering method.

The objects of the clustering method are day-patterns, and naturally are the targets of the data compression. The rationale of the data compression is simply to merge the experiences attained from outside into a compact data set, i.e. the day-pattern model. By this way, the clustering time can be effectively shortened by restraining the size of primitive clustering data in preparation. Also, the features of data can be preserved in a good condition at the same time. The day-pattern model is learning and adapting itself over time to evolve toward maturity.

EVALUATION RESULTS

Owing to the limitation of space, in this chapter the evaluations of UbiSrvInt are two folds: fault tolerance and context awareness. In this section, the performance of UbiSrvInt on fault tolerance will be furnished. As to context awareness of UbiSrvInt, small demo scenarios (as shown in Section 5.4) are exerted to show the functionality of UbiSrvInt on context awareness (as the precision of the reasoning is completely dependant on domain-specific knowledge and thus it is negligible to evaluate the reasoning precision). Those demo scenario depicts the vision of ad-hoc wireless service provision that provides personalized and contextualized tourist services according to a user's profile and his/her surrounding context. For complete details of the demo scenarios, please see (Chen et. al., 2004).

Since UbiSrvInt is unique in its capability of fault tolerance (as far as as-hoc wireless service provision is concerned), this section aims to investigate if the idea of FTM is feasible in WP2P service sharing networks.

- We first need to *justify that the benefit of the replication mechanism (physical redundancy of fault tolerance) devised and provided by FTM is greater than the overhead*

153

it generates. We also need to *find proper values of the replication factor (k – the dispatch number per request) to meet acceptable levels of availability and to avoid unnecessary high cost.*

- We then *examine if the Semi-Global mechanism indeed brings into full play the synergy of experience sharing of peers and make a decisive contribution to the success of FTM.*

For the aforementioned attempted investigations, several metrics are exerted to measure the overall service performance and overhead of UbiSrvInt. Performance is measured by *solvability* and *efficiency* of services. Overhead is then measured primarily by *load* along three dimensions: *network traffic, processing cost,* and *clustering cost.* The detailed explanation and calculation of these metrics are shown below:

- **Performance:** *Performance is generally regarded as the overall throughput of completed services that peers provide through time.* A service is defined as a task, which can be decomposed into several subtasks, i.e. lightweight services. A service is considered successful only if it is through a complete successful process of discovery, execution and integration of all the subtasks. We look at throughput from two perspectives:
  - *Service Solvability* is measured in the services success rate, which represents the effectiveness of the system. The success rate is defined as the percentage of successful services through time.

$$Service\ Solvability = \frac{Cumulative\ number\ of\ successful\ services}{Cumulative\ number\ of\ requested\ services}$$

- *Service Efficiency* is measured in the reciprocal of the service response time per successful service. For a successful service, we define the service response time as the time between when a formal request message is sent and when the first reply message of the request is received.

$$Service\ Efficiency = \frac{Cumulative\ number\ of\ successful\ services}{\sum(The\ time\ service\ received - The\ time\ service\ requested)}$$

- **Load:** *Load is conceptually regarded as the amount of efforts that peers must engage for attaining successful results.* One factor concerned in load measurement in networks is the flow of messages exchanged. Besides, the processing cost of service requests and the processing cost of clustering analysis are also considered. In examining the amount of efforts that peers must engage for attaining successful results, three perspectives are then unfolded to formulate the load measurements:
  - *Network traffic* is measured by counting the number of message sent by peers to the network. An overhead of network traffic incurred by peers with respect to the total resulting successful services is then defined as follows:

$$Relative\ Network\ Traffic = \frac{Cumulative\ number\ of\ forwarded\ messages}{Cumulative\ number\ of\ successful\ services}$$

- *Processing cost* is conceptually measured in the number[4] of subtasks executed by peers. An overhead of processing cost incurred by peers with respect to the total resulting successful services is defined as follows:

$$\text{Relative Processing Cost} = \frac{\text{Cumulative number of executed subtasks}}{\text{Cumulative number of successful services}}$$

○ *Clustering cost* is measured by calculating the total time spent on the core process of FTM, clustering analysis. An overhead of clustering cost incurred with respect to the total resulting successful services is defined as follows:

$$\text{Relative Clustering Cost} = \frac{\text{Cumulative time spent on clustering}}{\text{Cumulative number of successful services}}$$

The remainder of this section is unfolded as follows: (1) We first describe the parameters of the experiment setting, followed by a description of the experiment process (Section 4.1) (2) The feasibility analysis of FTM in UbiSrvInt is provided in Section 4.2. (3) The examination of the effect of the Semi-Global mechanism is then furnished in Section 4.3. Discussions of the performance of UbiSrvInt on fault tolerance will be then interspersed in the respective subsections.

Experiment Settings

The performance of FTM is affected by a wide range of parameters. We divide these parameters into global parameters and local parameters. A quick look at these parameters is shown Table 1.

Global parameters describe the background of environment used for running several miniature peers from a macro point of view. They are application dependent environment constants, which include the number of peers in the network, the total number of unique services that can be provided in the network, and the average

Table 1. Experimental parameters

Parameter	Value	Description
$T_{simulation}$	2 hr.	Total simulation time
$S_{network}$	20	Total network size
$\lambda_{mobility}$	0.02	Leave (Join) rate per peer per minutes
$S_{service}$	10	Total size of service space
$N_{subtask}$	4	Average number of subtask of a service
$S_{capacity}$	20	Service capacity per peer
$\lambda_{request}$	0.2	Request rate per peer per minute
$R_{choosing}$	0.1	Request choosing rate. ($R_{choosing} = 1/S_{service}$)
k		Dispatch number per request
λ	$[0, \lambda_{max}]$	Failure rate per peer per minute
λ_{repair}	2	Repair rate per peer per minute
T_{wait}	40 sec.	Respond timeout
$T_{abandon}$	4 min.	Service timeout
S_{window}	24 hr.	Size of sliding window
S_{slot}	1 hr.	Size of time slots in sliding windows

number of subtasks that must be done for a single service, *etc*.

On the other hand, local parameters are parameters specific to the functionalities of UbiSrvInt; the values of the parameters may differ from peer to peer. These parameters describe the behaviors of peer, which include the storage capacity of services for each peer, the average time to request for a service per peer, and the average time of failure and recovery of a peer, *etc*.

Due to space limitation, we only explain certain parameter value settings and their correlative assumptions in our experiments (for complete descriptions of the parameters, please see (Chen et. al., 2004)):

- The size of service space $S_{service}$ is set to 10. What we called a service space is a pre-existing collection of services allowing peer access. The services in the service space are all composed by several subtasks. We assume that the subtask number $N_{subtask}$ of a particular service follows a normal distribution with a mean of 4 and variance of 1 (without loss of generality). To reduce the effect of uncertain variables, the level of hierarchical service decomposition is set to 1. Thus a service only needs to be decomposed once by the request peer. We assume that peer can get the decomposition knowledge from outside world entities, such as provisioning servers or other peers.

- The service capacity $S_{capacity}$ denotes the number of subtasks a peer can provide. We assume that service capacity per peer follows a normal Distribution with a mean of 20 and variance of 4 (without loss of generality) for simulating the actual environment where the variety of mobile devices influences its capability of providing service.

- As to the behavior of peers, we assume that each peer process service requests with an exponentially distributed rate $\lambda_{request}$ of 0.2 per minutes (without loss of generaliza-

tion). That is to say, the average elapsed time to generate a demand of a service per peer is 5 minutes. Each service request R_i, $0 \leq i < S_{service}$, is chosen uniformly at random inside the service space. Thus, with the size of service space, $S_{service}$, of 10, the average choosing rate $R_{choosing}$ of a service request is 0.1.

- We simulate the failure occurrence for each peer with λ. To complement, we also set a repair rate λ_{repair} for a peer. Both rates are simulated according to exponential distributions. We assume that *each peer has a different failure rate λ_i, $0 \leq i < S_{network}$*. Accordingly, we set a range corresponding to different peer types, where that *top failure rates λ_{max} may be different in different experiments (denoting stability of ubiquitous service environments)*. The parameter λ_i is attained from the weighted effects of user characters, OS versions and releases, and device brands and types respectively as follow:

$$\lambda_i = \lambda_{max}(w_{user}E_{user} + w_{os}E_{os} + w_{device}E_{device})$$

$$w_{user} + w_{os} + w_{device} = 1, 0 \leq E_{user} \leq 1, 0 \leq E_{os} \leq 1, 0 \leq E_{device} \leq 1$$

in which E_{user} denotes the user effect, E_{os} denotes the OS effect, and E_{device} denotes the device effect. In the simulation, w_{user}, w_{os}, and w_{device} are set to 0.2, 0.3, 0.5 separately. As to the repair rate, the mean time is fixed to 0.5 minutes because we suppose that most mobile device have a speedy recovery capability.

- We assume that occurrences of events in the simulation are all *Poisson processes*, including the arrival requests, unexpected failures and the corresponding repairs from failures. A Poisson process is characterized by its rate function $\lambda(t)$, which is the expected number of "events" or "arrivals" that occur per unit time. Poisson processes are of the characteristics: (1) *Orderliness*: Events don't occur simultaneously. (2) *Memorylessness*: Any event occurring after time t is independent of any event occurring before time t. The exponential distribution is generally used to model Poisson processes, where events occur with constant probabilities per unit. Particularly, failures in an electronic device are usually memoryless and hence are well modeled by an exponential distribution.

In the simulation, the experiments will be conducted several times with different setting of configurations, which are defined by a set of global and local parameters as shown in Table 1. Most experiments are conducted given a simulation time $T_{simulation}$ of 2 hours. *In the experiments, we use the aforementioned metrics to evaluate the behavior of UbiSrvInt for a changing dispatch number (k), dynamic vs. stable environments, and with vs. without the Semi-Global mechanism respectively.*

The results of the experiments are primarily illustrated with cumulative time sequence dia-grams. That is, for each metric we accumulate observed values over time, and mark it on diagram every 10 minutes to draw a curve so as to see how trend changes. In other words, each data point on the curve denotes an overall value of the time point labeled on x-axis.

Feasibility Analysis of FTM

Since FTM is exerting physical redundancy for fault tolerance, FTM first determines a number of peer candidates (the dispatch number k) for duplicating a service and then execute the replication process (dispatching the service to the peer candidates). This section aims to *examine how the system behaves as the dispatch number k increases and then justifies the feasibility of FTM (i.e., to show the benefit is greater than the overhead).*

Since a higher k value denotes the higher level of replication in the mechanism of FTM, the mechanism exists only when k is greater than one. In the first set of experiments, we inject failures into each peer with a failure rate per peer per minute of λ_i which ranges from 0 to 0.1, i.e.

Figure 14. Performance results in dynamic ubiquitous service environments

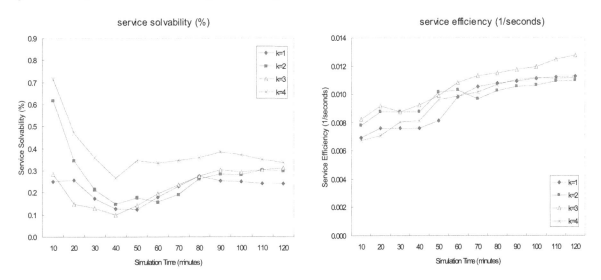

Figure 15. Load in dynamic ubiquitous service environments

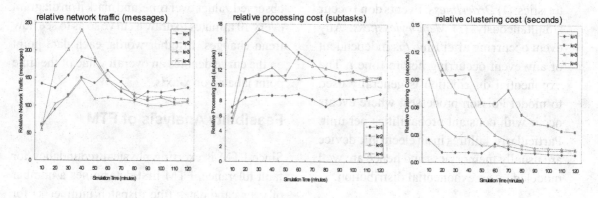

Figure 16. Performance results in stable ubiquitous service environments

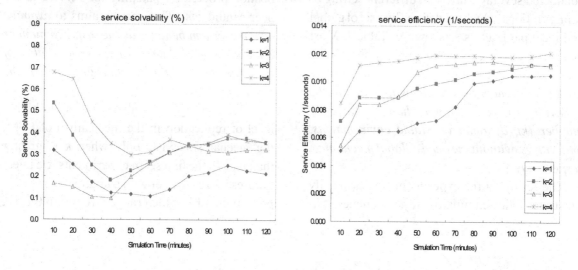

Figure 17. Load in stable ubiquitous service environments

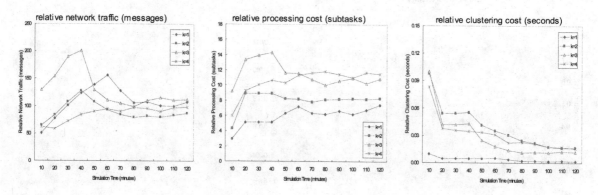

λ_{max} *is set to 0.1 (characterizing a fairly dynamic ubiquitous service environment).* Note that the actual λ_i of each peer depends on the peer type it belongs to. Each experiment is carried out with a different configuration of k value. In the second set of experiments, we then conduct a series of experiments resembling to the first set but *under relatively stable environments, where* λ_{max} *is 0.05.* Accordingly the failure rate λ_i per peer per minute lies in the range [0, 0.05]. The first and second sets of experiments are both conducted with the existence of the Semi-Global mechanism.

The evaluation results can briefly be itemized as follows:

- **Performance in *dynamic* ubiquitous service environments** (Figure 14):
  - Service solvability:
    —k=4 >> k=3 >> k=2 >> k=1 (The performance in service solvability grows in proportion to the magnitude of k.)
    —k=4 >> k=1 (The final overall service solvability in k value of 4 is more than 1.4^5 times higher than the one in k value of 1.)
    —k=4 >> k=1 (Under a total average of the final overall solvability of 0.3, the difference in proportion between both sides - k=4 and k=1 - is more than 32%, which is highly significant)
    Note: ">>" represents a relationship of outperforming (with respect to a designated metric or measurement) between two cases of experiments using two different replication factors (k).
  - Service efficiency:
    —k=3 >> (K=4 ≒ k=2 ≒ k=1) (In general, all curves are on the rise as the time passed by. At the ends of the experiments, the final overall service efficiency for all k values are almost equivalent except for the value of 3. It is apparent especially in k value of 4

and k value of 1. As to the k value of 3, it gains the distinctly highest final overall service efficiency of all).
Note: "≒" represents an indistinguishable relationship (with respect to a designated metric or measurement) between two cases of experiments using two different replication factors (k).

- **Load in *dynamic* ubiquitous service environments** (Figure 15):
  - Relative network traffic:
    —k=1 >> k=2 ≒ k=3 ≒ k=4 (In general, the relative network traffic curves are ordered in an inverse way against the service solvability curves. As the k value increases, the relative load came from network traffic goes down.)
    —k=1 >> Average of k=2,3,4 (The overheads of the final overall relative network traffic in the experiments with replication mechanism are close eventually in the experiments, which are lower than the overhead in k = 1 over 18%[6] on average at the ends of the experiments.)
  - Relative processing cost:
    —(k=4 ≒ k=3 ≒ k=2) >> K=1 (The overall relative processing cost has the lowest load when k value is set to 1. Besides, the final loads are about the same when the other k values are set.)
    —Average of k=2,3,4 >> k=1 for more than around 2 units of subtasks (The overhead of the overall relative processing cost incurred - for k of values other than 1 - is only around 2 units of subtasks per successful service request at the ends of the experiments. This is considerably low in our simulation environment.)
  - Relative clustering cost:
    —The difference between different values of k is only few milliseconds,

which is quite slight. Accordingly, we can neglect the impact of the clustering overhead on performance.

- **Performance in *stable* ubiquitous service environments** (Figure 16):
  - Service solvability:

    —(K=4 ≒ k=2) >> k=3 >> k=1 (In general, the overall performance of FTM still far outperforms the one without the replication mechanism, i.e. $k = 1$. But the level of replication in FTM has relatively limited impact on the performance in comparison with that of a dynamic environment. The experiment using a k value of 4 is still performs well above the others, but the difference between that using a k value of 2 is a nuance in the later half of the experimental durations. This might suggest a lower clustering number is good enough to maximum effect on the service efficiency and we will elaborate the discussion at the end of this section.)

    —k=4 >> k=1 (The final overall service solvability in k value of 4 is around 1.7 times higher than the one in k value of 1 at the ends of the experiments. Furthermore, the difference in proportion between both sides - k=4 and k=1 - has been raised up to around 46%.)

  - Service efficiency:

    —K=4 >> (k=3 ≒ k=2) >> k=1 (For growing the value of the dispatch number k, the performance of FTM is improved in terms of the absolute values of service efficiency throughout the simulation. The rationale is that less failure rates yield more dispatched peers contributing their provisions of subtasks and thus a request peer can acquire what it needs earlier from any one who is dispatched. The experiment using a k value of 4 then persistently has the best efficiency.)

    —k=4 >> k=1 (The overall service response time per successful service request in k value of 4 is at least 12.5 seconds faster than that in k value of 1 in the durations which represent at about 100 minutes faster in reality.)

- **Load in *stable* ubiquitous service environments** (Figure 17):
  - Relative network traffic:

    —K=3 >> k=1 >> k=4 >> k=2 (The overheads from network traffic under replication mechanism are relatively smaller than the one without replication mechanism in general, in spite of the different levels of replication.)

  - Relative Processing Cost:

    —K=4 >> k=3 >> k=2 >> k=1 (For higher values of the dispatch number

Figure 18. Summarized results of FTM's feasibility

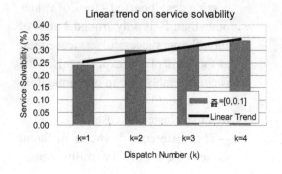

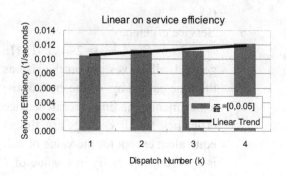

k, FTM gains higher processing costs relatively.)

—Increase is around 1.36 units per upgrading of *k*. (On average, the increase in the overall relative processing cost when upgrading a level of replication is around 1.36 units at the ends of the experiments. This is believed to be a reasonable tradeoff with processing cost for a higher efficiency.)

○ Relative clustering cost:

—Differences are only few milliseconds. (The average cost is slightly higher than that of *k* value being 1, although not a significant difference with only few milliseconds apart.)

—Average of k=4,3,2 is around 0.0147 seconds. (The costs for K being 4,3,2 start from a higher value and drop significantly to an average value of 0.0147 seconds per successful service at the ends of the experiments.)

From Figure 14-17, we can conclude the following observations (that subsequently justify the feasibility of FTM):

- **Under dynamic environments:** The feasibility of FTM is very positive because of the much better performance and the relatively lower overheads. Moreover, it shows that the efficiency of *k* = 3 is apparently higher then the others as its solvability is not far from *k* = 4, and its relative overheads are close to the others. The clustering number, i.e. *replication level, can best effect service solvability*, as the linear trend on the final overall service solvability as shown in Figure 18. This results from the fact that *higher failure rates yield less peers accomplishing task correctly. Hence the increase of number of dispatched peers results in the higher service solvability*. In the meanwhile, the

relative processing cost does not distinctly increase as *k* value increases.

- **Under stable environments:** The feasibility of FTM is affirmed once again since the enormous performance gained is sufficient to counteract the overhead involved in processing. The result in *k* = 2 is notable. We found that the solvability of *k* = 2 is almost as good as *k* = 4. And it has the lowest relative overhead of network traffic and a second lower relative processing cost (only slightly higher than *k* = 1). Moreover, *dispatch number k best effects service efficiency*, as the linear trend on the final overall service efficiency shown in Figure 18. The processing cost increases as *k* value increases. This results from the fact that *lower failure rates yield more peers performing task correctly*. Hence, we can manipulate the clustering number to maximum effect on the service efficiency by far.

- To extend the meaning of the results attained from stable environments, the quality of the replication is more effective than its quantity when the clustering data is relatively rich in contents. In stable environments, the behaviors of peers are more unobvious in terms of failure occurrence. Hence, a coarser failure correlation clustering is sufficient to classify peers into proper clusters to facilitate the replication mechanism. By contrast to dynamic environments, the quality of the replication will be more effective than its quantity if and only if a refined clustering performs, that is, plenty clustering data in content involved.

The Effects of the Semi-Global Mechanism

In this set of experiments, we follow the same configuration settings used in the first set of experiments (Section 4.2), except that the experiments are conducted without the Semi-Global

Figure 19. The positive effects of the semi-global mechanism

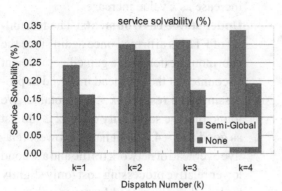

mechanism in order to examine its influence on FTM. For this reason, all the other parameters are set exactly the same: the top failure rate λ_{max} is set to 0.1 and the dispatch number k varies from 1 to 4.

In these experiments, the cumulative time sequence diagrams of the evaluation metrics are not deployed here one by one since we only interested in the final overall effect of the Semi-Global mechanism in this phase. Hence we only capture the final results obtained at the ends of the experiments, i.e. after 2 hours, to see the final overall performance and load in each experiment. And the experimental results are compared and illustrated with bar charts instead.

The evaluation results (as shown in Figure 19) can briefly be itemized as follows:

- Service solvability:
  —Average of K=4,3,2,1 with Semi-Global is 1.5 times more than that of no Semi-Global. (The mean of the final overall performances of service solvability in experiments with Semi-Global is around 1.5 times higher then the mean in experiments without Semi-Global at the ends of the experiments.)
  —k=3 with Semi-Global is 1.75 times better than that of no Semi-Global and it is 43% difference in proportion)

—k=4 with Semi-Global is 1.85 times better than that of no Semi-Global and it is 46% difference in proportion.

- Service efficiency:
  —k=3 with Semi-Global is 35 seconds faster than that of no Semi-Global. (The experiments with Semi-Global show the higher performance comprehensively in terms of service efficiency. Especially in the case of k = 3, the difference is about 35 seconds per successful service.)

Following the above experiment results, we can conclude the beneficial results of the Semi-Global mechanism. *The replication factor is ineffectual without the complement of the Semi-Global mechanism.*

The Semi-Global mechanism improves the accuracy of clustering so as to find the most appropriate peer candidates to dispatch subtasks and subsequently attain a better service performance. That is, by way of dispatching peers who have the lowest failure correlation from each other, service-sharing system can achieve higher solvability and efficiency in general. In other words, *this experience sharing of the Semi-Global mechanism (in combination with physical redundancy of the replication mechanism) empowers UbiSrvInt with a unique capability of fault tolerance for wireless service composition.*

Possible Application Scenarios of UbiSrvInt on Context Awareness

As a result of the rising and the flourishing of tourism, enormous capital has been invested in the tourist industry. It is highly suitable to have tourism applications implemented on a P2P platform because of the characteristic of mobile tourists longing for various information and services on the fly. It is highly valuable to tourists for tourist services being personalized, contextualized and capable of providing immediate access in an ad-hoc wireless manner for tourists. From system perspective, they must be lightweight and reliable. Let us envisage a possible scenario set in the future.

For instance, Amy is visiting a museum in her sightseeing tour. Her personal digital assistant (PDA) on hand with wireless support automatically downloads "visiting route" service provided by museum while she is buying an entrance ticket. *On her way to museum lobby, her PDA broadcasts the requests for "tourist distribution", "showroom information", "floor map" and "Chinese translation" services to nearby tourists. In a short while, her PDA has already collected those services it needs to compose a personalized service for Amy.*

Amy gets a "Chinese version of visiting route" service without manual operation. Amy follows the route showed on her PDA, noticing that there are some useful facilities marked on the route such as information desk and female washroom. *Her PDA requires and collects "art introduction" automatically while she is entering a different showroom. That is, Amy can always get the right information at the right time whenever needed.* Of course, if she likes, she can choose vocal introductions rather than written ones.

The preceding scenario illustrates an ad-hoc wireless service provision providing personalized and contextualized tourist services according to Amy's profile and surrounding context. Moreover, suppose that Amy goes into the second showroom,

one of the peers that provide "painting location", which is part of the "art introduction" service, is suddenly lost connection. The traditional fault-tolerance solution to this problem is to search for a candidate to re-execute the failed subtask and then compose them again. By that time Amy may leaved the second showroom already. In a WP2P environment and such a time critical situation, the time redundancy solution is unreasonable. *Exerting UbiSrvInt, the failure will be avoided by analyzing the dependability of peers as far as possible, therefore providing customized service without wasting any time.*

Alternative application scenario utilizing the social contexts (retained in the profiles of the users and processed by the BDI reasoning agent) extends the application scope of UbiSrvInt a step deeper. As follows shows a simple demonstration of the application:

1. Amy is a visitor (whose handheld profile is shown in Figure 20) of a museum in her sightseeing tour.

2. During Amy's visiting of the museum, the context information provided by museums provisioning server will be faithfully recorded and displayed on this Context Information Panel (as shown in Figure 21) to notify Amy. The Context Information Panel shows the current states of user's surrounding.

3. The BDI Reasoning Agent then obtains Amy's profile (as shown in the User Profile Setting Panel of Figure 20) and the context information (as shown in the Context Information Panel of Figure 21) to infer Amy's true intentions. The knowledge about reasoning rules can be downloaded from provisioning servers or nearby peers. And the results of reasoning will be presented in the Service Recommendation Panel for Amy's reference. (The Service Recommendation Panel can be set to automatic or manual. User can either authorize system to automatically reasoning while new context information is newly

Figure 20. Handheld profile setting panel (Automatic / Manual)

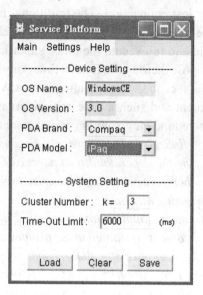

Figure 21. Context information panel (Automatic / Manual)

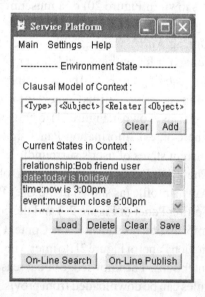

obtained, or choose a manual control to silence system when user needs undisturbed environments, such as during a meeting, taking a nap, *etc.*)

Figure 22. Service recommendation panel (automatic / manual)

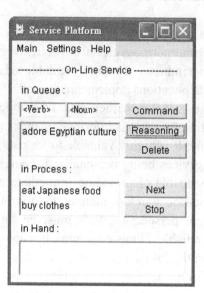

4. Amy's friend, Bob, makes an appointment with Amy in the museum, but he is late. Before Bob's arrival, Amy takes the opportunity to browse the gift shop and choose a birthday present for Candy, her classmate, because this morning Amy got a memorandum about Candy's birthday party from the PDA. Amy also sends a digital post-card of Egyptian culture downloaded from the museum to Eva, her younger sister, who is a college student with a major in Archeology with the recommendation of the BDI reasoning agent (shown in Figure 22). The social context information is also stored in Amy's PDA in the format of tuples such as:

(*<relationship> <Candy> <friend> <Amy>*)
(*<profile> < Candy > <born> <1977/5/20>*)
(*<relationship> <Eva> <sister> <Amy>*)
(*<profile> <Eva> <love> <Egyptian culture>*)

5. After Bob arrives the museum, his PDA gets an official welcome message from the

provisioning server resident in the museum. The message may look like such a tuple: (*<location> <user> <entering> <Palace Museum>*). The Reasoning Agent in Bob's system gets the newly arrival context information, thus starts the inference. The incoming context information is shown on the Context Information Panel. The agent notices that Bob is a Spaniard and has a date with Amy, thus sensibly guesses that Bob may need (i) a Spanish translation of the museum tour guide and museum catalogue and (ii) a note message to inform Amy that he has arrived. The two services will be then automatically shown on the Service Recommend Panel. If Bob dislikes that, he can manually stop it, otherwise the services will be provided after they are fulfilled. The fulfilled services will be also recorded on the Service Recommendation Panel for user reference.

RELATED WORKS

This section gives some exemplars of existing relevant works on the infrastructures of e-service provision emphasizing on either service integration or service adaptation or service replication. The works about service integration, in general, rely on complied knowledge (e.g., process schema, process template, or state charts) in terms of (semi-)centralized architectures. On the other hand, the works for service adaptation mostly are condition-based and those for service replication then quest for load balancing. UbiSrvInt is distinct from these works in service provision based on inference-based adaptation and fault-correlation-analysis service replication (in addition to UbiSrvInt being a pure peer-to-peer approach).

eFlow (Casati et. al., 2002) is a platform developed at HP Laboratories for specifying, enacting, and monitoring composite e-services in order to aid in e-commerce. In eFlow, a composite service is described as a process schema that composes other basic or composite services. A composite service is modeled by a flow structure, which defines the order of execution among the nodes in the process. The graph may include service, decision, and event nodes. Service nodes represent the invocation of a basic or composite service; decision nodes specify the alternatives and rules controlling the execution flow, while event nodes enable service processes to send and receive several types of events. A service process instance is an enactment of a process schema enacted by the eFlow engine.

The Ninja (Mao et. al., 2001) project aims to develop a software infrastructure to support the next generation of Internet-based applications. In the Ninja project, a dynamic service composition platform has been designed and implemented with the goals of automation, scalability and fault-tolerance through use of cluster computing platforms, identification of common patterns of ad-hoc, application-specific compositions, classification of services into a strongly typed system, redundant control mechanisms for monitoring and recovery, and a continuous optimization process with feedback. Central to the architecture is the concept of path. A path is a flow of Application Data Units through multiple services and transformational operators across the wide area. A mechanism, Automatic Path Creation (APC) service, plays an essential role by seamlessly supporting any new communication device in the infrastructure.

A SELF-SERV platform (Benatallah et. al., 2002) for rapid composition of Web services has been developed based on Java and XML, in which web services are declaratively composed, and the resulting composite services are executed in a P2P and dynamic environment. SELF-SERV employs a declarative language for composing services based on state charts which support the expression of control-flow dependencies such as branching, merging, concurrency, *etc*. A P2P service execution model, whereby the responsibility of coordinating the execution of a composite service, is distributed across several peer software components called *coordinators*. They are in charge of initiating, controlling, monitoring the associated services, and collaborating with their peers to manage service execution. The knowledge required while composing services is statically extracted from the state chart and represented in a simple tabular form.

Anamika (Dipanjan et. al., 2002) is a reactive service composition architecture for pervasive computing environments that is implemented over Bluetooth. Central to Anamika is the concept of a distributed broker that can execute at any node in the environment. A broker may be selected based on various parameters such as resource capability, geometric topology of the nodes and proximity of the node to the services that are required to compose a particular request. The architecture primarily deals with the discovery, integration and execution of the components of a composite request. The architecture introduces two distributed reactive techniques to carry out service composition in purely ad-hoc environments: Dynamic Broker Selection Technique, Distributed Brokering Technique. The former approach centers on a procedure of dynamically selecting a device to be a broker for a single request in the environment. And the latter approach distributes the brokering of a particular request to different entities in the system by determining their suitability to execute a part of the composite request.

PCAP (Sheng et. al., 2004) devises the design of a distributed, adaptive, and context-aware framework for personalized service composition in terms of users annotating existing process templates (leading to personalized service-based processes). Personalization is the like of execution constraints encompassing temporal and spatial constraints, which respectively indicate when and where the user wants to see a task executed. The execution policies include the service selec-tion policy and the service migration policy. For a specific task, users can specify how to select a service for this task. The service can be a fixed one (the task always uses this service), or can be selected from a specific service community or a public directory (e.g., UDDI) based on certain criteria (e.g., location of the mobile user).

ServiceGlobe (Keidl et. al., 2003) presents a generic dispatcher in web service provision for the purpose of load balancing and high service availability in terms of automatic service replication. The dispatcher performs load balancing (or load sharing) using several servers on the back-end with identically mirrored content and a dispatching strategy like round robin using load information about the back-end servers.

CONCLUSION REMARKS

In this chapter, a novel pure P2P approach solution (UbiSrvInt) for ad-hoc wireless service provision is presented. UbiSrvInt is unique in its context awareness and fault tolerance (that are fulfilled by the approach's components - Reasoning Agent and Fault-Tolerance Module - respectively). The aim of this chapter is to empower users with mobile wireless devices to access personalized and contextualized services composed within the reachable ad-hoc network of services in a pure Peer-to-Peer manner. Accordingly, we provide a general-purpose approach (UbiSrvInt) so as to facilitate the discovery, integration, and provision of a large cross-section of P2P mobile services. UbiSrvInt advances existing service provision infrastructures (centralized or mediator-based) by its capability in the removal of the bottlenecks of the centralized/mediator nodes (for reliability, scalability, extensibility, real-time information). Moreover, UbiSrvInt takes into account fault tolerance and context awareness (that are vital for attaining high usability of the approach for wireless service provision). As for the complexity of UbiSrvInt, it is still manageable because most of the computation exerted is fairly effective and with the Moore's Law the power of mobile devices would be aggressively improved (in terms of the capabilities of computation and capacity) as time goes.

The performance of UbiSrvInt on fault tolerance is three-fold: (1) Under unreliable environments, sufficient dispatch number (replication level) should be provided to seek for distinctly higher service solvability. (2) As to reliable environments, lower replication level is good enough to gain favorable solvability and replication level could be raised to seek for distinctly higher service efficiency (if the extra process cost is either unconcerned by or unaware to users). (3) For synergy of Semi-Global, in both kinds of environments Semi-Global should be enabled for complementing FTM so as to gain an overall higher performance in all aspects. As to the functionality of UbiSrvInt on context awareness, it has also been justified through relevant scenario demos of UbiSrvInt. In short, through the experiments and evaluations[7] UbiSrvInt is justified for its claimed distinctive features of context awareness and fault tolerance.

Our future work includes the application of the UbiSrvInt approach to myriad service domains (e.g., travel, learning, *etc.*) in order to attain domain dependent statistics (such as level of increased satisfaction, efficiency and activity volume). For FTM, certain further investigation can be conducted, such as granularity of time slots in a sliding window (the more exquisite the day-patterns the more segmented time slots), varied experiment parameters (e.g., network size), and advanced adaptability through personalized reasoning rules about a desired balance of accuracy and efficiency. We hope our work can shed light on further advanced platform development for contextualized P2P mobile service provision.

IMPLICATIONS FOR U-COMMERCE

For u-commerce, the nature of services focuses on actively sensing different customer's role through different specific contextual attributes (e.g., time, location, resources, customer profiles) (Fano et. al., 2002) in order to meet customers' needs and change the interactions with the customers (Varshney et. al., 2000) in terms of dynamic configurations of services and devices. To support u-commerce and the services, the environment features the ubiquitous networks that are full convergence, technologically heterogeneous, geographically dispersed, context sensing, architecturally flexible and without a centralized control mechanism (Banavar et. al., 2002). However, the ubiquitous networks, in reality, are not as reliable as the wired networks and thus the issue of fault tolerance has to be considered in addition to context awareness. To meet this end, this chapter provides an approach for P2P mobile service provision, which is not only robust to failure but also aware of the surrounding context in ubiquitous networks. In other words, the IT infrastructure required for u-commerce and the services, in nature, have some differences from those of traditional e-commerce or m-commerce in terms of the two kinds of supports required (fault tolerant and context awareness). On top of the needed infrastructure supports, the values of the u-commerce services could then be realized to the fullest extent (together with different directions of exploration on customers' needs in ubiquitous contexts).

REFERENCES

Agrawal, R., Lin, K, Sawhney, H., & Shim, K. (1995). Fast Similarity Search in the Presence of Noise, Scaling, and Translation in Time-Series Databases. *In Proceedings of the 21st International Conference on Very Large Databases (VLDB'95),* Zurich, Switzerland.

Banavar, G., & Bernstein, A. (2002). Software Infrastructure and Design Challenges for Ubiquitous Computing Applications. *Communications of ACM, 45*(12), 92-96.

Benatallah, B., Dumas, M., Sheng, Q., & Ngu, A. (2002). Declarative Composition and Peer-to-Peer Provisioning of Dynamic Web Services. *In 18th International Conference on Data Engineering (ICDE'02)*, San Jose, CA, USA.

Bratman, M., Israel, D., & Pollack, M. (1988). Plans and Resource Bounded Practical Reasoning. *Computational Intelligence, 4*(4), 349-355.

Casati, F., Ilnicki, S., Jin, L., Krishnamoorthy, V., & M. Shan. (2002). *Adaptive and Dynamic Service Composition in eFlow*. HP Lab Technical Report HPL-2000-39, Palo Alto: Software Technology Laboratory.

Chakraborty, D. (2001). *Service Composition in Ad-hoc Environments*. Ph.D Dissertation Proposal, Technical Report TR-CS-01-20.

Chakraborty, D., Perich, F., Joshi, A., Finin, T., & Yesha, Y. (2002). *A Reactive Service Composition Architecture for Pervasive Computing Environments*. Technical Report TR-CS-02-02, University of Maryland at Baltimore, USA.

Chen, F. Y., & Yuan, S. T. (2004). *A Study on Contextualized Fault-tolerant Service Composition in WP2P Environments*. Technical Report, Fu-Jen University, Taiwan.

Deng, D., & Kasabov, N. (2000). ESOM: An Algorithm to Evolve Self-Organizing Maps from On-line Data Streams. *In Proceedings of the IJCNN'2000 on Neural Networks Neural Computing: New Challenges and Perspectives for the New Millennium, 6*, 3-8.

Dialani, V., Miles, S., Morcan, L., Rourc, D., & luck, M. (2002). Transparent Fault Tolerance for Web Services Based Architectures. *In Proceedings of the 8th International Euro-Par Conference (EURO-PAR'02)*, Paderborn, Germany.

Dipanjan, C. *et al.* (2002). A Reactive Service Composition Architecture for Pervasive Computing Environments. *7th Personal Wireless Communications Conference*, Singapore.

Fano, A., & Gershman, A. (2002). The Future of Business Services in the Age of Ubiquitous Computing. *Communications of ACM, 45*(12), 63-87.

Gribble, S. D., Welsh, M., Brewer, E. A., & Culler, D. E. (1999). *The NINJA project pages*. http://ninja.cs.berkeley.edu.

Hartigan, J. A., & Wong, M. A. (1979). A K-Means Clustering Algorithm. J. Royal Statistical Society, Ser. C, *Applied Statistics, 28,* 100-108.

Jena, http://www.hpl.hp.com/semweb/jena.htm

Keidl, M., Seltzsam, S., & Kemper, A. (2003). Reliable Web Service Execution and Deployment in Dynamic Environments. *Lecture Notes in Computer Science, 2819*, 104-118.

Lamport, L., Shostak, R., & Pease, M. (1982). The Byzantine Generals Problem. *ACM Transactions on Programming Languages and Systems, 4*(3), 382-401.

Mao, Z., Brewer, E., & Katz R. (2001). *Fault-tolerant, Scalable, Wide-area Internet Service Composition*. Technical Report UCB/CSD-1-1129, Department of Computer Science and Electrical Engineering, University of Maryland, Baltimore County, USA.

Mennie, D., & Pagurek, B. (2000). An Architecture to Support Dynamic Composition of Service Components. *In Proceedings of the 5th International Workshop on Component-Oriented Programming (WCOP 2000)*, Sophia Antipolis and Cannes, France.

Powell, D., Verissimo, P., Bonn, G., Waeselynck, F., & Seaton, D. (1988). The Delta-4 approach to dependability in open distributed computing systems. *In Proceedings of The 18th International*

Symposium on Fault-Tolerant Computing, Tokyo, Japan.

Project JXTA. http://www.jxta.org

Ranganathan, A., & Campbell, R. (2003). A Middleware for Context-Aware Agents in Ubiquitous Computing Environments. *ACM/IFIP/USENIX International Middleware Conference,* Rio de Janeiro, Brazil.

Schlichting, R., & Schneider, F. (1983). Fail-stop Processors: An Approach to Designing Fault-Tolerant Computing Systems. *ACM Transactions on Computer Systems, 1*(3), 222-238.

Schuster, H., Georgakopoulos, D., Cichocki, A., & Baker, D. (2000). Modeling and Composing Service-based and Reference Process-based Multi-enterprise Processes. *In Proceedings of the International Conference on Advanced Information Systems Engineering (CAiSE2000),* Stockholm, Sweden.

Sheng, Q. Z., Benatallah, B., & Maamar, Z. (2004). Enabling Personalized Composition and Adaptive Provisioning of Web Services. *The 16th International Conference on Advanced Information Systems Engineering,* Riga, Latvia.

Sheng, Q., Benatallah, B., Dumas, M., & Mak, E. (2002). SELF-SERV: A Platform for Rapid Composition of Web Services in a Peer-to-Peer Environment. *In Proceedings of the 28th Very Large DataBase Conference (VLDB'2002),* Hong Kong, China.

Song, Q., & Kasabov, N. (2001). ECM - A Novel On-line, Evolving Clustering Method and Its Applications. *In Proceedings of the Fifth Biannual Conference on Artificial Neural Networks and Expert Systems (ANNES2001),* Dunedin, New Zealand.

Varshney, U., Vetter, R. J., & Kalakota, R. (2000). Mobile Commerce: A New Frontier. *IEEE Computer,* (pp. 32-38).

Weatherspoon, H., Moscovitz, T., & Kubiatowicz, J. (2002). Introspective Failure Analysis: Avoiding Correlated Failures in Peer-to-Peer Systems. *In Proceedings of the International Workshop on Reliable Peer-to-Peer Distributed Systems (SRDS'02),* Osaka , Japan.

ENDNOTES

[1]   L, M, H respectively indicates low, medium and high in the willingness of a user to host a specified function.

[2]   Peers of vicinity are referring to those mobile peers accessible through wireless communication (e.g., Bluetooth).

[3]   RDF is best thought of in the form of node and arc diagrams.

[4]   The number of subtasks is used to substitute for the total time of subtask execution because the services in the simulation are "virtual" and doesn't really be executed.

[5]   The value of 1.4 is attained from dividing the best final overall solvability, i.e. k=4, by the worst final overall solvability, i.e. k=1. (0.337/0.241)

[6]   The value of 18% is attained from dividing the difference between the highest final overall relative network traffic, i.e. k=1, and the average of the final overall relative network traffic of the others, i.e. k=2,3,4, by the highest final overall relative network traffic. ((133.5-108.9)/133.5)

[7]   Since UbiSrvInt is the first pure P2P approach solution for ad-hoc wireless service composition, instead of providing benchmark evaluations this chapter aims for justifying the usefulness and the effectiveness of the approach proposed. The usefulness is originated from the nature of fault tolerance and context awareness for ad-hoc wireless service provision. The effectiveness subsequently is confirmed from the feasibility affirmation of the Fault-Tolerance Module and the manifesting demo scenarios of Reasoning Agent.

Figure A2. UbiSrvInt's activity diagram

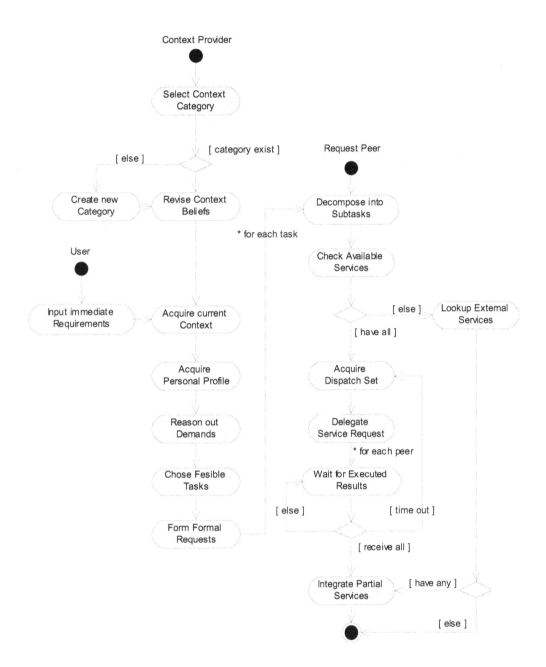

Section IV
Interacting with Mobile Devices

Chapter X
Perceptions of Mobile Device Website Design:
Culture, Gender and Age Comparisons

Dianne Cyr
Simon Fraser University, Canada

Milena Head
McMaster University, Canada

Alex Ivanov
Simon Fraser University, Canada

ABSTRACT

Anytime anywhere services offered through mobile commerce hold great potential to serve customers in wireless environments. However, there is limited understanding of how mobile Web site design is perceived by diverse users. This chapter explores how users who differ by culture, age, and gender perceive the design of a mobile device and their subsequent level of satisfaction with the device. Sixty subjects were tested in a controlled laboratory experiment on an Internet enabled phone. The results of a quantitative analysis were statistically inconclusive in terms of cultural and gender differences, but significant differences were found between older and younger users. However, an in-depth qualitative analysis of interview transcripts revealed some interesting differences among cultural, gender and age groups. Consistent with findings in the stationary Internet domain, design elements were found to impact satisfaction with mobile services.

INTRODUCTION

Organisations will be well served to not be complacent with their wireless site design efforts... [But] *before wireless site designers can address the usability challenge, and before organisations can leverage the commercial benefits of m-commerce, a deeper understanding of what aspects of usability is important to users and how they may differ in a wireless context is required.* (Venkatesh et al., 2003, p.56)

Mobile commerce[1] (or m-commerce) has huge potential to serve customers in wireless environments. The adoption of m-commerce is dependent on consumer acceptance of new and well-designed technologies (Ancker & D'Incau, 2002; Coursaris et al., 2003: Kim et al., 2002; Kumar & Zahn 2003; Nysveen et al., 2005; Perry et al., 2001; Schrott & Gluckler, 2004; Yang, 2005). It is expected design characteristics may influence user perceptions towards a mobile device. Congruent with work done by Cyr (2008), Information Design (ID), Navigation Design (ND), and Visual Design (VD) may all contribute to user adoption of a technology, as well as to satisfaction with a mobile technology.

Concerning user attitudes of handheld devices, it is also expected that diverse categories of users based on culture, gender, or age may react differently to using the device. There is growing literature on cross-cultural website design, mostly evaluated within the context of the stationary Internet (Becker, 2002; Chau et al., 2000; Cyr, 2008; Cyr et al., 2006; Cyr & Trevor-Smith, 2004; Marcus & Gould, 2000; Sun, 2001). More recently, research has examined culture and mobile data services (Choi et al., 2006). Investigations have likewise examined gender and design in the context of mobile devices, but research results are mixed (Anckar & D'Incau, 2002: Kwon & Chidambaram, 2000; Teo et al., 1999). Finally, research that examines cohorts by age (younger versus older users) is practically nonexistent when design is considered, although some studies have focused on special needs and preferences of older users (Goodman et al., 2005), or features of a mobile device perceived by user groups as adding value (Anckar & D'Incau 2002).

To explore the role of user differences concerning the perception of the design of a mobile device, users who differ on cultural, gender and age dimensions were tested on an Internet enabled cellular phone. Related to culture, Canadian and Chinese cultures were chosen due to acknowledged diversity (Hofstede, 1980). Between-group comparisons were conducted with respect to screen design (including information design, navigation design, and visual design), and satisfaction with the mobile device. In an exploration of these topics, the paper provides a review of relevant literature leading to the hypotheses for testing, the methodology used, an elaboration of results, and discussion of the findings. Given the increased diversity of mobile users, developing an expanded understanding of user perceptions and preferences not only has theoretical importance, but also serves to enhance the reengineering of devices to best meet consumer requirements.

MOBILITY AND DESIGN

In the realm of the stationary Internet, effective website design engages and attracts online consumers (Agarwal & Venkatesh, 2002; Fogg & Tzeng, 1999; Hui & Triandis, 1985; Morgan & Hunt, 1994; Schultz, 2003). According to Gommans et al. (2001), 'A website has to be designed for a targeted customer segment...' Chau et al. (2000) argue the modes of information presented on the Internet, and the quality of graphics has a significant impact on user experience. Research in design suggests various guidelines for effective Web navigation (Childers et al., 2001; Farkas & Farkas, 2000), criteria for optimal Web design (Bernard, 2002; Egger 2001), and how aesthetics and usability might be linked (Tractinsky, 1997).

The sensory experience of the website can help to determine if a user stays and shops at a site (Rosen & Purinton, 2004; Yoon, 2002).

The quality of handheld displays that favor enhanced information design and visual design is steadily increasing and affects user perceived effectiveness of the presentation (Rau et al., 2006). While mobile screens are much smaller than those available on the stationary Internet (Schmidt & Frick, 2000), various studies demonstrate comprehension rates on smaller screens are generally equivalent to their larger counterparts (Dillon & McKnight, 1990; Duchnicky & Kolers, 1983; Resiel & Shneiderman, 1987). Other researchers consider the smaller screens of mobile devices a 'serious obstacle to usability of the mobile Internet' (Chae & Kim, 2004, p. 165). Sarker & Wells (2003) examined interface characteristics and network capabilities that affect the implementation and acceptance of wireless phones. They discovered while users were 'quite forgiving of physical limitations of the device due to technological constraints, they were bothered by flaws in the interface of the devices' (p. 37).

In recent years there has been increased attention to mobile usage and in 2004 the *International Journal of Human-Computer Studies* devoted a special issue to this topic. The issue addressed mobile use in a variety of contexts including human characteristics and interface systems, although design aspects of the mobile website were not specifically considered. Further, in 2005 *Behaviour & Information Technology* devoted a special issue to mobility from a human computer interaction (HCI) perspective. Topics included navigation support, user acceptance and trust, and user evaluation of usability of mobile devices. In research in which interface design and usability are examined for wireless devices in m-commerce, Tarasewich (2003) suggests many current principles of interface design can be transferred to mobile devices. He examines various issues such as content, user interaction with the device, issues

of reading text on small screens, rapid serial visual presentation, and browser types.

Relevant to the current research, design categories for information design, navigation design, and visual design as suggested by Garrett (2003) were selected for systematic examination. A definition of each category follows.

a. **Information design:** Elements of the site that convey accurate or inaccurate information to a user. For instance, the location of an icon on the screen would be the domain of information architecture, but whether or not that icon conveys the right information to a user is the domain of information design. Clear and logical presentation of information about services or products is also a component of information design.

b. **Navigation design:** The navigational scheme used to help or hinder users as they access different sections of the site, such as the location and format of navigation aids.

c. **Visual Design:** Elements that deal with the balance, emotional appeal, aesthetics, and uniformity of the website overall graphical look. This includes colors, photographs, shapes, or font type.

These categories are represented in other work in design (Agarwal & Venkatesh, 2002; Yoon, 2002; Flavian et al., 2005; Palmer, 2002; Simon, 2001), and while not exhaustive are representative of key elements of website usability. The same categories were used by Cyr (2008) to study website design across cultures, and by Cyr and Bonanni (2005) regarding website design and gender. Further, in a study of mobile services Choi et al. (2006) consider three categories of user experience across cultures. These are content (similar to information design), information architecture (which includes navigation design), and graphical user interface (which is similar to visual design). In this research, information design, navigation design, and visual design are considered in the specific context of a mobile device.

Culture and Design

User preferences for website design features are known to vary across cultures (Barber and Badre, 2001; Cyr, 2008; Evers and Day, 1997; Nielsen and DelGaldo, 1996; Sun, 2001). Cyr and Trevor-Smith (2004) examined design elements for 30 municipal websites in each of Germany, Japan, and the United States. Significant differences were found across countries for use of symbols and graphics, color preferences, site features, language, and content. In a study in which user impressions were evaluated toward eight website design features, numerous differences were detected between collectivist Japanese and Chinese users with individualist British users (Hu et al., 2004). In the current investigation participants are tested who are either Canadian or Chinese. With respect to these cultures, Singh et al. (2003) compared domestic and Chinese versions of websites for 40 American-based companies and found differences in all the cultural categories examined.

Studies of m-commerce in different countries and considering different cultures are rare, although 'an understanding of the cultural dimensions of a market can aid marketers immensely in developing appropriate m-commerce services...' (Harris et al., 2005). In response, research in the area of culture and mobility is beginning to emerge. Cross-country differences were found for adoption of mobile applications in Hong Kong, Japan, and Korea (Kim et al., 2004), between the UK and Hong Kong (Harris et al., 2005), and between France and the USA (Carlson et al., 1999). Lee et al. (2002) compared Japan and South Korea in a study of m-commerce usage, and found significant cultural differences regarding value structures of the mobile Internet and their effect on users' satisfaction.

More specifically, and with respect to information design, research comparing user preferences in Canada, the U.S., Germany and Japan for perceived access and presentation of product information on a stationary computer uncovered few significant differences between the U.S., Canada, and Germany, but significant differences (p<.01) between these countries and a highly collectivist[2] culture like Japan (Cyr et al., 2005). Based on qualitative comments from the study, there appeared a desire on the part of Canadians, Americans, and Germans for utility - at least as far as obtaining site information is concerned. Choi et al. (2006) examined cultural characteristics and user experience attributes in mobile data services in Korea, Japan, and Finland. Based on qualitative findings, the authors found user experience attributes correlated to the user's culture and 'Finnish participants showed a cultural profile opposite to that of the Koreans' (p. 192). For example, in the area of information design Koreans and Japanese (both collectivists), preferred large amounts of information on a single screen while Finns (individualists) preferred direct, explicit communication and reacted negatively to large amounts of content. Related to the preceding studies, like the Finns, Canadians are individualists. Alternately, Chinese are collectivists in alignment with Koreans and Japanese.

H1a: *There will be differences between Chinese and Canadian users in the perception of information design of a mobile device. Canadian users will prefer utility in information design, while Chinese prefer more detail and depth of information presented in a mobile medium.*

Regardless of culture, users prefer easy to navigate websites. In an experiment using a stationary website, Simon (2001) found that North Americans prefer navigation that enhances movement and makes the interface simpler to use. In the study by Choi et al. (2006) in mobile data services as already mentioned, Koreans and Japanese liked clear and logical ordering of menu items, while Finns mentioned they most liked search facilities. Despite the paucity of prior research on navigation design across culture, and particularly in the context of mobile devices the following exploratory hypothesis is offered.

H1b. *There will be no differences between Chinese and Canadian users in the perception of navigation design of a mobile device. Both Canadians and Chinese will prefer simple and logical navigation formats.*

User preferences vary by culture with respect to visual design of the interface. Color varies by culture. Red means happiness in China, but danger in the US (Barber and Badre 2001). When applied to Web design, color may impact user expectations of the interface as well as overall satisfaction (Barber & Badre, 2001). In a cross-cultural study on website design, a Japanese respondent indicated a preference for more pictures and an "emotional approach" (Cyr et al., 2005). In other work specifically focused on images used in website design, in qualitative analyses Canadians perceived images to have aesthetic, affective and functional qualities while Japanese respondents focused only on affective qualities (Cyr et al., 2006). Sun (2001) found that users from cultures such as China or Japan have a strong preference for visuals and aesthetic beauty of the interface. In a mobile context, Koreans and Japanese preferred colorful screen design and Finns preferred simple screen design with less emphasis on color (Choi et al., 2006).

H1c. *There will be differences between Chinese and Canadian users in the perception of visual design of a mobile device. Chinese will be more concerned than Canadians with aesthetic beauty in visual design.*

Gender and Design

Gender is frequently used as a basis for segmentation, and researchers have attempted to understand the fundamental similarities and differences between the men and women for decades (Deaux &

Kite, 1987; Putrevu, 2001). Past empirical studies have shown significant gender differences across a variety of tasks and domains. For example, men often perform better than women on spatial orientation tasks, whereas females tend to score better on verbal or linguistic tasks (Simon, 2001; Deaux & Kite, 1987). Similarly, men and women differ in their reactions to visual images, affecting recall and recognition (Jones et al., 1998).

There are also gender differences in computer usage. Men and women diverge in Web acceptance, with perceived usefulness found to positively influence intention to use the Web more in men than women (Sanchez-Franco, 2006). Women use computers for collaboration and networking, while men view computers as a tool for obtaining and evaluating content (Gefen & Straub, 1997). Pearson et al. (2003) examined gender as a moderating variable to end-user computer efficacy, and found no differences between men and women although women were somewhat less confident to learn new computer applications. In other research, narrowing of differences between men and women has occurred concerning software use, anxiety, and enthusiasm (Rainer et al., 2003). Specific to mobile commerce, studies indicate that among Internet users men are predisposed to mobile adoption more than women (Yang, 2005; Brennan, 2000; Joines et al., 2003; Park & Jun, 2003; Rohm & Swaminathan, 2004). Contrary to these studies, gender differences were not detected in Spanish users related to shopping patterns and m-commerce adoption (Bigne et al., 2005).

It is anticipated the design of a website will impact user preferences, which in turn may produce different reactions between men and women (Chen & Dhillon, 2003). In one investigation in which gender and design are considered, Simon (2001) tests users' perceptions of a site, which refer to information richness, communication effectiveness, and communication interface. Women were found to have a less satisfied perception of the websites than men. Other work demonstrates differences between men and women for content and navigation (Maltby et al., 2003) and preference for color or graphics (Rodgers & Harris, 2003). In a study of website design, Cyr and Bonanni (2005) found specific information design elements (such as site organization and presentation of product information) were perceived more favorably by men than women. Further, men found the sites easier to navigate, and liked certain visual design aspects such as degree of interaction and animations more than women.

The above findings on a stationary website suggest there will be differences between the preferences of men and women for interface design in a mobile context. This assumption will be explored in the following hypotheses.

H2a. *There will be differences between men and women in the perception of information design of a mobile device.*

H2b. *There will be differences between men and women in the perception of navigation design of a mobile device.*

H2c. *There will be differences between men and women in the perception of visual design of a mobile device.*

Age and Design

Age is another common dimension used to segment consumer and user groups. There has been a growing level of interest and research in issues relating human computer interaction and age groups (Goodman & Lundell, 2005). Some researchers have focused on the unique design characteristics posed by older adults. Hawthorn (2000) lists various physical, sensory and cognitive limitations that may alter with increased age and their implications for interface design. Physical limitations, such as reduced dexterity and precision, can make the use of small and delicate input devices (as found on various mobile devices) more difficult. Sensory limitations can create limitations

for the design of computer output and cognitive limitations can affect the design of the interface itself. For example, cognitive spatial ability has predicted computer performance (Kelley and Charness 1995), and was demonstrated to decline with increasing age (Salthouse, 1992). In other research, age affected the retention of computer training (Brown, 2001), and confidence in learning new applications (Crosby et al., 2003). Older employees generally exhibited a less positive attitude towards computers (Brown, 2001), and were less satisfied users (Simmers & Anandarajan, 2001) than younger employees. It is expected that well designed visual cues such as text links and icons are able to support the needs of older users. The format for organizing Web contents and the amount of information appearing on a screen enable higher performance for older users as their visual search skills and selective attention diminish (Ellis & Kurniawan, 2000).

As with gender, studies that investigate mobile use or m-commerce with consideration of age or design are few. Stroetmann et al. (2002) found that 43% of elderly people surveyed had at least some difficulty with mobile devices and 21% had considerable difficulty because of some physical or cognitive impairment. In a study of Swedish teenagers, Weilenmann and Larsson (2000) reported that young people use a mobile phone in radically different ways from more mature adults. Younger users use a mobile device more for expression than for information, and for social purposes rather than for coordination or efficiency. In a study with Spanish users, younger people are more predisposed to m-commerce adoption than older Internet users (Bigne et al., 2005). In a report on mobile use in India (MACRO 2004), limited adoption of mobile devices among older users resulted from small buttons on the handset and tiny screens that impede user visibility. Goodman et al. (2005) found that text, speech, and photographs were all effective ways to present landmark information to older users using a mobile navigation aid.

In this investigation we are interested to examine design characteristics (such information design, navigation design, and visual design) as outlined by Garrett (2003) for a mobile device, in this case an Internet enabled phone. To our knowledge this is the first attempt to systematically examine these design features and how they may differ for older or younger mobile users. To develop some understanding in this area, the following exploratory hypotheses are offered.

H3a. *There will be differences between older and younger users in the perception of information design of a mobile device.*

H2b. *There will be differences between older and younger users in the perception of navigation design of a mobile device.*

H3c. *There will be differences between older and younger users in the perception of visual design of a mobile device.*

Design and Satisfaction

For many years customer satisfaction has been studied in physical environments (Balasubramanian et al., 2003; Parasuraman et al., 1988; Oliver, 1980 and 1999). More recently, research into consumer satisfaction has turned to the Web domain and examines 'stickiness' and 'the sum of all the website qualities that induce visitors to remain at the website rather than move to another site' (Holland & Baker, 2001). According to Anderson and Srinivasan (2002), e-satisfaction is defined as the contentment of the customer with respect to his or her prior purchasing experience with a given electronic firm. In the present research we adapt the definition for online satisfaction presented by Anderson and Srinivasan to suggest mobile satisfaction refers to contentment of the customer with the experience of using the mobile interface. However, there is no requirement for completion of a purchase in the current context. This defini-

tion is in alignment with Chae et al. (2002) who examined information quality related to user satisfaction for mobile Internet services.

Online satisfaction motivates online shoppers to stay at the site and return to the site in the future (Flavian et al., 2005; Bhattacherjee, 2001; Doll & Torkzadesh, 1988; McKinney et al., 2002) thus yielding a loyal customer outcome. In research into stationary websites, customer satisfaction is affected by content and context of the website (Flavian et al., 2005; Teo et al., 2003). More specific to information design, Szymanski and Hise (2000) discovered that product information and site design are critical to creating a satisfying customer experience. The experience of online shopping can be affected by the richness of product information presented (Palmer, 2002; McKinney et al., 2002), and is a dominant concern of the user (Kateranttanakul & Siau, 1999; Pitt et al., 1995; Zhang et al., 2000). A positive navigation experience and perception of a well-designed site may likewise result in online consumer satisfaction (Agarwal & Venketesh, 2002; Fogg & Tzeng, 1999; Palmer, 2002; Fogg et al., 2002; Hoffman & Novak, 1996; Koufaris, 2002; Nielsen, 2001), an enjoyable online shopping experience (Childers et al, 2001), and sales (Lohse & Spiller, 1999). Yoon (2002) found navigation functionality resulted in satisfaction, and induced Web visitors to remain at the site. Lohse and Spiller (1998) demonstrated that designing online stores with friendly user interfaces positively influences traffic and sales. Cyr (2008) found information design, navigation design, and visual design to all positively impact satisfaction for users from multiple countries.

While design research is limited within the mobile context, Tarasewich (2003) concluded: '[A]esthetics, along with usability, may also be part of designing an overall enjoyable user experience with mobile devices' (p. 12). Jiang and Benbasat (2003) found that mobile interface features can positively influence users' attitudes regarding product presentations. Graphical user interfaces, information architecture, and content

Figure 1. Research model for mobile services

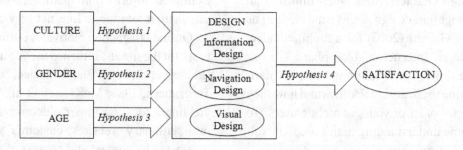

all contributed to differences in perceived satisfaction with mobile data services (Choi et al., 2006). The preceding considerations lead to the final hypotheses:

H4a. *Perception of information design of a mobile device will impact user perceived satisfaction with the mobile device.*

H4b. *Perception of navigation design of a mobile device will impact user perceived satisfaction with the mobile device.*

H4c. *Perception of visual design of a mobile device will impact user perceived satisfaction with the mobile device.*

The above hypotheses as examined in this research are visually depicted in Figure 1.

RESEARCH METHODOLOGY

Participants

Sixty participants were recruited who were either Chinese or Canadian in origin (30 in each category). These countries were chosen to represent diverse cultural characteristics as per Hofstede (1980). Refer to Table 1.

Participants were also categorized by gender and age. Consistent with Aarnio et al. (2002), younger participants were 34 and younger and

Table 1. Country comparisons (Source: based on Hofstede, 1980)

Country Dimension	Canada	China
Power Distance	Low (39)	High (80)
Uncertainty Avoidance	Low (48)	Medium (60)
Masculine	Medium (52)	Medium (50)
Individualism	High (80)	Very Low (20)
Long-Term Orientation	Very Low (23)	Very High (118)

older participants were 35 or older. A relatively small sample size of 30 was chosen for each group due to the individualized and in-depth requirements of the data collection process. To participate, individuals must have used a cell phone for at least one year. In fact, all participants in the study were experienced users, and had owned a cell phone for approximately 4.5 years. Demographics of the sample appear in Table 2.

Experimental Site and Device

Given the emphasis on aesthetics in usability, an attractive site was required, without interference from a slow or faulty live Internet connection. Most WAP sites in North America and Europe are primarily text based, however the Lonely Planet offered some visual treatment (www.lonelyplanet.com with access from a mobile phone at wap.lonelyplanet.com). Therefore the City Guide version of this site was chosen for the experiment and further enhanced. The site for this study featured a colored background and text cells, as

Table 2. Participant demographics

	Canadian (n=30)	Chinese (n=30)
Age	< 35 : 67% ≥ 35 : 33%	< 35 : 60% ≥ 35 : 40%
Gender	Male : 53% Female : 47%	Male : 43% Female : 57%
Highest level of education	High school : 40% Technical degree : 3% Undergraduate/College : 43% Masters/Doctorate : 13%	High school : 27% Technical degree : 3% Undergraduate/College : 53% Masters/Doctorate : 17%
Time spent online/week	22 hours	17.4 hours
Time owned a cell phone	4.8 years	4.4 years
Mobile Internet browsing experience	20%	17%
Use of the mobile Internet (if available)	Buy movie/concert tickets : 33% Download games/ring tones : 40% Check news : 50% Browse places to eat, shop, etc. : 47% Other: 33%	Buy movie/concert tickets : 30% Download games/ring tones : 60% Check news : 67% Browse places to eat, shop, etc. : 67% Other: 7%

well as photographs, maps and icons, among other features. Each version of the site was created in both English and Chinese. For the Chinese version, site contents were translated to Chinese, 'back-translated' from Chinese to English, and then this version was compared with the original English version to verify content equivalence. Screenshot pages appear in Appendix A. Testing occurred on a Nokia 6600 Internet enabled cell phone. This phone was considered very suitable to the aims of the investigation as it has one of the largest screens on the market and has a superior color display (65,536 TFT) capable of laptop quality images. The interface included a joystick option for easy navigation.

To prevent problems with download and browsing delays typical of a real website using WAP technology, website pages for the Lonely Planet were downloaded and saved locally on the cell phone. Based on feedback obtained from a pilot focus group (of 6), participants were not aware of this manipulation and perceived the connection to be '*real*'. Important to this study, saving the site locally allowed the content to be modified and the display speeds to be controlled.

Experimental Tasks

The pilot study with 6 participants was used to pre-test potential tasks and the experimental protocol including survey items and interview questions. Participants in the pilot study were initially asked to perform three information retrieval tasks: finding movie listings at a local theatre, choosing a restaurant in a different city, and booking a hotel in a different city. It was decided the restaurant task was most suitable because it was preferred by the pilot subjects and afforded excellent visual design opportunities. For the restaurant task, photos of the venue's interior as well as the map showing the location were included.

In the full study, each participant went through the experiment individually, under the supervision of a research investigator. For Chinese participants, all documents were translated and back translated, and a translator was available as required. The session began with a brief introduction and completion of a background data sheet, followed by familiarization with the Nokia 6600 device including a written summary of key functions. Once it was determined participants were comfortable with the device they were read the following narrative:

Imagine that you have just arrived in San Francisco to meet up with an old friend. Your friend has suggested that you select a restaurant on your cell phone, and call her back with the address. Use the bookmarked CityGuide site to accomplish this task. Spend as much time as you need browsing through the featured listings for San Francisco. There is no need to actually write down any information or make any calls. Just let me know what your selection is when you're finished.

The device was then handed to the participant with the browser opened at the introductory page of the site. The site listing for San Francisco featured four restaurants. Participants first completed the task, and then responded to a survey and were interviewed regarding their experience. At the end of the experiment, participants were debriefed and received a $20 honorarium for their time.

Survey Instrument

Following the completion of the experimental task, subjects were asked to complete a paper-based survey. In this section, we provide an overview of the survey measurement items, focusing on its content and construct validity.

Content validity considers how representative and comprehensive the items are in creating the experimental constructs. Validity is assessed by examining the process by which the construct items were generated (Straub, 1989). Constructs should draw representative questions (items) from a universal pool (Cronbach, 1971; Kerlinger, 1964). In this research, survey items were adapted from previously validated work on Information design (Cyr et al., 2004 and 2005), Navigation design (Cyr et al., 2004 and 2005), Visual design (Cyr et al., 2004 and 2005; van der Heijden, 2003), and Satisfaction (Cyr et al., 2004 and 2005). All items were constructed as agree-disagree statements on

a seven-point Likert scale. The complete survey appears in Appendix B.

Construct validity assesses the extent to which a construct measures the variable of interest. In other words, there should be high correlations between items of the same construct (convergent validity), and low correlations between items of different constructs (discriminant validity) (Straub, 1989). Results of the principal components analysis with varimax rotation appear in Table 3. The loadings for navigation design, visual design, and satisfaction construct items exceed recommended thresholds (Hair et al., 1998). However information design had two items (ID3 and ID4) that had high cross-loadings with items in the visual design construct. As such, ID3 and ID4 were removed from our analysis in order to maintain discriminant validity.

Discriminant validity can also be assessed by the average variance extracted (AVE) for each construct. As shown in Table II, the AVEs were all above the recommended 0.50 level (Fornell & Larcker, 1981), which meant that more than one-half of the variances observed in the items were accounted for by their hypothesized factors.

Construct reliability (internal consistency) of the four factors was examined using Cronbach's α-value. As shown in Table II, α-values ranged from 0.61 (for information design) to 0.89 (for visual design). Rivard and Huff (1988) suggest that this measure for reliability should be higher than 0.5 and ideally higher than 0.7. Navigation design, visual design and satisfaction α-values are well past this recommended threshold, and the α-value for information design (with its two items dropped) is also in an acceptable range. Therefore, our survey instrument encompassed satisfactory content validity (as evidenced from drawing construct items from existing validated literature); satisfactory convergent validity (as evidenced from high item loadings and construct reliability); satisfactory discriminant validity (as evidenced from low cross-loadings of factor items and the AVE for each factor); and satisfactory

Table 3. Principle components analysis and reliability

	ID	ND	VD	SAT
Cronbach alpha	.61	.84	.89	.84
AVE	.57	.68	.60	.56
Items				
ID1	**.775**	.221	.094	.101
ID2	**.730**	.020	.311	.245
ID3	.598	.271	.559	.176
ID4	.546	.227	.537	.300
ND1	.250	**.700**	.302	.175
ND2	.004	**.891**	.072	.249
ND3	.222	**.862**	.131	.039
VD1	.110	.093	**.859**	.146
VD2	.336	.157	**.833**	.182
VD3	.101	.122	**.601**	.510
VD4	.214	.200	**.789**	.291
SAT1	-.159	.240	.247	**.661**
SAT2	.326	.060	.223	**.857**
SAT3	.313	.102	.137	**.810**
SAT4	.408	.279	.290	**.646**

Notes: ID=Information Design; ND=Navigation Design; VD=Visual Design; SAT=Satisfaction

construct reliability (as evidenced from Cronbach's α-values).

Interviews

Following the completion of the survey, subjects were asked open-ended questions in a tape-recorded interview. The interview questions were meant to solicit additional information about the participants' experiences with the experimental task and interface. The questions probed how participants liked the design of the site, what they would change, and whether or not they found the device useful.

Responses were content analyzed and coded using Atlas.ti. This software provides an effective means to analyze qualitative data such as interview transcripts. The qualitative analysis process consisted of the following steps: (1) data preparation (i.e. interview transcription and formatting); (2) in vivo coding (use of participants' words as code labels) and open coding (use of arbitrary labels for code labels); (3) category and concept building in which semantic relationships between codes are identified to build higher conceptual abstractions; and (4) theory building based on interpretation of the results.

RESULTS

The descriptive statistics and correlations for the perceptual constructs are shown in Table 4. Each of the design variables (ID, ND and VD) was correlated to each other, as well as to overall

Table 4. Descriptive statistics and correlations

	Mean	Std. Dev.	ID	ND	VD	SAT	GEN	CUL	AGE
ID	5.43	1.04							
ND	5.73	0.90	.37***						
VD	5.28	1.09	.53****	.43***					
SAT	4.98	1.11	.49****	.43***	.59****				
GEN	----	----	.09	.01	.09	.08			
CUL	----	----	-.06	-.09	.02	.17	.10		
AGE	----	----	.04	.07	.26**	.18	-.10	.07	

Notes:
1 ID=Information Design; ND=Navigation Design; VD=Visual Design; SAT=Satisfaction
2. Descriptive statistics not provided for GEN, CUL and AGE, as these are dichotomous variables
3. * $p<.10$; ** $p<.05$; *** $p<.01$; **** $p<.001$

satisfaction. From the demographic variables, only age is positively correlated with visual design.

Overall, respondents have a rather favorable impression of the mobile interface, with mean scores of over 5 out of 7 for information design (ID), navigation design (ND), and visual design (VD). The mean score for satisfaction is 4.98, also indicating overall satisfaction with the site. To probe these results further, a word count was run on transcribed interviews using the atlas.ti software. The word 'easy' appeared 69 times, mostly in response to the question 'Try to describe the navigation experience on the site'. As such, the majority of users find the navigation of the device easy. One respondent elaborates, '[U]sing the joystick was pretty straightforward, once I remembered to go left and right to go up the links. It was more intuitive to use the scroll button up or down...'

Although information design receives a relatively high mean score (5.43), more than half the respondents thought there could have been more information about the restaurants on the site. This split into two category codes: one related to not enough information for each restaurant, which typically was lack of a menu (code *menu*) and two, not enough choice of restaurants (under the code *choice*). In terms of visual design of the

site, the following quote captures some of the favorable sentiments as expressed by a number of users: '[E]*asy to use, attractively displayed, something that awes people, this display is very graphically appealing. I really want to play with this.*' Another user comments: '*The colors were good. The colors were actually fairly robust. Resolution seemed to be pretty good.*'

Tests of Culture, Gender, and Age as Moderators

T-tests of differences between culture, gender, and age group means for design and satisfaction are shown in Tables 5, 6, and 7 respectively.

Additionally, interview data was coded using two methods: (i) in vivo (using the participant's exact words as the basis for a code), and (ii) open coding (using arbitrary labels to code the data). Interview responses were systematically categorized in each design area (information, navigation and visual design). Altas.ti was used to create a concept map for the design areas, highlighting the actual number of responses in each code based on gender and culture. Refer to Appendix C. Although the numbers are relatively low, they signify response trends between the groups. In addition, representative quotations are included. Further,

Table 5. T-test of differences between culture group means for design and satisfaction

	Group Means	t-value	p-value
ID	Can: 5.48 Ch: 5.37	0.433	.667
ND	Can: 5.81 Ch: 5.66	0.688	.507
VD	Can: 5.27 Ch: 5.32	-0.176	.861
SAT	Can: 4.80 Ch: 5.17	-1.279	.206

Notes: Can= Canadian; Ch=Chinese

Table 6. T-test of differences between gender group means for design and satisfaction

	Group Means	t-value	p-value
ID	M: 5.33 F: 5.52	-0.698	.488
ND	M: 5.72 F: 5.74	-0.076	.939
VD	M: 5.19 F: 5.39	-0.685	.497
SAT	M: 4.87 F: 5.06	-0.576	.567

Notes: M=Males; F=Females

Table 7. T-test of differences between age group means for design and satisfaction

	Group Means	t-value	p-value
ID	<35: 5.39 ≥35: 5.48	-0.277	.784
ND	<35: 5.68 ≥35: 5.82	-0.626	.534
VD	<35: 5.08 ≥35: 5.66	-2.274	.027**
SAT	<35: 4.83 ≥35: 5.25	-1.501	.139

*Notes: * $p < .1$; ** $p < .05$; *** $p < .01$*

more theoretical themes were created from the emerging concepts, across the design areas. The main themes from our interview data were:

- **Information breadth:** The number of alternative (restaurant) choices. This is encapsulated by comment such as 'choices are limited' and unmet expectations for 'a lot of restaurants represented'.
- **Information depth:** The amount of detail for each alternative (restaurant) choice. This is encapsulated by participants seeking 'detailed menus', 'prices', 'famous dishes', 'parking', 'exterior shots', 'reviews' and 'hours of operation'.
- **Visual ease:** Utilitarian view on the interface design's capability to facilitate the task. This is captured through comments such as 'adequate resolution', 'easy to read' and 'easy to look at'.
- **Visual beauty:** Hedonic view on the beauty of the interface design. This is captured through comments such as 'cute' design, 'should be more charming', 'put some music', and 'animation would be good'.
- **Navigation layout:** The layout of the information within the site. Captured by comments such as 'laid out in a logical way', and too much 'scrolling'.
- **Navigation challenges:** Navigation/interaction challenges mostly stemming from inexperience with the new technology. Encapsulated by comments such as 'counterintuitive joystick' and not convenient to 'press the left side to select the options'.

Table 8 summarizes the analysis of the interview transcripts across the above emerging themes and individual differences (culture, gender, age).

Based on the survey data, it is surprising no statistically significant differences are evident for culture or gender. However based on the qualitative analysis of the interview data some differences in these categories are indicated.

These results support H1a that Canadians prefer utility of information design, while Chinese prefer more detail and depth of information. Canadians

Table 8. Summary of interview analysis across culture, gender and age groups

Design Area	Culture	Gender	Age
Information Design	Canadian: focused on Information Breadth Chinese: focused on Information Depth	Male: no noticeable patterns Female: focused on Information Depth (in particular, Chinese females)	Young: focused on Information Breadth Old: commented on both Information Breadth and Information Depth, with more focus on Depth
Navigation Design	Canadian: commented on both Navigation Layout and Challenges (in particular, Canadian women focused on Navigation Challenges) Chinese: very few comments on navigation	Male: some comments on Navigation Layout. Female: focused on Navigation Challenges (in particular, Canadian women).	Young: very few comments on navigation Old: some comments on Navigation Challenges
Visual Design	Canadian: focused on Visual Ease (in particular, Canadian men) Chinese: focused on Visual Beauty (mostly providing suggestions to augment beauty)	Male: No men commented on Visual Beauty; Canadian men commented on Visual Ease Female: focused on Visual Beauty (in particular, Chinese females)	Young: some comments on Visual Ease Old: commented on both Visual Ease and Visual Beauty (females only for Visual Beauty).

were much more disappointed with the number of restaurant choices (Information Breadth) than Chinese, who focused on the lack of restaurant details (Information Depth). This Chinese focus on Information Depth was particularly evident among Chinese women. H1b was also generally supported in that both Canadians and Chinese prefer simple and logical navigation formats. In the case of Canadians they thought navigation could in fact be simpler, and the Chinese made few specific comments. Finally, qualitative results also support H1c. It was predicted Chinese would be more concerned with aesthetic beauty of the mobile interface than Canadians. In fact, Chinese (women only) even commented on how to augment the beauty of the interface, and Canadians focused more on visual ease.

It is interesting to note that no male from either culture made comments on the visual beauty or hedonic elements of interface design. However there were some cases where women not only commented on their hedonic preferences, but also made distinctions of what they prefer versus what they think men prefer. Overall, while our quantitative analysis rejects hypothesis 2 concerning differences in gender, our in-depth qualitative

analysis suggests there may be some interesting differences in these categories.

Some support is found for hypothesis 3. Using survey data, statistically significant differences exist between older users (35 or older) and younger users (under 35) for visual design, with older respondents indicating the design of the mobile interface more appealing. Generally speaking, older respondents seem more impressed with the novelty of the device and its design than the younger group. This is evidenced in the following comment from an older subject: '*The newness of it, it's captivating. Being efficient is fun sometime. Not having to wade through a whole bunch of stuff. Look at this, look at what it can do, you can do it really easily, and you can get the information before everybody else does.*'

Predicting Satisfaction

Regression analysis was performed to assess the determinants of satisfaction based on main effects and interaction effects of the variables in this research. Gender and culture categorization was straightforward, where dummy variables represented males/females and Canadian/Chinese participants. Age was also coded as a dichoto-

Table 9. Predicting satisfaction

	R²	ΔR²	β	Sig.
GENDER	.063	.013	.174	.551
AGE			.415	.171
CULTURE			.322	.270
ID	.422	.391	.220	.097*
ND			.230	.118
VD			.420	.002***
ID x GENDER	..031	-.021	-.120	.583
ND x GENDER			.192	.432
VD x GENDER			-.025	.924
ID x AGE	.175	.130	.061	.532
ND x AGE			-.111	.343
VD x AGE			.180	.122
ID x CULTURE	.071	.022	.306	.258
ND x CULTURE			-.105	.663
VD x CULTURE			-.104	.738
ID x GENDER x AGE	.018	-.035	-.005	.602
ND x GENER x AGE			.077	.654
VD x GENDER x AGE			.011	.948
ID x GENDER x CULTURE	.012	-.041	.086	.848
ND x GENDER x CULTURE			.181	.546
VD x GENDER x CULTURE			-.261	.573
ID x AGE x CULTURE	.131	.084	.361	.051*
ND x AGE x CULTURE			-.091	.636
VD x AGE x CULTURE			-.190	.448
ID x AGE x GENDER x CULTURE	.013	-.040	.166	.580
ND x AGE x GENDER x CULTURE			.116	.661
VD x AGE x GENDER x CULTURE			-.263	.452

Notes: 1. ID=Information Design; ND=Navigation Design; VD=Visual Design
2. * p < .1; ** p < .05; *** p < .01

mous variable for clarity in presentation (Morris et al., 2005). Participants who are 34 years of age or younger were categorized as 'younger', while those 35 or older were placed in the 'older' category (as per Aarnio et al., 2002). Morris et al. (2005) suggested that gender differences in technology perceptions are more pronounced among older workers, and the interplay between key demographic variables should be examined in addition to investigating isolated demographic characteristics. This notion is supported by others in the information systems field (Butler, 2000; Venkatesh et al., 2000), as well as the field of psychology (Nosek et al., 2002; Kubeck et al., 1996). Therefore, in Table 9 the regression analysis examines various combinations of three-way and four-way interactions between demographic variables (e.g., visual design X gender X age).

In general, results of the regression analysis in Table 9 support hypothesis 4 that design elements do impact satisfaction with mobile services.

The effect size of independent variables on a dependent variable can be determined by comparing the R^2 of the dependent variable with and without the presence of each independent variable (Chin, 1998). The calculation for effect size (f^2) is as follows:

$$f^2 = \frac{R^2_{\text{included}} - R^2_{\text{excluded}}}{1 - R^2_{\text{included}}}$$

The effect size of perceived information design, navigation design and visual design on satisfaction were $f^2=0.09$, $f^2=0.08$ and $f^2=0.23$, respectively. Cohen (1988) provides the following criteria for interpreting effect size: (i) for small effect size, $0.02<f^2\leq0.15$; (ii) for medium effect size, $0.15<f^2\leq0.35$; and (iii) for large effect size, $f^2>0.35$. Therefore, both information and navigation design were shown to have a small effect size on satisfaction, while visual design can be classified as having a medium effect size on satisfaction.

The only interaction effect shown to have a statistical impact on satisfaction is information design by age by culture. Not all groups were equally satisfied with information provided at the site. This is supported in our qualitative analysis. Canadians were primarily concerned about the limited number of restaurant options (Information Breadth), whereas Chinese sought more detailed information for each of the restaurant choices (Information Depth). As one Chinese participant noted, '*You need to know price of the restaurant, the surroundings, and what the location and street looks like, but maybe I would have to call them to get information and details*'. In contrast, a Canadian participant commented: '*I was expecting there would be a lot of restaurants represented. For San Francisco I would be disappointed, I wouldn't trust the source*'. This was particularly evident among the older participants.

DISCUSSION AND CONCLUSION

Egan (1998) makes the case for exploring individual differences in interface design, and claims 'differences among people usually account for much more variability in performance than differences in system designs or differences in training procedures' (p. 543). Individual differences may affect what users seek in a system's interface, and how they interpret such interfaces. Elements of a user interface appropriate for one group may not be appropriate for another.

For mobile devices, evidence of the impact of individual differences on design and satisfaction has been preliminary, scattered, and incomplete. In fact, the majority of previous research tends to examine the *adoption* of mobile devices by culture (Harris et al., 2005; Kim et al., 2004; Carlson et al., 1999), gender (Yang, 2005; Brennen, 2000; Joines et al., 2003; Park & Jun, 2003; Rohm & Swaminathan, 2004) or age (Wielenmann & Larsson, 2000) rather than based on design considerations.

In contrast, the current research explores user perceptions of mobile *design* by culture, gender and age. This has included a focus of information design, navigation design and visual design and how each impacts user satisfaction with an Internet enabled cellular phone. Our exploratory analysis using both quantitative and qualitative data reveals some interesting differences for culture and age between user groups related to our three mobile design dimensions and satisfaction. Equally interesting is that there are no gender differences for the mobile device as tested.

In the realm of information design, overall Canadian and Chinese users felt there was adequate information presented on the mobile device, but each group was attentive to different types of information. Canadians focused on 'Information Breadth' (more choice of alternative restaurants) and the utility of information design, while Chinese focused on 'Information Depth' (more detail about the existing choices). This finding is in alignment with the qualitative results of Choi et al. (2006) who discovered that collectivist Koreans and Japanese preferred large amounts of detail on a single screen. With respect to gender and information design, no specific patterns emerged for men however women tended to focus more on 'Information Depth', especially Chinese women. This finding suggests women more than men desire detailed information content, perhaps related to different modes of information processing (Maltby et al., 2003). With respect to age, younger participants focused on 'Information Breadth' while older users desired both breadth and depth of information, with more emphasis on depth. Taken collectively, younger Canadian users were most concerned with 'Information Breadth' while older Chinese females were most focused on 'Information Depth'. These results have implications for mobile interface designers who aim to best connect with users.

On the stationary Internet, there is evidence that preferences for visual design vary by culture (Cyr, 2008; Cyr & Trevor-Smith, 2004). Users from collectivist cultures such as China desire visuals and aesthetic beauty of the interface, with emphasis on "affective" qualities (Cyr et al., 2006). On a mobile interface Choi et al. (2006) similarly found that collectivist Koreans and Japanese preferred colorful screen design, while Finns preferred simpler, less colorful screen design. Results from the current investigation parallel these earlier studies. In the area of visual design, Canadians focused on Visual Ease (utilitarian elements of design) while Chinese commented more on the 'beauty' of the design. Related to gender, men in both cultures and age groups were more concerned with 'Visual Ease' while women were more interested in 'Visual Beauty' and more aesthetic elements of the interface.

Almost all participants found the mobile interface relatively easy to use and navigate. The sites are not deep, are laid out in a logical way, and the joystick is easy to master. Chinese participants had little to say about navigation, while Canadians women and older users generally commented on challenges of navigation the interface. This finding is aligned to other work in which women found stationary websites more difficult to navigate (Cyr & Bonanni, 2005), or where physical limitations may have implications for interface design with older users (Hawthorn, 2000).

Consistent with findings for the stationary Internet, it is not surprising that in this investigation design elements impact satisfaction in a mobile service context. Further, the current work is consistent with Chae et al. (2002) who found that information quality of mobile services contributed to satisfaction. However, Chae et al. examined different elements of the mobile interface than in our investigation. Collectively, these findings support the assertion that regardless of technology or device, the interface is often considered the most important component of the entire system to the end-user (Sarker & Wells, 2003), and plays an important role in user attitudes (Bidgoli, 1990). As such, further research related to effective mobile design has commercial implications for m-commerce and is aligned to investigations of effective website design in e-commerce (Agarwal & Venkatesh, 2002; Fogg & Tzeng, 1999; Hui & Triandis, 1985; Morgan & Hunt, 1994; Schultz, 2003).

This is an initial exploratory study with a limited sample size, representing only two cultures. Although participants are representative of the desired cultural groups, they may not fully represent the socio-economic group within their country. It is recommended that follow-up studies draw samples from larger populations, and from additional culture groups. Also, usability evaluations themselves may be culturally bound. As Yeo (2001) points out, participants from various cultures are prone to provide false statements during usability evaluations to allow the designer to 'save face'. Research is needed to develop usability and research methodologies that accurately reflect personal opinions and preferences across cultures. Further, designers tend to ignore the role culture may play in the design of the interface (Sheridan, 2001), in particular within the Web context (Jagne et al., 2005). While many studies have been inconclusive, cultural factors deserve further investigation (Kwon & Chidambaram, 2000). At the very least, researchers and designers will ideally seek to better understand design elements that promote cultural attractiveness.

It is noteworthy that only one mobile application (a restaurant selection) and only one WAP site (lonelyplanet.com) are used in this experiment. The site offered some visual treatment, but has a narrow structure and simple layout. A more complex site with a deeper hierarchy may reveal more pronounced differences across diverse groups. Future research should consider multiple designs across multiple mobile applications. A positive feature of this investigation is the application of design elements as outlined by the design community (Garrett's 2003 categorizations for information design, visual design, and navigation design) to a mobile treatment. Further, in a nascent area of study as represented here, a strong point

of the investigation is the use of both quantitative and qualitative methodologies. In addition to surveys, interview data was evaluated using atlas.ti software to provide a systematic evaluation of words or phrases into categories relevant to this investigation. The use of atlas.ti afforded deeper insights into the user experience than survey data alone can provide.

This research is an important first step in understanding the impact of individual differences on the design and satisfaction of mobile services. This relatively unexplored area is worthy of future attention. The quest for further knowledge as to how culture, gender and age impact technology use and satisfaction implies appreciation that these relationships are dynamic, and subject to continuous transformation (Simon, 2001). Enhanced understanding of subtle dimensions related to specific user groups will eventually enable fulfillment of expectations for optimal anytime and anywhere services.

REFERENCES

Aarnio, E. A., Heikkila, J., & Hirvola, S. (2002). Adoption and use of mobile services empirical evidence from a Finnish survey. In *Proceedings of 35th International Conference of System Sciences, Hawaii, USA.*

Agarwal, R., & Venkatesh, V. (2002). Assessing a firm's web presence: A heuristic evaluation procedure for measurement of usability. *Information Management Research, 13,* 168–121.

Anckar, B., & D'Incau, D. (2002). Value creation in mobile commerce: Findings from a consumer survey. *Journal of Information Technology Theory & Application, 4,* 43–64.

Anderson, R. E., & Srinivasan, S. S. (2002). E-satisfaction and e-loyalty: A contingency framework. *Psychology & Marketing, 20,* 123–138.

Balasubramanian, S., Konana, P., & Menon, N. (2003). Customer satisfaction in virtual environments: A study of online investing. *Management Science, 49,* 871–889.

Barber, W., & Badre, A. N. (2001). Culturability: The merging of culture and usability. In *Proceedings of 4th Conference on Human Factors and the Web.* New Jersey: Basking Ridge.

Becker, S. A. (2002). An exploratory study on web usability and the internationalization of US e-businesses. *Journal of Electronic Commerce Research, 3,* 265–278.

Bernard, M. (2002). *Criteria for optimal web design (Designing for usability).* Retrieved from: http://psychology.wichita.edu/optimalweb/print.htm

Bhattacherjee, A. (2001). Understanding information systems continuance: An expectation-confirmation model. *MIS Quarterly, 2,* 351–369.

Bidgoli, H. (1990). Designing a user-friendly interface for a decision support system. *Information Technology, 12,* 148–154.

Bigne, E., Ruiz, C., & Sanz, S. (2005). The impact of internet user shopping patterns and demographics on consumer mobile buying behavior. *Journal of Electronic Commerce Research, 6,* 193–209.

Brennan, M. (2000). *Dot-com flavor of the week or hand-held revolution?* Retrieved from: http://www.bizjournals.com/tampabay/stories/2000/10/09/focus5.html

Brown, K. (2001). Using computers to deliver training: Which employees learn and why? *Personnel Psychology, 54,* 271–296.

Butler, D. (2000). Gender, girls, and computer technology: What's the status now? *Clearing House, 73,* 225–229.

Carlson, P. J., Kahn, B. K., & Rowe, F. (1999). Organisational impacts of new communication technology: A comparison of cellular phone adoption in France and the United States. *Journal of Global Information Management, July,* (pp. 19–29).

Chae, M., & Kim, J. (2004). Do size and structure matter to mobile users? An empirical study of the effects of screen size, information structure, and task complexity on user activities with standard web phones. *Behaviour & Information Technology, 23,* 165–181.

Chae, M., Kim, J., & Ryu, H. (2002). Information quality for mobile internet services: A theoretical model with empirical validation. *Electronic Markets, 12,* 38–46.

Chau, P. K., Au, G., & Tam, K. Y. (2000). Impact of information presentation modes on online shopping: An empirical evaluation of a broadband interactive shopping service. *Journal of Organisational Computing Electronic Commerce, 10,* 1–22.

Chen, S. C., & Dhillon, G. S. (2003). Interpreting dimensions of consumer trust in e-commerce. *Information Technology and Management, 4,* 303–318.

Childers, T., Carr, C., Peck, J., & Carson, S. (2001). Hedonic and utilitarian motivations for online retail shopping behavior. *Journal of Retailing, 77,* 511–535.

Chin, W. W. (1998). The partial least squares approach to structural equation modeling. In G.A. Marcoulides (Ed.), Modern methods for business research (pp. 295–336). Mahwah: Lawrence Erlbaum Associates.

Choi, B., Lee, I., & Kim, J. (2006). Culturability in mobile data services: A qualitative study of the relationship between cultural characteristics and user-experience attributes. *International Journal of Human-Computer Interaction, 20,* 171–206.

Choi, B., Lee, I., Kim, J., & Jeon, Y. (2005). A qualitative cross-national study of cultural influences on mobile data service design. In *Proceedings of Computer-Human Interaction, Portland, Oregon, USA, 2-7 April.*

Cohen, J. (1988). *Statistical power analysis for the behavioral sciences.* 2nd ed. New York: Academic Press.

Coursaris, C., Hassanein, K., & Head, M. (2003). Understanding the mobile consumer. In S. Nansi (Ed.), *Wireless communications and mobile commerce* (pp. 132–165). Idea Group Inc.

Cronbach, L. J. (1971). Test validation in educational measurement. In R. L. Thorndike, (Ed.), 2nd ed. (pp. 443–507). Washington, D.C: American Council on Education.

Crosby, L. B., DeVito, R., & Pearson, J. M. (2003). Manage your customers' perception of quality. *Review of Business, 24.*

Cyr, D. (2008). Modelling website design across cultures: Relationships to trust, satisfaction and e-loyalty. *Journal of Management Information Systems, 24*(4), 47–72.

Cyr, D., Head, J., Larios, H., & Pan, B. (2006). Exploring human images in website design across cultures: A multi-method approach. In *Proceedings for the Fifth Pre-ICIS HCI Research in MIS Workshop 2006, Milwaukee, Wisconsin.* Nominated for Best Paper Award.

Cyr, D., Bonanni, C., Bowes, J., & Ilsever, J. (2005). Beyond trust: Website design preferences across cultures. *Journal of Global Information Management, 13,* 24–52.

Cyr, D., & Bonanni, C. (2005). Gender and website design in e-business. *International Journal of Electronic Business, 6,* 565–582.

Cyr, D., Bonanni, C., & Ilsever, J. (2004). Design and e-loyalty across cultures in electronic commerce. In *Proceedings of 6th International Conference on Electronic Commerce.*

Cyr, D., & Trevor-Smith, H. (2004). Localization of web design: An empirical comparison of German, Japanese, and U.S. website characteristics. *Journal of the American Society for Information Science and Technology, 55,* 1–10.

Deaux, K., & Kite, M. E. (1987). Thinking about gender. In B. B. Hess & M. M. Ferree (Eds.), *Analyzing gender: A handbook of social science research* (pp. 92–117). Newbury Park, CA: Sage Publications.

Dillon, R. J., & McKnight, C. (1990). The effect of display size and text splitting on reading lengthy text from the screen. *Behavior and Information Technology, 9,* 215–227.

Doll, W. J., & Torkzadesh, G. (1988). The measurement of end-user computing satisfaction. *MIS Quarterly, 12,* 259–274.

Doney, P. M., Cannon, J. P., & Mullen, M. R. (1998). Understanding the influence of national culture on the development of trust. *Academy of Management Review, 23,* 601–620.

Duchnicky, R. L., & Kolers, P. A. (1983). Readability of text scrolled on visual display terminals as a function of window size. *Human Factors, 25,* 683–692.

Egan, D. E. (1998). Individual differences in human-computer interaction. In M. Helander (Ed.), *Handbook of human-computer Interaction* (pp. 543–568). Amsterdam: Elsevier Science Publishers.

Egger, F. N. (2001). Affective design of e-commerce user interfaces: How to maximize perceived trustworthiness. In *Proceedings of International Conference of Affective Human Factors Design.* London Press.

Ellis, R. D., & Kurniawan, S. H. (2000). Increasing the usability of online information for older users: A case study in participatory design. *International Journal of Human-Computer Interaction, 12,* 263–276.

Evers, V., & Day, D. (1997). The role of culture in interface acceptance. In S. Howard, J. Hammond, & G. Lindegaard (Eds.), *Proceedings of Human Computer Interaction, INTERACT '97*. London: Chapman and Hall.

Farkas, K., & Farkas, J. B. (2000). Guidelines for designing web navigation. *Technical Communication, Third Quarter*, (pp. 341–358).

Flavián, C., Guinalíu, M., & Gurrea, R. (2005). The role played by perceived usability, satisfaction and consumer trust on website loyalty. *Information & Management, 42*, 719–729.

Fogg, B. J., Soohoo, C., & Danielson, D. (2002). *How people evaluate a web site's credibility?* Results from a large study. Persuasive Technology Lab, Stanford University. Retrieved from: www.consumerwebwatch.org/news/report3_credibilityresearch/stanfordPTL.pdf

Fogg, J., & Tseng, S. (1999). Credibility and computing technology. *Communications of the ACM, 14*, 39–87.

Fornell, C., & Larcker, D. F. (1981). Evaluating structural equation models with unobserved variables and measurement error. *Journal of Marketing Research, 18*, 39–50.

Garrett, J. J. (2003). *The Elements of user experience: User-centered design for the web*. Indiana, USA: New Riders Publications.

Gefen, D., & Straub, D. W. (1997). Gender differences in the perception and use of email: An extension to the technology acceptance model. *MIS Quarterly, 21*, 389–400.

Gommans, M., Krishan, K. S., & Scheddold, K. B. (2001). From brand loyalty to e-loyalty: A conceptual framework. *Journal of Economic and Social Research, 3*, 43–58.

Goodman, J., Brewser, S. A., & Gray, P. (2005). How can we best use landmarks to support older people in navigation? *Behaviour & Information Technology, 24*, 3–20.

Goodman, J., & Lundell, J. (2005). HCI and the older population: Editorial. *Interacting with Computers, 17*, 613–620.

Hair, F., Anderson, R. E., Tathan, R. L., & Black, W. C. (1998). *Multivariate data analysis*. Englewood Cliffs, N.J.: Prentice Hall.

Harris, P., Rettie, R., & Kwan, C. C. (2005). Adoption and usage of m-commerce: A cross-cultural comparison of Hong Kong and the United Kingdom. *Journal of Electronic Commerce Research, 6*, 210–224.

Hawthorn, D. (2000). Possible implications of aging for interface design. *Interacting with Computers, 12*, 507–528.

Hoffman, D. L., & Novak, T. P. (1996). Marketing in hypermedia computer-mediated environments: Conceptual foundations. *Journal of Marketing, 60*, 50–68.

Hofstede, G. (1980). *Culture's consequences: Comparing values, behaviors, institutions and organisations across nations*, 2nd ed. Thousand Oaks, CA: Sage Publication.

Holland, J., & Baker, S. M. (2001). Customer participation in creating site brand loyalty. *Journal of Interactive Marketing, 15*, 34–45.

Hu, J., Shima, K., Oehlmann, R., Zhao, J., Takemura, Y., & Matsumoto, K. (2004). An empirical study of audience impressions of B2C web pages in Japan, China and the U.K. *Electronic Commerce Research and Applications, 3*(2), 176–189.

Hui, C. H., & Triandis, H. C. (1985). Measurement in the cross-cultural psychology: A review and comparison of strategies. *Journal of Cross-Cultural Psychology, 16*, 131–152.

Jagne, J., Smith-Atatkan, S., Duncker, E., & Curzon, P. (2005). Cross-cultural factors of physical and e-shopping. In *Proceedings of the Eleventh International Conference on Human Computer Interaction*.

Jiang, Z., & Benbasat, I. (2003). The effects of interactivity and vividness of functional control in changing web consumers' attitudes. In *Proceedings 24th International Conference of Information Systems, Seattle, USA.*

Joines, J. L., Scherer, C., & Scheufele, D. (2003). Exploring motivations for consumer web use and their implications for e-commerce. *The Journal of Consumer Marketing, 20.*

Jones, M. Y., Stanaland, A. J., & Gelb, B. D. (1998). Beefcake and cheesecake: Insights for advertisers. *Journal of Advertising, Summer.*

Kateranttanakul, P., & Siau, K. (1999). Measuring information quality of web sites: Development of an instrument. In *Proceedings of International Conference of Information Systems, Charlotte, North Carolina* (pp. 279–285).

Kelley, C. L., & Charness, N. (1995). Issues in training older adults to use computers. *Behavior and Information Technology, 14,* 107–120.

Kerlinger, F. N. (1964). *Foundations in behavioral research.* New York: Holt, Rinehart, and Winston.

Kim, K., Kim, J., Lee, Y., Chae, M., & Choi, Y. (2002). An empirical study of the use contexts and usability problems in mobile Internet. In *Proceedings of 35th Annual Hawaii International Conference on System Sciences, Los Alamitos, CA.*

Kim, M. K., Park, C., & Jeong, D. H. (2004). The effects of customer satisfaction and switching barrier on customer loyalty in Korean mobile telecommunication services. *Telecommunications Policy, 28,* 145–159.

Knight, M., & Pearson, J. (2005). The changing demographics: The diminishing role of age and gender in computer usage. *Journal of Organisational and End User Computing, 17,* 49–65.

Koufaris, M. (2002). Applying the technology acceptance model and flow theory to online consumer behaviour. *Information Systems Research, 13,* 205–22.

Kumar, S., & Zahn, C. (2003). Mobile communications: Evolution and impact on business operations. *Technovation, 23,* 515–520.

Kubeck, E., Delp, N. D., Haslett, T. K., & McDaniel, M. A. (1996). Does job-related training performance decline with age? *Psychology of Aging, 11,* 92–107.

Kwon, H. S., & Chidambaram, L. (2000). A test of the technology acceptance model: The case of cellular phone adoption. In *Proceedings of 33rd Hawaii International Conference on System Sciences.*

Lee, Y., Kim, J., Lee, I., & Kim, H. (2002). A cross-cultural study on the value structure of mobile internet usage: Comparison between Korea and Japan. *Journal of Electronic Commerce Research, 3,* 227–239.

Lohse, G. L., & Spiller, P. (1999). Internet retail store design: How the user interface influences traffic and sales. *Journal for Computed-Mediated Communication, 5.*

Lohse, G. L., & Spiller, P. (1998). Electronic shopping. *Communications of the ACM, 41,* 81–88.

MACRO (2004). Mobile phone usage among the teenagers and youth in Mumbai. Report. Retrieved from: www.itu.int/osg/spu/ni/futuremobile/socialaspects/IndiaMacroMobileYouthStudy04.pdf

McKinney, V., Yoon, K., & Zahedi, F. M. (2002). The measurement of web-customer satisfaction: An expectation and disconfirmation approach. *Information Systems Research, 13,* 296–315.

Maltby, Chudry, F., & Wedande, G. (2003). Cyber dudes and cyber babes: Gender differences and internet financial services. *Journal of Financial Services Marketing, 8,*152–165.

Marcus, A., & Gould, E. W. (2000). Cultural dimensions and global web user interface design. *Interactions, July/August,* 33–46.

Morgan, R., & Hunt, S. D. (1994). The Commitment-trust theory of relationship marketing. *Journal of Marketing, 58,* 20–38.

Morris, G. M., Venkatesh, V., & Ackerman, P. L. (2005). Gender and age differences in employee decisions about new technology: An extension to the theory of planned behavior. *IEEE Transactions on Engineering Management, 52,* 69–84.

Nielsen, J. (2001). *Designing for web usability.* Indianapolis: New Riders Publications.

Nielsen, J., & Del Galdo, E. M. (1996). *International User Interfaces.* Wiley Computer Publishing, John Wiley & Sons, New York.

Nosek, B. A., Banaji, M. R., & Greenwalk, A. G. (2002). Harvesting implicit group attitudes and beliefs from a demonstration website. *Group Dynamics: Theory, Research, Practice, 6,* 101–115.

Nysveen, H., Pedersen, P. E., & Thorbjørnsen, H. (2005). Intentions to use mobile services: Antecedents and cross-service comparisons. *Journal of the Academy of Marketing Science, 33,* 330–346.

Oliver, R. L. (1980). A cognitive model of the antecedents and consequences of satisfaction decisions. *Journal of Marketing Research, 42,* 460–469.

Oliver, R. L. (1999). Whence consumer loyalty? *Journal of Marketing, 63,* 33–44.

Palmer, J. W. (2002). Website usability, design, and performance metrics. *Information Systems Research, 13,* 151–167.

Parasuraman, A., Zeithaml, V. A., & Berry, L. L. (1988). SERVQUAL: A multiple-item scale for measuring customer perceptions of service quality. *Journal of Retailing, 64,* 12–40.

Park, C., & Jun, J. K. (2003). A cross-cultural comparison of internet buying behavior: Effects of internet usage, perceived risks, and innovativeness. *International Marketing Review, 20,* 534–553.

Pearson, J. M., Crosby, L., Bahmanziari, T., & Conrad, E. (2003). An empirical investigation into the relationship between organisational culture and computer efficacy as moderated by age and gender. *Journal of Computer Information Systems, 43,* 58–70.

Perry, M., O'Hara, K., Sellen, A., Harper, R., & Brown, B.A.T. (2001). Dealing with mobility: Understanding access anytime, anywhere. *Transactions on Computer-Human Interaction, 8,* 323-347.

Pitt, L. F., Watson, R. T., & Kavan, C. B. (1995). Service quality: A measure of information systems effectiveness. *MIS Quarterly, 19,* 173–187.

Putrevu, S. (2001). Exploring the origins and information processing differences between men and women: Implications for advertisers. *Academy of Marketing Science Review, 10.* Retrieved from: http://www.amsreview.org/articles/putrevu10-2001.pdf

Rainer, R. K., Laosethakul, K., & Astone, M. (2003). Are gender perceptions of computing changing over time? *Journal of Computer Information Systems, 43,* 108–114.

Rau, P. P., Chen, J., & Chen, D. (2006). A study of presentations of mobile web banners for location-based information and entertainment information websites. *Behaviour & Information Technology, 25,* 253–261.

Resiel, J. F., & Shneiderman, B. (1987). Is bigger better? The effects of display size on program reading. In G. Salvendy (Ed.), *Social, ergonomic and stress aspects of work with computers* (pp. 113–122). Elsevier Science Publishers.

Rivard, S., & Huff, S. (1988). Factors of success for end user computing. *Communications of the ACM, 31,* 552–561.

Rodgers, S., & Harris, M. A. (2003). Gender and e-commerce: An exploratory study. *Journal of Advertising Research, 43,* 322–329.

Rohm, J., & Swaminathan, V. (2004). A typology of online shoppers based on shopping motivations. *Journal of Business Research, 57,* 748–757.

Rosen, D. E., & Purinton, E. (2004). Website design: Viewing the web as a cognitive landscape. *Journal of Business Research, 57,* 787–794.

Salthouse, T. A. (1992). Reasoning and spatial abilities. In F. I. M. Craik & T. A. Salthouse (Eds.), *The handbook of aging and cognition,* 3rd ed. (pp. 167–212). Hillsdale, NJ: Lawrence Erlbaum Associates.

Sanchez-Franco, M. J. (2006). Exploring the influence of gender on the web usage via partial least-squares. *Behaviour & Information Technology, 25,* 19–36.

Sarker, S., & Wells, J.D. (2003). Understanding mobile handheld device use and adoption. *Communications of the ACM, 46,* 35–40.

Schultz, L. (2003). Effects of graphical elements on perceived usefulness of a library. Masters thesis. Retrieved from: http://www.tarleton.edu/~schultz/finalprojectinternetsvcs.htm

Sheridan, E. F. (2001). Cross-cultural web site design: Considerations for developing and strategies or validating local appropriate online content. *MultiLingual Computing, 12.* Retrieved from: http://www.multilingual.com.

Schmidt, S. H., & Frick, O. (2000). WAP – designing for small user interfaces. In *Proceedings of Conference on Human Factors in Computing Systems.*

Schrott, G., & Gluckler, J. (2004). What makes mobile computer supported cooperative work mobile? Towards a better understanding of cooperative mobile interactions. *International Journal of Human Computer Studies, 60,* 737–752.

Simmers, S., & Anandarajan, M. (2001). User satisfaction in the internet-anchored workplace: An exploratory study. *Journal of Information Technology Theory and Application, 3,* 39–61.

Simon, S. J. (2001). The impact of culture and gender on web sites: An empirical study. *The Data Base for Advances in Information Systems, 32,* 18–37.

Singh, N., Xhao, H., & Hu, X. (2003). Cultural adaptation on the web: A study of American companies' domestic and Chinese websites. *Journal of Global Information Management, 11,* 63–80.

Straub, D. W., Loch, W., Aristo, R., Karahanna, E., & Strite, M. (2002). Toward a theory-based measurement of culture. *Journal of Global Information Management, 10,* 13–23.

Straub, D.W. (1989). Validating instruments in MIS research. *MIS Quarterly, 12,* 147–170.

Stroetmann, V. N., Husing T., Kubitschke L., & Stroetmann K. A. (2002). The attitudes, expectations and needs of elderly people in relation to e-health applications: Results from a European survey. *Journal of Telemedicine and Telecare, 8,* 82–84.

Sun, H. (2001). Building a culturally-competent corporate web site: An explanatory study of cultural markers in multilingual web design. In *Proceedings of SIGDOC'01,* 21-24, October (pp. 95–102).

Szymanski, D. A., & Hise, R. T. (2000). E-satisfaction: An initial examination. *Journal of Retailing, 76,* 309–322.

Tarasewich, P. (2003). Designing mobile commerce applications. *Communications of the ACM, 46,* 57–60.

Teo, H., Oh, L., Liu, C., & Wei, K. (2003). An empirical study of the effects of interactivity on web user attitude. *International Journal of Human-Computer Studies, 58,* 281–305.

Teo, T., Lim, V., & Lai, R. (1999). Intrinsic and extrinsic motivation in internet usage. *Omega International Journal of Management Science, 27,* 25–37.

Tractinsky, N. (1997). Aesthetics and apparent usability: Empirically assessing cultural and methodological issues. In *CHI Proceedings.*

van der Heijden. (2003). Factors influencing the usage of websites: The case of a generic portal in the Netherlands. *Information & Management, 40,* 541–549.

Venkatesh, V., Ramesh, V., & Massey, A. P. (2003). Understanding usability in mobile commerce. *Communications of the ACM, 46,* 53–56.

Venkatesh, V., Morris, G. M., & Ackerman, P. L. (2000). A longitudinal field investigation of gender differences in individual technology adoption decision-making processes. *Organisation Behavior Human Decision Process, 83,* pp. 33–60.

Weilenmann, A., & Larsson, C. (2000). Collaborative use of mobile telephones: A field study of Swedish teenagers. In *Proceedings of NordiCHI 2000, Stockholm, Sweden, 23–25 October.*

Yang, K. (2005). Exploring factors affecting the adoption of mobile commerce in Singapore. *Telematics and Informatics, 22,* 257–277.

Yeo, A. (2001). Global software development lifecycle: An exploratory study. In *CHI 2001 Conference on Human Factors in Computing Systems* (pp. 104–111). ACM Press.

York J., & Pendharkar, P. (2004). Human-computer interaction issues for mobile computing in a variable work context. *International Journal of Human-Computer Studies, 60,* 771–797.

Yoon, S. (2002). The antecedents and consequences of trust in online-purchase decisions. *Journal of Interactive Marketing, 16,* 47–63.

Zhang, X., Keeling, K. K., & Pavur, R. J. (2000). Information quality of commercial web site homepages: An explorative analysis. In *Proceedings of International Conference on Information Systems, Brisbane, Australia* (pp. 164–175).

ENDNOTES

[1] Throughout this paper the terms 'portable', 'handheld', 'mobile' and 'small-screen' refer to essentially the same type of device, typically called a 'smart phone'. Also, the term 'mobile Internet' refers to accessing the Web directly on a small-screen, handheld, or mobile device that may be connected to the Internet.

[2] The work by Geert Hofstede (1980) outlines 5 cultural dimensions: (1) Power distance - extent to which a society accepts unequal distributions of power in organizations and institutions. (2) Uncertainty avoidance - how societies accommodate high levels of uncertainty and ambiguity in the environment. (3) Masculinity-Femininity - in feminine societies there is an emphasis on quality of life and relationships; cultures that focus on material success and assertiveness are considered more masculine in orientation. (4) Individualism-Collectivism - in an individualist society individuals are expected to consider personal interests over interests of the group and individual decision-making is valued; in a collectivist culture the good of the group is more likely to be considered. (5) Time Orientation - whether the focus in on short-term vs. long-term considerations. For a further elaboration of Hofstede's cultural dimensions, refer to Hofstede (1980) or Simon (2001).

APPENDIX A. SCREEN SHOTS

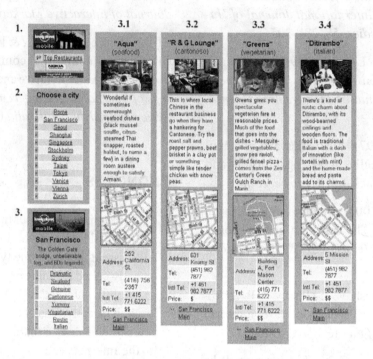

English Version: Numbers indicate different pages, or decks

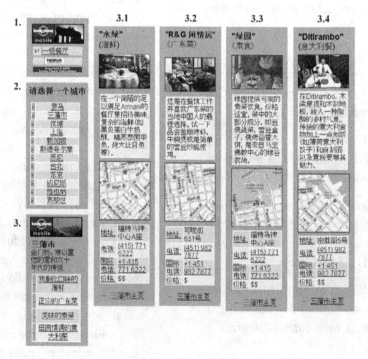

Chinese version: Numbers indicate different pages, or decks

APPENDIX B. DESIGN SURVEY

Following are the statement used in the survey. Each was answered on a 7-point Likert scale from strongly disagree to strongly agree.

Information Design [Sources: Cyr et al. 2005; 2004]

ID-1: I find the information logically presented.

ID-2: All service options, service attributes and restaurant information are well presented.

ID-3: I find the information to be well organized.

ID-4: The presentation of information is effective.

Navigation Design [Sources: Cyr et al. 2005; 2004]

ND-1: This browser provides good navigation facilities to information content.

ND-2: I can easily navigate the CityGuide site.

ND-3: I find the CityGuide site easy to use.

Visual Design [Sources: Cyr et al. 2005; 2004; van der Heijden 2003]

VD-1: The screen design (i.e. colors, boxes, menus, etc) is attractive.

VD-2: This site looks professionally designed.

VD-3: The graphics are meaningful.

VD-4: The overall look and feel of the site is visually appealing.

Satisfaction [Sources: Cyr et al. 2005; 2004]

S-1: This site appeals to me emotionally.

S-2: This service completely fulfills my expectations.

S-3: This service satisfies my needs well.

S-4: Using this service is satisfactory overall.

APPENDIX C: ATLAS.TI CONCEPT MAP

Note: C_M = Canadian male, C_F = Canadian female, CH_M = Chinese male, CH_F = Chinese female.

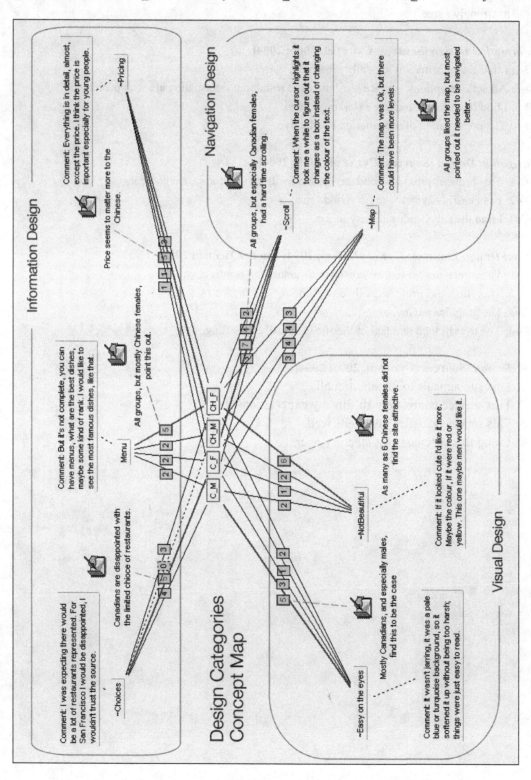

Chapter XI
The Exchange of Emotional Content in Business Communications:
A Comparison of PC and Mobile E-Mail Users

Douglass J. Scott
Waseda University, Japan

Constantinos K. Coursaris
Michigan State University, USA

Yuuki Kato
Tokyo University of Social Welfare, Japan

Shogo Kato
Waseda University, Japan

ABSTRACT

This study compared the exchange of emotional content in PC and mobile e-mail in business-related discussions. Forty American business people were divided into two groups (PC and mobile e-mail users) and were then assigned to anonymous discussion pairs who exchanged a total of six messages on a predetermined topic. When a message was sent, the writers completed two questionnaires related to 12 target emotions: One questionnaire assessed the emotions they experienced and another estimated their partner's emotional reaction. E-mail readers filled out similar questionnaires. Statistical analysis showed that when emotional exchange was successful, mobile e-mail users more accurately predicted positive emotions than did PC e-mail users. Conversely, when emotional exchange was unsuccessful, mobile e-mail users failed to accurately exchange negative emotions far more than their PC using counterparts. These findings indicate that the communication medium used may influence the exchange of emotional content in text-based communications.

INTRODUCTION

The unprecedented growth of mobile communication options and capabilities in recent years has drastically increased the flexibility in and opportunities for transacting business for both companies and customers. The widespread adoption of mobile communication devices facilitates communication within and between companies, and between producers and consumers. While such devices enable workers to largely overcome the limitations of time and place, this capacity presents its own set of challenges and potential problems. Among these are the challenges of accurately predicting the e-mail reader's emotional reactions and estimating the e-mail writer's state of mind.

Previous research on computer-mediated communications (CMC) indicates that the fewer paralinguistic cues in CMC limit the sender's ability to effectively and accurately transmit their intended emotions and meanings relative to face-to-face interactions (Kato, Y. & Akahori 2006). However, little or no research has been done on the relative ability of text-based communications (e.g. PC and mobile) to convey the effectively exchange emotional content. In order to address this gap, this chapter presents a study emotional exchange in mediated business communications, comparing computer-based e-mail (PC e-mail) and mobile phone-based e-mail messaging.

The current variety of available communication tools extends our ability to communicate at almost any time in almost any location. Modern business communications are no longer limited to traditional CMC contexts as the use of mobile communication devices has increased significantly. Internet-capable mobile phones have gone from being an executive status symbol to an essential business tool used by all levels in the organization. Monitoring e-mail traffic from any location at any time has become commonplace, if not expected, among users in many business sectors. However, the nature of mobile communication devices seems

different than the computer-based options. These differences include limited screen size, keyboard size, and data transfer rates that empirically result in shorter, less detailed communications.

The ease with which we are able to communicate makes it easy to overlook that these technologies are facilitating the interaction of complex human beings. One element that contributes greatly to our complexity is our emotions. Emotions are fundamental to human behavior and their transfer in face-to-face (FTF) contexts is challenging and previous research (Kato & Akahori 2004a, 200b) indicates that mediated communications, especially those without the benefit of non-verbal cues, complicates this process and increases misunderstandings over FTF communications.

The current study is based on a Japanese study (Kato, S., Kato, & Akahori 2006) that examined the transmission and interpretation of emotions in text-based communications between Japanese college students. That study, described in greater detail below, concluded that there is a tendency for negative or unpleasant emotions (like anger and anxiety) to increase when there is a lack of emotional cues in the transmission. Such a lack of cues increases the chances of misunderstanding between the communication partners.

However, Kato et al.'s (2006) conclusions were based on the study of a single type of text-based communications and compared successful emotional exchanges with unsuccessful emotional exchanges. The study presented here expands Kato et al.'s work, initially by comparing two common forms of mediated communications, in this case PC and mobile e-mail, to assess their relative ability to convey emotional content. In addition, the current study applies Kato et al.'s approach to a new cultural context (i.e. America rather than Japan) and examines the communications of a different demographic group (i.e. business people rather than college students).

Applying Kato et al.'s approach to a different cultural context is an important first step in what we hope will be a series of future research projects. Initially, by increasing the number of communication media to include PC e-mail and mobile phone e-mail, a comparison can be made between these two kinds of mediated communications commonly used in business contexts. This comparison may shed light on whether Kato et al.'s findings were a function of the nature of the communication medium, a function of the emotions themselves, or some combination of the two. In addition, the current study focused on participants from another culture and from a different life stage (i.e. working people as opposed to college students). Both of these elements should be studied independently in future research projects, namely, for instance, applying the current protocol to Japanese business people and American college students. These points will be addressed in greater detail in the final section.

BACKGROUND

One key element of the current study is emotional exchange in mediated communications, in this case, PC and mobile e-mail messages in a business context. Foundational research on computer-mediated communications (CMC) shows that advantages of CMC include the lack of temporal or spatial constraints (Kiesler, Siegel, & McGuire 1984; Kiesler & Sproull 1992; Kiesler 1997). This conclusion is based on a comparison between face-to-face (FTF) and computer-mediated communications, but mobile communications seem to have the potential to expand this advantage even further. Whereas the mediated communications of the 1980's and 1990's were largely tied to a desktop computer, mobile communications (such as mobile telephone e-mail) after the turn of the current century allow business people to continue their communications outside of the office, extending their range to any location that is covered by the wireless network.

Two central features of CMC (i.e. visual anonymity and text-based communication) have been linked to various interpersonal behaviors, both positive and negative (Dietz-Uhler & Bishop-Clark 2001). On the positive side, when compared to FTF communications, CMC is often more impersonal and free (Kiesler et al. 1984), more uninhibited (Siegel, Dubrovsky, Kiesler, & McGuire 1986; Sproull & Kiesler 1986, 1991), contains more disclosures of personal information (Joinson 1998, 2001; Kiesler & Sproull 1992), more equal-member participation (Sproull & Kiesler 1993), and more task-oriented interactions (Connolly, Jessup, & Valacich 1990). As a result, CMC often allows people to feel more comfortable and confident in their discussions (Sato & Akahori 2004). This final point is particularly germane to the current study as positive emotional states, such as comfort and confidence, might facilitate the effective transmission and interpretation of emotions in e-mail messages.

However, CMC has negative aspects as well. For instance, CMC discussions can also cause participants to feel uninhibited or depersonalized (Garton & Wellman 1995; Walther, Anderson, & Park 1994). In particular, it was found that CMC encouraged negative emotional communications, such as "flaming" (Nojima & Gill 1997; Dyer, Green, Pitts, & Millward 1995; McGuire, Kiesler, & Siegel 1987). Some models explaining the mechanism of flaming have been proposed, for example, the Reduced Social Cues Model (Sproull & Kiesler 1991) and the Social Identity and De-individuation (SIDE) Model (Lea 1992). While most of these studies focused on the sender of the inflammatory message, little work has been done of the emotions of the message receiver. The current study includes both assessments of one's own emotions (sender's and receiver's) and estimations of others' emotions (receiver's and sender's respectively) to address this gap.

While prior research on CMC focuses on the lack of nonverbal cues in mediated communications, other studies have suggested that a variety of nonverbal information is being transmitted. According to Walther (1992), CMC can transfer social-emotional information, including emotions. Walther & Burgoon (1992) found that CMC groups could adapt their verbally transmitted or textual messages to some degree of social-emotional content in CMC environments and improve to higher levels in some relational aspects coming close to levels similar to face-to-face groups. In CMC, many nonverbal cues exist which include individual differences, chronemics (time of sending and receiving a message), frequency and duration of messaging, primacy and recency effects, gender composition, group size, or paralinguistic cues (Liu, Ginther, & Zelhart 2001). In addition, other researchers, such as Reid (1995) and Thompsen & Foulger (1996), have consistently found the benefits of using pictographs or typographic marks and emoticons in CMC interaction because these marks can convey social emotions and reduce perceptions of flaming.

Starting from our first social interactions, we communicate primarily face-to-face (FTF). In business contexts, the balance between FTF and mediated communications has shifted somewhat, but we still rely primarily on direct, synchronous communications. Given our vast experience communicating directly with other people, it is unsurprising that in such contexts, we are highly effective in judging other people's characteristics, such as familiarity, gender, emotion, or temperament (Cheng, O'Toole, & Abdi 2001). Our ability to assess others' psychological states is an important aspect of human interpersonal communication as we employ all available information, including verbal and non-verbal cues (Patterson 1994).

Technology now mediates much of our daily communications including telephones, e-mail or video-conferences. Regardless of the technology being used, we must make do with limited cues to help us estimate other people's emotional states, dispositions, and personalities. This is especially important as CMC users cannot see each other and the CMC environment is restricted in terms of

nonverbal cues (Sproull & Kiesler 1991). A number of studies have been conducted to investigate judgment in CMC contexts (Gill & Oberlander 2003; Kato & Akahori 2004a, 2004b; Kato, Sugimura, & Akahori 2001; Markey & Wells 2002; Nass, Moon, Fogg, & Reeves 1995). In particular, Kato et al. (2001) focused on judgment of other's emotional states in e-mail communications, and found gaps between the sender's self-report of emotional states and the receiver's judgment of the sender's emotional states. In addition, Kato & Akahori (2004a, 2004b) have compared the accuracy of estimating one's partner's emotions during e-mail communication to FTF. Their findings showed that the judgment of emotions in e-mail communication lacks accuracy, and there is a tendency to misjudge the partners' negative emotions as hostile in e-mail communication.

RESEARCH METHOD

In a study of the ability to convey emotion in text-based communications, Kato, Kato, and Akahori (2006) used a measure of 12 emotions exchanged during the course of an online text-based discussion between study participants. Kato et al.'s (2006) participants used one questionnaire to assess the emotions they experienced when posting a message to an online discussion forum and another questionnaire to estimate the reader's emotional response to that message. In turn, e-mail recipients assessed the emotions they experienced when reading the message and the emotions they estimated the writer experienced while composing the message. These anticipated and realized emotions were compared to form the basis of the authors' conclusions that included a tendency for readers to inaccurately interpret some negative emotions while positive emotions were more accurately interpreted.

The current study built upon and expanded Kato et al.'s work. The basic approach remained the same, with pairs of participants exchanging text-based messages and completing questionnaires of emotions experienced and predicted. First, PC and mobile e-mail were selected as common forms of daily business communication. The increase from one to two communication technologies opened up the possibility of comparing their relative ability allow senders and receivers to effectively exchange emotions. Second, the current study focused on the experiences of American business people rather than Japanese college students.

45 business people in central Michigan were contacted and asked to volunteer for this study. Potential participants completed a demographic questionnaire that included their experiences with and access to different kinds of communication technologies. Based on this information, 40 people were assigned to anonymous discussion pairs, 20 of which would communicate using PC e-mail and 20 which would communicate with mobile e-mail. Participants were sent instruction packets (one for the first person to send a message and a different one to the partner who would receive that message) and asked to exchange a total of three e-mail messages each on a predetermined discussion topic. After writing or reading a message, participants were required to complete a pair of questionnaires, one assessing their own emotions and another estimating their partner's emotions. In all, 12 questionnaires were completed at the end of the discussion process. At the conclusion of the study, a total of seven PC e-mail pairs (for a total of 14 participants) and three mobile e-mail pairs (for a total of six participants) completed the entire discussion process. These data were analyzed and those results are presented below.

The discussion topic was presented as a role-playing scenario where participants were asked to respond to the following:

Your CEO has just announced that all employees will be given mobile telephones to support mobile communications. Discuss your reaction to this policy with a colleague. Consider the pros and cons of this policy and how it may help (or hurt) the way you work.

To avoid complicating this process with possible gender or power differences (e.g. a CEO communicating with a new hire), all pairings and communications were anonymous. Messages were sent to a prepared e-mail address controlled by the researchers. Message contents were then copied into a new e-mail message and sent to the recipient. While time- and labor-intensive, this method worked reasonably well and we believe helped us avoid unnecessary complications.

The questionnaires focused on the emotions the participants experienced directly and the emotions they thought their partners did or might experience. The emotions selected for use in this study are based on Izard, Libero, Putnam, & Haynes (1993) and include:

- Interest
- Enjoyment
- Surprise
- Sadness
- Anger
- Disgust
- Contempt
- Fear
- Guilt
- Shame
- Shyness
- Inward hostility

Discussion data were collected using four types of questionnaires that included the 12 emotions described above. Participants used a five-point scale ranging from "didn't experience" to "very strong" (see Tables 1-4) to self-report the emotions they experienced and estimate their partner's emotions. The questionnaires were to be filled out in a particular order depending on the participant's current role in the discussion process. For instance, when participants composed and sent an e-mail message, they were asked to complete a questionnaire of the emotions they experienced (or didn't experience) while writing the message (Table 1).

Table 1. Sample questionnaire: Emotions experienced while writing a message

Instructions: Below are 12 sentences that describe emotions you may have experienced while writing this message. Put an "X" in the box to the right that best describes how strongly you felt a particular emotion (if at all).	Didn't experience	Weak	Moderate	Strong	Very strong
1. **Interest**: How strongly did you feel <u>interest</u> when writing this message?					

Table 2. Sample questionnaire: Anticipating partner's emotions when reading a message

Instructions: Below are 12 sentences that describe emotions your partner may experience while reading this message. Put an "X" in the box to the right that best describes how strongly you think they may feel a particular emotion (if at all).	Didn't experience	Weak	Moderate	Strong	Very strong
1. **Interest**: How strongly will your partner feel <u>interest</u> when reading this message?					

Table 3. Sample questionnaire: Anticipating partner's emotions when writing a message

Instructions: Below are 12 sentences that describe emotions your partner may have experienced while writing this message. Put an "X" in the box to the right that best describes how strongly you think they felt a particular emotion (if at all).	Didn't experience	Weak	Moderate	Strong	Very strong
1. **Interest**: How strongly did your partner feel <u>interest</u> when writing this message?					

Table 4. Sample questionnaire: Emotions experienced while reading a message

Instructions: Below are 12 sentences that describe emotions you may have experienced while reading this message. Put an "X" in the box to the right that best describes how strongly you felt a particular emotion (if at all).	Didn't experience	Weak	Moderate	Strong	Very strong
1. **Interest**: How strongly did you feel <u>interest</u> when reading this message?					

Message writers also completed a second questionnaire which asked them to predict the emotions the receiver might experience when reading the e-mail message. An example of this questionnaire is shown in Table 2.

After receiving and reading the message, recipients completed the questionnaire shown in Table 3 as they attempted to assess their partner's emotional state when writing the message.

Finally, Table 4 shows an example of the questionnaire message readers would use to assess their own emotional reactions (or lack thereof) to the message they had received.

When all questionnaires were completed, the participants would have rated their own emotions when sending and reading e-mail messages and their partner's anticipated emotional reactions or estimated emotional states to the messages exchanged. Each pair generated a total of 12 questionnaires which were analyzed and the results are presented in the following section.

RESULTS

As described above, 40 participants were equally divided into two groups (PC e-mail and mobile e-mail users) and the groups were further divided into anonymous discussion pairs. Each pair was given a predetermined topic and asked to exchange a total of six e-mail messages. Immediately after writing or reading a message, participants completed two questionnaires to gauge their emotional state or the emotions they thought their partner did or might experience. Questionnaire order was different depending on whether the participant was initiating the discussion or receiving the initial message. However, by the end of the e-mail exchange, both participants completed the same number and type of questionnaires.

The 40 participants were assigned to anonymous discussion pairs, 10 pairs using PC e-mail and 10 pairs using mobile e-mail. In the end, complete data were available for 10 pairs: Seven PC and three mobile e-mail pairs. The following demographic information pertains to the messages exchanged and questionnaires completed by the final 20 participants.

Participants who completed the study ranged in age from 25 to 62 and their average age was 36.8. There were a total of six men and 14 women; men were slightly older on average (37.2) than women (36.6). The PC group (38.2 years) was somewhat older than the mobile e-mail group (33.2 years). Despite the larger number of women in the sample, the overall pairings were somewhat evenly distributed with men participating in about half of the groups; See Table 5 for the complete breakdown.

The PC and mobile e-mail user groups were roughly balanced on such demographic categories as length of computer use (18.6 years to 18.7 years), experience using the Internet (11.6 years to 9.7 years), and mobile phone use (10.3 years to 10.0 years). All participants have used both PC and mobile communication technologies for many years.

The following subsection describes the basic numerical characteristics of the messages exchanged for all participants. These counts include total words, punctuation, emoticons, and other distinctive message characteristics.

Message length was strikingly different for the two groups. PC e-mail users exchanged an average of 133.6 words per message. In contrast, mobile messages averaged roughly half as many (79.4) words per message.

Participants were originally asked to complete their online discussions within five business days.

Table 5. Gender distribution in the discussion pairs by communication technology used

PC E-mail Pairs			
No.	Gender (Age)	No.	Gender (Age)
PC1	Male (25)	PC2	Female (25)
PC3	Female (45)	PC4	Male (45)
PC5	Female (58)	PC6	Female (51)
PC7	Female (25)	PC8	Male (25)
PC9	Female (25)	PC10	Female (23)
PC11	Female (44)	PC12	Female (62)
PC13	Female (32)	PC14	Male (52)

Mobile E-mail Pairs			
No.	Gender (Age)	No.	Gender (Age)
M1	Male (26)	M2	Female (32)
M3	Female (40)	M4	Male (50)
M5	Female (25)	M6	Female (26)

Since the participants were working in different locations and had no direct contact with the researchers, this limit was difficult to enforce. Further delaying the message exchanges was the routing of all messages through the study's e-mail account. As explained above, the researchers acted as intermediaries (receiving, preparing, and sending all messages) to preserve participant anonymity. All told, PC e-mail groups took an average of 9.7 days to complete their discussions while mobile e-mail uses took just over five days (5.3).

The following subsection describes the results of the statistical analysis of the data collected. T-tests were conducted on PC and mobile e-mail participants' questionnaire responses and the results are presented in the following subsections.

Actual emotions experienced when writing messages: Writers for both groups (PC and mobile e-mail users) experienced various emotions while composing their e-mail messages. Writers used a questionnaire to assess the degree to which they experienced 12 different emotions while writing their message. A comparison of the means of both PC and mobile e-mail writers' responses is presented in Graph 1.

The first impression one gets from Graph 1 is the overall similarity of the responses from both PC and mobile e-mail writers. Nine of the 12 emotions show little to no difference between PC and mobile e-mail participants. There are three areas

of difference, and the only emotion that shows a statistically significant difference is mobile e-mail writers' assessment of the joy they experienced while writing their messages (t(64)=2.74, p<0.01). There seems to be strong tendencies that mobile e-mail writers experienced two additional emotions—willingness (t(64)=1.807, p<0.10) and guilt (t(64)=1.924, p<0.10)—to greater degrees than did their PC using counterparts. Thus, compared with PC e-mail writers, mobile message writers experienced both positive (i.e. joy and willingness) and negative emotions (e.g. guilt).

Expected emotional response when reading messages: After writing their message and completing the previous questionnaire, e-mail writers completed a second questionnaire which asked them to estimate the type and degree of emotions their partners might experience when reading the message. A comparison of the means of both PC and mobile e-mail writers' responses is presented in Graph 2.

Initial impressions of this graph indicate more areas of difference than seen in the previous graph. That is, mobile e-mail writers expected their partners to experience a greater variety of emotions and to a greater degree than did their PC using peers. In particular, mobile e-mail writers anticipated that their partners would experience six different emotions to a significantly greater degree than PC writers felt their readers would experience: Interest (t(64)=1.942, p<0.05)

Graph 1. Comparison of actual emotions experienced while writing PC and mobile e-mail

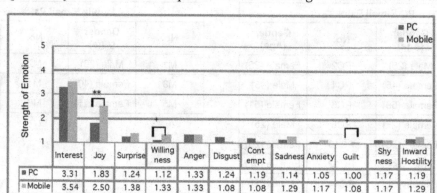

PC data n=42, Mobile data n=24
+ p<0.10, ** p<0.01

Graph 2. Comparison of expected emotional response when reading PC and mobile e-mail

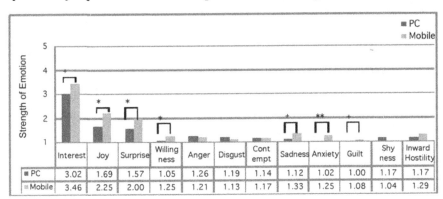

	Interest	Joy	Surprise	Willing ness	Anger	Disgust	Cont empt	Sadness	Anxiety	Guilt	Shy ness	Inward Hostility
PC	3.02	1.69	1.57	1.05	1.26	1.19	1.14	1.12	1.02	1.00	1.17	1.17
Mobile	3.46	2.25	2.00	1.25	1.21	1.13	1.17	1.33	1.25	1.08	1.04	1.29

PC data n=42, Mobile data n=24
*+ p<0.10, * p<0.05, ** p<0.01*

joy (t(64)=2.268, p<0.05), surprise (t(64)=2.111, p<0.05), willingness: t(64)=2.183, p<0.05) and anxiety (t(64)=3.022, p<0.01). In addition, there was a tendency for mobile message writers to anticipate their messages would elicit feelings of sadness (t(64)=1.807, p<0.10) and guilt (t(64)=1.924, p<0.10) to a greater degree than did PC message writers.

It is notable that for both graphs of e-mail message writers, there were no emotions that PC users experienced or anticipated their readers would experience to a greater degree than did mobile e-mail writers. Second, both graphs show that mobile e-mail writers experienced a roughly similar amount of positive emotions and negative emotions. Specifically, in Graph 1, they experienced joy, willingness, and guilt, and in Graph 2, they anticipated the readers would experience interest, joy, surprise, and willingness, and at the same time, the negative emotions of sadness, anxiety, and guilt. Thus, while PC writers didn't experience or anticipate emotions to a greater degree than did mobile e-mail writers, mobile writers experienced and expected both positive and negative emotions to a greater degree than did PC writers.

Actual emotions experienced when reading messages: The previous two graphs described

the emotions experienced and expected by e-mail message writers. The following two graphs focus on the message readers' experienced and expected emotions.

Readers in both groups (PC and mobile) experienced various emotions while reading their partner's e-mail messages. Readers used a questionnaire to assess the degree to which they experienced 12 different emotions while reading the message. A comparison of the means of both PC and mobile e-mail readers' responses is presented in Graph 3.

Three areas of significant difference were identified: Mobile message readers experienced significantly greater degrees of interest (t(64)=2.445, p<0.05), joy (t(64)=2.588, p<0.05), and willingness (t(64)=2.586, p<0.05) than did PC e-mail readers. Notably, all three of these emotions are positive and no differences for negative or hostile emotions were apparent.

Estimated emotional state when writing messages: After reading the message and completing the previous questionnaire, e-mail readers completed a second questionnaire which asked them to estimate the type and degree of emotions their partners might have experienced when composing the message. A comparison of the means of both PC and mobile e-mail readers' responses is presented in Graph 4.

Graph 3. Comparison of actual emotions experienced while reading PC and mobile e-mail

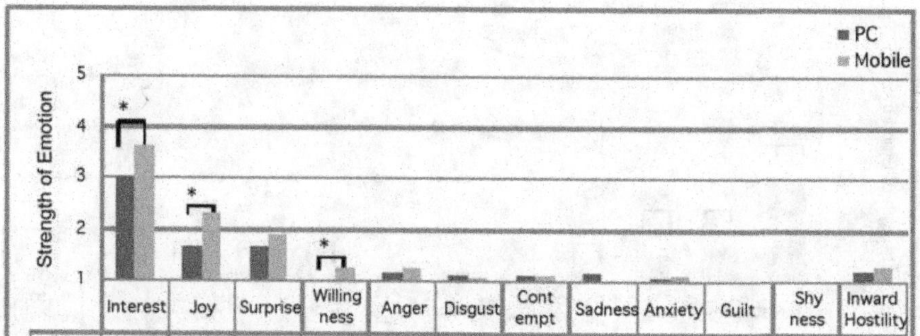

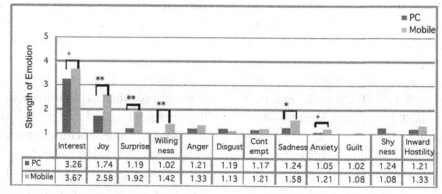

	Interest	Joy	Surprise	Willing ness	Anger	Disgust	Cont empt	Sadness	Anxiety	Guilt	Shy ness	Inward Hostility
■ PC	3.02	1.69	1.67	1.02	1.17	1.12	1.12	1.17	1.05	1.00	1.02	1.21
Mobile	3.63	2.33	1.92	1.25	1.25	1.08	1.13	1.04	1.13	1.04	1.00	1.29

PC data N=42, Mobile data N=24
* p<0.05

Graph 4. Comparison of estimated emotional state when writing PC and mobile e-mail

	Interest	Joy	Surprise	Willing ness	Anger	Disgust	Cont empt	Sadness	Anxiety	Guilt	Shy ness	Inward Hostility
■ PC	3.26	1.74	1.19	1.02	1.21	1.19	1.17	1.24	1.05	1.02	1.24	1.21
Mobile	3.67	2.58	1.92	1.42	1.33	1.13	1.21	1.58	1.21	1.08	1.08	1.33

PC data N=42, Mobile data N=24
+ p<0.10, * p<0.05, ** p<0.01

As seen in Graph 4, mobile e-mail readers perceived a variety of emotions to significantly greater degrees than did PC e-mail readers. Specifically, they perceived significantly greater joy (t(64)=3.816, p<0.01), surprise (t(64)=3.668, p<0.01), willingness (t(64)=3.432, p<0.01), and sadness (t(64)=2.060, p<0.05). They also perceived a strong tendency towards interest (t(64)=1.920, p<0.10) and anxiety (t(64)=1.792, p<0.10) in mobile e-mail writers.

Similar to the previous section, mobile e-mail readers experienced and perceived a greater range of emotions to a greater degree than did PC e-mail readers. Just as for writers, PC e-mail readers did not experience or perceive any emotion to a statisti-

cally significant degree. Unlike message writers, mobile e-mail readers' areas of greatest difference were more positive than negative: Mobile readers' actual experience included only positive emotions (i.e. interest and willingness), while the emotions they perceived in their partners' were both positive (i.e. interest, joy, surprise, and willingness) and negative (i.e. sadness and anxiety).

Correlation coefficient analyses: As noted above, each participant was asked to send three e-mail messages to their partner, resulting in a total of six e-mails exchanged within each pair. Correlation coefficients were computed for two sets of data: (1) the message sender's ability to predict their partner's emotional response to their e-mail message, and (2) the message reader's ability to predict the message writer's emotional state when composing the e-mail. These analyses focus on the degree of accuracy PC and mobile e-mail users showed in estimating the degree of emotions experienced by their partners.

When the writer's estimate of the reader's emotional response was accurate for the mean of all 12 emotions (with a correlation coefficient of 0.70 or greater), the e-mail exchange was categorized as a high-correlation exchange (HCE). Conversely, when the writer's estimate of the reader's emotional response was inaccurate for the mean of all 12 emotions (with a correlation coefficient of 0.69 or lower), the e-mail exchange was categorized as a low-correlation exchange (LCE).

High-correlation and low-correlation exchanges were then compared for each of the 12 emotions to see which, if any, were particularly successful or difficult to convey or predict.

Predicting readers' responses: Based on the average success in estimating their partner's emotional state for all 12 emotions, the following graphs break out and compare high-correlation exchanges (HCE) and low-correlation exchanges (LCE). The first two graphs below (Graphs 5 and 6) focus on PC e-mail exchanges, while Graphs 7 and 8 focus on mobile e-mail exchanges.

According to these data, while the high-correlation exchange group was, on average, more successful in predicting the readers' emotional reaction, they did not predict any of the 12 in-

Graph 5. Comparison of predicted emotions experienced while reading PC e-mail: HCE and LCE

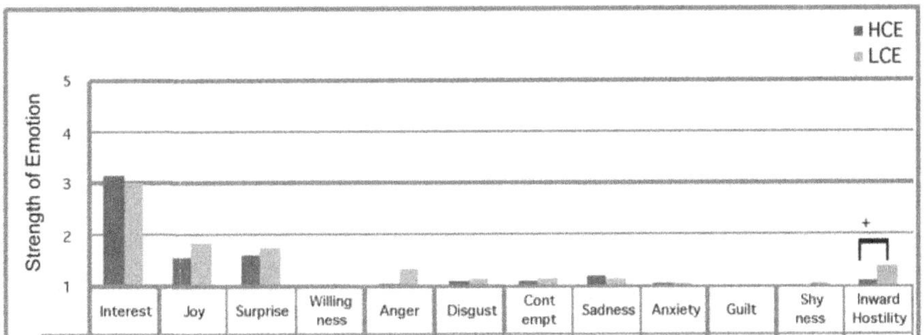

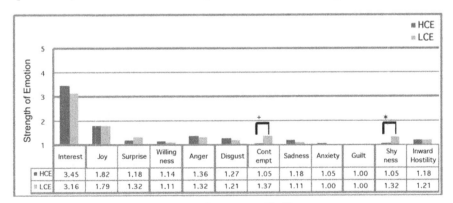

	Interest	Joy	Surprise	Willing ness	Anger	Disgust	Cont empt	Sadness	Anxiety	Guilt	Shy ness	Inward Hostility
■ HCE	3.14	1.59	1.64	1.00	1.05	1.09	1.09	1.18	1.05	1.00	1.00	1.09
▨ LCE	3.00	1.84	1.74	1.05	1.32	1.16	1.16	1.16	1.05	1.00	1.05	1.37

High-correlation group N=22, Low-correlation group N=19

Graph 6. Comparison of estimated emotions experienced while writing PC e-mail: HCE and LCE

	Interest	Joy	Surprise	Willing ness	Anger	Disgust	Cont empt	Sadness	Anxiety	Guilt	Shy ness	Inward Hostility
■ HCE	3.45	1.82	1.18	1.14	1.36	1.27	1.05	1.18	1.05	1.00	1.05	1.18
▨ LCE	3.16	1.79	1.32	1.11	1.32	1.21	1.37	1.11	1.00	1.00	1.32	1.21

High-correlation group N=22, Low-correlation group N=19

dividual emotions with significantly greater accuracy than the low-correlation exchange group. In contrast, the LCE group had somewhat more trouble predicting inward hostility (t(39)=1.928. p<0.10) than did the HCE group.

The results shown in Graph 6 are similar to those of Graph 5: PC e-mail readers in high-correlation exchanges (those who on average were more successful in estimating the writer's emotional state) did not accurately predict any individual emotions to a significantly greater degree than low-correlation exchanges. However, the low-correlation exchange group had significantly more trouble estimating the emotion of shyness (t(39)=2.029, p<0.05) and showed a strong tendency to have difficulty with the emo-

tion of contempt (t(39)=1.909, p<0.10) compared to the HCE group.

The previous graphs focused on PC e-mail users. The following two graphs describe the results of the mobile e-mail users.

Graph 7 indicates that high-correlation exchanges using mobile e-mail were significantly more successful in predicting interest (t(16)=3.474, p<0.01) and joy (t(16)=2.527, p<0.05). For their part, low-correlation exchanges showed a strong tendency to have difficulty predicting willingness (t(16)=1.849, p<0.10), anger (t(16)=1.978, p<0.10), and anxiety (t(16)=1.978, p<0.10). Thus, emotional exchanges that were generally successful (HCE) demonstrated significantly greater accuracy in predicting two positive emotions (i.e. interest and

Graph 7. Comparison of predicted emotions experienced while reading mobile e-mail: HCE and LCE

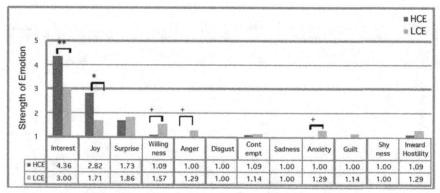

	Interest	Joy	Surprise	Willing ness	Anger	Disgust	Cont empt	Sadness	Anxiety	Guilt	Shy ness	Inward Hostility
HCE	4.36	2.82	1.73	1.09	1.00	1.00	1.09	1.00	1.00	1.00	1.00	1.09
LCE	3.00	1.71	1.86	1.57	1.29	1.00	1.14	1.00	1.29	1.14	1.00	1.29

High-correlation group N=11, Low-correlation group N=7

Graph 8. Comparison of estimated emotions experienced while writing mobile e-mail: HCE and LCE

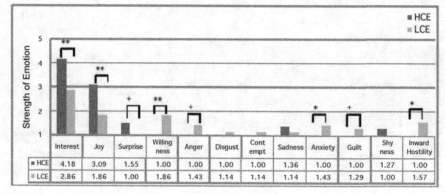

	Interest	Joy	Surprise	Willing ness	Anger	Disgust	Cont empt	Sadness	Anxiety	Guilt	Shy ness	Inward Hostility
HCE	4.18	3.09	1.55	1.00	1.00	1.00	1.00	1.36	1.00	1.00	1.27	1.00
LCE	2.86	1.86	1.00	1.86	1.43	1.14	1.14	1.14	1.43	1.29	1.00	1.57

High-correlation group N=11, Low-correlation group N=7

joy), while emotional exchanges that were generally unsuccessful (LCE) tended to have difficultly with one positive emotion (i.e. willingness) and two negative emotions (i.e. anger and anxiety).

Graph 8 shows that high-correlation exchanges using mobile e-mail were significantly more successful in predicting interest (t(16)=3.760, p<0.01) and joy (t(16)=3.266, p<0.01), and a strong tendency to accurate predict surprise (t(16)=2.075, p<0.10). Low-correlation exchanges showed significantly more problems predicting willingness (t(16)=4.195, p<0.01), anxiety (t(16)=2.708, p<0.05), and inward hostility (t(16)=2.453, p<0.05). They also demonstrated a tendency to have trouble estimating the writer's anger (t(16)=1.840, p<0.10) and guilt (t(16)=1.978, p<0.10). Thus, exchanges that were generally successful (HCE) demonstrated significantly greater accuracy in predicting three positive emotions (i.e. interest, joy, and surprise), while exchanges that were generally unsuccessful (LCE) tended to have difficultly with one positive emotion (i.e. willingness) and four negative emotions (i.e. anger, anxiety, guilt, and inward hostility).

Correlation coefficient comparison summary: The following table summarizes the results from the previous four graphs.

The upper half of this table (HCE group) shows PC and mobile e-mail exchanges that were generally accurate in predicting readers' emotional reactions and estimating writers' emotional states. For these high-correlation exchanges, PC e-mail users were no more accurate in predicting or estimating any of the 12 emotions than were low-correlation exchange PC e-mail users. In contrast, HCE mobile e-mail users were significantly more accurate in their prediction of readers' interest and joy, and in estimating writers' interest, joy, and to some extent, surprise.

The lower half of Table 6 (LCE group) shows PC and mobile e-mail exchanges that were less accurate in predicting readers' emotional reactions and estimating writers' emotional states. For low-correlation exchanges, PC e-mail users had somewhat greater difficulty in accurately predicting readers' reaction of inward hostility and estimating writers' shyness and, to a certain extent, contempt. For their part, LCE mobile e-mail users had some difficulty predicting readers' willingness, anger, and anxiety, and significantly more difficulty estimating writers' willingness, anxiety, and inward hostility, and some difficulty with the emotions of anger and guilt.

DISCUSSION AND CONCLUSION

This final section will summarize the key findings from the previous section, discuss their possible meaning for the broader topic of emotional

Table 6. Summary of correlation comparisons between HCE and LCE within PC and mobile e-mail users

Group	Method	Predicted reader's emotional reaction	Estimated writer's emotional state
HCE	PC E-mail	--	--
	Mobile E-mail	Interest (**) Joy (*)	Interest (**) Joy (**) Surprise (+)
LCE	PC E-mail	Inward Hostility (+)	Shyness (*) Contempt (+)
	Mobile E-mail	Willingness (+) Anger (+) Anxiety (+)	Willingness (**) Anxiety (*) Inward Hostility (*) Anger (+) Guilt (+)

t-test, ** p<.01, *p<.05, +p<.10

transmission in mediated communications, and conclude by considering future directions for this research topic.

Based on a study of Japanese college students' exchange of text-messages (Kato et al. 2006), this study examined the relative ability of PC and mobile e-mail to exchange emotions in two types of communication technologies. 40 participants were divided into two groups who used PC and mobile e-mail respectively to complete a short electronic discussion of a business scenario. Questionnaire about emotions experienced and emotional reactions anticipated were completed by both participants when each message was exchanged.

The first part of each exchange was the composing and sending of an e-mail message. The first two questionnaires of each exchange are from the message writer's perspective: The emotions they felt while writing the message and the emotions they anticipated the receiver would experience when reading the message. Data from the message writers' questionnaires indicates that there were no emotions that PC e-mail writers experienced or anticipated their readers would experience to a greater degree than did mobile e-mail writers. When mobile e-mail writers experienced greater emotions, they were roughly divided between positive and negative ones: Joy, willingness, and guilt when writing e-mail messages, and interest, joy, surprise, willingness, sadness, anxiety, and guilt when estimating their reader's emotional reaction. Thus, while PC writers did not experience or anticipate emotions to a greater degree than did mobile e-mail writers, mobile e-mail writers experienced and expected both positive and negative emotions to a greater degree than did PC e-mail writers.

The second half of each exchange was the reading of the message and completing two questionnaires on the emotions they experienced and the emotions they estimate the writer experienced when composing the message. The results are similar to those for message writers; mobile e-mail readers experienced and perceived a greater range of emotions to a greater degree than did PC e-mail readers. PC e-mail readers did not experience or perceive any emotion to a statistically significant degree more than their mobile e-mail counterparts. Unlike message writers, however, mobile e-mail readers' areas of greatest difference were more positive than negative: Their actual experiences included only positive emotions (i.e. interest and willingness), while the emotions they perceived in their partners' were both positive (i.e. interest, joy, surprise, and willingness) and negative (i.e. sadness and anxiety).

The next set of analyses looked at correlation between the relative ability of PC and mobile e-mail pairs to accurately predict their partner's emotional response (when reading) or emotional state (when composing). For successful exchanges, mobile e-mail pairs achieved greater success with more emotions than did their PC e-mail pairs. For successful pairs, the emotions that were better predicted and estimated where all positive (i.e. interest, joy, and surprise). When e-mail exchanges were unsuccessful, both PC and mobile users had trouble predicting or estimating certain emotions. Mobile e-mail exchanges were less successful for a wider range or emotions than was PC e-mail. Only one positive emotion (e.g. willingness) proved to be difficult to predict and estimate for mobile users while PC users did not have difficulties with any positive emotion. Negative emotions were difficult for both PC and mobile e-mail users, but mobile pairs had particular trouble with more than twice as many negative emotions as did PC pairs.

Thus, when PC e-mail exchanges are successful, they tend to be evenly successful for all emotions, positive and negative. When mobile e-mail exchanges are successful, they tend to be somewhat more successful for positive emotions, both when predicting readers' reactions and estimating writers' emotional states. When PC e-mail exchanges are unsuccessful, there is little difference in the prediction and estimation of positive emotions while a few negative emotions tend to be difficult to predict and estimate. In contrast, mobile e-mail exchanges that are unsuccessful show a greater number of negative emotions that are inaccurately predicted or estimated. Therefore, mobile e-mail shows a greater overall range of emotional predictions and interpretations, both good and bad, than does PC e-mail which seems somewhat more evenly balanced.

Past research by the authors indicated that positive emotions were more easily transmitted and interpreted while negative emotions were more easily misinterpreted (Kato & Akahori 2004a, 2004b; Kato et al. 2006; Kato, Kato, & Scott 2007). These conclusions were based on the analysis of an online discussion forum. The results for the current study are somewhat more complex. For instance, for PC e-mail users, there were no emotions—positive or negative—that were more easily exchanged, while there were three negative emotions that were particularly difficult for PC e-mail users to effectively exchange. Mobile e-mail users' results more closely matched those of Kato et al.: When mobile e-mail users had success exchanging emotions, they tended to be positive emotions ones like interest and joy. Conversely, when mobile e-mail users had difficulty exchanging emotional content, the emotions that were most challenging tended to be negative, similar to Kato et al.'s results.

There are three main conclusions from these results. The first is that through post facto study of e-mail messages, we can determine exchanges that are more (or less) effective at exchanging emotional content in text-based messages. Building upon that base, it may be possible that further research could help identify and define a set of abilities that promote successful emotional exchange. This understanding should enable us to create guidelines and training for the effective exchange of emotional content in text messages.

A second and related conclusion is that these preliminary results indicate that the communication technology used may play a role in the exchange of emotional content. Kato et al.'s results

for computer forum discussions were similar to our findings for mobile e-mail messages, while PC e-mail messages seemed less effective even for those users who were generally successful in exchanging emotional content. While such research is in its early stages, studies of three different communication media suggest there are differences in their users' ability to exchange emotional content and should be the focus of future research.

The third conclusion refers back to Table 6. We note that there is no overlap between the emotions that were particularly easy or difficult to predict or interpret in e-mail messages, both PC and mobile. If that is the case, it may be true that certain media lend themselves to the accurate transmission of particular emotions while limiting the ability to successfully exchange other emotions. If this tentative conclusion is developed in the future, one may be able to choose one medium to convey particular emotions, or avoid potential misunderstandings with another medium. Knowing the potential strengths and weaknesses of the range of available communication technologies can make us more effective users of these devices.

Lastly, and for a more explicit consideration of the implications for practice, the results of this study suggest that a corporate communication policy could potentially contribute to more effective communication exchanges and collaborations. Providing the infrastructure for corporate mobile communications could offer significant increases in productivity and in turn overall value. However, given the results of this study, communications with a greater degree of uncertainty, intensity, and/ or risk, such as conflict, may be better handled through non-mobile e-mail communications, as the likelihood of misinterpretation of transmitted emotions is high and may lead to a further escalation of the conflict in progress.

For instance, in the absence of a rich, face-to-face communication exchange, PC e-mail is the better medium than mobile e-mail for exchanges where negative emotions are being expressed.

For example, flaming (i.e. the hostile exchanges between interacting parties) may be more likely to occur during mobile e-mail exchanges than PC e-mail exchanges, consequent of such a misinterpretation of transmitted emotions. This study supports the warning issued by Nancy Flynn, who argued that "E-mail is very easy to misinterpret, which not only triggers flame wars but lots of litigation," (Leahy, 2006), and further qualifies it by showing that mobile e-mail is far more susceptible to these problems. Practitioners may be indifferent about minimizing the risk of flaming, but minimizing the risk of litigation through a prudent and effective communication policy is a measure that senior management should consider, because it is likely to generate a substantial return on investment during the organization's future operations. In addition, at the individual employee level and based on the results shown in Table 6 (i.e. the summary of correlation comparisons between HCE and LCE within PC and mobile e-mail users), professionals should take more care in considering the possibility of 'reading into' an e-mail excessively or simply misinterpreting the intended tone. This approach may prevent an unnecessary e-mail reply that would otherwise initiate conflict.

This study had a number of limitations and weaknesses. One limitation was this study's focus on participants' self-reports and estimates of emotions which did not include data that would help determine what caused or elicited the perceived emotions. Additional data on participants' reactions to various message elements (e.g. message length, wording, tone, inclusion of emoticons, etc.) could help us better understand the role of those elements in the exchange of emotional content.

Another challenge this study faced was the difficulty in recruiting participants and communicating with participants from a large number of geographically-dispersed businesses. Both participant recruitment and retention were un-doubtedly affected by the geographic distribution and our limited resources. Contacting potential participants electronically, while not ideal, was necessary given the participants' geographic distribution and the researchers' limited time and resources. On the other hand, taking the "glass is half full" perspective, the authors were able to employ mediated technologies to increase the sample size and include more participants than might have been possible relying on face-to-face access alone.

One alternative might be to could gain access to one large company where potential participants could be approached directly. In addition, with the cooperation of one company, participants could meet together (like Kato et al.'s college students) and complete the requisite e-mail exchanges in one session. Either adjustment would likely result in increased response rates and provide better results.

Emotions are fundamental to human interaction in general and play an important part in business communications in particular. The pace of modern society compels us to supplement our direct communications with various technologies that enable us to overcome the barriers of time and distance. However, these tools do not appear to posses similar attributes and depending on the user's needs, one tool may be more appropriate than another for a particular situation. Given the rapid pace with which new communication technologies are developed, introduced, and distributed, it is unsurprising that little research has been done of the relative advantages and limitations of even the most common communication tools. This study is one small step in the direction of better understanding our communication options. We look forward to developing this line of inquiry to help business people increase their communication effectiveness.

REFERENCES

Ben-Ami, O., & Mioduser, D. (2004). The affective aspect of moderator's role conception and enactment by teachers in a-synchronous learning discussion groups. *Proceedings of ED-MEDIA 2004* (2831–2837).

Bower, G. H. (1981). Mood and memory. *American Psychologist, 36,* 129–148.

Cheng, Y., O'Toole, A., & Abdi, H. (2001). Classifying adults' and children's faces by sex: computational investigations of subcategorial feature encoding. *Cognitive Science, 25,* 819–838.

Connolly, T., Jessup, L. M., & Valacich, J. S. (1990). Effects of anonymity and evaluative tone in idea generation in computer-mediated groups. *Management Science, 36,* 97–120.

Dietz-Uhler, B., & Bishop-Clark, C. (2001). The use of computer-mediated communication to enhance subsequent face-to-face discussions. *Computer in Human Behavior, 17,* 269–283.

Dyer, R., Green, R., Pitts, M., & Millward, G. (1995). What's the flaming problem? CMC – deindividuation or disinhibiting? In M. A. R. Kirby, A. J. Dix, & J. E. Finlay (Eds.), *People and computers.* Cambridge: Cambridge University Press.

Forgas, J. P. (1991). *Emotion and social judgments.* Oxford: Pergamon Press.

Garrison, D. R., & Anderson, T. (2003). *E-learning in the 21st Century: A Framework for Research and Practice.* London: Routledge Falmer.

Garton, L., & Wellman, B. (1995). Social impacts of electronic mail in organizations: a review of the research literature. In B. R. Burleson (Ed.). *Communication yearbook,18,* 434–453). Thousand Oaks, CA: Sage.

Gill, A. J., & Oberlander, J. (2003). Perception of e-mail personality at zero-acquaintance: Extraversion take care of itself; Neuroticism is a worry.

Proceedings of the 25th annual conference of the Cognitive Science Society (1–6).

Gunawardena, C. N. (1995). Social presence theory and implications for interaction and collaborative learning in computer conferences. *International Journal of Educational Telecommunications, 1,* 147–166.

Gunawardena, C. N., & Zittle, F. J. (1997). Social presence as a predictor of satisfaction within a computer-mediated conferencing environment. *The American Journal of Distance Education, 11,* 8–26.

Higgins, & Kruglanski, A. W. (Eds.), *Social psychology: Handbook of basic principles* (pp. 655–701). New York: The Guilford Press.

Izard, C. E., Libero, D. Z., Putnam, P., & Haynes, O. M. (1993). Stability of emotion experiences and their relations to traits of personality. *Journal of Personality and Social Psychology, 64,* 847–860.

Joinson, A. (1998). Causes and implications of disinherited behavior on the internet. In S. Kiesler (Ed.), *Culture of the Internet* (pp. 43–59). Mahwah, NJ: Erlbaum.

Joinson, A. (2001). Self-disclosure in computer-mediated communication: the role of self-awareness and visual anonymity. *European Journal of Social Psychology, 31,* 177–192.

Kato, S., Kato, Y., & Akahori, K. (2006). Emotional states and emoticons in e-mail communication using mobile phone. *Proceedings of World Conference on Educational Multimedia, Hypermedia and Telecommunications (ED-MEDIA) 2006,* 417-424.

Kato, Y., & Akahori, K. (2004a). E-mail communication versus face-to-face communication: perception of other's personality and emotional state. *Proceedings of ED-MEDIA 2004* (pp. 4160–4167).

Kato, Y., & Akahori, K. (2004b). The accuracy of judgment of emotions experienced by partners during e-mail and face-to-face communication. *Proceedings of ICCE 2004* (pp. 1559–1570).

Kato, Y., & Akahori, K. (2006). Analysis of judgment of partners' emotions during e-mail and face-to-face communication. *Journal of Science Education in Japan, 29*(5), 354-365.

Kato, Y., Kato, S., & Akahori, K. (2007). Effects of emotional cues transmitted in e-mail communication on the emotions experienced by senders and receivers. *Computers in Human Behavior, 23*(4), 1894-1905.

Kato, Y., Kato, S., & Scott, D. J. (2007). Misinterpretation of emotional cues and content in Japanese e-mail, computer conferences, and mobile text messages. In E. I. Clausen (Ed.), *Psychology of Anger*, (pp. 145-176). Hauppauge, NY: Nova Science Publishers.

Kato, Y., Sugimura, K., & Akahori, K. (2001). An affective aspect of computer-mediated Communication: analysis of communications by e-mail. *Proceedings of ICCE/SchoolNet 2001* (pp. 636–642).

Kato, Y., Sugimura, K. & Akahori, K. (2002). Effect of contents of e-mail messages on affections. *Proceedings of ICCE 2002* (pp. 428–432).

Kiesler, S. (1997). Preface. In S. Kiesler (Ed.), *Culture of the internet* (ix–xvi). Mahwah, NJ: Erlbaum.

Kiesler, S., & Sproull, L. (1992). Group decision making and communication technology. *Organizational Behavior and Human Decision Processes, 52*, 96–123.

Kiesler, S., Siegel, J., & McGuire, T. W. (1984). Social psychological aspects of computer mediated communication. *American Psychologist, 39*, 1123–1134.

Krauss, R. M., & Fussell, S. R. (1996). Social Psychological models of interpersonal communication. In E. T. Higgins & A. W. Kruglanski (Eds.), Social psychology: *Handbook of basic principles* (pp. 655–701). New York: The Guilford Press.

Kraut, R. E. (1978). Verbal and nonverbal cues in the perception of lying. *Journal of Personality and Social Psychology, 36*, 380–391.

Kruger, J., Epley, N., Parker, J., & Ng, Z. (2005). Egocentrism over e-mail: Can people communicate as well as they think? *Journal of Personality and Social Psychology, 89*, 925-936.

Lea, M. (Ed.). (1992). *Contexts of computer-mediated communication*. London: Harvester Wheatsheaf.

Leahy, S. (2006). *The Secret Cause of Flame Wars. Wired.* Published on February 13, 2006, Retrieved from http://www.wired.com/science/discoveries/news/2006/02/70179 on September 27, 2008.

Liu, Y., Ginther, D., & Zelhart, P. (2001). How do frequency and duration of messaging affect impression development in computer-mediated communication? *Journal of Universal Computer Science, 7*, 893-913.

Markey, P., & Wells, S. (2002). Interpersonal perception in internet chat rooms. *Journal of Research in Personality, 36*, 134–146.

McGuire, T., Kiesler, S., & Siegel, J. (1987). Group and computer-mediated discussion effects in risk decision making. *Journal of Personality and Social Psychology, 52*, 917–930.

Nass, C., Moon, Y., Fogg, B., & Reeves, B. (1995). Can computer personalities be human personalities? *International Journal of Human-Computer Studies, 43*, 223–239.

Nojima, H., & Gill, S. P. (1997). Cultural differences in evaluative communication. *The second Conference of The Asian Association of Social Psychology, 139*.

Patterson, M. L. (1994). Strategic functions of non-verbal exchange. In J. A. Daly & J. M. Wiemann (Eds.), *Strategic Interpersonal Communication* (pp. 273–293). Hillsdale, NJ: Erlbaum.

Reid, E. (1995). Virtual worlds: Culture and imagination. In S. G. Jones (Ed.), *Cybersociety: Computer-mediated communication and community* (pp. 164-183). Thousand Oaks, CA: Sage.

Sannomiya, M., & Kawaguchi, A. (1999). Cognitive characteristics of face-to-face and computer-mediated communication in group discussion: An examination from three dimensions. *Japan Journal of Educational Technology, 22*, 19–25.

Sato, K. & Akahori, K. (2004). Enhancing interactivity in face-to-face lecture by using "board mediated communication." *Proceedings of ED-MEDIA 2004* (146–153).

Short, J., Williams, E., & Christie, B. (1976). *The social psychology of telecommunications.* London: John Wiley & Sons.

Siegel, J., Dubrovsky, V., Kiesler, S., & McGuire, T. W. (1986). Group processes in computer-mediated communication. *Organizational Behavior and Human Decision Processes, 37*, 157–187.

Sproull, L., & Kiesler, S. (1986). Reducing social context cues: electronic mail in organizational communication. *Management Science, 32*, 1492–1512.

Sproull, L., & Kiesler, S. (1991). *Connections: New ways of working in the networked organization.* Cambridge, MA: MIT Press.

Sproull, L., & Kiesler, S. (1993). Computers, networks and work. In L. Harasim (Ed.), *Global Networks: Computers and International Communication* (pp. 105–120). Cambridge MA: MIT Press.

Thompsen, P. A. & Foulger, D. A. (1996): Effects of pictographs and quoting on flaming in electronic mail. *Computers in Human Behavior, 12*, 225-243.

Walther, J. B. (1992). Interpersonal effects in computer-mediated interaction: A relational perspective. *Communication Research, 19*(1), 52-90.

Walther, J. B., & Burgoon, J. K. (1992). Relational communication in computer-mediated interaction. *Human Communication Research, 19*, 50-88.

Walther, J. B., Anderson, J. F., & Park, D. W. (1994). Interpersonal effects in computer-mediated interaction. *Communication Research, 21*, 460–487.

Section V
International Perspectives
for Mobile and
Ubiquitous Commerce

Chapter XII
Mobile Internet Adoption by Spanish Consumers

Carla Ruiz-Mafé
University of Valencia, Spain

Silvia Sanz-Blas
University of Valencia, Spain

Adrian Broz-Lofiego
University of Valencia, Spain

Daniel Marchuet
University of Valencia, Spain

ABSTRACT

The chapter aims to present an in-depth study of the factors influencing Mobile Internet adoption. The authors analyse the influence of Internet use experience, compatibility, perceived financial risk, credibility and attitude towards Mobile Internet in the M-Internet adoption decision. After identifying the key drivers of M-Internet adoption, the second part of the chapter presents an empirical study of the Spanish market. Results based on a sample of 213 Internet users show that Internet use experience, M-Internet compatibility, credibility and attitude are positive key drivers of M-Internet adoption. Perceived financial risk influences negatively on M-Internet usage intention. This chapter will give managers and students insight into the M-Internet industry and the different factors that influence M-Internet adoption. In addition, these factors can be applied to the specific context of the Spanish market.

INTRODUCTION

Since its introduction, but particularly in recent years, Internet has become an effective, simple medium for providing information and services to millions of users. Internet has made it possible to tackle successfully two significant issues affecting consumers: time and space restrictions for carrying out their activities. The new technologies have enabled consumers and companies to build "connectivity" by transcending time and space limitations, increasing accessibility and expanding their social and commercial networks (Palen, 2002).

Technological progress is particularly noticeable in the area of mobile telephony which has gained importance with the rapid spread of mobile telephones throughout the world and the development of "wireless" technology. WAP (Wireless Application Protocol) technology has given rise to a new protocol of advanced Internet communications through the mobile phone and allows smaller cell terminals with larger screens to receive all the multimedia content offered on the Internet. Based on WAP technology supported by third generation mobile terminals (3G), multimedia mobile telephony has changed mere telephones into the equivalent of a laptop computer. The new terminals are a screen with an integrated intelligent television and digital radio decoder capable of receiving sound, television and video images on demand.

Wireless communications are enabled by the convergence of two technologies: Internet and wireless technology such as mobiles phones and personal digital assistants. With the explosive growth of the mobile phone population combined with the development of wireless technologies, usage of M-Internet services has increased in recent years. The proliferation of Internet via mobile devices will provide the ubiquity, convenience, localization and customisation for users participating in mobile communications and service activities (Lu et al., 2003). In this sense, it should be noted that service quality is very important when providing wireless services because the degree of perceived service quality and perceived value are key factors affecting consumer satisfaction with mobile services (Turel et al., 2006).

Hsu, Lu and Hsu (2007) define M-Internet as "mobile commerce activities, including mobile telecommunication, mobile content, entertainment service and E-commerce relying on a mobile platform". This chapter accordingly defines the M-Internet user as "the consumer who accesses Internet by using mobile access to computer-mediated networks with the help of an electronic device".

Internet navigation on mobile devices is taking us to a new spectrum of communications which is changing the shape of work activities and lifestyles. The proliferation of devices for wireless Internet connection is creating unprecedented commercial opportunities, increasing the benefits of mobility (Lu, Yu, Liu and Yao, 2003). In addition to basic mobile services such as communication and the sending of messages, it is also possible to navigate the Internet, access TV, radio services, videoconferencing services, chats and information services, among others.

Increased wireless communications usage in recent years is a clear example of the system's growth, significance and opportunities and it, therefore, merits special attention from researchers. Despite the importance of M-Internet, there is a lack of literature on the profile of M-Internet users and M-Internet adoption processes. M-Internet research will provide useful information for managers specially at this early stage of development and implementation. As the future commercial success of M-Internet depends to some extent on whether current Internet users also access this medium via mobile devices, it becomes crucial for managers to analyze which variables determine M-Internet adoption by Internet users in order to assign resources effectively to obtain competitive advantages.

Previous research into M-Internet has adopted a theoretical approach (Lu et al., 2003) or has mainly focused on adoption in the context of high E-commerce adoption rate regions such as Japan (Funk, 2005) and to a lesser extent in developing regions such as Taiwan and Korea (Cheong and Park, 2005; Hsu, Lu and Hsu, 2007). This study offers an insight into M-Internet adoption in Spain and a clear indication of marketing strategy to be deployed by service providers.

The chapter aims to present an in-depth study of the factors influencing M-Internet adoption. The chapter's specific goals are to:

1. Provide a holistic view of factors influencing M- Internet adoption.
2. Identify consumer segments more likely to adopt M-Internet services.
3. Analyse the impact of consumer perceived barriers (financial risk and credibility), psychological attitudes and Internet usage behaviour that encourage and discourage M-Internet services adoption and use the study's findings to develop strategies for managers on how to maximize the adoption rate.
4. Provide empirical research on the Spanish market that analyses the influence of Internet experience, compatibility, financial risk, credibility and attitude towards Mobile Internet, on the M-Internet adoption decision

BACKGROUND AND HYPOTHESES DEVELOPMENT

Past research has identified a number of psychological factors predetermining M-Internet adoption by consumers. This section shows a description of the impact of Internet experience, M-Internet compatibility, perceived financial risk, credibility and attitude on M-Internet adoption.

Internet Experience

The literature review shows that distance shoppers enjoy using direct shopping media (Park and Kim, 2003), are more innovative than non distance shoppers (Donthu and García, 1999) and often use other technologies as well (Eastlick and Lotz, 1999). Moreover, it should be remembered that an influential factor in consumer attitude to distance shopping is exposure to technology, with previous studies showing that as exposure to technologies increases, so does the likelihood of use Web portals (Yoon, Cropp and Cameron, 2002).

Rogers (1995) argues that the adoption of one new technology may trigger the adoption of several others in a cluster which consists of one or more distinguishable elements of technology that are perceived as being interrelated. The technology cluster concept has been used to examine the adoption of videotext (Etteman, 1984), cable television (La Rose and Atkin, 1992), E-Commerce (Eastin, 2002) and M-Commerce (Yang, 2005). This concept posits that consumers are likely to adopt a technology offering the same functions as those already adopted. As Coursaris and Hassanein (2002) indicated, M-commerce is an extension of E-commerce. Bigné, Ruiz and Sanz (2007) evidenced that previous Internet shopping experience positively influences M-shopping patronage.

In view of the above, we hypothesize that consumers with previous Internet experience will use more M-Internet than novice Internet users.

H1. *As Internet experience increases, so does M-Internet usage intention*

Compatibility

Innovation diffusion literature suggests that the following perceived innovation attributes have an impact on the rate of innovation diffusion: relative advantage, compatibility, complexity, divisibility (trialability) and communicability. These characteristics are used to explain the user adoption and decision making process. Results from previous studies found that compatibility, complexity and relative advantage are the most important predictors of innovation adoption (Agarwal and Prasad, 1998; Wu and Wang, 2005).

Compatibility has been defined as "the degree to which an innovation is consistent with adopters' behaviour patterns, life-styles and values" (Holak and Lehmann, 1990). Many empirical studies have confirmed that the perceived compatibility of an innovation has a positive influence on innovation adoption (Cooper and Zmud, 1990; Tan and Teo, 2000).

Previous research focused on M-services (Hsu et al., 2007, Wu and Wang, 2005) has posited a direct influence of compatibility on attitude. Research by Wu and Wang (2005) found that Mobile Commerce compatibility has a strong positive influence on M-commerce behavioural intention. Later research by Hsu et al., (2007) shows that M-Internet compatibility plays a role in MMS adoption for the early-majority and late majority groups of users.

We posit that if using M-Internet is perceived to be compatible with mobile user lifestyle and with the way they engage in online transactions (existing M-shopping habits), it is likely to induce future M-Internet use. Therefore, we hypothesize that,

H2. *Compatibility positively affects M-Internet usage intention*

Perceived Financial Risk

The concept of perceived risk suggests that consumer behavior involves a risk because the consumer cannot completely foresee the consequences of his or her behavior and those consequences may be disagreeable (Bauer, 1960; Mitchell, 1999).

According to Forsythe and Shi (2003) the perceived risk of online shopping is the Internet user's expectation of loss in a given electronic transaction. Therefore, the perceived risk for the M-Internet user can be defined as the expectation of loss in the pursuit of a desired outcome from using M-Internet services.

Several studies have considered perceived risk as a multidimensional construct which subdivides into several losses or risk factors, which together, explain the overall risk associated with the purchase of a product or service. This paper is focused on financial risk dimension as it has been cited a major obstacle to adopt Internet services (Forsythe and Shi, 2003; Lee et al., 2005; Sathye, 1999). Financial risk represents the perceived likelihood of not getting the best value for money (Mitchell, 1999). In general, it is the risk that the service purchased may not be worth the money paid for it.

Grewal et al, (1994) defines financial risk as the potential monetary outlay associated with the initial purchase price as well as the subsequent maintenance cost of the product. The cost of using M-Internet is twofold (Cheong and Park, 2005): initial investment in the device and the subscription charge. In developing a behavioural intention, customers compare service benefit and service cost and if the cost exceeds the benefit, they do not subscribe the service. Therefore, as Luarn and Lin (2005) pointed out, financial cost considerations may influence mobile users' behaviour. Other research (Cheong and Park, 2005; Mathieson, Peacock and Chin 2001; Wu and Wang, 2005; Luarn and Lin, 2005) has also found perceived financial resources to be a significant antecedent of the behavioural intention to use Mobile services.

Forsythe and Shi (2003) showed that the perceived financial risk of purchase is an important predictor of the future intention to purchase online, its effect being greater on non-purchasing users than on purchasers. A money-back guarantee may reduce this type of risk (Tan, 1999) although the higher the cost of the service, the greater this type of risk (Sweeney et al., 1999), especially if the consumer is not familiar with the service.

According to the literature review, perceived financial risk is expected to negatively influence the M-Internet adoption decision.

H3. *The perceived financial risk has a negative influence on M-Internet usage intention.*

Credibility

Consumer concerns surrounding connectivity involve the issues of security, reliability, download times and cost (Coursaris and Hassanein, 2002). Mobile Internet usage intention can be affected by users' security and privacy concerns.

Consumer fears regarding the safety of the information exchanged over a wireless network increases with the degree of interaction and the sensitivity of the information exchanged. Applications that require less interaction and are less personal (e.g. weather notifications) present a lower security concern than those applications involving increased interaction and containing personal information (e.g. mobile banking). Therefore, appropriate security features need to be implemented for each type of mobile application (Coursaris and Hassanein, 2002).

Another important barrier to E-services adoption is consumers' reluctance to provide personal details (Jacobs, 1997; Swaminathan et al., 1999). Swaminathan et al., (1999) found that consumers who habitually purchase products and services on the Internet are interested in the development of the legislation relating to protection of the privacy of data obtained via the web and that they are reluctant to continue providing their personal data.

Perceived credibility can be defined in our context as "the extent to which a person believes that the use of M-Internet will have no security or privacy threats" (Wang et al, 2003). Previous research (Wang et al., 2003; Luarn and Lin, 2005)

focused on online banking found that perceived credibility influences the behavioural intention to use Internet and Mobile banking services.

We posit that the perceived credibility that people have in the ability of M-Internet to conclude their transactions securely and to maintain the privacy of their personal information affects peoples' voluntary acceptance of M-Internet.

Therefore, we hypothesize that,

H4. *Credibility has a positive influence on M-Internet usage intention.*

Attitude

Attitude is an individual's positive or negative evaluation of a given object or behavior (Ajzen, 1991) and includes feelings or affective responses. It refers to the individual's general willingness to develop behavior. This attitude is the result of individual beliefs concerning the behavior, the results of that behavior and the importance attached to such beliefs.

Prior studies show that attitude has a direct, positive effect on Internet shopping intentions (Chen et al., 2002; Suh and Han, 2002). This relationship between attitude and intention/behaviour has already been tested in the area of M-commerce and a strong positive correlation was found between both variables (Liao *et al.*, 2007; Nysveen *et al*, 2005). Research by Kesti et al., (2004) also posits that perceptions and attitudes users get from testing mobile services affects their intention to use those kinds of services in the future.

H5. *Attitude towards M-Internet has a positive influence on M-Internet usage intention.*

The conceptual model of M-Internet adoption (see Figure 1) is an outcome of the literature review presented above.

Figure 1. Research model

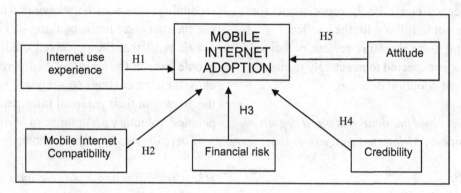

THE CASE OF SPANISH M-INTERNET USERS

After identifying the key drivers of Mobile Internet adoption, the second part of the chapter presents an empirical study of the Spanish market. Spain has been chosen because despite its medium B2C Internet adoption rate, the percentage of mobile phone users is noteworthy.

Analysis of the evolution of mobile penetration in Spain shows a substantial increase in user numbers since 2002. It is worth noting that over half of the contracts are postpaid, and this percentage has increased in recent years (see Table 1) as the result of improved contract conditions to gain user loyalty. This last aspect favours the adoption of different mobile services, as postpaid contracts include complementary services at prices lower than the prepaid rates.

At present, the Spanish mobile market has a penetration rate of 109% with 49 million mobile subscribers and 9.8 million 3G services sub-

scribers (Netsize, 2008). Furthermore, 20.3% of Internet users access wireless Internet using mobile phones (AIMC, 2008). This rate suggests that there may be significant business opportunities for employing M-Internet related services. In terms of mobile operators, Spain is similar to the European average with a total of four mobile operators –Movistar, Vodafone, Orange and Yoigo. With over 22.4 million users and a market share of 59.2% in 2007, Telefonica MoviStar dominates the Spanish market, followed by Vodafone (31.5%) (Netsize, 2008).

Specific analysis of Internet navigation in the field study by AIMC (2008) shows that mobile access is the third connection equipment to access Internet, after desktop and laptop Internet access.

Mobile Internet access frequency is still low, as it is shown on Table 3.

There is no doubt that the Spanish mobile telephony market has enormous potential and is moving towards a new business model where

Table 1. Mobile penetration in Spain (Source: CMT, 2007)

	2000	2001	2002	2003	2004	2005	2006
Mobile	24.265.059	29.655.729	33.530.997	37.219.839	38.622.582	42.693.832	46.152.022
Postpaid	8.528.403	10.384.261	12.657.346	15.592.659	18.555.948.	21.980.367	25.271.063
Prepaid	15.736.656	19.271.468	20.873.651	21.627.180	20.066.634	20.713.465	20.880.959
Others	63.081	43.732	37.816	29.582	24.214	18.869	17.402
Total	24.328.140	29.699.461	33.568.813	37.249.421	38.646.796	42.712.701	46.169.424

Table 2. Internet connection equipment (Source: AIMC, 2008)

Equipment	Internet users	%
Desktop computer	46.805	94,7%
Laptop computer	25.435	51,5%
Television	777	1,6%
Landline phone with screen	207	0,4%
Mobile telephone	**10.107**	**20,5%**
Electronic agenda (PDA)	4.608	9,3%
Video console	4.097	8,3%
Other Equipment	785	1,6%
Don't knows	34	0,1%

Table 3. Frequency of Internet access via mobile devices (Source: AIMC, 2008)

Frequency of Internet access	Internet users	%
Several times a day	1.220	2,5%
Everyday or almost everyday.	1.164	2,4%
Several times a week	2.318	4,7%
Once a week	1.516	3,1%
Twice a month	3.653	7,4%
Once a month	2.072	4,2%
Less than once a month	6.383	12,9%
Never or hardly ever	30.770	62,3%
Don't knows	322	0,7%

users can enjoy a wide variety of services with a growing level of signification. In this context, M-Internet navigation has a high potential determined by the low participation of people who connect to Internet through this type of equipment and because of the low frequency of service use, despite the flexibility it provides. That is why it is very important to understand the key drivers of M-Internet adoption.

The quantitative analysis will provide answers to the following research questions:

1. How does perceived financial risk influence M-Internet adoption?
2. How important is credibility as a barrier to M-Internet adoption for Spanish consumers?
3. How does online experience influence Mobile Internet adoption?

4. Are some consumers 'more compatible' with M-Internet than others? / Does that compatibility influence M-Internet adoption?

METHODOLOGY

For the quantitative research, we examined data from 213 personal interviews given to Spanish Internet users, aged 14 years and over. The study collected information using quota sampling on the basis of gender and age determined by the Red. es study (2007). This study is the most important directory of Internet users in Spain and uses random sampling method. The field work was done in January 2008.

The research instrument employed to obtain the information was a survey with close-ended questions. The questionnaire was developed and tested with 5 focus groups -PhD students, professors of Marketing at the University of Valencia and professionals focused on Marketing and Information System activities- to examine the dynamics of M-Internet users with different levels of previous experience and familiarity with the new mobile technologies. The pre-test instructed respondents to fill out the questionnaire and report any feedback. As a result of the pretests, some redundant questions were eliminated and some of the scales were adapted in order to facilitate understanding and avoid erroneous interpretations.

A research instrument with close-ended questions was used for this study. Questionnaires were delivered to and collected from volunteer participants over the age of 14. A total of 250 consumers were contacted during the survey; 219 agreed to participate in this study. Among the questionnaires

Figure 2. Sample description: gender

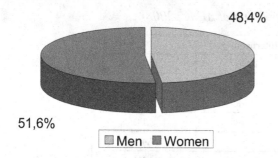

Figure 3. Sample description: age

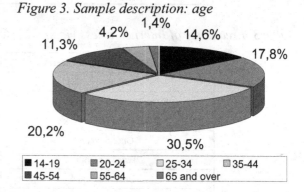

Figure 4. Sample description: education

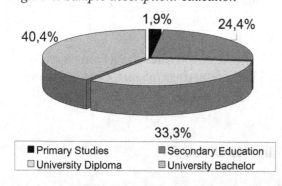

Figure 5. Sample description: occupation

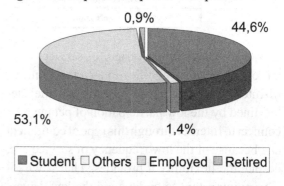

Figure 6. Sample description: income statement

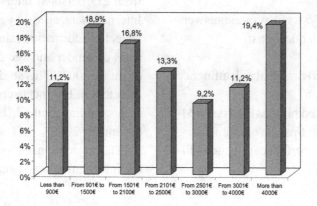

Figure 7. Internet experience in years

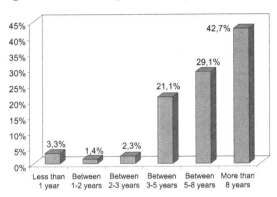

Figure 8. Internet access

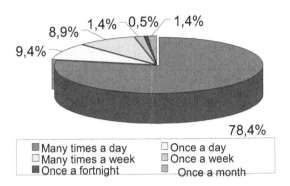

received, 213 were completed and analysed. Only 27% of the sample have not previous M-Internet experience. 34.3% of the sample have purchased something online and and 20.6% have purchased Mobile services.

Demographics are shown in Figures 2 to 6.

The average age of the sample is 32 years old, with 48.4% men and 51.6% women. Of the sample considered, 73.7% have completed university studies, and 24.4% have completed secondary school. Also, 53% of the participants were employed and 44.6% were students.

Around 93% of the sample have more than 3 years' experience of Internet (see Figure 7). Additionally, as shown in Figure 8, 87.8% of the sample uses Internet at least once a day.

MEASURES

The constructs used in our study were adapted from previous studies and measured by multiple item 5-point Likert-type scales, with the exception of Internet use experience (1 item) and M-Internet adoption (1 item), as shown in more detail in Table 4.The scale items for perceived financial risk were adapted from the measurement defined by Cheong and Park (2005) and Featherman and Pavlou (2003). Credibility was measured using Luarn and Lin's (2005) scale. M-Internet compatibility was measured via a two item scale based on research

by Wu and Wang (2005). Internet use experience was measured following other research work (Goldsmith, 2002) that uses variables relating to seniority with media use to measure this concept. Attitude was measured adapting Zaichkowsky's scale (1994) to the context of this study. M-Internet adoption was measured by the response to the question: would you use wireless Internet via mobile devices in the coming year?.

RESULTS

The perceived financial risk, credibility, attitude and M-Internet compatibility scales were analysed statistically, verifying their multidimensionality and compliance with the psychometric properties established by the literature.

After evaluating the psychometric properties of the measurement instrument, a logistical regression (N=213) was used to test the proposed model. For the regression, Mobile Internet adoption was coded as a dichotomous variable including Internet users who would use Mobile Internet next year (n=106) against those who said they will never use Mobile Internet (n=107). Independent variables included Internet use experience, perceived financial cost, credibility and M-Internet compatibility (see Table 5).

Hypothesis testing of the significance of the regression coefficients (β) gave the following results (see Table 7):

Table 4. Measurement of the variables

Concept	Items	Source
CREDIBILITY	Using mobile Internet would not divulge my personal information I would find mobile Internet secure in conducting my communications	Adapted from Luarn, and Lin (2005)
COMPATIBILITY	Using Mobile Internet is compatible with most aspects of my online transactions Using Mobile Internet fits my lifestyle Using Mobile Internet fits well with the way I like to engage in online transactions	Adapted from Wu and Wang (2005)
PERCEIVED FINANCIAL RISK If I used M-Internet…	I would be worried that the M-Internet service was not worth the price I would be worried that the M-Internet service didn't provide the advantages listed by the provider I would be worried that the use of M-Internet would lead to a financial loss for me	Adapted from Cheong and Park (2005); Featherman and Pavlou (2003).
INTERNET EXPERIENCE	Under 6 months Between 6 & 12 months Between 1 & 2 years Between 2 & 3 years Between 3 & 5 years Between 5 & 8 years More than 8 years	Adapted from Goldsmith (2002)
ATTITUDE TO M-INTERNET (5 point Likert Scale) Using M-Internet…	…is appealing …is convenient …is involving …is fascinating …is interesting …is valuable …is exciting …is secure …is needed …is a good idea	Adapted from Zaichkowsky (1994)
FUTURE M-INTERNET USE INTENTION Would you use wireless Internet via mobile devices in the coming year?	1. Yes, definitely 2. Probably 3. Indifferent 4. Probably not 5. No, definitely not	Adapted from Bigné, Ruiz and Sanz (2007)

Table 5. Logistic regression for predicting mobile banking adoption

Variable	B	SE	Wald	Sig.	Exp(B)
Financial risk	-0.428	0.140	9.365	0.002	0.651
Credibility	0.191	0.102	3.506	0.046	1.210
Compatibility	0.602	0.128	22.119	0.000	1.825
Attitude	0.868	0.170	26.070	0.000	2.382
Internet Experience			8.859	0.115	
Internet Experience (1)	1.156	1.168	0.980	0.322	3.176
Internet Experience (2)	0.063	1.442	1.908	0.965	1.065
Internet Experience (3)	2.249	1.215	3.426	0.065	.9.478
Internet Experience (4)	0.528	0.474	1.240	0.266	1.696
Internet Experience (5)	0.721	0.378	3.638	0.044	2.056
Intercept	2.142	0.920	5.420	0.020	8.516

- The greater the online use experience, the more likely is M-Internet adoption. Mobile Internet adoption is 2.056 times more likely if the consumer online use experience is more than 8 years than if it is less than 6 months (H1 accepted) and it is 1.825 times more likely if the users are compatible with the service being offered (H2 accepted). On the other hand, it is 0.651 times less likely they will use online financial services if they perceive financial risk (H3 accepted).
- The results also show that it is 1.210 times more likely that Internet users will use M-Internet if they have confidence in the service (H4 accepted).
- Attitude is another significant variable in the model. Thus, it is 2.382 times more likely that the interviewee will use M-Internet if his/her attitude toward M-Internet use is positive than if it is negative.

Having checked the statistical significance of the estimated logistic regression coefficients, we proceed to verify the overall significance of the model using the Chi-Square test with Hosmer and Lemeshow. The empirical value of Chi-square (Chi-Square =3.213, df= 8 ; p= 0.920), stated that model fit is good. Furthemore, the model presents very good predictive capacity: 77.9% of the cases are correctly classified given a cut-off value of 0.5.

CONCLUSION AND MANAGERIAL IMPLICATIONS

The main academic contribution of this chapter is that it will give insight into the different factors that influence M-Internet adoption. In addition these factors can be seen applied to the specific context of the Spanish market. Specifically, this study analyses the impact of the consumer perceived barriers (perceived financial risk and credibility), psychological attitudes and Internet

usage behaviour that encourage and discourage M-Internet services adoption and will improve managers' understanding of how to maximize the M-Internet adoption rate.

Logistic regression analysis on the set of variables analyzed has highlighted the important role that attitude plays in the model proposed because is the variable with the greatest influence on the M-Internet adoption decision. The influence of attitude on the use of M-Internet is consistent with previous studies done in other countries as Taiwan or Finland which show that attitude is one of the main precursors to present and future intention to use M-services (Cheong and Park, 2005; Nysveen et al., 2005).

M-Internet adoption is more likely in consumers who have high Internet use experience, possibly due to the fact that these consumers value the advantages and usefulness of the M-Internet service more. Therefore, greater online experience leads to improved relations with M-Internet services, as the individual is more familiar with the medium and values its benefits more. The central role of Internet user experience (seniority) as an antecedent to M-Internet usage intention confirms the importance of general Internet use in the population as the prior step to growth in E-commerce (Yoon et al., 2002; Park and Kim, 2003) and M-commerce (Bigné et al., 2007). Similarly, in the study of Liao and Cheung (2001) about E-shopping behavior in Singapore, IT education and Internet experience were significant antecedents in the development of people's intention to E-shopping.

The positive influence of Internet use experience on M-Internet use intention is also consistent with previous studies done in other countries using the technology cluster concept that concludes the adoption of new communication technologies is best predicted by the adoption of functionally similar technologies and user perception toward them (Rogers, 1995; Yang, 2005). Yang's study (2005) done using a sample of Singapore students evidenced that consumer past adoption of technologies related to M-commerce influences positively on M-commerce perceptions. Eastin's study (2002) done in US that analyze four E-commerce activities (i.e., online shopping, banking, investing, and electronic payment system) found that prior technology adoption is one of the key drivers of the adoption decision. Research by Cheong and Park (2005) also evidenced that Internet experience influences positively on consumer beliefs of M-Internet. Therefore, Mobile users who have been using Internet for a long time, seem to be more inclined towards trying to use all the features in a given device (the mobile phone).

Credibility is also a key driver of M-Internet adoption. Previous studies (Kruck et al., 2002; Lardner, 1999), have found credibility to be the most influential factor for consumer confidence in Internet services. Our results revealed that M-Internet services will be used more when they are considered to be secure and not violate users' privacy. This is consistent with previous studies that have also highlighted the importance of personal privacy and transaction security for mobile users (Rao and Troshani, 2007; Wu and Wang, 2005). Our findings also support previous research done in Taiwan that evidences the appropiateness of using credibility as an antecedent of M-services usage intention (Luarn and Lin, 2005) and Internet services usage intention (Wang et al., 2003). Perceived credibility is a dimension of trust, therefore, our results agree with research by Lu et al., (2008) that suggests wireless mobile trust awareness is a significant antecedent of wireless mobile data services usage intention for chinese consumers.

Our results evidenced the influence of life-style compatibility in general and the shopping method in particular on M-Internet adoption and highlight the importance of psychological factors in M-Internet adoption. This results agree with previous studies (Rao and Troshani, 2007; Wu and Wang, 2005) that show high compatibility will lead to preferable adoption. Furthermore, the study suggests there is a close relationship

between the mobile device and the person using it, so that improved compatibility of the service with user lifestyles has a very positive impact on all M-service use, including Internet access. For example, adopters' lifestyle in terms of degree of mobility is likely to have a strong impact on their decision to adopt M-Internet.

The influence of financial risk on the future Mobile Internet use decision is consistent with previous research done in other countries that highlights the influence of perceived risk in M-services usage decision (Luarn and Lin, 2005; Wu and Wang, 2005; Cheong and Park, 2005).

This chapter can help managers to develop effective strategies to attract Mobile Internet users and, therefore, to gain competitive advantages.

Firstly, we suggest that companies give priority to the Internet medium to promote M-Internet use, because this would attract Internet users more likely to want to use the mobile service (early adopters). In this sense, it would be advisable to advertise in portals and websites mainly visited by expert Internet users. That would reach users who are more likely to use M-Internet, as they would probably be the target public of early adopters.

Companies should provide information on M-Internet services and possibilities and how they can adapt to individuals' different lifestyles and situations. This would have a favourable influence on perceived compatibility of access and consequently on the service use intention. For example, an advertisement could show a young couple who have just finished a meal in a top class restaurant and while she goes to the ladies' room, he buys tickets for the film they want to see using M-Internet. This advertising message relates compatibility of M-Internet access and lifestyle. The idea is that the communication axis should underline the privacy and freedom of M-Internet and compatibility with certain lifestyles of these early adopters.

It is also recommended that communication campaigns show that M-Internet is secure and reliable, emphasising that it is a totally private, personal and individual form of access which travels with users wherever they go, making the mobile device into something personal which nobody can access except the owner.

Finally, companies should offer reliable services which provide the benefits individuals expect by incurring the cost of using the service. So, companies which use the mobile phone as a shopping channel should be able to offer new, innovative services and contents with added value to reduce perceived financial risk. Moreover, companies should offer special promotions through the mobile such as: reduced rates or discount packages where the price advantages of mobile Internet are clearly explained. This type of action will help to awaken interest in the service in more price-sensitive users.

In terms of the limitations of this study, there are complementary aspects not included in the questionnaire which could be relevant to analyze. For example, we have not analyzed the impact of affinity to mobile devices and innovativeness on M-Internet adoption. For this reason, and bearing in mind the lack of research in this field, we are considering, as a line of research, proposing and empirically testing a general model of M-Internet adoption behaviour that includes the antecedents of these external variables.

In this paper we have noted that compatibility has a significant influence on the M-Internet acceptance decision. Therefore, another future line of research would be to analyse the life-styles of individuals who declare themselves most compatible with M-services.

This study has focused on measuring attitudes (future M-Internet usage intention) which do not always become behaviours. Thus, a possible future line of research would be to contrast the proposed model with a sample of M-Internet users to see if these results remain valid.

The consumer's cultural background is one of the aspects which can influence the creation of a favourable climate for developing and consolidating Internet services usage (Van Birgelen,

De Ruyter, De Jong and Wetzels, 2002). For this reason, we consider that another interesting line of research would be to contrast the validity of the proposed behavioural model with samples of consumers from other cultures and compare the results obtained.

REFERENCES

Agarwal, R., & Prasad, J. (1998). A conceptual and operational definition of personal innovativeness in the domain of information technology. *Information Systems Research, 9*(2), 204-301.

AIMC (2008). *Navegantes en la Red. 10ª encuesta AIMC a usuarios de Internet.* http://www.aimc.es

Ajzen, I. (1991). The Theory of Planned Behavior. *Organizational Behavior and Human Decision Processes, 50*, 179-211.

Anderson, J. C., & Gerbing, D. W. (1988). Structural Equation Modeling in Practice: A Review and Recommend Two-Step Approach. *Psychological Bulletin, 103*(3), 411-423.

Bauer, R. A. (1960). Consumer behavior as risk-taking. In R. S. Hancock (Ed.). *Dynamic marketing for a changing world* (pp. 389–398). In Chicago: American Marketing Association.

Bagozzi, R., & Yi, Y. (1988). On the evaluation of structural equation models. *Academy of Marketing Science, 16*(1), 74-94.

Bentler, P. M. (1995). *EQS structural equations program manual.* Multivariate Software Inc., C.A., USA.

Bigné, E., Ruiz, C., & Sanz, S. (2007). Key drivers of mobile commerce adoption. An exploratory study of Spanish mobile users. *Journal of Theoretical and Applied Electronic Commerce Research, 2* (2), 48-60.

Chen, L.; Gillenson, M., & Sherrell, D. (2002). Enticing on-line consumers: an extended technology acceptance perspective. *Information and Management, 39*, 705–719.

Cheong, J., & Park M. C. (2005). Mobile Internet Acceptance in Korea. *Internet Research, 15*(2), 125-140.

Cooper, R. B., & Zmud, R. W. (1990). Information Technology Implementation Research: A Technological Diffusion Approach. *Management Science*, (pp. 123-139).

Coursaris, C., & Hassanein K. (2002). Understanding m-Commerce: A Consumer-Centric Model. *Quarterly Journal of Electronic Commerce, 3*(3), 247-272.

Donthu, N., & García, A. (1999). The Internet Shopper. *Journal of Advertising Research, 39*(3), 52-58.

Eastin, M. S. (2002). Diffusion of e-commerce: An analysis of the adoption of four e-commerce activities. *Telematics and Informatics, 19*, 251-267.

Eastlick, M. A., & Lotz, S. (1999). Profiling Potential Adopters and Non-Adopters of an Interactive Electronic Shopping Medium. *International Journal of Retail and Distribution Management, 27*(6), 209-223.

Etteman, J. (1984). Three phrases in the creation of information inequities: An empirical assesment of a prototype videotex system. *Journal of Broadcasting, 28*, 293-385.

Flavián, C., & Guinalíu, M. (2006). Consumer trust, perceived security and privacy policy: Three basic elements of loyalty to a web site. *Industrial Management & Data Systems, 106*(5), 601-620.

Fornell, C., & Larcker, D. (1981). Structural Equation Models with Unobserved Variables and Measurement Error. *Journal of Marketing Research, 36*(3), 39-50.

Forsythe, S., & Shi, B. (2003). Consumer patronage and risk perceptions in Internet shopping. *Journal of Business Research, 56*(11), 867-875.

Funk, J. (2004). Key technological trajectories and the expansion of mobile Internet applications. *The journal of policy, regulation and strategy for telecommunications, 6*(3), 208-215.

Grewal, D., Iyer, G., & Levy, M. (2004). Internet retailing: enablers, limiters and market consequences. *Journal of Business Research, 57*, 703-713.

Goldsmith, R. (2002). Explaining and Predicting Consumer Intention to Purchase Over the Internet: An Exploratory Study. *Journal of Marketing, 66*(Spring), 22-28.

Hair, J. F., Anderson, R. E., Tatham, R. L., & Black, W. C. (1999). *Multivariate data analysis*. New Jersey, USA: Prentice Hall.

Holak, S. L., & Lehmann, D. R. (1990). Purchase Intentions and the Dimensions of Innovation: An Exploratory Model. *Journal of Product Innovation Management, 7*(1), 59-73.

Hsu, C. L., Lu, H. P., & Hsu, H. H. (2007). *Adoption of the mobile Internet: An empirical study of multimedia message service (MMS)*. Omega, *35*(6), 715-726.

Jacobs, P. (1997). Privacy: what you need to know. *Infoworld, 19*(44), 111-112.

Kesti, M., Ristola, A., Karjaluoto, H., & Koivumäki, T. (2004). Tracking consumer intentions to use mobile services: empirical evidence from a field trial in Finland. *E-Business Review, 4*, 76-80.

Kruck, S. E., Gottovi, D., Moghadami, F., Broom, R., & Forcht, K. A. (2002). Protecting personal privacy on the Internet. *Information Management & Computer Security, 10*(2), 77-84.

Lardner, J. (1999). I know what you did last summer and fall. *US News & World Report, 126*(15), 55.

Larose, R., & Atkin, D. (1992). Audiotext and the reinvention of the telephone as a mass medium. *Journalism Quarterly, 69*, 413-421.

Lee, E., Kwon, K., & Schumann, D. (2005). Segmenting the non-adopter category in the diffusion of internet banking. *International Journal of Bank Marketing, 23*(5), 414-37.

Liao, Z., & Cheung, M. (2001). Internet-based e-shopping and consumer attitudes: an empirical study. *Information and Management, 38*(5), 299-306.

Liao, S., Shao, Y., Wang, H., & Chen, A. (1999). The adoption of virtual banking: an empirical study. *International Journal of Information Management, 19*, 63-74.

Lu, J.; Liu, Ch.; Yu, Ch., & Wang, K. (2008). Determinants of accepting wireless mobile data services in China. *Information & Management, 45*, 52-64.

Lu, J., Yu, C.S., Liu, C. & Yao, J.E. (2003). Technology acceptance model for wireless Internet. *Internet Research: Electronic Networking Applications and Policy, 13*(3), 206-222.

Luarn, P., & Lin H. H. (2005). Toward an understanding of the behavioral intention to use mobile banking. *Computers in Human Behavior, 21*(6), 873-891.

Mathieson, K., Peacock, E., & Chin, W. W. (2001). Extending the technology acceptance model: the influence of perceived user resources. *The Data Base for Advances in Information Systems, 32*(3), 86-112.

Mitchell, V. W. (1999). Consumer perceived risk: conceptualizations and models. *European Journal of Marketing, 33*(1/2), 163-195.

Netsize (2008). *The Netsize guide 2008. Mobile 2.0, you are in control. Mobile Industry Report.* http:// www.netsize.com.

Nysveen, H., Pedersen, P. E., & Thorbjornsen, H. (2005). Intentions to Use Mobile Services: Antecedents and Cross-Service Comparisons. *Academy of Marketing Science Journal, 33*(3), 330-346.

Nunnally, J. C., & Bernstein, I. H. (1994). *Psychometric theory (3rd Ed.).* New York, USA. McGraw-Hill.

Park, C., & Kim, Y. (2003). Identifying key factors affecting consumer purchase behaviour in an online shopping context. *International Journal of Retail and Distribution Management, 31*(1), 16-29.

Palen, L. (2002). Mobile telephony in a connected life. *Communications of the ACM, 45*(3), 78-82.

Rao, S., & Troshani (2007). A Conceptual Framework and Propositions for the Acceptance of Mobile Services. *Journal of Theoretical and Applied Electronic Commerce Research, 2*(2), 61-73.

Red.es (2007). *Estudio sobre Comercio Electrónico B2C 2007.* http://observatorio.red.es/estudios/documentos/b2c.pdf.

Rogers, E. (2003). *The Diffusion of Innovation.* Fifth Edition. New York, USA. Free Press.

Satorra, A., & Bentler, P. M. (1988). Scaling corrections for chi-square statistics in covariance structure analysis. American Statistical Association. *Proceedings of Business and Economics 14*, 308–313. Alexandria, VA: American Statistical Association.

Sathye, M. (1999). Adoption of Internet banking by Australian consumers: an empirical investigation. *International Journal of Bank Marketing, 17*(7), 324-34.

Swaminathan, V.; Lepkowska-White, E., & Rao, B. (1999). Browsers or Buyers in Cyberspace? An Investigation of Factors Influencing Electronic Exchange. *Journal of Computed-Mediated Communication, 5*(2) http://jiad.org/vol5/no2/swaminathan (08.03.04).

Sweeney, J. C., Soutar, G. N., & Johnson, L. W. (1999). The role of perceived risk in the quality-value relationship: a study in a retail environment. *Journal of Retailing, 75*(1), 77-105.

Suh, B., & Han, I. (2003). The impact of customer trust and perception of security control on the acceptance of electronic commerce. *International Journal of Electronic Commerce*, (pp. 135-161).

Tan, S. (1999). Strategies for reducing consumer's risk aversion in Internet shopping. *Journal of Consumer Marketing, 16*(2), 163-180.

Tan, M., & Teo, Thompson, S. H. (2000). Factors influencing the adoption of Internet Banking. *Journal of Association for Information Systems, 1*(5), 1-41.

Taylor, S., & Todd, P.A. (1995). Understanding Information Technology Usage: A test of Competing Models. *Information Systems Research, 6(2)*, 144-176.

Turel, O., & Serenko, A. (2006). Satisfaction with mobile services in Canada: An empirical investigation. *Telecommunications Policy 30*(5-6), 314-331.

Van Birgelen M., De Ruyter, K., De Jong, A., & Wetzels, M. (2002). Customer evaluations of alter-sales service contact modes: an empirical analysis of national culture's consequences. *International Journal of Research in Marketing, 19*(19), 43-64.

Wang, Y. S., Wang, Y. M., Lin, H. H., & Tang, T. I. (2003). Determinants of user acceptance of Internet banking: an empirical study. *International Journal of Service Industry Management, 14*(5), 501-519.

Wu, J. H., & Wang, S. C. (2005). What drives mobile commerce? An empirical evaluation of the revised technology acceptance model. *Information & Management, 42*(5), 719-729.

Yang, K. C. (2005). Exploring factors affecting the adoption of mobile commerce in Singapore. *Telematics and Informatics, 22*, 257-277.

Yoon, D., Cropp, F., & Cameron, G. (2002). Building Relationships with Portal Users: the Interplay of Motivation and Relational Factors. *Journal of Interactive Advertising, 3*(1). http://jiad.org/vol3/no1/yoon (08.03.04).

Chapter XIII
Framework for Mobile Payment Systems in India

Mahil Carr
Institute for Development and Research in Banking Technology, India

ABSTRACT

This chapter introduces concepts, frameworks and possible models for introducing mobile payments in India. The introductory section defines mobile payments, outlines its characteristics and identifies the stakeholders. Ideally, mobile payments have to be simple and usable, universal, interoperable, secure, private, affordable and be available within the country wide as well as globally. There are various stakeholders in this context: the customer, the merchant, banks, mobile network operators, software and technology service providers, mobile device manufacturers and the government. The technology considerations are addressed in a technological landscape with a wide variety of possibilities for implementing mobile payments. Implementations can be based on different access channels to the mobile device such as SMS, USSD or WAP/GPRS. The relative advantages and disadvantages each of these channels for mobile payments are discussed. Generic architectures that employ these technologies are modeled. The mobile phone carrying debit or card information (Track 2) within the device can act as a payment instrument. It can be used to extend the present day card based payment systems. This requires an independent entity called as a Trusted Service Manager (TSM) who provides the necessary hardware and software for handling transactions. The TSM is an intermediary between the financial institutions (banks) and the mobile network operators (telecommunications industry). Essentially the TSM accepts the information from the customer owning a mobile and it routes the financial transaction to the bank or an inter-bank clearing and settlement system (using an electronic interface—a financial switch) or to a payment systems operator (in the case that the customer is using a credit card). Possible models for one TSM in the country or having several independent TSMs are outlined. The TSMs may commu-

nicate with the financial system using the ISO 8583 messaging standards. Finally, technical standards and security issues are addressed. A symmetric encryption scheme (based on Triple DES or AES) can offer confidentiality of mobile payment transactions. However, for assuring integrity, authentication and non-repudiation a PKI scheme is required. Cost wise a PKI enabled scheme would be more than twice as costly as a symmetric scheme due to overheads in digital certificate transmission. Low value transactions may use the symmetric encryption standards whereas high value transactions can be done using asymmetric encryption standards.

INTRODUCTION

Definition and Scope of Mobile Payments

Mobile commerce is a natural successor to electronic commerce. The capability to pay electronically coupled with a website is the engine behind electronic commerce. Electronic commerce has been facilitated by automatic teller machines (ATMs) and shared banking networks, debit and credit card systems, electronic money and stored value applications, and electronic bill presentment and payment systems. Mobile payments are a natural evolution of e-payment schemes that will facilitate mobile commerce. A mobile payment or m-payment may be defined, for our purposes, as any payment where a mobile device is used to initiate, authorize and confirm an exchange of financial value in return for goods and services (Au and Kauffman, 2008). Mobile devices may include mobile phones, PDAs, wireless tablets and any other device that connect to mobile telecommunication network and make it possible for payments to be made (Karnouskos and Fokus, 2004). The realization of mobile payments will make possible new and unforeseen ways of convenience and commerce. Unsuspected technological innovations are possible. Music, video on demand, location based services identifiable through mobile handheld devices—procurement of travel, hospitality, entertainment and other uses are possible when mobile payments become feasible and ubiquitous. Mobile payments can become a complement to cash, cheques, credit cards and debit cards. It can also be used for payment of bills (especially utilities and insurance premiums) with access to account-based payment instruments such as electronic funds transfer, Internet banking payments, direct debit and electronic bill presentment.

Several mobile payment companies and initiatives in EU have failed and many have been discontinued (Dahlberg *et al.*, 2008). In Europe and North America with few exceptions such as Austria, Spain and Scandinavian countries the development of mobile payments have not been successful. However, mobile payment services in Asia have been fairly successful especially in South Korea, Japan and other Asian countries (e.g., Mobile Suica, Edy, Moneta, Octopus, GCash). NTT DoCoMo has 20 million subscribers and 1.5 million of them have activated credit card functionality in Japan. There are 100,000 readers installed in Japan (Ondrus and Pigneur, 2007). The main difference between successful implementations of mobile payment services in the Asia Pacific region and failure in Europe and North America is primarily attributed to the 'payment culture' of the consumers that are country-specific.

This chapter discusses a generic technical architecture for mobile payments. First a literature review framework outlines the broad context in which mobile payments operate. Following this we outline the general characteristics of mobile payments. The technology considerations of mobile payment solutions bring out the differing communication channels that a mobile device has and its implications for mobile payment solutions. The generic architecture provides a framework to understand how the mobile payment model works internally. Systemic issues such as the need for a clearing and settlement arrangement are highlighted. Finally, security and standards are touched upon. The final section concludes the chapter.

Background: Literature Review

Mobile payments services market primarily combines the efforts of various players such as consumers, merchants, financial institutions and telecom operators. Dahlberg *et al.* (2008) have arrived at a competitive factors strategy model for mobile payments based on Porter's framework (1998) by making a substantial review of literature. Figure 1 shows the framework Dahlberg *et al.* propose of factors impacting on mobile payment service markets and is discussed below.

There are outer four contingency factors (changing social/cultural, commercial, technical and legal/regulatory/standards). Four inner competitive inner factors—consumer power, merchant power, traditional payment systems and new payment systems drive the market.

The first contingency factor is the cultural and lifestyle factors that have influenced mobile payment market. Most Japanese payment services have been successful since a large number of commuters used mobile services (Srivastava, 2004). The second factor changing commercial environments includes the development of the Internet and the telecommunication infrastructures that have influenced the way commerce is done. In the technological developments mobile phones are becoming functionally rich, versatile and user-friendly facilitating payment services. New advances in architecture, security and trust and transaction protocols have made mobile payments technically feasible. As mobile payments are emerging and there are several solutions proposed by different service providers that raises

Figure 1. Framework of factors impacting on mobile payment services market (Based on Dahlberg et al., 2007)

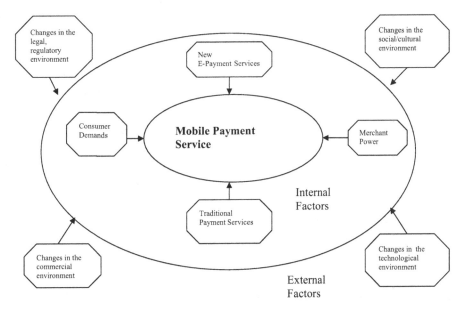

the issue of standardization. Moreover, as mobile payments emerge as a new type of payment and settlement system the need arises for new regulatory measures to be instituted to protect the interests of the users.

Mobile payment adoption/diffusion models and technology acceptance models study various factors that influence consumer demands. Specific factors include cost, trust and security, social influence, ease of use and privacy concerns. If mobile payments are to be successful merchants need to adopt the provision of mobile payment services. Current barriers to adoption have been studied (Malllat and Tuunaien, 2005, Teo et al., 2005). The major inhibiting factors are high costs, lack of relative advantage, complexity (ease of use) and low compatibility. Mobile payments have to compete with existing traditional payment systems such as cash, cheques, demand drafts, credit and debit cards. Finally, mobile payment systems also have to compete with newer electronic payment systems such as Internet banking, electronic funds transfers and new payment intermediaries such as PayPal.

Mobile Payment Characteristics

A mobile payment service in order to become acceptable in the market as a mode of payment the following conditions have to be met (Karnouskos and Fokus, 2004):

- **Simplicity and usability:** The m-payment application must be user friendly with little or no learning curve to the customer. The customer must also be able to personalize the application to suit his or her convenience.
- **Universality:** M-payments service must provide for transactions between one customer to another customer (C2C), or from a business to a customer (B2C) or between businesses (B2B). The coverage should include domestic, regional and global environments. Payments must be possible in terms of both low value micro-payments and high value macro-payments.

- **Interoperability:** Development should be based on standards and open technologies that allow one implemented system to interact with other systems.
- **Security, privacy and trust:** A customer must be able to trust a mobile payment application provider that his or her credit or debit card information may not be misused. Secondly, when these transactions become recorded customer privacy should not be lost in the sense that the credit histories and spending patterns of the customer should not be openly available for public scrutiny. Mobile payments have to be as anonymous as cash transactions. Third, the system should be foolproof, resistant to attacks from hackers and terrorists. This may be provided using public key infrastructure security, biometrics and passwords integrated into the mobile payment solution architectures.
- **Cost:** The m-payments should not be costlier than existing payment mechanisms to the extent possible. A m-payment solution should compete with other modes of payment in terms of cost and convenience.
- **Speed:** The speed at which m-payments are executed must be acceptable to customers and merchants.
- **Cross border payments:** To become widely accepted the m-payment application must be available globally, word-wide.

Stakeholders

There are many different stakeholders in the process of implementing mobile payments. They are (Karnouskos and Fokus, 2004):

- Consumers
- Merchants
- Mobile Network operators
- Mobile device manufacturers
- Financial institutions and banks

- Software and technology providers
- Government

Each player has different incentives and strategies. Sometimes these interests and strategies between different players may be in conflict e.g., the telecommunications network provider would like to maximize revenues through each m-payment transaction whereas customers and merchants would like to minimize costs for each m-payment transaction. The expectations of each of the stakeholders are outlined below.

Consumer Expectations

- Personalized service
- Minimal learning curve
- Trust, privacy and security
- Ubiquitous—anywhere, anytime and any currency
- Low or zero cost of usage
- Interoperability between different network operators, banks and devices
- Anonymity of payments like cash
- Person to person transfers

Merchant

- Faster transaction time
- Low or zero cost in using the system
- Integration with existing payment systems
- High security
- Being able to customize the service
- Real time status of the mobile payment service

Banks

- Network operator independent solutions
- Payment applications designed by the bank
- Exceptional branding opportunities for banks

- Better volumes in banking—more card payments and less cash transactions
- Customer loyalty

Telecom Network Providers

- Generating new income by increase in traffic
- Increased Average Revenue Per User (ARPU) and reduced churn (increased loyalty)
- Become an attractive partner to content providers

Mobile Device Manufacturer

- Large market adoption with embedded mobile payment application
- Low time to market
- Increase in Average Revenue Per User (ARPU)

Software and Technology Providers

- Large markets

Government

- Revenue through taxation of m-payments
- Standards

TECHNOLOGY CONSIDERATIONS

Mobile Payment Solutions

Mobile payment solutions may be classified according to the type of payment effected, and based on the technology adopted to implement the solution. There are a variety of combinations of these frameworks—technology adopted and mode of payment, a survey of which would constitute a study in itself. There are three different models available for m-payment solutions on the basis of payment (Lim, 2008):

1. Bank account based
2. Credit card based
3. Telecommunication company billing based

Bank Account Based Mobile Payments

Banks have several million customers and telecommunication operators also have several million customers. If they both collaborate to provide an m-payment solution it is a win-win situation for both industries. In this model, the bank account is linked to the mobile phone number of the customer. When the customer makes an m-payment transaction with a merchant, the bank account of the customer is debited and the value is credited to the merchant account.

Credit Card Based Mobile Payments

In the credit card based m-payment model, the credit card number is linked to the mobile phone number of the customer. When the customer makes an m-payment transaction with a merchant, the credit card is charged and the value is credited to the merchant account. Credit card based solutions have the limitation that it is heavily dependent on the level of penetration of credit cards in the country. In India, the number of credit card holders is 15 million. Only this small segment of the population will benefit in the credit card based model. Though limited in scope, there may be high demand within this segment for a payment solution with credit cards and also, may provide high volumes of transactions.

Telecommunication Company Billing of Mobile Payments

Customers may make payment to merchants using his or her mobile phone and this may be charged to the mobile phone bills of the customer. The customer then settles the bill with the telecommunication company (Zheng and Chen, 2003).

This may be further classified into prepaid airtime (debit) and postpaid subscription (credit).

Technologies for Mobile Payments

The mobile technology landscape provides various possibilities for implementing m-payments. Essentially, a GSM mobile phone may send or receive information (mobile data service) through three possible channels—SMS, USSD or WAP/GPRS. The choice of the channel influences the way m-payment schemes are implemented. The merits and demerits of each channel are discussed. Secondly, the m-payment client application may reside on the phone or else it may reside in the subscriber identity module (SIM). We briefly describe NFC technology as another possibility.

Short Message Service (SMS)

This is a text message service that enables short messages (140-160 characters) that can be transmitted from a mobile phone. Short messages are stored and forwarded by SMS centers. SMS messages have a channel of access to phone different from the voice channel (Valcourt, Robert and Beaulieu, 2005). SMS can be used to provide information about the status of one's account with the bank (informational) or can be used to transmit payment instructions from the phone (transactional).

Advantages of SMS for Mobile Payments
An SMS message can interact with a client application. The client wallet resident either on the SIM or the phone can carry credit or debit card information (Track 2). Therefore this can make the mobile device as a bankcard instrument that can be presented for payments through the electronic card based payment system. Moreover, the private key of a user can be stored in the SIM, which makes it possible to send digitally signed messages by the mobile device user.

Disadvantages of SMS for Mobile Payments

Since SMS is a store and forward service there is no guaranteed delivery of messages. At times messages may be dropped and this can cause transaction failure. Another cause for concern is that SMS messages are stored on the phone. In case the mobile device is lost, the information stored in the SMS messages can become a source for fraud as it leaves a trace. SMS leaves a lot of residual data in its communication path.

In face-to-face contexts where immediate payments need to be made an SMS based m-payment system may not be suitable. However, in the context of remote m-payments where transaction time is not a critical issue, an SMS based m-payment service is ideal. Secondly, SMS can be used to carry digital certificates and exchange digitally signed messages in PKI enabled transactions. It is suitable for high-value transactions that need a high degree of security.

Unstructured Supplementary Services Delivery (USSD)

Unstructured Supplementary Service Data (USSD) is a technology unique to GSM. It is a capability built into the GSM standard for support of transmitting information over the signaling channels of the GSM network. USSD provides session-based communication, enabling a variety of applications. USSD is session oriented transaction-oriented technology while SMS is a store-and-forward technology. Turnaround response times for interactive applications are shorter for USSD than SMS. Applications are server-based.

Advantages of USSD for Mobile Payments

The first advantage of USSD is that since it is server-based device independent convenience can be given to the customer (like Internet banking). Secondly, since it is a session-oriented protocol the problems faced with SMS of failed transactions due to communication failure do not arise.

Moreover, it offers the possibility of providing multilingual service.

Disadvantages of USSD for Mobile Payments

Applications that use USSD are uploaded from a server and that application cannot converse with any other client application on the phone. Therefore, USSD is not suitable in contexts where some data elements need to be supplied from the mobile device. USSD is a service that is available only on the GSM network. Seventy five per cent of the subscribers in India are GSM customers. The rest are CDMA subscribers[1].

USSD applications are particularly suitable where both payer and payee belong to the same service provider and the business model is mobile network operator centric or bank centric (similar to PayPal). In other cases also, a server side wallet can be used for remote transactions hence any merchant can be part of the eco-system but the payer will have to belong to the network which provides USSD access.

WAP/GPRS

General Packet Radio Service (GPRS) is a mobile data service available to GSM users. GPRS provides packet-switched data for GSM networks. GPRS enables services such as Wireless Application Protocol (WAP) access, Multimedia Messaging Service (MMS), and for Internet communication services such as email and World Wide Web access in mobile phones.

Advantages of GPRS for Mobile Payments

GPRS users can avail of all Internet banking facilities—balance enquiry, funds transfer, bill payments etc. It is possible to do all electronic commerce transactions using GPRS.

Disadvantages of GPRS for Mobile Payments

GPRS requires expensive, high-end mobile devices. The user needs to subscribe for bandwidth.

It is relatively less user friendly compared to traditional Internet banking.

GPRS caters to a small segment (20 million, about 10% of all mobile subscribers) of the market currently and in future more powerful mobile devices may make it possible for its wider acceptance as a payment medium.

Phone-based Application (J2ME/BREW)

The client m-payment application can reside on the mobile phone of the customer. This application can be developed in Java (J2ME) for GSM mobile phones and in Binary Runtime Environment for Wireless (BREW) for CDMA mobile phones. Personalization of the phones can be done over the air (OTA).

SIM-based Application

The subscriber identity module (SIM) used in GSM mobile phones is a smart card i.e., it is a small chip with processing power (intelligence) and memory. The information in the SIM can be protected using cryptographic algorithms and keys. This makes SIM applications relatively more secure than client applications that reside on the mobile phone. Also, whenever the customer acquires a new handset only the SIM card needs to be moved (Card Technology Today, 2007). If the application is placed on the phone, a new handset has to be personalized again.

Near Field Communication (NFC)

NFC is the fusion of contactless smartcard (RFID) and a mobile phone. The mobile phone can be used as a contactless card. NFC enabled phones can act as RFID tags or readers. This creates opportunity to make innovative applications especially in ticketing and couponing (Ondrus and Pigneur, 2007). The 'Pay-Buy Mobile' project launched by the GSM Association (fourteen mobile operators are part of the initiative) targets 900 million mobile

users with a common global approach using NFC (Card Technology Today, 2007).

Dual Chip

Usually the m-payment application is integrated into the SIM card. Normally, SIM cards are purchased in bulk by telecom companies and then customized for use before sale. If the m-payment application service provider has to write an m-payment application in the SIM card, this has to be done in collaboration with the telecommunications operator (the owner of the SIM). To avoid this, dual chip phones have two slots one for a SIM card (telephony) and another for a payment chip card. Financial institutions prefer this approach as they can exercise full control over the chip and the mobile payment process (Karnouskos and Fokus, 2004). But, customers would have to invest in dual chip mobile devices.

Mobile Wallet

A m-payment application software that resides on the mobile phone with details of the customer (and his or her bank account details or credit card information) which allows the customer to make payments using the mobile phone is called as a mobile wallet. Customers can embed and use several debit or credit payment instruments as part of a single wallet. Several implementations of wallets that are company-specific are in use globally.

A GENERIC ARCHITECTURE FOR MOBILE PAYMENTS

Following are simple, illustrative conceptual models that describe the relationship between the major participants in an m-payment scenario. There is the payer (customer or a person) and the payee (merchant or a person) who would like to use an m-payment service. The mobile network operator carries the information exchanges between the parties. There are banks—card-issuing bank (CIB) for the customer and it is presumed that the beneficiary (payee) also has a bank account. The financial part of the transaction can be handled through an electronic interface (financial switch) of the Inter-bank Clearing and Settlement System (ICSS). The Trusted Service Manager (TSM) is an independent entity that provides the necessary technical infrastructure (hardware and software) to facilitate m-payments and acts as an intermediary between the financial institutions and mobile network operators. The TSM registers users who would like to avail of the m-payment service. The users (customers and merchants or persons) have to be registered with the TSM prior to using the service. At the time of registration the TSM collects the bank account details of the registering party. The users are provided with a client m-payment application (mobile wallet) that is either resident on their phones or else in the SIM card. This application may be provided over the air to the users. The CIB provides the Track 2 information to the user using secure communication. The mobile wallet will normally interact with the TSM server. We discuss two cases—the first case using the m-payment service for a purchase

transaction and the second case for funds transfer between two individuals.

Purchase Transaction Model

A mobile phone user communicates with a Merchant and makes an economic transaction (e.g., buying a ticket from an airline over the phone). The Merchant obtains the phone number of the Customer and initiates the m-payment transaction request stating the services offered. The Customer makes a choice of the service he or she would like to avail (e.g., choosing an airline and a particular flight). The Merchant presents the bill. The Customer confirms the request and authorizes payment (for this illustration we presume that the Customer is using the debit card). The TSM receives the authorization and verifies the authenticity of the Customer. The TSM then debits the Customer account and credits the Merchant account by interacting with the bank (if both parties belong to the same bank). Once the electronic funds transfer is successful a confirmation message is sent to the customer (transaction receipt) and the merchant advising them of the debit and credit respectively. The steps are outlined below for Figure 2:

Figure 2. Purchase transaction model

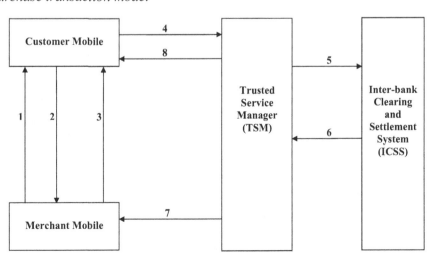

1. **Merchant → Customer:** Services Available
2. **Customer → Merchant:** Choice of service
3. **Merchant → Customer:** Presentation of bill
4. **Customer → TSM:** Authorization of payment
5. **TSM → ICSS:** Debit Customer account and credit Merchant Account
6. **ICSS → TSM:** Status of transaction information: success (or failure)
7. **TSM → Merchant:** Payment confirmation
8. **TSM → Customer:** Payment receipt

Funds Transfer Model

In the funds transfer model, funds are transferred from one individual to another. Figure 3 illustrates this scenario. It is assumed that both parties are registered with the TSM. The steps are detailed below for transfer of funds from Aruna to Bob:

1. **Aruna → TSM:** Authorization of payment to Bob
2. **TSM → ICSS:** Debit Aruna's account and credit Bob's Account
3. **ICSS → TSM:** Status of transaction information: success (or failure)
4. **TSM → Aruna:** Payment receipt
5. **TSM → Bob:** Payment confirmation

Mobile Payment System Models

Several possible models have been identified and we have a look at two of them based on different technologies and different approaches to payments.

Mobile Extension of the Card-Based Payment System

In this model (Figure 4), the SIM card of the mobile user carries bankcard information (credit or debit card). Instead of a customer presenting a card at a POS Terminal or an ATM, the mobile device (carrying the Track 2 information) presents the 'card' to the electronic payment network (through the mobile network operator) using encrypted SMS. In the case of a customer using the debit card, if both the customer and merchant belong to the same bank, the TSM routes the messages to the bank switch. In case the customer and merchant belong to different banks the TSM handles the financial transaction through the electronic interface (a financial switch) to the inter-bank clearing and settlement system. Else, if the customer uses a credit card the TSM interacts with the payment systems operator (e.g., VISA/MasterCard etc.).

Figure 3. Funds transfer model

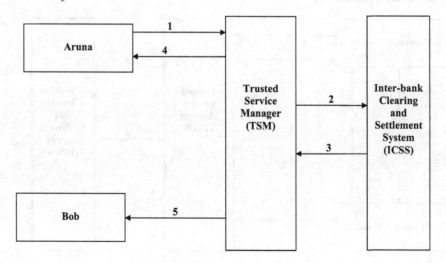

Figure 4. Mobile extension to card based payment system

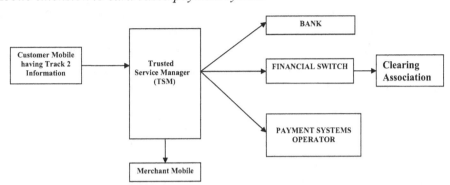

The communication between the TSM and the electronic financial system may be handled using the ISO 8583 messaging standard (please refer to Appendix II for details).

Mobile Extension of Basic Services

In the model described above the bankcard details are held in the mobile device. However, we can have an alternative scenario where the TSM server itself can have the information in its database. A bank may adopt the function and role of TSM. In this case we presume that customers and merchants all belong to one closed user group i.e. all are customers of the same bank. The bank server will have all the account information. The basic services of bank using a core-banking solution can be extended to the mobile context. Using USSD, funds transfer or purchase transactions can be made within the closed user group. This model can be understood as a variant of Internet banking for the mobile scenario. The advantage of using USSD is that device independent service can be rendered for the users.

Clearing and Settlement for Mobile Payments

The mobile payment scheme outlined in this section transfers value between a merchant and a customer or enables a peer-to-peer funds transfer. When an electronic transaction happens only the respective accounts are credited or debited. There has to be an actual transfer of monetary value between the parties. This needs an infrastructure for the clearing and settlement process (refer to Appendix). The mobile phone becomes a payment instrument where the user initiates the payment process after authentication of the mobile phone user and authorization by the user (using PIN/digital certificates). Through the telecommunications network the TSM routes the card and account information to inter-bank clearing and settlement system (in the case of a debit card) where the transactions are not in-house. In the case of a credit card the information is routed to the payment systems operator who has an in-built clearing and settlement procedure. The mobile payments system for using a debit card requires an electronic interface to the inter bank clearing and settlement system. One possibility is the use of existing ATM switches to handle the interface. The serious limitation arises that the ATM transactions are netted on a daily basis and settled on the next day. Moreover, ATM switches can be used only to make debits on accounts (pull information) but cannot be used to credit accounts (push). This means the funds transfer will only take place the following day (T+1) using a separate procedure to credit the payee's account. The real infrastructure solution would necessitate a financial switch that can do both debit and credit of bank accounts to permit payments and funds transfer on a real-time basis.

Architectural Model of Multiple Trusted Service Managers

The TSM has to be appropriately positioned within the banking and financial system. One may think of having one TSM as a national body. Or else, one can think of a scenario where several independent TSMs operate with appropriate licensing from a regulatory authority. This raises the issue of interoperability between customers and merchants who belong to different TSMs. One needs to introduce an additional inter-service provider switch to handle this scenario. Figure 5 shows the model. Let us assume that the Customer belonging to a TSM_x and a Merchant belonging to a TSM_y. The TSM_x needs to have the beneficiary bank details from TSM_y in order to carry out the financial transaction with the financial system. This is obtained through the inter-service provider switch. The merchant has to specify his or her mobile number as well as the TSM identity to which he or she belongs to the Customer (this is similar choosing a particular bank before giving the account details while making an electronic payment through the Internet).

SECURITY ISSUES AND STANDARDS

Standards

Mobile payments lack cohesive technology standards that can provide a universal mode of payment. Consolidation of standards in the mobile commerce arena is critical and it will enable producers and consumers to make investments that produce value. The lack of standards will give rise to lot of local and fragmented versions of m-payments offered by different stakeholders (network operator centric models and bank centric models). Standards need to address security and privacy concerns of consumers as well as interoperability between various implementations. Standards formation is a process of negotiation between various stakeholders; it is rather more political negotiations in nature rather than technical discussions. First movers benefit from this situation by creating *de facto* standards and major market share. There is no consensus among the players in terms of m-payments standards setting. Certain start up companies have proposed standards and they hope to make these *de facto* by being first movers with strategic advantage and early market selection. The battle over standards occurs at the firm level and at the inter-consortia level (Lim, 2008). We discuss technical standards for achieving secure mobile transactions in the following section.

Security for Mobile Payments

For widespread use and customer acceptance of m-payment services, both perceived and technical levels of security should be high. For customers, privacy should not be compromised and there should be no possibility of financial losses. For businesses, customer authentication is important. As per the general framework of any secure messaging system - confidentiality, integrity, non-repudiation and authentication should be guaranteed by the m-payment services (Misra and Wickamasinghe, 2004). The transport layer security offered by GSM/CDMA networks sufficiently guarantees confidentiality (that messages cannot be read by anyone else) and message integrity (the assurance that the message has not been altered in transit). GSM algorithms for secure transaction (A3/A8 and A5) have been challenged[2]. However, a Triple DES or Advanced Encryption Standard (AES) symmetric encryption can provide sufficient guarantees for privacy. Authentication (identifies the author of the

Figure 5. Architectural model of multiple trusted service managers

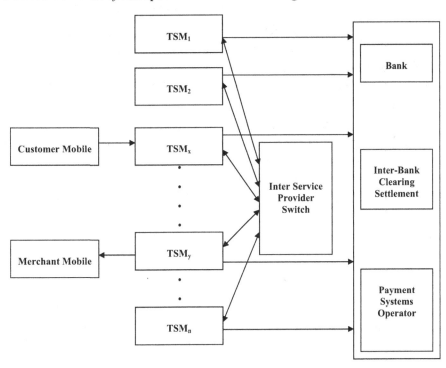

transaction) and non-repudiation (makes sure that any of the users in the system cannot later deny the message they sent) can only be guaranteed with the help of wireless public key infrastructure (WPKI) and digital certificates. Hassinen, Hyppönen and Trichina (2007) suggest that secure mobile payment transactions can be implemented using existing national public key infrastructure, which is independent of financial institutions, mobile network operators and mobile payment application service providers but can be used by all of them. Their proposed technological solution to provide secure mobile payment transaction is briefly described below.

Public Key Infrastructure and SIM Cards

Every user of the system is listed in a publicly available directory. Aruna would like to send a message to another user Bob. Aruna first obtains Bob's public key from the directory and encrypts the message using it. Since only Bob has the private key only he can read the message (after decryption) and no one else. Further Aruna can digitally sign the message. In this scheme anybody can verify that Aruna did indeed send the message and the message was not altered during transmission. A Certification Authority (CA) maintains the publicly available directory, which is responsible for issuing and revoking digital certificates. A digital certificate contains the public key of a user in the system. This framework is known as public key infrastructure (PKI).

A user normally maintains his or her private key confidentially in a personal secure environment. SIM cards have the ability to store and process private keys. In terms of key management, there must be an administrative system to issue key pairs to genuine citizens in a country.

Protocols

A sample protocol that describes the transaction between a customer and a merchant, each using his or her mobile phone and a m-payment Trusted Service Manager as an intermediary (cf. generic architecture for mobile payments in section 3 above) is outlined in this section. It is assumed that customer and merchant are registered as users with the m-payment TSM (with their respective bank account details) and both of them have valid digital certificates. The protocol is detailed below.

1. **Service request**
    Customer → Merchant:
    Customer makes a service request to the merchant
2. **Product options**
    Merchant → Customer:
    Merchant sends his product options and his certificate
3. **Product selection**
    Customer → Merchant:
    Customer selects a product; the selection is signed by the customer's private key
4. **Payment request**
    Merchant → Trusted Service Manager (TSM) → Customer:
    The payment request (containing the invoice amount) is signed using merchant's private key. Customer can verify that the merchant is genuine by using his certificate (sent earlier in step 2). The TSM also authenticates the merchant before passing the payment request to the customer.
5. **Payment authorization**
    Customer → TSM:
    The customer authorizes the payment request by digitally signing the authorization using the customer's private key. The TSM transfers the money from the buyer's account to the seller's account by communicating to the bank(s).
6. **Payment confirmation**
    TSM → Merchant:
    TSM informs merchant of successful payment
    TSM → Customer:
    TSM confirmation of payment is made to the customer
    The customer and the merchant can verify their respective bank accounts as to whether payment has been made.

Symmetric and Asymmetric Encryption

A PKI enabled mobile payment is relatively more costly (more than twice, since digital certificates have to be transmitted) operationally than a simple symmetric encryption framework (using Triple DES/AES). Also, the customer has to bear the cost of the digital certificate. While low value transactions within a certain threshold or limit may use the symmetric scheme, high value transactions need to be secured using PKI-enabled mobile payment scheme. A PKI based scheme will also have legal protection under the IT Act 2000, as authentication is possible and repudiation is not possible.

Regulatory Issues

Although mobile payments may allow parties to make economic exchanges, it is not *legal tender* in the sense it lacks the status of other payment instruments such as cash, which is a medium of exchange that is authorized, adopted and guaranteed by the government (Au and Kauffman, 2008). At best mobile payments will have to be backed by the issuer's promise to pay. To overcome this problem legislation may have to be put in place that will make mobile payments legal tender.

CONCLUSION

This chapter has enumerated the various technologies and models that can be used to implement mobile payments in India. Technical standards and security issues have been addressed especially in the context where GSM networks are not secure enough to handle mobile payments. A symmetric encryption scheme (based on Triple DES or AES) can offer confidentiality of mobile payment transactions. However, for assuring integrity, authentication and non-repudiation a PKI scheme is required. Cost wise a PKI enabled scheme would be more than twice as costly as a symmetric scheme due to overheads in digital certificate transmission. Low value transactions may use the symmetric encryption standards whereas high value transactions can be done using asymmetric encryption standards.

The introduction of mobile payments is at the design stage in India. The rollout and implementation will take place shortly. This will enable mobile phone users vast convenience. Considering that more than one fourth of the Indian population have mobile access this would create a tremendous impact in India.

REFERENCES

Au, Y.A., & Kauffman, R. J. (2008). The economics of mobile payments: Understanding stakeholder issues for an emerging financial technology application. *Electronic Commerce Research and Applications*, 7(2), 141-164.

Committee on Payment and Settlement Systems (2000). *Clearing and settlement arrangements for retail payments in selected countries.* Basel, Switzerland: Bank for International Settlements. Retrieved March 3, 2009, from http://www.bis.org/publ/cpss40.htm

Dahlberg, T., Mallat, N., Ondrus, J., & Zmijewska, A. (2008). Past, present and future of mobile payments research: A literature review. *Electronic Commerce Research and Applications*, 7(2), 165-181.

Hassinen, M., Hyppönen, K., & Trichina, E. (2008). Utilizing national public-key infrastructure in mobile payment systems, *Electronic Commerce Research and Applications*, 7(2), 214-231.

Karnouskos, S., & Fokus F. (2004). Mobile payment: A journey through existing procedures and standardization initiatives. *IEEE Communications Surveys and Tutorials*, 6(4) 44-66.

Lim, A. S. (2008). Inter-consortia battles in mobile payments standardization. *Electronic Commerce Research and Applications,* 7(2), 202-213.

Mallat, N., & Tuunainen, V. K. (2005). Merchant adoption of mobile payment systems. *Proceedings of the Fourth International Conference on Mobile Business* (ICMB), Sydney: IEEE Computer Society.

Misra, S. K., & Wickamasinghe, N. (2004). Security of mobile transaction: A trust model, *Electronic Commerce Research and Applications,* 4(4) 359-372.

Ondrus, J., & Pigneur, Y. (2007). An assessment of NFC for future mobile payment systems. *Sixth International Conference on the Management of Mobile Business*, (pp. 43-53) Washington, DC: IEEE Computer Society.

Porter, M. (1998). *Competitive Strategy.* New York: Free Press.

Srivastava, L. (2004). Japan's ubiquitous mobile information society. *Journal of Policy, Regulation and Strategy for Telecommunications*, 6(4) (2004) 234–251.

Teo, E., Fraunholz, B., & Unnithan, C. (2005). Inhibitors and facilitators for mobile payment adoption in Australia: a preliminary study. *Proceedings of the Fourth International Conference on Mobile Business (ICMB)*, Sydney: IEEE Computer Society.

Valcourt, E. Robert, J., & Beaulieu, F. (2005). Investigating mobile payment: supporting technologies, methods, and use. *IEEE International*

Conference on Wireless And Mobile Computing, Networking And Communications, (pp. 29-36). Montreal: IEEE Computer Society.

Zheng, X., & Chen, D. (2003). Study of mobile payments systems. *IEEE International Conference on E-Commerce*, (pp. 24—27) Newport Beach: IEEE Computer Society.

(2007). GSM Association aims for global mobile payments using NFC. *Card Technology Today*, *19*(2), 1-3.

ENDNOTES

[1]   Total number of subscribers in India 213,009, 843. GSM—160,013,642, CDMA - 2,996,201 as on 31st October 2007. (Source: http://www.india-cellular.com/Cellular-Subscribers.html)

[2]   Source: GSM Security (http://www.gsm-security.net/)

APPENDIX: CLEARING AND SETTLEMENT

This section (Adapted from Committee on Payment and Settlement Systems, 2000) briefly explains the clearing and settlement process for retail payment services such as cheques, card payments (i.e., credit and debit cards) and ATM withdrawals that give debits on bank accounts. Then we will consider the appropriate infrastructure arrangements for making mobile devices as payment instruments. The use of payment instruments mentioned above necessitates validation of the payment instrument, the exchange of information between the payee and payer's financial institutions and the final exchange of funds between these institutions when a payment transaction is made.

If both parties to a payment belong to the same financial institution then it is normally considered as in-house and the phases in the clearing and settlement occurs within the same institution. Inter-bank arrangements are needed if both parties have accounts in different financial institutions. In this case the institutions need to interact to complete a payment process. In many cases this requires the final settlement of funds on the books of the central bank.

The Payment Process

The payment process consists of a number of detailed steps. If a cheque or a debit card (information) is used the payee will submit it to his or her financial institution. The instrument or the information needs to be exchanged with the payee's financial institution through a clearing arrangement. From the end users' point of view a payment process ends when the payer's account is debited and the payee's account is credited with the payment amount. However, finally inter-bank settlement has to be made between the financial institutions.

The payment transaction process involves the following steps:

1.   Verification of the identity of the parties
2.   Validation of the payment instrument
3.   Verification of the ability to pay
4.   Authorization of funds transfer by the payee's and payer's financial institutions
5.   Communication of information by the payer's financial institution to payee's financial institution
6.   Processing of the transaction

Clearing Process

The clearing process consists of two steps:

1.   The exchange of payment instrument or information between the payer's and the payee's financial institutions.
2.   The calculation of claims for settlement.

This validates the payment to the payer and provides a claim for the payer's institution on the payee's institution.

The procedures may consist of several detailed steps such as:

1. Matching the transactions
2. Sorting of the transactions
3. Data collection
4. Data aggregation
5. Sending of relevant data.

The settlement claims are made up of:

1. Calculation of gross claims
2. Calculation of net or aggregated claims to be settled.

There are four types of arrangements for clearing of a payment process.

1. In-house transactions.
2. Bilateral arrangements between the institutions themselves.
3. A common third party may be employed as a correspondent to handle contracts negotiated bilaterally.
4. Multilateral clearing arrangements e.g., a clearinghouse, or else a clearing association may be employed for coordinating and facilitating clearing among institutions.

Settlement Process

During settlement the valid claim on the payer's institution is discharged by means of a payment from the payer's institution to the payee's institution. The specific steps are:

1. Collection and integrity check of the claims to be settled.
2. Ensuring availability of funds for settlement.
3. Settling the claims between the institutions.
4. Logging and communication of settlement to the parties concerned.

Large value settlement usually takes place in central bank money and may use automated procedures such as Real Time Gross Settlement (RTGS). Retail payments such as ATM transactions are batched and netted for settlement each day using a private correspondent bank or a clearing association.

Section VI
Additional Selected Readings

Chapter XIV
Mobile Code and Security Issues

E. S. Samundeeswari
Vellalar College for Women, India

F. Mary Magdalene Jane
P. S. G. R. Krishnammal, India

ABSTRACT

Over the years computer systems have evolved from centralized monolithic computing devices supporting static applications, into client-server environments that allow complex forms of distributed computing. Throughout this evolution limited forms of code mobility have existed. The explosion in the use of the World Wide Web coupled with the rapid evolution of the platform independent programming languages has promoted the use of mobile code and at the same time raised some important security issues. This chapter introduces mobile code technology and discusses the related security issues. The first part of the chapter deals with the need for mobile codes and the various methods of categorizing them. One method of categorising the mobile code is based on code mobility. Different forms of code mobility like code on demand, remote evaluation and mobile agents are explained in detail. The other method is based on the type of code distributed. Various types of codes like Source Code, Intermediate Code, Platform-dependent Binary Code, Just-in-Time Compilation are explained. Mobile agents, as autonomously migrating software entities, present great challenges to the design and implementation of security mechanisms. The second part of this chapter deals with the security issues. These issues are broadly divided into code related issues and host related issues. Techniques like Sandboxing, Code signing and Proof carrying code are widely applied to protect the hosts. Execution tracing, Mobile cryptography, Obfuscated code, Co-Operating Agents are used to protect the code from harmful agents. The security mechanisms like language support for safety, OS level security and safety policies are discussed in the last section. In order to make the mobile code approach practical, it is essential to understand mobile code technology. Advanced and innovative solutions are to be developed to restrict the operations that mobile code can perform but without unduly restricting its functionality. It is also necessary to develop formal, extremely easy to use safety measures.

INTRODUCTION

Mobile code computation is a new paradigm for structuring distributed systems. Mobile programs migrate from remote sites to a host and interact with the resources and facilities local to that host. This new mode of distributed computation promises great opportunities for electronic commerce, mobile computing, and information harvesting. There has been a general consensus that security is the key to the success of mobile code computation.

Distributed applications involve the coordination of two or more computers geographically apart and connected by a physical network. Most distributed applications deploy the client/server paradigm. There are certain problems with the client/server paradigm such as the requirement of a high network bandwidth and continuous user-computer interactivity. Hence the mobile code paradigm has been developed as an alternative approach for distributed application design.

In the client/server paradigm, programs cannot move across different machines and must run on the machines they reside on. The mobile code paradigm, on the other hand allows programs to be transferred among and executed on different computers. By allowing code to move between hosts, programs can interact on the same computer instead of over the network. Therefore, communication cost can be reduced. Besides, one form of mobile code is a program that can be designed to work on behalf of users autonomously. This autonomy allows users to delegate their tasks to the mobile code, and not to stay continuously in front of the computer terminal.

With the growth of distributed computer and telecommunications systems, there have been increasing demands to support the concept of "mobile code", sourced from remote, possibly untrustworthy systems, but executed locally.

MOBILE CODE

Mobile code consists of small pieces of software, obtained from remote systems outside the enclave boundary, transferred across a network, and then downloaded and executed on a local system without explicit installation or execution by the recipient.

The mobile code paradigm encompasses programs that can be executed on one or several hosts other than the one that they originate from. Mobility of such programs implies some built-in capability for each piece of code to travel smoothly from one host to another. A mobile code is associated with at least two parties: its producer and its consumer – the consumer being the host that runs the code.

Examples of mobile code include a Java script embedded within an HTML page, a Visual-Basic script contained in a WORD document, an HTML Help file, an ActiveX Control, a Java applet, a transparent browser plug-in or DLL, a new document viewer installed on demand, an explicitly downloaded executable binary, etc. Since mobile code runs in the execution context of the user that downloads the code, it can issue any system calls that the user is allowed to make, including deleting files, modifying configurations or registry entries, ending emails, or installing back-door programs in the home directory. The most common type of malicious mobile code is email attachment.

Mobile code systems range from simple applets to intelligent software agents. These systems offer several advantages over the more traditional distributed computing approaches like flexibility in software design beyond the well established object oriented paradigm and bandwidth optimization. As usual, increased flexibility comes with a cost that is increased vulnerability in the face of malicious intrusion scenarios akin to Internet. Possible vulnerabilities with mobile code fall in one of two categories: attacks performed by a mobile program against the remote host on

257

which the program is executed as with malicious applets or ActiveX programs, and the less classical category of attacks due to the subversion of the mobile code and its data by the remote execution environment.

Advantages of Mobile Code

Here are some possible advantages of mobile code:

- Eliminates configuration, installation problems and reduces software distribution costs of desktop applications
- The code is potentially portable to many platforms
- Enhances the scalability of client/server applications
- Achieves performance advantages
- Achieves interoperability of distributed applications

Categories of Mobile Code

One method of categorising the mobile code is based on code mobility (Ghezzi & Vigna, 1997). Different forms of code mobility are *code on demand*, *remote evaluation* and *mobile agents*. *Code on demand* is the downloading of executable content in a client environment as the result of a client request to a server. In *remote evaluation* the code is uploaded to a server, where this code is executed. Multi-hop migration of code across the network and autonomous execution on many different hosts is termed as *mobile agent*.

Code on Demand

In the code on demand paradigm, the client component owns the resources needed for the execution of a service, but lacks the know-how needed to use them in performing the service. The corresponding code component can be retrieved from a remote server component, which acts as

a code repository and subsequently executed, thus providing enhanced flexibility by allowing the server to change dynamically the behavior of the client. This is the scheme typically employed by Web applets, or by the parameter passing mechanism in Java/RMI.

Remote Evaluation

In the remote evaluation paradigm, the client component owns the know-how about the service that must be executed, but lacks the resources needed to perform the service, which are owned by the server component. A sort of enhanced client-server interaction takes place, where the client sends a request to the server, but includes also the code component required to perform the service. After the code component is received on the server, the interaction proceeds as in the client-server paradigm, with the code component accessing the resources now co-located with it, and sending the results back to the client. This reduces network traffic by executing a computation close to the resources located at the server's side. Common example is SQL servers performing queries on a remote database.

Mobile Agents

In the mobile agent paradigm the mobile components explicitly relocate themselves across the network, preserving their execution state (or part thereof) across migrations. It is therefore associated with many security issues needed for 'safe' execution. The mobile agents offer new possibilities for the e-commerce applications, creating new types of electronic ventures from e-shops, e-auctions to virtual enterprises and e-marketplaces. The agent helps to automate many electronic commerce tasks such as simple information gathering tasks, all tasks of commercial transactions, namely price negotiation, contract signing and delivery of (electronic) goods and services. Such agents are developed for diverse business areas, e.g., contract negotiations, service brokering, stock trading and many others. Examples of systems supporting this type of mobility are Telescript (Telescript, 1995), Aglets (IBM Aglets, 2002), and JADE (Java Agent DEvelopment Framework, 2005).

The first two forms, code on demand and remote evaluation can be classified as weak-mobility forms as it involves the mobility of code only. Since the mobile agent involves the mobility of computation, it is commonly known as strong mobility form.

The other method of categorising 'mobile code' technologies is based on the type of code distributed (Tennenhouse et al., 1996):

- Source Code
- Intermediate Code
- Platform-dependent Binary Code
- Just-in-Time Compilation

Source Code

The first approach is based on distributing the source for the 'mobile code' unit used. This source will be parsed and executed by an interpreter on the user's system. The interpreter is responsible for examining the source to ensure it obeys the required syntactic and semantic restrictions of the language; and then for providing a safe execution 'sand-box' environment. The safety of this approach relies on the correct specification and implementation of the interpreter.

The main advantages of the source code approach is the distribution of relatively small amounts of code; the fact that since the user has the full source, it is easier to check the code; and that it is easier for the interpreter to contain the execution environment. Disadvantages include the fact that it is slow, since the source must first be parsed; and that it is hard to expand the core functionality, since the interpreter's design limits this. Examples are Programmable MUDs, JavaScript etc.

Intermediate Code

A second approach to providing 'mobile code' is to have the programs compiled to a platform-independent intermediate code which is then distributed to the user's system. This intermediate code is executed by an interpreter on the user's system. Advantages are that it is faster to interpret than source since no textual parsing is required and the intermediate code is semantically much closer to machine code. The interpreter provides a safe execution 'sand-box' and again, the safety of the system depends on the interpreter. The code in general is quite small and the user's system can check the code to ensure it obeys the safety restrictions. Disadvantages of this approach are its moderate speed since an interpreter is still being used and the fact that less semantic information is available to assist in checking the code than if source was available. Java is a very good example for this category.

Table 1. Summary of mobile code techniques

Type of mobility	Category	Mobility of Code	Resources	Processor
Weak	Code on demand	Remote to Local (Pull)	Local side	Local side
	Remote evaluation	Local to Remote (Push)	Remote side	Remote side
Strong	Mobile agent	Migration	Remote side	Agent's originator

Where **Resource**s represent the information and other resources for code execution
Processor is the abstract machine that holds the state of computation

Native Binary Code

The third category of code distribution uses native binary code which is then executed on the user's system. This gives the maximum speed but means that the code is platform-dependent. Safe execution of binary code requires the restricted use of instruction set and the restricted address space access. Approaches to ensuring this can rely upon:

- Traditional heavy address space protection that is costly in terms of system performance and support
- The verified use of a trusted compiler that guarantees to generate safe code that will not violate the security restrictions
- The use of 'software fault isolation' technologies that augment the instruction stream, inserting additional checks to ensure safe execution.

A combination of verified use of a trusted compiler and the software fault isolation approach has created considerable interest, especially when used with a Just-in-Time Compiler.

Just-in-Time Compilation

Just-in-Time Compilation (JIT) is an approach that combines the portability of intermediate or source code with the speed of binary code. The source or intermediate code is distributed, but is then compiled to binary on the user's system before being executed. If source is used, it is slower but easier to check. If intermediate code is used, then it is faster. Another advantage is that users can utilise their own trusted compiler to verify code, and insert the desired software fault isolation run-time checks. Individual procedures are translated on a call-by-call basis. This approach is being used with Java JIT compilers.

PROPERTIES OF MOBILE CODE

- Comes in a variety of forms
- Often runs unannounced and unbeknownst to the user
- Runs with the privilege of the user
- Distributed in executable form
- Run in multiple threads
- Can launch other programs

SECURITY ISSUES OF MOBILE CODE PARADIGMS

In this section, some possible security attacks to different mobile code paradigms and possible mechanisms against these attacks are discussed.

A security attack is an action that compromises the security requirements of an application. Applications developed using different paradigms are subject to different attacks. In the conventional client/server model, the local computer is usually assumed to be fortress for code and data. Therefore the sources of security attacks are outsiders of the local machine. The main possible attacks are *masquerading* (pretending the server or the client), *eavesdropping* on the communication channel and *forging messages* to the client or the server.

The security model of the client/server paradigm also applies to the *remote evaluation* and *code-on-demand* approaches, with the additional concern that the code receiving side must make sure the code is not harmful to run. In remote evaluation, the code receiving side is the remote side, while it is the local side in code-on-demand. *Mobile agent*, on the other hand, is the most challenging area of mobile code security, due to the autonomy of agents. Mobile agent security is usually divided into two aspects: *host security* and *code security*. Host security (Loureiro S. et al., 2000) deals with the protection of hosts against malicious code / agent, whereas code security deals with the protection of code / agents against malicious hosts or other agents.

HOST SECURITY AGAINST MALICIOUS CODE

In the interconnected world of computers, mobile code generated by a malicious outsider, has become an omnipresent and dangerous threat. Malicious code can infiltrate hosts using a variety of methods such as attacks against known software flaws, hidden functionality in regular programs, and social engineering.

From the host perspective a secure execution environment is necessary to protect itself from such types of code. The first step towards a secure environment is to simply limit the functionality of the execution environment in order to limit the vulnerabilities. Techniques for protection of hosts now evolve along two directions (1) executing mobile codes in a restricted environment (2) a mobile code infrastructure that is enhanced with authentication, data integrity and access control mechanisms. The following section details both the aspects.

Sandboxing

Sandboxing is a software technique used to protect hosts from malicious mobile code. In an execution environment, local code is executed with full permission and has access to crucial system resources. On the other hand, mobile code is executed inside a restricted area called a "sandbox" which restricts the code to operating system functionality. A Sandboxing mechanism enforces a fixed security policy for the execution of the mobile code. The policy specifies the rules and restrictions that mobile code should confirm to. A mechanism is said to be secure if it properly implements a policy that is free of flaws and inconsistencies

Figure 1. Sandboxing technique

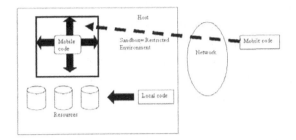

To contain mobile code within a sandbox, extensive type checking is used. Also memory accesses and jump addresses are checked at runtime. If these addresses do not fall within the sandbox then they are redirected to a location within the sandbox. The error however, is contained within the sandbox and cannot affect the rest of the system. Sandboxing can also be used for restricting access to file systems and limiting the ability to open network connections.

The most common implementation of Sandboxing is in the Java interpreter inside Java-enabled web browsers. A Java interpreter contains three main security components: ClassLoader, Verifier, and Security Manager. The ClassLoader converts mobile code into data structures that can be added to the local class hierarchy. Thus every remote class has a subtype of the ClassLoader class associated with it. Before the mobile code is loaded, the Verifier performs a set of security checks on it in order to guarantee that only legitimate Java code is executed .The mobile code should be a valid virtual machine code, and it should not overflow or underflow the stack, or use registers improperly . Additionally, remote classes cannot overwrite local names and their operations are checked by the Security Manager before the execution.

The main problem with the sandbox is that any error in any security component can lead to a violation of the security policy. The sandbox also incurs a high runtime overhead. A downside of the Sandboxing technique is that it increases the execution time of legitimate remote code

Code Signing

In the "Code Signing" technique a digitally signed piece of software identifies the producer who created and signed it. It enables the platform to verify that the code has not been modified since it was signed by the creator. Code Signing makes use of a digital signature and one-way hash function where a private key is used to sign code, both ensuring transmission integrity and enabling policy defined by trust in the signer. Code Signing enables the verification of the code producer's identity but it does not guarantee that they are trustworthy.

The platform that runs mobile code maintains a list of trusted entities and checks the code against the list. If the code producer is on the list, it is assumed that they are trustworthy and that the code is safe. The code is then treated as local code and is given full privileges; otherwise the code will not run at all. An example is Microsoft's Authenticode system for ActiveX.

There are two main drawbacks of the Code Signing approach. Firstly, this technique assumes that all the entities on the trusted list are trustworthy and that they are incorruptible. Mobile code from such a producer is granted full privileges. If the mobile code is malicious, it can use those privileges not only to directly cause harm to the executing platform but also to open a door for other malicious agents by changing the acceptance policy on the platform. Moreover, the affects of the malicious agent attack may only occur later, which makes it impossible to establish a connection between

Figure 2. Code signing technique

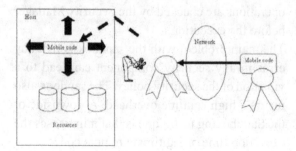

the attack and the attacker. Such attacks are referred to as "delayed attacks". Secondly, this technique is overly restrictive towards agents that are coming from unrecognized entities, as they do not run at all.

Code Signing and Sandboxing Combined

This technique combines the advantages of both Code Signing and Sandboxing. If the code consumer trusts the signer of the code, then the code will run as if it were local code, that is, with full privileges being granted to it. On the other hand, if the code consumer does not trust the signer of the code then the code will run inside a Sandbox The main advantage of this approach is that it enables the execution of the mobile code produced by untrustworthy entities. However, this method still suffers from the same drawback as Code Signing, that is, malicious code that is deemed trustworthy can cause damage and even change the acceptance policy. The security policy is the set of rules for granting programs permission to access various platform resources. The "black-and-white" policy only allows the platform to label programs as completely trusted or untrusted. The combination of Code Signing and Sandboxing implemented in JDK 1.2 incorporates fine-grained access control where it allows a user to assign any degree of partial trust to a code, rather than just "trusted" and "untrusted".

There is a whole spectrum of privileges that can be granted to the code. In JDK1.2 all code is subjected to the same security policy, regardless of being labelled as local or remote. The run-time system partitions code into individual groups called protection domains in such a way that all programs inside the same domain are granted the same set of permissions. The end-user can authorize certain protection domains to access the majority of resources that are available at the executing host while other protection domains may be restricted to the Sandbox environment. In between these two, there are different subsets of privileges that can be granted to different protection domains, based on whether they are local or remote, authorised or not, and even based on the key that is used for the signature

Proof Carrying Code

Proof Carrying Code (PCC) (Proof-Carrying Code. 2002) strikes an effective balance between security and flexibility. The process, pioneered by Necula and Lee (1998) involves the code producer attaching additional data to a piece of code. This data can be interpreted as a proof that a particular property holds for the piece of code.

In this technique the code producer is required to provide a formal proof that the code complies with the security policy of the code consumer. The code producer sends the code together with the formal safety proof, sometimes called machine-checkable proof, to the code consumer. Upon receipt, the code consumer checks and verifies the safety proof of the incoming code by using a simple and fast proof checker. Depending on the result of the proof validation process, the code is proclaimed safe and consequently executed without any further checking, or it is rejected. PCC guarantees the safety of the incoming code providing that there is no flaw in the verification-condition generator, the logical axioms, the typing rules and the proof-checker.

PCC is considered to be "self-certifying", because no cryptography or trusted third party is required. It involves low-cost static program checking after which the program can be executed without any expensive run-time checking. In addition, PCC is considered "tamper-proof" as any modification done to the code or the proof will be detected. Other applications include active networks and extensible operating systems. Proof Carrying Code also has some limitations which include the potential size of the proof and the time consumed in the proof-validation process.

MOBILE CODE SECURITY AGAINST MALICIOUS HOST

While a mobile agent is roaming among host platforms, it typically carries information such as code, static data, data collected from other hosts that were visited and the execution state of the mobile agent. The execution state is a dynamic data created during the execution of the agent at each host. Agents may be susceptible to observation of execution or any other information it possesses.

The possible attacks by the host platform on mobile agents are extracting sensitive information such as encryption keys, credit card information, corrupting or modifying the execution state and code information and denial of service. The data collected by the agent from other hosts or from the host's own database is manipulated to report false information to the user. Similarly the agent's code and execution sequence is manipulated to learn about the information the user is interested in and make the agent to perform something illegitimately. Denial of service includes terminating the agent without executing it, ignoring the agent's request for services and resources, providing insufficient resources, making it very difficult for the agent to complete execution in a timely fashion, or assigning continuous tasks to the agent so that it will never reach its goal. A malicious agent may assume the identity of another agent in order to gain access to platform resources and services, or simply to cause mischief or even serious damage to the platform. Likewise, a platform can claim the identity of another platform in order to gain access to the mobile agent data. This type of attack is known as masquerading.

It is intrinsically more difficult to protect the agents located on potentially untrusted hosts since the environment has a total control over the mobile code (otherwise, protecting the host would be impossible). Three categories of solutions exist to protect agents (Sanders and Tschudin 1998a, Sanders and Tschudin 1998b and Chan and Anthony 1999) – Agent tampering avoidance, detection and prevention. In avoidance technique, a closed network is established by sending the agents only to trusted hosts, such as intra-organizational applications, or on a third party hosted network that is trusted by all parties involved. Such an arrangement is effective but obviously satisfies system openness. The attacks can be detected using techniques such as forward integrity and execution tracing. These techniques are not suitable for very critical actions, for which detection may be too late. The attacks can be prevented either by making the tampering difficult or expensive. This can be achieved either by digitally signing the agent state and the data or encrypting them with a public key of the targeted host or by obfuscated code. In co-operating agents technique, the agent code /state is duplicated to recover from an agent termination attack. These prevention techniques are not well developed and are of current research issue.

Tampering Detection Techniques

Execution tracing (Vigna, 1997) is a technique that enables the detection of any possible misbehaviour by a platform. It is based on cryptographic traces that are collected during an agent's execution at different platforms and attached to the agent itself. Traces are the logs of actions performed by the agent during its lifetime and can be checked by the agents' owner to see if it contains any unauthorized modifications. This technique has some limitations such as the potential large size and number of logs to be retained and, the owner has to wait until it obtains suspicious results in order to run the verification process. Tracing is only triggered on suspicion that malicious tampering of an agent has occurred during its itinerary and is too complicated to be used for multi-threaded agents. A variation of this technique is by assigning the trace verification process to a trusted third party, the verification server, instead of depending on the agent's owner. These techniques assume that all

the involved parties own a public and private key that can be used for digital signatures to identify the involved parties. Another variation of this technique uses a list of secret keys provided by the agent's originator. For each platform in an agent's itinerary, there is an associated secret key. When an agent finishes an execution at a certain platform in its itinerary, it summarizes the results of its execution in a message for the home platform, which could be sent either immediately or later. The agent erases the used secret key of the current visited platform before its migration to the next platform. Destroying the secret key ensures the "forward integrity" of the encapsulation results. Forward integrity guarantees that no platform to be visited in the future is able to modify any results from the previously visited platform.

Tampering Prevention Techniques

Mobile Cryptography
This technique (Sanders and Tschudin, 1998 a) is based on executing the agent in its encrypted form. It is not the code which is encrypted but the function this code executes. The major challenge here is to find encryption schemes for expressing a program of arbitrary functions or login. An approach that uses the mobile cryptography is a time limited blackbox (Hohl, 1998). It defines the blackbox as an agent which performs the same task as the original agent but has a different structure. The agent has the blackbox property if its code and data cannot be read or modified. The agent holds the blackbox property for a known time interval, which should be sufficient to perform the required task. After this time the agent is invalidated, and the attacks have no effect. Various means of code obfuscation and authentication techniques are proposed to achieve this time limited blackbox.

Obfuscated Code
Obfuscation (Motlekar, 2005) is a technique of enforcing the security policy by applying a behaviour preserving transformation to the code

before it is being despatched to different hosts. It aims to protect the code from being analysed and understood by the host, thereby making the extraction and corruption of sensitive data, code or state very difficult. Different obfuscating transformations are Layout obfuscation – remove or modify some information in the code such as comments and debugging information, Data obfuscation – modifying the data and data structures in the code without modifying the code itself and Control obfuscation – altering the control flow in the code without modifying the computing part of the code. Code mess up is a variation of this approach where by the code is rendered to look illogically, use irrelevant variable names, have odd data representation- decomposing the variables bit-by-bit and to reassemble then into the actual values during execution, add a small amount of dead code that may appear to be active in the program. It is not sufficient to scramble the code only once, as the code may be reconstituted and comprehended by a malicious observer. The agent must have a new structure for each dispersal from the home origin. Obfuscation concentrates on protecting the code from decompilers and debuggers. It could delay, but not prevent the attacks on agent via reverse engineering.

Co-Operating Agents

This technique distributes critical tasks of a single mobile agent between two co-operating agents. Each of the two co-operating agents executes the tasks in one of two disjoint sets of platforms. The co-operating agents share the same data and exchange information in a secret way. This technique reduces the possibility of the shared data being pilfered by a single host. Each agent records and verifies the route of its co-operating agent. When an agent travels from one platform to another, it uses an authenticated communication channel to pass information about its itinerary to its co-operating agent. The peer agent takes a suitable action when anything goes wrong. The drawbacks of this technique are the cost of setting

up the authenticated communication channel for each migration; care should be taken to assign the two agents to disjoint platforms and never assigned to the same malicious host.

SECURITY MECHANISMS

Developing sound, reliable security mechanisms is a non-trivial task, and a history of vulnerable and/ or incomplete implementations of these mechanisms led to the idea that mobile code systems are inherently insecure, too complex, and very difficult to deploy. To overcome these problems, the mobile code system must rely as much as possible on the security mechanisms already provided by the language used for developing and the underlying operating system. By doing this, it is possible to develop, with reduced effort, security services that rely on well-known, well-understood, and well-tested security mechanisms. Also, by describing the security of the mobile code system in terms of the language and OS security mechanisms, system administrators can better evaluate the security implications of deploying the system.

Language Support for Safety

The features of the language needed to ensure that various code units do not interfere with each other, and with the system are given below.

- Heavy address space protection mechanisms
- Type-safe feature to ensure that arrays stay in bounds, pointers are always valid, and code cannot violate variable typing (such as placing code in a string and then executing it)
- Designing a modular system, separating interfaces from implementations in programs, and with appropriate layering of libraries and module groups, with particular care being taken at the interfaces between security boundaries.

- Replace general library routines which could compromise security with more specific, safer ones. For example a general file access routine can be replaced with one that can write files only in a temporary directory.
- Granting Access to Resources -Determining exactly which resources a particular code unit is to be granted access to. That is, there is a need for a security policy, which determines what type access any "mobile code" unit has. This policy may be:

1. **Fixed for all "mobile code" units:** very restrictive but easy, and the approach currently is used to handle applet security in web browsers such as Netscape.
2. **User verifies each security related access requests:** relatively easy, but rapidly gets annoying, and eventually is self-defeating when users stop taking notice of the details of the requests. Whilst there is a place for querying the user, it should be used exceedingly sparingly.
3. **Negotiate for each "mobile code" unit:** much harder, as some basis is needed for negotiation, perhaps based on various profiles, but ultimately this is likely to be the best approach.

OS Level Security

The types of events to be monitored in association with the agent execution are very similar to those audited for the system's users. Moreover, the agents can be easily grouped and differentiated within the system. In addition to extensive authentication and authorization mechanisms, accounting and auditing mechanisms should be implemented.

In system like "Distributed Agents on the Go"- DAGO (Felmetsger V. & Vigna G., 2005), a mobile agent is viewed as an ordinary system's

user who logs in to the host and uses some of the system's resources for its own needs. Every incoming mobile agent is given an individual account and a unique user identifier (UID) for the duration of its execution on a host. This approach allows the hosting OS to apply to mobile agents the same set of rules and policies that are applied by the OS to all of its users.

In Unix a number of logging, auditing and accounting mechanisms are available to monitor the action of its users and the status of its resources. These tools can work at the system call level and can be configured based on different types of events, such as opening and closing of files, reads and writes, programs executed and so on. They also can allow one to specify groups of system objects to be monitored for certain activities and can track system usage by recording the statistics about CPU and memory usage, I/O operations, running time and other forms of system resource usage along with the user IDs of the processes involved. These tools can be easily leveraged and extended to a multi-agent environment.

A variety of customizable tools such as SNARE – System iNtrusion Analysis and Reporting Environment (SNARE, 2005), BSM – Basic Security Module provide a greater degree of security assurance. SNARE is a dynamically loadable kernel nodule that can be used as a stand-alone auditing system or as a distributed tool. The tool can be configured to monitor events associated with certain groups of users, filter the monitored events with specific "search expressions", and submit reports in different formats and time frames. The type of events monitored can be either defined by a category (for example, system calls) or by an identifier (such as "denied access").

Safety Policies for Mobile Code Programs

A safety policy is a set of restrictions placed upon locally run untrusted code to ensure that the program does not behave in a manner that is detrimental to the system or to the system security. At the very least, a safety policy should guarantee the following fundamental safety properties (Muller, 2000):

- **Control Flow Safety:** The program should never jump to and start executing code that lies outside of the program's own code segment. All function calls should be to valid function entry points and function returns should return to the location from where the function was called.
- **Memory Safety:** The program should never be allowed to access random locations in memory. The program should only access memory in its own static data segment, live system heap memory that has been explicitly allocated to it and valid stack frames.
- **Stack Safety:** The program should only be allowed to access the top of the stack. Access to other areas of the stack should be completely restricted.

These three properties combined offer the minimum nontrivial level of security for mobile code. More complicated security policies are possible depending on the application.

Trust

Security is based on the notion of trust. Basically, software can be divided into two categories, namely software that is trusted and software that is not, separated by an imaginary trust boundary. All software on our side of the trust boundary is trusted and is known as the trusted code base.

All security implementations rely on some trusted code. As a result, a trust model of a particular implementation can be made. The trust model basically specifies which code is to be included in the trusted code base and which code lies outside of the trust boundary. At the very least, the trusted code base should include the local operating system kernel, but

can also include other items of trusted software like trusted compilers or trusted program run-time environments (e.g. the Java interpreter). It is desirable, however, to keep the trusted code base as small as possible to reduce the security vulnerabilities.

Performance and Security

Unfortunately, as it is in most applications, performance is sacrificed for increased security. It would, however, be profitable to have applications that are both secure and perform well at the same time. For this reason, there is much research concerned with resolving the conflict between these concepts in some way.

CONCLUSION

The purpose of this chapter is to raise readers' awareness of mobile code and various approaches to addressing security of mobile code and agents. All of the techniques discussed in this chapter offer different approaches to combating malicious mobile code. However the best approach is probably a combination of security mechanisms. The sandbox and code signing approaches are already hybridized. Combining these with firewalling techniques such as the playground gives an extra layer of security. PCC is still very much in the research and development phase at present.

In order to make the mobile code approach practical, it is essential to develop advanced and innovative solutions to restrict the operations that mobile code can perform but without unduly restricting its functionality. It is also necessary to develop formal, extremely easy to use safety languages to specify safety policy

Organizations relying on the Internet face significant challenges to ensure that their networks operate safely and that their systems continue to provide critical services even in the face of attack. Even the strictest of security policies will not be able to prevent security breaches. Educating users in social engineering attacks based around mobile code is also necessary.

REFERENCES

Alfalayleh M. & Brankovic L. (2004). An Overview Of Security Issues And Techniques In Mobile Agents. http://sec.isi.salford.ac.uk/cms2004/Program/CMS2004final/p2a3.pdf

Brown L. (1996). Mobile Code Security. [Electronic version]. http://www.unsw.adfa.edu.au/~lpb/papers/mcode96.html

Chan Hing Wing & Anthony. (1999). Secure Mobile Agents: Techniques, Modeling and Application. www.cse.cuhk.edu.hk/~lyu/student/mphil/anthony/term3.ppt

Felmetsger V. & Vigna G. (2005). Exploiting OS-level Mechanisms to Implement Mobile Code Security. www.cs.ucsb.edu/~vigna/pub/2005_felmetsger_vigna_ICECCS05.pdf

Ghezzi C. & Vigna G.(1997). Mobile Code Paradigms and Technologies: A Case Study. In Kurt Rothermet, Radu Popescu-Zeletin, editors, Mobile Agents, First International Workshop, MA'97, Berlin, Germany, April 1997, Proceedings, LNCS 1219, p. 39-49, Springer.

Hefeeda M. & Bharat B. On Mobile Code Security. Center of education and Research in Information Assurance and Security And Department of Computer Science, Purdue University West Lafayette, IN 47907, U.S.A. http://www.cs.sfu.ca/~mhefeeda/Papers/OnMobileCodeSecurity.pdf

Hohl F. (1998). Time Limited Blackbox Security: Protecting Mobile Agents From Malicious Hosts. http://citeseer.ist.psu.edu/hohl98time.html

Hohl F. (1998). Mobile Agent Security and Reliability. Proceedings of the Ninth International Symposium on Software Reliability Engineering (ISSRE '98).

Hohl F. (1998). Time Limited Blackbox security: Protecting Mobile Agents from Malicious Hosts. Mobile Agents and Security, Vol. 1419 of LNCS. Springer-Verlag.

Hohl, F. (1997). An approach to solve the problem of malicious hosts. Universität Stuttgart, Fakultät Informatik, Fakultätsbericht Nr. 1997/03, 1997. http://www.informatik.uni-stuttgart.de/cgi-bin/ncstrl_rep_view.pl?/inf/ftp/pub/library/ncstrl.ustuttgart_fi/TR-1997-03/TR-1997-03.bib

IBM Aglets. (2002). http://www.trl.ibm.com/aglets/.

Jansen W., Karygiannis Tom (NIST Special Publication 800-19 – Mobile Agent Security http://csrc.nist.gov/publications/nistpubs/800-19/sp800-19.pdf

Java Agent DEvelopment Framework (2005) http://jade.tilab.com/.

Karjoth, G., Lange, D.B. & Oshima, M. (1997). A Security Model for Aglets. IEEE Internet Computing, 1(4) 68-77. [Electronic version] http://www.ibm.com/java/education/aglets/

Loureiro S., Molva R. & Roudier Y. (2000). Mobile Code Security. Proceedings of ISYPAR 2000 (4ème Ecole d'Informatique des Systems Parallèles et Répartis), Code Mobile, Toulouse, France, February. http://www.eurecom.fr/~nsteam/Papers/mcs5.pdf

Lucco, S., Sharp, O. & Wahbe, R. (1995). Omniware: A Universal Substrate for Mobile Code. Fourth International World Wide Web Conference, MIT. [Electronic version] http://www.w3.org/pub/Conferences/WWW4/Papers/165/

McGraw G. & Morrisett G. (2000). Attacking Malicious Code http://www.cs.cornell.edu/Info/People/jgm/lang-based-security/maliciouscode.pdf

Mobile Code and Mobile Code Security. (2005). http://www.cs.nyu.edu/~yingxu/privacy/0407/main.html.

Mobile Code Security and Computing with Encrypted Functions [Electronic version] http://www.zurich.ibm.com/security/mobile

Mobile Code Security. (1996). [Electronic version] http://www.unsw.adfa.edu.au/~lpb/papers/mcode96.html.

Motlekar S. (2005). Code Obfuscation. http://palisade.paladion.net/issues/2005Aug/code-obfuscation/

Muller A. (2000). Mobile Code Security: Taking the Trojans out of the Trojan Horse http://www.cs.uct.ac.za/courses/CS400W/NIS/papers00/amuller/essay1.htm.

Necula G.C. & Lee, P. (1998). Safe, Untrusted Agents using Proof-Carrying Code. Lecture Notes in Computer Science N. 1419. Springer-Verlag.

Oppliger, R. (2000). Security technologies for the World Wide Web. Computer Security Series, Artech House Publishers.

Proof-Carrying Code. (2002). http://raw.cs.berkeley.edu/pcc.html.

Robust Obfuscation. (2005). http://www.cs.arizona.edu/~collberg/Research/Obfuscation/

Roger A. G. (2001). Malicious Mobile Code- Virus Protection for Windows [Electronic version]. O'Reilly & Associates, Inc.

Rubin, A. D., Geer, D. E. (1998). Mobile Code Security. IEEE Internet Computing.

Sander T. & Tschudin C. (1998 a). Towards Mobile Cryptography. Proceedings of the IEEE Symposium on Security and Privacy.

Sander, T. & Tschudin C. (1998 b). Protecting Mobile Agents Against Malicious Hosts. [Electronic version] Mobile Agents and Security Lecture Notes in Computer Science, 1419, G. Vigna, ed., Springer-Verlag, 44-60. http://citeseer.ist.psu.edu/article/sander97protecting.html

SNARE—System iNtrusion Analysis and Reporting Environment (2005). [Electronic version] http://www.intersectalliance.com/projects/Snare.

Telescript Language Reference. (1995). http://citeseer.ist.psu.edu/inc95telescript.html.

Tennenhouse, D. L. & Wetherall , D. J. (1996) Towards an Active Network Architecture. Computer Communication Review. http://www.tns.lcs.mit.edu/publications/ccr96.html.

Vigna Giovanni. (1997). Protecting Mobile Agents Through Tracing. Proceedings of the 3rd ECOOP Workshop on Mobile Object Systems, Jyväskylä, Finland, June. http://www.cs.ucsb.edu/~vigna/listpub.html.

This work was previously published in Web Services Security and E-Business, edited by G. Radhamani and G. Rao, pp. 75-92, copyright 2007 by IGI Publishing (an imprint of IGI Global).

Chapter XV
Finland:
Internationalization as the Key to Growth and M–Commerce Success

Tommi Pelkonen
Satama Interactive and Helsinki School of Economics, Finland

ABSTRACT

This chapter describes the Finnish mobile telecommunications industry trends and prospects. In addition, it presents two theoretical frameworks based on the Finnish companies' experiences in the turbulent m-commerce markets. First, the internationalization framework is targeted to facilitate m-commerce actors to position themselves in the global telecom business. Second, the mobile media framework is targeted to facilitate analyses related to the emerging mobile media markets. Furthermore, the chapter presents five mini-cases of Finnish m-commerce companies and concludes with theoretical and managerial implications to m-commerce actors.

INTRODUCTION: FINLAND, THE MOBILE PIONEERING COUNTRY

As a small North European country with only 5.1 million inhabitants, Finland is a very unlikely country to be the homeland for the mobile telecom industry giant, Nokia. Yet, since early 1990s, Nokia has been one of world's leading companies in creating and orchestrating the m-commerce industry. Finnish telecom industry has a long and fascinating background, having links to the Russian Czar and nationalistic movement in the late 19th century and pioneering scrambled radio communications solutions for the Finnish Army in WW-II. Nokia's outstanding business performance in the 1990s and early 21st century, as such, offers an attractive subject of analysis for this book. Additional interest in this Northern tiny country stems from the fact that very few economies globally have become so rapidly linked to the success of one single homegrown multinational company.

This chapter illustrates the status of the Finnish mobile industry in the early 2005. The key objective of the chapter is to assess how *a small m-commerce related company originating from a small and open economy* (SMOPEC, see Luostarinen 1979) *has a significant need to start planning its internationalization strategy and operations nearly from day one of its business operations*. In addition, the chapter aims to illustrate the international interorganizational networks a leading m-commerce company has to enmesh in, to succeed in the contemporary world. The following questions are addressed in this chapter:

1. How can an m-commerce industry actor analyze its position in dynamic and global mobile telecommunications markets?
2. What kind of challenges is the global mobile telecommunications industry likely to face based on the pioneering Nordic experiences of Finland, and particularly Nokia?
3. What kind of impacts does a single multinational corporation, such as Nokia, have globally on the development of fruitful and successful m-commerce business environments?

In this analysis, the companies originating from small domestic markets, such as Finland, are seen to relate to the "born global/international"-category (BG) of companies (Madsen and Servais, 1997). BG companies have right from the inception a strong ambition to operate their businesses internationally.

The chapter has five main parts. First, selected *basic facts* of Finnish markets are presented. Second, an *analysis framework* to help to position companies within the global m-commerce value creation networks (Pelkonen and Dholakia 2004) is formed and described. Third, as one of the core areas for mobile commerce—at least in 2005—is *mobile media content*, the chapter presents a model to evaluate various elements of mobile media development. Fourth, some interesting *success*

cases are presented to illustrate the impact Nokia has had on small companies wanting to expand from the marginal domestic markets to the major global markets. Finally, some *conclusions and recommendations* are drawn from the cases and models presented.

HISTORICAL OVERVIEW OF FINNISH DEVELOPMENT

The Finnish telecom industry dates back to 19th century when the first telecom networks were built in the country, initiated by the Russian Czar and the Finnish autonomous government. Until the 1980s, because of very limited capital resources available in the country, local telecom companies and cooperatives dominated the Finnish telecommunications markets. Yet, the nearly 300 local telephone companies had very talented personnel and Finland's telecom industry, led by the national monopoly company Telecom Finland (now part of Swedish-Finnish TeliaSonera), gradually developed one of the most sophisticated networks in Western Europe. Liberalization and digitization of the telecom network, strongly initiated and steered by the Finnish government, boosted the sophistication of the networks. In addition, the Finnish Technology Agency, TEKES, supported strongly the formation of the Finnish mobile cluster with several technology programs and networking events.

In the early 1990s, Nokia—the Finnish industrial conglomerate making major losses (business areas: paper and pulp, car tires, rubber boots, consumer electronics)—changed its strategy to divest all other operations except mobile and fixed telecommunications equipment and manufacturing and services. The company took major risks in investing most of its available resources into GSM-technology development and commercialization (see Pulkkinen, 1997). Nokia's devotion and capability to develop, sell, and delivery high quality digital mobile telephony enabled it to become the global market leader by the turn of the century.

Nokia's success created strong opportunities for Finnish startup companies to leverage their local strong relationship with this global market leader. Despite the IT "dotcom" crash of 2000, several venture financiers were still actively seeking investment opportunities from Finland in 2001. Of course, not all such venture investments succeeded. Finnish business scene experienced some dramatic bankruptcies of pioneering, high-end m-commerce start-ups (such as Riot Entertainment or WapIt, see Pelkonen and Dholakia, 2004). By 2005, the technology markets revived and the survivors of the crash, as well as new start-ups, became active in technology and market development.

In 2004, the success of content-driven m-commerce companies started shaping the m-commerce business. Neogames, the Finnish initiative for boosting mobile game development and commercialization, supported strongly again by TEKES, enabled Finnish mobile game-related companies to emerge as top actors in international markets (see, e.g., Pelkonen, 2004). We will take a closer look at some of these companies later in this chapter.

Key figures and facts about European mobile telecommunication markets are available at multiple websites (see, e.g., www.netsize.com, www.stat.fi, www.mintc.fi). Since markets evolve constantly, only the key facts about the Finnish markets are summarized here (see Table 1).

In the late 1990s, the early years of m-commerce, the markets were still emerging and mobile operators as well as pioneering application developers were investing continually and strongly into "future" solutions and trials, even when immediate demand growth and returns were not forthcoming. *Innovation, R&D and technological capability and compatibility*, and *relationships with Nokia*—these were the key competitive factors for Finnish m-commerce companies. Pioneering companies attracted investments and were seen as future winners.

In 2005, the markets became mature and highly competitive for Finnish companies. There were multiple reasons for this. First, the globalized Nokia Corporation was *sourcing its partners worldwide*, not just from Finland or Nordic nations. Second, *Japan and East Asia* overtook the Nordic nations in many aspects of mobile commerce innovation and solution development. Third, there is an emerging consensus that mobile solutions need to be tested with end users in large, core markets—Central Europe, United States, UK, Japan, China, etc. It is no longer sufficient to build solid business cases based on technology trials in small marginal markets such as Finland. Fourth, *Media- and brand-driven mobile solutions* have become increasingly common—and the major media and brands are located outside

Table 1. Selected facts about the Finnish Mobile Markets in 2003 (Source: Netsize, 2004 and Statistics Finland, 2004)

Number of mobile subscribers (2004): 4.7 millions (91% of total population), telephony (wired/wireless) 98 %, more wireless subscriptions than wired.	**Status of 3G**: Operations started in 2003, still marginal. **Terminals**: 0ver 50 % color screens, 65 % Java-enabled	**Other characteristics**: Strong impact of Nokia on market development Many start-ups with an international focus. Home of multiple trials and technology programs
Key operators: TeliaSonera, Elisa, DNA Finland, Saunalahti	**Most successful value-adding services**: Ringtones, Logos and Images; also recently downloadable interactive applications for mobiles	**Total value of value-added services markets (2003)**: 188 million euros

Finland. Finally, there is fierce *price and market power competition* as well as strategic leveraging of *relationships throughout global mobile value networks*. Therefore, it is no longer easy to innovate merely by working from a small domestic country, even with the advantageous proximity of Nokia. M-commerce companies have little choice but to internationalize.

INTERNATIONALIZATION FRAMEWORK FOR M-COMMERCE COMPANIES

As the global markets for m-commerce solutions get crowded with companies offering solutions (media, software, transactions, middleware technology etc), it is fruitful to create a model to facilitate the understanding of linkages between various kinds of market actors. In their analysis of the Finnish mobile telco markets, Pelkonen and Dholakia (2004) leveraged the Scandinavian network-research models (Johansson and Matson, 1986) to illustrate the prevailing strong market dynamics within the mobile telecom industry. The key objective for market actors, they argued, is to *gain as strong position within their business network* that consisted of various types of mobile telecom market actors and market activities. The strategic goal for leaders was to obtain *strong control over the core assets*, various tangible and intangible resources in the mobile telecom markets. This model is developed further for the purpose of this chapter. The analysis to follow shows how challenging it is for a mobile solution company originating from a small local market (such as Finland) to penetrate major global markets.

In the model presented in Figure 1, there are two main value chains leading up to the end-users

Figure 1. Internationalization framework for m-commerce companies

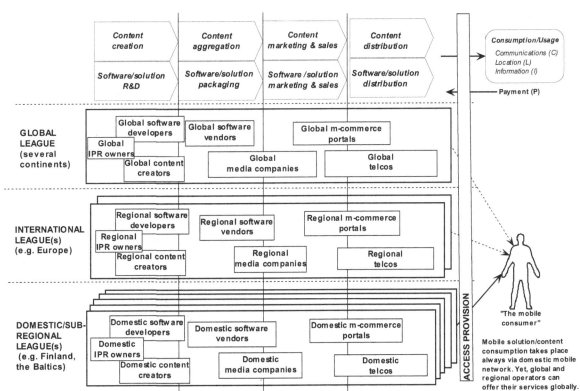

of mobile solutions. The focus in this framework is mainly on B2C solutions and markets. First is the content creation value chain, commonly referred to as the core process in the media business (see e.g. Baubin et al., 1996). Second is the consumer software development and commercialization value chain, commonly known as the software (mobile or computer-based) industry functional structure (see Pelkonen, 2003). Both value-adding processes lead up to the adoption and usage of the solution/media and generate payments from the end-users—the ultimate source of all the earnings logics within mobile telecoms. The CLIP-framework presented earlier suits perfectly to this picture. Mobile content/software product is communicated (C) at a specific location (L) to the consumers who obtain it through the access networks (I). Providers obtain the payment (P) from the consumers.

The bottom part of the framework is distributed into three main layers: global, international and domestic/sub-regional leagues. These three layers of international business underscore the fact that mobile telecoms represent one of the most internationalized fields of contemporary business. Mobile consumers move and travel with their devices and the global telcos (such as Vodafone or T-Mobile) constantly seek new opportunities for additional revenues. Consumers expect to have their services available wherever they move at any time of the day or year. The walled-garden strategy (limiting the access to services of only one operator or geographic location) may in the long run become a major obstacle for the industry development.

A developer/vendor of m-commerce solutions—content or software—from a small domestic market such as Finland would have to, at a minimum, partner with domestic operators and m-commerce portals. If domestic business potential for the solution is only marginal, the only way to grow and develop the business is to expand operations abroad (see Luostarinen and Gabriels-

son, 2004). To succeed in this, the developer will have to obtain access to the content/distribution portals of 1) other domestic markets, 2) regional markets, and/or 3) global markets. Developer/content creator with this kind of ambitions is required not only to expand its geographical reach, but also to ensure that all the elements within the CLIP-setup (e.g. communications and international payment systems) are expanded to support the targeted expansion. Relationships with global manufacturers such as Nokia become crucial for such operational expansion. Furthermore, the domestic company can expand via international/global alliances entailing partnerships, mergers, or acquisitions. This can take place either horizontally in the value chain or vertically within the internationalization layers.

MOBILE MEDIA AS THE SOURCE FOR INNOVATION AND GROWTH OF M-COMMERCE

As a third main are of analysis in this chapter, we examine one of the key developing areas in the m-commerce business: mobile media. Mobile phones are developing from a communications-only device into true portable mini-computers and media consumption devices. The increasing penetration of high-speed transmission networks (3G/UMTS/Wi-Fi), increased computing power and storage capacity (hard drives) in the devices, as well as the changing consumption habits for mobile media users have created an interesting landscape for mobile content and media innovation. The analysis that follows is based on the experiences that Finnish companies have had in the early years of mobile media. Such analysis contributes also to the broader understanding of what mobile media are and what kind of innovations can be expected in the coming years.

Mobile media, by definition, reside at the *interface* between two major business areas: *media pub-*

lishing and *telecommunications*. The two sectors have their own legacy and earnings logics, which make the "mobile media" industry innovations face continual pressures from two established and conventional sectors. Based on the author's research in the North European m-commerce markets, mobile media can be categorized into four main categories. The categories are based on the content creator's origin and a combined category termed "the meta-data". The main categories are: 1) publisher-originated content; 2) personal and person-to-person content; 3) community-created content and 4) content related to spaces and locations. In the overlaps and interstices of these four content areas lie the meta-data driven innovation areas, with key focus on the question: "What is new, relevant, and matches the consumption needs and contexts of the mobile end-user?"

The mobile media framework along with some of the up-to-date technology area buzzwords is presented in Figure 2. The technology areas are not explained in detail in this article: details can be obtained via simple Internet searches. For example, Kymäläinen (2004) has published a

very thorough analysis of the whole mobile entertainment (media) markets in a recent project, M-Gain (www.m-gain.org). This EU-funded analysis gives detailed insights into the areas of this framework.

In analyzing the future potential for m-commerce innovations, this framework helps understand the challenges an innovator may face in commercializing its solutions. If the innovation is related to something in the traditional publishing sector (top-left corner), the business model will have to reflect somehow the content publishing models: earnings by transaction or subscription or by advertising. On the other hand, the personal mobile content sector reflects the value and models controlled traditionally by telcos: business revenues generated by communications time and volume. In 2005, the newcomers to the mobile content consumption seem to arrive from the broadcast business—mobile television markets seem to emerging (see e.g. www.mobiletvforum. com).

Comparing the publisher-driven and personal-driven content areas indicates that the content

Figure 2. Mobile Media Solution and Innovation Areas (Source: Author's own research and Satama Interactive, 2005)

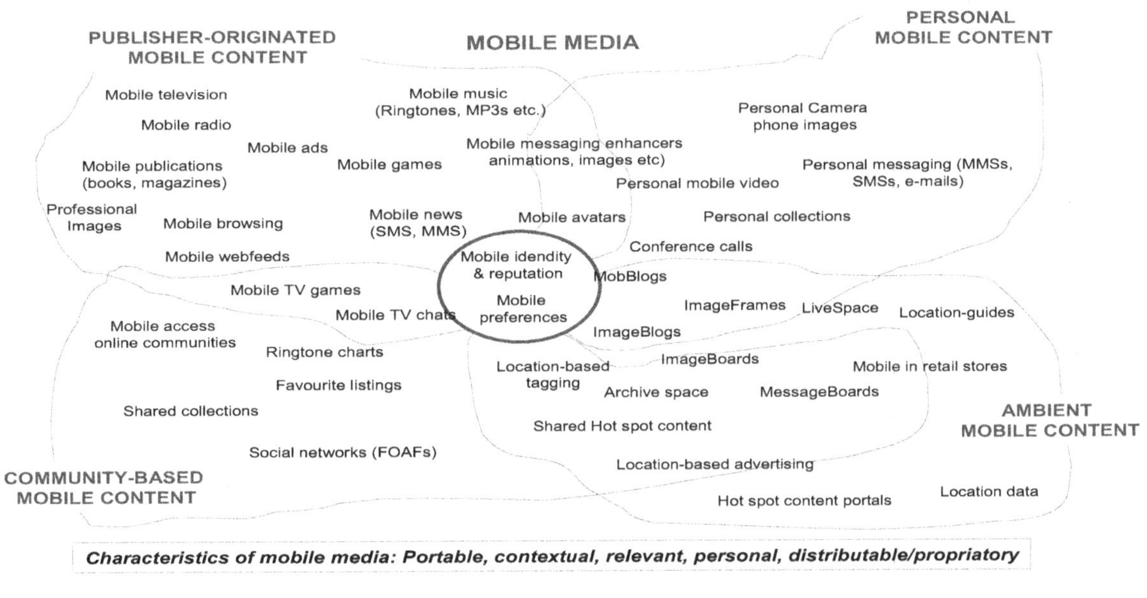

possessing the highest perceived value for the end-users is very often in the personal segment. Images taken, for example, from family events; important messages from cared ones—these usually constitute the most valuable elements for mobile consumers. Yet, profit margins for media companies and content producers from such person-to-person content are nearly nonexistent. Telcos and various mobile portals that offer storage capacity are in somewhat favorable market positions to gain from this segment. In late 2004, the power of the personal media content production was clearly shown during the Asian Tsunami catastrophe: individuals' digital cameras and mobile device recordings became the most authentic reports of the wave's attack. As a consequence of this, media companies were willing to pay major sums for these personal content files. The similar case was even stronger with the July 2005 London bombings. User-generated online sites such as Flickr.com and Wikipedia.org are starting to play an increasingly significant role in journalism and mobile phone is becoming a key enabler for this new wave of "citizen" journalism.

The two remaining sectors provide very interesting sources for innovations. Solutions designed to facilitate communications between individuals' social networks may become a surprisingly important element in m-commerce/mobile media revenue generation. Apple's iTunes listings and favorites-sharing functionalities have shown that there is major value in community-oriented media consumption. Moreover, the success of real-time TV chats and games via text messaging with mobile phones (see e.g. www.waterwar. tv) have proven that Andy Warhol's 15 minutes of fame have turned into 15 seconds of fame via consumer's message appearing on live TV chat discussion.

Location, as the keynote chapter of this book clearly indicated, is one of the core elements in the emerging m-commerce as well as mobile media consumption environment. The common term that researchers and mobile telco industry in Finland are using to characterize solutions designed for spaces and locations is "ambient media". In early 21st century, Nordic mobile operators and software producers have been active in testing and developing location-based concepts and their commercial potential is starting to become a reality. In urban areas, such innovations appear to be especially feasible. The near-GPS-accurate location possibilities of installed cellular networks have enabled location-based cellular gaming (see, e.g., Swedish website www.itsalive.com). Furthermore, solutions combining urban area maxi screens and SMS/MMS-based interaction are becoming popular (see, e.g., www.satama. com: MMS-board). Interesting opportunities may also occur in the areas of tourism. For example, MMS-photos taken of famous sights under perfect weather conditions could soon become available to the visitors trying to take photos at less good conditions. A professional photographer—in fact anyone with a camera phone—could take these photos.

Regardless of the origin of the mobile media solution, the end-user needs an intelligent "sensor" device that can become "aware" of the mobile media solution/content/access possibility. Until recently, mobile phones have been the dominant device for mobile media interaction. Yet, Finnish sport equipment manufacturer Suunto (www. suunto.com) has demonstrated—in cooperation with Microsoft—that other kinds of devices can be used for mobile media consumption. Suunto's M3 wrist-top computer receives data (e.g., weather forecasts) based on the user's settings. Combined with Suunto's special expertise in physical performance measurement, such devices can "sense" both the environment as well as the individual's movements, and share such data with preferred target groups. In the near future, this kind of new generation of mobile media information and consumption may open up interesting opportunities for mobile companies.

SUCCESSFUL MINI-CASES IN FINLAND'S MOBILE SECTOR

To bring more clarity to the two frameworks presented in the previous section of this chapter, we turn to some Finnish mini-cases. Each of the companies has their own solutions for benefiting from the internationalization opportunities, and the media-consumption driven future for m-commerce.

Sulake Labs, www.sulake.com

Year of founding: 1999

Short Description of Activities

Springing from the hobby of its multimedia-enthusiastic founders, Sulake Labs created one of the first truly profitable "virtual goodie" environments. Their concept "Habbohotel" is a virtual 3D community in which registered members can interact, move, chat, play games, dance, etc. Furthermore, users can create their own rooms in which they can purchase virtual furniture and other decorations with their mobile phones. Surprisingly, the concept has proven to be very successful and Habbohotel has several thousand active members. The original Finnish operation, "Hotel Kultakala", is offered in cooperation with Finnish telecom operator and has become profitable for both parties. In addition, the solution has won several awards in international digital design contests.

Status as of Early 2005

Sulake continues to develop its technology solutions. It has opened its Fuse software solution for developers worldwide. Sulake has also expanded into international markets with operations in the U.K. and elsewhere. In January 2004, Sulake collected in additional financing of 18 million euros for its international expansion. The company has set targets to become one of best-known global brands among young mobile consumers. Sulake employed nearly 160 people and had a turnover of about 15 million euros in 2004.

Sumea, www.sumea.com

Year of founding: 1999

Short Description of Activities

Sumea started as one of pioneering companies to produce professionally miniature digital games for mobile devices. The company benefited strongly from Nokia's need to have well-functioning, attractive and compact games to promote its devices. Sumea's games were just in the correct format and the company's timing to develop the games was just perfect. Sumea's games became immediate hits in 2002-2003 and have been among the most sold mobile games globally. Sumea attracted many financiers to invest in it, but in June 2004 was acquired by a US-based mobile game-focused developing company, Digital Chocolate (DC). DC was formed by one the gaming industry giants Electronic Arts' founders, Trip Hopkins.

Status as of Early 2005

Sumea/Digital Chokolate is still located in Helsinki, employs over 100 people and operates as the European headquarters for Digital Chocolate. Sumea has currently about 40 mobile game titles and its games are sold in 50 countries. The company earns its main revenues from direct sales via operators' mobile portals.

Digia, www.digia.com

Year of founding: 1997

Short Description of Activities

Originally founded as an e-learning and digital media service company in early 1990s, Digia changed its strategy radically in 2000. It was faced with profitability challenges and decided to focus all of its resources into Symbian-based software solution development. Symbian, of course, is the popular operating system for mobile devices. The risky but bold strategy has propelled Digia to become one of powerhouse in global Symbian production. Despite the global IT-crash in 2001, Digia kept on growing and has been able to produce both customized and standardized software solutions for its clients.

Status as of Early 2005

Digia is one of the leading producers of Symbian solution in the world. It hired 260 software professionals and had a turnover of 21 million euros in 2004. Company's key clients include Nokia and TeliaSonera. In early February 2005, Digia announced its plans to merge with another Finnish IT-company, Sysopen, forming a relatively large Nordic IT-actor: Digia Sysopen with about 570 professionals and a turnover of over 47 million euros.

Sofia Digital, www.sofiadigital.fi

Year of founding: 2000

Short description of activities

Having its origins in FutureTV, a research project led by the Helsinki University of Technology, Sofia Digital (SD) became the first company to produce commercial interactive software for the MHP-standard-based (Multimedia Home Platform) digital television solution network. SD created the national user interface for the Finnish digital terrestrial TV program guide. Besides television applications, SD has been able to expand its line of operations to include mobile interaction with television broadcasting. In 2004, Sofia acquired the Finnish market leader in mobile TV game production, Outerrim, to benefit from this growing field of business.

Status as of early 2005

Sofia Digital is among the leading European companies producing interactive applications for digital television. It employs 40 television and software professionals. Sofia's key customers include Antenna Hungaria, Czech Telecom, Helsinki Televisio, Mediaset, MTV3, Nelonen, Nokia, Nordea, ST Microelectronics, Sun Microsystems Italia, Veikkaus and YLE. Company's MHP expertise is of high standard and it has expertise also in cross-media solution design and implementation. SD's future within the field of television-based interaction is strongly tied to popularity of interactive set-top-boxes as well as to the penetration of text-message-based interaction among television broadcasters.

Satama Interactive, www.satama.com

Year of founding: 1997

Short description of activities

As the leading Finnish creator of digital solutions for Finnish companies, Satama has mobile Internet-related operations since 1999. Satama has been actively helping its customers to promote and commercialize mobile applications. Satama's special expertise in mobility business has been in mobile event and maxi-screen interaction solution design. Satama's core business has been in digital marketing communications and solution design, but mobile solutions have started to play an increasingly important role in the revenue generation.

Status as of Early 2005

In late 2004, Satama acquired a small Finnish software company, Mind-on-Move, to increase its presence and expertise in downloadable mobile application markets. Satama currently employs about 300 digital media professionals. In 2004, it had a turnover of about 23 million euros and had offices in Finland and in the Netherlands as well as network partners in Sweden and Germany. Satama's key customers include mobile industry companies such as Nokia, Vodafone, KPN and TeliaSonera.

Movial, www.movial.fi

Year of founding: 2001

Short Description of Activities

Movial's founders have their background in the dotcom-era high-end consulting company, Adcore. The founders sold their Linux-technology-focused software and consulting company to the Swedish-led Adcore coalition in 1999. Adcore expanded extremely rapidly globally and had, at its peak in 2001, operations in 13 countries and employed over 2000 IT-professionals. After radical restructuring, Adcore was left with operations only in Stockholm and 300 employees. The Finnish entrepreneurs left Adcore coalition in late 2001 to form two companies, Creanor, focusing on digital design, and Movial focusing on mobile application design and implementation. From the originally 25 employees in 2002, Movial has grown rapidly employing with 90 IT-professionals at end of 2004.

Status as of Early 2005

Movial is constantly expanding its expertise and product portfolio in both customized and standardized mobile software production. The company had a turnover of almost 5 million euros in 2004 and its main customers were Nokia, Blueberg Digital Ltd and Buscom. The founders own the company and are constantly leveraging

their experiences gained from the Adcore's rapid internationalization efforts as well as the expertise and cost-efficiency obtained by Linux-based server solutions.

TECHNOLOGICAL AND MANAGERIAL LESSONS FROM FINLAND'S MOBILE EXPERIENCE

Though its pioneering moves have been overshadowed to some extent by Asian developments, the Finnish case in the global m-commerce business is still very relevant for business analyses of mobile markets. Nokia's transformation from an industrial diversified manufacturer into one of the leading high-tech companies in a bit over a decade is unparalleled in global economic history. Nokia's massive growth has given a kick-start to multiple Finnish small start-up companies and enabled a much higher role for these companies than companies originating from comparably small, high-tech countries. Finnish governmental support has been strong in supporting the visionary and risk-taking strategy that Nokia and its partners adopted.

The major challenge for any company or economy performing excellently for several succeeding years is to keep up with pace of the innovation. Nokia's failures to foresee the demand for clamshell-shaped mobile phones caused it to lose its market share in 2004. Yet, the industry giant was able to react to the need and streamline its operations, design, and R&D—and rapidly developed the models needed to keep up with the constantly intensifying rivalry. In contrast to earlier crises, Nokia sought solutions from all global units of the company. For the Finnish economy, especially the ICT-sector, Nokia's global sourcing willingness creates greater challenges. Without stronger internationalization, small actors—previously dependent on Nokia—may risk of losing markets and revenues.

Similar situations prevail also in other smaller economies. The Swedish ICT-sector was strongly dependent on the activities and initiatives of Ericsson, which has now become the more global Sony-Ericsson. As the globalization of ICT firms continues apace, relying on a single large domestic partner becomes increasingly risky. Nokia Vice President Kosonen, for example, has presented some key criteria for a multinational corporation to seek partners and business operation locations. His approach (see Figure 3) sums up succinctly and supplements the issues presented earlier in this chapter and in the mini-cases.

Kosonen's criteria show clearly the kind of elements that governments, start-ups, financiers and other actors in the turbulent m-commerce markets should focus their actions on to serve global mobile actors. The Finnish success case of 1990s demonstrates clearly how positive development can take place when all the elements are present. Furthermore, Nokia's more recent capability to expand beyond conventional national boundaries demonstrates how challenging it is for small and open economies to sustain the positive development year after year.

The Finnish mini-cases demonstrate that for m-commerce start-ups originating from small domestic economies, dependence on a local "locomotive" (such as Nokia) may be a very fruitful strategy in the early phases. Yet to succeed on a larger scale, these companies need to expand their customer base rapidly to new markets and segments that are independent of the success of the "door-opener/locomotive" company like Nokia. The small and medium enterprises (SMEs) need to expand their internationalization networks (Johansson and Matsson, 1988) and establish positions in business areas and markets that that let them develop their operations regardless of the activities the "godfather/door-opener/locomotive" company.

Convergence of mobile communication technology into consumer electronics is bringing the m-commerce industry to another turning point. As media are starting to be consumed via networked mobile devices, mobile telcos, start-ups and equipment manufacturers are faced with the challenge of cooperating with media-driven companies. In 1990s, the boom for mobile communications was driven by technology innovation and provision of additional technology features to mobile phones. By contrast, the boom of the second half of first decade in the 21st century may well be led by *mobile content.*

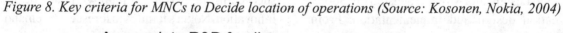

Figure 8. Key criteria for MNCs to Decide location of operations (Source: Kosonen, Nokia, 2004)

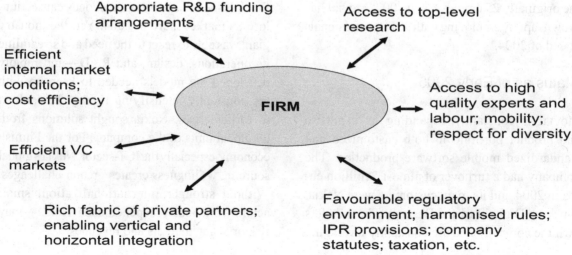

Consumers' preferences are about to switch *from technological attractiveness to media consumption-driven models*. In the next few years, portable gadgets such as mobile phones will be purchased to consume content, not just communicate. In these evolving markets, time will show which of the winners of the 1990s, mobile telcos and manufacturers, would continue to triumph and which new players would carve out significant market shares. Based on the Finnish case, the mobile companies are in a solid but at the same time turbulent situation. Competition from Southeast Asia is strong and traditional consumer electronics is strong. Regardless of the outcome, for the incumbent m-commerce actors, one thing is sure: there are, once more, great and emergent opportunities for innovations in the m-commerce markets.

QUESTIONS FOR DISCUSSION

1. What kind of strategies can m-commerce companies in Finland use to expand the geographical business reach for their products and services?
2. What challenges does international expansion create for m-commerce companies, especially for companies from small but innovative nation such as Finland?
3. How can mobile portals benefit from user-generated content in their content and service offerings?
4. What kind of business strategies and conditions are needed to make location-based mobile solutions break into mainstream markets?

DEDICATION

This article is dedicated to the memory of D.Sc. (Econ.) Matti Pulkkinen, my former research supervisor and honored colleague and to all the victims of the December 2004 Tsunami in Asia.

REFERENCES

Baubin, T, Bruck, P. Hofbauer T. (1996). Electronic publishing—Strategic developments for the European publishing industry the towards the year 2000. ECSC-EEC-EAEC, Brussels-Luxembourg.

Gabrielsson, M. and Gabrielssson, P. (2003), Global Marketing Strategies of Born Globals and Globalising Internationals in the ICT field. Journal of Euromarketing, Vol 12 No 3-4, pp. 123-145.

Johanson J. and Mattsson, L.-G. (1986). International Marketing and Internationalization Processes - Network approach. In Turnbull, P. W. and Paliwoda, S. J., Research in International Marketing. Croom Helm, New Hampshire, 234-265.

Johanson, J. and Mattsson, L.-G. (1988). Internationalization in industrial systems: A network approach. In Hood, N. and Vahlne, J.-E. (eds). Strategies in global competition. Croom-Helm, New York, pp. 287-314.

Luostarinen, R. (1979), Internationalisation of the Firm. Thesis for the degree of Doctor at the Helsinki School of Economics.

Luostarinen, R. and Gabrielsson, M. (2004). Born Globals of Small and Open Economies (SMOPECs)—A New Entrepreneurial Challenge. In Dana, L. P. (Ed), Handbook of Research on International Entrepreneurship. Edward Elgar, Cheltenham.

Madsen, T. and Servais, P. (1997). The Internationalization of Born Globals-An Evolutionary Process. International Business Review, Vol 6 No 6, pp. 1-14.

Kosonen, M. (2004). Global competitiveness of MNCs. Presentation at EIBA academic conference. 2004. Llubljana. Slovenia

Kymäläinen, P. (ed.). (2004). Mgain: Mobile Entertainment Industry and Culture. Helsinki University of Technology. www.m-gain.org

Netsize Guide. (2004). Developing the mobile multimedia market. Netsize. www.netsize.com

Pelkonen, T. (2003). Value creation patterns and current trends in digital media service creation: A case study of the Finnish digital media industry. Europrix Scholars Conference paper, November 13, 20003. Tampere, Finland (www.mindtrek. org/sc).

Pelkonen, T. (2004) Mobile Games markets. ACTen E-Content Report 3. http://www.acten.net/ cgi-bin/WebGUI/www/index.pl/mobile_games

Pelkonen, T. and Dholakia, N. (2004). Understanding Emergent M-Commerce Services by Using Business Network Analysis: The Case of Finland. In Wireless Communications and Mobile Commerce, Nan Si Shi (ed.), Hershey PA: Idea Group Publishing, 105-131.'

Pulkkinen, M. (1997). The Breakthrough of Nokia Mobile Phones. Doctoral Dissertation. Helsinki School of Economics. HeSePrint, Helsinki.

Satama Interactive, (2005). Satama Insight: Mobile Media as an business opportunity. Company internal material. Helsinki, Finland.

In addition to the mentioned sources the following online news database were used in this article:

Case company websites; news from www.it-viikko.fi, www.tietoviikko.com, www.talentum. com, www.rekaksois.com, www.digitoday.fi ; several statistics and analyses from www.stat.fi and www.mintc.fi

Chapter XVI
Mobile Workforce Management in a Service–Oriented Enterprise:
Capturing Concepts and Requirements in a Multi–Agent Infrastructure

Dickson K.W. Chiu
Dickson Computer Systems, Hong Kong

S.C. Cheung
Hong Kong University of Science and Technology, Hong Kong

Ho-fung Leung
The Chinese University of Hong Kong, Hong Kong

ABSTRACT

In a service-oriented enterprise, the professional workforce such as salespersons and support staff tends to be mobile with the recent advances in mobile technologies. There are increasing demands for the support of mobile workforce management (MWM) across multiple platforms in order to integrate the disparate business functions of the mobile professional workforce and management with a unified infrastructure, together with the provision of personalized assistance and automation. Typically, MWM involves tight collaboration, negotiation, and sophisticated business-domain knowledge, and thus can be facilitated with the use of intelligent software agents. As mobile devices become more powerful, intelligent software agents can now be deployed on these devices and hence are also subject to mobility. Therefore, a multiagent information-system (MAIS) infrastructure provides a suitable paradigm to capture the concepts and requirements of an MWM as well as a phased development and deployment. In this book chapter, we illustrate our approach with a case study at a large telecommunication enterprise. We show how to formulate a scalable, flexible, and intelligent MAIS with agent clusters. Each agent cluster comprises several types of agents to achieve the goal of each phase of the workforce-management process, namely, task formulation, matchmaking, brokering, commuting, and service.

INTRODUCTION

The advancement of mobile technologies has resulted in an increasing demand for the support of mobile-workforce management (MWM) across multiple platforms anytime and anywhere. Examples include supply-chain logistics, group calendars, dynamic human-resources planning, and postal services. Existing solutions and proposals often treat the workforce as passive-moving resources and cannot cope with the current requirements for the knowledge-based economy and services, such as technical-support teams (e.g., computer- or network-support engineers and technicians).

Recent advances in hardware and software technologies have created a plethora of mobile devices with a wide range of communication, computing, and storage capabilities. New mobile applications running on these devices provide users with easy access to remote services at anytime and anywhere. Moreover, as mobile devices become more powerful, the adoption of mobile computing is imminent. The Internet is quickly evolving toward a wireless one, but the wireless Internet will not be a simple add-on to the wired Internet. New challenging problems arise from the handling of mobility, handsets with reduced screens, and varying bandwidth. Moreover, the business processes involving the workforce tends to get complicated with requirements from both within the organization's management and external Web services (e.g., tracking and logistics integration). New mobile applications running on these devices provide users easy access to remote services regardless of where they are, and will soon take advantage of the ubiquity of wireless networking to create new virtual worlds. Therefore, the main challenge of MWM is to provide an effective integration of the ever-increasing disparate business functions in a unified platform not only to management, but also to the mobile professional workforce.

An additional challenge to MWM in service-oriented enterprises (such as telecom and computer vendors) is the provision of personalized assistance and automation to the mobile professional workforce, whose members each have different capabilities, expertise, and support requirements. Often, consultations and collaborations are required for a task. Because of their professional capabilities and responsibilities, members of the workforce have their own job preferences and scheduling that cannot be flexibly managed in a centralized manner. As mobile devices become more powerful, peer-to-peer mobile computing becomes an important computation paradigm. In particular, intelligent software agents can now run on these mobile devices and can adequately provide personalized assistance to the mobile workforce. Under the individual's instructions and preferences, these agents can be delegated to help in the negotiating and planning of personalized tasks and schedules, thereby augmenting the user's interactive decisions. In addition, agent-based solutions are scalable and flexible, supporting variable granularities for the grouping of workforce management.

We have been working on some related pilot studies related to MWM, such as constraint-based negotiation (Chiu, Cheung, et al., 2004), m-service (mobile-service) adaptation (Chiu, Cheung, Kafeza, & Leung, 2003), and alert management for medical professionals (Chiu, Kwok, et al., 2004). Based on these results, we proceed to a larger scale case study, and the contributions of this chapter are as follows. First we formulate a scalable, flexible, and intelligent multiagent information-system (MAIS) infrastructure for MWM with agent clusters in a service-oriented enterprise. Then we propose the use of agent clusters, each comprising several types of agents to achieve the goal of each phase of the workforce-management process, namely, task formulation, matchmaking, brokering, commuting, and service. Next we formulate a methodology for the analysis and design of MWM in the context of enterprise service integration with MAIS. Finally, we illustrate our approach with an MWM case study in a large service-oriented telecom enterprise, highlighting typical requirements and detailing architectural design considerations. This book chapter is an extension of our previous work (Chiu, Cheung, & Leung, 2005). It refines our previous MAIS infrastructure and relates that to the believe-desire-intention (BDI) agent architecture (Rao & Georgeff, 1995). The application of the refined MAIS infrastructure is illustrated by a case study based on a large service-oriented telecom enterprise.

The rest of the chapter is organized as follows. First we introduce background and related work. Next we explain an overview of an MAIS and a development methodology for MWM. After this, we highlight the MWM process requirements. The next section details our MAIS architecture and implementation framework. Then we evaluate our approach from different stakeholders' perspectives. We conclude this chapter with our plans for further research.

BACKGROUND

Users under mobile or wireless computing environments are no longer constrained by working at a fixed and known location where wired connection is available. Users of a workforce-management system can collaborate at anywhere and anytime. This facilitates timely and location-aware decision making. Although a mobile system shares many characteristics with a distributed system, it imposes new challenges (Barbara, 1999) to computing applications, including workforce management. First, communication between parties in a mobile system is no longer symmetric. The downstream data rates are much wider than upstream data rates. Some two to three orders of magnitude differences are generally expected. As such, mobile applications need to be designed with care to minimize the upstream data transfer.

Second, mobile communication channels are more liable to disconnection and data-rate frustration. Message exchanges should be designed to be as idempotent as possible. As a result, mobile process flows must support exception handling and be able to adapt to environmental changes. Third, the screen sizes of mobile devices are usually small and vary across different models. This affects how information can be effectively disseminated and displayed to users. Fourth, mobile or wireless networks are ad hoc in nature. A wireless connection infrastructure typically consists of thousands of mobile nodes whose communication channels can be dynamically reconfigured. To reduce overheads, channel reconfiguration generally requires limited network management and administration. The availability of mobile ad hoc networking technology imposes challenges to effective multihop routing, mobile data management, congestion control, and dynamic quality-of-services support. The autonomy of mobile nodes is desired (Shi, Yang, Xiang, & Wu, 1998). Fourth, mobile nodes have stringent constraints on computational resources and power. Expensive computations as required by asymmetric encryption or video encoding should not be performed frequently.

Advanced work-flow-management systems (WFMSs) are mostly Web enabled. Recently, researchers in work-flow technologies have been exploring cross-organizational work flows to model these activities, such as Grefen, Aberer, Hoffner, and Ludwig (2000), Kim, Kang, Kim, Bae, and Ju (2000), and the Workflow Management Coalition (1995, 1999). In addition, advanced WFMSs can provide various services such as coordination, interfacing, maintaining a process repository, process (work flow) adaptation and evolution, matchmaking, exception handling, data and rule bases, and so on, with many opportunities for reuse. With the advance in mobile and wireless technologies, mobile workforce management has become more and more decentralized, with involved components becoming increasingly autonomous, and location and situation awareness being incorporated into system design (Karageorgos, Thompson, & Mehandjiev, 2002; Lee, Buckland, & Shepherdson, 2003; Thompson & Odgers, 2000).

A business process is carried out through a set of one or more interdependent activities, which collectively realize a business objective or policy goal. Work flow is the computerized facilitation or automation of a business process. WFMSs can assist in the specification, decomposition, coordination, scheduling, execution, and monitoring of work flows. In addition to streamlining and improving routine business processes, WFMSs help in documenting and reflecting upon business processes. Often, traditional WFMSs can only coordinate work flows within a single organization. However, contemporary WFMSs can now interact with various types of distributed agents over the Internet.

Intelligent agents are considered autonomous entities with abilities to execute tasks independently. He, Jennings, and Leung (2003) present a comprehensive survey on agent-mediated e-commerce. An agent should be proactive and subject to personalization, with a high degree of autonomy. In particular, due to the different limitations on different platforms, users may need different options in agent delegation. Prior research studies usually focus on the technical issues in a domain-specific application. For example, Lo and Kersten (1999) present an integrated negotiation environment by using software-agent technologies for supporting negotiators. However, all of these works did not support their models on different platforms.

This problem is further complicated by the dynamicity of the mobile e-commerce environment brought about by wireless communication channels and portable computing devices. Mobile-agent technology is a promising solution to the problem (Kowalczyk et al., 2003). Various studies have been made to integrate mobile and wireless technologies into agents (Bailey &

Bakos, 1997; Kotz & Gray, 1999; Kowalczyk & Bui, 2000; Lomuscio, Wooldridge, & Jennings, 2000; Papaioannou, 2000).

However, the problem of MWM and the deployment of agents for this purpose are rarely studied. Research in mobile computing mainly focuses on the enabling technologies at communication layers instead of the deployment of applications such as MWM on the application layer. Guido, Roberto, Tria, and Bisio (1998) point out some MWM issues and evaluation criteria, but the details are no longer up to date because of the fast-evolving technologies. Jing, Huff, Hurwitz, Sinha, Robinson, and Feblowitz (2000) present a system called WHAM (workflow enhancements for mobility) to support the mobile workforce and applications in work-flow environments, with emphasis on a two-level (central and local) resource-management approach. Both groups did not consider distributed agent-based, flexible, multiplatform business-process interactions or any collaboration support. Although there have been studies on related technologies for MWM, there have not been in-depth studies on how to integrate these technologies for a scalable MWM MAIS.

The emergence of MAIS dates back to Sycara and Zeng (1996), who discuss the issues in the coordination of multiple intelligent software agents. In general, an MAIS provides a platform to bring together the multiple types of expertise for any decision making (Luo, Liu, & Davis, 2002). For example, F. R. Lin, Tan, and Shaw (1998) present an MAIS with four main components: agents, tasks, organizations, and information infrastructure for modeling the order-fulfillment process in a supply-chain network. Furthermore, F. R. Lin and Pai (2000) discuss the implementation of MAIS based on a multiagent simulation platform called Swarm. Next, Shakshuki, Ghenniwa, and Kamel (2000) present an MAIS architecture in which each agent is autonomous, cooperative, coordinated, intelligent, rational, and able to communicate with other agents to fulfill the users' needs. Choy, Srinivasan, and Cheu (2003) propose the use of mobile agents to aid in meeting the critical requirement of universal access in an efficient manner. Chiu et al. (2003) also propose the use of a three-tier view-based methodology for adapting human-agent collaborative systems for multiple mobile platforms. In order to ensure interoperability of an MAIS, standardization on different levels is highly required (Gerst, 2003). Thus, based on all these prior works, our proposed MAIS framework adapts and coordinates agents with standardized mobile technologies for MWM.

E-collaboration (Bafoutsou & Mentzas, 2001), being a foundation of WFM, supports communication, coordination, and cooperation for a set of geographically dispersed users. Thus, e-collaboration requires a framework based on strategy, organization, processes, and information technology. Furthermore, Rutkowski, Vogel, Genuchten, Bemelmans, and Favier (2002) address the importance of structuring activities for balancing electronic communication during e-collaboration to prevent and solve conflicts. For logic-based collaboration, Bui (1987) describes various protocols for multicriteria group-decision support in an organization. Bui, Bodart, and Ma (1998) further propose a formal language based on first-order logic to support and document argumentation, claims, decisions, negotiation, and coordination in network-based organizations. In this context, a constrain-based collaboration can be modeled as a specific case of the Action-Resource Based Argumentation Support (AR-BAS) language.

Wegner, Paul, Thamm, and Thelemann (1996) present a multiagent collaboration algorithm using the concepts of belief, desire, and intention. In addition, Fraile, Paredis, Wang, and Khosla (1999) present a negotiation, collaboration, and cooperation model for supporting a team of distributed agents to achieve the goals of assembly tasks. However, this paper mainly focuses on the overall integration of MWM support with MAIS.

Another foundation of MFM is meeting scheduling. There are some commercial products, but they are just calendars or simple diaries with special features, such as availability checkers and meeting reminders (Garrido, Brena, & Sycara, 1996). Shitani, Ito, and Sycara (2000) highlight a negotiation approach among agents for a distributed meeting scheduler based on the multiattribute-utility theory. Lamsweerde, Darimont, and Massonet (1995) discuss a goal-directed elaboration of requirements for a meeting scheduler, but do not discuss any implementation frameworks. Sandip (1997) summarizes an agent-based system for an automated distribution meeting scheduler, but it is not based on BDI agent architecture. However, all these systems cannot support manual interactions in the decision process or any mobile support issues.

In summary, none of the existing works consider an MAIS infrastructure for MWM as a solution for integration and personalized workforce support. Scattered efforts have looked into subproblems but are inadequate for an integrated solution. There is neither any work describing a concrete implementation framework and methodology by means of a portfolio of contemporary enabling technologies.

MAIS INFRASTRUCTURE

An MAIS provides an infrastructure for the exchange of information among multiple agents as well as users under a predefined collaboration protocol. Agents in the MAIS are distributed and autonomous, each carrying out actions based on their own strategies. In this section, we explain our MAIS infrastructure and metamodel in which the computational model of an agent can be described using a BDI framework. Then, we summarize our methodology for the design and analysis of an MAIS for MWM.

MAIS Layered Infrastructure for MWM

Figure 1 summarizes our layered infrastructure for MWM. Conventionally, services and collaboration are driven solely by human representatives. This could be a tedious, repetitive, and error-prone process, especially when the professional workforces have to commute frequently. Furthermore, agents facilitate the protection of privacy and security. The provision of computerized personal assistance to individual users across organizations by means of agents is a sensible choice. These agents, acting on behalf of their delegators, collaborate through both wired and wireless Internet, forming a dynamic MAIS over an enterprise information system (EIS). Such repeatable processes can be

adequately supported, and the cost of developing the infrastructure is well justified.

The BDI framework is a well-established computational model for deliberative intelligent agents, as summarized in Figure 2. A BDI agent constantly monitors the changes in the environment and updates its information accordingly. Possible goals are then generated, from which intentions to be pursued are identified. A sequence of actions will be performed to achieve the intentions. BDI agents are proactive by taking initiatives to achieve their goals, yet adaptive by reacting to the changes in the environment in a timely manner. They are also able to accumulate experience from previous interactions with the environment and other agents.

Internet applications are generally developed with a three-tier architecture comprising the front,

Figure 1. A layered infrastructure for MWM

Personal Assistance	Information/Service Resources	Planning	...
Mobile Workforce Management			
Multiagent Information System			
BDI Agents			
		Collaboration Protocol	
EIS Three-Tier Implementation Architecture (Interface Tier/Application Tier/Data Tier)			

Figure 2. BDI conceptual model

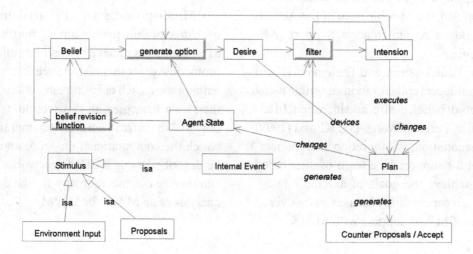

application, and data tiers. Though the use of a three-tier architecture in the agent community is relatively new, it is a well-accepted pattern to provide flexibility in each tier (Chiu et al., 2003) and is absolutely required in the expansion of e-collaboration support. Such flexibility is particularly important to the front tier, which often involves the support of different solutions on multiple platforms. In our architecture, users may either interact manually with other collaborators or delegate an agent to make decisions on their behalf. Thus, users without agent support can still participate through flexible user interfaces for multiple platforms.

MAIS Metamodel

Figure 3 describes the metamodel of an MAIS system in a class diagram of UML (Object Management Group [OMG], 2001), which is widely used for visualizing, specifying, constructing, and documenting the artifacts of a software-intensive system. It summarizes our mapping between the components of a BDI agent to individual tiers of a three-tier system hosted by an organization. A BDI agent is made up of three major components: input and output, functions, and data sets. It acts on behalf of a user in an organization and inter-

acts with other agents according to a predefined collaboration protocol. The agent receives inputs and generates outputs through the front tier. The agent's functions and the protocol logic can be implemented at the application tier. The data tier can be used to implement the various data sets of an agent.

A BDI computational model is composed of three main data sets: belief, desire, and intention. Information or data are passed from one data set to another through the application of some functions. Once a stimulus is sensed as input, the belief-revision function (BRF) converts it to a belief. The desire set is updated by generating some options based on the data in the belief set. Options in the desire set are then filtered to become the new intentions of the agent, and a corresponding plan of action can then be generated. As such, the BDI agent mimics an assistant for decisions on behalf of a human user, which is particularly useful for collaborations.

Though an agent can receive signals from the environment (such as user location), the stimulus inputs are mainly incoming requests and responses from other agents and users. These inputs are usually associated with a set of constraints and/or options (solutions) to a proposal. As a result, the belief set contains several sets of constraints

Figure 3. Metamodel of an MAIS in a UML (unified modeling language) class diagram

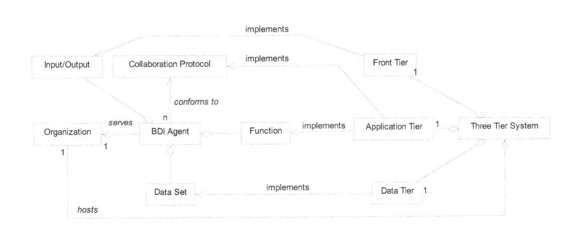

representing the requirements of a proposal. All solutions or even future options should satisfy these sets of constraints. As such, acceptable workforce service and collaboration arrangements are solved by mapping the constraints generated to the well-known constraint-satisfaction problem (CSP; Tsang, 1993), where efficient solvers are available.

MAIS Analysis and Design Methodology for MWM

Based on our previous experience in constraint-based negotiation, m-service adaptation, and alert management for mobile medical professionals, we proceed in this study to generalize and scale up our framework to a MAIS for MWM. We advocate the system analysis and design methodology to be carried out in two parts. Part 1 deals with the overall architectural design. That is, we have to analyze high-level requirements and formulate an enterprise MAIS infrastructure and system integration aspects that are specific for a particular purpose (MWM here) and to a particular domain (service-oriented enterprises here). The application of MWM for service-oriented enterprises has not been studied before and is therefore the focus of this chapter. The steps for Part 1 are as follows.

1. Identify different categories of services and objectives for the workforce in the enterprise. The identification can make use of available service ontologies, such as those defined in Semantic Web services.
2. Identify the life cycle (i.e., different phases) for the management of a typical service task, from task request to completion.
3. For each phase, identify the major agent to represent it and then the interactions required based on the process requirements.
4. Further identify minor agents that assist the major agents in carrying out these functionalities. As a result, clusters of different types

of agents (instead of a single monolithic pool of agents) constitute the MAIS.
5. Identify the interactions required for each minor agent type.
6. Design the basic logics for all these agents.
7. Identify the (mobile) platforms to be supported and where to host different types of agents. See if any adaptation is required.

Only after successful high-level requirement studies and the design of the overall architecture can we proceed to the next part. Part 2 deals with the detail design of agents, and the methodology has been preliminarily studied in our previous work (Chiu, Cheung, et al., 2004). It should be noted that the actual detailed design for each type of agent in the MWM domain has high potentials for further research because of its emerging adoptions. Here, we summarize the steps as follows for conveying a more complete picture of the required effort.

1. Design and adapt the user interface required for users to input their preferences. Customize displays to individual users and platforms.
2. Determine how user preferences are mapped into constraints and exchange them in a standardized format.
3. Consider automated decision support with agents. Identify the stimulus, collaboration parameters, and output actions to be performed by a BDI agent.
4. Partition the collaboration parameters into three data sets: belief, desire, and intention. Formulate a data subschema for each of these data sets. Implement the schema at the data tier.
5. Derive transformations amongst the three data sets. Implement these transformations at the application tier.
6. Enhance the performance and intelligence of the agents with various heuristics gather-

ing during the testing and pilot phase of the project.

MWM REQUIREMENTS OVERVIEW

This study is based on the requirements of a large service-oriented telecom enterprise, in which sales, technical, and professional workforces are mobile. We first highlight the requirements of the users and management before introducing the service-task categories. Then we present the workforce services and process overview.

User and Management Requirements

The main target users of the MWM are the mobile sales, technical, and professional workforces. Their main job functions are to carry out quality consultations and customer services, with commitments in improving customer relationships (thereby increasing sales). Users employ MWM systems to assist their work. The provision of anytime and anywhere connections is essential because the workforce tends to become mobile, especially for professionals such as physicians, service engineers, and sales executives as well as other staff who need to travel. In particular, the flexibility of supporting multiple front-end devices increases users' choice of hardware and therefore their means of connectivity. Agent automation helps reduce tedious collaboration tasks that are often repeated, including meeting scheduling as well as negotiations with standardized parameter (Chiu, Cheung, Hung, et al., 2005).

For management, it is expected that the MWM can integrate disparate heterogeneous organizational applications. In addition, MWM can locate mobile workforce members and therefore improve staff communications. Though this may not be in the interest of the workforce, the MWM infrastructure helps management to control and manage them, such as for location-dependent job allocation. Also, agents help improve the quality

and consistency of decision results through pre-programmed intelligence through the BDI-agent architecture. In addition, an integration approach reduces development costs through software reuse and the time required for development.

Service-Task Categories

To effectively support mobile workforces in fulfilling their tasks and in particular services, we have to understand different types of service requirements. We analyze the characteristics of tasks, and each task may have one or more of the following characteristics.

A collaboration task requires more than several workforce members; that is, the availability of more than one person at the same time. As such, there is a subproblem similar to a well-known and nontrivial collaboration problem: meeting scheduling. In practice, scheduling is a time-consuming and tedious task. It involves intensive communications among multiple persons, taking into account many factors or constraints. In our daily life, meeting scheduling is often performed by ourselves or by our secretaries via telephone or e-mail. Most of the time, each attendee has some uncertain and incomplete knowledge about the preferences and the diaries of the other attendees. Historically, meeting scheduling emerged as a classic problem in artificial intelligence and MAIS.

An on-site task requires the workforce member(s) to travel to a specific location. This is typical for sales representatives, construction-site supervisors, field engineers, medical professionals, and so on. They often need to visit numerous locations in a day. Thus, a route advisory system (possibly supported by a third party or public services) can help them find the viable routes to their destinations. This could also help the organizations save time and costs by providing the fastest and most economical routes, respectively. However, if an organization has its own transportation vehicles for their workforce, further integration of the vehicles with the workforce-management system is required.

A personal task requires one or more specific members of the workforce to fulfill the tasks (say, because of job continuity). Otherwise, a flexible task allows the capability requirements of the task to be specified instead so that the system can select the best possible candidate(s).

A remote task requires communications support. The user, workforce, or agent involved has to be connected to the EIS or portals from remote sites for effective work. Information transcoding or even process adaptation may be required (Chiu et al., 2003).

Workforce Services and Processes Overview

Tracing the overall process from the placement of a customer service call or visit plan to its completion, we identify the following phases of a typical MWM service task.

1. The task-formulation phase concerns the creation of a task request and its specification from various sources inside and outside the enterprise.
2. The matchmaking phase concerns the tactical identification of the possible workforce capable of the task and ranks a subset of them for consideration in the brokering phase

Figure 4. MAIS architecture overview for MWM

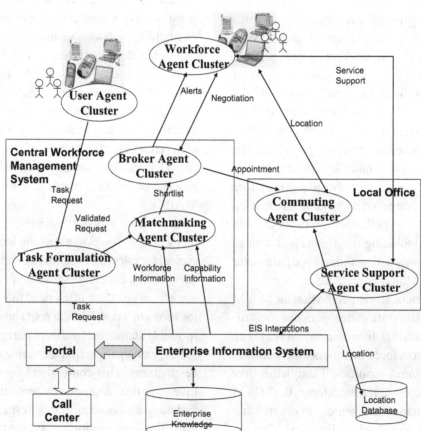

by using protocols such as the contract net (Smith, 1980).

3. The brokering phase concerns negotiation with a short list of the workforce to pick the best available one for a suitable appointment time according to schedule, location, and preferences.

4. The commuting phase concerns the travel of the workforce (if necessary), their vehicles (if any), and their locations.

5. The service phase concerns the actual execution of the task and the necessary support for the remote workforce.

SYSTEM ARCHITECTURE AND IMPLEMENTATION

We employ an MAIS design in our infrastructure for MWM (as shown in Figure 4) because of the requirements of mobile users as well as application flexibility and scalability. In particular, local offices can maintain their own commuting agent clusters and service-support agent clusters. This approach not only off-loads the central MWM, but also facilitates the maintenance of local knowledge. We discuss in subsections below each major agent cluster, which corresponds to various phases of a task-management life cycle.

Task-Formulation Agent Cluster

The task-formulation agents are assisted by a cluster of agents (as summarized in Table 1) to carry out the functions for the task-formation phase of the MWM process. There are many possible sources for a service-task request, such as (a) call centers, (b) customer Web portals, (c) management orders, (d) regular service schedulers, (e) service follow-ups, (f) customer relationship management (CRM) systems, (g) EIS triggers, and so on. Because of the diversity of request formats from existing systems, request-translation agents are built as the front end for each of these sources to map these requests into a common compatible format. Important request attributes include the task category expressed in the enterprise's ontology, urgency, importance, budget, resource requirement, location, requestor, related customer, and so on. However, requests from call centers and Web portals are often (problem) case reports, and are currently diagnosed by customer-services specialists and engineers. To reduce cost and increase efficiency, automation with report-diagnosis agents should be developed in the next stage of the system deployment.

Task-validation agents then attempt to fill in unspecified or implied attributes for requests with various heuristics. For example, the urgency and importance of tasks are often not specified clearly. These requests are then validated against a rule base of constraints, which specifies the rules and policies of the enterprise as well as various units. In particular, request authorization and budget are validated. Rejected tasks are passed back to the requestors clearly stating the violations and problems so that they can revise their request effectively. In the next stage of the system deploy-

Table 1. Key agents in the task-formulation agent cluster

Agents	Functions
Task Formulation	Main agent formulates a task requirement from requests
Request Translation	Translate requests into a common format
Task Validation	Fill in unspecified or implied task attributes and check task validity
Requirement Negotiation	Negotiate requests with requestors
Report Diagnosis	Diagnose requests and calls

ment, requirement-negotiation agents should be developed to handle failed requests in a more effective manner.

Validated task requests are recorded in the enterprise case base and then forwarded to the matchmaking agents for the next phase as well as the monitor agents for monitoring.

Matchmaking Agent Cluster

The matchmaking agents are assisted by a cluster of agents (as summarized in Table 2) for the matchmaking phase of the MWM process. They identify the possible workforce members who are capable of carrying out the task. The overall approach is based on our earlier work on capability and role modeling for work flows (Chiu et al., 1999). We separate the matchmaking and brokering phases because they deal with the operational and tactical allocation of workforces, respectively. In particular, a centralized management personal schedule of all workforce members together with intelligent task allocations based on such massive information is infeasible.

After receiving a validated task request, a capability-analysis agent analyzes the request to identify the detailed breakdown of the capability requirements according to the enterprise's ontology.

If the task request has personal specification, the capability of the workforce member is validated against the elicited capability requirements. Otherwise, the matchmaking agent has to select a preliminary short list of candidates from the workforce database according to the capability requirements. Though we do not consider complete schedules of the workforce here, we can still filter the workforce according to duty rosters and avoid those marked busy. Some preliminary algorithms are presented by Chiu et al. (1999). However, for a comprehensive MWM, we have to consider the workforce locations as well as the possibilities of a composition workforce for a task. For example, we have to decide between two engineers who each have one of the two required capabilities or a senior engineer with the two capabilities.

Workforce locations are determined by locations agents, which retrieve location contexts that are streamed continuously from spatial sensitive signals, such as those delivered by the global positioning system (GPS). More sophisticated location agents may also compute position and orientation based on signal strengths received from nearby wireless transmission stations for mobile communications.

The preliminary short list of the workforce is then passed to the cost-evaluation agent for estimating the cost of service. If there are many valid combinations, the final short list of combinations has to be pruned according to various search heuristics. In addition, the salary cost, the travel cost, and the cost incurred due to the travel time must be considered among other heuristic components of cost functions. The final short list, together with the estimated costs, is then forwarded to the broker agents for the next phase.

Table 2. Key agents in the matchmaking agent cluster

Agents	Functions
Matchmaking	Main agent identifies the possible workforce members capable of carrying out the task
Capability Analysis	Break down the capability requirements of a task
Location	Determine the location of workforce members
Cost Evaluation	Estimate cost of service

Table 3. Key agents in the broker agent cluster

Agents	Functions
Broker	Main agent negotiates and picks the best available short-listed workforce
Appointment	Negotiate with workforce members for appointment
Alert	Keep track of alert messages to the workforce members

Broker Agent Cluster

The broker agents are assisted by a cluster of agents (as summarized in Table 3) for the brokering phase of the MWM process. They have to negotiate with the short list of workforce to pick the best available one for a suitable appointment time, according to schedule, location, and preferences.

An appointment agent first obtains the update locations of the short-listed workforce and then contacts them for a possible appointment. As detailed in our recent work (Chiu et al., 2003), we advocate the use of constraints for time and place negotiation because the collection of complete personal schedules can be avoided for efficiency, privacy, and communication costs. An additional requirement over our previous protocol is that not all the contacted workforces are appointed; preferences should be given to those at the top of the short list. It should be noted that in the case of a personal task, we still have to carry out the negotiation for selecting the best appointment time and location. In addition, if customers are involved, customer preferences should be considered a priority over those of the workforce.

Furthermore, alert agents tackle messaging on behalf of appointment agents for task requests with an alert mechanism (Chiu, Kwok, et al., 2004). This is particularly important if a target user (such as an external customer) without agent support is involved in the appointment. Manual responses have to be tracked. In the case of no reply, the alert agent has to resend the message and/or inform the appointment agent to raise the urgency or consider other alternatives.

When an appointment is confirmed, the workforce members go into the commuting phase if traveling is required; otherwise, they go directly into the service phase.

Commuting Agent Cluster

The commuting agent cluster (as summarized in Table 4) plays a main role in the commuting phase. These agents take care of the traveling needs of the workforce if they have to travel to work on site. Location agents track the location of each workforce member.

Transport-advisory agents search for a suitable route from public transport for a commuting workforce member. In developing countries or crowded large cities, even professional workforce members may not have their own vehicles unless they are senior employees or are usually traveling with a

Table 4. Key agents in the commuting agent cluster

Agents	Functions
Commuting	Main agent manages the traveling needs of workforce members
Location	Determine the location of workforce members
Transport Advisory	Search for a suitable route from public transport for a commuting workforce member
Vehicle	Manage vehicles used by workforce members

lot of equipment. For those with vehicles owned by the enterprise, vehicle agents help plan the route for the vehicles to their service destinations and track vehicle locations. Transport-advisory agents also consult nearby vehicle agents for possibilities of picking up colleagues to take them to their destinations.

If the workforce and vehicles are mobile in a large metropolis, the main challenge is performance and efficiency because of the large number of public transport routes (for example, more than 1,000 in Hong Kong) and locations. In addition, both travel time and cost may have to be considered. We are working on an agent-based mobile route-advisory system for public-transport networks to address this problem (Chiu, Lee, et al., 2005).

Service-Support Agent Cluster

The service-support agent cluster (as summarized in Table 5) supports the workforce in the service phase. These agents take care of the communication needs of the workforce when connection to remote collaborators or systems is required.

Collaboration-session agents maintain widgets such as shared desktops and blackboards for collaborating workforce members. For example, the workforce on the same project may edit the same document concurrently even if they are located in different sites. These collaboration-session agents must therefore coordinate and consistently reflect changes in shared widget properties. In the past, there were two approaches to coordinating communications among individual groupware widgets. The first approach is to have the coordi-

nation handled by specialized applications. This inevitably complicates the application logistics and limits the reuse of groupware widgets. The second approach is to provide a set of generic groupware widgets with built-in logistics for communications among individual widgets. However, prebuilt groupware widgets may not be easily customized to suit various user needs. Generic groupware widgets tend to be bulky and accompanied by many unused features.

With collaboration-session agents, many groupware widgets can just mirror the functionality of their single-user counterparts, except for the additional logistics to synchronize shared properties. Collaboration-session agents communicate with one another through registered connections to update the widgets of all the users in the collaboration section with the changes in the shared properties, say, with a callback mechanism. Thus, widget designers only need to determine the set of properties by which a group of widgets should be synchronized and to what extent they are synchronized. These properties collectively define the coupling among a group of widgets as a coupling portfolio among the collaboration-session agents. The dynamic modification of coupling portfolios is thus supported by on-the-fly reconfiguration of multicast groups through negotiation among these agents.

Remote EIS agents enable the workforce to connect to the EIS for information relevant to their task. Security is the main concern and therefore EIS agents act as guards and filters to allow only the authorized users to connect to the authorized EIS resources. Additional filtering is necessary to screen sensitive information for security as well as for conserving bandwidth.

Table 5. Key agents in the service-support agent cluster

Agents	Functions
Collaboration Session	Maintain widgets for collaborating workforce members
Remote EIS	Connect to EIS for required information
Monitor	Keep track of the progress of tasks

Table 6. Key agents in the workforce and user agent cluster

Agents	Functions
Calendar	Maintain individual's schedule and negotiates appointment
Reminder	Remind of upcoming events and interact with alert agents
Preference	Maintain individual's preferences
Interface	Transform input and output to conform with individual's device

Monitor agents keep track of the progress of all tasks. In particular, they are interested in when a workforce member or group commits to a task and when a task is completed. If deadlines are missed or exceptions are reported by the workforce or their agents, the monitor agents will report the cases to relevant supervisors or management.

Workforce and User Agent Cluster

Each workforce member has a workforce agent cluster (as summarized in Table 6) to assist with daily work. As the workforce (especially senior ones) can schedule meetings and arrange work for their subordinates, workforce members are also users. For external users or customers, we only need to limit them to a subset of agents and functions from a security perspective. Thus, we discuss these two types of agent clusters together.

Calendar agents maintain their personal schedules and act on their user's behalf for appointment negotiation. Reminder agents help the calendar agents to remind users of their upcoming schedules (especially the important ones) and urgent alerts received from alert agents. Preference agents provide interfaces for users to input their requests and preferences.

Interface agents transform the extended markup language (XML) output from other agents to the current user platform with XML stylesheet language (XSL) technologies. For example, different hypertext markup language (HTML) outputs are generated for Web browsers on desktop PCs (personal computers) and PDAs (personal digital assistants), while wireless ac-

cess protocol (WAP) markup language (WML) outputs are generated for mobile phones (Y. B. Lin & Chlamtac, 2000).

DISCUSSIONS

In this section, we evaluate the applicability of our implementation framework and methodology with respect to the major stakeholders, including users, management, and system developers. The issues considered are based on the research framework on nomadic computing proposed by Lyytinen and Yoo (2002).

User's Perspective

Users employ MWM systems to assist in their work. In particular, agents help improve the reliability and robustness of workforce collaboration by retrying upon unsuccessful attempts, searching for alternatives, and so on. Agent-based adaptation of collaboration-protocol design for different operating environments improves the ease of use. This helps overcome the impact of expanding system functionalities and operation environments. Our proposed infrastructure also increases the chances to connect to the EIS and to interoperate with systems of other organizations. Thus, the main problem of integration and personalized assistance can be archived.

Our proposed way of applying constraint technologies helps achieve a balance of the performance and privacy of the workforce because they need not send all or part of their private information to a designated agent. This also avoids too much unnecessary data being sent, which wastes bandwidth and is not suitable for mobile users or agents.

Management's Perspective

A major concern of management is the costs against the benefits of the MWM system. In particular, if any of the improvements to the workforce as discussed in the previous subsection can significantly help improve their productivities, the costs can be justified. MWM provides tangible benefits for organizations by allowing information sharing among the mobile workforce. In addition, MWM usually implies the ability of locating mobile workforce members, therefore improving staff communications. Though this may not be in the interest of the workforce, the MWM infrastructure helps management to control and manage them, such as for location-dependent job allocation.

The incorporation of MWM helps improve customer relationships due to improved communications and service. Indirectly, business opportunities may increase, too. The disparity of heterogeneous organizational applications has created inflexible boundaries for communicating and sharing information and services among the mobile workforce, management, and customers. Therefore, MWM provides a standardized way to share the information through information agents and services among various heterogeneous applications.

Agents help improve the quality and consistency of decision results through preprogrammed intelligence. The BDI-agent architecture mimics the human practical deliberation process by clearly differentiating among the mental modalities of beliefs, desires, and intentions. Flexibility and adaptation are achieved by the agent's means- and ends-revising capabilities. As such, costs to program into the agent the operation and even the

management knowledge elicited are minimized. Also, expertise to handle practical problems can be incorporated into the options function to generate desires and the filter function to determine intentions.

As for cost factors, our approach is suitable for the adaptation of existing systems by wrapping them with communication and information agents. Through software reuse, a reduction in not only the total development cost but also training and support cost can be achieved. For security, as explained in the previous subsection, constraints help reduce the need of revealing unnecessary information in collaborations and therefore improve security.

System Developer's Perspective

System developers are often concerned about the system-development costs and subsequent maintenance efforts. These concerns can be addressed by systematic, fine-grained requirements elicitation of the functions of various agent types. Thus, with loosely coupled and tightly coherent intelligent software modules encapsulated in agents, system complexity can be managed. Agents are highly reusable and can be maintained with relative ease. Furthermore, it should be noted that the use of XSL technologies and database views as the main mechanism for user-interface adaptation by presentation agents facilitates software maintenance at the application tier. This can significantly shorten the system-development time, meeting management expectations in a competitive environment.

Recent advances in technologies have resulted in fast-evolving mobile-device models and standards. MWM systems require much greater extents of adaptations to keep up. Agents are readily adaptable to cope with new technologies and can further help reduce uncertainties through adequate testing and experimentations of new technologies.

Some system functions have been implemented using entry-level PDAs, HP iPAQs®, each equipped with a 200MHz StrongArm® processor and 32MB SDRAM. The implementation aimed at exploring the feasibility of supporting agents on PDA platforms. The BDI-agent model and the associated constraint solver were written in Microsoft®-embedded Visual C++® and executed under Windows CE®. We found that an agent could comfortably solve 100 constraints with 200 to 300 variables in a second. This is a comfortable problem size for daily applications. As such, there is no need to rely on powerful computational servers to solve these constraints. In fact, a distributed solution of agents favors not only privacy, but also scalability. It further eases the programming of captured knowledge as explained in the previous subsections.

As constraints can be used to express general planning problems, including those involving higher order logic (Tsang, 1993), we anticipate that this approach can be applied in different domains for solving different problems related to MWM.

CONCLUSION

This chapter has presented a pragmatic approach to developing an MWM system with an MAIS infrastructure. We have also explained a metamodel of MAIS and a layer-infrastructure framework that supports multiple platforms (in particular, wireless mobile ones) and their integration with the EIS. We have summarized our experience in the analysis and design of an MAIS for MWM. We have also explained an overview of MVM requirements and process life cycle. We have further detailed the design of each agent cluster corresponding to each phase of the MWM process life cycle. Finally, we have explained the merits and applicability of our approach from the perspectives of major system stakeholders. As such, we are addressing the main challenge of MWM for a service-oriented enterprise, which is the integration of disparate business functions for the mobile professional workforce and management with a unified infrastructure, together with the provision of personalized assistance and automation.

With this solid foundation, we can proceed to study or reexamine the technical and management perspectives of each phase and functions of the MWM process in detail. We also anticipate this framework can serve as a reference model for this new MWM application area. We believe that only after task management for mobile workforces has been adequately studied can the problem of managing a complete mobile work flow be tackled.

ACKNOWLEDGMENT

The work described in this chapter was supported by a grant from the Research Grants Council of the Hong Kong Special Administrative Region, China (Project No. CUHK4190/03E).

REFERENCES

Bafoutsou, G.., & Mentzas, G. (2001. A comparative analysis of Web-based collaborative systems. In *Proceedings of the 12th International Workshop on Database and Expert Systems Applications* (pp. 496-500).

Bailey, J., & Bakos, Y. (1997). An exploratory study of the emerging role of electronic intermediaries. *International Journal of Electronic Commerce, 1*(3), 7-20.

Barbara, D. (1999). Mobile computing and databases: A survey. *IEEE Transactions on Knowledge and Data Engineering, 11*(1), 108-117.

Bui, T. X. (1987). *Co-oP: A group decision support system for cooperative multiple criteria group decision making* (LNCS 290). Berlin, Germany: Springer-Verlag.

Bui, T. X., Bodart, F., & Ma, P.-C. (1998). ARBAS: A formal language to support argumentation in network-based organization. *Journal of Management Information Systems, 14*(3), 223-240.

Chiu, D. K. W., Cheung, S. C., Hung, P. C. K. Chiu, S. Y. Y., & Chung, K. K. (2005). Developing e-negotiation process support with a meta modeling approach in a Web services environment. *Decision Support Systems, 40*(1), 51-69.

Chiu, D. K. W., Cheung, S. C., Hung, P. C. K., & Leung, H.-F. (2004). Constraint-based negotiation in a multi-agent information system with multiple platform support. In *Proceedings of the 37th Hawaii International Conference on System Sciences (HICSS37),* Waikoloa, Big Island, HI [CD-ROM]. IEEE Computer Society Press.

Chiu, D. K. W., Cheung, S. C., Kafeza, E., & Leung, H.-F. (2003). A three-tier view methodology for adapting M-services. *IEEE Transactions on System, Man and Cybernetics, Part A, 33*(6), 725-741.

Chiu, D. K. W., Cheung, S. C., & Leung, H.-F. (2005). A multi-agent infrastructure for mobile workforce management in a service oriented enterprise. *Proceedings of the 38th Hawaii International Conference on System Sciences (HICSS38),* Waikoloa, Big Island, HI [CD-ROM]. IEEE Press.

Chiu, D. K. W., Kwok, B., Wong, R., Kafeza, E., & Cheung, S. C. (2004). Alert driven e-services management. In *Proceedings of the 37th Hawaii International Conference on System Sciences (HICSS37),* Waikoloa, Big Island, HI [CD-ROM]. IEEE Computer Society Press.

Chiu, D. K. W., Lee, O., & Leung, H.-F. (2005). A multi-modal agent based mobile route advisory system for public transport network. In *Proceedings of the 38th Hawaii International Conference on System Sciences (HICSS38),* Waikoloa, Big Island, HI [CD-ROM]. IEEE Computer Society Press.

Chiu, D. K. W., Li, Q., & Karlapalem, K. (1999). A meta modeling approach for workflow management system supporting exception handling. *Information Systems, 24*(2), 159-184.

Choy, M. C., Srinivasan, D., & Cheu, R. L. (2003). Cooperative, hybrid agent architecture for real-time traffic signal control. *IEEE Transactions on System, Man and Cybernetics, Part A, 33*(5), 597-607.

Fraile, J.-C., Paredis, C. J. J., Wang, C.-H., & Khosla, P. K. (1999). Agent-based planning and control of a multi-manipulator assembly system. In *Proceedings of the IEEE International Conference on Robotics and Automation, 2,* 1219-1225.

Garrido, L., Brena, R., & Sycara, K. (1996). Cognitive modeling and group adaptation in intelligent multi-agent meeting scheduling. In *Proceedings of the 1st Iberoamerican Workshop on Distributed Artificial Intelligence and Multi-Agent Systems* (pp. 55-72).

Gerst, M. H. (2003). The role of standardisation in the context of e-collaboration: ASNAP shot. In *Proceedings of the 3rd Conference on Standardization and Innovation in Information Technology* (pp. 113-119).

Grefen, P., Aberer, K., Hoffner, Y., & Ludwig, H. (2000). CrossFlow: Cross-organizational workflow management in dynamic virtual enterprises. *International Journal of Computer Systems Science & Engineering, 15*(5), 277-290.

Guido, B., Roberto, G., Tria, P. di, & Bisio, R. (1998). Workforce management (WFM) issues. In *Proceedings of the IEEE Network Operations and Management Symposium (NOMS 98), 2,* 473-482.

He, M., Jennings, N. R., & Leung, H.-F. (2003). On agent-mediated electronic commerce. *IEEE TKDE, 15*(4), 985-1003.

Jing, J., Huff, K., Hurwitz, B., Sinha, H., Robinson, B., & Feblowitz, M. (2000). WHAM: Supporting mobile workforce and applications in workflow environments. In *Proceedings of the 10th International Workshop on Research Issues in Data Engineering (RIDE 2000)* (pp. 31-38).

Karageorgos, M., Thompson, S., & Mehandjiev, N. (2002). Agent-based system design for B2B electronic commerce. *International Journal of Electronic Commerce, 7*(1), 59-90.

Kim, Y., Kang, S., Kim, D., Bae, J., & Ju, K. (2000). WW-flow: Web-based workflow management with runtime encapsulation. *IEEE Internet Computing, 4*(3), 56-64.

Kotz, D., & Gray, R. (1999). Mobile agents and the future of the Internet. *ACM Operating Systems Review, 33*(3), 7-13.

Kowalczyk, R., & Bui, V. (2000). On constraint-based reasoning in e-negotiation agents. In F. Dignum & U. Cortés (Eds.), *Agent mediated electronic commerce III* (LNAI 2003, pp. 31-46). London: Springer-Verlag.

Kowalczyk, R., Ulieru, M., & Unland, R. (2003). Integrating mobile and intelligent agents in advanced e-commerce: A survey. In *Proceedings of Agent Technology Workshops 2002* (LNAI 2592, pp. 295-313). Berlin, Germany: Springer-Verlag.

Lamsweerde, A. van, Darimont, R., & Massonet, P. (1995). Goal-directed elaboration of requirements for a meeting scheduler: Problems and lessons learnt. In *Proceedings of the 2nd IEEE International Symposium on Requirements Engineering (RE '95)* (pp. 194-203).

Lee, H., Buckland, M. A., & Shepherdson, J. W. (2003). A multi-agent system to support location-based group decision making in mobile teams. *BT Technology Journal, 21*(1), 105-113.

Lin, F.-R., & Pai, Y.-H. (2000). Using multi-agent simulation and learning to design new business processes. *IEEE Transactions on System, Man and Cybernetics, Part A, 30*(3), 380-384.

Lin, F.-R., Tan, G. W., & Shaw, M. J. (1998). Modeling supply-chain networks by a multi-agent system. In *Proceedings of HICSS31* (Vol. 5, pp. 105-114).

Lin, Y.-B., & Chlamtac, I. (2000). *Wireless and mobile network architectures.* New York: John Wiley & Sons.

Lo, G., & Kersten, G. K. (1999). Negotiation in electronic commerce: Integrating negotiation support and software agent technologies. In *Proceedings of the 29th Atlantic Schools of Business Conference* [CD-ROM].

Lomuscio, A., Wooldridge, M., & Jennings, N. (2000). A classification scheme for negotiation in electronic commerce. In F. Dignum & C. Sierra (Eds.), *Agent-mediated electronic commerce: A European perspective* (LNCS 1991, pp. 19-33). London: Springer-Verlag.

Luo, Y., Liu, K., & Davis, D. N. (2002). A multi-agent decision support system for stock trading. *IEEE Network, 16*(1), 20-27.

Lyytinen, K., & Yoo, Y. (2002). Research commentary: The next wave of nomadic computing. *Information Systems Research, 13*(4), 377-388.

Object Management Group (OMG). (2001). *Foreword UML specification 1.4.* Retrieved from http://www.omg.org/cgi-bin/doc?formal/01-09-67

Papaioannou, T. (2000). Mobile information agents for cyberspace: State of the art and visions. In *Proceedings of Cooperating Information Agents (CIA-2000)* [CD-ROM].

Rao, A. S., & Georgeff, M. P. (1995). BDI agents: From theory to practice. *Proceedings of the 1st International Conference on Multiagent Systems* (pp. 312-319).

Rutkowski, A. F., Vogel, D. R., Genuchten, M. van, Bemelmans, T. M. A., & Favier, M. (2002). E-collaboration: The reality of virtuality. *IEEE TPC, 45*(4), 219-230.

Sandip, S. (1997, July-August). Developing an automated distributed meeting scheduler. *IEEE Expert, 12*(4), 41-45.

Shakshuki, E., Ghenniwa, H., & Kamel, M. (2000). A multi-agent system architecture for information gathering. In *Proceedings of the 11th International Workshop on Database and Expert Systems Applications* (pp. 732-736).

Shi, M., Yang, G., Xiang, Y., & Wu, S. (1998). Workflow management systems: A survey. In *Proceedings of the IEEE International Conference on Communication Technology*, S33.05.01-S33.05.06.

Shitani, S., Ito, T., & Sycara, K. (2000). Multiple negotiations among agents for a distributed meeting scheduler. In *Proceedings of the 4th International Conference on MultiAgent Systems* (pp. 435-436).

Smith, R. G. (1980). The contract net protocol: High-level communication and control in a distributed problem solver. *IEEE Transactions on Computers, C-29*(12), 1104-1113.

Stroulia, E., & Hatch, M. P. (2003). An intelligent-agent architecture for flexible service integration on the Web. *IEEE Transactions on System, Man and Cybernetics, Part C, 33*(4), 468-479.

Sycara, K., & Zeng, D. (1996). Coordination of multiple intelligent software agents. *International Journal of Cooperative Information Systems, 5*(2-3), 181-212.

Thompson, S. G., & Odgers, B. R. (2000). Collaborative personal agents for team working. In *Proceedings of the 2000 Artificial Intelligence and Simulation of Behavior (AISB) Symposium* (pp. 49-61).

Tsang, E. (1993). *Foundations of constraint satisfaction*. London; San Diego, CA: Academic Press.

Wegner, L., Paul, M., Thamm, J., & Thelemann, S. (1996). Applications: A visual interface for synchronous collaboration and negotiated transactions. *Proceedings of the Workshop on Advanced Visual Interfaces* (pp. 156-165).

Workflow Management Coalition. (1995). *The workflow reference model* (WFMC-TC-1003, 19-Jan-95, 1.1). Retrieved from http://www.wfmc.org/standards/model.htm

Workflow Management Coalition. (1999). *Terminology and glossary* (WFMC-TC-1011, 3.0). Retrieved from http://www.wfmc.org/standards/model.htm

This work was previously published in Enterprise Service Computing: From Concept to Deployment, edited by R. Qiu, pp. 105-131, copyright 2007 by IGI Publishing (an imprint of IGI Global).

Chapter XVII
Bringing Secure Wireless Technology to the Bedside:
A Case Study of Two Canadian Healthcare Organizations

Dawn-Marie Turner
DM Turner Informatics Consulting Inc., Canada

Sunil Hazari
University of West Georgia, USA

ABSTRACT

Wireless technology has broad implications for the healthcare environment. Despite its promise, this new technology has raised questions about security and privacy of sensitive data that is prevalent in healthcare organizations. All healthcare organizations are governed by legislation and regulations, and the implementation of enterprise applications using new technology is comparatively more difficult than in other industries. Using a configuration-idiographic case-study approach, this study investigated challenges faced by two Canadian healthcare organizations. In addition to interviews with management and staff of the organizations, a walk-through was also conducted to observe and collect first-hand data of the implementation of wireless technology in the clinical environment. In the organizations under examination, it was found that wireless technology is being implemented gradually to augment the wired network. Problems associated with implementing wireless technology in these Canadian organizations are also discussed. Because of different standards in this technology, the two organizations are following different upgrade paths. Based on the data collected, best practices for secure wireless access in these organizations are proposed.

INTRODUCTION

Technology, the Internet, and healthcare reform are converging to change the healthcare environment and create a seamless integrated healthcare network. This seamless network will facilitate the flow of information from multiple sources to multiple healthcare providers, administrators, patients, and other support services 24 hours a day, seven days a week, among multiple sites (Masys & Baker, 1997). Implementing and managing such a network within the healthcare environment poses unique challenges. First, medical and health information is highly sensitive; therefore security and privacy of the information must be a top priority. Security and privacy in healthcare is governed by legislation and regulation. In Manitoba, this means the Personal Health Information Act (PHIA). PHIA specifies how medical information can be accessed, by whom, and for what purposes. It also states the security and privacy regulations for all health information systems used within the province. Second, unlike other industries, medical care is not delivered in the same place even by the same healthcare professional, necessitating the need for multiple access points (APs) for the same information. For example, a physician on rounds moves from one patient to another, each of whom may reside in a different room, necessitating the need for network access in each room to record and receive data and communicate with other needed services such as pharmacy or nursing.

The challenge in creating a seamless network in healthcare is how to provide information to multiple users at the point in which they will require the information to deliver effective patient care. A wireless network may offer the opportunity to meet this challenge and provide significant benefits to the healthcare system. A wireless local area network (WLAN) offers improved accuracy and efficiency for documenting nursing care, decreased preventable medication error through better point-of-care medication-administration

systems, an increase in patient satisfaction, and efficiency in admission and discharge and other health administration processes (Sims, 2004). Additional technical benefits include lower costs, less cabling, availability of the network in locations not accessible with a wired connection, and the ability to adapt to growth easier.

The implementation of a WLAN is not without its challenges. Some challenges such as performance, speed, and accessibility are similar to those of a wired network, but others such as limited battery power of the devices, necessitating the need for an electrical source if the device is required for extended use; higher risk of equipment loss; and interference with medical equipment are unique to the WLAN environment (Karygiannis & Owens, 2002). Multiple standards and the fact that a WLAN does not usually replace a wired network but augments it increases the complexity of the management and compatibility of new systems (Drew, 2003). However, security is the biggest challenge facing a healthcare organization contemplating a wireless network. Wireless networks pose an increased risk of eavesdropping, hackers, and rogue devices (Sims, 2004). Securing a WLAN and the perception of its security may be one of the most limiting factors in the widespread use of WLAN in healthcare today (Campbell & Durigon, 2003).

Objectives of the Study

The objectives of this study were the following:

a.   To gain an understanding of wireless-technology standards and their application within healthcare.
b.   To articulate the security issues of wireless technologies within healthcare.
c.   To identify the potential for best practice in the implementation of wireless technology in healthcare using a case-study methodology.

Wireless Technology in Healthcare

As the development and use of the electronic patient record progresses, mobile devices will become more common. Healthcare providers will begin to use these devices to access information previously only available in the paper-based chart or record. The increased use of wireless will help to stabilize wireless communication standards (Campbell & Durigon, 2003). Currently there are three standards used for wireless networking, wireless fidelity (Wi-Fi), mobile communications (cell phones), and Bluetooth. Wi-Fi was the standard used in the case studies in this research, therefore it is the standard discussed in this literature review.

The Wi-Fi standard encodes the data and then sends them over a selected channel using radio-wave frequencies. The connection is made through the use of a wireless network card within the device and a connection to an access point creating a wireless LAN. If the access point is connected directly to the corporate network or the Internet, the wireless user will have direct access to the corporate network or Internet (Campbell & Durigon, 2003). The standard for Wi-Fi (802.11) has been established by the Institute of Electrical and Electronics Engineers (IEEE), a professional organization of engineers, students, and scientists. This standard (802.11) was the original standard set for wireless computing and established the protocols to be used between a wireless device and access point, or two wireless devices (Drew, 2003). Revisions and updates to 802.11 have resulted in several versions of the 802.11 standard. Prior to implementing WLAN, a healthcare organization needs to select the variation of the Wi-Fi standard it will use. Choosing which variation will depend on the data-transmission needs, cost, and the number of devices accessing the network. Three variations of the 802.11 standard currently being used by the case studies within this chapter will be discussed (802.11a, 802.11b, 802.11g).

Specification 802.11b, completed in 1999, is probably the most widely used standard. It is a physical-layer standard and operates in the 2.4 GHz frequency, providing users with 11Mbs throughput between the wireless device and the AP, depending on the distance between the device, the number of users, and any other interference. This standard has three available radio channels (Campbell & Durigon, 2003; Drew, 2003). One disadvantage to 802.11b is it operates in the same frequency as most medical devices such as ultrasound, sterilizers, and treatment or diagnostic devices. Therefore using a wireless device at this frequency requires all devices to be tested for potential interference with existing medical equipment sharing the same frequency, special consideration to the placement of the access nodes, and frequent retesting for possible interference.

Specification 802.11a also completed in 1999 provides users with a faster throughput at 54Mbs using the 5 GHz frequency spectrum. In addition to its faster throughput, 802.11a offers two advantages over 802.11b. First, the 5 GHz frequency is not shared by other commonly used devices such as microwaves, cellular phones, and medical monitoring equipment, making interference from these devices less of an issue. Second, 802.11a opens more channels, making the network more available; with eight vs. three channels, it offers better protection against possible interference from neighboring access points (Campbell & Durigon, 2003). However, its disadvantage is the need for more access points because the higher throughput is gained at the cost of a shorter transmission distance, making 802.11a more expensive to implement, something that must be considered when choosing which standard to use. 802.11a is also not backward compatible. This means a healthcare organization that has already implemented a wireless network using 802.11b must replace their access nodes for compatibility with 802.11a. One solution for this is the use of dual-band access points that are certified to work with

802.11b and 802.11a, allowing organizations to leverage existing technology when upgrading to the new standard (Karygiannis & Owens, 2002). The newest standard, 802.11g, was developed in 2001 as a direct result of the compatibility issues between 802.11b and 802.11a. It provides the throughput of 802.11a but is backward compatible with 802.11b (Campbell & Durigon). As such, organizations that have already invested in 802.11b technologies without the use of dual-band access points can upgrade to the new standard without the expense of new hardware.

Authentication is a very important component for healthcare organizations. It refers to the ability to verify the identity of client stations or individuals accessing health data over a network, and deny access to those not providing the correct electronic credentials. The Wired Equivalent Privacy (WEP) protocol defines two types of authentication: open-system and shared-key authentication. Open-key authentication is not a true authentication process because it only requires a one-way channel. Access points using open-system authentication will accept a mobile device on the basis of it having a media access control (MAC) address and does not verify if it is an authenticated address within the network. Shared-key authentication requires a two-way interchange between the access point and the device based on cryptography. In this scenario, the client requesting access to the WLAN sends a message to the access point, and the access point responds with a challenge to the client requesting it to identify itself using its special key. The access point then decrypts the message and if it matches the values allowed, the client is authenticated to the network. The WEP protocol only requires open-system authentication, creating a potential security risk if shared-key authentication is not also implemented within the organization (Newman, 2003). The need for authentication of wireless devices within a healthcare facility is extremely important because of the number of transient population (e.g., patients, visitors) that has the potential to tap into the health informa-tion network and have access to sensitive patient records.

Confidentiality or privacy refers to protecting the data from eavesdropping either intentionally or unintentionally through cryptographic techniques. (Privacy issues in healthcare are discussed later.) The WEP protocol uses the Rivest Cipher 4 (RC4) symmetric key, stream cipher algorithm to generate a pseudo-random data sequence supporting a 40-bit encryption for the shared key. This is a weak encryption system and on a busy network could be cracked in a matter of hours (Sims, 2004). Integrity ensures messages sent are not modified during transmission. The service was developed to reject any messages that appeared to have been modified during transmission. The technique used within the WEP is "a simple encrypted cyclic redundancy check (CRC) approach that after sealing the packet encrypts it for transmission where on receipt of the packet, it is decrypted and compared to the original. If they are not equal, an error message is sent. Unfortunately, CRC, unlike a hash code or message authentication code, is not cryptographically secure. Although the WEP provides security services, it is clear they are not sufficient to provide the level of security required for the sensitive information being transmitted within a healthcare institution (Berghel & Uecker, 2005).

It appears clear from this discussion that standards alone will not create a secure network, and controls are also needed. Controls are the mechanisms that reduce or eliminate threats to the organization's computer systems and network (Fitzgerald & Dennis, 2002). There are typically three types of controls. Preventative controls, as the name implies, prevents or mitigates the chance of a security breach such as the use of passwords and locking the computer equipment (such as those located in areas like nursing stations and administrative offices). Detective controls are those strategies and mechanisms used to identify when a security breach has occurred such as identifying when an unknown address has tried to gain entry (such as by implementing an intrusion-detection system on the hospital's internal network). Detection controls usually include reporting and may include an alarm function to alert network personnel of potential threats. Corrective controls correct or fix an unwanted event or threat. Controls should be used to develop specific countermeasures to address the vulnerabilities with using a WLAN. The application of specific countermeasures minimizes the risks to create a more secure network. As with wired networks, risks cannot be completely eliminated, but through the appropriate application of countermeasures and the use of controls, risk can be reduced to a level that is acceptable to the organization. Countermeasures can be divided into three broad areas: management, operational, and software.

Management countermeasures usually focus on the preventative level. They start with a comprehensive security policy outlining such things as who has access to the network, authorization levels, the installation of access points, configuration management, and the reporting of loss or stolen wireless devices. In Manitoba, the security policy must also include a signed confidentiality agreement between the user and the organization outlining what constitutes a breach and the consequences of any breaches.

Operational countermeasures offer both preventative and detection controls. These include the physical security measures taken to ensure only authorized personnel have access to the devices and networks through such things as identification badges, locking the equipment, security guards and video cameras, the use of passwords or biometrics, and the use of site survey tools for mapping access points and ensuring coverage remains within the intended range. It should also include logging and auditing of all accesses and attempted access to the network to identify if unauthorized use has occurred.

Technical countermeasures include the use of software and hardware to protect the network such as proper access-point configurations, software

patches and upgrades, authentication, intrusion-detection systems, encryption, the use of a virtual private network (VPN), firewalls, and public-key infrastructure (PKI). The use of a VPN within a wireless network can afford the same level of protection it does within the wired environment. Like in a wired environment, a VPN creates an encrypted secure channel between the user's wireless device and the network, thus hiding the transmission (Kilpatrick, 2003). A firewall is one of the most formidable lines of system defense because it prevents unauthorized users and creates an invisible wall to potential intruders (Campbell & Durigon, 2003; Derba & Siegal, 2003). The goal is to ensure that only authorized individuals are able to view an individual's healthcare record.

Implementing a wireless network in any healthcare environment should be considered carefully with a clear business need. It must also consider the highly sensitive nature of the information being transmitted coupled with the risk of any potential breach of the system. Once the decision has been made to implement wireless, a careful assessment of capabilities must be matched to the goals and objectives for the wireless network. Only then can related decisions about standards, hardware, and software be made.

Privacy Issues in Healthcare

The significance of information privacy will continue to escalate in proportion to the value of information (Rust, Kannan, & Peng, 2002). Information privacy in healthcare organizations is related to information security. It is important to note that an organization may have information security without privacy, but it is not possible to have privacy without having information security controls (preventative, detective, or corrective as discussed earlier). While wireless technology offers convenience and potential that shows promise for improving healthcare delivery, the right to privacy for patients must be protected. In wireless transmission, data is not being confined to a physical medium so that it remains secure when being transmitted from node to node. Therefore, it is necessary that healthcare organizations should develop and implement system security and privacy strategies to protect data and information stored in research and clinical databases. According to Huston (2001), confidentiality and security of a patient's health information has always been important, and with the ease of access afforded electronically, security will likely be more difficult to provide without advanced planning.

As healthcare organizations move toward converting paper-based records and communication processes to digital formats that can be easily stored and manipulated for administrative decision making, intranets and extranets are established within and outside the boundaries of the healthcare organization. There needs to be a strategic aspect to maintaining security, privacy, and standardization of networks that carry data and information within and outside the organization. A common example is the use of a networked decision-support system that is specially developed for supporting decision making related to the solution of a particular healthcare-management problem (Turban, 1993). This type of system ties in with centralized databases so effectively, controls need to be present in these databases to ensure confidentiality, integrity, and availability of data.

Government regulations (e.g., PHIA in Canada, and HIPAA [Health Insurance Portability and Accountability Act] in USA) have provided guidelines to healthcare organizations to maintain privacy and security aspects of the transmission and maintenance of patient records. Healthcare organizations previously outsourced services such as transcriptions, which made it possible to identify patient data. Regulations now hold providers responsible for auditing policies and procedures of contracted firms (Walker & Spencer, 2000). This was done in an effort to safeguard the privacy of patient data. Similarly, policies and procedures for handling patient data that were previously written for the "paper world" are

being revised to comply with electronic storage, access, sharing, and transmission of data (Shortell & Kaluzny, 1994).

METHODOLOGY

The case study is a widely used method of qualitative research within information systems and is an effective design for understanding the organizational context of information-technology innovations. A case study is defined as "an empirical enquiry that investigates a contemporary phenomenon within its real-life context, especially when the boundaries between phenomenon and context are not clearly evident and it relies on multiple sources of evidence" (Darke, Shanks, & Broadbent, 1998, p. 273). Case-study research is often used to describe, test, or develop theory. This type of case-study research is called the configuration-idiographic study, which is used to describe events and their circumstances to identify relationships but not necessarily generate theoretical interpretations (Smith, 1990). As the purpose of this study was explanatory, case selection was based on the available cases offering the greatest explanatory power.

Two midsize healthcare organizations in Canada using a WLAN were approached and agreed to participate in the case study. Both organizations provide inpatient and outpatient treatment facilities and clinics. One organization's WLAN extended beyond the physical boundaries of the institution, enabling wireless access to the corporate network in two satellite facilities approximately 2 to 5 km away. Interviews were conducted using a semi-structured interview format with one or all of the following personnel: the network manager, and IT security and systems analysts. The interview questions were developed to identify the characteristics of the network and current practices used to secure the organization's wireless network and devices. In addition to the interviews, a walk-through was conducted at one of the sites to view the wireless device within the clinical environment.

The interview questions from each case study were analyzed using a qualitative inductive approach. The goal of this approach was to explore and analyze existing practices of the organizations within the context of recommendations, practices, and standards identified in the literature. There was no effort made to quantify results or compare one organization with the other. The responses to the interview questions were analyzed to answer each of the research questions. Responses to the first research question were assessed against the three primary wireless threats (identified in the literature): malicious hackers, eavesdropping (war driving), and rogue wireless devices. Best practice was assessed using the National Institute of Standards and Technology (NIST) steps for a secure wireless LAN and the fit with current organizational practices to these recommendations. Data was also collected to assess the rationale for selecting wireless technology, the current standard implemented, and the location of wireless within the organization. These areas were not categorized but will be discussed.

Findings

Both organizations in the case study indicated wireless was not a stand-alone network but augmented the existing wired network to provide healthcare professionals with point-of-care access to patients' electronic records housed on the corporate network. Wireless was also implemented to reduce overall costs and ease the management of providing point-of-care access because the wireless technology allowed multiple users to use the same equipment vs. requiring the purchasing of a laptop for each user. Additionally, IEEE 802.11b was the current standard within both organizations. However, future upgrades were split with one organization choosing to upgrade to 802.11a and the other choosing 802.11g. An increased volume of users in one organization was the rationale for the planned upgrade to 802.11a. Although

prior implementation of dual-band access nodes meant compatibility with the existing network was not an issue, the increased cost due to the greater number of required access nodes was slowing down the rate of growth. The need for higher transmission rates and compatibility with the existing WLAN was the second organization's rationale for upgrading to 802.11g.

In both organizations, interference with medical equipment was a consideration and required all wireless devices to be tested for compatibility by the biomedical engineering department. Although no issues were found in either organization, one organization had implemented a policy that dictated wireless devices were not permitted in areas with highly critical medical monitoring equipment such as the intensive care units. Each organization identified their first step in securing wireless for healthcare was to enable security within the wireless standard, usually WEP. However, it was identified that this level of security was not enough as one network specialist indicated: "It is not enough to use the security that comes with the system. You need to layer your security; the default settings are not secure enough."

Securing and protecting the wireless network from eavesdropping, malicious hackers, and rogue devices or access points was approached in both organizations from four perspectives: securing the wireless network, securing the device, protecting the data, and protecting the larger corporate network. Securing the wireless network was accomplished through the configuration of the MAC addresses requiring authentication to the network (access nodes will only talk to addresses they know), and hiding the name of the network was also done through the configuration. As one organization indicated, this means "anyone scanning for a network might still find it, but because they don't know its name, it will be inaccessible." In addition to authentication of the MAC address, one organization installed a firewall between the WLAN and the corporate network; the firewall actively scanned the airwaves for unrecognized MAC addresses and when it detected something, it sent a warning that unidentified addresses had attempted access to the system. Additionally, the firewall provided the organization with end-to-end 128-bit encryption and authentication between the WLAN and the corporate network. Furthermore, protection of the network was provided through software monitor switches that looked for and detected unauthorized access nodes. Unauthorized nodes were immediately removed and the organization maintains a strict policy regarding the installation of unapproved access points.

Securing the devices was accomplished in both organizations first through a security policy that specified who could use a wireless device, what authorization level they had, and what their access level was. Second, each device was inventoried and a hardware log was maintained. Finally, the devices themselves were secured. Both organizations in this study use computers on wheels (COWS) as the wireless devices. These are laptop computers secured to a cart or mobile station allowing for easy movement within the organization, but making it difficult to remove from the property. Consideration was given to the use of other wireless devices such as personal digital assistants (PDAs); however, these were considered to pose an increased security risk due to their lack of direct connectivity to the network and the need to store personal health information (even temporarily) on the device. As one organization noted, "When personal health information resides on the device, the loss or theft of a device jeopardizes the confidentiality of the information stored on that device." The storage of personal health information on the device even for a short time also prevented real-time access to information by the health professional. The need to synch the device created a time lag between when the device recorded the information and when it is was entered into the network and available to another healthcare professional.

Protecting health and medical information residing on the corporate network was done through enhanced 128-bit encryption that was centrally controlled and configured for end-to-end data encryption. As one network manager stated, "We made the assumption that people may break in, so we make the data stream unreadable...essentially they get garbage." One organization also indicated the wireless network is treated as a hostile environment, therefore without the proper authentication; even someone that manages to get into the wireless network cannot access the corporate network. As indicated previously, authentication was a two step process, authenticating first to the wireless network and then to the LAN. Finally, access to the corporate network in both organizations was role based as defined by PHIA, giving access to the corporate network only to the level required for the user to deliver safe patient care.

BEST-PRACTICE WIRELESS IN HEALTHCARE

NIST outlined eight steps for maintaining a secure wireless network (Karygiannis & Owens, 2002). A further analysis of the data collected from the case studies appears to support these eight steps as a foundation on which to build best practice for a secure wireless network in a healthcare organization. A review of each of these steps is presented in Table 1 with an indication of how the case-study organizations addressed each one. Alone, these eight steps were not enough. For the organizations reviewed in this study, best practice also included a strict and well-published security policy, the use of 128-bit encryption end to end, the use of a firewall between the WLAN and the corporate network, strong authentication of both the device and the user, and the use of a virtual private network for wireless transmission.

Limitations

The availability of suitable cases is one difficulty in case-study methodology (Darke et al., 1998). The slower growth of information technology within healthcare (and in particular wireless) coupled with the highly sensitive nature of the topic (security) limited the number of cases available for study. Only two sites were used for this study, and one site

Table 1. Establishing best practice for wireless in healthcare

	Wireless Security Steps	Case-Study Findings
1.	Maintain a full topology of all wireless connections and access points	Prior to implementation of the network, an access coverage map was drawn to identify the placement of nodes and allow for the straddling of frequencies.
2.	Label and maintain an inventory of all wireless devices	All wireless equipment was inventoried. The security policy prohibits the use of personal wireless devices, e.g., PDAs and laptops. An inventory and table of all authorized MAC addresses was retained.
3.	Create regular backups	No data were stored on wireless devices; they were all contained within the corporate network. The WLAN serves only as an access mechanism to the corporate network or electronic patient record. Routine back up of servers is done daily.
4.	Perform regular security tests of network and devices	All equipment was tested at the time of deployment. Penetration tests were completed routinely (no indication of frequency was provided) and routine vulnerability testing by the third party were completed randomly as outlined in the security policy.
5.	Perform random but regularly timed audits	All access to the WLAN, LAN, and applications are logged and available for audit as specified in PHIA. Routine education of staff concerning proper use of WLAN and devices was conducted.
6.	Apply patches and security enhancements	Software monitors the switches to detect unauthorized access nodes. Antiviral software is installed and updated regularly on all devices. Current security patches apply in both organizations.
7.	Monitor the industry for new standards affecting security and new products to enhance security	802.1x security enhancements were explored.
8.	Monitor vigilantly for new threats and vulnerabilities	A firewall was installed for active monitoring of the airwaves. WLAN was treated as a hostile environment and appropriate controls were applied.

limited the amount of information it provided due to concerns about breaching security. Therefore generalizations are difficult. Another limitation of the study was that due to the time constraints of the study period, only the network manager and systems analyst were interviewed, and not the users of the wireless devices. Organizational security policies, although identified, were also not reviewed.

CONCLUSION

Wireless technology affords many advantages within the healthcare environment, but it also poses a greater risk if not implemented properly. As one participant noted, "You need to assume your system is vulnerable, then make the data stream unreadable through encryption and limit exposure to the rest of the network through the installation of a firewall between the wireless device and the enterprise network."

Is wireless secure enough for healthcare? Although it is difficult to generalize based on only two case studies, it appears a secure WLAN can be implemented to meet the unique requirements of healthcare. However, this research also demonstrated that the implementation of a secure WLAN needs more careful planning, evaluation, and reassessment of the risks and vulnerabilities than a traditional LAN in order to meet the security and privacy challenges within the healthcare environment. The challenge for any organization would be to maintain the confidentiality, integrity, and availability of data and information in a secure environment that makes it possible to provide the most efficient patient care. To achieve this, current technologies (such as wireless networks) offer healthcare practitioners and administrators the opportunity to positively impact the quality of healthcare not only in offices for administrative purposes, but more importantly clinically by the patients' bedside.

REFERENCES

Berghel, H., & Uecker, J. (2005). Wifi attack vectors. *Communications of the ACM, 48*(8), 21-28.

Campbell, R., & Durigon, L. (2003). Wireless communication in healthcare: Who will win the right to send data boldly where no data has gone before? *Healthcare Manager, 22*(3), 233-240.

Darke, P., Shanks, G., & Broadbent, M. (1998). Successfully completing case study research: Combining rigour, relevance and pragmatism. *Information Systems Journal, 8*, 273-289.

Derba, M., & Siegal, J. (2003). Wireless networks. *The CPA Journal, 73*(7), 18-21.

Drew, W. (2003). Wireless networks: New meaning to ubiquitous computing. *Journal of Academic Librarianship, 29*(2), 102-106.

Fitzgerald, J., & Dennis, A. (2002). *Business data communications and networking* (7th ed.). New York: John Wiley & Sons.

Huston, T. (2001). Security issues for implementation of e-medical records. *Communications of the ACM, 44*(9), 89-94.

Karygiannis, T., & Owens, L. (2002). *Wireless network security* (NIST special publication 800-48). Gaithersburg, MD: National Institute of Standards and Technology.

Kilpatrick, I. (2003, December). Are you indulging in unprotected wireless. *Logistics and Transport Focus, 5*(10), 20-21.

Masys, D. R., & Baker, D. B. (1997). *Patient-centered access to secure systems online: A secure approach to clinical data access via the World Wide Web*. Retrieved February 13, 2006, from http://www.saic.com/healthcare/sysint/pdf/amia1997.pdf

Newman, R. (2003). *Enterprise security*. Columbus, OH: Prentice-Hall.

Rust, R., Kannan, P., & Peng, N. (2002). The customer economics of Internet privacy. *Journal of the Academy of Marketing Science, 30*(1), 455-464.

Shortell, S. M., & Kaluzny, A. D. (1994). Healthcare management: Organization design and behavior (3rd ed.). New York: Delmar.

Sims, B. (2004). Moving from liability to viability. *Health Management Technology, 25*(2), 32-35.

Smith, C. (1990). The case study: A useful research method for information management. *Journal of Information Technology, 5*(3), 123-133.

Turban, E. (1993). *Decision support and expert systems: Management support systems* (3rd ed.). New York: Macmillan.

Walker, J., & Spencer, J. (2000). Ten deadly sins. *Health Management Technology, 21*(7), 10.

This work was previously published in Web Mobile-Based Applications for Healthcare Management, edited by L. Al-Hakim, pp. 167-180, copyright 2007 by IRM Press (an imprint of IGI Global).

Compilation of References

3UK. (2008). Retrieved Sep 05, 2008, from www.three. co.uk

Aarnio, E. A., Heikkila, J., & Hirvola, S. (2002). Adoption and use of mobile services empirical evidence from a Finnish survey. In *Proceedings of 35th International Conference of System Sciences, Hawaii, USA.*

ABI Research. (2007). *GPS-Enabled Mobile Devices— Key Drivers and Latest Trends Pushing GPS Penetration in CDMA, GSM and WCDMA Handsets* (White Paper).

AcbTaskMan. (2007). AcbTaskMan software. Retrieved Sep 05, 2008, from www.acbpocketsoft.com

Ackerman, L., Kempf, J., & Miki, T. (2003). Wireless Location Privacy Law and Policy. *Internet Society.* Retrieved February 6, 2008, from http://www.isoc.org/ briefings/015/index.shtml.

Afuah, A., & Tucci, C. T. (2000). *Internet Business Models and Strategies: Text and Cases.* McGraw-Hill Higher Education.

Agarwal, R., & Prasad, J. (1998). A conceptual and operational definition of personal innovativeness in the domain of information technology. *Information Systems Research, 9*(2), 204-301.

Agarwal, R., & Venkatesh, V. (2002). Assessing a firm's web presence: A heuristic evaluation procedure for measurement of usability. *Information Management Research, 13,* 168–121.

Agrawal, R., Lin, K, Sawhney, H., & Shim, K. (1995). Fast Similarity Search in the Presence of Noise, Scaling, and Translation in Time-Series Databases. *In Proceedings of the 21st International Conference on Very Large Databases (VLDB'95),* Zurich, Switzerland.

AIMC (2008). *Navegantes en la Red. 10ª encuesta AIMC a usuarios de Internet.* http://www.aimc.es

Ajzen, I. (1991). The Theory of Planned Behavior. *Organizational Behavior and Human Decision Processes, 50,* 179-211.

Albrecht, K., & MacIntyre, L. (2005). *Spychips: How Major Corporations and Government Plan to Track Your Every Move with RFID.* Nelson Current.

Alfalayleh M. & Brankovic L. (2004). An Overview Of Security Issues And Techniques In Mobile Agents. http://sec.isi.salford.ac.uk/cms2004/Program/CMS2004final/p2a3.pdf

Alt, R., & Zimmermann, H.-D. (2001). Introduction to special section-business models. *Electronic Markets, 11*(1).

American National Standard Institute. (2005). *X9.62-2005, Public Key Cryptography for the Financial Services Industry, The Elliptic Curve Digital Signature Algorithm (ECDSA).*

Anckar, B., & D'Incau, D. (2002). Value creation in mobile commerce: Findings from a consumer survey.

Journal of Information Technology Theory & Application, 4, 43–64.

Andersen, D., Bansal, D., Curtis, D., Seshan, S., & Balakrishnan, H. (2000). *System Support for Bandwidth Management and Content Adaptation in Internet Applications.* Paper presented at the 4th Symposium on Operating Systems Design and Implementation (OSDI), San Diego, CA, USA.

Anderson, J. C., & Gerbing, D. W. (1988). Structural Equation Modeling in Practice: A Review and Recommend Two-Step Approach. *Psychological Bulletin, 103*(3), 411-423.

Anderson, J. C., & Narus, J. A. (1998). Business Marketing: Understand What Customers Value. *Harvard Business Review, 76,* 53-65.

Anderson, R. E., & Srinivasan, S. S. (2002). E-satisfaction and e-loyalty: A contingency framework. *Psychology & Marketing, 20,* 123–138.

Andersson, C., Freeman, D., James, I., Johnston, A., & Ljung, S. (2006). *Mobile Media and Applications, From Concept to Cash: Successful Service Creation and Launch.* West Sussex, England: Wiley.

Angell, I., & Kietzmann, J. (2006). RFID and the End of Cash? *Communications of the ACM, 49*(12), 90-96.

Arthur, C. (2006). What is the 1% rule? Retrieved Sep 05, 2008, from http://technology.guardian.co.uk/weekly/story/0,1823959,00.html

Au, Y.A., & Kauffman, R. J. (2008). The economics of mobile payments: Understanding stakeholder issues for an emerging financial technology application. *Electronic Commerce Research and Applications, 7*(2), 141-164.

Aubert, B. A., Rivard, S., & Patry, M. (2004). A transaction cost model of IT outsourcing. *Information & Management, 41,* 921-932.

Australian Law Reform Commission. (2007). *Discussion Paper 72: Review of Australian Privacy Law (DP72).*

Bafoutsou, G.., & Mentzas, G. (2001. A comparative analysis of Web-based collaborative systems. In *Proceed-*

ings of the 12th International Workshop on Database and Expert Systems Applications (pp. 496-500).

Bagozzi, R., & Yi, Y. (1988). On the evaluation of structural equation models. *Academy of Marketing Science, 16*(1), 74-94.

Bailey, J., & Bakos, Y. (1997). An exploratory study of the emerging role of electronic intermediaries. *International Journal of Electronic Commerce, 1*(3), 7-20.

Balasubramanian, S., Konana, P., & Menon, N. (2003). Customer satisfaction in virtual environments: A study of online investing. *Management Science, 49,* 871–889.

Banavar, G., & Bernstein, A. (2002). Software Infrastructure and Design Challenges for Ubiquitous Computing Applications. *Communications of ACM, 45*(12), 92-96.

Barbara, D. (1999). Mobile computing and databases: A survey. *IEEE Transactions on Knowledge and Data Engineering, 11*(1), 108-117.

Barber, W., & Badre, A. N. (2001). Culturability: The merging of culture and usability. In *Proceedings of 4th Conference on Human Factors and the Web.* New Jersey: Basking Ridge.

Barkuus, A., & Dey, A. (2003, July). Location-Based Services for Mobile Telephony: a Study of Users' Privacy Concerns. *Proceedings of the INTERACT 2003, 9th IFIP TC13 International Conference on Human-Computer Interaction.*

Barnés, M. D., Gómez, D. S., Gómez-Skarmeta, A. F., Martínez, M., Ruiz, A., & Sánchez, D. (2005). *An Electronic Signature Infrastructure For Mobile Devices.* Securing Electronic Business Processes. Austria: Vieweg Verlag.

Barney, J. (1991). Special Theory Forum the Resource-Based Model of the Firm: Origins, Implications, and Prospects. *Journal of Management, 17,* 99-120.

Barney, J. (1999). How a Firm's Capabilities Affect Boundary Decisions. *Sloan Management Review, 40,* 137-145.

Baubin, T, Bruck, P. Hofbauer T. (1996). Electronic publishing—Strategic developments for the European publishing industry the towards the year 2000. ECSC-EEC-EAEC, Brussels-Luxembourg.

Bauer, R. A. (1960). Consumer behavior as risk-taking. In R. S. Hancock (Ed.). *Dynamic marketing for a changing world* (pp. 389–398). In Chicago: American Marketing Association.

Becker, S. A. (2002). An exploratory study on web usability and the internationalization of US e-businesses. *Journal of Electronic Commerce Research, 3,* 265–278.

Belamy, C. (2000). The politics of public information systems. In G. Garson (Ed.), *Handbook of Public Information Systems.* New York: Marcel Dekker, Inc.

Bellare, M., Al-Qayedi, A., Adi, W., Mabrouk, A., & Zahro A. (2004). Combined web/mobile authentication for Secure Web Access Control. *IEEE Wireless Communications and Networking Conference WCNC2004.* Atlanta.

Bellare, W., Hoornaert, F., M'Raihi, D., Naccache, D., & Ranen, O. (2005). *HOTP: An HMAC-Based One-Time Password Algorithm.* Network Working Group, Request for Comments: 4226.

Ben-Ami, O., & Mioduser, D. (2004). The affective aspect of moderator's role conception and enactment by teachers in a-synchronous learning discussion groups. *Proceedings of ED-MEDIA 2004* (2831–2837).

Benatallah, B., Dumas, M., Sheng, Q., & Ngu, A. (2002). Declarative Composition and Peer-to-Peer Provisioning of Dynamic Web Services. *In 18th International Conference on Data Engineering (ICDE'02),* San Jose, CA, USA.

Bennett, C. J., & Crow, L. (2005, June). Location-Based Services and the Surveillance of Mobility: An Analysis of Privacy Risks in Canada. *A Report to the Office of the Privacy Commissioner, under the 2004-5 Contributions Program.*

Bentler, P. M. (1995). *EQS structural equations program manual.* Multivariate Software Inc., C.A., USA.

Berghel, H., & Uecker, J. (2005). Wifi attack vectors. *Communications of the ACM, 48*(8), 21-28.

Bernard, M. (2002). *Criteria for optimal web design (Designing for usability).* Retrieved from: http://psychology.wichita.edu/optimalweb/print.htm

Bhattacherjee, A. (2001). Understanding information systems continuance: An expectation-confirmation model. *MIS Quarterly, 2,* 351–369.

Bicakci, K., & Baykal, N. (2003). *Design and Performance Evaluation of a Flexible and Efficient Server Assisted Signature Protocol. IEEE 8th Symposium on Computers and Communications.* Turkey: IEEE Press.

Bicakci, K., & Baykal, N. (2004). *SAOTS: A New Efficient Server Assisted Signature Scheme for Pervasive Computing.* 1st International Conference on Security in Pervasive Computing, LNCS No. 2802. Germany.

Bicakci, K., & Baykalb, N. (2005). Improved server assisted signatures. *Journal of Computer Networks, 47*(3), 351-366.

Bidgoli, H. (1990). Designing a user-friendly interface for a decision support system. *Information Technology, 12,* 148–154.

Bigné, E., Ruiz, C., & Sanz, S. (2005). The impact of internet user shopping patterns and demographics on consumer mobile buying behavior. *Journal of Electronic Commerce Research, 6,* 193–209.

Bigné, E., Ruiz, C., & Sanz, S. (2007). Key drivers of mobile commerce adoption. An exploratory study of Spanish mobile users. *Journal of Theoretical and Applied Electronic Commerce Research, 2* (2), 48-60.

Blake-Wilson, S., Karlinger, G., Kobayashi, T., & Wang, Y. (2005). *Using the Elliptic Curve Signature Algorithm (ECDSA) for XML Digital Signatures.* RFC 4050. http://www.ietf.org/rfc/rfc4050.txt

Bless, R., Hillebrand, J., Prehofer, C., & Zitterbart, M. (2004). Quality-of-Service Signaling for Next-Generation IP-Based Mobile Networks. *IEEE Communications Magazine, 42*(6), 72-79.

Bondi, A. B. (2000). Characteristics of scalability and their impact on performance. *Proceedings of the 2nd International Workshop on Software and Performance* (pp. 195-203). Ontario, Canada.

Booth-Thomas, C. (2003). The See-It-All-Chip, *Time Online Edition.*

Bower, G. H. (1981). Mood and memory. *American Psychologist, 36,* 129–148.

Bowman, C., & Ambrosini, V. (2000). Value Creation Versus Value Capture: Towards a Coherent Definition of Value in Strategy. *British Journal of Management, 11,* 1-15.

Bratman, M., Israel, D., & Pollack, M. (1988). Plans and Resource Bounded Practical Reasoning. *Computational Intelligence, 4*(4), 349-355.

Brennan, M. (2000). *Dot-com flavor of the week or hand-held revolution?* Retrieved from: http://www.bizjournals.com/tampabay/stories/2000/10/09/focus5.html

Brooks, R. (1991). Comparative Task Analysis: An Alternative Direction for Human-Computer Interaction Science. In J. Carroll (Ed.), *Designing Interaction: Psychology at the Human Computer Interface* (pp. 50-59). Cambridge: Cambridge University Press.

Brown L. (1996). Mobile Code Security. [Electronic version]. http://www.unsw.adfa.edu.au/~lpb/papers/mcode96.html

Brown, K. (2001). Using computers to deliver training: Which employees learn and why? *Personnel Psychology, 54,* 271–296.

Buchholz, W., & Bach, N. (2001). *The Evolution of Netsourcing Business Models.* Giessen, Germany: University of Giessen, Chair of business administration II.

Bui, T. X. (1987). *Co-oP: A group decision support system for cooperative multiple criteria group decision making* (LNCS 290). Berlin, Germany: Springer-Verlag.

Bui, T. X., Bodart, F., & Ma, P.-C. (1998). ARBAS: A formal language to support argumentation in network-based organization. *Journal of Management Information Systems, 14*(3), 223-240.

Bults, R., Wac, K., van Halteren, A., Konstantas, D., & Nicola, V. (2005). *Goodput Analysis of 3G wireless networks supporting m-health services.* Paper presented at the 8th International Conference on Telecommunications (ConTEL05), Zagreb, Croatia.

Buschken, J. (2004). *Higher Profits Through Customer Lock-In:* Thomson Texere.

Butler, D. (2000). Gender, girls, and computer technology: What's the status now? *Clearing House, 73,* 225–229.

Cairncross, F. (1997). *The Death of Distance.* Boston, Mass: Harvard Business School Press.

Calvo, M., Rodríguez, C., & Dillinger, M. (2004). *Business models for reconfigurable communication systems.* Paper presented at the 13th IST Mobile & Wireless Communications Summit, Lyon, France.

Campbell, R., & Durigon, L. (2003). Wireless communication in healthcare: Who will win the right to send data boldly where no data has gone before? *Healthcare Manager, 22*(3), 233-240.

Campbell, S. (2003). *Supporting Digital Signatures in Mobile Environments.* International Workshop on Enabling Technologies: Infrastructure for Collaborative Enterprises.

Camponovo, G., & Pigneur, Y. (2003). *Business model analysis applied to mobile business.* Paper presented at the 5th Intl Conference on Enterprise Information Systems (ICEIS03), Angers, FR.

Cap Gemini Ernst & Young (2004). *Survey on Electronic Public Services in Europe.*

Carbo, T., & Williams, J. (2004). Models and Metrics for Evaluating Local Electronic Government Systems and Services *Electronic Journal of e-Government, 2*(2), 95-104.

Carlson, P. J., Kahn, B. K., & Rowe, F. (1999). Organisational impacts of new communication technology: A comparison of cellular phone adoption in France and the United States. *Journal of Global Information Management, July,* (pp. 19–29).

Carter, L., & Belanger, F. (2004). The influence of Perceived Characteristics of Innovating on e-Government Adoption *Electronic Journal of e-Government, 2*(1), 11-20.

Casati, F., Ilnicki, S., Jin, L., Krishnamoorthy, V., & M. Shan. (2002). *Adaptive and Dynamic Service Composition in eFlow.* HP Lab Technical Report HPL-2000-39, Palo Alto: Software Technology Laboratory.

Chae, M., & Kim, J. (2004). Do size and structure matter to mobile users? An empirical study of the effects of screen size, information structure, and task complexity on user activities with standard web phones. *Behaviour & Information Technology, 23,* 165–181.

Chae, M., Kim, J., & Ryu, H. (2002). Information quality for mobile internet services: A theoretical model with empirical validation. *Electronic Markets, 12,* 38–46.

Chakraborty, D. (2001). *Service Composition in Ad-hoc Environments.* Ph.D Dissertation Proposal, Technical Report TR-CS-01-20.

Chakraborty, D., Perich, F., Joshi, A., Finin, T., & Yesha, Y. (2002). *A Reactive Service Composition Architecture for Pervasive Computing Environments.* Technical Report TR-CS-02-02, University of Maryland at Baltimore, USA.

Chalmers, D., & Sloman, M. (1999). A survey of Quality of Service in mobile computing environments. *IEEE Communications Surveys and Tutorials, 2*(2).

Chan Hing Wing & Anthony. (1999). Secure Mobile Agents: Techniques, Modeling and Application. www.cse.cuhk.edu.hk/~lyu/student/mphil/anthony/term3.ppt

Chau, P. K., Au, G., & Tam, K. Y. (2000). Impact of information presentation modes on online shopping: An empirical evaluation of a broadband interactive shopping service. *Journal of Organisational Computing Electronic Commerce, 10,* 1–22.

Chen, C., Chen, C., Liu, L., & Horng, G. (2007). A server-aided signature scheme for mobile commerce. *In Proceedings of the 2007 international conference on Wireless communications and mobile computing,* (pp. 565-570). Honolulu, Hawaii, USA: ACM.

Chen, F. Y., & Yuan, S. T. (2004). *A Study on Contextualized Fault-tolerant Service Composition in WP2P Environments.* Technical Report, Fu-Jen University, Taiwan.

Chen, L.; Gillenson, M., & Sherrell, D. (2002). Enticing on-line consumers: an extended technology acceptance perspective. *Information and Management, 39,* 705–719.

Chen, S. C., & Dhillon, G. S. (2003). Interpreting dimensions of consumer trust in e-commerce. *Information Technology and Management, 4,* 303–318.

Chen, W. T., & Shu, Y. Y. (2005). *Active application oriented vertical handoff in next-generation wireless networks.* Paper presented at the Wireless Communications and Networking Conference (WCNC05).

Cheng, Y., O'Toole, A., & Abdi, H. (2001). Classifying adults' and children's faces by sex: computational investigations of subcategorial feature encoding. *Cognitive Science, 25,* 819–838.

Cheong, J., & Park M. C. (2005). Mobile Internet Acceptance in Korea. *Internet Research, 15*(2), 125-140.

Chesbrough, H. W. (2003). *Open Innovation.* Boston: Harvard Business School Press.

Childers, T., Carr, C., Peck, J., & Carson, S. (2001). Hedonic and utilitarian motivations for online retail shopping behavior. *Journal of Retailing, 77,* 511–535.

Chin, W. W. (1998). The partial least squares approach to structural equation modeling. In G.A. Marcoulides (Ed.), Modern methods for business research (pp. 295–336). Mahwah: Lawrence Erlbaum Associates.

Chiu, D. K. W., Cheung, S. C., & Leung, H.-F. (2005). A multi-agent infrastructure for mobile workforce management in a service oriented enterprise. *Proceedings of the 38th Hawaii International Conference on System Sciences (HICSS38),* Waikoloa, Big Island, HI [CD-ROM]. IEEE Press.

Chiu, D. K. W., Cheung, S. C., Hung, P. C. K. Chiu, S. Y. Y., & Chung, K. K. (2005). Developing e-negotiation process support with a meta modeling approach in a Web services environment. *Decision Support Systems, 40*(1), 51-69.

Chiu, D. K. W., Cheung, S. C., Hung, P. C. K., & Leung, H.-F. (2004). Constraint-based negotiation in a multi-agent information system with multiple platform support. In *Proceedings of the 37ʰ Hawaii International Conference on System Sciences (HICSS37)*, Waikoloa, Big Island, HI [CD-ROM]. IEEE Computer Society Press.

Chiu, D. K. W., Cheung, S. C., Kafeza, E., & Leung, H.-F. (2003). A three-tier view methodology for adapting M-services. *IEEE Transactions on System, Man and Cybernetics, Part A, 33*(6), 725-741.

Chiu, D. K. W., Kwok, B., Wong, R., Kafeza, E., & Cheung, S. C. (2004). Alert driven e-services management. In *Proceedings of the 37ʰ Hawaii International Conference on System Sciences (HICSS37)*, Waikoloa, Big Island, HI [CD-ROM]. IEEE Computer Society Press.

Chiu, D. K. W., Lee, O., & Leung, H.-F. (2005). A multi-modal agent based mobile route advisory system for public transport network. In *Proceedings of the 38ʰ Hawaii International Conference on System Sciences (HICSS38)*, Waikoloa, Big Island, HI [CD-ROM]. IEEE Computer Society Press.

Chiu, D. K. W., Li, Q., & Karlapalem, K. (1999). A meta modeling approach for workflow management system supporting exception handling. *Information Systems, 24*(2), 159-184.

Choi, B., Lee, I., & Kim, J. (2006). Culturability in mobile data services: A qualitative study of the relationship between cultural characteristics and user-experience attributes. *International Journal of Human-Computer Interaction, 20,* 171–206.

Choi, B., Lee, I., Kim, J., & Jeon, Y. (2005). A qualitative cross-national study of cultural influences on mobile data service design. In *Proceedings of Computer-Human Interaction, Portland, Oregon, USA, 2-7 April*.

Choy, M. C., Srinivasan, D., & Cheu, R. L. (2003). Co-operative, hybrid agent architecture for real-time traffic signal control. *IEEE Transactions on System, Man and Cybernetics, Part A, 33*(5), 597-607.

Chung, W. W. C., Yam, A. Y. K., & Chan, M. F. S. (2004). Networked enterprise: A new business model for global sourcing. *International Journal of Production Economics, 87,* 267-280.

Cilingir, D., & Kushchu, I. (2004). E-Government and M-Government: Concurrent Leaps by Turkey. *Proceedings of the 4ʰ European Conference on E-Government*, (pp. 813-821).

Claessens, J., Preneel, B., & Vandewalle, J. (2001). Combining world wide web and wireless security. *Proceedings of IFIP I-NetSec*. Leuven (Belgium).

Claffy, K., Miller, G., & Thompson, K. (1998). *The nature of the beast: recent traffic measurements from an Internet backbone*. Paper presented at the International Networking Conference (INET98), Geneva, Switzerland.

Clegg, B. & Tan, B. (2007). Using QFD for e-business planning and analysis in a micro-sized enterprise. *International Journal of Quality &Reliability Management, 24,* 813-828.

Clulow, V., Barry, C., & Gerstman, J. (2007). The resource-based view and value: the customer-based view of the firm. *Journal of European Industrial Training, 31,* 19-35.

Cohen, J. (1988). *Statistical power analysis for the behavioral sciences*. 2nd ed. New York: Academic Press.

Committee on Payment and Settlement Systems (2000). *Clearing and settlement arrangements for retail payments in selected countries*. Basel, Switzerland: Bank for International Settlements. Retrieved March 3, 2009, from http://www.bis.org/publ/cpss40.htm

Connolly, T., Jessup, L. M., & Valacich, J. S. (1990). Effects of anonymity and evaluative tone in idea generation in computer-mediated groups. *Management Science, 36,* 97–120.

Cooper, R. B., & Zmud, R. W. (1990). Information Technology Implementation Research: A Technological Diffusion Approach. *Management Science*, (pp. 123-139).

Council for Excellence in Government and Accenture (2003). *The new e-government equation: Ease, engagement, privacy and protection.*

Coursaris, C., & Hassanein K. (2002). Understanding m-Commerce: A Consumer-Centric Model. *Quarterly Journal of Electronic Commerce, 3*(3), 247-272.

Coursaris, C., Hassanein, K., & Head, M. (2003). Understanding the mobile consumer. In S. Nansi (Ed.), *Wireless communications and mobile commerce* (pp. 132–165). Idea Group Inc.

Coursaris, C., Hassanein, K., & Head, M. (2008). Mobile technology and the value chain: Participants, activities and value creation. *International Journal of Business Science and Applied Management, 3.*

Cousins, K. C., & Robey, D. (2005). Human Agency in a Wireless World: Patterns of Technology Use in Nomadic Computing Environments. *Information and Organization, 15*(2), 151-180.

Cox, A. (1997). *Business success: a way of thinking about strategy, critical supply chain assets and operational best practice.* Winteringham: Earlgate Press.

Cronbach, L. J. (1971). Test validation in educational measurement. In R. L. Thorndike, (Ed.), 2nd ed. (pp. 443–507). Washington, D.C: American Council on Education.

Crosby, L. B., DeVito, R., & Pearson, J. M. (2003). Manage your customers' perception of quality. *Review of Business, 24.*

Cuevas, A., Moreno, J. I., Vidales, P., & Einsiedler, H. (2006). The IMS Platform: A Solution for Next Generation Network Operators to Be More Than Bit Pipes. *IEEE Commun. Mag., Advances in Service Platform Technologies, 44*(8), 75-81.

Cyr, D. (2008). Modelling website design across cultures: Relationships to trust, satisfaction and e-loyalty. *Journal of Management Information Systems, 24*(4), 47–72.

Cyr, D., & Bonanni, C. (2005). Gender and website design in e-business. *International Journal of Electronic Business, 6,* 565–582.

Cyr, D., & Trevor-Smith, H. (2004). Localization of web design: An empirical comparison of German, Japanese, and U.S. website characteristics. *Journal of the American Society for Information Science and Technology, 55,* 1–10.

Cyr, D., Bonanni, C., & Ilsever, J. (2004). Design and e-loyalty across cultures in electronic commerce. In *Proceedings of 6th International Conference on Electronic Commerce.*

Cyr, D., Bonanni, C., Bowes, J., & Ilsever, J. (2005). Beyond trust: Website design preferences across cultures. *Journal of Global Information Management, 13,* 24–52.

Cyr, D., Head, J., Larios, H., & Pan, B. (2006). Exploring human images in website design across cultures: A multi-method approach. In *Proceedings for the Fifth Pre-ICIS HCI Research in MIS Workshop 2006, Milwaukee, Wisconsin.* Nominated for Best Paper Award.

Dahlberg, T., Mallat, N., & Öörni, A. (2003). Consumer acceptance of mobile payment solutions—Ease of use, usefulness and trust. *Proceedings of the 2nd International Conference on Mobile Business* (pp. 211-218). Vienna, Austria.

Dahlberg, T., Mallat, N., Ondrus, J., & Zmijewska, A. (2008). Past, present and future of mobile payments research: A literature review. *Electronic Commerce Research and Applications, 7*(2), 165-181.

Dankers, J., Garefalakis, T., Schaffelhofer, R., & Wright, T. (2002). Public Key Infrastructure in mobile systems. *IEEE Electronics and Communications Engineering Journal, 14*(5), 191-204.

Dao, D., Rizos, C., & Wang, J. (2002). Location-Based Services: Technical and Business Issues. *School of Surveying and Spatial Information Systems.* The University of New South Wales, Sydney.

Darke, P., Shanks, G., & Broadbent, M. (1998). Successfully completing case study research: Combining rigour, relevance and pragmatism. *Information Systems Journal, 8*, 273-289.

Davis, F. (1989). Perceived Usefulness, Perceived Ease of Use and User Acceptance of Information Technology. *MIS Quarterly, 13*(3), 319-340.

Dawes, S., & Pardo, T. (2002). Building collaborative digital government systems. In W. Mciver & K. Elmagarmid (Eds.), *Advances in digital government. Technology human factors and policy.* Norwell, MA: Kluwer Academic Publishers.

De Vriendt, J., Laine, P., Lerouge, C., & Xu, X. (2002). Mobile Network Evolution: A Revolution on the Move. *IEEE Commun. Mag., 40*(4), 104-111.

Deaux, K., & Kite, M. E. (1987). Thinking about gender. In B. B. Hess & M. M. Ferree (Eds.), *Analyzing gender: A handbook of social science research* (pp. 92–117). Newbury Park, CA: Sage Publications.

Dekleva, S., Shim, J. P., Varshney, U., & Knoerzer, G. (2007). Evolution and emerging issues in mobile wireless networks. *Commun. ACM, 50*(6), 38-43.

Deng, D., & Kasabov, N. (2000). ESOM: An Algorithm to Evolve Self-Organizing Maps from On-line Data Streams. *In Proceedings of the IJCNN'2000 on Neural Networks Neural Computing: New Challenges and Perspectives for the New Millennium, 6*, 3-8.

Derba, M., & Siegal, J. (2003). Wireless networks. *The CPA Journal, 73*(7), 18-21.

Dialani, V., Miles, S., Morcan, L., Rourc, D., & luck, M. (2002). Transparent Fault Tolerance for Web Services Based Architectures. *In Proceedings of the 8th International Euro-Par Conference (EURO-PAR'02)*, Paderborn, Germany.

Dietz-Uhler, B., & Bishop-Clark, C. (2001). The use of computer-mediated communication to enhance subsequent face-to-face discussions. *Computer in Human Behavior, 17*, 269–283.

Digital Chocolate. (2008). Seize the Minute. Retrieved Sep 05, 2008, from www.digitalchocolate.com

Dillon, R. J., & McKnight, C. (1990). The effect of display size and text splitting on reading lengthy text from the screen. *Behavior and Information Technology, 9*, 215–227.

Ding, X., Mazzocchi, D., & Tsudik, G. (2002). *Experimenting with server-aided signatures.* Network and Distributed Systems Security Symposium.

Dipanjan, C. *et al.* (2002). A Reactive Service Composition Architecture for Pervasive Computing Environments. *7th Personal Wireless Communications Conference*, Singapore.

Directive 2002/58/EC of the European Parliament and of the Council concerning the processing of personal data and the protection of privacy in the electronic communications sector (Directive on privacy and electronic communications).

Doll, W. J., & Torkzadesh, G. (1988). The measurement of end-user computing satisfaction. *MIS Quarterly, 12*, 259–274.

Domingo-Ferrer, J., Posegga, J., Sebe, F., & Torra, V. (2007). Special Issue on Advances in Smart Cards. *Journal of Computer Networks, 51*.

Doney, P. M., Cannon, J. P., & Mullen, M. R. (1998). Understanding the influence of national culture on the development of trust. *Academy of Management Review, 23*, 601–620.

Donthu, N., & García, A. (1999). The Internet Shopper. *Journal of Advertising Research, 39*(3), 52-58.

Dood, A. (2005). *The Essential Guide to Telecommunications.* US: Prentice Hall PTR.

Dourish, P. (2001). *Where the action is: The foundations of embodied interaction*: MIT Press.

Drew, W. (2003). Wireless networks: New meaning to ubiquitous computing. *Journal of Academic Librarianship, 29*(2), 102-106.

Duchnicky, R. L., & Kolers, P. A. (1983). Readability of text scrolled on visual display terminals as a function of window size. *Human Factors, 25,* 683–692.

Durlacher Research (2001). *UMTS Report, an Investment Perspective.* [Online] Available: http://www.durlacher. com [Accessed: 30 Jul 2002].

Dyer, R., Green, R., Pitts, M., & Millward, G. (1995). What's the flaming problem? CMC – deindividuation or disinhibiting? In M. A. R. Kirby, A. J. Dix, & J. E. Finlay (Eds.), *People and computers.* Cambridge: Cambridge University Press.

Eastin, M. S. (2002). Diffusion of e-commerce: An analysis of the adoption of four e-commerce activities. *Telematics and Informatics, 19,* 251-267.

Eastlick, M. A., & Lotz, S. (1999). Profiling Potential Adopters and Non-Adopters of an Interactive Electronic Shopping Medium. *International Journal of Retail and Distribution Management, 27*(6), 209-223.

Egan, D. E. (1998). Individual differences in human-computer interaction. In M. Helander (Ed.), *Handbook of human-computer Interaction* (pp. 543–568). Amsterdam: Elsevier Science Publishers.

Egger, F. N. (2001). Affective design of e-commerce user interfaces: How to maximize perceived trustworthiness. In *Proceedings of International Conference of Affective Human Factors Design.* London Press.

Elfvengren, K., Kärkkäinen, H., Torkkeli, M., & Tuominen, M. (2004). A GDSS based approach for the assessment of customer needs in industrial markets. *International Journal of Production Economics, 89,* 275-292.

Elichirigoity, F. (2004). *Embedded Mobilities.* Paper presented at the The Life of Mobile Data: Technology, Mobility and Data Subjectivity, University of Surrey, UK.

Ellis, R. D., & Kurniawan, S. H. (2000). Increasing the usability of online information for older users: A case study in participatory design. *International Journal of Human-Computer Interaction, 12,* 263–276.

Eshghi, A., Haughton, D., & Topi, H. (2007). Determinants of customer loyalty in the wireless telecommunications industry. *Telecommunications Policy, 31*(2), 93.

ETSI (2003). *Mobile Commerce (M-COMM); Mobile Signature Service; Security Framework. TR 102 206.* European Telecommunications Standards Institute (ETSI) Specifications.

ETSI (2003). *Mobile Commerce (M-COMM); Mobile Signature Service; Business and Functional Requirements. TR 102 203.* European Telecommunications Standards Institute (ETSI) Specifications.

ETSI. (2006). *XML Advanced Electronic Signatures (XAdES).* TS 101 903 v1.3.2. European Telecommunications Standards Institute (ETSI) Specifications.

ETSI. (2007). *CMS Advanced Electronic Signatures (CAdES).* TS 101 733 v1.7.3. European Telecommunications Standards Institute (ETSI) Specifications.

Etteman, J. (1984). Three phrases in the creation of information inequities: An empirical assesment of a prototype videotex system. *Journal of Broadcasting, 28,* 293-385.

European Central Bank (2006). *Payment and securities settlement systems in the European Union and in the acceding countries.*

European Committee for Standardization. (2004). *Secure signature-creation devices EAL 4+ in CEN Workshop Agreement (CWA) 14169.* European Committee for Standardization. http://www.cen.eu.

European IST Project Wireless Trust mobile business. (2004). http://www.wireless-trust.org.

European Parliament. (2000). *Directive 1999/93/EC of the European Parliament and the council of December 1999 on a Community framework for electronic signatures.* Official Journal of the European Communities. Belgium.

Evers, V., & Day, D. (1997). The role of culture in interface acceptance. In S. Howard, J. Hammond, & G. Lindegaard (Eds.), *Proceedings of Human Computer Interaction, INTERACT '97.* London: Chapman and Hall.

Faber, E., Ballon, P., Bouwman, H., Haaker, T., Rietkerk, O., & Steen, M. (2003). *Designing business models for mobile ICT services*. Paper presented at the 16th BLED Electronic Commerce Conf.—eTransformations, Bled, Slovenia.

Facebook. (2007). A social utility that connects you with the people around you. Retrieved Sep 05, 2008, from www.facebook.com

Fano, A., & Gershman, A. (2002). The Future of Business Services in the Age of Ubiquitous Computing. *Communications of ACM, 45*(12), 63-87.

Farkas, K., & Farkas, J. B. (2000). Guidelines for designing web navigation. *Technical Communication, Third Quarter,* (pp. 341–358).

Felmetsger V. & Vigna G. (2005). Exploiting OS-level Mechanisms to Implement Mobile Code Security. www.cs.ucsb.edu/~vigna/pub/2005_felmetsger_vigna_ICECCS05.pdf

Finger, M., & Pecoud, G. (2003). From e-Government to e-Governance? Towards a model of e-Governance. *Electronic Journal of e-Government, 1*(1), 1-10.

Fitzgerald, J., & Dennis, A. (2002). *Business data communications and networking* (7th ed.). New York: John Wiley & Sons.

Flavián, C., & Guinalíu, M. (2006). Consumer trust, perceived security and privacy policy: Three basic elements of loyalty to a web site. *Industrial Management & Data Systems, 106*(5), 601-620.

Flavián, C., Guinalíu, M., & Gurrea, R. (2005). The role played by perceived usability, satisfaction and consumer trust on website loyalty. *Information & Management, 42,* 719–729.

Flint, D. J., & Woodruf, R. B. (1998). The Initiators of Changes in Customers' Desired Value. *Industrial Marketing Management, 30,* 321-337.

Flint, D. J., Woodruff, R. B., & Gardial, S. F. (1997). Customer Value Change in Industrial Marketing Relationships. *Industrial Marketing Management, 26,* 163-175.

Fogg, B. J., Soohoo, C., & Danielson, D. (2002). *How people evaluate a web site's credibility?* Results from a large study. Persuasive Technology Lab, Stanford University. Retrieved from: www.consumerwebwatch.org/news/report3_credibilityresearch/stanfordPTL.pdf

Fogg, J., & Tseng, S. (1999). Credibility and computing technology. *Communications of the ACM, 14,* 39–87.

Forgas, J. P. (1991). *Emotion and social judgments*. Oxford: Pergamon Press.

Fornell, C., & Larcker, D. (1981). Structural Equation Models with Unobserved Variables and Measurement Error. *Journal of Marketing Research, 36*(3), 39-50.

Forsythe, S., & Shi, B. (2003*).* Consumer patronage and risk perceptions in Internet shopping. *Journal of Business Research, 56*(11), 867-875.

Fraile, J.-C., Paredis, C. J. J., Wang, C.-H., & Khosla, P. K. (1999). Agent-based planning and control of a multi-manipulator assembly system. In *Proceedings of the IEEE International Conference on Robotics and Automation, 2,* 1219-1225.

Franks, J., Hallam-Baker, P. M., Hostetler, J. L., Lawrence, S. D., Leach, P.J ., Luotonen, A., & Stewart, L. (1999), *HTTP Authentication: Basic and Digest Access Authentication*. Network Working Group, Request for Comments: 2617.

Fritsch, L., Ranke, J., & Rossnagel, H. (2003). Qualified Mobile Electronic Signatures: Possible, but worth a try? *Information Security Solutions Europe (ISSE) Conference*. Vienna, Austria: Vieweg Verlag.

Funk, J. (2004). Key technological trajectories and the expansion of mobile Internet applications. *The journal of policy, regulation and strategy for telecommunications, 6*(3), 208-215.

Gabrielsson, M. and Gabrielssson, P. (2003), Global Marketing Strategies of Born Globals and Globalising Internationals in the ICT field. Journal of Euromarketing, Vol 12 No 3-4, pp. 123-145.

Gandolfi, K., Mourtel, C., & Olivier, F. (2001) Electromagnetic Analysis: Concrete Results. *Lecture Notes in Computer Science, 2162.* Springer-Verlag.

Gao, J., & Küpper, A. (2006). Emerging Technologies for Mobile Commerce. *Journal of Theoretical and Applied Electronic Commerce Research, 1*(2).

Gardner, B. (2001). What Do Customers Value? *Quality Progress, 34,* 41-48.

Garfinkel, S., & Rosenberg, B. (2006). *RFID: Applications, Security, and Privacy*: Addison-Wesley Professional.

Garrett, J. J. (2003). *The Elements of user experience: User-centered design for the web.* Indiana, USA: New Riders Publications.

Garrido, L., Brena, R., & Sycara, K. (1996). Cognitive modeling and group adaptation in intelligent multi-agent meeting scheduling. In *Proceedings of the 1st Iberoamerican Workshop on Distributed Artificial Intelligence and Multi-Agent Systems* (pp. 55-72).

Garrison, D. R., & Anderson, T. (2003). *E-learning in the 21st Century: A Framework for Research and Practice.* London: Routledge Falmer.

Garson, G. (2003). *Toward an information technology research agenda for public administration.* In G. Garson (Ed.), *Public information technology: Policy and management issues.* Hershey, PA: Idea Group Publishing.

Garton, L., & Wellman, B. (1995). Social impacts of electronic mail in organizations: a review of the research literature. In B. R. Burleson (Ed.). *Communication yearbook, 18,* 434–453). Thousand Oaks, CA: Sage.

Garvin, D. A. (1987). Competing on the eight dimensions of quality. *Harvard Business Review, 65,* 101-109.

Garvin, G., & Levesque, C. (2008), The Multiunit Enterprise, *Harvard Business Review,* June 2008, (pp. 106-117).

Gefen, D., & Straub, D. W. (1997). Gender differences in the perception and use of email: An extension to the technology acceptance model. *MIS Quarterly, 21,* 389–400.

Gefen, D., Karahanna, E., & Straub, D. (2003). Trust and TAM in Online Shopping: An Integrated Model. *MIS Quarterly, 27*(1), 51-90.

Gerpott, T. J., Rams, W., & Schindler, A. (2001). Customer retention, loyalty, and satisfaction in the German mobile cellular telecommunications market. *Telecommunications Policy, 25*(4), 249.

Gerst, M. H. (2003). The role of standardisation in the context of e-collaboration: A SNAP shot. In *Proceedings of the 3rd Conference on Standardization and Innovation in Information Technology* (pp. 113-119).

Ghezzi C. & Vigna G.(1997). Mobile Code Paradigms and Technologies: A Case Study. In Kurt Rothermet, Radu Popescu-Zeletin, editors, Mobile Agents, First International Workshop, MA'97, Berlin, Germany, April 1997, Proceedings, LNCS 1219, p. 39-49, Springer.

Gibson, J. J. (1977). The Theory of Affordances. In R. Shaw & J. Bransford (Eds.), *Perceiving, Acting, and Knowing,* .

Gill, A. J., & Oberlander, J. (2003). Perception of e-mail personality at zero-acquaintance: Extraversion take care of itself; Neuroticism is a worry. *Proceedings of the 25th annual conference of the Cognitive Science Society* (1–6).

Goldsmith, R. (2002). Explaining and Predicting Consumer Intention to Purchase Over the Internet: An Exploratory Study. *Journal of Marketing, 66*(Spring), 22-28.

Gomez, G., & Sanchez, R. (2005). *End-to-End Quality of Service over Cellular Networks: Data Services Performance Optimization in 2G/3G*: John Wiley & Sons, Ltd.

Gommans, M., Krishan, K. S., & Scheddold, K. B. (2001). From brand loyalty to e-loyalty: A conceptual framework. *Journal of Economic and Social Research, 3,* 43–58.

Gonzalez, M., Hidalgo, C. A., & Barabasi, A. (2008). Understanding individual human mobility patterns. *Nature, 453*(1), 779-782.

Goodman, J., & Lundell, J. (2005). HCI and the older population: Editorial. *Interacting with Computers, 17,* 613–620.

Goodman, J., Brewser, S. A., & Gray, P. (2005). How can we best use landmarks to support older people in navigation? *Behaviour & Information Technology, 24,* 3–20.

Gorlach, A., Heinemann, A., & Terpstra, W. (2004). *Survey on location privacy in pervasive computing.* Paper presented at the Workshop on Security and Privacy in Pervasive Computing (SPCC04) at PERVASIVE2004.

Grefen, P., Aberer, K., Hoffner, Y., & Ludwig, H. (2000). CrossFlow: Cross-organizational workflow management in dynamic virtual enterprises. *International Journal of Computer Systems Science & Engineering, 15*(5), 277-290.

Grewal, D., Iyer, G., & Levy, M. (2004). Internet retailing: enablers, limiters and market consequences. *Journal of Business Research, 57,* 703-713.

Gribble, S. D., Welsh, M., Brewer, E. A., & Culler, D. E. (1999). *The NINJA project pages.* http://ninja.cs.berkeley.edu.

Grillo, A., Lentini, A., Me, G., & Rulli, G. (2008). *Trusted SMS - A Novel Framework for Non-repudiable SMS-based Processes.* In L. Azevedo & A. R. Londral (Eds.), *HEALTHINF,* (1), 43-50. INSTICC - Institute for Systems and Technologies of Information, Control and Communication.

Gühring, P. (2006). *Concepts against Man-in-the-Browser Attacks.* Retrieved April 01, 2008, from http://www.it-observer.com/pdf/dl/concepts_against_mitb_attacks.pdf

Guido, B., Roberto, G., Tria, P. di, & Bisio, R. (1998). Workforce management (WFM) issues. In *Proceedings of the IEEE Network Operations and Management Symposium (NOMS 98), 2,* 473-482.

Gunawardena, C. N. (1995). Social presence theory and implications for interaction and collaborative learning in computer conferences. *International Journal of Educational Telecommunications, 1,* 147–166.

Gunawardena, C. N., & Zittle, F. J. (1997). Social presence as a predictor of satisfaction within a computer-mediated conferencing environment. *The American Journal of Distance Education, 11,* 8–26.

Gürgens, S., Rudolph, C., & Vogt, H. (2005). On the security of fair non-repudiation protocols. *International Journal of Information Security, 4*(4), 253-262.

Hair, J. F., Anderson, R. E., Tatham, R. L., & Black, W. C. (1999). *Multivariate data analysis.* New Jersey, USA: Prentice Hall.

Haller, N. et al. (1998). *The S/KEY One-Time Password System.* Request For Comments, 2289.

Hamel, G. (2000). *Leading the revolution.* Boston: Harvard Business School Press.

Han, Q., & Venkatasubramanian, N. (2006). Information Collection Services for QoS-aware Mobile Applications. *IEEE Transactions on Mobile Computing, 5*(5), 518-535.

Hansmann, U., Merck, L., Nicklous, M. S., & Stober, T. (2003). *Pervasive Computing: The Mobile World.* Heidelberg: Springer Verlag.

Harris, P., Rettie, R., & Kwan, C. C. (2005). Adoption and usage of m-commerce: A cross-cultural comparison of Hong Kong and the United Kingdom. *Journal of Electronic Commerce Research, 6,* 210–224.

Hartigan, J. A., & Wong, M. A. (1979). A K-Means Clustering Algorithm. J. Royal Statistical Society, Ser. C, *Applied Statistics, 28,* 100-108.

Hassinen, M., Hyppönen, K., & Haataja, K. (2006). An Open, PKI-Based Mobile Payment System. *In Emerging Trends in Information and Communication Security,* (pp. 86-100).

Hassinen, M., Hyppönen, K., & Trichina, E. (2008). Utilizing national public-key infrastructure in mobile payment systems, *Electronic Commerce Research and Applications, 7*(2), 214-231.

Karnouskos, S., & Fokus F. (2004). Mobile payment: A journey through existing procedures and standardization initiatives. *IEEE Communications Surveys and Tutorials*, *6*(4) 44-66.

Hawthorn, D. (2000). Possible implications of aging for interface design. *Interacting with Computers*, *12*, 507–528.

He, L., Zhang, N., He, L., & Rogers, I. (2007). Secure M-commerce Transactions: A Third Party Based Signature Protocol. *In Proceedings of the Third International Symposium on Information Assurance and Security*, (pp. 3-8). IEEE Computer Society.

He, M., Jennings, N. R., & Leung, H.-F. (2003). On agent-mediated electronic commerce. *IEEE TKDE*, *15*(4), 985-1003.

Hefeeda M. & Bharat B. On Mobile Code Security. Center of education and Research in Information Assurance and Security And Department of Computer Science, Purdue University West Lafayette, IN 47907, U.S.A. http://www.cs.sfu.ca/~mhefeeda/Papers/OnMobileCodeSecurity.pdf

Heinkele, C. (2003). *Überblick und Einordnung ausgewählter Mobile Payment-Verfahren*. Augsburg, Germany: University of Augsburg, Chair of Business Informatics and Systems Engineering.

Henkel, J. (2002). Mobile Payment. In G. Silberer, J. Wohlfahrt, & T. Wilhelm (Eds.), *Mobile commerce — Basics, business models and success factors* (pp. 327-351). Wiesbaden, Germany: Gabler.

Hevner, A. R., March S. T., Park J., & Ram S. (2004). Design science in information systems research. *MIS Quaterly, 28*(1), 75-100.

Higgins, & Kruglanski, A. W. (Eds.), *Social psychology: Handbook of basic principles* (pp. 655–701). New York: The Guilford Press.

Hoegg, R., & Stanoevska-Slabeva, K. (2005). *Towards Guidelines for the Design of Mobile Services*. Paper presented at the 18th BLED Electronic Commerce Conf., Bled, Slovenia.

Hoegg, R., Martignoni, R., Meckel, M., & Stanoevska-Slabeva, K. (2006). *Overview of business models for Web 2.0. communities*. Paper presented at the GeNeMe, Dresden, DE.

Hoffman, D. L., & Novak, T. P. (1996). Marketing in hypermedia computer-mediated environments: Conceptual foundations. *Journal of Marketing, 60*, 50–68.

Hofstede, G. (1980). *Culture's consequences: Comparing values, behaviors, institutions and organisations across nations*, 2nd ed. Thousand Oaks, CA: Sage Publication.

Hohl F. (1998). Mobile Agent Security and Reliability. Proceedings of the Ninth International Symposium on Software Reliability Engineering (ISSRE '98).

Hohl F. (1998). Time Limited Blackbox security: Protecting Mobile Agents from Malicious Hosts. Mobile Agents and Security, Vol. 1419 of LNCS. Springer-Verlag.

Hohl, F. (1997). An approach to solve the problem of malicious hosts. Universität Stuttgart, Fakultät Informatik, Fakultätsbericht Nr. 1997/03, 1997. http://www.informatik.uni-stuttgart.de/cgi-bin/ncstrl_rep_view.pl?/inf/ftp/pub/library/ncstrl.ustuttgart_fi/TR-1997-03/TR-1997-03.bib

Holak, S. L., & Lehmann, D. R. (1990). Purchase Intentions and the Dimensions of Innovation: An Exploratory Model. *Journal of Product Innovation Management, 7*(1), 59-73.

Hole, J. K., Moen, V., & Tjostheim, T. (n.d.). Case study: Online banking security. *IEEE Security and Privacy, 4*(2), 14-20.

Holland, J., & Baker, S. M. (2001). Customer participation in creating site brand loyalty. *Journal of Interactive Marketing, 15*, 34–45.

Hong, J. I., Boriello, G., Landy, J. A., McDonald, D. W., Schilit, B. N., & Tygar, J. D. (2003). Privacy and Security in the Location-enhanced World Wide Web. *In the Proceedings of the Workshop on Privacy at Ubicomp 2003*.

Höök, K., Benyon, D., & Monroe, A. J. (Eds.). (2003). *Designing Information Spaces: The Social Navigation Approach.* London: Springer-Verlag.

Housley, R. (2004). *Cryptographic Message Syntax.* RFC 3852.

Hsu, C. L., Lu, H. P., & Hsu, H. H. (2007). *Adoption of the mobile Internet: An empirical study of multimedia message service (MMS). Omega, 35*(6), 715-726.

Hu, J., Shima, K., Oehlmann, R., Zhao, J., Takemura, Y., & Matsumoto, K. (2004). An empirical study of audience impressions of B2C web pages in Japan, China and the U.K. *Electronic Commerce Research and Applications, 3*(2), 176–189.

Hui, C. H., & Triandis, H. C. (1985). Measurement in the cross-cultural psychology: A review and comparison of strategies. *Journal of Cross-Cultural Psychology, 16,* 131–152.

Huston, T. (2001). Security issues for implementation of e-medical records. *Communications of the ACM, 44*(9), 89-94.

Hutchison, D., Mauthe, A., & Yeadon, N. (1997). Quality-of-service architecture: Monitoring and control of multimedia communications. *Electronics & Communication Engineering Journal, 9*(3), 100.

IAIK - Institute for Applied Information Processing and Communication (2008). *IAIK JCE Micro Edition cryptography library for the Java™ Mobile Edition platform.* http://jce.iaik.tugraz.at/sic/products/mobile_security/jce_me. Accessed on: 25th September 2008.

IBM Aglets. (2002). http://www.trl.ibm.com/aglets/.

ITU. (2005). *The Internet of Things (Statistical Annex).*

ITU-T. (1993). General aspects of Quality of Service and Network Performance in Digital Networks, including ISDNs (Vol. I.350): ITU.

ITU-T. (2006). Framework for achieving end-to-end IP performance objectives (Vol. Y.1542): ITU.

ITU-T. (2007). Vocabulary for performance and quality of service: Appendix I—Definition of Quality of Experience (QoE) (Vol. P.10/G.100): ITU-T.

Izard, C. E., Libero, D. Z., Putnam, P., & Haynes, O. M. (1993). Stability of emotion experiences and their relations to traits of personality. *Journal of Personality and Social Psychology, 64,* 847–860.

Jacobs, P. (1997). Privacy: what you need to know. *Infoworld, 19*(44), 111-112.

Jaegar, P., & Thomson, K. (2003). E-government around the world: Lessons, challenges, and future directions. *Government Information Quarterly, 20*(4), 389-394.

Jaeger, P. (2003). The Endless wire: E-government as global phenomenon. *Government Information Quarterly, 20*(4), 323-331.

Jagne, J., Smith-Atatkan, S., Duncker, E., & Curzon, P. (2005). Cross-cultural factors of physical and e-shopping. In *Proceedings of the Eleventh International Conference on Human Computer Interaction.*

Jakobsson, M., & Wetzel, S. (2001). *Security weakness in Bluetooh.* Murray Hill, USA.

Jansen W., Karygiannis Tom (NIST Special Publication 800-19 – Mobile Agent Security http://csrc.nist.gov/publications/nistpubs/800-19/sp800-19.pdf

Java Agent DEvelopment Framework (2005) http://jade.tilab.com/.

Jena, http://www.hpl.hp.com/semweb/jena.htm

Jiang, Z., & Benbasat, I. (2003). The effects of interactivity and vividness of functional control in changing web consumers' attitudes. In *Proceedings 24th International Conference of Information Systems, Seattle, USA.*

Jing, J., Huff, K., Hurwitz, B., Sinha, H., Robinson, B., & Feblowitz, M. (2000). WHAM: Supporting mobile workforce and applications in workflow environments. In *Proceedings of the 10th International Workshop on Research Issues in Data Engineering (RIDE 2000)* (pp. 31-38).

Johanson J. and Mattsson, L.-G. (1986). International Marketing and Internationalization Processes - Network approach. In Turnbull, P. W. and Paliwoda, S. J., Research in International Marketing. Croom Helm, New Hampshire, 234-265.

Johanson, J. and Mattsson, L.-G. (1988). Internationalization in industrial systems: A network approach. In Hood, N. and Vahlne, J.-E. (eds). Strategies in global competition. Croom-Helm, New York, pp. 287-314.

Johnson, M., & Moore, S., (2007). *A New Approach to E-Banking*. Retrieved April 01, 2008, from http://mjj29.matthew.ath.cx/2007-Johnson-ebanking-full.pdf

Joines, J. L., Scherer, C., & Scheufele, D. (2003). Exploring motivations for consumer web use and their implications for e-commerce. *The Journal of Consumer Marketing, 20.*

Joinson, A. (1998). Causes and implications of disinherited behavior on the internet. In S. Kiesler (Ed.), *Culture of the Internet* (pp. 43–59). Mahwah, NJ: Erlbaum.

Joinson, A. (2001). Self-disclosure in computer-mediated communication: the role of self-awareness and visual anonymity. *European Journal of Social Psychology, 31,* 177–192.

Jones, M. Y., Stanaland, A. J., & Gelb, B. D. (1998). Beefcake and cheesecake: Insights for advertisers. *Journal of Advertising, Summer.*

Jorns, O., Quirchmayr, G., & Jung, O. (2007). A Privacy Enhancing Mechanism based on Pseudonyms for Identity Protection in Location-Based Services. *Australasian Information Security Workshop: Privacy Enhancing Systems (AISW)*. Ballarat, Australia.

Kakihara, M. (2003). *Hypermobility: Emerging Work Practices of ICT-Enabled Professionals*. London School of Economics and Political Science, London.

Kakihara, M., & Sørensen, C. (2001). Expanding the 'Mobility' Concept. *Siggroup Bulletin, 22*(3), 33-37.

Kalakota, R., & Robinson, M. (2002). *M Business: The Race to Mobility*: McGraw-Hill.

Kallinikos, J. (2001). *The Age of Flexibility*. Lund: Academia Adacta AB.

Karageorgos, M., Thompson, S., & Mehandjiev, N. (2002). Agent-based system design for B2B electronic commerce. *International Journal of Electronic Commerce, 7*(1), 59-90.

Karjoth, G., Lange, D.B. & Oshima, M. (1997). A Security Model for Aglets. IEEE Internet Computing, 1(4) 68-77. [Electronic version] http://www.ibm.com/java/education/aglets/

Kärkkäinen, H., & Elfvengren, K. (2002). Role of careful customer need assessment in product innovation management - empirical analysis. *International Journal of Production Economics, 80,* 85-103.

Kärkkäinen, H., Piippo, P., Puumalainen, K., & Tuominen, M. (2001). Assessment of hidden and future customer needs in Finnish business-to-business companies. *R&D Management, 31,* 391-407.

Karnouskos, S., Vilmos, A., Hoepner, P., Ramfos, A., & Venetakis, N. (2003). Secure Mobile Payment—Architecture and Business Model of SEMOPS. *Proceedings of the EURESCOM summit*. Heidelberg, Germany.

Karygiannis, T., & Owens, L. (2002). *Wireless network security* (NIST special publication 800-48). Gaithersburg, MD: National Institute of Standards and Technology.

Kateranttanakul, P., & Siau, K. (1999). Measuring information quality of web sites: Development of an instrument. In *Proceedings of International Conference of Information Systems, Charlotte, North Carolina* (pp. 279–285).

Kato, S., Kato, Y., & Akahori, K. (2006). Emotional states and emoticons in e-mail communication using mobile phone. *Proceedings of World Conference on Educational Multimedia, Hypermedia and Telecommunications (ED-MEDIA) 2006,* 417-424.

Kato, Y., & Akahori, K. (2004). E-mail communication versus face-to-face communication: perception of other's personality and emotional state. *Proceedings of ED-MEDIA 2004* (pp. 4160–4167).

Kato, Y., & Akahori, K. (2004). The accuracy of judgment of emotions experienced by partners during e-mail and face-to-face communication. *Proceedings of ICCE 2004* (pp. 1559–1570).

Kato, Y., & Akahori, K. (2006). Analysis of judgment of partners' emotions during e-mail and face-to-face communication. *Journal of Science Education in Japan, 29*(5), 354-365.

Kato, Y., Kato, S., & Akahori, K. (2007). Effects of emotional cues transmitted in e-mail communication on the emotions experienced by senders and receivers. *Computers in Human Behavior, 23*(4), 1894-1905.

Kato, Y., Kato, S., & Scott, D. J. (2007). Misinterpretation of emotional cues and content in Japanese e-mail, computer conferences, and mobile text messages. In E. I. Clausen (Ed.), *Psychology of Anger,* (pp. 145-176). Hauppauge, NY: Nova Science Publishers.

Kato, Y., Sugimura, K. & Akahori, K. (2002). Effect of contents of e-mail messages on affections. *Proceedings of ICCE 2002* (pp. 428–432).

Kato, Y., Sugimura, K., & Akahori, K. (2001). An affective aspect of computer-mediated Communication: analysis of communications by e-mail. *Proceedings of ICCE/SchoolNet 2001* (pp. 636–642).

Keidl, M., Seltzsam, S., & Kemper, A. (2003). Reliable Web Service Execution and Deployment in Dynamic Environments. *Lecture Notes in Computer Science, 2819,* 104-118.

Kelley, C. L., & Charness, N. (1995). Issues in training older adults to use computers. *Behavior and Information Technology, 14,* 107–120.

Kerlinger, F. N. (1964). *Foundations in behavioral research.* New York: Holt, Rinehart, and Winston.

Kesti, M., Ristola, A., Karjaluoto, H., & Koivumäki, T. (2004). Tracking consumer intentions to use mobile services: empirical evidence from a field trial in Finland. *E-Business Review, 4,* 76-80.

Khodawandi, D., Pousttchi, K., & Wiedemann, D. G. (2003). Akzeptanz mobiler Bezahlverfahren in Deutschland. *Proceedings of the 3rd Workshop on Mobile Commerce* (pp. 42-57). Augsburg, Germany.

Khu-smith, V., & Mitchell, C. J. (2002). *Enhancing ecommerce security using GSM authentication,* London, England.

Kiesler, S. (1997). Preface. In S. Kiesler (Ed.), *Culture of the internet* (ix–xvi). Mahwah, NJ: Erlbaum.

Kiesler, S., & Sproull, L. (1992). Group decision making and communication technology. *Organizational Behavior and Human Decision Processes, 52,* 96–123.

Kiesler, S., Siegel, J., & McGuire, T. W. (1984). Social psychological aspects of computer mediated communication. *American Psychologist, 39,* 1123–1134.

Kietzmann, J. (2008). Interactive Innovation of Technology for Mobile Work. *European Journal of Information Systems, 17*(3), 305-320.

Kietzmann, J. (2008). *The Dark Side of Mobile RFID and the Disappearing Computer.* Paper presented at the European Group for Organizational Studies, Amsterdam.

Kilpatrick, I. (2003, December). Are you indulging in unprotected wireless. *Logistics and Transport Focus, 5*(10), 20-21.

Kim, K., Kim, J., Lee, Y., Chae, M., & Choi, Y. (2002). An empirical study of the use contexts and usability problems in mobile Internet. In *Proceedings of 35th Annual Hawaii International Conference on System Sciences, Los Alamitos, CA.*

Kim, M. K., Park, C., & Jeong, D. H. (2004). The effects of customer satisfaction and switching barrier on customer loyalty in Korean mobile telecommunication services. *Telecommunications Policy, 28,* 145–159.

Kim, Y., Kang, S., Kim, D., Bae, J., & Ju, K. (2000). WWflow: Web-based workflow management with runtime encapsulation. *IEEE Internet Computing, 4*(3), 56-64.

Kleinrock, L. (1996). Nomadicity: Anytime, Anywhere in a Disconnected World. *Mobile Networks and Applications, 1,* 351-357.

Knight, M., & Pearson, J. (2005). The changing demographics: The diminishing role of age and gender in computer usage. *Journal of Organisational and End User Computing, 17,* 49–65.

Kortge, G. D., & Onkonkwo, P. A. (1993). Perceived Value Approach to Pricing. *Industrial Marketing Management, 22,* 133-140.

Kosonen, M. (2004). Global competitiveness of MNCs. Presentation at EIBA academic conference. 2004. Llubljana. Slovenia

Kothandaraman, P., & Wilson, D. T. (2001). The Future of Competition - Value-Creating Networks. *Industrial Marketing Management, 30,* 379-389.

Kotler, P. (2003). *Marketing Management.* Upper Saddle River, New York, USA: Pearson Education.

Kotz, D., & Gray, R. (1999). Mobile agents and the future of the Internet. *ACM Operating Systems Review, 33*(3), 7-13.

Koufaris, M. (2002). Applying the technology acceptance model and flow theory to online consumer behaviour. *Information Systems Research, 13,* 205–22.

Kowalczyk, R., & Bui, V. (2000). On constraint-based reasoning in e-negotiation agents. In F. Dignum & U. Cortés (Eds.), *Agent mediated electronic commerce III* (LNAI 2003, pp. 31-46). London: Springer-Verlag.

Kowalczyk, R., Ulieru, M., & Unland, R. (2003). Integrating mobile and intelligent agents in advanced e-commerce: A survey. In *Proceedings of Agent Technology Workshops 2002* (LNAI 2592, pp. 295-313). Berlin, Germany: Springer-Verlag.

Krauss, R. M., & Fussell, S. R. (1996). Social Psychological models of interpersonal communication. In E. T. Higgins & A. W. Kruglanski (Eds.), Social psychology: *Handbook of basic principles* (pp. 655–701). New York: The Guilford Press.

Kraut, R. E. (1978). Verbal and nonverbal cues in the perception of lying. *Journal of Personality and Social Psychology, 36,* 380–391.

Kreyer, N., Pousttchi, K., & Turowski, K. (2002). Standardized Payment Procedures as Key Enabling Factor for Mobile Commerce. *Proceedings of the EC-Web, E-Commerce and Web Technologies* (pp. 400-409). Aix-en-Provence, France.

Kristoffersen, S., & Ljungberg, F. (2000). Mobility: From Stationary to Mobile Work. In *Planet Internet* (pp. 137-156). Lund: Studentlitteratur.

Kruck, S. E., Gottovi, D., Moghadami, F., Broom, R., & Forcht, K. A. (2002). Protecting personal privacy on the Internet. *Information Management & Computer Security, 10*(2), 77-84.

Krueger, M. (2002). Mobile Payments: A Challenge for Banks and Regulators. *IPTS Report, 63,* 5-11.

Krueger, M., Leibold, K., & Smasal, D. (2006). *Online Payment Methods from the Viewpoint of Customers— Results of the Study IZV8.* Karlsruhe, Germany: University of Karlsruhe.

Kruger, J., Epley, N., Parker, J., & Ng, Z. (2005). Egocentrism over e-mail: Can people communicate as well as they think? *Journal of Personality and Social Psychology, 89,* 925-936.

Kubeck, E., Delp, N. D., Haslett, T. K., & McDaniel, M. A. (1996). Does job-related training performance decline with age? *Psychology of Aging, 11,* 92–107.

Kuchinskas, S. (2007). Is Privacy Where It's At. *Internet News.* Retrieved January 30, 2008, from http://www.internetnews.com/wireless/article.php/3718706.

Kumar, S., & Zahn, C. (2003). Mobile communications: Evolution and impact on business operations. *Technovation, 23,* 515–520.

Kushchu, I., & Boricki, C. (2004). A Mobility Response Model for Government. *Mobile Government Lab.* Retrieved 9 March 2006 from http://www.mgovlab.org.

Kushchu, I., & Kuscu, H. (2003). From E-government to M-Government: Facing the Inevitable. *Proceedings of the 3rd European Conference on e-Government,* (pp. 253-260).

Kwon, H. S., & Chidambaram, L. (2000). A test of the technology acceptance model: The case of cellular phone adoption. In *Proceedings of 33rd Hawaii International Conference on System Sciences.*

Kymäläinen, P. (ed.). (2004). Mgain: Mobile Entertainment Industry and Culture. Helsinki University of Technology. www.m-gain.org

Lamport, L., Shostak, R., & Pease, M. (1982). The Byzantine Generals Problem. *ACM Transactions on Programming Languages and Systems, 4*(3), 382-401.

Lamsweerde, A. van, Darimont, R., & Massonet, P. (1995). Goal-directed elaboration of requirements for a meeting scheduler: Problems and lessons learnt. In *Proceedings of the 2nd IEEE International Symposium on Requirements Engineering (RE '95)* (pp. 194-203).

Langheinrich, M. (2001). *Privacy by Design – Principles of Privacy-Aware Ubiquitous Systems.* Institute of Information systems, IFW, Zurich, Switzerland.

Lardner, J. (1999). I know what you did last summer and fall. *US News & World Report, 126*(15), 55.

Larose, R., & Atkin, D. (1992). Audiotext and the reinvention of the telephone as a mass medium. *Journalism Quarterly, 69*, 413-421.

Larsen, E., & Rainie, L. (2002). *The rise of the e-citizen: How people use government agencies' Web sites.* Washington DC: Pew Internet & the American.

Lea, M. (Ed.). (1992). *Contexts of computer-mediated communication.* London: Harvester Wheatsheaf.

Leahy, S. (2006). *The Secret Cause of Flame Wars. Wired.* Published on February 13, 2006, Retrieved from http://www.wired.com/science/discoveries/news/2006/02/70179 on September 27, 2008.

Lee, E., Kwon, K., & Schumann, D. (2005). Segmenting the non-adopter category in the diffusion of internet banking. *International Journal of Bank Marketing, 23*(5), 414-37.

Lee, H., Buckland, M. A., & Shepherdson, J. W. (2003). A multi-agent system to support location-based group decision making in mobile teams. *BT Technology Journal, 21*(1), 105-113.

Lee, S. F., & Ko, A. S. O. (2000). Building balanced scorecard with SWOT analysis, and implementing ``Sun Tzu's The Art of Business Management Strategies'' on QFD methodology. *Managerial Auditing Journal, 15,* 68-76.

Lee, Y., Kim, J., Lee, I., & Kim, H. (2002). A cross-cultural study on the value structure of mobile internet usage: Comparison between Korea and Japan. *Journal of Electronic Commerce Research, 3,* 227–239.

Lenk, K., & Traumuller, R. (2000). A framework for electronic government. *Proceedings of the 11th International Workshop on Database and Expert Systems Applications,* (p. 271). Baltimore, Maryland: ACM Publications

Li, F., & Whalley, J. (2002). Deconstruction of the telecommunication industry: from value chains to value networks. *Telecommunications Policy, 26,* 451-472.

Liao, S., Shao, Y., Wang, H., & Chen, A. (1999). The adoption of virtual banking: an empirical study. *International Journal of Information Management, 19,* 63-74.

Liao, Z., & Cheung, M. (2001). Internet-based e-shopping and consumer attitudes: an empirical study. *Information and Management, 38*(5), 299-306.

Lilischkis, S. (2003). *More Yo-yos, Pendulums and Nomads: Trends of Mobile and Multi-Location Work in the Information Society:* STAR.

Lim, A. S. (2008). Inter-consortia battles in mobile payments standardization. *Electronic Commerce Research and Applications, 7*(2), 202-213.

Lin, F.-R., & Pai, Y.-H. (2000). Using multi-agent simulation and learning to design new business processes. *IEEE Transactions on System, Man and Cybernetics, Part A, 30*(3), 380-384.

Lin, F.-R., Tan, G. W., & Shaw, M. J. (1998). Modeling supply-chain networks by a multi-agent system. In *Proceedings of HICSS31* (Vol. 5, pp. 105-114).

Lin, Y.-B., & Chlamtac, I. (2000). *Wireless and mobile network architectures.* New York: John Wiley & Sons.

Linck, K., Pousttchi, K., & Wiedemann, D. G. (2006). Security Issues in Mobile Payment from the Customer Viewpoint. *Proceedings of the 14th European Conference on Information Systems.* Gothenburg, Sweden.

Linz, J., & Stepan, A. (1996). *Problems of democratic transition and consolidation: Southern Europe, South America, and post-communist Europe.* Baltimore: John Hopkins University Press.

Liu, Y., Ginther, D., & Zelhart, P. (2001). How do frequency and duration of messaging affect impression development in computer-mediated communication? *Journal of Universal Computer Science, 7,* 893-913.

Ljungberg, F., & Sørensen, C. (2000). Overload: From Transaction to Interaction. In K. Braa, C. Sørensen & B. Dahlbom (Eds.), *Planet Internet* (pp. 113-136). Lund: Studentlitteratur.

Lo, G., & Kersten, G. K. (1999). Negotiation in electronic commerce: Integrating negotiation support and software agent technologies. In *Proceedings of the 29th Atlantic Schools of Business Conference* [CD-ROM].

Lockwood, S. E. (2004). Who Knows Where You've Been? Privacy Concerns Regarding the Use of Cellular Phones as Personal Locators. *Harvard Journal of Law & Technology, 18*(1), 307-317.

Lohse, G. L., & Spiller, P. (1998). Electronic shopping. *Communications of the ACM, 41,* 81–88.

Lohse, G. L., & Spiller, P. (1999). Internet retail store design: How the user interface influences traffic and sales. *Journal for Computed-Mediated Communication, 5.*

Lomuscio, A., Wooldridge, M., & Jennings, N. (2000). A classification scheme for negotiation in electronic commerce. In F. Dignum & C. Sierra (Eds.), *Agent-mediated electronic commerce: A European perspective* (LNCS 1991, pp. 19-33). London: Springer-Verlag.

Long, M. (2007, September). *Longitude and Latitude: location technologies and privacy concerns.* Paper presented at the 29th International Conference of Data Protection and Privacy Commissioners, Montreal.

Loureiro S., Molva R. & Roudier Y. (2000). Mobile Code Security. Proceedings of ISYPAR 2000 (4ème Ecole d'Informatique des Systems Parallèles et Répartis), Code Mobile, Toulouse, France, February. http://www.eurecom.fr/~nsteam/Papers/mcs5.pdf

Lu, J., Yu, C.S., Liu, C. & Yao, J.E. (2003). Technology acceptance model for wireless Internet. *Internet Research: Electronic Networking Applications and Policy, 13*(3), 206-222.

Lu, J.; Liu, Ch.; Yu, Ch., & Wang, K. (2008). Determinants of accepting wireless mobile data services in China. *Information & Management, 45,* 52-64.

Luarn, P., & Lin H. H. (2005). Toward an understanding of the behavioral intention to use mobile banking. *Computers in Human Behavior, 21*(6), 873-891.

Lucco, S., Sharp, O. & Wahbe, R. (1995). Omniware: A Universal Substrate for Mobile Code. Fourth International World Wide Web Conference, MIT. [Electronic version] http://www.w3.org/pub/Conferences/WWW4/Papers/165/

Luo, Y., Liu, K., & Davis, D. N. (2002). A multi-agent decision support system for stock trading. *IEEE Network, 16*(1), 20-27.

Luostarinen, R. (1979), Internationalisation of the Firm. Thesis for the degree of Doctor at the Helsinki School of Economics.

Luostarinen, R. and Gabrielsson, M. (2004). Born Globals of Small and Open Economies (SMOPECs)—A New Entrepreneurial Challenge. In Dana, L. P. (Ed), Handbook of Research on International Entrepreneurship. Edward Elgar, Cheltenham.

Lyytinen, K., & Yoo, Y. (2002). Issues and Challenges in Ubiquitous Computing. *Communications of the ACM, 45*(12), 6-65.

Lyytinen, K., & Yoo, Y. (2002). Research commentary: The next wave of nomadic computing. *Information Systems Research, 13*(4), 377-388.

M.I.S Trend S.A. (2007). *Study of use of mobile services in telecommunication (realized for Division of Telecommunication of the Federal Communication Office in Switzerland).* Lausanne, CH: Institute for market and opinion surveys study.

MACRO (2004). Mobile phone usage among the teenagers and youth in Mumbai. Report. Retrieved from:

www.itu.int/osg/spu/ni/futuremobile/socialaspects/IndiaMacroMobileYouthStudy04.pdf

Madsen, T. and Servais, P. (1997). The Internationalization of Born Globals-An Evolutionary Process. International Business Review, Vol 6 No 6, pp. 1-14.

Magretta, J. (2002). Why Business models Matter? *Harvard Business Review, 80,* 86-92.

Mahmoud, Q. H. (2004). *J2ME and Location-Based Services.* Retrieved June 21, 2008, from http://developers.sun.com/mobility/apis/articles/location/.

Malhotra, K., Gardner, S., & Mepham, W. (2008). A novel implementation of signature, encryption and authentication (SEA) protocol on mobile patient monitoring devices. *Technol. Health Care, 16*(4), 261-272.

Mallat, N., & Tuunainen, V. K. (2005). Merchant adoption of mobile payment systems. *Proceedings of the Fourth International Conference on Mobile Business* (ICMB), Sydney: IEEE Computer Society.

Maltby, Chudry, F., & Wedande, G. (2003). Cyber dudes and cyber babes: Gender differences and internet financial services. *Journal of Financial Services Marketing, 8,* 152–165.

Manhart, K. (2001). *Mobile digitale Signatur* (pp. 60-61). Germany: Funkschau.

Mann, S., & Niedzviecki, H. (2002). *Cyborg: Digital Destiny and Human Possibility in the Age of the Wearable Computer*: Doubleday Canada.

Manner, J., Burness, L., Hepworth, E., Lopez, A., & Mitjana, E. (2001). *Provision of QoS in heterogeneous wireless IP access networks.* Paper presented at the Intl Symposium on Personal, Indoor and Mobile Radio Communications.

Mansfield, G. M., & Fourie, L. C. H. (2004). Strategy and business models - strange bedfellows? A case for convergence and its evolution into strategic architecture. *South African Journal of Business Management, 35,* 35-44.

Mao, Z., Brewer, E., & Katz R. (2001). *Fault-tolerant, Scalable, Wide-area Internet Service Composition.*

Technical Report UCB/CSD-1-1129, Department of Computer Science and Electrical Engineering, University of Maryland, Baltimore County, USA.

Marcus, A., & Gould, E. W. (2000). Cultural dimensions and global web user interface design. *Interactions, July/August,* 33–46.

Markey, P., & Wells, S. (2002). Interpersonal perception in internet chat rooms. *Journal of Research in Personality, 36,* 134–146.

Martignoni, R., & Stanoevska-Slabeva, K. (2007). *Mobile Web 2.0.* Paper presented at the 20th BLED Electronic Commerce Conf.—eMergence, Bled, Slovenia.

Martin, B., & Byrne, J. (2003). Implementing e-Government: widening the lens. *Electronic Journal of e-Government, 1*(1), 11-22.

Masys, D. R., & Baker, D. B. (1997). *Patient-centered access to secure systems online: A secure approach to clinical data access via the World Wide Web.* Retrieved February 13, 2006, from http://www.saic.com/healthcare/sysint/pdf/amia1997.pdf

Mathieson, K., Peacock, E., & Chin, W. W. (2001). Extending the technology acceptance model: the influence of perceived user resources. *The Data Base for Advances in Information Systems, 32* (3), 86-112.

McCarthy, E. J. (1996). *Basic Marketing: A Managerial Approach.* Irwin, Homewood, Illinois, USA.

McCullough, M. (2004). *Digital Ground: Architecture, Pervasive Computing, and Environmental Knowing* (Vol. The MIT Press). Cambridge, Massachusetts.

McGraw G. & Morrisett G. (2000). Attacking Malicious Code http://www.cs.cornell.edu/Info/People/jgm/lang-based-security/maliciouscode.pdf

McGuire, T., Kiesler, S., & Siegel, J. (1987). Group and computer-mediated discussion effects in risk decision making. *Journal of Personality and Social Psychology, 52,* 917–930.

McKinney, V., Yoon, K., & Zahedi, F. M. (2002). The measurement of web-customer satisfaction: An expectation and disconfirmation approach. *Information Systems Research, 13,* 296–315.

Me, G., Strangio, M. A., & Dellutri, F. (2005). Local Authentication with Bluetooth enabled mobile devices. *Proceedings of IEEE International Conference on Autonomic and Autonomous Systems.*

Mennie, D., & Pagurek, B. (2000). An Architecture to Support Dynamic Composition of Service Components. *In Proceedings of the 5th International Workshop on Component -Oriented Programming (WCOP 2000),* Sophia Antipolis and Cannes, France.

Michael, K., Perusco, L., & Michael, M. G. (2006, October). *Location-Based Services and the Privacy-Security Dichotomy.* Paper presented at Proceedings of the 3rd International Conference on Mobile Computing and Ubiquitous Networking, London.

Michaut, F., & Lepage, F. (2005). Application-oriented network metrology: Metrics and active measurement tools. *IEEE Communications Surveys & Tutorials, 7*(2), 2-24.

Mikkonen, K., Hallikas, J., & Pynnönen, M. (2008). Connecting customer requirements into the multi-play business model. *Journal of Telecommunications Management, 1,* 177-188.

Minch, R. P. (2004). Privacy Issues in Location-Aware Mobile Devices. *Proceedings of the 37th Hawaii International Conference on System Sciences.*

Misra, S. K., & Wickamasinghe, N. (2004). Security of mobile transaction: A trust model, *Electronic Commerce Research and Applications, 4*(4) 359-372.

Mitchell, T. (1999). Machine Learning and Data Mining. *Communications of the ACM, 42*(11), 30-36.

Mitchell, V. W. (1999). Consumer perceived risk: conceptualizations and models. *European Journal of Marketing, 33*(1/2), 163-195.

MobiHealth. (2007). Putting care in motion. Retrieved Sep 05, 2008, from www.mobihealth.com

Mobile Code and Mobile Code Security. (2005). http://www.cs.nyu.edu/~yingxu/privacy/0407/main.html.

Mobile Code Security and Computing with Encrypted Functions [Electronic version] http://www.zurich.ibm.com/security/mobile

Mobile Code Security. (1996). [Electronic version] http://www.unsw.adfa.edu.au/~lpb/papers/mcode96.html.

Mobipay.com (2007). *How it works.* Retrieved May 11, 2007, from http://www.mobipay.com/en/home.htm

Moore, G., & Benbasati, I. (1991). Development of an instrument to measure the perceptions of adopting an information technology innovation. *Information Systems Research, 2*(3), 173-191.

Morgan, R., & Hunt, S. D. (1994). The Commitment-trust theory of relationship marketing. *Journal of Marketing, 58,* 20–38.

Morris, G. M., Venkatesh, V., & Ackerman, P. L. (2005). Gender and age differences in employee decisions about new technology: An extension to the theory of planned behavior. *IEEE Transactions on Engineering Management, 52,* 69–84.

Morris, M., & Venkatesh, V. (2000). Age Differences in Technology Adoption Decisions: Implications for a Changing Workforce. *Personnel Psychology, 53*(2), 375-403.

Motlekar S. (2005). Code Obfuscation. http://palisade.paladion.net/issues/2005Aug/code-obfuscation/

Mueller-Merbach, H. (1976). *The Use of Morphological Techniques for OR-Approaches to Problems. Operations Research '75* (pp. 127-139). Amsterdam, Holland: North-Holland Publishing Company.

Muir, A., & Oppenheim, C. (2002). National information policy developments worldwide I: electronic government. *Journal of Information Science, 28*(3), 173-186.

Muller A. (2000). Mobile Code Security: Taking the Trojans out of the Trojan Horse http://www.cs.uct.ac.za/courses/CS400W/NIS/papers00/amuller/essay1.htm.

Nahrstedt, K., Xu, D., Wichadakul, D., & Li, B. (2001). QoS-aware middleware for ubiquitous and heterogeneous environments. *IEEE Communication Magazine, 39*(11), 140-148.

Nass, C., Moon, Y., Fogg, B., & Reeves, B. (1995). Can computer personalities be human personalities? *International Journal of Human-Computer Studies, 43*, 223–239.

Necula G.C. & Lee, P. (1998). Safe, Untrusted Agents using Proof-Carrying Code. Lecture Notes in Computer Science N. 1419. Springer-Verlag.

Netsize (2008). *The Netsize guide 2008. Mobile 2.0, you are in control. Mobile Industry Report.* http:// www. netsize.com.

Netsize Guide. (2004). Developing the mobile multimedia market. Netsize. www.netsize.com

Newman, R. (2003). *Enterprise security.* Columbus, OH: Prentice-Hall.

Nielsen, J. (2001). *Designing for web usability.* Indianapolis: New Riders Publications.

Nielsen, J., & Del Galdo, E. M. (1996). *International User Interfaces.* Wiley Computer Publishing, John Wiley & Sons, New York.

Nojima, H., & Gill, S. P. (1997). Cultural differences in evaluative communication. *The second Conference of The Asian Association of Social Psychology, 139.*

Nokia. (2004). *Quality of Experience (QoE) of mobile services: Can it be measured and improved?*

Nosek, B. A., Banaji, M. R., & Greenwalk, A. G. (2002). Harvesting implicit group attitudes and beliefs from a demonstration website. *Group Dynamics: Theory, Research, Practice, 6*, 101–115.

NTRU (2008). *The NTRU Neo for Java.* http://www.ntru. com/products/index.htm. Accesed on: 25th September 2008.

Nunnally, J. C., & Bernstein, I. H. (1994). *Psychometric theory (3rd Ed.).* New York, USA. McGraw-Hill.

Nysveen, H., Pedersen, P. E., & Thorbjornsen, H. (2005). Intentions to Use Mobile Services: Antecedents and Cross-Service Comparisons. *Academy of Marketing Science Journal, 33*(3), 330-346.

O'Reilly, T. (2005). What is Web 2.0? Retrieved Sep 05, 2008, from www.oreillynet.com/pub/a/oreilly/tim/news/2005/09/30/what-is-web-20.html

Object Management Group (OMG). (2001). *Foreword UML specification 1.4.* Retrieved from http://www.omg. org/cgi-bin/doc?formal/01-09-67

Oliver, R. L. (1980). A cognitive model of the antecedents and consequences of satisfaction decisions. *Journal of Marketing Research, 42*, 460–469.

Oliver, R. L. (1999). Whence consumer loyalty? *Journal of Marketing, 63*, 33–44.

Ondrus, J., & Pigneur, Y. (2007). An assessment of NFC for future mobile payment systems. *Sixth International Conference on the Management of Mobile Business*, (pp. 43-53) Washington, DC: IEEE Computer Society.

Oppliger, R. (2000). Security technologies for the World Wide Web. Computer Security Series, Artech House Publishers.

Ortiz, S. (2007). 4G Wireless Begins to Take Shape. *IEEE Computer, 40*(11), 18-21.

Osterwalder, A., Ondrus, J., & Pigneur, Y. (2005). *Skype's Disruptive Potential in the Telecom Market: A Systematic Comparison of Business Models.* Lausanne, CH: University of Lausanne.

Osterwalder, A., Pigneur, Y., & Tucci, C. L. (2005). Clarifying Business Models: Origins, Present, and Future of the Concept . *Communications of AIS, 15*, 751-755.

Palen, L. (2002). Mobile telephony in a connected life. *Communications of the ACM, 45*(3), 78-82.

Palmer, J. W. (2002). Website usability, design, and performance metrics. *Information Systems Research, 13*, 151–167.

Papaioannou, T. (2000). Mobile information agents for cyberspace: State of the art and visions. In *Proceedings of Cooperating Information Agents (CIA-2000)* [CD-ROM].

Parasuraman, A., Zeithaml, V. A., & Berry, L. L. (1988). SERVQUAL: A multiple-item scale for measuring customer perceptions of service quality. *Journal of Retailing, 64,* 12–40.

Park, C., & Jun, J. K. (2003). A cross-cultural comparison of internet buying behavior: Effects of internet usage, perceived risks, and innovativeness. *International Marketing Review, 20,* 534–553.

Park, C., & Kim, Y. (2003). Identifying key factors affecting consumer purchase behaviour in an online shopping context. *International Journal of Retail and Distribution Management, 31*(1), 16-29.

Parno, B., Kuo, C., & Perrig, A. (2006). Phoolproof Phishing Prevention. In G. Di Crescenzo and A. Rubin (eds.), *Financial Cryptography and Data Security*, vol. LNCS of 4107 (pp. 1–19). Springer-Verlag. Retrieved April 01, 2008, from http://sparrow.ece.cmu.edu/_adrian/projects/phishing.pdf

Pascu, C., Osimo, D., Ulbrich, M., Turlea, G., & Burgelman, J. C. (2005). The potential disruptive impact of internet 2 based technologies. *First Monday—peer-reviewed Journal on the Internet.*

Patterson, M. L. (1994). Strategic functions of nonverbal exchange. In J. A. Daly & J. M. Wiemann (Eds.), *Strategic Interpersonal Communication* (pp. 273–293). Hillsdale, NJ: Erlbaum.

Pavlou, P. (2003). Consumer Acceptance of Electronic Commerce: Integrating Trust and Risk with the Technology Acceptance Model. *International Journal of Electronic Commerce, 7*(3), 69-103.

Pawar, P., Wac, K., van Beijnum, B. J., Maret, P., van Halteren, A., & Hermens, H. (2008). *Context-Aware Middleware Architecture for Vertical Handover Support to Multi-homed Nomadic Mobile Services.* Paper presented at the 23rd Annual ACM Symposium on Applied Computing (ACMSAC08), Ceará, Brazil.

Paybox.net (2003). *The Paybox Group restructures.* Retrieved May 15, 2007, from http://www.paybox.net/327_378.htm

Paybox.net (2007). *Paybox Money Mobiliser.* Retrieved May 15, 2007, from http://www.paybox.net/download/paybox_fact_sheets/paybox_Money-Mobiliser.pdf

Pearson, J. M., Crosby, L., Bahmanziari, T., & Conrad, E. (2003). An empirical investigation into the relationship between organisational culture and computer efficacy as moderated by age and gender. *Journal of Computer Information Systems, 43,* 58–70.

Peddemors, A. (2008). CoSPhere NAL software. Retrieved Sep 05, 2008, from http://cosphere.telin.nl/nal

Pelkonen, T. (2003). Value creation patterns and current trends in digital media service creation: A case study of the Finnish digital media industry. Europrix Scholars Conference paper, November 13, 20003. Tampere, Finland (www.mindtrek.org/sc).

Pelkonen, T. (2004) Mobile Games markets. ACTen E-Content Report 3. http://www.acten.net/cgi-bin/WebGUI/www/index.pl/mobile_games

Pelkonen, T. and Dholakia, N. (2004). Understanding Emergent M-Commerce Services by Using Business Network Analysis: The Case of Finland. In Wireless Communications and Mobile Commerce, Nan Si Shi (ed.), Hershey PA: Idea Group Publishing, 105-131.'

Perry, M., O'Hara, K., Sellen, A., Brown, B., & Harper, R. (2001). Dealing with Mobility: Understanding access anytime, anywhere. *ACM Transactions on computer human interaction (TOCHI), 8*(4), 323-347.

Phaos Micro Foundation (2008). *Cryptographic library fro J2ME CLDC and CDC environments.* http://www.phaos.com/resources/datasheets/pmf_datasheet.pdf. Accessed on: 15th August 2008.

Pisko, E. (2007). Mobile Electronic Signatures: Progression from Mobile Services to Mobile Application Unit. *6th IEEE International Conference on the Management of Mobile Business.* Toronto, Canada: IEEE Computer Society Press.

Pitt, L. F., Watson, R. T., & Kavan, C. B. (1995). Service quality: A measure of information systems effectiveness. *MIS Quarterly, 19,* 173–187.

Plant, S. (2001). *On the Mobile*. from http://www.motorola.com/mot/doc/0/234_MotDoc.pdf.

Porter, M. (1980). *Competitive Strategy: Techniques for Analyzing Industries and Competitors*. New York, USA: Free Press.

Porter, M. (1998). *Competitive Strategy*. New York: Free Press.

Pousttchi, K. (2003). Conditions for acceptance and usage of mobile Payment Procedures. *Proceedings of the 2nd International Conference on Mobile Business* (pp. 201-210). Vienna, Austria.

Pousttchi, K. (2004). An Analysis of the Mobile Payment Problem in Europe. *Proceedings of the Multikonferenz Wirtschaftsinformatik* (pp. 260-268). Essen, Germany.

Pousttchi, K. (2005). *Mobile Payment in Deutschland—Szenarienbasiertes Referenzmodell für mobile Bezahlvorgänge*. Wiesbaden, Germany: Deutscher Universitätsverlag.

Pousttchi, K. (2008). A modeling approach and reference models for the analysis of mobile payment use cases. *Electronic Commerce Research and Applications, 7*(2), 182-201.

Pousttchi, K., & Wiedemann, D. G. (2005). Payment Procedures for Electronic Government Services. *Proceedings of the 5th European Conference on e-Government (ECEG)*. Antwerp, Belgium, June 2005.

Pousttchi, K., & Wiedemann, D. G. (2007). Mobile Payment and the Charging of Mobile Services. In: Taniar, D. (Ed.): *Encyclopedia of Mobile Computing and Commerce*. Idea Group Inc., Clayton, Australia.

Pousttchi, K., Schießler, M., & Wiedemann, D. G. (2007). Analyzing the Elements of the Business Model for Mobile Payment Service Provision. *Proceedings of the 6th International Conference on Mobile Business* (pp. 201-210). Toronto, Ontario, Canada.

Pousttchi, K., Schießler, M., & Wiedemann, D. G. (2008). Proposing a comprehensive framework for analysis and engineering of mobile payment business models. *Information Systems and e-Business Management* (DOI 10.1007/s10257-008-0098-9) (in press).

Pousttchi, K., Wiedemann, D. G., & Schaub, J. (2006). Aktueller Vergleich mobiler Bezahlverfahren im deutschsprachigen Raum. *Studienpapiere der Arbeitsgruppe Mobile Commerce*. Bd. 1, Augsburg 2006, 50-96.

Powell, D., Verissimo, P., Bonn, G., Waeselynck, F., & Seaton, D. (1988). The Delta-4 approach to dependability in open distributed computing systems. *In Proceedings of The 18th International Symposium on Fault-Tolerant Computing*, Tokyo, Japan.

Prevelakis, V., & Spinellis, D. (2007). The Athens Affair. *IEEE Spectrum*. Retrieved April 01, 2008, from http://www.spectrum.ieee.org/jul07/5280

Pulkkinen, M. (1997). The Breakthrough of Nokia Mobile Phones. Doctoral Dissertation. Helsinki School of Economics. HeSePrint, Helsinki.

Putrevu, S. (2001). Exploring the origins and information processing differences between men and women: Implications for advertisers. *Academy of Marketing Science Review, 10*. Retrieved from: http://www.amsreview.org/articles/putrevu10-2001.pdf

Pynnönen, M., & Hallikas, J. (2008). Applying a Customer Value Model in Mobile Communication Business. *International Journal of Electronic Business, In Press*.

Pynnönen, M., Hallikas, J., & Savolainen, P. (2008). Mapping business: value stream based analysis of business models and resources in ICT service business. *International Journal of Business and Systems Research, 2*, 305-323.

Rainer, R. K., Laosethakul, K., & Astone, M. (2003). Are gender perceptions of computing changing over time? *Journal of Computer Information Systems, 43*, 108–114.

Ranganathan, A., & Campbell, R. (2003). A Middleware for Context-Aware Agents in Ubiquitous Computing Environments. *ACM/IFIP/USENIX International Middleware Conference*, Rio de Janeiro, Brazil.

Rankl, W., & Effing, W. (2004). *Smart Card Handbook* (3º ed., pp. 1120). Wiley.

Rao, A. S., & Georgeff, M. P. (1995). BDI agents: From theory to practice. *Proceedings of the 1st International Conference on Multiagent Systems* (pp. 312-319).

Rao, S., & Troshani (2007). A Conceptual Framework and Propositions for the Acceptance of Mobile Services. *Journal of Theoretical and Applied Electronic Commerce Research, 2*(2), 61-73.

Ratnasingam, P., & Phan, D. (2003). Trading Partner Trust in B2B E-Commerce: A Case Study. *Information Systems Management, 20*(3), 39-50.

Ratnasingam, P., Pavlou, P., & Tan, Y. (2002). *The Importance of Technology Trust for B2B Electronic Commerce.* Paper presented at the 15th BLED Electronic Commerce Conf.—eReality: Constructing the eEconomy, Bled, Slovenia.

Rau, P. P., Chen, J., & Chen, D. (2006). A study of presentations of mobile web banners for location-based information and entertainment information websites. *Behaviour & Information Technology, 25,* 253–261.

Reid, E. (1995). Virtual worlds: Culture and imagination. In S. G. Jones (Ed.), *Cybersociety: Computer-mediated communication and community* (pp. 164-183). Thousand Oaks, CA: Sage.

Resiel, J. F., & Shneiderman, B. (1987). Is bigger better? The effects of display size on program reading. In G. Salvendy (Ed.), *Social, ergonomic and stress aspects of work with computers* (pp. 113–122). Elsevier Science Publishers.

Rivard, S., & Huff, S. (1988). Factors of success for end user computing. *Communications of the ACM, 31,* 552–561.

Robles, T., Mitjana, E., & Ruiz, P. (2002). *Usage scenarios and business opportunities for systems beyond 3G.* Paper presented at the IST Mobile and Wireless Telecommunications Summit 2002, Thessaloniki, GR.

Rodgers, S., & Harris, M. A. (2003). Gender and e-commerce: An exploratory study. *Journal of Advertising Research, 43,* 322–329.

Roger A. G. (2001). Malicious Mobile Code- Virus Protection for Windows [Electronic version]. O'Reilly & Associates, Inc.

Rogers, E. (1995). *Diffusion of Innovations.* New York: The Free Press.

Rogers, E. (2003). *The Diffusion of Innovation.* Fifth Edition. New York, USA. Free Press.

Rohm, J., & Swaminathan, V. (2004). A typology of online shoppers based on shopping motivations. *Journal of Business Research, 57,* 748–757.

Rosen, D. E., & Purinton, E. (2004). Website design: Viewing the web as a cognitive landscape. *Journal of Business Research, 57,* 787–794.

Rossnagel H. (2004). *Mobile Qualified Electronic Signatures and Certification on Demand.* First European PKI Workshop: Research and Applications, EuroPKI. Samos Island, Greece.

Rossnagel, H., & Royer, D. (2005). *Making Money with Mobile Qualified Electronic Signatures. Trust, Privacy and Security in Digital Business.* Lecture Notes in Computer Science, vol. 3592.

RSA Laboratories. (1993). *PKCS #7: Cryptographic Message Syntax Standard.* ftp://ftp.rsasecurity.com/pub/pkcs/ascii/pkcs-7.asc.

RSA Laboratories. (1999). *PKCS #12 v1.0: Personal Information Exchange Syntax.* ftp://ftp.rsasecurity.com/pub/pkcs/pkcs-12/pkcs-12v1.doc.

RSA Laboratories. (2000). *PKCS #15 v1.1: Cryptographic Token Information Syntax Standard.* ftp://ftp.rsasecurity.com/pub/pkcs/pkcs-15/pkcs-15v1_1.doc.

RSA Laboratories. (2002). *PKCS #1 v2.1: RSA Cryptography Standard.* ftp://ftp.rsasecurity.com/pub/pkcs/pkcs-1/pkcs-1v2-1.doc.

Rubin, A. D., Geer, D. E. (1998). Mobile Code Security. IEEE Internet Computing.

Ruiz-Martínez, A., Sánchez-Martínez, D., Martínez-Montesinos, M., & Gómez-Skarmeta, A. F. (2007). A survey of electronic signature solutions in mobile devices. J. Theor. Appl. Electron. Commer. Res., 2(3), 94-109.

Rust, R., Kannan, P., & Peng, N. (2002). The customer economics of Internet privacy. *Journal of the Academy of Marketing Science, 30*(1), 455-464.

Rutkowski, A. F., Vogel, D. R., Genuchten, M. van, Bemelmans, T. M. A., & Favier, M. (2002). E-collaboration: The reality of virtuality. *IEEE TPC, 45*(4), 219-230.

Saaty, T. (1999). *Decision Making For Leaders: The Analytic Hierarchy Process for Decisions in a Complex World.* Pittsburgh: RWS Publications.

Salthouse, T. A. (1992). Reasoning and spatial abilities. In F. I. M. Craik & T. A. Salthouse (Eds.), *The handbook of aging and cognition,* 3rd ed. (pp. 167–212). Hillsdale, NJ: Lawrence Erlbaum Associates.

Salvi, A. B., & Sahai, S. (2002). Dial M for Money. *Proceedings of the 2nd ACM International Workshop on Mobile Commerce.* Atlanta, USA.

Sanchez, A., Carro, B., & Wesner, S. (2008). Telco Services for End Customers: European Perspective. *IEEE Commun. Mag., 46*(2), 14-18.

Sanchez-Franco, M. J. (2006). Exploring the influence of gender on the web usage via partial least-squares. *Behaviour & Information Technology, 25,* 19–36.

Sánchez-Martinez, D., Marín-López, I., & Jiménez-García, T. (2008). *Electronic Document Management in the University of Murcia.* 14th European University Information Systems Conference. EUNIS 2008.

Sander T. & Tschudin C. (1998). Towards Mobile Cryptography. Proceedings of the IEEE Symposium on Security and Privacy.

Sander, T. & Tschudin C. (1998). Protecting Mobile Agents Against Malicious Hosts. [Electronic version] Mobile Agents and Security Lecture Notes in Computer Science, 1419, G. Vigna, ed., Springer-Verlag, 44-60. http://citeseer.ist.psu.edu/article/sander97protecting.html

Sandip, S. (1997). Developing an automated distributed meeting scheduler. *IEEE Expert, 12*(4), 41-45.

Sannomiya, M., & Kawaguchi, A. (1999). Cognitive characteristics of face-to-face and computer-mediated communication in group discussion: An examination from three dimensions. *Japan Journal of Educational Technology, 22,* 19–25.

SANS Institute. (2001). *An overview of Bluetooth security.* Retrieved April 01, 2008, from http://whitepapers.techrepublic.com.com/whitepaper.aspx?docid=143972, 2001.

Sarker, S., & Wells, J.D. (2003). Understanding mobile handheld device use and adoption. *Communications of the ACM, 46,* 35–40.

Satama Interactive, (2005). Satama Insight: Mobile Media as an business opportunity. Company internal material. Helsinki, Finland.

Sathye, M. (1999). Adoption of Internet banking by Australian consumers: an empirical investigation. *International Journal of Bank Marketing, 17*(7), 324-34.

Sato, K. & Akahori, K. (2004). Enhancing interactivity in face-to-face lecture by using "board mediated communication." *Proceedings of ED-MEDIA 2004* (146–153).

Satorra, A., & Bentler, P. M. (1988). Scaling corrections for chi-square statistics in covariance structure analysis. American Statistical Association. *Proceedings of Business and Economics 14,* 308–313. Alexandria, VA: American Statistical Association.

Schlichting, R., & Schneider, F. (1983). Fail-stop Processors: An Approach to Designing Fault-Tolerant Computing Systems. *ACM Transactions on Computer Systems, 1*(3), 222-238.

Schmidt, S. H., & Frick, O. (2000). WAP – designing for small user interfaces. In *Proceedings of Conference on Human Factors in Computing Systems.*

Schneier, B. (1995). Applied cryptography (2nd ed.): protocols, algorithms, and source code in C (pág. 758). John Wiley & Sons, Inc.

Schneier, B. (1999). Attack trees. *Dr. Dobb's J., 24*(12), 21-29.

Schneier, B. (2005). *Schneier on Security: The Failure of Two-Factor Authentication.* Retrieved April 01, 2008, from http://www.schneier.com/blog/archives/2005/03/the_failure_of.html

Schnell, R., Hill, P., & Esser, E. (1999). *Methoden der empirischen Sozialforschung.* Munich, Germany: Oldenbourg.

Schrott, G., & Gluckler, J. (2004). What makes mobile computer supported cooperative work mobile? Towards a better understanding of cooperative mobile interactions. *International Journal of Human Computer Studies, 60,* 737–752.

Schultz, L. (2003). Effects of graphical elements on perceived usefulness of a library. Masters thesis. Retrieved from: http://www.tarleton.edu/~schultz/finalprojectinternetsvcs.htm

Schuster, H., Georgakopoulos, D., Cichocki, A., & Baker, D. (2000). Modeling and Composing Service-based and Reference Process-based Multi-enterprise Processes. *In Proceedings of the International Conference on Advanced Information Systems Engineering (CAiSE2000),* Stockholm, Sweden.

Seitz, N. (2003). ITU-T QoS standards for IP-based networks. *IEEE Communications Magazine, 41*(6), 82-89.

Shakshuki, E., Ghenniwa, H., & Kamel, M. (2000). A multi-agent system architecture for information gathering. In *Proceedings of the 11th International Workshop on Database and Expert Systems Applications* (pp. 732-736).

Sheng, Q. Z., Benatallah, B., & Maamar, Z. (2004). Enabling Personalized Composition and Adaptive Provisioning of Web Services. *The 16th International Conference on Advanced Information Systems Engineering*, Riga, Latvia.

Sheng, Q., Benatallah, B., Dumas, M., & Mak, E. (2002). SELF-SERV: A Platform for Rapid Composition of Web Services in a Peer-to-Peer Environment. *In Proceedings of the 28th Very Large DataBase Conference (VLDB'2002),* Hong Kong, China.

Shepherd, D., Scott, A., & Rodden, T. (1996). Quality-of-Service Support for Multimedia Applications. *IEEE MultiMedia, 03*(3), 78-82.

Sheridan, E. F. (2001). Cross-cultural web site design: Considerations for developing and strategies or validating local appropriate online content. *MultiLingual Computing, 12.* Retrieved from: http://www.multilingual.com.

Shi, M., Yang, G., Xiang, Y., & Wu, S. (1998). Workflow management systems: A survey. In *Proceedings of the IEEE International Conference on Communication Technology,* S33.05.01-S33.05.06.

Shitani, S., Ito, T., & Sycara, K. (2000). Multiple negotiations among agents for a distributed meeting scheduler. In *Proceedings of the 4th International Conference on MultiAgent Systems* (pp. 435-436).

Short, J., Williams, E., & Christie, B. (1976). *The social psychology of telecommunications.* London: John Wiley & Sons.

Shortell, S. M., & Kaluzny, A. D. (1994). Healthcare management: Organization design and behavior (3rd ed.). New York: Delmar.

Siegel, J., Dubrovsky, V., Kiesler, S., & McGuire, T. W. (1986). Group processes in computer-mediated communication. *Organizational Behavior and Human Decision Processes, 37,* 157–187.

Simmers, S., & Anandarajan, M. (2001). User satisfaction in the internet-anchored workplace: An exploratory study. *Journal of Information Technology Theory and Application, 3,* 39–61.

Simon, S. J. (2001). The impact of culture and gender on web sites: An empirical study. *The Data Base for Advances in Information Systems, 32,* 18–37.

Sims, B. (2004). Moving from liability to viability. *Health Management Technology, 25*(2), 32-35.

Singh, N., Xhao, H., & Hu, X. (2003). Cultural adaptation on the web: A study of American companies' domestic and Chinese websites. *Journal of Global Information Management, 11,* 63–80.

Smith, C. (1990). The case study: A useful research method for information management. *Journal of Information Technology, 5*(3), 123-133.

Smith, R. G. (1980). The contract net protocol: High-level communication and control in a distributed problem solver. *IEEE Transactions on Computers, C-29*(12), 1104-1113.

Soh, W. S., & Kim, H. S. (2003). QoS Provisioning in Cellular Networks Based on Mobility Prediction Techniques. *IEEE Commun. Mag., 41*(1), 86-92.

Song, Q., & Kasabov, N. (2001). ECM - A Novel On-line, Evolving Clustering Method and Its Applications. *In Proceedings of the Fifth Biannual Conference on Artificial Neural Networks and Expert Systems (ANNES2001),* Dunedin, New Zealand.

Sørensen, C., Fagrell, H., & Ljungstrand, P. (2000). Traces: From Order to Chaos. In K. Braa, C. Sørensen & B. Dahlbom (Eds.), *Planet Internet.* Lund, Sweden: Studentlitteratur.

Spiekermann, S. (2004). General Aspects of Location-Based Service. In J. Schiller & A. Voisard (Eds.), *Location-Based Services* (pp. 9-25). Morgan Kaufman.

Sproull, L., & Kiesler, S. (1986). Reducing social context cues: electronic mail in organizational communication. *Management Science, 32,* 1492–1512.

Sproull, L., & Kiesler, S. (1991). *Connections: New ways of working in the networked organization.* Cambridge, MA: MIT Press.

Sproull, L., & Kiesler, S. (1993). Computers, networks and work. In L. Harasim (Ed.), *Global Networks: Computers and International Communication* (pp. 105–120). Cambridge MA: MIT Press.

Srivastava, L. (2004). Japan's ubiquitous mobile information society. *Journal of Policy, Regulation and Strategy for Telecommunications, 6*(4) (2004) 234–251.

Srivastava, L., Fahey, L., & Christensen, H. K. (2001). The resource-based view and marketing: The role of market-based assets in gaining competitive advantage. *Journal of Management, 27,* 777-802.

Staehler, P. (2001). *Geschäftsmodelle in der digitalen Ökonomie.* Lohmar, Cologne, Germany.

Stahl, C. (2005). The Paradigm of E-Commerce in E-Government and E-Democracy. In W. Huang, K. Sisiiau, & K. Wei, (Eds.), *Electronic Government Strategies and Implementation,* (pp. 1-19). Hershey PA: Idea Group Publishing.

Stein, A., Hawking, P., & Sharma, P. (2005). A Classification of U-Commerce Location Based Tourism Applications. *Centre for Hospitality and Tourism Research.* Victoria University, Australia.

Straub, D. W., Loch, W., Aristo, R., Karahanna, E., & Strite, M. (2002). Toward a theory-based measurement of culture. *Journal of Global Information Management, 10,* 13–23.

Straub, D.W. (1989). Validating instruments in MIS research. *MIS Quarterly, 12,* 147–170.

Stroetmann, V. N., Husing T., Kubitschke L., & Stroetmann K. A. (2002). The attitudes, expectations and needs of elderly people in relation to e-health applications: Results from a European survey. *Journal of Telemedicine and Telecare, 8,* 82–84.

Stroulia, E., & Hatch, M. P. (2003). An intelligent-agent architecture for flexible service integration on the Web. *IEEE Transactions on System, Man and Cybernetics, Part C, 33*(4), 468-479.

Suh, B., & Han, I. (2003). The impact of customer trust and perception of security control on the acceptance of electronic commerce. *International Journal of Electronic Commerce,* (pp. 135-161).

Sun Java Specifications. (2007). *Security and Trust Services API for J2ME (SATSA); JSR 177.* http://jcp.org/aboutJava/communityprocess/mrel/jsr177/index.html

Sun, H. (2001). Building a culturally-competent corporate web site: An explanatory study of cultural markers in multilingual web design. In *Proceedings of SIGDOC'01,* 21-24, October (pp. 95–102).

Svantesson, D. (2005). Geo-identification – Now They Know Where You Live. *Privacy Law and Policy Reporter.*

Swaminathan, V.; Lepkowska-White, E., & Rao, B. (1999). Browsers or Buyers in Cyberspace? An Investigation of Factors Influencing Electronic Exchange. *Journal of Computed-Mediated Communication, 5*(2) http://jiad.org/vol5/no2/swaminathan (08.03.04).

Sweeney, J. C., Soutar, G. N., & Johnson, L. W. (1999). The role of perceived risk in the quality-value relationship: a study in a retail environment. *Journal of Retailing, 75*(1), 77-105.

Sycara, K., & Zeng, D. (1996). Coordination of multiple intelligent software agents. *International Journal of Cooperative Information Systems, 5*(2-3), 181-212.

Szajna, B. (1996). Empirical Evaluation of the Revised Technology Acceptance Model. *Management Science, 42*(1), 85-92.

Szymanski, D. A., & Hise, R. T. (2000). E-satisfaction: An initial examination. *Journal of Retailing, 76,* 309–322.

Tachikawa, K. (2003). A Perspective on the Evolution of Mobile Communications. *IEEE Commun. Mag., 41*(10), 66-73.

Taga, K., & Karlsson, K. (2004). *Arthur D. Little Global M-Payment Report.* Arthur. D. Little Austria GmbH, Vienna, Austria.

Tan, M., & Teo, Thompson, S. H. (2000). Factors influencing the adoption of Internet Banking. *Journal of Association for Information Systems, 1*(5), 1-41.

Tan, S. (1999). Strategies for reducing consumer's risk aversion in Internet shopping. *Journal of Consumer Marketing, 16*(2), 163-180.

Tan, S. (2004). *Evolution of mobile technology and business models (technical report)*: Center for Information and Communication Technologies, Lyngby, DK.

Tapscott, D., & Williams, A. D. (2006). *Wikinomics: How Mass Collaboration Changes Everything.* New York, USA: Portfolio.

Tarasewich, P. (2003). Designing mobile commerce applications. *Communications of the ACM, 46,* 57–60.

Taylor, S., & Todd, P.A. (1995). Understanding Information Technology Usage: A test of Competing Models. *Information Systems Research, 6*(2), 144-176.

Telescript Language Reference. (1995). http://citeseer.ist.psu.edu/inc95telescript.html.

Tennenhouse, D. L. & Wetherall , D. J. (1996) Towards an Active Network Architecture. Computer Communication Review. http://www.tns.lcs.mit.edu/publications/ccr96.html.

Teo, E., Fraunholz, B., & Unnithan, C. (2005). Inhibitors and facilitators for mobile payment adoption in Australia: a preliminary study. *Proceedings of the Fourth International Conference on Mobile Business (ICMB)*, Sydney: IEEE Computer Society.

Teo, H., Oh, L., Liu, C., & Wei, K. (2003). An empirical study of the effects of interactivity on web user attitude. *International Journal of Human-Computer Studies, 58,* 281–305.

Teo, T., Lim, V., & Lai, R. (1999). Intrinsic and extrinsic motivation in internet usage. *Omega International Journal of Management Science, 27,* 25–37.

Thomke, S., & von Hippel, E. (2002). Customers as Innovators: A New Way to Create Value. *Harvard Business Review, 80,* 74-81.

Thompsen, P. A. & Foulger, D. A. (1996): Effects of pictographs and quoting on flaming in electronic mail. *Computers in Human Behavior, 12,* 225-243.

Thompson, S. G., & Odgers, B. R. (2000). Collaborative personal agents for team working. In *Proceedings of the 2000 Artificial Intelligence and Simulation of Behavior (AISB) Symposium* (pp. 49-61).

Thompson, S. H. T., & Yuanyou, Y. (2004). Online buying behavior: a transaction cost economics perspective. *The International Journal of Management Science, 33,* 451-465.

Thomson Reuters. (2008). *Turkcell's Award-Winning Mobile Signature Service: Success Powered by*

Valimo. http://www.reuters.com/article/pressRelease/idUS125351+25-Jan-2008+PRN20080125. Accessed on: 10th September 2008.

Timmers, P. (1998). Business Models for Electronic Markets. *Journal on Electronic Markets, 8*(2), 3-8.

Timmers, P. (2000). *Electronic Commerce - Strategies and models for business-to-business trading.* London: John Wiley & Sons Ltd.

Tornatky, L., & Klein K. (1982). Innovation characteristics and innovation adoption-implementation: A meta-analysis of findings. *IEEE Transactions on Engineering Management, 29*(1), 28-45.

Tractinsky, N. (1997). Aesthetics and apparent usability: Empirically assessing cultural and methodological issues. In *CHI Proceedings.*

Tsalgatidou, A., & Pitoura, E. (2001). Business models and transactions in mobile electronic commerce: requirements and properties. *Computer Networks, 37*(2), 221-236.

Tsang, E. (1993). *Foundations of constraint satisfaction.* London; San Diego, CA: Academic Press.

Turban, E. (1993). *Decision support and expert systems: Management support systems* (3rd ed.). New York: Macmillan.

Turban, E., Lee, J. K., King, D., McKay, J., & Marshall, P. (2008). *Electronic Commerce 2008: A Managerial Perspective.* Fifth Edition, Pearson - Prentice Hall.

Turel, O., & Serenko, A. (2006). Satisfaction with mobile services in Canada: An empirical investigation. *Telecommunications Policy 30*(5-6), 314-331.

Turowski, K., & Pousttchi, K. (2004). *Mobile Commerce.* Heidelberg, Germany: Springer-Verlag.

Ulaga, W., & Chacour, S. (2001). Measuring Customer-Perceived Value in Business Markets. *Industrial Marketing Management, 30,* 525-540.

University of Murcia & Telefónica. (2007). *Firma electrónica móvil de actas digitales en la Universidad de Murcia.* Sociedad de la Información, pp 48-49.

http://www.socinfo.info/contenidos/pdf40sep07/p30-50empresas.pdf.

Valcourt, E. Robert, J., & Beaulieu, F. (2005). Investigating mobile payment: supporting technologies, methods, and use. *IEEE International Conference on Wireless And Mobile Computing, Networking And Communications,* (pp. 29-36). Montreal: IEEE Computer Society.

Van Birgelen M., De Ruyter, K., De Jong, A., & Wetzels, M. (2002). Customer evaluations of alter-sales service contact modes: an empirical analysis of national culture's consequences. *International Journal of Research in Marketing, 19*(19), 43-64.

van der Heijden. (2003). Factors influencing the usage of websites: The case of a generic portal in the Netherlands. *Information & Management, 40,* 541–549.

van Halteren, A., Bults, R., Wac, K., Konstantas, D., Widya, I., Dokovsky, N., et al. (2004). Mobile Patient Monitoring: The MobiHealth System. *The Journal on Information Technology in Healthcare, 2*(5), 365-373.

van Heck, E., & Vervest, P. (2007). Smart business networks: how the network wins. *Commun. ACM, 50*(6), 28-37.

Van Slyke, C., Belanger, F., & Comunale, C. (2004). Factors Influencing the Adoption of Web-Based Shopping: The Impact of Trust. *ACM SIGMIS Database, 35*(2), 32-49.

Varshney, U., & Vetter, R. (2002). Mobile commerce: framework, applications and networking support. *Mobile Networks and Applications, 7*(3), 185-198.

Varshney, U., Vetter, R. J., & Kalakota, R. (2000). Mobile Commerce: A New Frontier. *IEEE Computer,* (pp. 32-38).

Venkatesh, V., Morris, G. M., & Ackerman, P. L. (2000). A longitudinal field investigation of gender differences in individual technology adoption decision-making processes. *Organisation Behavior Human Decision Process, 83,* pp. 33–60.

Venkatesh, V., Ramesh, V., & Massey, A. P. (2003). Understanding usability in mobile commerce. *Communications of the ACM, 46,* 53–56.

Vigna Giovanni. (1997). Protecting Mobile Agents Through Tracing. Proceedings of the 3rd ECOOP Workshop on Mobile Object Systems, Jyvälskylä, Finland, June. http://www.cs.ucsb.edu/~vigna/listpub.html.

Voelckner F (2006). An empirical comparison of methods for measuring consumers' willingness to pay. *Marketing Letter, 17*(2), 137-149.

von Hippel, E. (1986). Lead Users: A Source of Novel Product Concepts. *Management science, 32,* 791-805.

Voss, C., Tsikriktsis, N., & Frohlich, M. (2002). Case research in operations management. *International Journal of Operations & Production Management, 22,* 195-219.

Vrechopoulos, A., Siomkos, G., & Doukidis, G. (2001) Internet Shopping Adoption by Greek Consumers. *European Journal of Innovation Management, 4*(3), 142-152.

W3C. (2008). *XML Signature Syntax and Processing (Second Edition).* W3C Recommendation. http://www.w3.org/TR/xmldsig-core/.

Wac, K. (2006). *QoS-predictions service: infrastructural support for proactive QoS- and context-aware mobile services.* Paper presented at the On the Move to Meaningful Internet Systems 2006: OTM Workshops, Intl Workshop on Context-Aware Mobile Systems (CAMS), Monpellier, France.

Wac, K., Hilario, M., Konstantas, D., & van Beijnum, B. J. (2008). Data Mining on Application-level QoS Traces: the MobiHealth System Case Study (forthcoming). *IEEE Trans. on Mobile Computing.*

Walker, J., & Spencer, J. (2000). Ten deadly sins. *Health Management Technology, 21*(7), 10.

Wallis Consulting Group Pty Ltd. (2007). *Consumer Attitudes to Privacy 2007, prepared for the Office of the Privacy Commissioner, Australia.* Retrieved on April, 21 2008, from http://www.privacy.gov.au/publications/rcommunity07.pdf .

Walther, J. B. (1992). Interpersonal effects in computer-mediated interaction: A relational perspective. *Communication Research, 19*(1), 52-90.

Walther, J. B., & Burgoon, J. K. (1992). Relational communication in computer-mediated interaction. *Human Communication Research, 19,* 50-88.

Walther, J. B., Anderson, J. F., & Park, D. W. (1994). Interpersonal effects in computer-mediated interaction. *Communication Research, 21,* 460–487.

Wang, Y. S., Wang, Y. M., Lin, H. H., & Tang, T. I. (2003). Determinants of user acceptance of Internet banking: an empirical study. *International Journal of Service Industry Management, 14*(5), 501-519.

Warkentin, M., Gefen, D., Pavlou, P., & Rose, G. (2002) Encouraging Citizen Adoption of e-Government by Building Trust. *Electronic Markets, 12*(3), 157-162.

Weatherspoon, H., Moscovitz, T., & Kubiatowicz, J. (2002). Introspective Failure Analysis: Avoiding Correlated Failures in Peer-to-Peer Systems. *In Proceedings of the International Workshop on Reliable Peer-to-Peer Distributed Systems (SRDS'02),* Osaka, Japan.

Wegner, L., Paul, M., Thamm, J., & Thelemann, S. (1996). Applications: A visual interface for synchronous collaboration and negotiated transactions. *Proceedings of the Workshop on Advanced Visual Interfaces* (pp. 156-165).

Weilenmann, A., & Larsson, C. (2000). Collaborative use of mobile telephones: A field study of Swedish teenagers. In *Proceedings of NordiCHI 2000, Stockholm, Sweden, 23–25 October.*

Wernerfelt, B. (1984). A Resource-based View of the Firm. *Strategic Management Journal, 5,* 171-180.

Wireless Communications: Voice and Data Privacy. *Privacy Rights Clearinghouse.* Retrieved April, 11 2008, from http://www.privacyrights.org/fs/fs2-wire.htm.

Wirtz, B. W. (2000). *Electronic Business.* Wiesbaden, Germany: Gabler.

Witten, I., & Frank, E. (2005). *Data Mining: Practical Machine Learning Tools and Techniques*: Morgan Kaufmann.

Workflow Management Coalition. (1995). *The workflow reference model* (WFMC-TC-1003, 19-Jan-95, 1.1). Retrieved from http://www.wfmc.org/standards/model.htm

Workflow Management Coalition. (1999). *Terminology and glossary* (WFMC-TC-1011, 3.0). Retrieved from http://www.wfmc.org/standards/model.htm

Wu, J. H., & Wang, S. C. (2005). What drives mobile commerce? An empirical evaluation of the revised technology acceptance model. *Information & Management, 42*(5), 719-729.

Wu, M., Garfinkel, S., & Miller, R. *Secure web authentication with mobile phones.* MIT Computer Science and Artificial Intelligence Lab.

Xiao, X., & Ni, L. M. (1999). Internet QoS: a big picture. *IEEE Network, 13*(2), 8-18.

Yang, K. C. (2005). Exploring factors affecting the adoption of mobile commerce in Singapore. *Telematics and Informatics, 22*, 257-277.

Yeo, A. (2001). Global software development lifecycle: An exploratory study. In *CHI 2001 Conference on Human Factors in Computing Systems* (pp. 104–111). ACM Press.

Yin, R. K. (1994). *Case Study Research; Design and Methods.* (Second edition) (vol. 5) London and New Delhi: Sage Publications.

Yoon, D., Cropp, F., & Cameron, G. (2002). Building Relationships with Portal Users: the Interplay of Motivation and Relational Factors. *Journal of Interactive Advertising, 3*(1). http://jiad.org/vol3/no1/yoon (08.03.04).

Yoon, S. (2002). The antecedents and consequences of trust in online-purchase decisions. *Journal of Interactive Marketing, 16*, 47–63.

York J., & Pendharkar, P. (2004). Human-computer interaction issues for mobile computing in a variable work context. *International Journal of Human-Computer Studies, 60*, 771–797.

Younes-Fellous, V. (2007). Privacy and data protection in Europe (art. 29 Working Party representative). *Commission nationale de l'informatique et des libertés.* Retrieved on April, 21 2008, from ec.europa.eu/information_society/activities/esafety/doc/esafety_2007/data_privacy_ws_13feb/younnes_ppt.pdf.

Yu, B., & Kushchu, I. (2004). The value of Mobility for e-government. *Proceedings of the 4th European Conference on E-Government,* (pp. 887-899).

Zalesak, M. (2003). Overview and opportunities of mobile government. *Mobile Government Lab.* Retrieved 9 March 2006 from http://www.mgovlab.org.

Zhang, X., Keeling, K. K., & Pavur, R. J. (2000). Information quality of commercial web site homepages: An explorative analysis. In *Proceedings of International Conference on Information Systems, Brisbane, Australia* (pp. 164–175).

Zheng, X., & Chen, D. (2003). Study of mobile payments systems. *IEEE International Conference on E-Commerce,* (pp. 24—27) Newport Beach: IEEE Computer Society.

Zhou, J. (2001). *Non-Repudiation in Electronic Commerce* (1º ed., pp. 234). Artech House Publishers.

Zmijewska, A., & Lawrence, E. (2005). Reshaping the Framework for Analysing Success of Mobile Payment Solutions. *International Conference on E-Commerce,* Porto, Portugal

Zmijewska, A., & Lawrence, E. (2006). *Implementation models in mobile payments.* In Proceedings of the 2nd IASTED international conference on Advances in computer science and technology (págs. 19-25). Puerto Vallarta, Mexico: ACTA Press.

Zmijewska, A., Lawrence, E., & Steele, R. (2004). Classifying mpayments—a user-centric model. *Proceedings of the Third International Conference on Mobile Business.* New York, USA.

About the Contributors

Milena M. Head is the associate dean and an associate professor of information systems at the De-Groote School of Business, McMaster University. She received her BMath from the University of Waterloo and her MBA & PhD from McMaster University. Specializing in electronic business (e-business) and human computer interaction (HCI), Dr. Head has published over 65 papers in peer-reviewed academic journals, books and conferences. Her research interests include trust, privacy and adoption in electronic commerce, interface design, mobile commerce, identity theft, cross-cultural issues in electronic commerce and human computer interaction, e-retailing, and web navigation. She has published in journals such as MIS Quarterly, Information & Management, International Journal of Human-Computer Studies, Interacting with Computers, International Journal of Electronic Commerce, Group Decision and Negotiation, among others. For further information, please browse Dr. Head's website at http://www.business.mcmaster.ca/IS/head/.

Eldon Y. Li is the University Chair Professor of the Department of Management Information Systems at the National Chengchi University, Taiwan and an emeritus professor of California Polytechnic State University (Cal Poly), San Luis Obispo, California, USA. He is also the director of NCCU Innovation and Incubation Center and Center for Service Innovation. He was a professor and the dean of the College of Informatics, and the director of the Graduate Institute of Social Informatics at the Yuan Ze University, Taiwan; a member of the research grant review board for the National Science Council of R.O.C. (2004-2005); a member of university evaluation committee for the Ministry of Education in Taiwan (2005); a senior professor of management area (1982/1-2007/3) and the coordinator of MIS program (1986-1989; 2001-2003) at the Orfalea College of Business, Cal Poly; the professor and founding director of the Graduate Institute of Information Management at the National Chung Cheng University in Chia-Yi, Taiwan (1994-1996); a visiting scholar of The Chinese University of Hong Kong (1999-2000). He holds a bachelor degree in international trade from National Chengchi University in Taiwan and MS and PhD degrees in information systems and quantitative sciences from Texas Tech University. Dr. Li has published in journals such as *Communications of the ACM, Computers & Education, Information & Management, Information Resources Management Journal, Journal of Computer Information Systems, Journal of Management Information Systems,* among others. He is the editor-in-chief of *International Journal of Electronic Business* and *International Journal of Information and Computer Security*. His research areas include human factors in information technology (IT), strategic IT planning, electronic business management, service science, software engineering, total quality management, IT management, business integration, and e-entrepreneurship.

* * *

Michail Batikas holds a BSc from University of Crete , Greece, in computer science and a MBA from Athens University of Economics and Business, Greece. Now, he is a 3rd year PhD student in the Department of Information and Communication Technologies of Universitat Pompeu Fabra, Barcelona, Spain. His main research interests are free/libre open source software, diffusion of innovation, IT adoption, and innovation management. Currently, he is a member of Network Technologies and Strategies Research Group of Universitat Pompeu Fabra. With his doctoral dissertation he tries to investigate the motivations of firms to contribute to FLOSS communities. He has published to several conferences like ECIS (European Conference on Information Systems), and ITS (International Telecommunication Society) Regional Conferences. Also, he is a reviewer of the ICIS (International Conference on Information Systems).

Adrian Broz-Lofiego (PhD student in marketing, Universidad de Valencia, Spain) is assistant professor in the Department of Marketing and Social Sciences, Faculty of Economics, Universidad de La Florida and part-time teacher at the Universidad Nacional de Rosario (Argentina). He has a degree in economics at the Universidad de Buenos Aires, a master's degree in economics at the Centro de Estudios Macroeconómicos de la República Argentina (CEMA) and a master's degree in marketing and market research at the Universidad de Valencia. His primary research interests include e-commerce, mobile commerce, Internet banking and international economics. He has presented some papers at Luso-Spanish Conference on Management.

Richard Bults holds a masters degree (cum laude) in telematics and a bachelor degree in technical computer science. He is a researcher in the remote monitoring and treatment section of the Bio Signals and Systems research group at the University of Twente, the Netherlands. His research interests are design of mobile telemedicine systems and QoS evaluation and control of these systems. Richard is also one of the Mobihealth BV founding fathers and the CTO of this privately owned company. MobiHealth's mission is to give patients full mobility during remote health monitoring sessions while staying in touch with their care professional. He is responsible for the company's product portfolio and tele-monitoring solutions consultancy.

Mahil Carr has a bachelor's degree in mathematics from the American College, Madurai Kamaraj University, Madurai, a master of computer applications from St. Joseph's College, Bharathidasan University, Trichirapalli and was awarded a doctoral degree in information systems from the City University of Hong Kong. At present, he is assistant professor at the institute and is the research & development coordinator for the institute since December 2007. Prior to joining the institute, he held the position of director (in-charge), Department of Computer Science, American College, Madurai, for over three-and-a-half years. His current research interests are in the areas of software engineering, information systems security and electronic/mobile commerce. He has published research papers in several conferences and in *Information Technology and Management*, the *Journal of Services Research*, *CAB Calling*, *Journal of Systems and Software*, and the *Journal of Information System Security*. Dr. Carr is on the editorial board of the *International Journal of E-Services and Mobile Applications* (IJESMA) and the *International Journal of Information Systems and Social Change* (IJISSC).

Fang-Yu Chen received her master from information management department of Fu-Jen University in Taiwan. Her research interests include mobile commerce, handheld technologies, *etc.* She is now working under the AsusTeK Computer Inc., Taiwan and actively engages in the R&D activities for Asus new mobile platforms and applications.

Hong Chen obtained his PhD from Erasmus University, Rotterdam School of Management. His research focused on individual tariffs and service personalization. He received MSc degree (cum laude) in computer science in 2003 from University of Twente, the Netherlands. He studied telecommunications engineering in Beijing University of Posts and Telecommunications from 1995 to 1999. From 1999 to 2001, he worked in Huawei Technologies as an engineer. Since August 2008, he had joined Altran CIS as a consultant specialized in telecom business.

Shing-Chi Cheung was born in 1962. Before joining the Hong Kong University of Science and Technology, he worked for the Distributed Software Engineering Group at the Imperial College in a major European ESPRIT II project on distributed reconfigurable systems. His effort led to the development of REX, which was adopted by various European firms like Siemens and Stollman to build in-house distributed software systems. More recently, he has been working on various research and industrial projects on object-oriented technologies and services computing. Dr. Cheung is an associate editor of *IEEE Transactions on Software Engineering*. He actively participates in the organization and program committees of many leading international conferences on software engineering and distributed computing, including ICSE, FSE, ASE, ISSTA, ICDCS, ER, and SCC. He is interested in technology transfer and has provided technical consultancy to various organizations, including banks, public organizations, and engineering companies on the use of object-oriented and component-based technologies.

Dickson K. W. Chiu is the founder of Dickson Computer Systems. Besides being an experienced consultant, he also teaches part time at universities. He was born in Hong Kong and received the BSc (honors) degree in computer studies from the University of Hong Kong in 1987. He received the MSc (1994) and the PhD (2000) degrees in computer science from the Hong Kong University of Science and Technology, where he worked as a visiting assistant lecturer after graduation. He also started his own computer company while studying part time. From 2001 to 2003, he was an assistant professor at the Department of Computer Science at the Chinese University of Hong Kong. His research interests include information-systems engineering and service computers with a cross-disciplinary approach, involving Internet technologies, software engineering, agents, work flows, information-system management, security, and databases. His research results have been published in over 70 technical papers in international journals and conference proceedings, such as *IEEE Transactions*, *Information Systems*, and *Decision Support Systems*. He served in program committees of several international conferences, such as the IEEE International Conference on Web Services; IEEE International Conference on e-Technology, e-Commerce and e-Services; and International Conference on Web-Age Information Management. He received a best-paper award at the 37th Hawaii International Conference on System Sciences in 2004. Dr. Chiu is a senior member of the IEEE as well as a member of the ACM and the Hong Kong Computer Society.

Constantinos Coursaris is an assistant professor in the Department of Telecommunication, Information Studies, and Media, and the Usability and Accessibility Center at Michigan State University. His formal training consists of a BEng in aerospace, an MBA in e-business, and a PhD in information systems with a concentration on electronic business (e-business) and mobile commerce (m-commerce).

During his academic career he has received many accolades in business analysis and e-business research and development. Coursaris has been involved in the instruction of over 40 university courses over the last seven years. He has been consulted on Web content management, Web site development, online and offline marketing, and event organizing. His current research interests lie in the intersection of usability and mobile devices for the purpose of health and/or commercial applications. The results of his research efforts can be found in his numerous publications and conference presentations.

Dianne Cyr is an associate professor in the faculty of business at Simon Fraser University in Vancouver. She earned a PhD from the University of British Columbia, a masters degree from the University of New Brunswick, and a bachelors degree from the University of Victoria. Her research is focused on how trust, satisfaction, and loyalty are built in online business environments through website design. Dr. Cyr is the author of five books and over 80 research articles in journals, books and conference proceedings. Her research appears in journals such as *Journal of Management Information Systems, Information & Management, Journal of the American Society for Information Science and Technology, Interacting with Computers,* and *Journal of Global Information Management.* Additional career and research information may be found at www.diannecyr.com and www.eloyalty.ca

Jukka Hallikas (DSc, Tech) is a professor of supply management at the school of business of the Lappeenranta University of Technology, Finland. His research interests focus on the management of value networks, risk management in supply networks and learning in interfirm relationships. He has published several scientific articles, books and book chapters on interfirm relationships and supply management.

Sunil Hazari is associate professor in the Department of Management and Business Systems, Richards College of Business, University of West Georgia. His teaching and research interests are in the areas of information security, infrastructure design of e-commerce sites, web usability, and organizational aspects of e-learning. He has authored several peer-reviewed journal publications in information and instructional technology areas, has presented papers at national conferences, and is editorial board member of information system journals.

Alex Ivanov is a PhD candidate at the School of Interactive Arts and Technology at Simon Fraser University, Canada. His research interests are in the area of information visualization and design for interactive environments. Alex holds a master of arts degree in advertising from The University of Texas at Austin, a BA in journalism from Bulgaria, and has five years experience in the marketing communications industry. For further information, please browse Alex's website, collabographics.com.

Mary Magdalene Jane received her MCA degree from Gobi Arts College, Gobi, India and the MPhil degree from Manonmaniam Sundaranar University, Tirunelveli, India. She is a lecturer in computer science, P.S.G.R.Krishnammal College for Women, Coimbatore, India. Her research interests focus on mobile computing and security in computing. She is a member of Computer Society of India.

Yuuki Kato is an assistant professor in the school of education at Tokyo University of Social Welfare in Japan. He earned a PhD from Tokyo Institute of Technology in 2005. His general research interests include educational technology; the application of behavior science, psychology, and information and communication technology (ICT) to educational scenes. Dr. Kato is particularly interested in the emotional aspects in technology-mediated human communications.

Shogo Kato is an assistant researcher in the school of human sciences, Waseda University in Japan and a part-time instructor in the faculty of economics, Dokkyo University in Japan. He earned a PhD from Tokyo Institute of Technology in 2005. His general research interests include educational technology; the application of behavior science, psychology, and information and communication technology (ICT) to educational scenes. Dr. Kato is particularly interested in the emotional aspects in virtual community, such as Internet bullying.

Jan Kietzmann received his PhD in 2007 from the London School of Economics and joined Simon Fraser University's Faculty of Business in 2008. Jan's research interests involve the intersection of mobility of work and wireless computing. Of particular interest are current developments that surpass well-established mobile interaction and communication technologies (ICTs). Jan studies how mobile radio-frequency identification, as one of many emerging "smart" technologies, invites the participation of physical objects into previously people-dominated mobile interaction. As objects gain an increasingly loud and clear voice in organizational information flows, Jan aims to understand the role of the artifact, the transformation of the individual and the changing relationship of the mobile worker, her colleagues, superiors and customers. In light of the emerging pervasiveness of mobile ICTs and their impact on the firm, Jan further studies participatory innovation processes that connect organizations with the mobile communities that form their future target audiences, both users and customers.

Dimitri Konstantas is professor and vice-dean at the Faculty of Social and Economic Sciences of the University of Geneva (CH), department of information systems, heading the Advanced Systems Group (ASG). He was previously professor and chair of the APS group at the University of Twente, The Netherlands. For the last 20 years he is active in research in the areas of object oriented systems, agent technologies, multimedia applications and e-commerce services, with numerous publications in international conferences, journals, books and book chapters, a long participation and leadership in many European projects and with many nominations as consultant and scientific expert for several international companies and governments. Since 2002 his main research areas are mobile and wireless multimedia services and applications, with special interest in mobile health and location based services.

Adrian Lawrence is a partner with the technology, communications and commercial group of Baker & McKenzie, Sydney. Adrian specialises in all aspects of online operations, including the major regulatory issues facing ecommerce such as privacy, content regulation, online contracting, intellectual property protection and new media regulation. Adrian's current research interests include the regulation of e-commerce and privacy across jurisdictional boundaries and the future of online copyright. Adrian lectures in the media, communications and information technology masters specialisation at the University of New South Wales and is the author of a leading looseleaf publication on e-commerce law, *The Law of Ecommerce.*

Ho-fung Leung is currently an associate professor in the Department of Computer Science and Engineering at the Chinese University of Hong Kong. He leads theoretical and applied research projects on intelligent agents, multiagent systems, game theory, artificial intelligence, and agent-mediated electronic-commerce technologies, and offers postgraduate courses in game theory and multiagent systems. He is a participating member of the Center for the Advancement of E-Commerce Technologies (AECT) of the engineering faculty. Leung reviews for many major journals and has served on the program committee of many conferences. Currently, he is serving on the program committees of CEC06 and EEE06, EDOC 2006, ISA2006, and PRIMA 2006. Leung was the chairperson of the ACM (Hong Kong chapter) in 1998. He serves as the university's nominee in the HKCE Computer and Information Technology Subject Committee of the Hong Kong Examinations and Assessment Authority. Leung is a professional member of the ACM, a senior member of the IEEE, a chartered member of the BCS, and a chartered IT professional. He is a chartered engineer registered by the ECUK and was awarded the designation of chartered scientist by the Science Council of the United Kingdom. Leung received his BSc and MPhil degrees in computer science from the Chinese University of Hong Kong, and his PhD degree and DIC (diploma of Imperial College) in computing from the Imperial College of Science, Technology and Medicine, University of London.

Daniel Marchuet-Martinez (PhD student in marketing, Universidad de Valencia, Spain) is a software engineer. He has a degree in business in economics and a degree in computer engineering and a master's degree in marketing and market research. His primary research interests include e-commerce, mobile commerce, viral marketing and consumer behaviour.

Antonio Ruiz Martínez received the MSc degree in Computer Science from University of Murcia (Spain). In 2000, he started as researcher staff in the Department of Information Engineering and Communications, University of Murcia, where he has been involved in various research projects in the field of electronic commerce and electronic government. From 2005, he is working as a full time assistant lecturer of the Department of Engineering and Communications. He has published several papers in national and international conference proceedings and journals. At present, he is involved in the integrated project eCoSPACE, in the field of collaborative environments. His main research areas are electronic commerce, payment systems, digital rights management, (mobile) electronic signature, Web services and service oriented architectures.

Daniel Sánchez Martínez obtained his computer science degree from the University of Murcia. Currently, he is working in projects related to security services based on smart cards and web services, such as electronic signature and authentication system for e-Government. He is also a member of the information and communications engineering department of the University of Murcia, where his is an assistant professor. His current research interests also include security infrastructures and mobile signature.

Gianluigi Me, PhD is adjunct professor of computer system security in the Università di Roma "Tor Vergata" computer science engineering department and in the Università di Roma "La Sapienza", criminology department. He holds a wealth of experience in managing training for law enforcement high tech crime units and government agencies. Furthermore, he is author of more than 50 scientific publications and he is Since 2005 he is consultant for the European Commission in the scope of the Safer Internet Plus program. He holds few patents in the area of security products and is the author of MIAT forensic toolkit and VirtualParent. His research interests include mobile computing applications and security, digital forensics, electronic/mobile payments and game theory.

Karri Mikkonen joined TeliaSonera's corporate strategy department in 2003, when TeliaSonera was created from the merger of Sonera and Telia, incumbents of Finland and Sweden. He holds an MSc in industrial management from Tampere University of Technology, and has also studied cognitive artificial intelligence and philosophy at the University of Utrecht in The Netherlands. He is continuing his PhD studies in the strategy area, with a special interest in changing ICT value networks and business models, while keeping his research focus on market timing of integrated offerings.

María Martínez Montesinos received the MSc degree in computer science from University of Murcia (Spain). She has collaborated with the engineering and computer technology department of the University of Murcia in 2001 developing her master thesis in "Integration of Payment Standards Based on Smart Card in E-Commerce Systems". Since 2003, she has worked in projects related to security services based on smart cards, such as electronic signature and authentication systems, including mobile systems, and a Telco company developing applications and software for electronic signature for mobile phones (J2ME) and Pocket PC. In 2005, she received a DEA (diploma of advanced studies) in new technologies of information and communications from Murcia University.

Wolfgang Palka is an analyst at the wi-mobile research group, University of Augsburg, business informatics/systems engineering, since 2006. To this day he studies the motivations, attitudes, and behaviors of consumers engaged in mobile viral marketing. Therefore he has executed several studies with qualitative and quantitative approaches. Since 2007 he has expanded his research on mobile payment. In this research area he focuses his analyses on business models in the context of the EU project on a Secure Mobile Payment System (SEMOPS). He was awarded for the best research on the International Conference on Mobile Business in Barcelona (2008) for a contribution on mobile viral marketing.

Tommi Pelkonen is a doctoral student at the Helsinki School of Economics. In his professional career he works as management consultant specializing in mobile telecommunications, internationalization, and business strategy formulation at Satama Interactive (www.satama.com), a European digital services firm. He has worked on multiple mobility-related business projects and currently focuses on interactive television solutions at Satama Amsterdam. Prior to Satama, Tommi Pelkonen worked as project manager and senior researcher in LTT-Research Ltd (www.ltt-tutkimus.fi) analyzing the developments in the Finnish interactive service provision markets. This topic forms also the theme of his doctoral dissertation. Pelkonen holds an MSc (Econ.) and has authored several publications of the Finnish and European digital media landscape. In addition, Mr. Pelkonen has worked as IT-project supervisor and lecturer in the information technology program (ITP) at the Helsinki School of Economics (itp.hkkk.fi).

Daniele Pirro graduated in computer science engineering in 2003 at University of Rome "Tor Vergata", where he has also got a MSc in software engineering in 2006. He has four years of experience in a major consulting IT company as a consultant and software engineer. He has worked in information systems designing and development in a wide variety of environments and technologies. He has been mainly involved in the public administration and utilities sectors, managing complex tasks for many important customers. His major areas of expertise are web technologies and mobile computing. At present time, he is attending an MBA at SDA Bocconi in Milan.

Key Pousttchi heads the wi-mobile research group at the University of Augsburg, business informatics/systems engineering. Following the special movements of the mobile industry, his group combines academic with applied research and employs the results in strategic consulting projects for major companies. Prior to this position he worked as a researcher at the University of the Federal Armed Forces Munich. As a nationally and internationally recognized expert for mobile markets, especially mobile financial services and mobile business processes, he has been involved in numerous projects including being the head of the National Roundtable M-Payment of the German banks and mobile operators, and a member of the m-enterprise advisory body for the German Ministry of Economics and Technology. He published eight books, frequently serves as a media commentator on mobile markets and has also been a visiting scholar to the Universities of Frankfurt and of Zurich/Switzerland.

Mikko Pynnönen is project manager at the Technology Business Research Center at Lappeenranta University of Technology. He holds a DSc (Econ.) degree from Lappeenranta University of Technology. His main research interests include business models and value networks in ICT industry. He has published several scientific articles on networked business models and customer value in ICT industry.

Carla Ruiz-Mafé (PhD in business and economics, Universidad de Valencia, Spain) is assistant professor in the Department of Marketing, Faculty of Economics, Universidad de Valencia. Her primary research interests include e-commerce, mobile commerce, communication, interactive marketing and consumer behaviour and she has articles published in *Internet Research, Online Information Review, Journal of Electronic Commerce Research, Journal of Consumer Marketing, Journal of Theoretical and Applied Electronic Commerce Research* and the best Spanish refereed journals. She has also presented some papers at AM and EMAC Conferences.

Samundeeswari E.S. received her MCA degree from P.S.G. College of Technology, Coimbatore, India and the MPhil degree from the Bharathiar University, Coimbatore, India. She is currently doing research in process management. She is a lecturer (selection grade) in computer science, Vellalar College For Women, Erode, India. Her current research interests are concurrent engineering, process model and workflow. She is a member of ISTE, New Delhi, India.

Silvia Sanz-Blas (PhD in business and economics, Universidad de Valencia, Spain) is associate professor in the Department of Marketing, Faculty of Economics, Universidad de Valencia. Her primary research interests include communication, sales, e-commerce, interactive marketing and consumer behaviour she has articles published in *Internet Research, Online Information Review, Journal of Electronic Commerce Research, Journal of Consumer Behaviour, Journal of Consumer Marketing, Journal of Vacation Marketing* and the best spanish refereed journals. She has also presented numerous papers at AM, AMS and EMAC Conferences.

Roberto Sarrecchia, holds MBA at Luiss in Rome in 2007, MSc in software engineering in 2006 at University of Rome "Tor Vergata" and graduated in computer science engineering in 2003 at "Politecnico of Milan". He worked as contractor for Booz Allen Hamilton and as product manager for Seat Pagine Gialle. Furthermore he worked in information systems designing and development (Microsoft Certified Datatabase Administrator since 2002). His major areas of expertise are Web technologies, data warehousing, advanced communication systems and security related issues. At present time, he is working for the Italian Government Department of Public Security–Crisis Unit.

Petri Savolainen is ICT expert at Technology Business Research Center at Lappeenranta University of Technology. He holds MSc (Tech.) degree from Lappeenranta University of Technology. He is specialized in content management, value network analysis and ICT industry analysis.

Douglass J. Scott is an associate professor at Waseda University, School of Human Sciences, human informatics and cognitive sciences department. Scott's academic background is in Japanese culture and society (MA University of Michigan, 1987) and educational foundations and policy (PhD University of Michigan, 1997). Prior to his doctoral studies, Dr. Scott worked as the director of a small Japanese company in Tokyo where he developed an interest in international communications and education. He later worked as an assistant professor at Michigan State University and as the resident director of the Japan Center for Michigan Universities before joining Waseda University in 2001. Dr. Scott's research interests include gender and intercultural differences in the use of communication technologies. His current research projects include emotional transfer in Japanese young people's text messages and the comparative study of Japanese and American young people's use of communication technologies.

Antonio F. Gómez Skarmeta. He received the MS degree in computer science from the University of Granada and BS (Hons.) and the PhD degrees in computer science from the University of Murcia Spain. Since 1993 he is professor at the same department and University. Gómez-Skarmeta has worked on different research projects at regional, national and specially at the European level in areas related to advanced services like multicast, multihoming, security and adaptative multimedia applications in IP and NGN networks. He has published over 50 international papers.

Bert-Jan van Beijnum received his MSc and PhD in electrical engineering from the University of Twente, the Netherlands. He is an assistant professor in the remote monitoring and treatment section of the Bio Signals and Systems research group at the University of Twente, the Netherlands. His research is embedded in the projects of the Centre for Telematics and Information Technology and the Institute of Biomedical Technology. His research interests include autonomic computing, mobile virtual communities, telemedicine, information systems, ICT management, task assignment systems and algorithms, application layer mobility handover mechanisms and QoS.

Dawn-Marie Turner is president of DM Turner Informatics Consulting Inc. She has twenty years experience in health and information technology. Her experience in health has included direct patient care, health administration and management, and health programming. Her experience in information technology has included project management, business process redesign, executive coaching and change management/transition planning.

Adam P. Vrechopoulos is assistant professor at the Athens University of Economics and Business (AUEB), Department of Management Science and Technology and Scientific Coordinator of the Interactive Marketing and Electronic Services (IMES) research group at the ELTRUN Research Center at AEUB. His research interests are digital marketing and electronic retailing. He holds a PhD from Brunel University at UK, an MBA from ALBA, and a BSc in information systems from AUEB. He has participated in many funded research projects and acted as researcher at the Electronic Business Interaction Research Group at Brunel University and at the ELTRUN Research Center at AUEB. He has published more than 70 papers in peer reviewed journals and academic conferences, and has acted as a reviewer for several international journals, member of conferences' scientific committees and books' editor. He is the 2002 Gold Award winner of the ECR Europe Academic Partnership Award. Before starting his academic career he worked in the industry in marketing, sales and project management positions.

Katarzyna Wac is a PhD candidate at University of Geneva, Switzerland conducting research in area of quality of service (QoS) in mobile applications. She is also a research staff member at the University of Twente, the Netherlands, where she is affiliated with the MobiHealth BV spin-off company. She has received her BSc and MSc degrees (cum laude) in computer science from Wroclaw University of Technology, Poland, and her MSc in telematics (cum laude) from University of Twente. Her current research interests include mobile applications and services with special emphasis on supporting adaptive multimedia protocols and end-to-end QoS mechanisms, especially in a mobile healthcare domain.

Dietmar Georg Wiedemann is a project leader at the wi-mobile research group, University of Augsburg, business informatics/systems engineering, since 2003. He is an expert in B2C-mobile-commerce. He has executed many studies with a qualitative and quantitative approach in mobile payment and mobile marketing. Since 2007 he is the project leader for the German part of the EU project on a secure mobile payment system (SEMOPS). He was awarded for the best research on the International Conference on Mobile Business in Barcelona (2008) for a contribution on mobile viral marketing.

Jane Williams is a senior associate at Baker & McKenzie in Sydney, Australia, and is a member of the firm's technology, communications and commercial group. Jane advises on a range of issues relating to information technology, e-commerce and privacy law, and assists with the preparation of a broad range of commercial contracts for technology and telecommunications companies. Jane also has experience in general commercial and intellectual property litigation. The focus of Jane's practice is privacy law, and she regularly advises on privacy compliance, assists with the handling of privacy complaints, and drafts privacy policies and data transfer agreements.

Soe-Tsyr Yuan is a professor of information management of National Chengchi University in Taiwan. She received his PhD in computer science from Oregon State University in USA. Her research interests include service science, mobile and ubiqutious commerce, service-oriented computing, business intelligence management, intelligent agents, knowledge discovery and data mining, *etc*. She has served as member of various programme and editorial committees for international conferences and journals (such as *International Journal of Web Services Research, International Journal of E-Business Research, Service Oriented Computing and Applications, etc.*).

Index

design and culture 174, 175, 176, 177, 189,
190, 192, 197, 319
design and gender 173, 174, 175, 177, 178,
320, 180, 184, 185, 186, 328, 188, 189,
195, 335, 196, 336, 197, 338, 339, 342
design and satisfaction 173, 314, 174, 176,
177, 319, 179, 320, 180, 322, 182, 184,
185, 186, 187, 328, 188, 191, 332, 193,
194, 334, 195, 196, 339, 341
detective control 306
diffusion of innovations 63, 65, 69

E

electronic government (e-government) 64, 65,
66, 67, 68, 69, 319, 71, 73, 74, 75, 76,
344
electronic product codes (EPC) 6
electronic signature (e-signature) 116, 117,
118, 119, 120, 121, 123
e-mail, mobile 201, 202, 203, 205, 207, 208,
209, 210, 211, 212, 213, 214, 215, 327,
216, 328, 217, 218
e-mail, PC 201, 202, 203, 205, 207, 208, 209,
210, 211, 212, 213, 214, 215, 216
enterprise information system (EIS) 288
EIS triggers 293
ethernet networking technologies 114
extensible markup language (XML) 297
XML stylesheet language (XSL) 297

F

face to face (FTF) interaction 202, 203, 204
fault tolerance 135, 137, 138, 139, 144, 149,
150, 153, 155, 157, 162, 166, 167, 169
firewalls 114, 307, 310
flaming 203, 204, 216, 219, 341

G

general packet radio service (GPRS) 108, 112,
114
global positioning system (GPS) 294
global system for mobile communications
(GSM) 105, 112, 113, 114, 328
government to business (G2B) initiatives 67
government to citizen (G2C) initiatives 67, 68,
75

government to government (G2G) initiatives
67

H

healthcare 304
healthcare environment 303
healthcare network 304
healthcare organization 306
Health Insurance Portability and Accountability
Act (HIPAA) (1996) 308
human computer interaction (HCI) perspective
175, 192, 193, 319, 324
hypertext markup language (HTML) 104, 114,
297
hypertext transfer protocol (HTTP) 109, 111,
113, 114, , 322
HTTP over secure socket layer (HTTPS) 109,
114

I

implementation 293
information design (ID) 174, 183, 184, 185,
187, 199
information flow 1, 2
Institute of Electrical and Electronics Engineers
(IEEE) 305, 309
integrated offering 49, 60
Internet 304–305

J

Java mobile edition platform (J2ME) 111, 114,
120, 123, 132, 133, 134, 335, 340
Java platform 102, 105, 111, 114

L

local area network (LAN) 114, 305
location information 16, 17, 18, 19, 20, 21, 22,
23, 24, 25, 26
location information, privacy issues of 15, 16,
17, 18, 19, 20, 21, 22, 25, 26
location information, privacy issues of: collection 16, 17, 19, 20, 21, 22, 23
location information, privacy issues of: disclosure 19, 20, 21, 22, 23, 24